Norms in a Wired World

Social order is regulated from above by the law, but its foundation is built on norms and customs, informal social practices that enable people to make meaningful and productive uses of their time and resources. Despite the importance of these practices in keeping the social fabric together, very little of the jurisprudential literature has discussed these norms and customs.

In *Norms in a Wired World*, Steven A. Hetcher argues that the traditional conception of norms as rulelike linguistic entities is erroneous. Instead, norms must be understood as patterns of rationally governed behavior maintained in groups by acts of conformity. Using informal game theory in the analysis of norms and customs, Hetcher breaks new ground by applying his theory of norms to tort law and Internet privacy laws.

This book will appeal to students and professionals in law, philosophy, and political and social theory.

Steven A. Hetcher is Professor of Law at Vanderbilt Law School.

Cambridge Studies in Philosophy and Law

Some other books in the series:

Norms in a Wired World

Steven A. Hetcher

Vanderbilt University

CAMBRIDGE
UNIVERSITY PRESS

PUBLISHED BY THE PRESS SYNDICATE OF THE UNIVERSITY OF CAMBRIDGE
The Pitt Building, Trumpington Street, Cambridge, United Kingdom

CAMBRIDGE UNIVERSITY PRESS
The Edinburgh Building, Cambridge CB2 2RU, UK
40 West 20th Street, New York, NY 10011-4211, USA
477 Williamstown Road, Port Melbourne, VIC 3207, Australia
Ruiz de Alarcón 13, 28014 Madrid, Spain
Dock House, The Waterfront, Cape Town 8001, South Africa

http://www.cambridge.org

First published 2004

Printed in the United States of America

Typeface Times Roman 10/12 pt.   *System* LATEX 2$_\varepsilon$ [TB]

A catalog record for this book is available from the British Library.

Library of Congress Cataloging in Publication Data

Hetcher, Steven A. (Steven Anthony), 1958–
Norms in a wired world / Steven A. Hetcher.
p.   cm. – (Cambridge studies in philosophy and law)
Includes bibliographical references and index.
ISBN 0-521-45436-0 (hb)
1. Customary law – Philosophy.   2. Torts – Philosophy.   3. Privacy, Right of – Philosophy.
4. Cyberspace – Philosophy.   5. Social norms – Philosophy.   I. Title.   II. Series.
K282 .H48   2003
306–dc21

2002038842

ISBN 0 521 45436 0 hardback

This book is dedicated to my mother, Melva K. Hetcher,
my brother, Nick L. Hetcher,
and the memory of my father, V. Louis Hetcher.
They taught me to love. All else is icing on the cake.

Contents

Acknowledgments

This book has been many years in the making. It has grown and evolved over a twelve-year period. I became interested in the philosophy behind norms while completing my dissertation at the University of Illinois-Chicago. My interest became infused with notions of rational actor theories from further graduate studies at the University of Chicago. The legal influence began with my work at the Yale Law School, and has continued the past six years while teaching at Vanderbilt Law School.

As with any project of this duration, the influences are many and the debts too extensive to be fully acknowledged, let alone repaid. Nevertheless, an attempt needs to be made. I wish to thank my dissertation committee, Gerald Dworkin, Charles Chastain, Richard Kraut, and especially Russell Hardin, both for his work on the committee and for the reading group on rational actor theory that he led, and Shelley Kagan, who served as chair of the committee and devoted uncounted hours to the project. Others whose arguments in various venues advanced my learning and understanding of the project include Randy Barnett, Brian Barry, Ann Bartow, Gary Becker, Emily Budziak, Paul Bullen, Guido Calabresi, Martha Chamallas, Tom Christiano, John Christman, James Coleman, Ingrid Creppel, Patrick Croskery, John Deigh, Robert Ellickson, Jon Elster, Heidi Feldman, Mark Geistfeld, Steve Gilles, Walter Grinder, Jim Johnson, Greg Keating, Jack Knight, Bill Landes, Tony Kronman, Mark Lemley, Leonard Luggio, Richard McAdams, Tom Palmer, Stephen Perry, Eric Posner, Richard Posner, Adam Pritchard, Tony Sebok, Ed Sherline, Ken Simons, Cass Sunstein, and Ben Zipursky. Vaious colleagues have read parts and in many cases all of prior drafts of the book and have shared their comments. These include Mark Brandon, Lisa Bressman, Jon Bruce, Barry Friedman, John Goldberg, Erin O'Hara, David Partlett, Bob Rasmussen, Suzanna Sherry, Kent Syverud, Randall Thomas, Bob Thompson, Don Welch, Christopher Yoo, and Nick Zeppos. Many students at Vanderbilt Law School served ably as research assistants. These students are Robert Brewer, Derek Edwards, Kimberly Gilman,

Catherine Hora, Aaron Kamlay, Mark Plotkin, Linda Potapova, Ryan Raforth, Tatjana Stoljarova, Beth Thomas, Angela Vitale, and Phillip Young. Invaluable assistance also came from librarians and staff, including Alycia Buford, Martin Cerjan, Janet Hirt, Stephen Jordan, Kathleen Kennedy-Jones, Abigail Larimer, Emily Urban, and Kelley Walker.

Finally, this book would not have been completed without the continued and unflagging guidance and inspiration of Jules Coleman.

Introduction

Social order may be regulated from above by the law, but its foundation is built on norms and customs which combat social disarray, allowing people to make meaningful and productive uses of their time and resources. The law's ability to promote a just social order can never be fully understood without taking account of the concurrent influence of these informal social practices. In spite of this, much jurisprudential writing has been devoid of sustained discussion of norms and customs, focusing instead on individuals and governments. Individuals are thought to be the locus of moral responsibility and rational decision making, while governments are thought to be the source of legal obligations that form the institutional backdrop against which moral and rational behavior occur. In concentrating on the small individual below and the vast, looming state above, those mid-sized objects of the social world – norms and customs – have been neglected.[1]

Recently, legal theorists have begun to pay attention to social norms.[2] The new legal literature draws on important work emanating from the social sciences as well as from moral and political philosophy, evolutionary biology, and anthropology.[3] Nearly all the new work by legal scholars utilizes rational choice methodology. This book also presents an analysis in the rational choice tradition albeit one that incorporates moral theory into the analysis as well. One of the underlying themes in this book is the compatibility of rational and moral analysis.

The present work seeks an equilibrium between theory and legal application.[4] Part One develops a philosophical conception of norms, which is then put to the test by applying it to tort law, first at an intermediate level of analysis in Part Two and then at a micro level of analysis in Part Three.[5]

Part One develops what will be called the *pattern conception* of social norms. First, I argue that the traditional conception of norms as rulelike linguistic entities is faulty. Instead, norms must be understood as patterns of rationally governed behavior maintained in groups by acts of conformity. Even though rules understood as linguistic entities still play a role in the pattern conception, patterned, conformative behavior is the essence of a norm.

Informal game theory, which characterizes human behavior in terms of strategic relationships between pairs or groups of people, will be utilized in the analysis of norms and customs. Peoples' patterns of behavior are modeled as *iterated games* among *players*. By showing how these players might rationally conform to certain practices, informal game-theoretic models offer a mechanism for explaining how these practices may be maintained over time. This is significant as plausible mechanisms of this sort are in short supply in social science and social theory.[6]

Structurally speaking, social norms are either strategic or nonstrategic. I divide strategic norms into two groups: those consisting of patterns of behavior maintained by sanctions and those consisting of patterns of behavior maintained without sanctions. The former are *sanction-driven norms* and the latter are *coordination norms*.

The sanction-driven norm is a broader structure than the Prisoner's Dilemma or collective action norm. The collective action problem is considered by some to represent one of the fundamental paradoxes of rationality.[7] The paradox is thought to reside in the fact that there is a divergence between individual and collective rationality; the collective of individuals will each do better if all contribute toward the production of certain important collective goods such as lighthouses, military defense, and roads, than if no one does, and yet for each individual it is rational to defect from cooperation. Individual defection is a *dominant strategy*, that is, each does better by not cooperating, regardless of the choice made by others. Consequently, a rational actor will attempt to *free ride* on the efforts of others. But because each has this preference, all will free ride, and the collective good will not be produced. The focus here is not on collective goods that are physical objects such as lighthouses but rather on norms and customs. Norms and customs are not goods in the usual sense; nevertheless, their provision may constitute a collective action problem.

Sanction-driven norms may solve collective action problems. They may solve a wider array of problems as well, such as the game of Chicken, or Ellickson's Specialized Labor Game.[8]

Norms scholars in the legal academy have shown a particular interest in sanction-driven norms, though not under that rubric. Ellickson provides an account of how close-knit groups can develop efficient norms resulting from the mutual sanctioning that is made possible by the repeated and overlapping interactions among members of a close-knit group. Richard McAdams develops an esteem-based account of sanctioning. Esteem sanctions are essentially free and are thus capable of solving the second-order collective action problem that is widely understood to arise with respect to the use of sanctions to solve a first-order collective action problem. Eric Posner argues that norms help solve iterated collective action problems by allowing people with low discount rates to identify one another by means of signaling. What these accounts have in common under the theory of norms that will be developed in Part One is that each description of the process of norm emergence or maintenance integrally involves sanctions, and so the resulting norm is a sanction-driven norm.

In turn, the coordination norm is a broader structure than the convention. According to David Lewis, conventions have the strategic structure of *proper coordination equilibria* because everyone benefits from participating, and everyone benefits still more from the participation of others.[9] The first feature, Lewis suggests, explains why conventions are self-maintaining. The second explains why conventions become norms. Lewis claims to capture the idea of conventions as first discussed at length by Hume. I will argue, however, that Hume's fundamental insight about the deeply conventional structure of social institutions should be formalized in a more complex manner than Lewis suggests. On my account, proper coordination equilibria are but a subset of *coordination norms*. Coordination norms are patterns of behavior made up of act-types performed to achieve a *coordination benefit*. A coordination norm – though not a proper coordination equilibrium, a coordination equilibrium, or even an equilibrium – may be maintained.

I also postulate a third category of norms, *epistemic norms*, which are best understood in terms of informational economy rather than in strategic terms. People often conform for epistemic reasons, that is, they conform to a preexistent social practice, rather than expending the effort to gather new information, in order to economize on the cost of information.[10] Other theories have not incorporated strategic and nonstrategic norms into a single account. This approach will be defended against leading norms accounts, such as those of David Lewis, Edna Ullmann-Margalit, Robert Ellickson, Richard McAdams, and Eric Posner.[11]

A fundamental if implicit tenet of much social theory is that conformity to prominent social customs substantially explains human conduct; *Homo sociologicus* is a conforming animal.[12] The notion of conformity scarcely makes an appearance in the work of rational choice theorists.[13] The instinct of these theorists is to view conformity as suspect. The appeal of the rational choice approach is substantially diminished, however, if it cannot be shown to be compatible with the supposition of widespread conformity to norms, as conformity is a fairly straightforward social phenomenon. To paraphrase the epigram from Francis Bacon that begins Part One, while people may have a variety of diverse thoughts running through their heads, the lion's share of their behavior is best explained by reference to reigning norms and customs. The pattern conception of social norms reconciles rational choice with conformative behavior. In other words, *Homo economicus* is also shown to be a conforming animal.

In addition, the pattern conception integrates moral motivation into the rational choice model of norms. Many moral theorists and sociologists have rejected the rational choice approach outright because they have assumed that once moral motivation is postulated, the rational choice framework loses coherence. At root, people are either moral or egoistic, but the twain shall never meet.

In fact, however, in ordinary morality, it is permissible to behave over a wide range of activities in a self-regarding manner. There is then a significant overlap between self-interested behavior and moral behavior. In addition, I will argue that norms, once they are up and running, may generate a variety of moral obligations and other moral relationships, depending on the type of norm at issue, and the moral commitments of the participants.

To the extent that they look at morality at all, rational choice theorists uniformly focus on consequentialist motivation.[14] Rational actors seek to maximize; their utility functions just happen to include the interests of others. An exclusive focus of consequentialist tendencies leads, however, to a cramped conception of moral behavior. By contrast, the theory developed here allows deontological, virtue-theoretic, and everyday moral motivation into the model of norm functioning, along side consequentialist motivation. This assumption has the virtue of realism.

Along with rational choice theorists, moral theorists have neglected to acknowledge the importance of conformity in the lives of ordinary people, for whom Kantian, Aristotelian, or utilitarian reflection is rare, while conformity to dominant moral practices is pervasive. The result is a sterile conception of morality with only a glancing connection to the complex normative texture of most people's lives. The notion of conformity has played almost no role in traditional moral theory. Conformity is suspect. One might easily suppose that conformers are not moral at all; they are merely conforming. The fundamental question then is whether moral actors can consistently conform to norms. If conformity is central to norms, and if norms are to be maintained by moral individuals, conformity must be acceptable to the moral individual.

I will argue that norm conformity, properly construed, is antithetical neither to ordinary morality nor to most critical moral theories. I will make this argument for the first best world from the perspective of the critical theorist, which is the world in which the population of actors share her moral outlook, and for the second best world, the real world, in which the moral actor comes in constant contact with heterogeneous norms constituted of conforming actions by people who represent a variety of moral and nonmoral outlooks.

The moral analysis leads to a typology of norms that parallels the one that emerges from the study of rational norms. There are three basic types: coordination moral norms, saction-driven moral norms, and epistemic moral norms. This parallel structure demonstrates unity of the normative.

Chapter One defends the pattern conception against the dominant *rule conception*. Because norms and customs are behavioral patterns rather than linguistic rules, they have rational structures rather than grammatical structures. Chapter Two develops an account of these structures based on a Hobbesian assumption of narrow self-interest.[15] Chapter Three maintains this motivational assumption but examines the various norm structures from the normative perspective of utilitarian moral theory. Chapter Four then develops an account based on a broader Humean conception of rationality, one that is consistent with the existence of genuinely moral motivation.[16] This position is called *predominant egoism*.[17] On this motivational assumption, genuinely moral norms may emerge as a result of norm conformity. Finally, Chapter Five examines the potential for norm maintenance based on the motivational assumptions of leading critical moral-theoretic approaches.

In combination, the chapters of Part One will seek to set out an account of norms that unifies rational actor and moral theoretic truths into a coherent whole. The goal is not to defend one particular set of normative assumptions over others. Quite the opposite, the goal is to develop a conception of norms and customs that is not dependent on any particular set of normative assumptions, either assumptions regarding the normative motivations of the actors or assumptions regarding the critical normative goals of the overall system. In Part One, I develop a theory of norms and customs, and in the remainder of the book I test the theory by plugging it into substantive legal debates. If the theory is a good one, it should work well in these applied contexts, serving to illuminate important applied areas of the law. Alternatively, if the account contains wrinkles that need to be ironed out, or is fundamentally wrongheaded beyond repair, these facts should become apparent once we have the opportunity to see the theory in action.

A number of scholars have drawn attention to dysfunctional properties of norms.[18] In Parts Two and Three, the legal norms I examine will be seen to display some significant dysfunctional characteristics. In Part Two, I explore the manner by which norms of significance to tort law, that is, norms that revolve around injury-producing behavior, may emerge and be maintained, despite possessing significantly dangerous characteristics. Part Three looks at a different sort of dysfunctionality, norms that allow for websites to falsely signal respect for user informational privacy, thereby fooling consumers.

Part Two will apply the pattern conception to tort law. Two connected issues will be examined: the proper role for custom in determining negligence, and, the role of the jury in injecting its norms into substantive applications of the reasonable person test. These are the two most significant roles played by custom in tort law.

In this epoch of accelerating change, it might be thought that custom was no longer capable of playing a prominent role in the maintenance of a safe social order, for how can customary practices evolve quickly enough to keep pace with the rapid changes that characterize modern society. In law in particular, it might seem that traditional, informal solutions should be rejected in favor of more rationalized and centralized means of affecting social order.

Just this sort of rejection of the dead hand of the past seems to be the lesson at the heart of the best-known tort case dealing with the rule of custom, *The T. J. Hooper*. In this case, Judge Learned Hand famously observed that industry customs may lag behind what is required by due care.[19] The fact that tug boat operators customarily did not use radios was not legally dispositive of the issue of negligence, as the whole tug boat industry may have negligently failed to adopt the use of radios as a means of avoiding storm loss. In other words, custom may be evidence as to the proper standard of care, but it is not the standard itself.[20] This standard must be independently ascertained by rational evaluation of all the competing interests involved. Hand seems clearly to be throwing off the yoke of the past as a sure guide to future conduct. Instead, the course of the law's development must be opened to rational appraisal if society is to prevail over the blind prejudices of the past.

It turns out, however, that custom runs deeper in tort law than is suggested by the rendition of Hand just alluded to. While the role of custom in tort has not diminished, it has changed. Part Two begins in Chapter Six with a look at the historical and jurisprudential underpinnings of the rule of custom. The shifting relationship between custom and law is first examined. At one time, certain customs were law itself – customary law. Custom no longer has this exalted status; nevertheless, customs may serve as sources of law. Chapter Six examines the historically important example of customary easements in land. Looking at the strategic structures of some prominent examples of customary land usages, we will see that the norms motivating the courts' decisions regarding these usages appear to be a mixture of consequentialist and nonconsequentialist impulses. In particular, in certain sorts of situations involving induced detrimental reliance on the part of customary users of land, courts have been inclined to find customary easements. The role of custom in this instance is striking; what would otherwise be a tortuous trespass instead becomes a use by right.

Chapters Seven through Nine explore the development of the modern *rule of custom*. The rule of custom has played a venerable role in tort doctrine. Modern tort law mainly follows the negligence standard according to which one will be found liable only if one acted negligently in causing an injury. Negligence is the failure to exhibit due care or ordinary care. Leading early cases established the connection between "ordinary" behavior and "customary behavior."[21] Ordinary behavior is simply customary behavior. Courts look to whether an injurious action conformed to an accepted custom or social norm in determining whether an action was negligent. Injurers attempt to establish their conformity to custom as evidence of due care while victims attempt to establish the injurer's failure to conform as evidence of negligence.

Leading decisions by Holmes and Hand expanded the role of custom by holding that custom may not only be dispositive regarding the question of negligence but also convey less powerful yet relevant *evidence* regarding negligence.[22] This finding in effect expanded the options of courts to apply the rule of custom in a more nuanced fashion. Modern tort law has alternatively endorsed two main rules of custom, which I label the *per se* and the *evidentiary* rules. The introductory doctrinal discussion in Chapter Seven focuses on the manner in which the older per se rule, whereby conformity to custom established the fact of due care, was replaced by an evidentiary rule, which holds that conformity may be evidence of, but is not dispositive of, due care.

Understanding why the evidentiary rule won out will be helpful in gaining a larger perspective on the relationship between custom and tort, as an adequate account of why courts have gravitated toward the evidentiary rule has remained elusive. Chapter Seven considers two initially plausible candidates. The first, developed in the classic article, *Custom and Negligence*, by Clarence Morris, argues that juries will be less biased against defendants in their deliberations when they are made to appreciate that the defendant's injurious behavior conforms to widespread industry practices.[23] The second account is the traditional, positive economic account of Landes and Posner, which predicts that the per se rule will be found in situations in which there is actual or potential bargaining between the parties, but not otherwise.[24] When parties are able to bargain, they will be able to reach welfare-maximizing agreements on their own, and these agreements will be represented in customary practices. Accordingly, courts should insulate the practices by means of the per se rule.

I will argue that each of these accounts fails to explain the emergence of the evidentiary rule as the dominant modern rule. Morris' account fails to explain why there may be genuine reasons that conformity to custom has epistemic value with regard to the issue of negligence, once concerns regarding jury bias have been factored in. Landes and Posner's account wrongly predicts that the per se rule will prevail in bargaining contexts. I will demonstrate that the evidentiary rule is the dominant modern rule in both bargaining and non-bargaining contexts. Moreover, Landes and Posner's account does not explain the main exception to the modern rule of custom, which applies the per se rule to the injuries caused by physicians and other professionals, despite the fact that they are neither more nor less likely than nonprofessionals to engage in the sort of bargaining discussed by Landes and Posner. By contrast, I will offer an explanation for this phenomena that draws on the important rational structure of tort law. I will argue that the norms of physicians and other professionals are often given strong deference, due to the *superior epistemic warrant* possessed by those knowledgeable in a field requiring expert training. In other words, my account relies on the supposition that certain important norms of professionals have epistemic structures.

In the process of evaluating Landes and Posner's account, it will become apparent that informal game theory helps to provide a better explanation of negligence law's use of social custom. On the account that I will set out, there are four relevant modalities of the rule of custom. The per se rule may be justified when the custom at issue is thought to be efficient, as this rule will protect the conforming action from going to the jury where the injurer might be found to be negligent. The evidentiary rule will make more sense when the custom at issue is not optimal but welfare-enhancing nevertheless, as this rule encourages juries to give deference to the custom, while at the same time allowing the jury to find negligence if a superior custom appears attainable. The evidentiary rule may take a weak form under which conformity is evidence of due care or a strong form under which conformity serves as a rebuttable presumption of due care. Finally, the rule that accords conformity no priority may be suitable if the custom at issue is either neutral or detrimental to the production of welfare.

The goal will be to determine the efficiency conditions for the sorts of norms and customs that matter to tort law. This task is complex for not only are there four versions of the rule of custom, but there are also three different rational structures of customs to which these versions may apply. Practically all previous applications of informal game theory to law have focused on the Prisoner's Dilemma (PD) or collective action problem.[25] One would naturally suppose that tort law would take an interest in PD-structured customs because tort law is concerned with injuries, and many PD customs present a situation in which a person is repeatedly in a position to cause injury to others, either by failing to conform to a safe PD custom or by conforming to a dangerous PD custom. While PD customs, and sanction-driven customs more generally, are indeed of great interest, the examples I consider will demonstrate that epistemic customs and coordination customs may also be important sources of injuries and so are equally of concern to tort law.

In order to determine whether a custom in a particular case is efficient, courts will need to know which type of custom is involved, as different sets of *welfare-maximization markers* apply to each of the three types of custom. Factors such as whether the incidence of injury falls on conformers or third parties, whether either or both of these groups are close-knit, whether the conformer has superior epistemic warrant, whether the Kaldor-Hicks test favors conformers, and whether an optimizing alternative practice is available matter differentially depending on the type of custom at issue.

Combining various possible rules of custom, various possible rational structures of custom, and the various welfare markers, thirty-seven distinct modalities of tort custom will be identified in Chapter Nine. The development of this schema calls into doubt the basic justification of the dominance accorded to the evidentiary rule by Holmes, Hand, and their modern followers. After all, only eight of the thirty-seven applications of the rule of custom call for the evidentiary rule. The per se rule is preferable for nineteen of the situations; the no-priority rule, for ten of the situations; and the presumption-shifting rule, for eight of the situations.

The conclusion will be irresistable, then, that welfare-maximizing courts will need to pay attention to a number of features of customs, and not simply whether there was a bargaining situation between the parties or a sanctioning situation surrounding the parties. In general, courts have not demonstrated a sophisticated understanding of the relevant complexities of customs. Although courts have to some extent accorded different legal treatment to some of the different types of custom, to all appearances they have done so by means of an intuitive methodology that fails to articulate explicitly the rationale for applying particular rules to particular structures.

The analysis in Chapters Seven through Nine labors under the assumption that courts are intent to maximize welfare in their decisions regarding the choice of the particular version of the rule of custom to apply in particular cases. Notice that this assumption is neutral regarding the motivations of the various other actors besides the judges. The lay members of the community may all be narrowly self-interested utility maximizers, they may be predominant egoists, or they may exhibit some other species of motivation entirely. The last two chapters of Part Two will develop a more substantive account with regard to the motivations of at least some of the participants other than judges, namely, the jurors. I will argue that jurors, and their norms and customs, play a crucial yet generally underappreciated role in negligence law, at least as judged by the two dominant accounts, the economic account and the corrective justice account.

The power of either litigant to request a jury is both a practically universal and a practically unique feature of American tort law. Despite the fact that most cases settle, the prospect of a case going to trial is always in the background, influencing litigation tactics, expected outcomes, and therefore settlement negotiations.[26] In Chapter Ten, I develop a five-stage account of the jury's role in a tort suit that makes its way through trial. I will argue that the practice of tort law gives the informal social norms of jurors an essential role in constituting the actual substance of the negligence standard. As a causal matter, it is this de facto standard, serving as an instantiation of the abstractly formulated formal standard promulgated by the judge via the jury instructions, that determines the final outcome in tort suits.

Because the de facto standard plays an essential role in the outcome of tort litigation, any entitlement created by the litigation is causally influenced in its creation from below by juror norms, as well as from above by the jury instructions conveying the formal liability standard. The bottom/up component of this bidirectional causal process will be referred to as the *jury norm effect*. Chapter Ten will provide an account of the particular substantive normative forces that are typically unleashed by means of the jury norm effect. These forces will be seen to include everyday analogs of strict liability and direct causation, comparative negligence and redistribution. In their efforts to provide a unified normative account, the dominant paradigms fail to notice these sui generis normative forces that fill out the substantive content of negligence determinations.

Given the jury's important role in the actual practice of tort law, there is a puzzle; why is so little attention paid to the jury in the dominant accounts of negligence? I will argue that the answer to this question is that these accounts exhibit a bias that in another context Robert Ellickson has labeled "legal centralism."[27] Legal centralists wrongly focus on top/down formal explanations of the source of liability entitlements at the expense of bottom/up explanations that would take account of the casual impacts of informal social norms, such as those that might flow from the deliberations of juries.

Chapter Eleven will look in greater detail at the dominant accounts of tort – the economic account and the corrective justice account – and the means by which each fails to pay proper attention to the important role played by juror norms. The economic conception receives its fullest expression in the *Restatement* (Third) of Torts.[28] The *Restatement* only countenances a role for social norms in the special situation in which there is an instantiated custom in place, such that either the defendant pleads conformity as a defense or the plaintiff seeks to demonstrate lack of conformity as evidence of negligence. What is missing is any acknowledgment of the prevasive role that social norms play in providing grist for the jury's concrete application of the reasonable person standard. This process may occur not only in situations in which custom is explicitly introduced as evidence by one of the parties, but in all situations in which lay juries deliberate.

The *Restatement*'s account is misguided, apparently due to its legal centralism, which leads the restaters to assume, largely without argument, the dominant causal efficacy of the Hand Test interpretation of the reasonable person standard on the deliberations of juries, and hence on the outcomes of negligence suits. Based on the analysis and empirical evidence examined in Chapter Ten, I will argue to the contrary that there is every reason to suppose that jurors do not engage in Hand Test analysis but instead draw from their heterogeneous array of everyday norms and customs when providing concrete substance to the abstract reasonable person standard in order to come to a decision on the issue of negligence. This discussion will conclude with an examination of an innovative attempt by Stephen Gilles to insulate the dominant conception from the line of criticism I offer. Gilles argues that, properly understood, the Hand Test actually involves a morally attractive Hand Norm that will tend to be expressed as a result of factor balancing by juries. Despite the attractiveness of this *First Restatement* approach as compared to the *Restatement* approach, it will in the end be rejected as well.

Next, Chapter Eleven will examine the corrective justice approach to negligence, focusing on Jules Coleman's influential account. Coleman sets out to provide a pragmatic explanation of tort law that is sensitive to the two-party structure of litigation and the justice concerns raised by one party's injury of the other party. The jury plays no role in Coleman's account. It thus remains to be explained why real-world juries would promote solely or mainly corrective justice norms.

I will conclude that there is a need for a new negligence account that accords the jury conceptual space commensurate with its role in the actual legal institution of tort law as practiced in America. The jury norm effect allows the norms of ordinary people to exert a direct causal effect over formal, legal outcomes. From the perspective of democratic theory, this is an anti-elitist, liberal feature of American tort law, which distinguishes it from its counterparts abroad.[29] According to one core tenet of pragmatist jurisprudence, important legal practices should be analyzed in order to uncover the normative principles embodied in the practices.[30] Tort jury practices arguably embody important liberal principles of political participation, value pluralism, and separation of powers.[31] In its focus on welfarist concerns or justice between the litigants, the dominant accounts fail to countenance these important values embodied in American tort law.

As noted, law and norms theory is developed in the book at three levels; pure theory, intermediate-level, and micro-level analysis. Part Three takes the analysis down to a micro level, looking at the specific issue of the formal and informal regulation of online personal data collection. Because this is one of the most pressing contemporary public policy concerns, it poses a serious challenge to the theory of law and norms.

Norms and customs are patterns of behavior. Patterns of behavior have traditionally existed in physical space. With the creation and ongoing construction of cyberspace, an increasingly rich new world is coming into being. Physical space plus cyberspace equals a wired world – and, increasingly, an unwired world as well – in which manifold social norms will emerge in the future. Injuries will increasingly occur in this world. The most significant type of injury to emerge thus far is injury to one's interest in personal data privacy. Incursions on one's online privacy do not currently rise to the level of a tort. This will likely change over time, either because of increasingly intrusive activities or because sensibilities change. The paucity of formal regulation of online personal data collection has been conducive to the emergence of informal online norms to regulate this activity. Part Three studies the emergence of these norms.

Over the past few years, the norms governing personal data interactions between consumers and certain websites have changed significantly, albeit unevenly. There is an increasing moral sensitivity on the part of many websites regarding the commercial collection and use of personal data. In general, the *social meaning* of personal data collection has changed from a morally neutral to a morally charged status.[32] Consumers now perceive a general right to privacy in cyberspace that includes respectful treatment of personal data.[33] This change arose not by accident or necessity, but from the intentional behavior of actors possessing an interest in promoting online privacy. Some of these actors seek to maximize their own welfare, and consumer privacy is merely a means to this end, while other actors appear to have genuine moral regard for the data privacy of others. The former are *privacy norm entrepreneurs*. I will designate the latter actors as *privacy norm proselytizers*.[34] For reasons they themselves accept, privacy norm proselytizers seek to arouse the moral consciousness of consumers vis-à-vis websites' collection and use of their personal data.[35]

In Part Three, I develop a supply and demand model of the emergence of website privacy norms. Chapter Twelve first examines the industry's initial efforts at self-regulation. These efforts, by and large, failed. Self-regulation failed at first because of the strategic structure of the relationship between consumers and websites on the one hand, and websites with one another, on the other hand. Specifically, websites are in a coordination game with one another, not an iterated collective action problem. Efforts to educate websites on the importance of privacy to consumers, and on the connection between allaying consumer privacy fears and the promotion of consumer confidence, did not work to change website behavior in the manner desired by the FTC. Nor will consumers be able to band together to demand more respectful privacy practices on the part of websites owing to the large-scale collective action problem they face in organizing their efforts. A number of commentators concluded that the failure of self-regulation mandated that the government step in and take a more direct role in requiring respectful informational practices on the part of websites. As the discussion in Chapters Thirteen and Fourteen will indicate, however, little direct government regulation of website practices has occurred thus far. Nevertheless, norms between websites and consumers have emerged. Some sites have begun genuine efforts to provide respect for user privacy, but many more sites have changed nothing, or worse, simulated respect in a cynical effort to get something for nothing.

Chapter Thirteen develops the demand side analysis. The chapter looks at how privacy norm proselytizers changed the social meaning of data collection through education, legislative efforts, and attempts to change consumers' moral outlook on the practices of websites. The set of concepts that increasingly surround the practice in popular discourse is evidence that consumers are developing a more complex normative understanding. Notably, interactions between websites and their visitors are now frequently framed in terms of privacy. Not long ago, the concept of informational privacy did not exist in either popular discourse or the moral theory lexicon, but increasingly, a consumer's entitlement to control her personal data is generally recognized. In economic terms, these events can be viewed as an increase in the demand for personal data privacy. The increase in demand in turn has led to an increase in supply, which will be the topic of Chapter Fourteen.

As consumers increasingly perceive an entitlement, there is a corresponding tendency for them to feel moral outrage at websites that fail to respect data privacy. Consumers who feel that they are disrespected may seek to punish websites by taking their business elsewhere, reciprocating the disrespect by providing the website with false personal information,[36] or sanctioning the website through negative gossip.[37] Because of this pressure, numerous websites have been inclined to increase the supply of respectful privacy treatment. I will utilize the account of rational norms developed in Part One of the book to model these interactions between websites and consumers. What we find is a strategic interaction of respect and trust, in which websites may be interested in exchanging respectful treatment toward consumers for trust on the part of these consumers.[38]

While some websites have begun to cooperate, as already noted, the vast majority of websites have to date displayed no genuine regard for the privacy interests of users. This raises an interesting question; why has a substantial increase in demand not created a substantial increase in supply? In answer to this question, I will argue in Chapter Fourteen that the simulation of respect is plausibly in the narrow self-interest of many sites, as compared to their provision of genuine respect.

Chapter Fourteen will explore two accounts as to why many websites might think it was sensible to simulate respect rather than provide the real thing. These accounts are derived as applications of two of the theories of norms explored in Part One. On Eric Posner's theory, as already noted, norms are sets of individual signaling acts, each of which is meant to communicate that the signaler has a low discount rate and so is a good type with whom to enter into cooperative relationships. On my theory, norms are patterns of rationally motivated conforming behavior. Each of these conceptions of a norm provides a distinct explanation of the dubious quality of most extant website privacy norms. Posner's signaling model would hold that websites are signaling their cooperative type but that all actual cooperation will occur in the future. On my theory, depending on the sorts of strategic considerations outlined in Part One, many websites are best viewed as already engaging in the cooperative activity of providing genuine respect for user privacy in exchange for trust on the part of their users. Thus, Posner's account fails to explain the emergence of these norms. Nor can McAdams's esteem-based emergence account provide an explanation, as websites are companies, not people, and it would appear that they would not value esteem. Last, the online personal data collection environment is not plausibly characterized as close-knit, and so Ellickson's account will not provide insight into the emergence of the new data collection norms.

Finally, after the conclusion of the analysis in Part Three, the book's conclusion will seek to provide an overall evaluation of the book's effort to develop the pattern conception of norms and customs and then test the theory's mettle by applying it to tort law and informational privacy law. I will conclude that the overall effect of these applications is to indicate that the conception of norms as patterns of behavior makes the most sense of the role that norms and customs have played in these important areas of the law. This is evidence that the pattern conception is the best conception of norms and customs.

PART ONE

THE PATTERN CONCEPTION
OF NORMS

Men's thoughts are much according to their inclinations; their discourse and speeches according to their learning and infused opinions; but their deeds are after as they have been accustomed.[†]

Francis Bacon

[†] Quoted in CARLETON KEMP ALLEN, *Law in the Making* 64 (6th ed. 1958) (1927).

1

Rule Conception Versus Pattern Conception

Practice has introduced rules rather than rules have directed practice.[1]

Samuel Johnson

Introduction

In part due to the diversity of disciplinary approaches to the topic of norms, a number of definitions of the term *norm* circulate. This first chapter will defend what I will call the *pattern conception* of a norm. On this view, a norm is a *pattern of rationally governed behavior, instantiated in a group, maintained by acts of conformity*. In contrast, on the dominant conception, norms are inherently rulelike, that is, norms are statements that individuals and groups generate and promulgate to guide their conduct. I will refer to this as the *rule conception* or *rule view*. This chapter will argue that the rule conception is deficient and, in the end, beyond repair.

Because norms and customs are behavioral patterns and not linguistic rules, they have rational structures rather than grammatical structures. The next two chapters develop an account of these structures based on a Hobbesian assumption of narrow self-interest. Subsequently, Chapter Four develops an account based on a broader Humean conception of rationality, one that is consistent with the existence of genuinely moral motivation. This position is called *predominant egoism*. On this motivational assumption, moral norms may emerge as a result of norm conformity.

Finally, Chapter Five will examine the potential for norm maintenance based on the motivational assumptions of leading critical moral-theoretic approaches. In this manner, the chapters of Part One will successively layer moral theory on top of rational theory, going from the purely rational to the purely moral.

I. The Received View: Norms as Rules

The rule conception will first be stated in outline form; then representative passages from the scholarly literature that support the various tenets of the account will be examined. Next, the intuitive plausibility of this account will be considered. Finally, the rule conception will be argued to be faulty, despite its initial plausibility.

The account developed here will not attempt to provide the necessary and sufficient conditions for a norm based on the rule conception. Nor will the account necessarily coincide exactly with the views of any one rule theorist. Instead, the following analysis will seek to capture the characteristics found most broadly in the literature regarding norms. These various elements will then be combined into a hybrid account. This is a desirable approach as there is currently no canonical definition of the term *norm* in either the social scientific or philosophical literature. Subsequently this hybrid account will be attacked and then replaced by the pattern conception.

In this first section, the five major tenets of the rule view will be discussed; then, two tenets, which are subsidiary to the first five, will be added.

A. The Rule Conception

TENETS OF THE RULE CONCEPTION OF NORMS

1. Norms are linguistic or verbal entities capable of being called up as occurrent or spoken thought.
2. Norms are prescriptive.
3. Norms are normative.
4. Norms are shared.
5. Norm obedience is maintained through sanctions.

The first tenet specifies that norms are linguistic or verbal entities that may manifest as occurrent or spoken thought. The notion of *occurrent thought* may be understood as thought that occurs as a verbal string of words, internally rather than externally. For example, if one recites the lyrics to a song in one's head without moving one's vocal chords, one is experiencing the song as occurrent thought. On the rule view, people experience, or are capable of experiencing, as occurrent thought the norms to which they contemplate allegiance.

The rule conception fits with one of Western thought's central orthodoxies, namely, that people willfully choose the actions they take. A free act of acceptance is, after all, one that is deliberated consciously. In order to consciously accept a norm, one must, to invoke a common metaphor, hold the norm before the mind's eye and then make a decision as to whether the underlying practice is worth following.[2] Conforming to norms may become routine in that the process of conscious reflection may be circumvented; nevertheless, this highly intentional model is the paradigm case on the rule account.[3]

The second and third tenets of the rule conception are that norms are prescriptive and that norms are normative. These two tenets are best discussed together.

Although the concepts of prescriptivity and normativity are often used in an overlapping manner, it will help to better understand the rule conception if these notions are kept separate. Though not acknowledging this distinction as such, rule theorists typically take norms to be both prescriptive and normative.

The act of prescribing simply involves one person telling another how to behave with the intention of thereby influencing her behavior. On this view, prescriptive language has an inherently rhetorical or persuasive function.[4] It need not have a normative function, however. Usually, one only prescribes behavior that one believes is rational or moral, either for oneself or for the person to whom one is prescribing. This need not be the case however.

If one thinks a certain type of behavior ought to be performed, it is sensible to tell others to perform it, that is, to prescribe the behavior. But in principle, one can tell others to behave in a manner that one does not think is either rational or moral, and one can think others ought to act in a certain manner without telling them that they should do so. Thus, prescriptivity does not entail normativity, and vice versa.

The normativity tenet holds that norms are statements describing behavior of a certain sort, namely, behavior that *ought* to be performed. This conception is neutral between various kinds of oughts, although the ought of rationality and the ought of morality are the concern of the present work. The same idea may be expressed by means of the notion of acceptance of a norm. When one accepts a norm, one thinks it ought to be acted on.

The fourth tenet of the rule conception is that norms are shared. This simply means that the rules are accepted not merely by individuals but rather by groups of individuals. Even though the rule must be shared or common to the group, it is not necessary that it be acted on in order to count as a norm. It is enough that the rule be shared in the sense that the members think it ought to be acted on.

The fifth and final of the major tenets of the rule conception is that norms involve sanctions. Sanctions may be positive or negative, that is, agents may be rewarded for conforming to norms or penalized for not conforming. A distinction is commonly drawn between *informal* and *formal sanctions*. Informal sanctions include verbal admonishments, exclusion from groups, and damage to reputation. Formal sanctions include fines and imprisonment. Different rule theorists place different weight on the role of sanctions. For some, it is because of sanctions that people conform to norms, while sanctions play a secondary role on other accounts. Those who think that sanctions are always necessary conceive of norm following as inherently onerous. Other theorists recognize, however, that some norms are conformed to, apart from the existence or efficiency of sanctions.

The following two tenets are implied by the five main tenets.

6. Norm acceptance occurs through transmission of the verbal rule.
7. It is unproblematic to detect which norms are accepted.

Tenet Six falls out easily from the preceding characterization of the rule conception. Because norms are linguistic entities, they may be spread through a population simply by stating them, either in spoken or written form. Others may be inclined to adopt the behavior described by the rule, either out of the relevant normative considerations or to avoid the sanctions that will often accompany the prescription.

Tenet Seven, which states that norms are detected unproblematically, is generally not discussed by rule theorists as such. But they write as if it is the case. One sees easily why rule theorists should think that norms are detected unproblematically. Norms are simple in nature, as witnessed by the fact that they are able to be examined occurrently or expressed to others. Thus, detecting them in particular situations should pose no problems. One simply listens to what prescriptions are uttered, or looks to the regularities of behavior, and infers which rules condone such behavior.

The next part will take a concentrated look at representative passages from important rule theorists to test the accuracy of the preceding characterization.

B. Defenders of the Rule Conception

Max Weber, one of early modernity's most prescient social theorists, defines the validity of a norm in terms of whether it is followed by a sufficient number of people. Implicit in this conception is the notion that a norm that does not have sufficient support is not valid, but is a norm nonetheless. Thus for Weber, behavior is not necessary for the definition of a norm. The norm is the linguistic entity contemplated by the members of the group, who may or may not enshrine it as valid by means of their collective behavior.[5]

Talcott Parsons, Weber's most-noted American follower, explicitly defines a norm as a linguistic entity. He writes: "A norm is a verbal description of a concrete course of action . . . regarded as desirable, combined with an injunction to make certain future actions conform to this course."[6] Parsons's short definition contains three of the five major tenets of the rule conception. Norms are seen as "verbal," which captures the occurrent linguistic tenet; norms are regarded as "desirable," which captures the normativity tenet; and finally, norms are delivered with an "injunction," that is, they are prescribed behavior.

George Homans provides the following characterization. A norm is an "idea in the minds of the members of a group, an idea that can be put in the form of a statement."[7] In Homans's mention of ideas, each capable of being expressed as a "statement," we have a clear expression of the thesis that norms are linguistic entities capable of occurrent expression, for if norms may be stated externally, they may be stated internally. His mention of norms as residing in the "members of a group," captures the fourth tenet, which holds that norms are shared. Elsewhere, Homans claims that norms, "are not behavior itself but what people think behavior ought to be."[8] This is a clear expression of the normativity thesis.

Another clear statement of the rule conception comes from Robin Williams: "Norms . . . are rules of conduct; they specify what should and should not be done by various kinds of social actors in various kinds of situation."[9] This characterization explicitly equates norms with "rules." In addition, by containing a clear expression of the conception of norms as statements telling agents how they ought to behave, it emphasizes the normativity tenet.

Before giving her own conception of a norm, Francesca Cancian says, "norms can be loosely defined as shared conceptions of appropriate or expected action. . . . Most definitions also include the idea that people are rewarded if they conform to norms and are punished if they deviate."[10] This short passage touches on three of the tenets of the rule conception. The notion of "shared conceptions" captures the tenet that holds that norms are shared; the mention of "appropriate or expected behavior" captures the normativity tenet; and the reference to people being "rewarded" or "punished" touches on the sanctions tenet.

The cited volume is an analysis based on Cancian's field studies of Mayan Indians. Her research methodology provides us with insight into her conception of a norm. She sees herself as coming to possess the list of norms held by the Mayan community under study by the method of having individuals list the norms they accept. Implicit in this method is the belief that norms are essentially the statements written down in the course of this procedure. Apparently then, she holds a view of norms consistent with the tenet that states that norms are capable of accessible linguistic expression.

Along with the preceding explicitly definitional remarks about norms, the following writers make comments about norms that support the rule conception. The political theorist, Michael Taylor, writes: "I shall take it that a norm is generally conformed to and is such that nonconformity, when observed, is generally punished."[11] The notion that norms are "generally conformed to" is close to the idea that norms are shared. Taylor's mention of punishment for nonconformity touches on tenet five which holds that norms involve sanctions. Similarly, John Finley Scott defines norms as "patterns of sanctions."[12]

Consider the following characterizations of a norm by philosophers. Allan Gibbard writes, "A norm, we might say, is a linguistically encoded precept."[13] Later, he adds, "By the norm itself, I suggest, we should mean simply a prescription or imperative that gives the rule a sophisticated observer could formulate."[14] Here Gibbard deviates from tenet one slightly, for his view is not that norm following necessarily involves the occurrent consideration of the norm, but just that such an occurrent formulation is possible. He clearly holds to the prescriptivity tenet, however, as witnessed by his mention of a norm as a prescription or imperative.

Edna Ullman-Margalit provides the following "rough characterization" of a social norm: "A social norm is a prescribed guide for conduct or action which is generally complied with by members of a society."[15] This notion of a norm as a "prescribed guide" is roughly an amalgam of the prescriptivity and normativity tenets. Elsewhere, Ullmann-Margalit makes it clear that she has in mind a linguistic conception of the "prescribed guide," which is in line with the first tenet, which holds that norms are verbal in nature. Finally, her mention of general compliance reflects the notion that norms are shared.

Ellickson defines norms as one of the five types of "rules" that make up a system of social control. Rules are categorized based on the source of the "rules of behavior and [the] sanctions that back up those rules."[16] First-party control comes from within the actor and is enforced by self-sanction. Second-party control is exerted by the other party with whom the primary actor is dealing and is enforced by personal self-help. Norms are one example of third-party control. They are enforced by nonhierarchical third-party enforcers.[17] The other sources of third-party control are private organizations and government. Private organizations provide organizational rules and sanctions, while government provides legal rules backed by state enforcement.

Richard McAdams writes, "[B]y norm I mean a decentralized behavioral standard that individuals feel obligated to follow, and generally do follow."[18] McAdams here says norms are standards. A standard is a linguistic entity. Norms are behavioral standards of a certain sort, ones that people feel obligated to follow. McAdams states, "I follow the literature that views norms as obligations."[19] An obligation is not a pattern of behavior or a social regularity. An obligation has an intentional, mental, abstract, or subjective existence. Obligations do not exist physically in the manner that a pattern of behavior does. McAdams's view is that norms are behavioral standards that govern behavior.[20]

The preceding examination demonstrates that there is a good amount of uniformity in the various characterizations of a norm, whether they come from social scientists or philosophers. The key consideration is that norms are essentially like rules; they are prescribed by individuals who believe they and others ought to follow them, and who see fit to sanction those who do not.

C. Intuitive Plausibility of the Rule Conception

The seven tenets of the rule conception taken as a whole present a plausible and intuitively attractive account of norms. To see why this is so, one must keep in mind the role that norms are thought to play in social theory. Generally speaking, social theorists think norms play an important role in explaining how societies are held together, how they maintain continuity over time, and which beliefs they hold most dear. Norms can only plausibly be seen to play this role if they can be undergirded by an account that explains their emergence and maintenance. The rule view is an intuitively plausible model for explaining the emergence and maintenance of norms.

On the rule view, a norm receives its start in life in the following manner. Of all the possible rules, some stand out to particular actors as worthy of allegiance or acceptance. To accept a rule is to think that the behavior prescribed by the rule should occur. In other words, one thinks the rule ought to be acted on, either for rational or moral reasons. Typically, one will think the rule should be acted on by other people in addition to oneself. Thus, it will be natural to try to get others to conform. This is easy – one simply prescribes the rules to others, that is, one utters the rule in their presence in such a manner that it has rhetorical force. Some people will accept the rule because they will see that it ought to govern their behavior. They may also prescribe it to others. Some people will not initially think the rule should direct their behavior but may be persuaded to conform by the presence of sanctions. They may also prescribe the behavior to others, again due to the presence of sanctions. Through such chains of prescriptions and sanctions, acceptance of the rule may spread. Thus, a community may come to share a rule in the sense that most or all of the members accept it internally and prescribe it externally. A shared rule of this sort is a norm.

All people conform to norms to some degree. Many norms are conformed to by individuals beginning at a very early age. Thus, a theory of norms must explain how the process of norm inculcation can be easy enough to be capable of mass participation and early inculcation. The rule account provides a simple and powerful explanation of how this may occur, as even the very young have enough mastery over language to understand simple rules and to be responsive to sanctions.

Perhaps the most significant accomplishment of the rule conception is its ability to explain in a simple and plausible manner the means by which values receive expression in the behavior of social groups. The possession of values by individuals and groups is in general not a well-understood phenomenon. The preceding model demystifies this process. Members of a group accept certain norms, which typically means that the rules are prescribed, taught to newcomers, and acted on, with defections being sanctioned. Norms accepted in this sense are the values of a group or community.

Thus, the rule conception is a very plausible and intuitively attractive account of norms. It is capable of providing answers to many of the key questions that arise for any theory of norms. In spite of the plausibility of the rule conception, a series of arguments for abandoning it will be presented next.

II. Arguments Against the Rule Conception

Five of the seven tenets of the rule conception are false and must be discarded. The normativity tenet and the tenet that holds that norms are shared will not be criticized, as each is an element of the correct view of a norm. The first three objections each serve to undermine the first tenet, which states that norms are linguistic entities capable of being called up as occurrent or spoken statements. This tenet and the prescriptivity tenet are the heart of the rule view. But this first tenet will receive the most attention as it is the most difficult to refute.

A. Critique of the Occurrent Linguistic Entity Tenet

The term *norm statement* will be used to refer to the occurrent or spoken expression of a norm. On the rule theorist's account, the norm statement is equivalent to the norm. On my account, they differ. In the early state of the analysis, I will use the term neutrally as between these competing conceptions.

1. THE COUNTING OBJECTION. There are two versions of the *counting objection* to the tenet that norms are linguistic entities. The first is that we sometimes seem to have one norm statement present when intuitively it seems that there are two norms. The second is that sometimes we have two norm statements present when intuitively only one norm is present. In each of these cases, there is behavior and a norm statement, and we are intuitively inclined to say that the behavior is the norm.

Consider, for example, the norm, *Turn the other cheek*. It might be the case that two separate patterns of behavior regarding the proper interpretation of this biblical injunction exist in two separate communities. In the first community, turning the other cheek is taken fairly literally to mean that if someone strikes you, you should do nothing to prevent them from striking you again. In the second community, the expression is taken to mean that if someone strikes you, you do not return the aggression, but neither do you allow yourself to remain open to further aggression.

Imagine that two distinct patterns of behavior develop in line with these two interpretations of the injunction. On the rule theorist's account, since norms are just the occurrent or spoken thoughts, there is only one norm instantiated in these two communities. Yet it is more intuitively plausible to suppose that each of these communities has its own distinct norm. Thus, norms cannot be identified with norm statements.

The example can also be run in the other direction. Suppose that distinct norm statements are characteristically uttered in each of the two communities but that the same pattern of behavior is found in each. For example, one community might accept the norm statement, *Turn the other cheek*, while the other might accept, *Do not fight back*. Despite the divergent verbiage, if the behavior is the same in both communities, we will be inclined to say that the same norm is found in both communities.

The rule theorist has a ready response to the counting objection in either version. She will point out that, though it is the short spoken phrase that ostensibly counts as the norm, in fact, this short statement is merely a convenient handle for a longer phrase that is actually what is accepted by the members of the group. A fitting term for the more complex item might be *internal representation*. Though we might not have complete or easy access to such internal representations, they underwrite our ability to obey norms and to detect norm deviations. I was quibbling about the rule at the merely verbal level, but the rule theorist is interested in rules *qua* internal representations, where these may or may not be readily accessible to agents.[21]

In the first example of two communities and two patterns of behavior but one norm statement, the rule theorist will contend that if the statements are more fully specified for each of the two groups, they will not be identical. Thus, the rule theorist has an explanation for why we are intuitively inclined to think that these communities have diverse norms regarding the general notion of turning the other cheek. The reason is that the groups have diverse rules, though this only becomes apparent when the rules are more fully spelled out. Consequently, the rule theorist will fail to be persuaded by the counting objection. She will claim that it is an exaggeration of her view to hold that she is committed to thinking that norms that are accepted by agents are fully captured by the content of the words they utter.

This defense fails, however. It is false to say that the rule theorist's view is exaggerated. Rather, the analysis takes rule theorists at their word, as captured in the explicit definitions of norms examined earlier in the chapter. It is simply a fact that rule theorists identify the norm with the linguistic or verbal statement.

In addition to explicit definitions, the linguistic conception is also evident in Tenet Six, the rule theorist's account of how norms are shared. As earlier discussion indicated, the rule theorists' account of norm transmission relies mainly on a linguistic model involving the teaching of rules by means of speech. This model is not apt for internal representations, however, for it is impossible that complex internal representations could be readily taught by means of speech. In addition, Tenet Seven, which states that norms are easily detected, seems inconsistent with norms as internal representations, for once again, it is far from clear how one would go about detecting another person's internal representations.

Rule theorists sometimes make remarks that appear to be at odds with the rule view of norms and more compatible with the view I will offer. This indicates that there is a degree of inconsistency between their actual use of the term and their explicit attempts to characterize it. If we assume for a moment that I am right and the rule conception is wrong, then it should be no surprise that many of the insights that the rule theorists have about norms will be in tension with their explicit characterizations of norms. Drawing a parallel will clarify this point.

In *Naming and Necessity*, Saul Kripke famously seeks to replace the dominant *description theory* of reference with the *causal theory*.[22] As he observes, if he is right that the description theory is wrong and the causal theory is right, it should be no surprise that many insights of description theorists fit nicely into the causal theory framework. But this does not mean that the description theorists are right in the manner in which they think reference works. Rather, it is hard for a false theory to be a seamless web; the truth will show through. This attacks the rule theorist's explicit account of norms, and what they think norms are when they actually try to say what norms are. It should be obvious that it is desirable that this should dovetail with what they in practice take norms to be.

The rule theorist's response involves a shift away from the claim of Tenet One, that a norm is an occurrent or spoken linguistic expression. This is acceptable as a reasonable retreat for the moment, as long as it is kept in mind that the further the rule theorist moves away from the view that the norm is the spoken rule, the harder it will be to maintain Tenets Six and Seven. The next objection creates similar tensions between various tenets of the rule theorist's position.

2. **THE COMPLEXITY OBJECTION.** Some norms are so complex that it is completely implausible to suppose that the content of the norm is captured by a linguistic rule capable of occurrent retrieval. For example, there are pervasive norms in this and other cultures regarding sexuality among extended family members. These sets of practices are jointly referred to as the *incest taboo* in the sociological literature. The taboo applies to much more than the simple prohibition of overt sexual relations among family members. In this culture, for example, aspects of the taboo regulate dating among cousins, what types of intimacy are permissible among siblings, whether flirtation may take place among extended family members, and myriad other subtle yet potent prohibitions and permissions. Casual empirical observation suggests that these more subtle aspects of the norm are rarely discussed. It is an objection to the rule view that a norm such as this is so complex that it is implausible to suppose that agents are capable of calling it up as occurrent thought, or learning of it through the speech process.

Consider another example. It is the norm in job talks in many academic disciplines that the speaker, if male, is to wear a coat and tie. With such a norm, we again see that the view on which norms are the spoken rule is not adequate. The rule theorist would say that the rule here is something like: *Men should wear a coat and tie for academic job talks.* But it is false that this is precisely the norm. It is rather that this verbal characterization approximates the norm, as surely there is more involved. For example, the agent could not wear a Hawaiian shirt or sneakers with the suit and tie, nor could he wear an inappropriate tie. All this will be understood by an agent of reasonable intelligence who has grown up in this culture, yet this thicker content is not captured in the norm statement.

The rule theorist will offer a reply similar to the one offered to rebut the counting objection. With the coat and tie example, for instance, we saw that the norm is more complex than just the rule offered in conversation. The rule theorist may grant this but observe that her theory can provide an explanation. What matters, the rule theorist will contend, is that the rule is known to the agent, not that it is fully capturable in an occurrent passage. It is only natural that the rule is indexed or coded for convenience in terms of some shortened version such as, *Wear a coat and tie,* but it is just as sure that the agent has the more complex rule internally represented as she clearly knows not to wear a Hawaiian shirt. Once again, the rule theorist must retreat from the claim that the norm is the spoken or occurrent phrase in order to avoid an objection. But as observed earlier, this move has its costs in terms of creating a tension with Tenets Six and Seven.

Summing up, then, the counting and complexity objections argue effectively against the supposition that a norm is to be identified with occurrent or spoken thought. It may still be true, however, that the norm is some type of complex, linguistic expression such as an internal representation. Thus, norms may still be conceived of as linguistic in a broad sense, to reside in the head of the agent, as it were. The following objection will provide reason to doubt this view.

3. THE HYPOCRISY OBJECTION. Suppose that some particular norm statement is recurrently uttered in a community and the members of the community claim that they accept this as a rule that ought to govern their behavior. Yet, there is no corresponding pattern of behavior to go along with the rule. The example of turning the other cheek is again appropriate. Suppose that people think they ought to turn the other cheek and teach their children to turn the other cheek. In spite of this, it might be the case that there is no extant pattern of behavior to which the various members of the community conform that correlates with the norm statement. They talk about turning the other cheek, but this simply is not captured in any sort of regularity of behavior.

In such a case, there cannot exist some second rule, either a simple one or a complex internal representation, that the rule theorist may say is really the norm. Rather she must say that the norm is the norm statement, *Turn the other cheek*. But this is just wrong. There is no norm in this community. The mere fact that the members of the community are in the habit of making a certain type of utterance does not mean that there is a norm. The norm simply cannot be equated with a norm statement.

Consider where the discussion up to this point has led. In response to the counting and complexity objections, the rule theorist was forced to retreat from Tenet One in favor of a view on which norms are internal representations. This is a more plausible view in that it allows for norms to have a more complex content, which is necessary if they are to overcome the objections. The hypocrisy objection demonstrated, however, that the retreat to the view of norms as complex internal representations is not always open to the rule theorist. The rule theorist is forced to accept that the norm is the rule accepted by the community even when there is no correlative behavior whatsoever. Intuitively, we are not willing to count this as a norm. Thus, Tenet One must be rejected.

Though the rule theorist is wrong to identify the norm with the norm statement, this is an understandable mistake. For many of the important norms that govern social behavior, it will be the case that a norm statement exists and is commonly mentioned. Thus, it is understandable that this norm statement can be mistaken for the norm itself.

B. Critique of the Prescriptivity Tenet

We have seen that the rule theorist may retreat to the view of norms as internal representations. This is one reason norms should not be thought of as rulelike, for intuitively, rules are short, linguistic items capable of being called up occurrently and spoken, while internal representations are not. Nevertheless, one might think it appropriate to talk of norms as rules, since these internal representations may be prescriptive, and prescriptivity is a feature of rules. But as the following paragraph will argue, prescriptivity is not necessary for norms. Hence, there will no longer be any reason to equate norms with rules.

The reason prescriptivity is not essential to a norm is quite simple; norms may exist though no one prescribes them. Norms may go unprescribed or underprescribed for a variety of reasons. For example, people may not want to bother with prescribing a norm, or they may not be able to, or it may not be in their interest. Prescriptions are not necessary to convey the content of norms as agents may receive this information in other ways. For example, people are often able to detect what would count as conformity to a norm through simple observation of the behavior of others.

On the conception of a norm developed in the next section, what matters for a norm is that there is a rationally governed pattern of behavior that is not coincidental, that is, a regularity that is caused by the actions of various agents seeking to conform to the norm. Such a regularity may be maintained though no one prescribes the conforming acts. What ultimately matters is that acts of conformity occur, not that people entertain particular linguistic items.

C. Critique of the Sanctions Tenet

Contrary to the received view, it turns out that sanctions are not necessary for norms. Sanctions are only necessary if people would never have the desire to conform to norms but for the desire to avoid sanctions. Some types of norms may be maintained due to other motives, however. For example, consider many customs of physicians. Conformity to accepted medical practices is an important part of a typical physician's mode of operating, as it would be impossible for each doctor to independently research each medically important procedure she needs to use.[23] These norms do not have a structure such that doctors only conform under the pressure of other doctors who benefit from their conformity and suffer from their defection. Instead, doctors conform as a means of economizing on the costs of information. They freely choose to do so and are glad to have the opportunity. Hence sanctions are not necessary for this conformity.

The claim that linguistic structure, prescriptivity, and sanctions are not part of the definition of a norm may seem a strange claim. How could other theorists be so off the mark? It is not the case that other definitions of norms are completely off the mark, however. Rather, they mistake contingent features of norms for necessary features. Norms are often stated explicitly, prescribed, and sanctioned. But this need not be the case. There is an important difference between supplying a definition of a concept, which entails providing its necessary features, and merely supplying its characteristic or normally concomitant features.[24]

D. Critique of the Verbal Transmission Tenet

The sixth tenet of the rule view is that norm acceptance occurs through verbal transmission of the norm statement. We have seen that this is an attractive feature of the rule view, for since the norm equals the norm statement, the rule view provides for a straightforward explanation of how norms may come to be shared throughout a community, which is that people simply hear the norm statement uttered and decide whether or not to accept it. When such acts of acceptance become widespread, a shared norm will exist in the community. But what can be made of Tenet Six given the rule theorist's retreat to the view of norms as internal representations? When one utters the norm statement, it is no longer the case that the full content of the norm is thereby transmitted. How then can another person come to accept and share the norm, that is, the full content of the norm, when only part of it is transmitted verbally? This appears to be an insurmountable problem for the rule conception.

E. Critique of the Ease of Detection Tenet

Tenet Seven states that it is unproblematic to detect which norms are accepted. Although this is not a necessary feature of the rule theorist's view, it is easy to understand why rule theorists generally have not seen norm detection as a problem. Their conception of norms is one of simple rules, and so it should not be difficult to detect if a particular situation is a case in which a particular rule comes into play. Perhaps the reason that rule theorists write as if norms are detected unproblematically is because they focus on the vivid examples set by important norms. They write as if all norms were like the Decalogue, and hence easy to detect because the norm statements are regularly explicitly stated.

In this regard, it is revealing to consider Cancian's method for eliciting the norms of the Mayan community she studied. As mentioned earlier, she simply asked participants to state or write down the norms they accepted.[25] Similarly, if one wanted to detect the norms of this community without asking people to participate, Cancian's model suggests that all one would need to do is spend time in the community and write down the norm statements one hears expressed in the course of people's daily interactions.

The reality of the situation, however, is that norms are often very difficult to detect. Consider, for example, the British upper class fondness for indirect uses of language.[26] The complexity of the linguistic norms involved is a barrier to easy detection. Thus, only those brought up in the fold are able to appreciate the subtleties fully. Others may wish to follow these norms but find it difficult or impossible to detect them fully. This is an extreme case, but even in less extreme circumstances, it will often be difficult to detect norms. This general phenomenon is most easily seen when one travels to exotic places, where many subtle norms will resist immediate comprehension. One might fail altogether to detect the presence of some norms. Even when in their home culture, most people are insensitive to some norms. Thus, Tenet Seven of the rule conception, which holds that norms are easily detected, must be rejected.

This section will conclude with a summary of the findings and some conclusions. The first tenet of the rule view, that norms are linguistic entities capable of occurrent or spoken expression, was shown to be untenable. The most plausible response on the part of the rule theorist was to retreat to the view that norms are instead more complex internal rules, so-called internal representations. This retreat was seen to create new problems, however, as the once plausible transmission tenet became implausible, and the formerly problematic ease-of-detection tenet became even more problematic. In addition, the rule view was seen incorrectly to take prescriptions and sanctions to be necessary to norms. In sum, then, the rule conception of norms is faulty in a number of important respects. In the next section, I develop an alternative conception of norms, one that focuses not on something internal to agents, such as rules, but rather on something external, namely behavior, as the key to understanding norms.

III. Norms as Patterns of Behavior

The goal of developing a new definition of a norm is to avoid the problems that face the dominant rule conception. The new view must also remain close enough to our intuitive sense of a norm, however, if we are to sensibly extend the term to include the preferred definition. The following conception fulfills both of these criteria. First, the reformed definition of a norm will be stated, then each of the important constituent elements will be examined.

A. The Definition of a Norm

DEFINITION: *A norm is a pattern of rationally governed behavior, instantiated in a group, maintained by acts of conformity.*

1. BEHAVIOR. A norm is a pattern of human *behavior*. The term *behavior* is ambiguous in the following important manner. Brute physical movements such as the motion of one's left arm up and down count as behavior. But we also commonly take more complex actions as constituting behavior. For example, when a parole board decides to release a convict early because of good behavior, what constitutes her good behavior cannot be understood or described at the level of gross bodily movements. It is necessary to distinguish between brute behavior and action, where action is understood to contain elements of intention or deliberation. Whereas behavior in the sense of gross bodily movements was of interest to the classical behaviorists, both kinds of behavior are grist for the theory of norms.[27]

A fundamental question arises as to the inclusion of *behavior* in the definition of a norm. As the term *norm* is understood by the rule theorist, behavior is not necessary for the existence of a norm. Why is it preferable to define a norm in terms of behavior? One reason is for conceptual clarity. Generally, a distinction is not drawn between rules and norms. The term *rule* is used for the notion of a verbal or linguistic entity created by an individual or institution and transmitted among individuals and institutions. The term *norm* is often used synonymously with this conception of a rule. But the term *norm* is also used to refer to the actual pattern of behavior that accords with the rule. It is worthwhile to keep clear on this distinction between the rule and the behavior of the group that accords with it. There is currently no term in the academic literature that is reserved solely for this second item. The term *norm* best describes this second element.

We will often wish to distinguish rules and norms. For example, we may want to say that while the rule is *Brush after every meal*, the actual norm is that most people brush their teeth twice a day. Ordinary usage allows for this ambiguity between the rule and the behavior in the use of the term *norm*. Generally, we are able to pick up on the difference in use due to contextual clues. But for purposes of more rigorous theoretical work, the difference should be captured terminologically.

2. PATTERNS. A norm is a *pattern* of behavior. Few definitions explicitly discuss the notion of a pattern. An exception is Scott's definition of a norm as a "pattern of sanctions," which was mentioned earlier. Although Gibbard does not fit the notion of patterns into his definition of a norm, nevertheless he realizes that norms are somehow about patterns. In describing how the higher animals may have norms, Gibbard writes: "As in the human case, these animal interactions follow certain regular patterns, and the patterns seem, in a way, to have a rationale. . . . Now a norm prescribes a pattern of behavior, and to internalize a norm, I want to say, is to have a motivational tendency of a particular kind to act on that pattern."[28] Thus, although Gibbard and I disagree about the definition of a norm, we do agree in thinking that normative behavior is essentially about patterns of behavior.[29]

A pattern is comprised of multiple instantiations of an act type. An act type is a particular kind of behavior which may be imitated by more than one person. When a norm exists, members of a group will exhibit behavior of the act type. Thus, each individual shares a property in common, that of performing conforming acts, each of which is a token of the given act type. This common behavior is not only distinct from other kinds of behavior but also different from random behavior.

There are homogeneous act types and heterogeneous act types. A *homogeneous act type* is one in which the bits of behavior that constitute it are similar in the sense that the bits are members of a natural kind. For example, a group of friends all meet up at one of their houses and all take off their shoes. Each individual has the property of taking off her shoes. The act type is shoe removal under such and such circumstances, a natural kind of sorts.

A *heterogeneous act type* is one in which there is not one simple act type but a set of act types that fit together to form a complex of group behavior. For example, there is a type of behavior in our culture that could be called the handshaking norm. There are different variants in different contexts. For example, the norm is different in a professional as compared to a nonprofessional, personal context. In a personal context, how one behaves typically depends heavily on one's gender (this is changing in some subcultures in response to larger norms calling for unisex or androgynous behavior). Roughly, the norm is that men are to shake firmly with other men, and are to wait for a woman to offer her hand, and to shake at the same degree of firmness as the woman, if and when her hand is offered. Women are to choose whether or not to offer their hands to be shaken when interacting with men, and are not to offer their hands to other women but to hug, kiss, or touch instead.

The female and male manner of behaving together make up the handshaking norm. It is only the fact that the different behavior types all count as proper conforming behavior under the general description of *handshaking norm* that unites them as a single act type. For simplicity, the remainder of this work treats act types that make up norms as homogeneous, unless it matters in some specific context to note otherwise.

There is an ambiguity as to whether the norm is the set of bits of conforming behavior of a specific act type, or alternatively, whether the norm is the instantiated pattern. I contend that it is the latter. An argument that the norm is the instantiated pattern and not the collection of bits of behavior is that all of the particular bits of behavior could be replaced and the norm might still exist. For example, a community of Amish might rigorously adhere to a norm practiced by their first forebears in America. We would have no trouble saying that they follow the same norm even though the particular bits of behavior that constitute the norm have changed. What matters for norm identity appears to be that the current behavior, the act type, is similar to its forebears, and that there is a causal continuation of the norm over time. This argument shows that a norm is not to be identified with a particular set of bits of behavior. The particular bits come and go, yet the norm remains.

One might suppose that if the norm is not to be identified with the particular set of bits, then it must be an abstract, platonic object. But this is not the only option. Consider the ship that retains its identity even though all its planks rot away and are replaced over time. It is not an abstract, Platonic object. Likewise, we need not suppose that norms are Platonic objects just because they are not to be identified with the particular bits of behavior of which they are constituted at a particular time.

3. NORMATIVE GOVERNANCE. Norms are constituted by patterns of behavior of a particular sort; the behavior must be *rationally governed*. This just means that the conforming acts must be performed by agents who believe they *ought* to behave in such a manner. The ought may be the ought of rationality, in the sense of narrow self-interest, or the ought of morality. Norms are not merely patterns of behavior, then, but patterns that people think ought to exist, or, at any rate, that ought to be conformed to.

What one feels one ought to do will depend on one's values or motives, whether these be completely egoistic, completely altruistic, or some mix of the two. Norms might be maintained by a group who possess a variety of values and motives, some people conforming for mainly egoistic reasons and others for mainly moral reasons. Defining norms so as to include normativity does not depend on the truth of any particular assumption about the nature of human motivation. If people are at bottom egoists, then we should expect to see norms that reflect this, and if people are at bottom at least partially non-egoistic, we should expect norms that reflect this. Chapter Four examines in greater detail the role of *predominant egoism* in the emergence of new norms.

4. INSTANTIATION. A norm is not a norm if it is not in place. Norms thus differ in an important way from rules, maxims, and laws, which can exist without being captured in the actual, instantiated behavior of a group. For example, there could be a law that proscribed homosexual behavior and yet many members of a group could be practicing homosexuals. This latter fact would not call into question the existence, per se, of the law or rule proscribing the action. Norms, on the other hand, must be instantiated in the behavior of a group in order to exist. If we go to strange new lands and inquire into the norms of the people, we are inquiring into the actual behavior of the community, not the behavior to which the group aspires or to which it pays lip service. Putative norms should not be confused with norms.

An individual or group may wish to instantiate a norm, and it may be that the best way to do so is by promulgating a rule or law, but unless this individual or group can get some substantial portion of the members of the community to actually follow the rule, there will be no norm. Along these lines, recall the hypocrisy objection discussed earlier where it was seen that hypocritical utterances of a group regarding turning the other cheek are not sufficient to count as a norm. If there is no behavior, there is no norm. The instantiation condition, then, is an important point of disagreement between the rule conception and the pattern conception.

5. GROUPS. The next term in the reformed definition of a norm is that of a *group*. A norm is a pattern of normatively governed behavior instantiated in a group. Exactly what percentage of the group need act in accordance with the norm for it to be a norm will vary with the type of norm and with the group. The group may not, however, consist of one person, that is, the present account does not allow for the existence of personal norms. This appears to agree with ordinary language. For it does not seem correct to talk in terms of personal norms. These are habits or routines, but not norms. Norms exist across persons, not across different time slices of the same person. Whereas one might say, *Normally, I swim on alternate afternoons*, one would not say, *The norm is that I swim on alternate afternoons*.[30] Thus, we see that the pattern must be instantiated across different persons, not solely different time slices of the same person.

The norm conformers must be active over the same range of time. For example, it does not seem to be possible for the popes, or the U.S. presidents, or the chief justices of the Supreme Court to have had norms with other members of their respective job types.[31]

Summarizing the last two points, the formation of norms requires more than one individual. Furthermore, these individuals must create and maintain the norm over the same range of time. The implication would seem to be that interaction is necessary for the existence of a norm. It appears, however, that this interaction need not be face to face. For example, an office worker and an after-hours janitor may coordinate over time on some norms, such as those dealing with where recycling should be left, even though they would not recognize one another were they to meet in the elevator. What seems to matter, then, is the structuring of one's own behavior to accord with the behavior of another, or a number of others, who are doing the same, over the same range of time.

6. CONFORMITY. We have seen that a norm is a pattern of rationally governed behavior instantiated in a group. But it cannot be rationally governed behavior of just any sort. It must be conforming behavior. Conforming behavior is individual behavior that instantiates a specific act type, and for which part of the best explanation of the individual act is the existence of the instantiated act type in the community.[32] This is a causal condition: the instantiated norm must be at least a partial cause of the particular bit of behavior. To adopt a piece of philosophical jargon, we might say that the agent must *track* the instantiated norm.[33] The nature of this causal condition will here be left in a fairly imprecise state. Thus, I will not attempt to provide necessary and sufficient conditions for a conforming act. It will be worthwhile, however, to look at a few examples to get a better sense of the different ways the causal condition may be met.

A straightforward and pervasive example of conforming behavior is tipping. Norms regarding tipping are complex and vary widely. When people travel to places in which they are unsure of the norm, the common thing to do is ascertain the norm through observation and then abide or at least gauge one's behavior by it. In this manner, a partial causal determinant of the person's action of tipping or not tipping is the behavior of others in similar circumstances. This satisfies the causal condition and thus counts as a conforming act. Another example in which one tries explicitly to do what others are doing is when giving presents. For example, if one takes a job in which there is a holiday present exchange where one's partner is determined by drawing names, one will want to give a gift in the same price range as others give.

Some regularities that may count as norms as far as our ordinary language intuitions go will not satisfy the causal condition. A simple example is that it is a norm that people eat everyday. Yet eating, as such, is not a regularity of behavior maintained by conformity; that is, people do not eat in order to conform to the behavior of others.[34] Thus, the proper causal connection is not present in order for this to count as an example of conformity.

Notice that conformity is not necessarily a conscious or intentional process. One may track the behavior of others without being conscious that one is doing so. For example, the postures people assume when walking often vary across groups and cultures. It seems likely that part of the explanation for these regularities has to do with people conforming their behavior to that of others, though without realizing that they are. In other cases, the conformity involves fairly little occurrent processing because the behavior is part of the agent's routine. Initially, perhaps, the choice to conform to the behavior of others was more deliberate, but such conscious effort may no longer be necessary.

It is difficult to determine precisely what type of causal connection is adequate for conformity. With some norms, the connection is very direct. For example, in the case of tipping, one explicitly looks at what others are doing in order to replicate it. In other cases, the causal connection is circuitous. As will be discussed in Chapter Two, some norms are only conformed to because of the presence of sanctions. In these cases, the behavior of others causes the sanctions to work so as to increase the likelihood of producing the same type of behavior. For example, the sanction against driving on the left is due to the fact that others drive on the right. Thus, the behavior type explains the sanction, which in turn is an element in the cause of more behavior of the same type.

In other cases, the causal connection will be yet more indirect. The fact that one lives in a culture in which coffee, instead of tea, is the norm will have a causal effect on the chances of one's drinking coffee as compared to tea. But the causal influence does not seem straightforward; that is, one does not choose to drink coffee after considering the behavior of others in the way one does in deciding whether to tip. Although it accords with ordinary language to say that coffee drinking is the norm in America, it is unclear whether this connection is too indirect to count as conformity.[35] For now, I will rest content with the general notion that conformity depends on one's behavior being partially caused by the like norm-conforming behavior of others. In the remaining chapters of

Part One, we will see that conformity, even as understood at this fairly general level, may pose serious problems for the theory of norms.

There is an instructive parallel example from the philosophy of language. The causal theory of reference pioneered by Saul Kripke and Hilary Putnam holds that, as Putnam quips, "meanings ain't in the head."[36] By this it is meant that reference from terms in the language to objects in the world is determined not by the set of descriptions – the intentional content – in the heads of particular agents, but rather by causal chains leading back from speakers to objects. Analogously, just as meanings are not in the head, neither, I argue, are norms. Agents may have heterogeneous internal representations in the head, yet all may be taking part in the same norm. What matters instead is that there be the right sort of causal connection between oneself and the norm in order for one's behavior to count as following this norm.

B. The Intuitive Plausibility of the Pattern Conception

The previous section explicated the various elements that, as a group, make up the reformed definition of a norm. For brevity, we may say that on this view, norms are patterns of behavior. This is in contrast to the received view on which norms are rules. Earlier we saw that despite the attractiveness of the rule view, it has a host of problems that, taken as a whole, force us to reject it. What remains is to give some sense as to how the various pieces of the pattern conception fit together to form a convincing whole.

Recall the previous discussion of the role of norms in social theory. Norms are thought to play an important role in explaining how societies are held together, and how they maintain continuity over time. It was observed that norms can only play this role if norms themselves can be undergirded by an account that explains their emergence and maintenance. The pattern conception provides an attractive and plausible picture of norms capable of fulfilling these requirements.

Norms emerge in groups as a result of people conforming to the behavior of others. Thus, the start of a norm occurs when one person acts in a particular manner in a particular situation because she thinks she ought to. Others may then conform to this behavior for a number of reasons. The person who performed the initial action may think that others ought to behave as she behaves in situations of this sort. Thus, she may prescribe the behavior to them by uttering the norm statement in a prescriptive manner. Alternately, she may communicate that conformity is desired in other ways, such as by gesturing. In addition, she may threaten to sanction them for not behaving as she wishes. This will cause some to conform to her wishes and act as she acts. But some others will not need to have the behavior prescribed to them. They will observe the regularity of behavior and decide on their own that they ought to conform. They may do so for either rational or moral reasons. By processes such as these, a rationally governed pattern of behavior may emerge in a community. It will satisfy the conformity condition if at least a partial reason for the conformity of each is the conformity of others.

The attractiveness of the pattern conception is highlighted when contrasted with the rule conception. The main puzzle in explaining the emergence and maintenance of norms is the issue of how norms are spread through a community. The problem with the received view is that it cannot explain how complex norms come to be accepted. The transmission story works nicely but only for simple norms that are adequately captured in brief norm statements. Yet as we saw, to handle complex content the rule theorist must move to the view on which norms are internal representations. This causes the transmission account to become untenable, as such complex content cannot be transmitted verbally, and so cannot explain the acceptance of these norms by others.

The pattern view, on the other hand, can easily account for complex norms. Because norms are patterns of behavior, complex norms are complex patterns of behavior. But complex as they may become, they are nonetheless observable and subject to imitation. Thus, their complexity does not preclude their spread throughout the community. It will take a greater effort on the part of people to detect the subtleties of complex norms. But this is a virtue of the account for it accords with our intuitive understanding of norms, which holds that some norms are harder to detect than others.

Conclusion

Summarizing the chapter, then, we have seen that the rule view of norms is problematic for a number of reasons. To avoid the criticisms of Tenet One, that norms are linguistic entities capable of occurrent retrieval, the rule theorist must retrench to a view on which norms are internal representations. But this view creates tensions with other tenets of the rule view. Thus, on either account, norms as rules cannot adequately perform the work in social theory for which they are needed. In contrast, we have seen that norms understood as patterns of behavior can. This, then, is the preferable conception of norms. The next chapter examines the rational structure of these norms.

2

Rational Norms

Now all forms of community are like parts of the political community; for men journey together with a view to some particular advantage, and to provide something they need for the purposes of life.[1]

Aristotle

Introduction

While Chapter One explicated the essential requirements for a norm, it did not explicitly appraise the rationality of the acts of conformity that make up the norms. This chapter does. The next step, taken in subsequent chapters, will be to make an appraisal of the morality of the acts of conformity making up moral norms. These analyses will then be integrated to better understand the role of norms and customs in particular real-world legal and policy debates.

On some accounts, the term *rational norm* is an oxymoron as the element of raw conformity necessary for norms to persist is thought to be in tension with the reflection and calculation necessary for rational action. In fact, however, many norms are best viewed as deep expressions of the heights to which our rationality may attain. Other norms do indeed appear to be hopelessly irrational.

The previous chapter argued that conformity is necessary for norms to exist. Norms are maintained in groups and societies because people conform to the behavior of other people. There is a difficulty with the notion of conformity, however. As it is often understood, conformity amounts to blind following or rote imitation of the behavior of others. Such a model of human behavior is clearly in tension with the rational choice model.

The Chicago sociologist James Coleman characterizes this tension in the following manner: "Especially for theories based on rational choice, invoking a norm to explain behavior constitutes an almost diametrically opposed approach. The rational choice theorist sees action as the result of choice made by a purposive actor; the social-norm theorist sees behavior as the result of conformity to norms."[2] If the type of behavior necessary for norms to be maintained cannot be reconciled with the picture of human motivation inherent in rational choice theory, norms can be of no further use to this dominant theoretical approach.[3] This, then, is a central problem for norms theory, reconciling conformity to norms with rational choice theory. This chapter will demonstrate that conformity to each of the three different types of norms set out below may indeed be rational.

Whether conformity may be reconciled with rationality depends on the circumstances in which the possibility of conformity arises. Three types of circumstances produce the three different norm types. First, circumstances in which free coordination is possible; second, those in which sanctions are necessary to solve collective action problems; finally, those circumstances in which savings on the cost of information may be achieved by conformity. The first two types of circumstance are strategic in the game-theoretic sense, while the third is nonstrategic. Different circumstances and different motivations combine to produce the different norm types. Strategic circumstances may produce *coordination norms* or *sanction-driven norms* while nonstrategic circumstances may produce *epistemic norms*. Strategic norms are more complex and so will occupy a greater portion of the following discussion.

I. Coordination Norms

The term *coordination norm* was coined by Edna Ullmann-Margalit.[4] Though I will borrow her term, I will argue that it is necessary to develop an alternative account of coordination norms. Ullmann-Margalit's account of a coordination norm is itself a generalization of David Lewis's account of *convention*.[5] It will be necessary to examine their treatments of the topics of coordination and convention in some detail as the present analysis is best understood by seeing how it builds on their contributions.

Problems in achieving basic coordination will first be discussed. These are *coordination problems*. Norms may serve as solutions to coordination problems. These are coordination norms. The complexities of coordination norms will then be explored.

A. Basic Coordination and the Coordination Problem

The simplest sort of coordination situations are easily solved. In this regard, consider the single equilibrium coordination game as represented in the payoff matrix in Figure 2.1.[6] For rational agents informed of the structure of the payoffs, reaching the outcome 1, 1 will be trivial. Each player will only get her preferred payoff of 1 if both she and the other player choose A. Each will also expect the other to choose A, as each will expect the other to make the rational choice. For each there is no reason to choose action B, as no matter what the other does, one gets a payoff of 0. Whereas, with the choice of A,

Column-Chooser

		A	B
		A	B
Row-Chooser	A	1, 1	0, 0
	B	0, 0	0, 0

Figure 2.1 Single Equilibrium Coordination Game

Column-Chooser

		A	B
		A	B
Row-Chooser	A	1, 1	0, 0
	B	0, 0	1, 1

Figure 2.2 The Pure Coordination Game

one may get 0 or one may get 1, depending on what the other player does. So unless one knows the likelihood of getting 1 is zero, which one will typically not know, then the expected utility of choice A must be greater than zero, and so greater than choice B, and so the preferred choice. Accordingly, there will be no problem in the actors achieving the rationally preferred outcome of 1, 1, as each will do the correct action on her own. It is for this reason that Lewis stipulates that coordination problems must have a minimum of two proper coordination equilibria or else the solution will be trivial, that is, there is no real problem of achieving coordination in the first place.[7]

Consider next a matrix representing the simplest type of coordination game, the so-called pure coordination game (Figure 2.2).[8] Pure coordination games contain no element of conflict. But unlike the single equilibrium coordination game, there are two coordination points for the players rather than one. In terms of the matrix, the coincidence of interests among the players means that they will have the same preference ranking for the list of possible outcomes. Row-chooser and Column-chooser will do best if they can produce either of the pairs with the payoff of 1, 1, that is, the northwest or southeast cells. Neither agent prefers one of these pairs over the other and both prefer these outcomes to the outcomes with the payoffs of 0, 0, the southwest and northeast cells. This is

Column-Chooser

		A	B
		A	B
Row-Chooser	A	2, 1	0, 0
	B	0, 0	1, 2

Figure 2.3 Simple Coordination and Conflict Game

a situation of interdependent decision as Row's best choice depends on what she expects Column to choose, and Column's best choice depends on what she expects Row to choose. In other words, if Row expects Column to choose A, then her best choice is A, and if she expects Column to choose B, then her best choice is B. Column's choices are equally dependent on her expectations of Row's choices.

Consider next the situation in Figure 2.3 where there is a mixture of coordination and conflict. Row-chooser's most preferred outcome is 2, 1, the northwest cell, as she gets 2, whereas Column-chooser's most preferred outcome is 1, 2, the southeast cell, as she gets 2. Thus, there is an element of conflict in this game because Row and Column each has a first preference for different outcomes. Yet, there is also an incentive to coordinate as each does better if settling for coordination on the other's preferred outcome than in the two situations in which they fail to coordinate on either of the preferred outcomes, the northeast and southwest cells, in which each receives 0.

Before continuing, some terminology must be introduced. *Equilibria* are combinations of choices in which each player has done as well as she can, given the choices of the other players. No player will regret her choice given the choices of the others, but she may be indifferent. A combination of choices is a *proper equilibrium* if each player prefers her choice to other choices she might have made, given the choices of the others. A *coordination equilibrium* is a combination of choices such that no one would have been better off had any one player, either herself or someone else, acted otherwise. A *proper coordination equilibrium* is a combination of actions such that no one would have been as well off had any one player acted differently, either herself or someone else.[9] Figures 2.2 and 2.3 represent strategic situations that have two proper coordination equilibria, namely, the outcomes 1, 1 and 1, 1 in Figure 2.2 and 2, 1 and 1, 2 in Figure 2.3.

When there are two equilibria, coordination may not be straightforward. Consider the matrix in Figure 2.2. Row and Column are indifferent as to which of the equilibrium outcomes is produced. But how do they arrive at one or the other? For each, the best choice is conditional on what she expects the other to do. If Row and Column can communicate, it will be easier for them to play this game to their mutual advantage; they may be able to agree on one of the two equally preferred outcomes, and each will consequently do her part to bring it about. But when communication is not possible, arriving at one of the two mutually preferred outcomes will not be so easy. Row will want to do what she expects Column to do, and Column will want to do what she expects Row to do. But how will either be able to form a reliable expectation of what the other will do? How can either act in such a manner as to guarantee coordination on one or the other of the mutually preferred outcomes?

Thomas Schelling argues that in coordination games, players may be able to coordinate their choices if the game happens to present the players with an outcome that stands apart from other outcomes for some reason, making it the salient choice on which to coordinate.[10] For example, consider the following coordination problem.

You and I must meet after work, but we are both unsure where the meeting should take place as we failed to come to a prior agreement on a location. Say, for example, that we had planned to meet at a restaurant near work, but it was closed, and for some reason it is not possible or convenient to meet in front. We both desire to coordinate on the same location but have a problem in separately arriving at the same choice to bring about the coordination. Each wants to go where she expects the other to go. Each knows that the other's choice is dependent on her own. We seek to arrive at what Lewis calls "concordant mutual expectations," that is, we want our expectations to accord with one another.[11] I will go where I expect you to go, but I know you will go where you expect me to go. You share this desire. If we are able to coordinate at all, it will most likely be because we are both able to zero in on a prominent or salient choice among the field of relevant possibilities.

For example, if the short list of possibilities for meeting consists of three establishments, the Oak, the Hawk and Dove, and Layla's, and your name is Laura and mine is Laurel, it might occur to each of us separately that Layla's is the salient choice. We might notice the slightly peculiar fact that each of our first initials are the same as those of one of these establishments and further that this establishment is named after a person while the others are not. These facts may be enough to single out this location in each of our minds. Each must expect that the other may also notice this particular fact, and each must expect the other to expect herself to notice this fact. Under these conditions, each will go to Layla's more than half expecting to meet the other. In such a manner, the coordination problem may be solved.

With this preliminary understanding of coordination problems and the means of their solution in mind, we are in a position to understand recurrent coordination problems and the means of their solution, namely, coordination norms and conventions.

B. Coordination Norms as Solutions to Recurrent Coordination Problems

Two people might repeatedly find themselves facing a need to coordinate in similar circumstances. In such situations, a convention may emerge to solve the recurrent problem.[12] Just as in the case of the one-shot game considered earlier, the problem may be solved with or without communication. When communication is possible, the solution should be trivial in situations of pure coordination for the same reason it was in single-shot games, that is, players will simply agree ahead of time on which of the outcomes on which to coordinate in future instances of the problem. In an iterated game, the agreement will create expectations on the part of each that the other will act in the predetermined manner when future cases arise, thus giving each a reason to act in this manner, as she expects the other to. But how are recurrent coordination problems solved when communication is not possible? Just as in the simple game, the answer comes through the notion of salience.

In an example such as the foregoing, we will in all likelihood be able to coordinate on Layla's as the solution to a repeated coordination problem and thus establish a convention of meeting at Layla's. The first case of coordination came about due to the fortuitous fact that the situation presented a salient choice that each of us could opt for with reasonable confidence that the other would also make the same choice. On a second occasion, we might both recognize that we face the same coordination problem as in the past; each of us now has a double reason to choose Layla's. First, for the same reason it was chosen the first time, namely, because of our names, and now, for the additional reason that it has added prominence since it has acquired *precedence*. Precedence is, for Lewis, a type of salience. He refers to "coordination by precedence."[13] If yet a third occasion for meeting arises, the precedent will be that much stronger. With each new situation that calls for us to meet, the reason to choose Layla's becomes stronger, while no countervailing reason to choose the Oak or the Hawk and Dove need surface.

It might of course dawn on one of us to mention to the other that we should plan to meet at Layla's if we should have the need to meet on any future occasions. Although this might nail down each other's expectations with greater certainty, it might not be necessary, and more importantly, it might not come up in conversation. Without consciously reflecting on it, each might have expectations based on the first few coordinations, which are strong enough that the issue never arises. If a third friend wishes to meet us after work, and if she knows that we meet at Layla's, this is where she will go. The same will hold for a fourth person, and so on. Thus, in a simple case such as this, it is fairly straightforward how a convention may emerge to solve a coordination problem. Perhaps, by such a process, certain bars and restaurants become the *in* places among members of a certain social circle.

Emergence accounts of norms are sometimes distinguished from *maintenance accounts*. In the present case, however, the distinction is largely unnecessary. Understanding how Layla's emerges as the place to meet is just to understand why it will tend to be maintained as the place to meet. For salience and precedence create the expectations that allow it to emerge. Salience and precedence will often continue and indeed strengthen, perhaps evolving into a minor custom or tradition. For example, though perhaps all the original members to the convention are dead, the Billy Goat in Chicago's Loop remains a drinking establishment where many of Chicago's journalists gather. There was never a point at which the emergence of this coordination solution ended and its maintenance began.

Before continuing, a terminological point must be made. Lewis talks about conventions as solutions to recurrent coordination problems. As we will see later, he thinks conventions become norms. Ullmann-Margalit accepts Lewis's account and introduces the term *coordination norm* for essentially the same phenomena.[14] Thus, it is appropriate to refer to the *Lewis/Ullmann-Margalit account* of conventions or coordination norms. On this account, a coordination norm is a solution to a recurrent coordination problem with two proper coordination equilibria.[15] I will argue that coordination norms, properly understood, are a broader category than the one explicated by Lewis and Ullmann-Margalit.

C. The Coordination Benefit

Lewis and Ullmann-Margalit contend that conventions or coordination norms serve as solutions to recurrent coordination problems.[16] On my account, a coordination problem is simply a strategic structure in which a coordination benefit may be produced. To count as a solution to a coordination problem, however, the occurrences of the numerous coordination benefits making up the norm cannot accrue by accident. Rather, a causal condition must be met such that the potential for benefit explains the conformity. In cases in which a coordination problem is recurrent, it may be solved by a coordination norm.

The coordination benefit is actually the important case of a more general phenomenon, the *coordination effect*. The coordination effect is a term I introduce for the change in utility experienced by one or more actors due to other actions that are of the same type as the action under consideration. The coordination effect may be positive or negative. Cases of the former will be called *coordination benefits*, and cases of the latter, *coordination losses*. Rational people seek coordination benefits and seek to avoid coordination losses. Coordination benefits are, however, the more important concern for our purposes, as it is their pursuit that may prompt people to conform to norms freely and of their own accord. The coordination benefit, at its simplest, may be represented in the game matrix in Figure 2.4.

In this situation, Row receives a coordination benefit if Row and Column coordinate on the choice of A. It must be the case that there is coordination on

Column-Chooser

		A	B
	A	1, 0	0, 0
Row-Chooser			
	B	0, 0	0, 0

Figure 2.4 The Coordination Benefit

a certain type of behavior by both parties for the coordination benefit to result. It is not enough, for example, that Row benefit from some action of Column's that Row did not help produce. Nor is it enough that Row produce the benefit by acting in a certain manner on her own. It must be the case that the benefit results from both acting in the same manner. With coordination benefits, defection by either party would cause Row to lose the benefit.

This is not to say, however, that each party must intend to or want to coordinate with the other. Consider the example of Dante and Beatrice described in *La Vita Nuova*. Dante goes where he expects Beatrice to go because of the deepened feelings of love he experiences in her presence. This situation might have the structure of Figure 2.4 in which Dante is represented by Row and Beatrice is represented by Column. Dante benefits from coordinating on the same location as Beatrice, but she is neutral as to his presence.

Thus, this example is one in which the coordination benefit accrues to only one of the coordinators. In reality, however, many cases of coordination have a structure such that both parties receive the coordination benefit. This is perhaps the case we would ordinarily expect to see, since it is otherwise unclear why Column would coordinate. In a case of mutual benefit, the payoffs to each player would be 1, 1. Coordination that results in benefits to both parties is part of the common notion of coordination, and, as we saw, an element of the Lewis/Ullmann-Margalit model. Yet the case of unilateral benefit represented in Figure 2.4 is not only possible but also of theoretical interest, as we will later see.

Though they are of less interest, coordination losses are captured in the game matrix in Figure 2.5. In this situation, if both players perform action A, Row loses out because her doing A is in coordination with Column's doing A. An example of such a case would be if you happen to coordinate on the same establishment as the local bully who is out to get you. (Imagine that for some reason the bully is no threat if you both end up at location B; say it is the bar of your good friend, who happens to be a bigger bully.)

Column-Chooser

		A	B
	A	0, 1	1, 1
Row-Chooser	B	1, 1	1, 1

Figure 2.5 The Coordination Loss

Column-Chooser

		A	B
	A	0, 2	1, 1
Row-Chooser	B	1, 1	1, 1

Figure 2.6 Coordination Benefit and Loss

The two matrices in Figures 2.4 and 2.5 illustrate the simplest cases of the coordination benefit and coordination loss. They may also occur together, as modeled in the matrix in Figure 2.6. In this situation, Row loses from coordination and Column benefits. An example is where the bully has the preference that he end up at the same place as you as long as it is location A. In this instance of coordination, there are two coordination effects, one positive and one negative.

Some examples will demonstrate the importance of the coordination benefit. A variety of examples will be offered to give a sense of how pervasive coordination benefits are. Subsequently, the role that the coordination benefit plays in the maintenance of coordination norms will be discussed.

1. Suppose I wish to take my children on a camping trip where they will have the opportunity to meet and play with other children. My success will depend on the extent to which I am successful in choosing a campground where other parents bring their children.

2. Suppose that I am a member of an aristocratic family and travel in an elite social circle of similar families. Suppose further that I wish the same for my

offspring. My success will to some extent depend on my ability to coordinate with other similarly situated parents on choice of schooling, socializing, and the like for our children.

3. Suppose I wish to routinely drive through traffic lights that are yellow. The extent to which I am able to adopt this practice with relative impunity will depend on the extent to which I am successful in finding a community in which others also drive through yellow traffic lights, as the prevalence of this action will reduce the likelihood of my apprehension by the authorities, given the plausible assumption that widespread breaches breed indifference on the part of the law.

4. Suppose I am deciding whether or not to become a vegetarian. The merits of this decision will depend on the number of vegetarians in the community. If there are few vegetarians, I will have difficulties finding appropriate foods in stores, ordering in restaurants, and finding a compatible mate. Thus, other things equal, I will want to coordinate with the eating habits of others in my community.

5. Suppose I am planning to move from a city to a small town and that I am currently in the market for an automobile. There will be a positive coordination effect if I can coordinate my choice of an automobile with that of other members of the community which I am entering. For example, suppose I buy a Volvo and no one else drives one. There will be no dealers to service the car, parts stores will not carry replacement parts, and mechanics will have less experience with the specific sorts of problems that may arise. Thus, other things equal, I will get more utility from buying a particular type of auto if others make the same choice.

6. Suppose I am in the process of launching a political career, and anticipate the need to have a position on the issues of abortion and capital punishment although I am in fact indifferent. There will be a positive coordination effect such that it will be in my interest to choose the positions that have the greater number of advocates in my community.

The preceding examples illustrate the coordination benefit in which the utility I receive for performing a type of action depends on others also performing the same action. Understanding the coordination benefit is instrumental to understanding how recurrent coordination problems may be solved.

D. Solving Recurrent Coordination Problems

A coordination problem is a game in which one or more individuals can achieve a coordination benefit. This is a wider definition of a coordination problem than that given by Lewis. As already mentioned, a coordination problem for Lewis exists only when there are at least two proper coordination equilibria. Because there are two or more equilibria to choose from, agents may have a problem in

TABLE 2.1. *Four Basic Coordination Norm Types*

Rational Type	Description	Example
(1) Non-equilibrium	Some agent would have gained had she alone acted otherwise.	Fashion Game
(2) Equilibrium	No agent would have gained had she alone acted otherwise.	Lawyer's Summer Vacation Game
(3) Coordination equilibrium	No agent would have gained had any agent alone acted otherwise, either herself or someone else.	Suit-wearing Game
(4) Proper coordination equilibrium	No one would have been as well off had any agent acted differently, either herself, or someone else.	Driving Game

coordinating on one of them. On my use of the term, such situations count as coordination problems. But other situations will also count that will not count for Lewis, as coordination benefits may be achieved in a variety of situations that are not proper coordination equilibria.[17]

Table 2.1 represents the various relevant possibilities regarding types of coordination norms. In each of the steps from (1) to (4), the requirements for the norm type become more complex as additional requirements are added on. It makes most sense to begin discussion with (4) as this structure is what Lewis takes as required for a convention. In fact, Lewis requires not one but two proper coordination equilibria for a coordination problem. Later, I will first argue that Lewis is right that situations of two or more proper coordination equilibria may indeed constitute coordination problems potentially solvable by coordination norms. I will show, however, that even with two equilibria, they do not necessarily need to be proper coordination equilibria or coordination equilibria. Despite these structural dissimilarities to a convention, these coordination problems may nevertheless result in coordination norms when they recur.

Consider first why a Lewisian convention would count as a coordination norm. Specifically consider the convention of meeting at Layla's. We can see that this convention is a norm on my definition, as articulated in Chapter One. It is clearly a pattern of rationally governed behavior instantiated in a group and maintained by conformity. In this case, the conformers are motivated by their rational desire to be with their confreres at Layla's.

The next issue is whether the pattern of behavior is maintained by rational acts of conformity. Recall that coordination norms must satisfy a causal condition in that the conformity must be caused by the existence of the coordination benefit. There is clearly no conformity taking place on the first play of the game in which the parties manage to meet at Layla's. On the second play, it still seems a bit forced to speak of the players conforming to their actions of the previous round. But hereafter, it seems more and more natural to say on each new occasion that the players conform to the emerging pattern of behavior of the group in order to

Child B

		Goes	Doesn't Go
	Goes	1, 1	0, 0
Child A			
	Doesn't Go	0, 0	0, 0

Figure 2.7 The Rock Quarry Game

secure the coordination benefit of meeting up with their friends. Clearly, then, a convention in Lewis's sense can pass the conformity requirement to qualify as a coordination norm.[18]

Next, consider a coordination problem with only one equilibrium, as in Figure 2.1. An example of this would be a situation in which two children separately choose to go to the one rock quarry in town to swim (Figure 2.7). Each will benefit from going only if the other also goes because each of them is interested in following the parental order each has received not to swim alone.

The first point to note is that this structure is not an example of a coordination problem on Lewis's definition because there is only one proper coordination equilibrium, the outcome 1, 1. It is a coordination problem, however, albeit a rather simple one. In this situation, there is the potential for a coordination benefit for both of the parties. If each child, as a rational actor aware of the payoff matrix (if only implicitly), goes to the swimming hole expecting to find the other there because they were able to form concordant mutual expectations, then on my account, this counts as the solution of a coordination problem.

As each is indifferent toward going to the swimming hole when not expecting to meet the other, they might happen to chance upon one another at the swimming hole. This does not count as solving the coordination problem, however, because the achievement of the coordination benefit is accidental. As we see from the payoff structure, neither has a preference for not going to the swimming hole if the other does not go.[19] This might plausibly be the case if, for example, the swimming hole is out of the way and thus requires extra effort to reach, but at the same time there is some other compensating pleasure such as the chance of spotting deer along the trail.

It is worth noting, however, that solving a coordination problem and thus producing a coordination benefit is not enough for a norm. Recall the case of Dante and Beatrice, as represented in Figure 2.4. The situation is that he benefits from coordination but she is neutral. In such a case, she has no motivation to coordinate with Dante. But the pure cases of norms which are the topic of this study are ones in which all the conformers have motivation to conform. Thus, even if the game between Beatrice and Dante were iterated, it would not count

Actress

	New York	Los Angeles
New York	1, 0	0, 0
Los Angeles	0, 0	0, 1

Actor

Figure 2.8 The Being-Seen-with-the-Right-Person Game

as a norm. Satisfying the conditions for a norm is yet more difficult as even if each actor has the motivation to conform, it may still not be enough for a norm. Consider the matrix in Figure 2.8.

It might be that two people each benefit from coordinating with the other, but the coordination points are not the same. Suppose, for example, that an actor and an actress each benefit from being seen with the other. For the actress, it only matters if they are seen in Los Angeles, while for the actor, it only matters if they are seen in New York. The situation presents each with a coordination problem. Yet a norm of behavior may not emerge since each cannot simultaneously solve the problem, as each prefers to coordinate in a different city. Thus, we see that it is not enough that there be a coordination point for every player. Rather, a norm will exist only when there is one coordination point for all players.

Consider what would be the case if the children manage to establish a pattern whereby they meet at the quarry on the way home from their separate schools each afternoon. Suppose further that after a time other children begin showing up also, each expecting to find others there. Such a situation would constitute a pattern of rationally governed behavior maintained in a group by conformity. The conformity is explicated in terms of coordinating with the like behavior of the others, namely, going to the swimming hole after school in order to benefit from having others with whom to swim. It is therefore appropriate to talk of a coordination norm. This example drives a wedge between the notion of a coordination norm and that of a convention in Lewis's sense of this term, as this coordination norm emerges in a situation with only one proper coordination equilibrium.

The next two examples demonstrate that a coordination norm need not be a proper coordination equilibrium. Recall that a coordination equilibrium is a combination of the agents' chosen actions such that no one agent wishes any agent – either herself or someone else – to have acted differently, that is, no one would have been better off had any one agent chosen a different action. A proper coordination equilibrium is a coordination equilibrium in the strong sense, that

Most Others

		Suit	No Suit
	Suit	1, 1	0, 1
Me			
	No Suit	0, 1	1, 1

Figure 2.9 The Suit-Wearing Game

is, a coordination equilibrium such that all the agents would have been *worse off* had anyone alone acted differently. Thus, in a convention, the conformers to the convention prefer that others conform also since a convention has two proper coordination equilibria. In the next example, a coordination norm wherein the conformers are indifferent as to the conformity of particular individuals other than themselves will be presented. This is a coordination equilibrium, but not a proper coordination equilibrium. In the example after this, the conformers prefer that individuals other than themselves not conform. This is an equilibrium, but not a coordination equilibrium.

Both Lewis and Ullmann-Margalit cite modes of dress as conventions.[20] Their analyses of conventions do not fit their examples, however, for typically others are indifferent as to the conformity of particular individuals. Thus, the situation does not have the structure of a proper coordination equilibrium because it is not the case that the conformers would have been worse off had some particular person not conformed. Yet, conformity still may occur due to the possibility of coordination benefits. As an example, consider the Suit-Wearing Game (Figure 2.9).

If most others wear a suit to job interviews, then I will benefit from doing so as well (northwest cell). And if most others do not wear a suit to job interviews, then I will benefit from not doing so (southeast cell). For if I do not do what most others do, I will be conspicuous, and this could hurt my chances of being hired. Thus, I benefit from coordinating with the behavior of others. But most others who also wear suits to interviews are indifferent to my doing so, as it has no effect on them, that is, they receive the same payoff whether I coordinate with them or not.

There is a puzzle here. Coordination problems are structures in which the coordination benefit may be achieved. The coordination benefit is the benefit I receive from coordinating with others. But if I benefit from coordinating with others, then how can I be indifferent as to whether particular others cooperate? And since each player is in a parallel situation, why are the others indifferent as to my conformity to the suit norm? Perhaps Lewis and Ullmann-Margalit are right that coordination problems have two proper coordination equibria. The puzzle dissolves, however, with the realization that although the conformity of the other player matters in two-party cases, the situation becomes more complex for multiparty coordination situations.

Consider the following distinction. There are two separate conditions under which defection by others may hurt me. The first is the stronger of the two. It is when defection by any *one* of the others hurts me. But there is also the weaker case in which defection by most or all would hurt me, but not defection by any one. The Suit-Wearing Game is an example in which the second condition holds but not the first. It is not the case that defection by any particular agent hurts me. In fact, the opposite is true; I will more easily get the job if I am wearing a suit and a few others are not. But if most others defect from wearing suits, then I will be hurt as I will stand out. The crucial point is that the fact that I will be hurt by the defection of most does not imply that I will be hurt by the defection of each. Thus, this is not a proper coordination equilibrium because conformers do not prefer that each particular agent conform also. Yet it is a situation in which I benefit from conformity to the norm. Because the other players are in the same position, the norm may be maintained over time by these acts of conformity.

To really bring this point home, it is instructive to contrast the Suit-Wearing Game with the favorite example of game theorists, the convention of driving on one side of the road or the other. Their analysis of driving as a convention that represents a proper coordination equilibrium seems correct. For it does matter to each of the conformers that all the others also drive on the same side of the road. If there is less than total conformity, everyone's life is in danger. But the same fact does not hold for wearing suits and other similar practices for which people are indifferent as to whether conformity is universal. These are thus examples of coordination equilibria that are not proper coordination equilibria. Recall that in a proper coordination equilibrium, everyone does worse if anyone acts differently, whereas in a coordination equilibrium, it is only that no one does better if anyone acts differently. In the Suit-Wearing Game, others are indifferent. It is not that the rest would have done worse by one person's defection, it is just that no one would have done better by such a defection.

The suit-wearing norm would not count as a coordination norm according to Lewis and Ullmann-Margalit as it lacks the requisite proper coordination equilibria. Intuitively, however, it is clear that we would count this as a coordination norm because it is a regularity of behavior that is maintained by people rationally seeking to coordinate their behavior with others. More specifically, my account captures why this example should be considered a coordination norm, as the conformity is explained by the possibility of achieving the coordination benefit.

Next, consider an example in which conformers actually prefer that others not conform. This is not a coordination equilibrium, but simply an equilibrium. At many law firms, there is a divergence between the official policy regarding

Others

	Two Weeks	Three Weeks
Two Weeks	3, 1	1, 4
Three Weeks	2, 2	4, 3

Me

Figure 2.10 The Associates Vacation Game

vacation time for associates and the actual practices of associates. Consider the example of what could be called the Associates Vacation Game in Figure 2.10.

In this situation, I prefer to do what others are doing. If they all take two weeks vacation, then I also want to take two weeks, so as not to stand out as a slacker. If they take three weeks, I prefer this also, so as to enjoy the longer vacation and so as not to be ostracized by my peers as obsequious. My co-workers, on the other hand, prefer that I do whatever they are not doing. If they take two weeks, they prefer I take three weeks so as to stand out as a slacker and thereby make them look better. And if they all take three weeks, they prefer I take two weeks so as to stand out as obsequious. Thus, my best choice of action is dependent on that of the others. I will receive the coordination benefit for taking two weeks if they take two weeks, or for taking three weeks if they take three weeks. But the others lose out due to my coordination; they suffer a coordination loss.

Consider a scenario in which associates take two weeks. This situation is in equilibrium because each person cannot do better, given what the others are doing. Given that the others are taking two weeks, each prefers that she also take two weeks. Thus the regularity will persist; the lawyers have reached equilibrium. But this is not a coordination equilibrium because it is not the case that no agent wishes any one agent – either herself or someone else – to have alone acted differently. Rather, each agent wishes any other agent to alone act differently from the rest.

Yet such a game is a coordination norm on my account. It is a pattern of rationally governed behavior instantiated in a group and maintained by conformity. The conformity is explained by the rational desire to achieve the coordination benefit. Intuitively, it is clear that the lawyers' conformity should count as a norm as it would be quite natural to remark that the norm in this scenario is for the associates is to take two weeks of vacation. Thus, it is a virtue of the present account that it shows why it should be included as such.

Though prescriptions and sanctions are characteristically present with norms, it is obvious why they will not be present in situations such as the

Associates Vacation Game. Prescriptions and sanctions usually serve to enhance the likelihood of conformity by changing the payoffs in favor of conformity. But in this example, the associates do not wish to increase the others' likelihood of conformity since their own interests are thereby harmed. It is because of the possibility of norms such as this that I argued in Chapter One that sanctions and prescriptions should not be built into the definition of norms. A similar point holds for the Suit-Wearing Game. Since others are indifferent to the defection of particular individuals, they will have no motive to prescribe conformity or sanction defection.[21]

We have seen that coordination norms may exist when there is not a proper coordination equilibrium, or even a coordination equilibrium. The next coordination norm to be considered is not in equilibrium at all. A game is in equilibrium when all players are satisfied with their choice, given the choices of others. No one prefers that she had acted otherwise, given the actions of others. If a norm is in equilibrium, the fact that new members join the group will not affect the conforming behavior of the current members. For example, if the norm currently has ten members, and if on the next round, five new members conform along with the original ten, if the norm is in equilibrium, then all fifteen conformers will be satisfied with their conformity, given the conformity of the others, and thus all will conform on the third round.

For example, the driving norm is in equilibrium. The fact that each year a new crop of teens become legal drivers and drive on the right has no tendency to affect the choice of current drivers to drive on the right. In the previous example, though each of the two-week vacationers wishes that one of the others had chosen three weeks, nonetheless, the choice of two weeks by the others has no tendency to cause the two-week vacationers to defect from the norm of choosing two weeks.

But with some norms, as new members enter the group, some of the current members no longer want to conform. This may lead to constant migration into and out of the norm. As long as the change is not drastic, we are inclined to say that the coordination norm continues to exist through changes of this sort, rather than saying that the old norm ceases to exist. Norms of fashion seem to have this character. A fashion might be a coordination norm in that it is a pattern of normatively governed behavior, instantiated in a group and maintained by conformity. Agents conform to achieve the coordination benefit, which is the positive utility one derives from looking like certain others. But this additional conformity may cause some of the previous conformers to wish to defect, that is, they receive a coordination loss from the conformity of the followers.

Imagine a fashion hub in the center of an urban area. The concentric circles around it represent the outer city, the suburbs, small towns and finally the countryside. Imagine a new fashion norm which starts at the hub. As those in the closest concentric band conform, those just outside the outer edge of this band begin to conform. This causes those at the inner edge to defect as they do not

Trend Setters

	New Fashion	Newer Fashion
New Fashion	2, 0	1, 2
Newer Fashion	0, 2	0, 1

Slaves to Fashion

Figure 2.11 The Fashion Game

want to be part of a fashion that has too many followers. In this manner, the concentric band of conformity might move out from the center of the city to the countryside. In such a case, it seems natural to say that the coordination norm continues to exist during the transition from being a norm of the avant-garde to becoming an outdated bumpkin norm of those who reside in the country. Thus, we see that a norm may stay in existence although it is not in equilibrium. Call this norm the *Fashion Game*. It has the strategic structure shown in Figure 2.11.

Slaves to fashion are those just outside the current outer edge of the band of conformity. The trend setters are those at the inner edge of the band of conformity. Their current conformity is precarious; they will defect if any new conformers join the fashion norm. The slaves to fashion wish to coordinate with all the current conformers. So the fact that their conformity causes the trend setters to defect will not be something they like, nor will it be enough to make them defect or not conform in the first place.

Summing up the preceding discussion, we have seen in the examples discussed that coordination norms may arise for three types of equilibria and also for the non-equilibrium case. In contrast, for Lewis and Ullmann-Margalit, conventions or coordination norms may arise only for one of these four categories, proper coordination equilibria. In addition, they require that there be a minimum of two of this type of equilibria, whereas we saw with the example of the Rock Quarry that one equilibrium is enough.

On the account developed previously, what is essential to a coordination norm is that one conform with the norm because of the coordination benefit. The agent benefits from coordination with the behavior of the others. The others need not benefit, however. For the other players, it matters that some others are acting as they are acting, but it need not matter that each additional person act in this manner. The dictionary captures this ambiguity in the notion of coordination. Coordination may occur when one coordinates one's activities with ongoing activities, or it may occur when two agents act together. The latter only is the sense captured by Lewis in his notion of actors forming "mutually concordant expectations" and then acting on them.[22] Coordination may persist, however, even when people are not mutually concordant. Games of coordination in the sense of Lewis and Ullmann-Margalit are then a special case of the larger topic of coordination in order to achieve the coordination benefit.

II. Sanction-Driven Norms

Sanction-driven norms (SD norms) are the second type of strategic norm. Just as was the case with coordination norms, a variety of related structures all count as sanction-driven norms. What the family of SD norms have in common is that the acts of conformity making up the norm are performed to avoid sanctions rather than out of natural inclination. This is in contrast to coordination norms for which conformity – and so the norms themselves – could exist in a world without the presence of sanctions.

An SD norm of particular interest is the type of norm that may emerge as the solution to what has been variously called the iterated Prisoner's Dilemma, collective action problem or public goods problem. As the Prisoner's Dilemma is now well known across a variety of academic disciplines and to some extent in the general population as well, this is a good place to begin.

A. One-Shot and Iterated Prisoner's Dilemmas

As will already be familiar to many, the Prisoner's Dilemma derives its name from the classic example of two prisoners and the dilemma each faces in individually deciding whether to cooperate with the other in withholding information from the authorities. The story is customarily told in the following manner. Two prisoners are charged with a crime. Though in fact both prisoners are guilty, the authorities do not have enough evidence to convict each of the full offense. There is enough evidence, however, to convict each of a lesser offense. Thus, if the prisoners can manage to keep silent, each will receive a shorter sentence than would be possible giving the severity of the offense, as the sentences will be based on this less incriminating evidence. If either alone confesses, however, thereby implicating the other, the prisoner who confesses will get the shortest possible sentence or be released on probation while the other will get an even stiffer sentence than if both were convicted of the full charge.

In this example, there are four possible lengths of sentence each of the prisoners might serve. Given that each prisoner may independently choose between confessing and not confessing, there are four possible outcomes. The ranking of the prisoners' preferences is captured in Figure 2.12.

In the language of informal game theory, refusal to confess counts as *cooperation* (or "C") while confession counts as *defection* (or "D"). Cooperation here does not mean cooperation with the authorities, but rather cooperation with the other prisoner in maintaining the mutually beneficial silence. Defection means

Prisoner B

		Not Confess (C)	Confess (D)
Prisoner A	Not Confess (C)	3, 3	1, 4
	Confess (D)	4, 1	2, 2

Figure 2.12 The Prisoner's Dilemma

defection from this silence. If A confesses while B does not (the southwest cell), then A receives 4, her most preferred outcome (shortest possible sentence or probation), and B receives 1, her least preferred outcome (the most severe sentence). If B confesses while A does not (the northeast cell), B receives 4, her most preferred outcome, and A receives 1, her least preferred outcome. If both confess (the southeast cell), each receives 2, the second least preferred outcome (the second most severe sentence) while if both refrain from confessing (the northwest cell), each receives 3, the second most preferred outcome (the second lightest sentence).

The so-called Prisoner's Dilemma arises due to the following features of this situation. If rational, each prisoner will notice that no matter what the other prisoner does, it is in her own interest to confess. For example, if B confesses, and A also confesses, A receives 2, whereas if A does not, she receives 1, thus preferring to confess. If B does not confess, and A confesses, A receives 4, whereas if she does not, she receives 3, thus, again preferring to confess. The same situation holds for B – whatever A does, it is better for B to confess. In the language of informal game theory, confession in this situation is the *dominant strategy*; each prefers it regardless of what the other person does.

The result is that each of the prisoners, if rational, will confess. The problem is that this will put them in the southeast cell, giving each the second worst outcome, whereas if both had held back the information from the authorities, each would have ended up in the northwest cell, giving each the second best outcome. Thus, when each chooses the individually rational strategy, both end up worse off than if they had been able to restrain themselves and choose the action that would provide for the jointly preferred outcome. This situation constitutes one of the so-called paradoxes of rationality, as behavior that is individually rational or optimal turns out to be collectively suboptimal.[23]

For single-shot Prisoner's Dilemmas, it is generally agreed that no solution to the problem is available. It is simply a cruel fact about the world that individually optimal choices may lead to collectively suboptimal results. This cruel fact will only be alarming if Prisoner's Dilemma situations are pervasive. Unfortunately, they are.[24] Not only do Prisoner's Dilemma problems arise often, but, like nightmares, they may recur. In the language of informal game theory, these are called *iterated Prisoner's Dilemmas*.

B. Norms as Solutions to Iterated Prisoner's Dilemmas

Fortunately, iterated Prisoner's Dilemmas contain the makings of their own solution. For although the Prisoner's Dilemma captures the strategic structure of the direct payoffs to agents in the types of situations under consideration, the fact that the situations recur may change the strategic structure of the situation as it exists over time, such that a cooperative strategy may become preferable to each of the players. If one player defects in a Prisoner's Dilemma situation and consequently her partner receives the worst payoff, she may decide not to cooperate with the first person in future play. This failure to achieve future cooperation may be more costly in the long run than the immediate gain from defection. All things considered, the best choice may be to cooperate. In addition, the disappointed person may harm the first person's reputation by telling others of her proclivity to defect. They too may then be reluctant to cooperate with this person in situations with the structure of an iterated Prisoner's Dilemma. So, by defecting in iterated Prisoner's Dilemma situations, a person may gain in the short run but lose overall.[25]

Consider an example, borrowed from David Hume, of stealing property from other people. Hume writes:

It is only a general sense of common interest; which sense all the members of society express to one another, and which induces them to regulate their conduct by certain rules. I observe, that it will be for my interest to leave another in the possession of his goods, provided he will act in the same manner with regard to me. He is sensible of a like interest in the regulation of his conduct. When this common sense of interest is mutually expressed, and is known to both, it produces a suitable resolution and behavior.[26]

If I steal from you and you do not steal from me, then I am better off and you are worse off. If we each steal from one other, then you are not as bad off as when I steal from you and you do not steal from me, and I am not as well off as when I alone am a thief. On the other hand, if we both refrain from stealing, we are both better off than when we both steal from one another, though neither is as well off as when he alone partakes of thievery. This is analogous to the situation in which we both refrain from confessing to the authorities. In the case of the prisoners, facing the situation once as they do, it is hard to see how an egoist could resist confessing. But this may not be the case with stealing. For, whereas the prisoners will only be in this situation once, people are often in a position to steal repeatedly from one another. Unlike one-shot situations, when agents are in the same situation repeatedly, it will sometimes be rational to cooperate with one another if doing so will allow each to achieve the jointly preferred outcome.

The reason is obvious. If we continue to steal from each other time after time, each is a loser, whereas if we can both summon up restraint, each will benefit. You will know that I will restrain from stealing your goods only if you restrain from stealing mine, and vice versa. Thus, each may practice restraint in order to induce restraint on the part of the other in the future.

This mutual practice of restraint may become a norm. The normative governance in this case would consist of the rational desire of each to give the other no reason to stop cooperating in future games and no reason to denigrate the other's reputation. The norm, then, represents a solution to the iterated Prisoner's Dilemma that the two people in Hume's example faced with respect to one another. A norm that serves as a solution to an iterated Prisoner's Dilemma is appropriately called a *Prisoner's Dilemma norm*, or *PD norm* for short.

C. Public Goods Problems

Norms may serve as solutions to public goods problems. Public goods have two defining features: *jointness of supply* and *impossibility of exclusion*.[27] When a good is in joint supply, consumption of the good by one person does not lessen the amount available to others. When a good has the property of impossibility of exclusion, if it is available to be consumed by one, it is available to be consumed by all. A common example of a public good is street lighting. One person's consumption of this good does not lessen the amount of light available to others, such that if street lighting is available to one member of the community it is available to all members.

Contrast the consumption of a public good with the consumption of a private good such as a can of soda. When one person consumes a soda from the refrigerator, there is less soda available for others. In the language of public goods, there is no jointness of supply. In addition, consumption of soda can be restricted, as for example by putting a lock on the refrigerator. In other words, exclusion is possible.

Of these two defining features of public goods, the one most relevant for our purposes is the second, impossibility of exclusion. The fact that it is impossible or infeasible to exclude others from consuming public goods once they are provided is the key to understanding the public goods problem. This feature makes free riding on the efforts of others possible, since, if the public good is provided by others, the rational actor may also reap the benefits without contributing, as she cannot be excluded. It might be true that her contribution will raise the probability that the good will be provided, or raise the level of provision of the good somewhat. But in situations with the structure of a public goods problem, these effects will not be pronounced enough to countervail the incentive to defect. Thus, free riding will be rational. The difficult problem with public goods provision is not that there might be some free riding at the margin, but that all actors may be in the position in which it is rational not to contribute to the production of the good. The result may be that no one will contribute, even though, if all were to contribute, all would be better off.

Political theorists have seen the provision of benefits from the state in terms of the public goods problem. Hobbes argued that a strong state, a Leviathan, is needed to provide the basic societal requirements of peace and security.[28] A number of writers have observed that peace and security are public goods because when they are provided for some, they are provided for all, and consumption by one does not diminish the amount available to others.[29] The typical public goods discussed have the feature that the good is a physical object such as a lighthouse. Lighthouses are in joint supply because one boater's benefit from a lighthouse does not diminish the ability of another boater to benefit. Second, it is practically impossible to exclude particular boaters from benefiting from the lighthouse, should they decide to do so, once it is in existence.

Of more interest in the present context, however, are not physical objects that may serve as public goods, but rather norms and customs that sometimes have structures that qualify them as public goods. Recall from Chapter One that a norm is not a rule but a pattern of rationally governed behavior instantiated in a community that is maintained by conformity. As such, norms have associated payoff structures, and these are sometimes fairly seen as public goods. The benefits flowing from the practice are such that it is not practically possible to exclude others, and the good, once produced, is in joint supply such that one person's benefit from the good does not diminish the ability of others to benefit.

Consider a few examples. The practice whereby the members of a group do not litter has the structure of a public goods problem. In this strategic situation, one faces off against all the other participants in the practice. The social practice whereby people refrain from littering is represented by the outcome in the northwest cell of Figure 2.13 in which each person receives a payoff of 3. It is apparent from the matrix why the maintenance of the practice may be problematic, for each person would prefer if the outcomes represented by the southwest cell instead existed.

		Others	
		Not Littering	Littering
You	Not Littering	3, 3	1, 4
	Littering	4, 1	2, 2

Figure 2.13 The Littering Game

Practices with structures whereby they embody a solution to a public goods problem appear prevalent. The practice whereby people refrain from stealing from one another can be seen in this light. The egoist prefers that others respect property but that she have the ability to show selective disrespect. The egoist wishes for others to show respect for two reasons. First, her own property will be safe, and, second, if there is a general respect for property, she will more easily be able to get away with her own transgressions (e.g., thieves may sometimes have an easier time in small communities due to the presence of fewer precautions).

Consider a few more examples. The egoist wants others to conform to a practice whereby passing motorists come to the aid of stranded motorists, for such a practice ensures that she will get help where she needs it. However, she has no desire to aid others. The egoist prefers that others refrain from driving while intoxicated so that she will be safer on the road. But she may sometimes prefer to be able to drive when intoxicated herself. The egoist prefers that the population at large use condoms as this reduces the pool of people with disease who might infect her. She may prefer, however, not to use them in some circumstances.

All these situations share the feature that the egoist wishes for some particular regularity of behavior to exist in a community so that she can benefit from it, but she wishes not to conform to the regularity herself, or only to conform selectively. It might seem apparent that these regularities could not exist in a world of egoists because all would have the same preference that others maintain them but not they themselves. This would be disappointing for the egoists involved, as each prefers that the regularity exist and that she adhere to it over the state of affairs in which the norm does not exist. And yet by each acting in her narrow self-interest, the latter results.

D. PD Norms as Solutions to Public Goods Problems

Consider the last five examples of the public goods problem. If somehow the proper norms were in place in these situations, then there would in fact be no failure of collective action. For the norm is just the pattern of conforming behavior. For example, if the norm is that no one violates another person's property, then in spite of the structure of the recurrent situation, in fact, the public good is provided. The public good in this case is the state of affairs in which everyone's possessions are safe from theft. In the example of littering, if there is a norm extant in the community whereby no one litters, then in spite of the structure of the situation, the public good of an attractive environment is provided. The public good is the attractive environment.

What then is the relation between SD norms and public goods? In some cases, the norm is the means to the public good. For example, in the case of littering, the public good is an attractive environment. The pattern of non-littering behavior is the means to the good. In other cases, the connection is more intimate. It seems fair to claim that in the aiding strangers example, the public good is simply the pattern of behavior. The public good is that one can expect to receive help when stranded. When the regularity of behavior is such that people stop for stranded motorists, the public good is therefore provided in virtue of others stopping. Thus the regularity of behavior is the public good. We see then that norms are a particular kind of public good. They are not objects like lighthouses or bridges but rather patterns of behavior instantiated in groups. If groups or communities can somehow manage to follow these patterns of behavior, they will have managed to provide the relevant public goods.

Public goods problems have an additional feature. The good cannot have the property that it is in the interest of some one person or a few persons to supply it. For example, there will not be a public goods problem in the case of the lighthouse if one particularly powerful shipper finds it in her interest to provide the good on her own. According to Olson, we can assume that the good will be provided in such a case.[30] The relevance of this for the present discussion is that in cases in which a public good is provided by one or some small number of individuals, this will not be an instance of a norm serving as a public good. Norms are patterns of behavior instantiated in a group. If the good is provided by one individual, thus making the group pattern of behavior unnecessary, the problem is solved, but not by a norm. For example, a wealthy environmentalist might find litter so repellent that she pays a crew to continually pick it up. The public good of an attractive environment is available to all, but it is not provided by a norm.

Note that even the extreme measures of the wealthy environmentalist cannot provide the good as well as a simple norm can. For the crew can only do their job after the littering has occurred and thus after people have suffered its unsightliness. If the norm against littering is extant, however, the litter will never hit the ground. Consider condom use in this light. The public good of decreased viral transmission is a function of the proportion of the group that conform to the norm. It is hard to imagine a realistic manner in which a single person could provide this good with anything close to the efficiency of a group whose members conform to safe sex norms. In this example, practically speaking, an individual cannot provide the good, only a norm can. The same holds for the threat drunk driving poses for driver safety. The public good is a less risky driving environment. Any manner by which a single person could ensure this good to a group would seem less efficient than if the group simply conforms to sober driving practices.

E. PD Norms Versus SD Norms

Ullmann-Margalit introduced the term *PD norm* to cover the types of examples I call SD norms. My term is appropriate because all the examples share the feature that conformity is only forthcoming as a result of sanctions; hence, these norms are driven by sanctions. Ullmann-Margalit might respond, however, that her term is equally appropriate because all the cases she considers have an iterated Prisoner's Dilemma structure. I will now go on to establish that what is at issue is actually a more general notion than the Prisoner's Dilemma.

What matters for an SD norm is that conformity is rational only when sanctions are present. In other words, with SD norms, the agent's most preferred outcome, sanctions aside, is one in which she is not conforming. This makes SD norms a broader category of norms than Prisoner's Dilemma norms as this notion is set out by Ullmann-Margalit because there are norms that exist only as a result of sanctions but that do not have the structure of an iterated Prisoner's Dilemma. This then is the second type of norm for which Ullmann-Margalit's explication of the concept is not sufficiently broad. With coordination norms, what mattered was whether a *coordination benefit* was available, not whether the situation presented multiple coordination equilibria. With the sort of situation in which a sanction-driven norm may arise, the player conforms because there is a strategic effect to conforming but it is negative, that is, one receives a *coordination loss* for conforming. It is only the presence of a sanction that makes it the case that, all things considered, the conformity results in a coordination benefit. These features are true of norms with a variety of strategic structures. What these structures share is that the first preference is not to conform. The rankings of the other preferences do not matter for present purposes. This is most easily seen by looking at another well-known game in the rational choice literature, the game of Chicken. The game of Chicken has the strategic structure shown in Figure 2.14.

Hume provides an example of two people who wish to drain a meadow.[31] As he describes it, the structure of this situation appears to be that of a Prisoner's Dilemma as each neighbor prefers to abandon the project (mutual defection) rather than to do the work on her own (unilateral cooperation). In a similar situation, however, the effects of leaving the meadow undrained might be so disastrous that each neighbor would prefer to do it on her own rather than leaving

Column-Chooser

		Cooperate	Defect
	Cooperate	3, 3	2, 4
Row-Chooser			
	Defect	4, 2	1, 1

Figure 2.14 The Game of Chicken

it undone.[32] This situation would have the structure of a game of Chicken, as is captured in Figure 2.14. Each prefers most that the other does the work, prefers next that both do the work, prefers next that she alone do the work, and finally, prefers least that the meadow is left undrained. Thus, unlike the Prisoner's Dilemma in which if one defects the other prefers to defect also, if the first defects in Chicken, the second prefers to cooperate.

It is plausible to suppose that in circumstances such as these, as in the Prisoner's Dilemma, one may be able to get the other to cooperate in mutual or reciprocal provision of the good through threat of defection. Each prefers that the other provide the good, which creates an incentive to somehow bind oneself to not helping drain the meadow so that the other person is forced to do it by herself if she wants it done at all. But each knows that it is dangerous to simply not cooperate as the other may reason in a similar manner, which would produce the worst outcome for each.

In such circumstances, it may be rational for each to try to sanction the other into cooperation. This might be accomplished by threatening not to cooperate in other spheres of interaction if the other does not cooperate with regard to the meadow. One's threat may bring about the worst outcome, however, if it fails to elicit cooperation on the part of the other. But this chance may be worth taking if the long-run benefits of mutual rather than unilateral provision of the good are large enough. If the meadow drainage problem is recurrent, a cooperative practice may develop. Such a norm is maintained through sanctions and so is fairly denominated an SD norm, yet it is not a PD norm.

Chicken and the Prisoner's Dilemma are alike in one important respect, however. The cooperative practice achieved through sanctions is preferred to the situation in which cooperation is not achieved at all. Thus, sanctions serve a useful role in iterated Chicken just as they do in the case of the iterated Prisoner's Dilemma, for it is the possibility of sanctioning one another that makes mutually beneficial cooperative practices possible. But not all sanction-driven norms have this feature. Consider a strategic structure in which people prefer mutual defection to mutual cooperation. Call it the game of Heroism. The payoff matrix in Figure 2.15 is similar to that for the Prisoner's Dilemma in other respects except that mutual defection is preferred to mutual cooperation, that is, the southeast cell provides a higher payoff to each of the players than does the northwest cell.

An example of the game of Heroism might be heroic behavior in a military unit. Each prefers most that others abide by the norm of heroism but that she defect. In such a situation, the war may be more easily won, and her life might even be saved by one of the heroic acts. This is similar to the Prisoner's Dilemma in that one's first preference is to free ride on a norm of cooperation. Unlike the Prisoner's Dilemma, however, the second preference of each is that no one act heroically, rather than the situation in which all are heroic. This might be a plausible preference for an egoist given the dangers of heroism. She would

Column-Chooser

		Heroism	No Heroism
	Heroism	2, 2	1, 4
Row-Chooser			
	No Heroism	4, 1	3, 3

Figure 2.15 The Game of Heroism

rather that the war not go so well and take her chances in terms of not being saved by others, rather than behaving as a hero herself. If this is the case, we should not expect egoists sanctioning defectors to be a means of eliciting cooperation by all.

Sanctions of a different sort, however, might be imposed to bring about conformity. If, for example, the military high command creates sanctions to alter the payoffs so that mutual cooperation is preferred to mutual defection, regular practices centered around heroism might come about. In the game of Chicken and the Prisoner's Dilemma, the agents themselves provide sanctions in order to bring about cooperation by others; in the game of Heroism, an outside source provides the sanctions.

In Chicken and PD, the sanctions allow the agents to reach a mutually preferred outcome that is otherwise unobtainable. Thus there is a sense in which sanctions are desirable to these agents. In the best of all possible worlds, the egoist has an endless supply of fresh cooperators to sucker. But if this world cannot be found, it is better to live in a world of rational egoists with whom one can reach cooperative solutions through sanctions than in a world where one is not able to do so. The same does not hold for the game of Heroism, however. Here, the sanctions cause the actors to settle on the outcome, which is mutually inferior to the outcome they would otherwise settle on. Other things equal, egoists prefer that sanctions of this sort not exist (at least where they are the ones being sanctioned). We might say that sanctions arising in the game of Chicken and the Prisoner's Dilemma are *welcome sanctions*, while those arising in the game of Heroism are *unwelcome sanctions*.

In the preceding examples, the welcome sanctions arise from within the norm group, whereas the unwelcome sanctions arise from outside the group. But this is purely a contingent matter. As groups become larger, it is increasingly difficult for sanctioning techniques like threats to reputation to work. Thus, the group may develop institutional techniques for sanctioning, such as a legal system. Once such sanctions are in place, it is as if the sanctions come from outside the group of conformers. Yet, this does not mean that the sanctions are unwelcome from the point of view of the egoist. For even though the sanctions are administered by an institution, they may nevertheless help to produce mutually preferred outcomes. We see then that what matters is the effect; do the sanctions bring about the preferred modes of behavior for the sanctioned group? If they do, they are welcome; if not, they are unwelcome.

A similar issue may be raised with regard to so-called internal sanctions. In their accounts of the working of norms, sociologists and moral theorists have noted the existence of self-imposed or internal sanctions.[33] The general idea is that, as a result of socialization, actors will internalize norms, that is, they will come to accept that behavior in accordance with the norm is morally required of them. Consequently, actors will be inhibited from deviation from the norm by self-imposed sanctions. Well-socialized persons subject to internal sanctioning may feel guilt and shame even at the thought of defection. The relevant question in the current context is whether such sanctions are best seen as welcome or unwelcome.

Before this question can be answered, we must consider whether the notion of internal sanctions even makes sense in the context of perfectly rational actors. It would appear that for perfectly rational actors, internal sanctions are inherently unacceptable because punishing oneself is costly and is hence irrational. Consequently, the authors cited earlier who talk about internal sanctions are implicitly bringing in a moral conception of the individual that violates the assumption of *Homo economicus*.

This objection is not sound, however. What matters to *Homo economicus* is doing the best for herself. If internal sanctions cause her to move to an individually superior outcome, then they are welcome, and if they cause her to move to an otherwise inferior outcome, they are unwelcome. For example, if internal sanctions cause two agents to seek the cooperative outcome in a Prisoner's Dilemma, then they are each better off for having the sanctions in place. Whereas if internal sanctions cause those in the game of Heroism to adopt the cooperative solution, they are worse off because of these sanctions. Thus, whether internal constraints are rationally desirable depends on the contingent issue of how often and to what degree one benefits from their presence versus how often and to what degree one is hurt by their presence. In the abstract, then, we cannot say whether internal sanctions are rational or not. Rather, they will be welcome in some cases and unwelcome in others.[34]

Before leaving this topic, the following objection to the very idea of SD norms must be discussed. It might be wondered whether acting in accordance with a norm out of the motive to avoid a sanction is really best thought of as an act of conformity. After all, the action is motivated by the sanction and not by the existence of the norm, per se. Remember, conformity, on my account, is a causal notion; part of the reason for behaving in a certain manner must be the fact that others are behaving in that manner. But this does not appear to be the case when the reason for a certain behavior is a sanction.

This objection appears to be valid in some instances and not in others. It will depend on the cause of the sanctions. The proper causal condition necessary for conformity is present when at least part of the cause of the sanctions is the conforming behavior of the others. For example, in the game of Heroism, it is plausible to suppose that unless the military authorities can count on a fairly high degree of conformity to their dictate of heroic behavior, the sanctions will not be imposed. In such a case, the conformity to the norm is a partial cause of the sanctions which in turn cause conformity by particular actors. Thus, behavior of a certain sort is the indirect cause of more behavior of the same sort; hence, the causal requirement is satisfied, although indirectly.

In sum, from the discussion in the previous section, we are able to see the two respects in which the notion of an SD norm is a generalization of the notion of a PD norm. The first relates to the strategic structure of the circumstances of conformity. It was shown that SD norms may be maintained in situations with strategic structures other than the Prisoner's Dilemma or collective action problem. This was seen for two cases, the game of Chicken and the game of Heroism. The second manner in which SD norms are a more general notion than PD norms has to do with the manner in which sanctions bring about conformity, in particular, norms may be maintained by welcome as well as by unwelcome sanctions.

III. Epistemic Norms

As mentioned at the outset of the chapter, the three types of rational norms emerge either in strategic or nonstrategic contexts. The previous two sections looked at the two types of strategic norms – coordination norms and sanction-driven norms. It is now time to consider nonstrategic norms. Indeed, on the surface, it is puzzling why norms would come about in nonstrategic contexts. With nonstrategic norms, the agent does not receive a greater payoff for performing an action of a certain type as a function of others also performing actions of this type. Why then would someone conform to the actions of others, if doing so does not have any beneficial effect for her? In spite of initial appearances, however, it is indeed often rational to conform to norms in nonstrategic contexts. The reason people sometimes conform to norms in such situations is to economize on information costs. Rather than expending the costs to gather the information to make a fully informed decision on her own, each agent may instead conform to what others who are similarly situated are doing. Because such acts of conformity are driven by epistemic considerations, the resulting patterns of behavior are properly labeled *epistemic norms*.[35] With such norms, it is not that they are a substitute for information, rather epistemic norms are a source of information.

In general, for rational actors, the right thing to do will depend on the circumstances. But as circumstances change, it will take work to discover the objectively rational thing to do. Fortunately, conformity to the behavior of others sometimes affords a short-cut. Given that others around you are in a comparable situation, and are intelligent, you may infer that what they are doing is the right thing for you also. In other words, you can borrow the expertise of others by conforming to their behavior. It is not difficult to imagine how such behavior might grow into a norm. With each new person who conforms, the total number of people performing a particular type of behavior in a particular circumstance grows. This allows a greater number of people to witness that this type of behavior is performed by others in these circumstances, which opens the door for still more conformity. At some point in this growth process, it will become natural to conclude that a norm has emerged.[36]

The concept of an epistemic norm may be clarified with a few examples. Suppose my neighbor is a child psychologist who in general seems to exhibit good judgment and common sense in our occasional interactions. Under the circumstances, I might be sensible to conform to my neighbor's behavior regarding the treatment of children, especially if I am ill informed and do not have ready access to other sources of information. There are no rules as such that I follow. Rather, I observe her behavior and conform to it. For example, if frequently she talks to her young infant in the backyard, I may take this as evidence that this is a preferred form of behavior. If she reprimands her toddler with a harsh tone or an occasional mild spanking, I may take this as appropriate or at least acceptable behavior.

I do what my neighbor does because she does it, that is, I allow my behavior to conform to hers. My conformity is nonstrategic as the outcome I wish to produce is not dependent on any choice of hers. As it stands, these are examples of single acts of rationally motivated conformity in a nonstrategic situation. But similar conforming acts might be performed by other parents in the neighborhood, also in response to the behavior of the respected child psychologist. In such a manner, a norm or set of norms could grow throughout the neighborhood. A new family might move in to a part of the neighborhood such that they could not observe the behavior of the child psychologist directly, but could observe the behavior of some of the families that are already conforming their child-rearing practices to those of the child psychologist. The new family might deem the behavior of the other families worthy of imitation. Over time enough such acts of conformity might occur such that it would be natural to say that a new set of child-rearing practices had emerged in the neighborhood.

Consider a second example. It has become something of a norm among certain cultural groups in America to buy foreign automobiles. Such purchasers appear to commonly believe that these automobiles are a better value than those manufactured in America. While there are objective sources of information one can consult to determine which automobiles are the best value, many buyers probably do not do so. Rather, they rely on the judgment of those better informed, and then conform to their choices. As the expression says, *go with the smart money.*

A third example of behavior that might lead to an epistemic norm is breast feeding, which in the last generation has made a comeback in the United States. It is almost certainly the case that many of the women who have chosen to breast feed do not have hard evidence that it is preferable to formula. Rather, they conform to those who appear better informed about the issue and who have chosen to breast feed. They economize on the cost of gathering information by conforming their actions to those of persons perceived to be more knowledgeable.

Long before certain states began adopting seat belt laws, the advisability of their use was debated. Many thought that seat belts saved lives. Others, however, cited instances in which people lived because they were not belted in. Instead of deciding on one's own who was right, one might very well have chosen to conform to the behavior of those who seemed better informed and better able to evaluate social scientific data. Thus, one might decide to wear seat belts because this was the trend among those who seem to exhibit good judgment about such matters. Through repeated instances of conformity of this sort, a norm of wearing seat belts might come about.

Each of the preceding examples shares the feature that a norm may come about and be maintained by actions, each of which is motivated by the desire to conform to the actions of others, instead of becoming fully informed on one's own. In such scenarios, the like actions of others play an important causal role in the best explanation of the choice of particular individuals to act likewise. Accordingly, such practices would satisfy the causal condition for a norm as first set out in Chapter One. In other respects, these practices also count as norms because they are patterns of normatively governed behavior instantiated in groups. The normative governance in the case of epistemic norms comes from the rational choice of each particular conformer to promote her interest in the context of a nonstrategic social setting. Finally, it is also clear that each of the preceding practices counts as a norm; it would be quite natural, for instance, to say that breast feeding is again the norm in some circles in the United States.

Note that in contrast to sanction-driven norms considered in the previous section, sanctions are not necessary for the maintenance of epistemic norms. Consider, for example, the norm of brushing one's teeth after every meal. One might rationally decide to conform to this norm instead of determining for oneself the optimal amount of times per day to brush one's teeth. Yet one will not be sanctioned for failing to conform to the norm. Even setting aside the problem of detecting one's deviation, the reason why others will not sanction one in this example is obvious; by and large, others do not care whether or not one brushes after every meal.[37] Yet the norm may be maintained by acts of conformity, nonetheless (seemingly, the conformity will tend to run along family lines). Thus, we see that like coordination norms, but unlike SD norms, sanctions are not necessary for the maintenance of epistemic norms.

Though sanctions are not necessary, they will often be present in an attenuated form. This was seen earlier to also be true for coordination norms. For example, with the coordination norm of wearing a coat and tie to interviews, one will not be sanctioned for deviations by the world at large, yet those who take one's interests to heart or have something at stake themselves may prescribe such behavior and sanction deviations. The same may hold for epistemic norms such as the norm of brushing after meals. Parents will often take an interest in their children conforming to this norm and sanction non-conformity. This is an important point to note as there appears to be an implicit albeit erroneous assumption at work in the sociological literature that all norms are equally sanctioned by society at large.

The next section looks briefly at some of the leading accounts of norms by law and norms scholars. These accounts will be explored in greater depth in Parts Two and Three of the book in applied legal contexts. The purpose of the following introduction is to see from a bird's-eye view where these accounts fit into the conceptual apparatus developed in Part One.

IV. Norms in the Theory of Law and Norms

The most striking fact about the conceptions of norms held by legal theorists is that they all involve sanction-driven norms, although they do not always go by that name. But within this type, these accounts are importantly distinct from one another. Discussion should begin with Robert Ellickson's account, which has been the dominant influence in law and norms scholarship.

Over the course of his book, *Order Without Law*, and in a series of articles, Ellickson has developed the leading argument in the legal literature for the efficiency of social norms that function as solutions to iterated collective action problems. Ellickson develops his position at greatest length in *Order Without Law*. In the context of a modern day ranching and farming community in Shasta County, California, Ellickson examines damage to crops, motorists, and automobiles by wandering cattle, and damage to cattle by motorists.[38]

One of Ellickson's leading examples involves practices that have developed with regard to boundary fences that are erected to control the wandering of animals. Each party will benefit from the fence, but each prefers the other to bear the cost of erecting and maintaining it, as fences are expensive.[39] Generalizing somewhat from the particular facts of the example, Ellickson calls this the Specialized Labor Game and characterizes it with the payoff matrix shown in Figure 2.16.[40]

The residents of Shasta County are able to reach the welfare-maximizing social practice as represented in the northeast quadrant. Ellickson argues that

Player B

		Build Fence	Shirk
	Build Fence	3, 3	0, 7
Player A			
	Shirk	7, −2	1, 1

Figure 2.16 Specialized Labor Game

it is the "close-knittedness" of the community that allows it to solve its fencing problem. In this scenario, the problem is solved when one person does all the work in providing the fence. Ellickson writes: "[M]embers of a close-knit group develop and maintain norms whose content serves to maximize the aggregate welfare that members obtain in their workaday affairs with one another."[41] Neighbors who share a common boundary may often be particularly close-knit since they live physically close together and are thus likely to have repeated interactions over a variety of everyday concerns. This may be especially true for the ranchers and farmers in Ellickson's study, as they earn a living off their land and move about it often. Such multiplex[42] social relationships allow members of the community to sanction one another so that conformity to the socially preferred practice becomes individually rational.[43] Ellickson contends that "the more close-knit a group, the more successful it will be at generating and enforcing utilitarian norms to govern informal disputes."[44]

The Specialized Labor Game is an example of a sanction-driven norm. While Ellickson does not discuss sanction-driven norms as such, sanctions are nevertheless crucial to his account of welfare maximization among close-knit groups. Repeated interaction and overlapping social networks afford the participants the opportunity to credibly threaten to sanction in future play for making dispreferred choices in current play.

Note that on Ellickson's account, the sanctions are utilized by one agent in an attempt to influence the behavior of other agents. Briefly consider Robert Cooter's account next. Cooter focuses on the role of "internal" sanctions.[45] Cooter's account is distinctive in that not only is the norm internalized, but the sanctions inducing conformity come from within as well. That is they are internal sanctions, in contrast to the external sanctions imposed by others, as is the case with sanction-driven norms. Once internalized, people will tend to feel guilty if they fail to conform to the norm.

For Cooter, internalization is essential to a norm. He writes, "a social norm is ineffective in a community and does not exist unless people internalize it."[46]

According to Cooter, those who internalize a norm will be willing to bear small costs to enforce it against others.[47]

Next, consider Richard McAdams's esteem-based account of the origin and development of norms. McAdams takes on the daunting task of explaining how norms initially arise.[48] This has been the single most vexing question in the theoretical literature on norms.[49] Understanding McAdams's account requires understanding the so-called second-order collective action problem. On the orthodox rational choice approach, norm maintenance requires sanctions. But sanctions are costly to administer. Therefore, a second-order collective action problem presents itself; rational actors will have an interest in free riding on the provision of sanctions, as the marginal benefit *to them* from the effect of this sanctioning on cooperation will almost surely be outweighed by the cost to them of this sanctioning activity.

McAdams's theory proposes a means of overcoming the second-order collective action problem. In short, McAdams argues that norms arise because people seek the esteem of others.[50] McAdams argues that under certain conditions, withholding esteem can be a costless means of inflicting costs on others.[51] McAdams fully accepts that these costs to people of others withholding esteem are often extremely small.[52] But he argues that a number of forces can cause a weak desire for esteem to produce powerful norms.

McAdams argues that people compete for the esteem of others.[53] This is because how one is esteemed will depend on how one stands next to others in regard to those properties that make one esteem worthy or disesteem worthy.[54] McAdams argues that under the right conditions, the desire for esteem produces a norm. McAdams Specifies three conditions for such an event:

For some behavior X in some population of individuals, a norm may arise if (1) there is a consensus about the positive or negative esteem worthiness of engaging in X (that is, either most individuals in the relevant population grant, or most withhold, esteem from those who engage in X); (2) there is some risk that others will detect whether one engages in X; (3) the existence of this consensus and risk of detection is well-known within the relevant population. When these conditions exist, the desire for esteem necessarily creates costs of or benefits from engaging in X, a norm will arise if, for most people, the esteem costs exceed the benefits of engaging in X.[55]

According to McAdams, if individuals desire esteem, and if the above conditions exist, it necessarily follows that one who violates a consensus incurs a cost. McAdams argues that if the consensus is that behavior X is commendable and the absence of X is deplorable, and the consensus is well known, then A will deduce that others will think less of her if they detect her failure to do X.[56] The esteem cost is the probability that a violation of the consensus will be detected multiplied by the value of the esteem that would then be lost.[57] According to McAdams, a norm arises when, for most individuals in the population, this esteem cost exceeds the cost of following the consensus.[58]

Thus, McAdams argues that if most group members prefer bearing the cost of doing X to the esteem cost of failing to do X, most members will do X.[59] Under these circumstances, we can say there is an esteem-based norm obligating individuals to do X.

McAdams argues that certain mechanisms magnify the power of esteem sanctions.[60] All of these arise due to the fact that esteem is a relative good. McAdams argues that there is a feedback effect whereby people competing to be "well thought of" compared to others discover that the cost of their non-compliance increases as compliance increases:[61] Not surprisingly, the status gain from compliance decreases as compliance increases. But individuals may nevertheless seek to achieve high status ("hero status").[62] Second, McAdams argues that esteem sanctioning can produce material sanctioning.[63] He plausibly claims that when people disapprove of those who approve norm violators, they produce secondary norms obligating enforcement of primary norms by disapproving primary norm violators.[64] The pursuit of hero status and the feedback effect generally can cause individuals to incur costs inflicting material sanctions on norm violators.[65] The end result of the competition for relative esteem under these mechanisms is that a weak behavioral standard may be transformed into a very demanding one.[66]

As this brief description of McAdam's theory of norm emergence indicates, his account of norms is, like Ellickson's and Cooter's, sanction-driven. In particular, his account is driven by esteem sanctions.

Finally, consider Eric Posner's signaling account of norms. I will first set out the core features of his account. Like that of McAdams, Posner's account ambitiously takes on the difficult topic of setting out a general theory of the emergence and maintenance of social norms. Posner argues that social norms are sets of rational acts whereby individuals seek to signal to others that they have low discount rates and hence that they would be good cooperative partners.[67] In general, signaling models seek to explain the manner by which words and deeds can serve a signaling function.[68] In a textbook-signaling example, the signal is used to communicate information regarding something about which there is *nonverifiable information*.[69] For example, warranties may be used to communicate that a product is of high quality. The signal works because the sellers of the higher quality products are able to send the signal more cheaply.[70] In the warranty example, Baird, Gertner, and Picker explain: "High quality sellers may be able to signal their type by selling goods with a warranty. Because their goods break down less often, these sellers can offer a warranty more cheaply than low-quality sellers."

According to Posner, individuals need to signal that they value the future sufficiently such that they would be willing to forego the immediate benefits of defecting in order to derive the future benefits of a sustained cooperative relationship. Posner emphasizes that signaling is a distinct form of activity from cooperative behavior itself. He writes, "Defection in cooperative endeavors is deterred by fear of reputational injury but the signaling behavior independently gives rise to forms of collective action that can be of great significance. People who care about future payoffs not only resist the temptation to cheat in a relationship; they signal their ability to resist the temptation by conforming to styles of dress, speech, conduct, and discrimination."[71]

As this quote indicates, on Posner's account, signaling allows actors to communicate to others that they have the "ability to resist the temptation" to defect in the current game. Thus, signaling is logically prior to actual rational acts of cooperation. It is signaling that may afford actors better opportunities for cooperative relationships at some later date.[72] Whether cooperation occurs will in part depend on the discount rates of the actors. The more one discounts the future, the less likely one is to forego the immediate one-time benefit gained from the defection in favor of the delayed benefit of future cooperation. Posner's model makes crucial use of the concept of discount rates. He refers to those with low discount rates as "good types" and those with high discount rates as "bad types."[73]

To distinguish themselves from bad types, good types engage in actions that are called "signals." Signals reveal type if only the good types, and not the bad types, can afford to send them, and everyone knows this. Because a good type is one who values future returns more than a bad type does, one signal is to incur large, observable costs prior to entering a relationship. For example, if a good type values a future payoff of 10 at a 10 percent discount and a bad type values the same payoff at a 30 percent discount, the good type can distinguish himself by incurring an otherwise uncompensated cost of 8.

The goal in searching for cooperative partners by means of being a signal watcher is to find people with low discount rates. Those with populations for high discount rates will be sanctioned by others' lack of interest in cooperating with them. Accordingly, actors will seek to convince others that they have low discount rates. Thus, sanctions play a crucial role in Posner's account just as they do in the accounts of Ellickson, Cooter, and McAdams. By the lights of the pattern conception of norms, signaling norms are then another instance in the more general category of sanction-driven norms. Signaling, according to Posner, is a means of establishing a reputation as a cooperator. He writes: "One wants a general reputation as a 'cooperator,' a person with a low discount rate, and one establishes that reputation both by declining to cheat in repeated games and by sending signals at every opportunity."[74]

On Posner's account, signals are arbitrary in the sense that any behavior could potentially come to serve as a signal as long as the behavior is observable and has an associated cost.[75] Posner seeks to fit a wide variety of behaviors into this model of arbitrary signals: engagement rings, deferred sex and unprotected sex, obedience to law, voting, patriotic displays, self-censorship, race discrimination, and nationalism. Posner argues that it is through norm entrepreneurs that these signals become established. He discusses a variety of actors who sometimes play this role: arbiters of taste, sellers of commercial goods, consultants, protocol experts, academics, journalists, politicians, and political activists.[76]

Because the signal is costly, it will mean that some actors – the bad types – will be prudentially excluded from sending it. The result will be a *separating equilibrium* in which good types act in one manner and bad types act in another manner.[77] For example, a good type may be willing to incur a greater cost from giving a gift in the early period of a relationship.[78] The less one discounts the future benefits of the relationship, the more one is willing to spend early on in order to signal one's low discount rate in order to foster a cooperative relationship. Social norms then on Posner's account are simply the patterns of behavior that result as the equilibrium outcomes of various signaling games such as the game of gift giving.

The discussion in this section has demonstrated that the leading law and norms accounts have previously focused on one of the three types of rational norms. Ellickson, Cooter, McAdams, and Posner all develop accounts that involve sanction-driven norms. Each of these accounts contains an element of truth. Esteem is desired and its pursuit may cause people to act in a cooperative manner, particularly toward those whose esteem they especially value. Conformity to norms may sometimes serve a signaling function. And close-knit communities may allow repeat players to share beneficial social practices. What I dispute is the comprehensiveness claimed for these accounts. All are sanction-driven accounts, but the world of norms and customs is a world with three types of rational custom, not one. The importance of this will be seen throughout the book. We will see norms that are plausibly seen as welfare-enhancing despite the fact that they are not maintained in close-knit communities. We will see important norms that are not plausibly seen as combinations of signaling acts. And we will see norms that are not plausibly the result of the desire for esteem.

I contend that each of the three accounts fails as a general account of the emergence of norms. In my view, no full account has been set out thus far. While I do not think there currently exists a general *emergence* account of norms (in Part One I develop a *maintenance* account) nevertheless I think that one can, by means of thick description, set out an emergence account for particular norms. This is precisely what I do in Part Three, where I will provide a detailed account of the emergence of website privacy norms.

V. Irrational Norms

The preceding discussion has set out three types of rational norms. It will be of interest to end the discussion with a brief consideration of what irrational norms might be like, by the lights of the theory set out herein.[79] Norms are patterns of rationally governed behavior instantiated in groups, maintained by conformity. What makes a norm rational is that the constitutive conforming acts are rational.

Irrational norms, then, if they exist, would be patterns of rationally governed behavior in which the agents conforming acts are irrational. In other words, the agents conform for irrational reasons.[80] It is unclear whether there are any irrational norms, for although it is certain that particular individuals sometimes do irrational things, it is far less certain that people act irrationally in the sort of systematic and patterned manner that would be necessary for norms to be maintained. Irrational actions might be fairly common, but not irrational norms. The existence of irrational norms entails the existence of irrational actions, but the reverse does not hold.

Rationality and irrationality are not uncontested concepts. On some views, there is little that is irrational. For example, on one extreme view, it would not be irrational to turn on the cold tap if one had a preference for a hot shower as the preference for tap turning and the preference for water temperature are logically distinct preferences, such that one could have these two distinct preferences without violating any of the axioms of decision theory. But one need not radically narrow the scope of irrational action in such a manner in order to question the existence of irrational norms. Consider the following model of irrational action, which will be called the *failure model*. It is arguably the most plausible general model for understanding irrationality. On this model, it is doubtful that irrational norms would exist.

People are not perfect. They are neither perfectly rational nor perfectly moral. It need not be the case that when one fails to be perfectly moral it is because one is being rational, or that when one fails to be perfectly rational it is because one is being moral. One may simply suffer from a failure to act either perfectly morally or perfectly rationally, that is, from a mere breakdown in the decision-making mechanism. In such cases, we may say that one acts irrationally, at least when the failure of morality or rationality is egregious. On this model, perhaps it is best said that irrationality is a failing rather than a true type of motivation. The existence of irrational acts need not contradict the assumption that people are rational and moral; it is just that they are not perfectly so. In fact, if one assumes that people are basically rational and moral, it is hard to see what larger role "irrational motivation" can play other than serving as a label for the failure of these positive types of motivation.

Seeing irrational acts as failures is instructive for understanding why irrational acts need not lead to irrational norms. If irrational conforming acts are merely failures, there need be no more than a random chance that they should occur together. Regression toward the mean should lead away from irrational acts of conformity being found in the patterns necessary to constitute norms. As an analogue, consider the manufacture of automobiles. Suppose one in every thousand parts that goes into an automobile is defective. If the defective parts randomly occur, we should not expect the same part to be defective in all the cars. So too, if irrational acts randomly occur, we should not expect the same irrational act type to be produced by a number of people. But this is what is needed for an irrational norm to exist; many people must perform the same irrational act type. Hence, we should not expect to see irrational norms on the failure model of irrational acts. Thus, if all irrational action is best explained in terms of the failure model, we would not expect to see irrational norms. Failures occur randomly, so a pattern should not be expected.

But all irrational action may not be random. Perhaps one type of irrationality is blind conformity, that is, conformity to the behavior of others without good reason.[81] Suppose such behavior exists. Under the best circumstances, it seems reasonable to suppose such irrational conforming acts may combine into norms. Consider the following example. The Illinois Lottery Commission has in the past waged an ad campaign to convince people to bet on their "lucky number." On many views, it is irrational to bet on lucky numbers. Suppose the lottery commission is successful in convincing a number of people to acquire a lucky number and bet on it each payday. This pattern of behavior might catch on such that after some time many people bet on their lucky numbers largely because other people are betting on their lucky numbers. It has become the thing to do. It could then be truthfully said that in Illinois there is a norm such that people bet on their lucky number each payday. At least on some views, this would count as an irrational norm as the constitutive acts are conforming acts, and they are irrational. How prevalent one thinks such norms are will depend on how prevalent one thinks blind conformity is.

A second type of action that is widely agreed to be irrational is called *shooting the messenger*. Shooting the messenger is blaming the bearer of bad news even when this person had no causal role in producing the bad news. This phrase stems from the example of Cleopatra who is said to have killed the bearer of the news of Caesar's defeat. Suppose it became the norm among a group to blame the bearer of bad news as indeed it may have been in the classical world of this example. People would look to others to determine what constituted being the bearer of bad news and the appropriate scope and form the blame should take. Such a norm seems a clear-cut case of an irrational norm.

In working out the boundaries of what counts as irrational, it should be noted that there may exist norms that are in some sense caused by irrational behavior but that are not themselves irrational norms. For example, weakness of will is a form of behavior that is widely regarded as irrational. There may be a norm against offering drinks to a recovering alcoholic. This norm may be the result of weakness of will in the sense that the norm need not exist and probably would not exist were individuals not tempted to act against their own long-term preferences out of weakness of will. Nonetheless, this is not an irrational norm as the acts of conformity of not offering drinks to recovering alcoholics are not themselves irrational acts.

There is yet another means by which norms that are otherwise irrational might come about among rational actors. This is through the imposition of sanctions. For example, a dictator might impose severe sanctions that have the effect of making it in the interests of a group to practice a pattern of behavior they would otherwise find irrational. Agents might find it desirable to conform to others' behavior as the means of best satisfying the dictator. In such a case, an SD norm would be present. In one sense of the term, however, we might wish to say that the norm of behavior for this group is irrational. This is similar to the norms of heroism imposed on the unwilling group due to sanctions from the military authorities considered in the section on SD norms. In each case, the norm is unwelcome to the group. The difference is that in the case of heroism, the sanctioned behavior was previously individually undesirable, whereas, in the present case, the sanctioned behavior was previously irrational.[82]

Conclusion

We have seen that social norms may be rational or irrational, strategic or non-strategic, and strategic but maintainable with or without sanctions. Coordination norms and SD norms have strategic structures, while epistemic norms do not; however, coordination norms and epistemic norms would exist in a world free of sanctions, while SD norms would not. This typology of norms and customs is broader than previous accounts, which have tended to either develop strategic or nonstrategic accounts but not one account combining both elements.

Previous accounts have not adequately bridged the gap between strategic and nonstrategic norms and customs, but the discussion in this chapter demonstrates that there is no reason not to have a bridge as the concepts are compatible. What cuts across both strategic and nonstrategic norms is the basic act of rational conformity. Conformity may be rationally motivated in one of two ways. In strategic situations, the motivation is to achieve the coordination benefit. In nonstrategic circumstances, the motivation is to economize on the cost of information. Both of these motivations for conformity to norms satisfy the dictate of methodological individualism. Accordingly, the account of conformity developed here does not fall prey to the sorts of criticisms that rational choice theorists make of sociological accounts of conformity. The test will come when this typology is applied to the law in order to determine which types of customs in fact have played a role. If it turns out that the law has importantly incorporated norms and customs of all three types, this will serve as a sort of empirical justification or confirmation of the felicity of the set of theoretical distinctions set out in this chapter.

3

Norm Utilitarianism

It looks as if a working moral code must comprise a set of specific directives like, 'No cigar smoking!' These directives might not guide people to do exactly what ideally anyone would like them to do, but they are the best that can be done by the instrument of a moral code.[1]

Richard Brandt

Introduction

The connection between utilitarianism and the rational actor account of norms developed in the chapter is deep and fundamental. Utilitarianism has a completely instrumental theory of right action. Right action is simply that which maximizes the good. The utilitarian should take note of the fact that there are three structures of norms. Rational actors' conformity to these norms is evidence of their welfare-producing capabilities.

In general, utilitarians have paid little attention to the theory of norms. The discussion in Chapter One suggests a possible explanation. Utilitarians, like the social theorists discussed in Chapter One, have been distracted from a proper examination of norms by their focus on rule-based accounts. This chapter will examine the role that norms should properly play in utilitarianism, and more generally in any critical normative approach to law that gives a prominent role to weighing consequences.

I. Norms Versus Rules in Utilitarian Theory

For the utilitarian, the fundamental question for practical ethics is how best to maximize utility. Rules have been the answer most often given by utilitarians. The utility-maximizing society will be the one built on the best set of moral and social rules. I will argue that this is incorrect. Rather, the society that incorporates the best set of norms will be the utility-maximizing society. I will first argue for the thesis that utilitarianism should be supplemented by the theory of norms. After the likely utilitarian response to this argument is entertained and rejected, I will argue for the stronger *Supplementary Thesis*, which is the thesis that norms should displace rules as the linchpin of practical utilitarian behavior.

Norms are important to utilitarianism simply because norms are important determinants of consequences. Though norms may have a positive or negative effect on consequences, I will here concentrate on the positive. Given the analysis of the previous chapter, it is not surprising that there are three main means by which norms generate utility. The first and simplest is that they reduce calculation costs. In addition, norms help solve recurrent coordination problems and Prisoner's Dilemmas. Calculation savings will be examined first.

From its inception, utilitarianism has been criticized for requiring an unacceptable amount of calculation as a prelude to each decision.[2] It is indeed true that calculating is an expensive activity. Norms, however, make much of the need for calculation redundant in cases where certain act types are easily seen to be positively correlated with utility payoffs. It is then not necessary to perform a calculation each time a situation of a recognizable type arises. The stronger the correlation, the more confident one can be in the absence of calculation. For example, consider the act type of opening doors for the elderly and disabled. It appears likely that there is a strong positive correlation between tokens of this type and utility generation. It is then utile to forgo calculating and proceed with the behavior on each occasion in which the relevant situation arises. This is not yet a norm for thus far only one agent is involved. But just as there is no reason for a particular person to calculate at each decision juncture, so too there is no reason for a particular person to calculate even the first time around. She may simply follow the norm that is extant in the culture and that is therefore relatively costlessly brought before her mind as a ready prescription for action. Thus the existence of the norm in the culture has a general tendency to reduce calculation costs and hence is utile.

A related point is that norms have the tendency to reduce calculation errors when they are well adapted to their environment, as they often are. The norm, if followed, will be more utile than what would tend to be produced by agents acting on their own, even agents who performed the requisite calculations. This is because agents on the whole will be likely to produce more errors in calculating than will be produced by a process of norm selection, either invisible hand or explicit. The best examples of this claim are norms that are influenced by experts. Norms of smoking behavior are changing quickly in this society. To all appearances, they are tracking facts determined by experts regarding health risks from primary and now secondary smoking. If agents do not have these norms to consult as possible prescriptions for behavior, but instead must perform calculations on their own, there will be greater errors. Individual agents are less able to evaluate evidence expertly and are thus more prone to error. It is worth keeping in mind that the reduction of calculation errors is just a special case of the reduction of calculation costs. For example, it would be possible in principle for each agent to become a medical expert on the effects of smoking, if not for the prohibitive costs in practice. Nonetheless, it is instructive to emphasize the manner in which norms allow for a greater level of expertise or distilled wisdom to pervade decision making.[3]

There is a finer point that can be added to the general discussion of norms and calculation costs. Norms sometimes become second nature to such an extent that one follows them without trying. One is able to conform with a minimal amount of attention just as one may drive inattentively for great stretches across the Great Plains. The ability of the mind to focus on particular thoughts, feelings, and tasks is precious. If it is squandered on myriad trivial decisions and calculations, it will not be available for more important tasks. Norms make room for innovative uses of the mind by making behavior routine. One can view the increasing complexity of Western technological society as the successive normalizing of more and more complex patterns of behavior.[4]

Along with economizing on calculation, norms generate utility by bringing about social coordination. The most cited example of a convention in the rational choice literature is that regarding the choice of which side of the road to drive on. The choice is conventional because it does not matter which side we choose as long as we coordinate on the same choice. A widely followed – though rarely discussed – norm is its pedestrian equivalent: the norm of walking on one side of sidewalks, hallways, and the like. The walking norm is not so straightforward as the driving norm. Roughly, it is as follows: *Walk wherever you want, except when someone is approaching, then move to the right, unless you see that they are not moving to their right, in which case, try to coordinate with what they are doing so as to avoid collision.* This norm has the strategic structure of a coordination norm. This is a norm of behavior to which nearly all people conform, sanctioning defectors if only by means of a sidelong glance. One easily sees the difficulty of getting about in the absence of a norm to regulate walking.

At this most basic level, norms like this are welfare-enhancing simply because they coordinate social interaction. Social coordination cannot be explained or reduced to the benefit of reducing calculation costs. In the preceding example, more information about the person one is approaching will not do any good. This is not a calculation problem; in the absence of a norm, there is no correct side of the sidewalk. Each person's choice is dependent on what the other does. This can be inefficient. We do not want people bumping into one another, nor do we want them stopping dead in their tracks, each waiting for the other to choose a side.

Another example of the phenomenon of social coordination is that of language. One can best understand language as a set of interrelated conventions that functions to make our lives easier by facilitating communication. Life would be intolerable if not impossible without the ability to communicate with shared language. But the patterns of understanding by which we communicate can be seen not merely as conventions but also as norms. To the extent that we explicitly teach language to children, we do so in a normative manner, letting them know that they should speak in certain ways. And to the extent that proper usage is maintained among adults, it is done by implicitly communicating that defectors will be punished through loss of opportunity, ridicule, and censure.

A third means by which norms may generate utility is that they allow groups to solve iterated collective action problems or Prisoner's Dilemmas. In a world in which self-interest operates, bringing about a social optimum is difficult. The utilitarian prefers mutual cooperation. The problem is that self-interested agents may have no reason to cooperate on any particular play. But if an ongoing norm that creates the needed motivation for cooperation can be established, self-interest can be reconciled with the utilitarian desiderata. As discussed in Chapter Two, there are a variety of means by which it may come to be in an agent's interest to cooperate in iterated Prisoner's Dilemmas.[5] If any of these means can be effected, then each agent gets what she wants without defecting. If no one defects, the best situation obtains for the group as a whole, which is as the utilitarian would want. With this last example, we have seen three main means by which norms generate utility. First, they reduce calculation costs; second, they allow for social coordination; and third, they allow for the solution of collection action problems.

In general, it can be said of norms that by coordinating individual behavior into social patterns, they create an environment of stable expectations that are efficient because agents act with greater assurance of the outcomes. Agents know how other agents will act in certain situations and know that other agents know how they will act. A widely accepted justification of the rule of law is that it provides stability of expectations.[6] Because patterns of legal decision are consistent across time and to some extent across geographical space, agents can proceed with their plans with a greater grasp of likely contingencies than they could were the law in flux. Using informal rather than formal sanctions, nonlegal norms function in a parallel manner. If an agent is in an environment in which particular norms are widely extant, she is better able to predict and strategically reason about the behavior of others.

A reasonable response to the demonstration that norms are utility generators might be the following. Norms such as walking on one side of sidewalks are insignificant. Though in principle such norms are utility generators, in practice little utility is actually at issue. Thus, such norms are of no real interest to the utilitarian.[7]

Two points are relevant for rebutting this objection. First, it cannot be generalized that all norms are of no interest to utilitarians simply because some norms are insignificant. Consider for example the previously mentioned norms that make up the common language of a culture. These norms are undoubtedly significant contributors to social welfare. Second, although it may be true that many norms are best seen as moral minutiae, what matters is the sheer number of such norms. Once one begins to notice norms, one will see that there is a very great number of them. Taken as a group, they largely determine the course of our social lives. Thus, it is true that many norms considered in isolation have only a marginal impact on the commonweal, but that norms taken as a set have a great impact.

One reason norms may not receive the credit they deserve is that norms are often taken for granted. We tend not to notice that everyone is acting in a certain manner, precisely because everyone is acting in a certain manner. Sometimes, one only becomes aware of a norm when traveling in a culture in which different norms hold, making it immediately obvious that something is different. The natural response is to search for the new culture's patterns. With the norm of walking on the right, for example, perhaps one will discover an alternative norm, or perhaps no norm. The Tower of Babel is a metaphor for social chaos. An absence of shared behavior, a normative chaos, would affect not only a group's speech from the Tower but also a group's actions on the ground. Such a lack of coordination would be tremendously disutile.

Having seen that norms are indeed significant generators of utility, the first premise of the argument for the Supplementary Thesis is established. The second premise of the argument is simply the claim that utilitarians have neglected to study or assimilate the theory of norms. This is self-evident from a study of the utilitarian literature, which contains almost no discussion of social norms. Norms are important to utilitarianism, but utilitarians have previously neglected them. Thus, the theory needs supplementation.

II. Rules: The Tail That Wags the Dog

The utilitarian will respond to the preceding argument as follows. Norms are indeed important to utilitarianism, but they have already been incorporated into the theory under the guise of rules; norms are just the causal downstream of rules.[8] Utilitarians do not think that rules in a vacuum are felicitous. Utility is generated only when rules are acted upon in a population. And rules that are acted upon are norms. Following the position of the rule theorist as set out in Chapter One, the utilitarian might argue that for every norm there is a rule, and focusing on rules is most interesting. As evidence for this claim, traditional utilitarians will contend that the utilitarian virtues I cited for norms – they save on calculation costs, promote social coordination, and solve collective action problems – can be accomplished with rules. Agents who follow rules need not calculate on each occasion. And when rules are common knowledge, agents will be able to act in a unified manner, promoting social coordination and solving collective action problems. Thus premise two is false. Utilitarians have not neglected norms; they have previously incorporated them into their theory under another guise.

It is false, however, that for each norm there is a corresponding rule. Consider the example discussed earlier of walking on the right. This is a norm for which no one is taught a rule. The norm is maintained by a process of conformity that does not involve rules. Examples of norms to which no rule is attached are bountiful in social life.

The rule proponent will grant that although utilitarians characteristically talk as if all rules were expressly stated or occurrently formulated, in principle the utilitarian need not make this strong claim. All she need claim is that for each norm there is a rule that could be formulated; these are the unwritten rules that pervade our lives. To take the walking norm as an example, though people do not explicitly state it, the rule they follow is obvious and could be stated: *One should walk on the right.*

This move does not solve all difficulties for the rule theorist. For it is simply false that peoples' behavior is governed by rules of this sort. As discussed in Chapter One, while rules are short linguistic phrases such as *Do not lie* or *Walk on the right*, the actual norms that people follow are much more complex. There are all sorts of exceptions to rules that are commonly understood and that form the details of the normative fabric of groups, differentiating one group from another. But these subtle differences are not captured in the rules, whether they are explicit or implicit.

The utilitarian, however, has a ready answer to this objection. It is that the real rule, the underlying rule, or as I will hereafter call it, the *Ideal Rule*, is much more complex than the rules that can be quickly formulated, explicitly or implicitly. The ideal rule will contain all sorts of exception clauses and qualifying conditions that suit it to the actual subtleties of the real world.[9]

While it is indeed open to the utilitarian to make this adjustment, it is important to note that these ideal rules are no longer anything like rules as they have traditionally been discussed by utilitarians. Utilitarians have characteristically offered what I will call the Commandment conception of rules. That is, rules are like the popular conception of the Ten Commandments.

Before we can fully understand the significance of the rule proponent's shift from this traditional conception of rules to the Ideal Rule conception, it is necessary to examine the traditional conception more closely. Given the central importance that utilitarians give rules, it is surprising that these features have not previously been explicitly discussed in detail. There are six central features of the Commandment conception of rules. The first two elements are characteristics of the rules themselves, that they are pithy and apply universally. The third element is a feature of the set of rules, specifically that the set contains a relatively small number of rules. The last three features address the role that rules play in determining action, specifically, how they are formulated, how they are transmitted, and how they are applied to particular situations.

A. The Commandment Conception of Rules

1. **PITHINESS.** By the pithiness of moral rules, I refer to the common conception of them as brief, linguistic statements that capture the essential content of behavior that is either prescribed or proscribed. Among utilitarians, Brandt is unusually explicit in discussing the pithiness of moral rules. Yet, this feature is characteristic of the rules utilitarians typically cite and is implicit in their discussion of them. In *On Liberty*, Mill, for instance, provides the following examples: "Keep promises," "Do not murder" and "Tell no lies."[10] In *Utilitarianism*, he says that one should not "rob or murder, betray or deceive."[11]

John Austin, one of Mill's tutors, clearly conceives of moral rules as pithy, linguistic items. He writes:

The inferences suggested to our minds by repeated experience and observation are, therefore, drawn into principles, or compressed into maxims. These we carry about us ready for use, and apply to individual cases promptly or without hesitation: without reverting to the process by which they were obtained; or without recalling, and arraying before our minds, the numerous and intricate considerations of which they are handy abridgments.[12]

In Austin's talk of inferences that are "compressed into maxims" or "handy abridgments," we have good evidence that he implicitly understood moral rules as pithy statements.

In developing his utilitarian conception of the "Ideal Moral Code," Brandt makes the following comment, "It looks as if a working moral code must comprise a set of specific directives like, 'No cigar smoking!' These directives might not guide people to do exactly what ideally anyone would like them to do, but they are the best that can be done by the instrument of a moral code."[13] In this passage, we see an example of a pithy rule, which, as Brandt admits, is not the ideal specification of the appropriate behavior. Brandt says that this is the best that can be expected of a moral code but provides no explanation for this remark. We will find the explanation later in his account of rule transmission. The idea is that these rules must be brief if they are to be taught and memorized. In addition, moral rules must be pithy if they are to be universal and generally applicable. This connection is alluded to in the following passage from Richard Hare: "The prima facie [rules] are general in two connected senses; they are rather simple and unspecific, and they admit of exceptions, in the sense that it is possible to go on holding them while allowing that in particular cases one may break them."[14]

2. UNIVERSALITY. Utilitarians take it as given that the correct set of moral rules will apply universally (within a society). First, it is necessary to understand *universality*, as it applies to rules, as there is a sense in which any rule, no matter how context dependent, is universally applicable. For example, the Soliz family in West El Paso may have a moral rule that says the last person home at night should walk the dog, close the garage door and lock up. This rule can be seen as universally applicable; the full statement of the rule is, "For any individual, if you are a member of the Soliz family and you are the last one in at night. . . ." This rule applies vacuously to all members of the society who do not meet the antecedent condition of belonging to the Soliz family. Clearly, however, this is not the sense of *universal* that utilitarians have in mind. Mill speaks of the "ethical creed"[15] to which all of mankind can agree. This, according to Mill, is composed of "rules of morality for the multitude."[16] A parallel conception resurfaces in Brandt's "Social Moral Code," which is meant to guide the behavior of all members of society.[17] For example, "Do not lie," is a rule everyone should follow. The "ethical creed," and "social moral code" are meant to consist of moral rules that are general enough to apply substatively to all citizens.

3. SMALL NUMBERS. The third element of the Commandment conception is that there are relatively few rules. This feature is connected to the feature of universality. If rules are to apply substantively to all people, there cannot be too many of them because people do not have enough features in common. A second reason is that the need to teach the moral code limits its size. Brandt comments:

> [The moral code] must not contain items too numerous to be taught by the methods (e.g. classical conditioning) which must be used to interiorize moral principles; so it will probably restrict itself to matters of some importance in the society. . . . We might then select some of these principles – the more important ones for that group – and teach them as the moral code for that society.[18]

So according to the Commandment conception, rules are pithy, universal, and relatively small in number. Consider now how these rules are thought to function.

4. RULE FORMATION AND TRANSMISSION. Rule formation and transmission are best explicated together. In the utilitarian literature, two different means of rule formation are discussed. Rules are either developed by average, private utilitarian agents or formed by experts representing the state, church, academia, and so on. Rules formed by private citizens are allowed to be *idiosyncratic*, while rules formed by experts are meant to be *common* to all. (An idiosyncratic rule is accepted by the agent who formulates it, while a common rule is accepted by all agents.) If all rules in society are idiosyncratic, the theory does not need an account of rule transmission. Each agent simply forms and acts on her own rules. But if rules are to be common, a process is needed to transmit them.

Although utilitarians sometimes write as if there is nothing to rule following but creating one's rules and acting on them, rule commonality and hence rule transmission must be a part of any plausible account of the best utilitarian society. Without it, maximal utility generation is impossible. Recall the three main types of utility benefit that purportedly may be derived from rules: reduced calculation costs, social coordination, and resolution of collective action problems. If rules are idiosyncratic, time will be saved because one need not calculate on each occasion. But an initial calculation to determine the rule still will be necessary. If rules are common, however, even that first calculation is unnecessary because one will have learned the rule from family or friends. In addition, and obviously enough, if all rules are idiosyncratic, social coordination and consonant collective action will be difficult to achieve because each agent will be marching to the beat of a different drummer. Even though common rules are necessary, both types can coexist. Some rules may be generated by experts and transmitted to the citizenry, while other rules are privately formulated and either remain idiosyncratic or come to reign within some limited domain.

Mill appears to think that for the most part individuals do not formulate their own rules. He writes, "all rational creatures go out upon the sea of life with their minds made up on the common questions of right and wrong."[19] Where, then, does Mill think rules come from? He does not precisely answer the question, but we may come closest to discovering what he has in mind by considering the following passages: "There has been ample time, namely, the whole past duration of the human species. During all that time, mankind has been learning by experience the tendencies of actions; on which experience all the prudence, as well as all the morality of life, are dependent."[20] The picture seems to be that somehow the rules are passed down from one generation to the next. Mill does not, however, provide a precise mechanism for how this process takes place. More importantly, he does not say where the rules originate. The closest he comes to specifying the origin is in the following remark: "Mankind must by this time have acquired positive beliefs as to the effects of some actions on their happiness; and the beliefs which have thus come down are the rules of morality for the multitude, and for the philosopher until he has succeeded in finding better."[21] With the claim that philosophers are to play a part in formulating better rules, we see that at least to some extent Mill endorses the expert conception of rule formation.

In the following passage from Anthony Quinton, rules are implicitly understood as resulting from explicit or "reflective" formulation in order to serve a common purpose:

This argument applies the principle of the division of labour to the domain of moral activity. It holds that the reflective task of elaborating general rules of beneficial conduct should be undertaken on the one hand by specially qualified people, that is to say moralists, or, on the other, during periods of time that are free from exigencies of action. In this way a stock of ready-made rules will be made available for moral agents confronted with the need for choice.[22]

Brandt's scattered comments regarding the source of rules do not reveal a coherent theory. For example, he refers to the "codebuilder"[23] at one point but a few pages later remarks, "Nothing prevents us, however, from learning more about the optimal specific rules; philosophers, psychologists, and other social scientists could co-operate in determining what a welfare-maximizing moral code would be. Indeed, it is not clear why much greater effort is not being made in this direction."[24] Whether these experts should convene a congress or advocate for a presidential commission to choose the rules is left to the reader's imagination. Apparently, what matters to Brandt are not these administrative details but that an ideal moral code can be developed on high and then brought down for public dissemination. While Brandt does not discuss precisely how dissemination or transmission work, the remarks he makes in passing reveal the picture he has in mind. He mentions the "teachers of morality – the parents, educators in the early grades."[25] He also discusses, "publically espousing such a system."[26] Like Brandt, Mill repeatedly emphasizes the importance of education for instilling the proper rules. As he says, the rules of morality should be "taught to the young, and enforced by law and opinion."[27]

In general, utilitarians seem to think that rules are taught by parents, teachers and the like or are embodied in the black-letter law of society. Teaching takes the form of uttering or writing commandments, which the listener hears, memorizes, and then passes along to others. That other possibilities are not explicitly discussed in the literature indicates the degree to which such a view is assumed. No other options seem worth mentioning, or even possible. Sometimes, writers suggest that rules are learned in a more subtle way, by observation of behavior.[28] But given the way the Commandment conception is built into the more explicit discussions, one presumes that the authors believe that rules picked up in this more subtle way are nonetheless pithy linguistic items.

5. RULE FOLLOWING. The Commandment conception of rule following has it that one hears the commandment, memorizes it, and then applies it to particular situations. Mill implicitly assumes this view in the following passage: "for the customary morality, that which education and opinion have consecrated, is the only one which presents itself to the mind with the feeling of being *in itself* obligatory.... [The moral agent] says to himself, I feel that I am bound not to rob or murder, betray or deceive."[29] Apparently, Mill believes that the agent applies rules by entertaining them occurrently. From the statements in the previous section on pithiness, we know these rules are in the form of "Do not rob" and the like. After calling up the brief statement internally, according to

Mill, the agent then goes on to determine whether it covers a specific situation. If it does, she acts accordingly.

Austin's remark regarding the pithiness of moral rules, which was quoted earlier, also speaks to the manner in which these rules arc applied. He writes:

The inferences suggested to our minds by repeated experience and observation are, therefore, drawn into principles, or compressed into maxims. These we carry about us ready for use, and apply to individual cases promptly or without hesitation: without reverting to the process by which they were obtained; or without recalling, and arraying before our minds, the numerous and intricate considerations of which they are handy abridgments.[30]

It is clear from this passage that Austin believes that we occurrently entertain pithy phrases in order to see whether they apply to the situation at hand. He also makes a connection between rule application and the property of pithiness. Though it is not crystal clear from the passage, the idea seems to be that rules can only be easily memorized and occurrently called up if they are "handy abridgments."

The three phases of rule functioning have now been examined. These, combined with the Commandment conception of the structure of rules, constitute the rule proponent's overall view of the role rules play in utilitarian moral theory.[31]

B. The Shift to Ideal Rule Theory

Recall where the discussion broke off before the traditional or Commandment conception of rules was examined. I had argued that utilitarianism must be supplemented with the theory of norms. The rule proponent responded that this is not necessary because rules can do all the work of norms and are already present in utilitarian theory. But I was able to show that rules, as traditionally understood, cannot do everything that norms can do. In particular, rules cannot account for the complexity of the normative structure of the social world. The rule proponent's response was to claim that if we shift to the Ideal Rule conception, then rules can do the job.

The problem with this response is that the shift to ideal rules is not costless for the rule proponent. If rules are to be complex items that exhaustively characterize all the subtleties of the actual norms, then they cannot be pithy, universally applicable, and few in number. As a result, they cannot be easily formulated, transmitted, and applied, at any rate, not in the manner rule proponents propound. For example, consider the norms regarding lying as they exist in this culture. It would take a good deal of social scientific work to discover the detailed contents of these norms, and the contents will vary from group to group within the culture. Even if these norms can be fully captured by complex ideal rules, surely they cannot be easily formulated in a pithy phrase, nor easily transmitted or applied.[32] This is not to say that it is impossible to provide some other account of how these processes work, but whatever these processes are, they are not the ones that utilitarians have proffered. Thus, for the rule proponent to shift to ideal rules, she also will need to provide new accounts of the nature of these rules and how they function. But these accounts will just be additions to the incomplete theories we currently possess regarding the nature of norms and how they function.

The point of the detailed discussion of the traditional conception of rules in the previous section is that it allows us to appreciate how much work needs to be done to revamp this conception. In the rest of this section, I provide a sketch of the needed Ideal Rule account.

1. **NONPITHINESS.** Ideal rules are a means of capturing the complexity of actual norms. Thus, they must contain the subtle exceptions and fine discriminations that characterize real norms. Consider for example the incest taboo. At a quick glance, it seems to proscribe only sexual intercourse within the immediate family. But actually it is more complex, governing not only the immediate family but the extended one, and not only intercourse, but also flirtation, physical contact, inappropriate discourse, and so on. Such complex normative content cannot be adequately described by a pithy, linguistic phrase such as, *Incest is prohibited.*

2. **NONUNIVERSALITY.** If ideal rules are to capture all of a norm's content, they must be very specific, making them inapplicable to all agents. For example, the Soliz family's norms discussed earlier are not captured by a society-wide ethical creed, yet they surely generate utility. The same holds for the incest taboo: its deep content is specific to particular subcultures.

3. **LARGE NUMBERS OF RULES.** The set of rules cannot be small if it is to describe our normative reality adequately. Large societies contain millions of people whose interactions are governed by countless different norms. Their numbers are so great that they could never be compiled into a list that could be used as an *ethical creed*, or *social moral code*.

4. **IDEAL RULE FORMATION.** As discussed earlier, the standard utilitarian conception of rule formation involves both idiosyncratic and common models. On each model, rules are explicitly formulated. But this will not work for ideal rules. It is implausible to suppose that a rule created by an agent, either for her to follow, or to disseminate to the public, will be complex enough to be the Ideal Rule that should accompany a norm.

The Ideal Rule as it actually is constituted must reflect many of the contingencies of the world that could not be accurately predicted by a rule creator at the start. Consider an architect's blueprint. No matter how much effort goes into creating it, contingencies may arise during construction that call for modification of the original plan. The same holds for norms (and consequently for the Ideal Rules that overlay them). The difference is that norms, of course, are generally not designed.

Rather than being explicitly formulated, many norms emerge spontaneously as the result of processes not yet well understood.[33] Bernard Mandeville and the Scottish Enlightenment philosophers – David Hume, Adam Smith, and Adam Ferguson – all contributed to the development of so-called invisible hand explanations for the emergence of functional social features such as norms.[34] Norms function so well that it looks as if they could only be the result of intentional design. Yet, they are perhaps best explained as resulting unintentionally from other social processes.

The scant literature that currently exists in the social sciences regarding the emergence of norms is the most relevant.[35] Yet there are problems in fitting this literature to utilitarians' needs. Utilitarians generally believe people are capable of some degree of unselfish behavior, an assumption captured in the common and idiosyncratic models. In the common model, the assumption appears to be that if we can just discover and promote the optimal set of rules, agents will follow them. In the idiosyncratic model, agents are motivated on their own to search for utility-maximizing rules. What is assumed is that agents want to discover utility-maximizing rules. But the emergence models in the social sciences assume narrow self-interest. How these models can be connected to utilitarians' needs has yet to be investigated adequately.

5. IDEAL RULE TRANSMISSION. On the traditional utilitarian account, rules are transmitted through teaching or command, either verbal or written. Even when the rule is transmitted by observation, what is observed is a pattern that implies a pithy, linguistic item. But if the utilitarian wants to become an Ideal Rule proponent, this model must be changed. Clearly, complex rules with many clauses are not what is transmitted verbally or in writing. Once again, though it is presumably possible to account for how such complex rules are transmitted, utilitarians have not done so.

Norms often are transmitted by observation, then imitation. The pithy, linguistic item that is communicated verbally does not carry the full content of the norm but rather serves to denote the thick pattern of behavior. In other words, we use verbal and written rules to point to the norm. The receiver must be in a position to see what the norm is; she cannot comprehend its full complexity in the propositional content of the linguistic rule. This difference is subtle but can be understood by contrasting the following two cases.

Consider a father who wants to send his daughter to the store by a route that she does not know. He writes directions for her on a piece of paper. The propositional content of the directions must contain all the information that is needed to get her to the store, for there is no other source available. But working norms function differently. For example, one occasionally hears the general incest taboo explicitly stated, and as a child one may have heard more specific exhortations from parents. But this is not enough. One learns the appropriate behavior in all its subtlety from observation. In this way, normative culture is passed on largely through observation and imitation, not through words. The pithy statement is used to denote the pattern of behavior. Perhaps the Ideal Rule utilitarian can provide a similar account, by arguing that the explicit or unwritten rule serves to denote the Ideal Rule.[36]

6. IDEAL RULE FOLLOWING. As we saw earlier, in the utilitarians' account of rule following the agent internalizes a pithy, linguistic item that takes the form of a generalized prescription, and then she applies it to particular cases. But if the rule proponent is to promote the Ideal Rule view, this account will not do. For complex ideal rules cannot be easily memorized and quickly called up. Nor does it appear that such a process is necessary if we consider the example of norm following. Conformity to norms is best understood as perceiving what the norm requires in particular situations. What is at issue here is a certain kind of objectivity. Extant norms and what they demand in particular circumstances can be seen or observed in a straightforward sense. Norms may become second nature so that one may follow them with little conscious effort. It is clear that explicit rules are not a necessary part of this process as prelinguistic children, as well as animals, are capable of the normative learning necessary for conformative behavior.[37]

The preceding six subsections on ideal rules represent the start on the path that the rule proponent must follow if she is to become an Ideal Rule proponent. We see that by suitably modifying her account, the rule proponent may be able to save the rule view. But an insurmountable problem arises when the utilitarian moves from advocating rules to advocating ideal rules. Recall that the reason for showing that rules are the tail that wags the dog is to rebut the second premise of the Supplementary Thesis, which claims that utilitarians have neglected the study of norms. The response was to say that this is false because norms have already been incorporated into utilitarian theory as the causal fallout of rules, which, of course, are already part of utilitarians' theoretical repetoire. But as we just saw, to move from the rule to the Ideal Rule view, the utilitarian must do much new theorizing to establish accounts of ideal rule formation, transmission and following and to eliminate the features of pithiness, universality, and existence in a small set.

These new demands on the utilitarian are parallel to those I made on the rule theorist in the social sciences in Chapter One: better accounts of norm formation, transmission, and following and a general characterization of the nature of norms. What is crucial is that given this need for new theorizing, the second premise of the Supplementary Thesis is true because, whether called norms or rules, they have been neglected. Thus, we see that the second premise is maintained regardless of which of the two possible moves the utilitarian makes. Either she maintains the standard rule view and misses the subtleties of norms, thereby neglecting them, or she moves to the Ideal Rule view, in which case much new theorizing is needed to spell out how such ideal rules work. But developing an account of ideal rules is tantamount to developing an account of norms. Thus the second premise is affirmed: norms have been neglected. Combining it with the first premise, we arrive at the Supplementary Thesis, which states that utilitarianism must be supplemented with the theory of norms.

Having seen how much work is involved in the shift from the rule view to the Ideal Rule view, we may wonder why it is worthwhile to call the new account a rule view at all. Since the account will completely overlap the theory of norms, why not use the term *norm view* and reserve the term *rule view* for the distinct theory that already exists? Utilitarians must admit that if a completely new account of rules and their function is needed, then the previous theory has been gutted. What reason could there be to hold onto the name of the old theory, other than to save the old theory in name?

An objection could be raised that I have been unfair to utilitarians. It might be claimed that they did not mean to talk about all rules, only moral rules. Thus I cannot legitimately take them to be talking about all norms, only moral norms. And they may argue that their analyses of these are adequate.

My response works on two levels. First, it is insignificant that they did not mean to talk about all rules. By their own lights, they should be interested in all rules, to the extent that these are important generators of utility. Consider the utility generated by having norms regulating how we communicate, walk, and so on. These have an important impact on utility and so should be of interest. But even if it is conceded for the sake of argument that utilitarians are not to be faulted for focusing exclusively on moral rules, their conception of moral rules is also inadequate. The Commandment conception is inadequate even to the task of capturing the complexities of moral rules, as will be seen next.

What I have developed so far is still a live-and-let-live thesis. We need norm theory, but we still have rule theory, which has only been impugned to the extent that it purports to explain the entire realm of patterned, normative activity. Rule theory is founded on the very plausible claim that rules understood as commandments improve utility production. Surely utilitarians can make a good argument for this position.

Take the Ten Commandments. These are rules that were formulated and now are transmitted and followed just as utilitarians suppose. The expert model provides the best characterization of their historical formulation (an understatement of sorts). They are transmitted through the written and spoken word by pithy, linguistic statements. And arguably, once internalized, they are retrieved and applied to particular cases and are followed. Such a procedure would seem to generate more utility than were each agent to make her own calculations for each decision. Hence, rules are plausibly seen as utility generators. Apparently then norms and rules are distinct utility generators. The question that naturally arises is: Which of the two is more important for utility?

There is a measurement problem, however, in trying to determine whether norms or rules are more important to utilitarianism. How are we to measure the constellation of norms' causal impact on utility compared to that of rules? The norm proponent has an argument for her account, however, that vitiates the need for the complex measurement. She claims that the rule proponent was illicitly trading on norms throughout her argument for the causal significance of rules.

Consider how the norm proponent can argue for this priority of norms over rules. As a simple example, consider the rule, *Do not lie*. If people literally followed this rule, much less utility and perhaps net disutility might be produced in comparison to the more complex norm that is actually followed. On the surface, it looks as if the pithy rule is transmitted and followed. But given the foregoing discussion, a more plausible explanation is that when one hears the rule, *Do not lie*, one looks to one's community or group to better understand what the speaker means. This process determines how one should act. Simply put, the actual behavioral norms instantiated in the community are acting as a guide. Thus, it is not the rule but the norm that smooths the way for the flow of utility. Norms remain hidden beneath rules, but they are doing the lion's share of the work in generating utility.

Given the preceding discussion, it appears that norms should replace rules as the linchpin of practical behavior for the utilitarian, that is, the utilitarian should ask not which rules should be followed, but which norms. In asmuch as consequences matter in nearly all moral theories, this point will be of significance more generally. Good consequences matter morally, and so the best means to obtaining them also matters morally. It was correct to look to rules as having an important role in the production of good consequences; it was incorrect to assign them the crucial role. For once norms are introduced, we see that they are the social structure that undergirds the rule, performing the real work. Often, rules are a part of norms and perhaps multivariate analysis could indicate the extent of the impact that rules as such have on consequences. But rules, understood as they are described in the literature as pithy, linguistic items, are only one component in the more complex structure that produces utility.

Conclusion

As stated in the book's introduction, the moral-theoretic analysis will be layered on top of the rational choice analysis. From the angle of this distinction, this chapter and the last are transition chapters. Each serves to erect conceptual bridges between rationality and morality. The present chapter continued with the moral motivational assumption of narrow self-interest. Moral analysis comes in from the perspective of critical moral theory. Utilitarian critical moral theorists can judge the moral bona fides of a community or society regardless of the particular motivational assumption that is made regarding the population of actors. Note that there is consistency in the moral analysis and the rational analysis because the moral analysis does not take odds with the Hobbesian motivational assumption at the core of rational choice analysis. In the next chapter, a degree of genuinely moral motivation will be layered onto the account, although Hobbesian motivation will continue to play an important role.

4

Emergent Moral Norms

To some philosophers the notion that moral phenomena – rights and duties or obligations – can be brought into existence by the voluntary action of individuals has appeared utterly mysterious; but this I think has been so because they have not clearly seen how special the moral notions of a right and an obligation are, nor how peculiarly they are connected with the distribution of freedom of choice; it would indeed be mysterious if we could make actions morally good or bad by voluntary choice.[1]

H. L. A. Hart

Introduction

Chapters Two and Three discussed rational norms, which are norms conformed to by rational actors. Moral norms, by contrast, are norms conformed to by moral actors. Economists and game theorists typically assume that people are rational actors and moral theorists and sociologists typically assume that people are moral actors. While neither assumption is fully realistic, each can be useful and lead to interesting results.

Starting with a rational choice account is in keeping with the dominant thrust of the literature out of which the previous discussion grew, for generally the rational choice or economic approach has been the dominant framework theorists have applied to analyze the structure of norms. The narrow self-interest account is flawed, however, because it fails to account for the strong evidence of the reality of genuine moral motivation in the workings of social practices. Accepting the reality and potency of moral motivation does not, however, mean one must see these influences as dominant. The most interesting results come from combining the assumptions of rational and moral motivation.

Chapter Two demonstrated that rational actors would find themselves in a world consisting of three types of norms, conformity to each of which having been shown to be fully consistent with the dictates of methodological individualism, a grounding tenet of rational choice theory. Any theory of moral norms must overcome a similar hurdle if it is to get off the ground, for just as the notion of conformity must be reconciled to the notion of rational action, so too must it be reconciled to the notion of moral action, for while rational choice theorists and moral theorists disagree about the basic goodness of humanity, they do agree that people are purposeful, willful actors. The notion of purposeful, willful behavior seems inherently in tension with the notion of conformitive behavior.

In moral theory, before anything else, people are choosers. To act morally is to choose freely an action in circumstances in which one is morally motivated and one sees the action as required by morality. This general description is true on the Kantian, utilitarian, and virtue theory approaches. Certainly, conformity is not one of moral theory's most cherished notions. Instead, one thinks of such concepts as goodness, rightness, justice, liberty, or fairness. Conformity is suspect; one might easily suppose that conformers are not really moral at all, they are just conforming. If this apparent incompatibility cannot be resolved, moral theorists may have to conclude that so-called moral norms are out of bounds, such that truly moral individuals cannot participate in norms to reap their benefits as conformity does not satisfy minimal standards of moral deliberation.

Some accounts try to make conformity more understandable by emphasizing the role of sanctions; conformity to norms is justified because the forces of socialization carry sanctions for defection. In this scenario, we are all conformers because we are all sanctioners. But this merely pushes the issue of blind conformity one step back, which solves nothing, as blind sanctioning is antithetical to any moral theory that comes to mind, whether it be one of various critical moral theories or ordinary morality.

Social theorists who reject the rational choice tradition have an interest in seeing the problem of moral conformity resolved. Their strategy for rebuking economists has been to point to the existence of moral norms as evidence of peoples' non-egoistic motivation.[2] But if the problem of moral norms cannot be resolved, this strategy against the economists will not work. Moral theorists and sociologists will not be able to use moral norms as evidence of moral motivation if they cannot explain how moral motivation genuinely may lead to the acts of conformity necessary for norms. Without such an account, their cherished norms will appear to be pseudo-moral, patterns of behavior maintained by a kind of pale, lifeless conformity. Both for moral theory and the social sciences, then, it is important to determine whether conformity can be reconciled with morality.[3]

Whereas there is arguably only one type of rational motivation, there are a variety of types of moral motivation. What counts as moral motivation is of course a matter of controversy. It is not the concern of the present work to determine the true or best account of morality, and then, derivatively, to determine which are the true moral norms. Instead, I will use the term *morality* broadly so as to include morality as conceived by a variety of moral theories and as instantiated in a variety of cultures and subcultures. On this purely descriptive use, moralities that are little more than manifestations of group self-interest will count as moral, as long as they cannot be completely reduced to narrow self interest.[4] This broad conception of morality and moral motivation will mean a broad conception of what counts as a moral norm.[5] In the following discussion, the moral account will be layered on top of the rational account. The concept of *predominant egoism* creates a consistency between these two accounts. Finally, the next chapter will be solely concerned with norms made up of the conforming actions of moral actors who share a moral outlook. Modeling norms in this manner will be of interest because we will see that participation in norms is consistent with the grounding principles of leading critical moral theories.

First, however, the present chapter will consider how norms are structured in the real world, not the theoretical world populated by ideally rational or ideally moral people, but instead the world we live in, where people are predominantly, albeit not completely, self-interested. The law evolved over many hundreds of years in a manner so as to reflect the moral complexion of the society out of which it grew. The best interpretation of the customs and practices that have played a role in the law must pay serious attention to the moral currents running through the culture out of which the law grew.

I. Predominant Egoism

Predominant egoism is the social scientific claim that people are character-istically mostly narrowly self-interested in their behavior. There is a world of difference between being mostly self-regarding and being completely self-regarding. This is the world of morality; not the ideal, well-scrubbed morality of moral theory, but the ordinary morality of people as they actually live out their lives.[6] SD norms, coordination norms, and epistemic norms may all reflect the fact that they are made up of the conforming actions of predominant egoists, rather than the pure egoists of standard economic analysis or the highly morally motivated persons of critical moral theory.

There is fundamental disagreement across the various disciplines about the nature of human motivation. Olson, Barry, Williamson, and Ellickson all draw the fundamental divide as between economists and sociologists.[7] These cat-egories can readily be expanded to lump rational choice theorists with the economists, and moral theorists, learning theorists, and cultural anthropolo-gists with the sociologists.

Roughly, the issue comes down to whether or not one accepts the fairly pes-simistic assumption about human nature as captured in the idea of economic man, or *Homo economicus*. Most economists and game theorists accept the as-sumption and most other social theorists do not. This apparent divide between the disciplines presents a problem for the further development of interdisci-plinary theory, for it would seem that a theory must come down on one side or

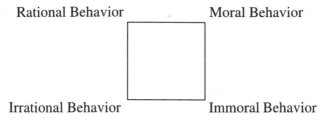

Figure 4.1 Fundamental Categories of Human Behavior

another of this divide, and hence appear automatically unacceptable to those on the other side, as beginning from a faulty core assumption. Fortunately, however, we will see that the divide is neither as deep nor as unbridgeable as is often thought.

It will be helpful at this point to schematize human motivation. Figure 4.1 displays the most relevant breakdown of human behavior.[8]

It is common for theorists to speak as if human motivation lies somewhere on the continuum between the narrowly rational and the moral. A more comprehensive account, however, must come to terms with irrationality and immorality as motivational types as well. The question arises as to whether it is ultimately most fruitful to see these as distinct types of motivation, or rather as mere failures to live up to the demands of rationality and morality. This complex issue cannot be settled here, so as an expository device, irrationality and immorality will be treated as separate categories from rationality and morality.

It is often said that economists and rational choice theorists have a cynical or pessimistic view of human nature, as their accounts emphasize peoples' self-interested nature. This chart shows that while economists may indeed be pessimistic along one dimension, along another dimension they are optimistic, as these theorists think that people are highly rational rather than somewhere on the continuum between the rational and the irrational.[9] Recently, however, psychologists such as Amos Tversky have provided accounts of irrational tendencies that seem more like modifications of the rational choice approach than outright rejections.[10] This type of work continues to make inroads, such that it perhaps can be said that many rational choice theorists now see human motivation as somewhere on the continuum between the rational and the irrational, though decidedly near the rational end.

The issue of immorality occupies a similar, ambiguous position in moral theory. Moral theorists tend to pay little attention to immorality per se, as distinct from self interest. There are notable exceptions, such as those writers who have tried to come to terms with evil.[11] But, starting with Plato, the dominant tradition has been to conceive of morality as fundamentally threatened by narrow self-interest rather than immorality. We see then that both moral theorists and rational choice theorists have tended to view the wellsprings of human motivation as lying somewhere along the top of the graph on the continuum between the rational and the moral.

The most extreme rationalist position holds that all behavior is narrowly rational. Because this is sometimes thought to have been Hobbes's position, I will refer to holders of this view as *Hobbesians*.[12] These theorists characteristically offer accounts of how patterns of behavior that seem to be moral on their face really result from the subtle machinations of enlightened self-interest. Impressionistic evidence strongly suggests, however, that few rational choice theorists who explicitly discuss the matter defend this extreme position.

The assumption that people are narrowly self-interested must be distinguished from the assumption that people are instrumentally rational, which is a weaker assumption. Economists and other rational choice theorists sometimes say that all they are committed to is the assumption that people seek to maximize their utility function, where this may include the interests of others. This concession is made in principle; nevertheless, these theorists evidently think other-regarding behavior is marginal in the real world as economists continue to provide self-interested explanations of seemingly morally infused practices such as voting, tipping, and giving to public radio. (Without the Hobbesian starting point there would be no need for reinterpretations of these practices because the people involved would be seen as merely behaving according to a utility function that incorporated the interests of others, the fellow citizens, waitpersons, and radio listeners.)[13]

Another group of rational choice theorists, while also delighting in debunking conventional understandings of many practices, nevertheless are willing to grant the real though limited existence of genuinely moral motivation.[14] Typically, these theorists appear to think that although morality cannot be entirely forgotten, it is, nevertheless, marginal so that, for most purposes, straightforward rational choice analysis is still the best approach. This position is historically best associated with Hume, who took a view of the world that gave pride of place to narrowly rational motivation, but who also thought that natural human sympathy could be a source of genuinely other-regarding behavior.[15] I will refer to holders of this view as *Humeans*.

Moral motivation has typically been incorporated into rational actor models in two manners. One is to model behavior in terms of narrow self-interest, and then, as an addendum, to mention morality in one form or another. The other is to incorporate moral motivation more directly, as, for example, by constructing payout matrices that assume a mixed population of actors, some of whom are moral and some of whom are narrowly rational, or a uniform population of actors who have a mixture of moral and narrowly rational motives. The first approach is more common.

As representatives of the first approach, Barry and Hardin argue, for example, that it is best for methodological reasons to do analysis in terms of narrow self-interest. They maintain, however, that human behavior is, in fact, more complex.[16]

In the camp of those who incorporate moral motivation more explicitly, Howard Margolis develops an approach whereby people are best understood as having two utility functions, one rational and the other altruistic.[17] This model is a more sophisticated version of one first offered by John Harsanyi.[18] Margolis tries to model what he refers to as, "the feeling of psychological equilibrium associated with the fair-share notion."[19] He says this can be intuitively captured in the so-called FS allocation rule, which Margolis characterizes in the following manner: "The larger the share of my resources I have spent unselfishly, the more weight I give to my selfish interests in allocating marginal resources. On the other hand, the larger benefit I can confer on the group compared with the benefit from spending marginal resources on myself, the more I will tend to act unselfishly."[20] Margolis is here making a social scientific claim about an aspect of ordinary morality, specifically that people are more or less altruistic depending on the amount of impersonal good they have done in the past, and on the relative degree of benefit they can do for others versus the relative cost to themselves. Margolis is not specific as to the absolute amount of moral motivation that is characteristically present, yet, between the lines, he appears more bullish than Harsanyi, who claims that the "impersonal attitude" necessary for altruistic behavior appears only in "rare moments."[21]

Gregory Kavka argues for a position he calls "predominant egoism."[22] Like Margolis, Kavka is explicit in his attempt to incorporate moral motivation into a predominantly economic model. Kavka conceives of his position as a modification of the strong Hobbesian view but still in the Hobbesian tradition of holding a fairly pessimistic view of human nature.[23] Kavka sees predominant egoism as the conjunction of the following four propositions:

1. For most people in most situations, the "altruistic gain/personal loss" ratio needed to reliably motivate self-sacrificing action is *large*.
2. The *number of people* for whom altruism and other non-self-interested motives normally override self-interested motives is *small*.
3. The *number of situations*, for the average person, in which non-self-interested motives override personal interest is *small*.
4. The *scope of altruistic motives* that are strong enough to normally override self-interest is, for most people, *small*, that is, confined to concern for family, close friends, close associates, or particular groups or public projects to which the individual is devoted.[24]

Notice that with Proposition 1 in particular, Kavka offers a kind of proportionality principle of the sort Margolis discusses. The intuitive idea is that people are more inclined to do good when they can get the most altruistic benefit for their dollar. Kavka appears to leave the door open for other moral notions when he mentions, "other non-self-interested motives," in proposition 2, but he never spells out what he has in mind here. Rather, the proportionality principle is emphasized.

There has been little discussion in the literature as to whether the Margolis/Kavka approach is better than the pure Hobbesian approach. While this is an important issue to explore, the answer need not be determined here. It is significant to note that the Margolis/Kavka approach does not in any way on its face assume a greater degree of moral motivation as a ratio of all behavior than the Barry/Hardin approach. Both Kavka and Margolis think that the lion's share of behavior is motivated by narrowly self-interested reasons.

For all these theorists have told us, then, there is no reason to think there is more at issue than various attempts to best model or describe a state of affairs that all basically agree on. In a nutshell, all these theorists hold that human behavior is for the most part, though not totally, self-regarding or narrowly self-interested. These views are nevertheless usefully contrasted with those of Harsanyi who thinks that non-egoistic behavior is rare. It is probably fair to say that most theorists tend more toward one version or another of predominant egoism as compared to the narrow Hobbesian position, if only implicitly. The predominant egoist position is more reasonable and realistic on its face than the strong Hobbesian position. It is also more compatible with the sorts of positions taken by those who do not accept rational choice theory because many moral theorists readily acknowledge and incorporate into their writings the potency of the human impulse toward narrowly self-interested behavior.[25] With rare exceptions, however, moral theorists do not hold the Hobbesian starting point to be most accurate as a matter of social science. But it is probably fair to say that moral theorists as a group tend to have a stereotype of rational choice theorists as more toward the strong egoist or Hobbesian position than, in fact, appears to be the case. The preceding discussion shows that the various widely held positions may be closer on the continuum between purely moral motivation and narrowly rational motivation than is commonly thought.

The previous section established the plausibility of adopting predominant egoism as a starting point for explanatory social theory. A full-scale examination of the moral impulses that interact with rational impulses is beyond the scope of the present project. Of interest here are those moral impulses that play a special role in the story of norms and customs. With a couple of important exceptions, this topic has failed to receive the attention in the literature that it deserves. It turns out that the morality of participation in practices is more complex than the simple proportionality principle of rational versus moral motivation offered by Margolis and Kavka. The moral relationships that emerge from practices will be seen to vary in their thick content depending on the structure of the underlying practice, that is, depending on whether the practice is an SD norm, a coordination norm, or an epistemic norm. Section I of the chapter explores the most important of these emergent moral relationships. Parts Two and Three of the book examine some of the most important emergent moral relationships that have appeared in a legal context.

II. Practice-Driven Emergent Moral Relationships

The following account will focus on three central moral impulses that emerge out of the interactions of groups of norm conformers. The first is a principle or duty that may arise in interactions that have the strategic structure of n-person Prisoner's Dilemmas. The second and third principles arise in interactions that have the strategic structure of coordination norms. To all appearances, these emergent moral principles are sui generis. There may also be other moral impulses that emerge, but the account presented here will focus on the core three only, rather than attempt to provide an exhaustive account. The most important point is to understand the process whereby these moral impulses emerge from the interactions of norm conformers. This will facilitate a better understanding of parallel processes whereby moral impulses may emerge in more explicitly legal settings, as will be discussed in Parts Two and Three.

A. *Lewis and Ullman-Margalit on Conventions as Norms*

It will be of interest to begin with a look at the normative arguments of Lewis and Ullman-Margalit. Both Lewis and Ullmann-Margalit think conventions may become norms. Lewis makes the following claim: "Conventions may be a species of norms: regularities to which we believe one ought to conform. I shall argue that they are." Lewis then lists a series of five propositions, which follow from the definition of a convention. From the five, the following two are implied: "(6) I have reason to believe that my conforming would answer to my own preferences. (7) I have reason to believe that my conforming would answer to the preferences of most other members of P involved with me in S; and that they have reason to expect me to conform."[26] Lewis makes the following remarks regarding these two propositions:

(6) and (7), when true, are presumptive reasons why I ought to conform. For we may presume, other things being equal, that one ought to do what answers to his own preferences. And we presume, other things being equal, that one ought to do what answers to others' preferences, especially when they may reasonably expect one to do so. For any action conforming to any convention, we would recognize these two (probable and presumptive) reasons why it ought to be done. . . . This is what I mean by calling conventions a species of norms.[27]

We see that on Lewis's account, conventions may be said to be norms in two different ways. In short, conventions are norms because they provide one with a rational reason why one ought to conform, and because they provide one with a moral reason why one ought to conform. Though Lewis says no more to clarify what background theory he thinks might justify the claim that such situations provide one with moral reasons, his comments lend themselves to a broadly utilitarian reading, as the preferences of others appear to be what matters. Yet he also refers to the fact that others will have reasonable expectations, which sounds like an appeal to fairness.

Ullmann-Margalit takes a similar approach to that of Lewis. She observes that the nature of recurrent coordination problems is such that conforming actions satisfy the preferences of the actor, as well as the expectations and preferences of the others involved.[28] In such situations, she claims, the expectations will become "deontic."

Ullmann-Margalit writes: "Where a coordination problem is recurrent, and where there emerges a regularity which solves it, and where there is room for speaking of precedents, these expectations tend rapidly to assume the character of deontic ones; i.e. to be more than mere predictions: to constitute mutual demands."[29] Ullmann-Margalit goes on to make the following remarks in which she, like Lewis, makes her one moral claim of the book:[30]

The claim that expectations upholding regularities tend to become deontic is, as such, an empirical generalization. But conjoin it to the previous point made, namely that an action in conformity with a regularity which solves a recurrent coordination problem is one that gratifies both the actor's and the other participants' interests, and you will have an independent justification why this will be so.[31]

In this passage, Ullmann-Margalit is apparently claiming that these expectations become deontic, and that it is right or morally correct that they should.

Both writers think it natural that sanctions and prescriptions will arise in the sorts of circumstances outlined here. Both Lewis and Ullmann-Margalit make the claim that the members of the group will exact moral sanctions against defectors. Lewis writes:

So if they see me fail to conform, not only have I gone against their expectations; they will probably be in a position to infer that I have knowingly acted contrary to my own preferences and their reasonable expectations. They will be surprised, and they will tend to explain my conduct discreditably. The poor opinions they form of me, and their reproaches, punishment, and distrust are the unfavorable responses I have evoked by my failure to conform to the convention.[32]

Ullmann-Margalit makes similar comments regarding sanctions.[33] Unlike Lewis, who does not discuss prescriptions,[34] Ullmann-Margalit provides a fairly lengthy discussion. She provides three benefits that accrue when a regularity takes on the status of an explicitly prescribed norm. The first benefit is that if the norm is explicitly prescribed, newcomers to the group will not threaten its regularity. The problem, as she sees it, is that current members will be able to follow regularities, but newcomers may not see them unless told.[35] Second, and relatedly, is the problem that a past regularity might be characterized by several different unique descriptions, which might all agree on the past instances but diverge on some future instance. An explicit norm, Ullmann-Margalit claims, may solve this problem, as it provides a "unique fitting description" of the regularity, "which provides unique guidance" in future cases.[36] Third, she remarks that norms have a higher degree of articulation and explicitness than mere regularities. Thus, they offer the safest solution to coordination problems.[37] We see that according to Lewis and Ullmann-Margalit, the reason why nonconformers will be sanctioned and have conformity prescribed is that the conformers prefer that the others conform, and it is in their interest that conformity be forthcoming.

But, as we saw in some of the examples of coordination norms examined in Chapter Two, conformers do not always prefer that the nonconformers conform. In the case of the conforming lawyer, the others actually prefer that the individual not conform. In many other cases, rational actors will be indifferent, as we saw in the example of wearing a suit. Given that most others act in certain ways, it will behoove one to do so as well. But others are neither harmed nor benefited by one's conformity. As we saw, it is deceptive to focus on the example of driving. For this is indeed a norm in which others are harmed by an individual's nonconformity. But with many social customs and traditions, this is not the case. If others fail to conform, they will stand out as being atypical, but their behavior, as such, is harmless. Thus, there will be no reason to prescribe conformity or punish defectors.[38] And this is in line with what we observe. For typically, one is not punished by others for failing to dress in a conventional manner, which would be in one's self-interest, in the same way that one is punished for acts of nonconformity, which are harmful to others, such as driving on the wrong side of the road.

In what sense then are these patterns of behavior norms? They are norms on my definition because they are rationally governed patterns of behavior, motivated by conformity that produces benefits. In the cases just discussed, the benefit of my coordinating only accrues to me and thus the others have no reason to sanction and prescribe because they do not have a potential to either benefit or suffer from doing so.

Sanctions and prescriptions may be forthcoming, however, from those who take an interest in one's welfare. Thus, parents sanction and prescribe behavior to make their children conform to prevalent coordination norms. But this is because they take an interest in the child's achievement of the coordination benefit. Another source may be those close to one whose welfare is a function of one's welfare. So for example a spouse may prescribe and sanction to induce conformity to prevalent coordination norms so that the other spouse may do better, so that the first spouse will indirectly do better. But this is consistent with it being the case by and large that people are indifferent. We see then that though sanctions and prescriptions may be present in the case of coordination norms, they need not be. This is precisely why we should not build them into the definition of norms.

B. Reciprocity and Fairness Relations as Created by Participation in PD Norms and Customs

When one benefits from an SD norm, one may incur obligations to reciprocate participation in order that other members of the group may also benefit. This basic moral intuition has been debated, though in a different context than here, by some of the century's foremost normative theorists. The so-called fairness argument was first developed by H.L.A. Hart, then amended by John Rawls, and attacked by Robert Nozick.[39] These theorists explored the fairness intuition in the context of political obligation. The focus here is on whether informal norms and customs may engender similar fairness obligations. Nevertheless, it will be useful to begin by seeing how the parallel intuition has been handled in the literature on political obligation. Some of the more controversial features of the fairness argument for political obligation are less troublesome in the context of informal norms.

As Hart sees it, obligations may emerge among persons taking part in co-operative social endeavors, or as Hart calls them, "joint enterprise[s] according to rules." Such participation may bring into existence "special rights" of the participants who submit to the scheme to receive a similar submission from those participants who have benefited.[40] Hart writes:

A third very important source of special rights and obligations which we recognize in many spheres of life is what may be termed mutuality of restrictions, and I think political obligation is intelligible only if we see what precisely this is and how it differs from the other right-creating transactions (consent, promising) to which philosophers have assimilated it. In its bare schematic outline it is this: when a number of persons conduct any joint enterprise according to rules and thus restrict their liberty, those who have submitted to these restrictions when required have a right to a similar submission from those who have benefited by their submission.[41]

This brief account is Hart's main statement of his argument for how a practice can create rights and obligations. The basic idea is that a person may take on obligations to contribute to a joint enterprise out of fairness, simply due to benefiting from the arrangement. With this duty is the correlative right that each of the contributors has that one submit. Crucially, Hart's account seeks to bypass consent as a requirement for the incursion of the obligation, while maintaining a requirement of voluntary participation in the joint enterprise. This distinguishes his approach from a contractarian account, which would require consent as a basis of obligation. A theory of political obligation that avoided consent as a requirement would avoid the difficulty that all contract theorists face, namely, spelling out a notion of consent that makes it more than a fiction of one sort or another.[42]

Though Hart does not mention the free-rider problem, per se, it is implicit in his discussion of the special obligation that emerges among beneficiaries to submit themselves to the restrictions needed to maintain the joint enterprise. These restrictions would not be necessary if people did not consider conformity onerous, and prefer instead to defect. Broadly speaking, the idea seems to be that many elements of society can be viewed as having the structure of a collective action problem; there are mutual benefits to be had if people cooperate in joint enterprises, but there is a threat of free riding, as people would prefer to be carried along by the efforts of others. Thus, writ large, it is the dominant strategic structure of society and one's relationship to it as a beneficiary that may create an obligation.

As Hart notes in the quoted passage, a special sort of obligation is most relevant; political obligation. This argument asks us to think of the state provision of goods as being similar to a cooperative venture that has the strategic structure of a collective action problem. Each prefers to free ride on the cooperative efforts of others, and so it is only fair that if the good is to be made available to all, that all should contribute, because it is only then that no one is able to benefit for free while others contribute.

It is by this means that the argument from political obligation leads to the argument for political coercion. The argument at its essence is that state coercion can be justified because the contributions are themselves only fair, since the person who is compelled to make them is the beneficiary of collective goods produced by the state, and since the contributions are fair and the only way to get them is through coercion, the coercion is justified.

Rawls picks up Hart's argument and adds more detail and analysis, as well as two labels: the "principle of fair play" and the "principle of fairness."[43] Rawls' statement of the principle is even more evocative of the free rider problem. He writes:

The principle of fair play may be defined as follows. Suppose there is a mutually beneficial and just scheme of social cooperation, and that the advantages it yields can only be obtained if everyone, or nearly everyone, cooperates. Suppose further that cooperation requires a certain sacrifice from each person, or at least involves a certain restriction of his liberty. Suppose finally that the benefits produced by cooperation are, up to a certain point, free: that is, the scheme of cooperation is unstable in the sense that if any one person knows that all (or nearly all) of the others will continue to do their part, he will still be able to share a gain from the scheme even if he does not do his part. Under these conditions a person who has accepted the benefits of the scheme is bound by a duty of fair play to do his part and not to take advantage of the free benefits by not cooperating.[44]

The conditions Rawls gives here for the emergence of the fairness principle are strikingly similar to those for a collective action problem or Prisoner's Dilemma; cooperation is a sacrifice and enough others are cooperating such that one may be able to get away without cooperating, without threatening to bring down the enterprise. These are the conditions in which we would expect to see narrowly rational people attempting to free ride. In these conditions, the duty of fairness requires that one should not defect from a mutually beneficial pattern of behavior simply because it is in one's self-interest to do so, if one has already incurred benefits and so taken on obligations. Barry and Hardin refer to this as the "anti-free-rider" principle.[45]

Though Rawls's position is very similar to Hart's, there are differences. Whereas Hart talked about a "joint enterprise," Rawls talks about a "mutually beneficial and just scheme of social cooperation."[46] For Hart, it appears to be enough that a person benefits from the scheme (although some sort of voluntary involvement is required), whereas, for Rawls, there must be an acceptance of the benefits.[47] In spite of these differences, the arguments are similar and may be treated as one argument for present purposes. With the basics of the argument on the table, we are ready to see how it applies, if at all, in the context of norms.

First, note that concern with norms is a more limited issue than is the concern with political obligation. Hart and Rawls are concerned with all public goods provided by the state, which would include goods such as national defense. Such a good is not the result of conformity to norms by some contributing group. Rather, taxes are levied, and the money is then used to hire and train specialists who provide the good.[48]

The heart of the controversy over the fairness argument as applied to the state has revolved around the issue of voluntariness. Both Hart and Rawls want the participation in the scheme and the receipt of the benefits to be in some appropriate sense voluntary. The controversy has been over whether a plausible story can be told whereby the average citizen's relation to goods provided by the state is one of voluntary acceptance. Voluntariness seems a fiction, however, because the state provides what it does regardless of what one personally voluntarily does.[49] This would not be an improvement over social contract theory, then, as one argument based on an illicit fiction would be done away with, only to be replaced by another.

The important point for present purposes, however, is that what might make for a dubious argument for state coercion may still make for an attractive argument for a type of special moral relationship that emerges among smaller groups, like groups of conformers to a practice. What is striking is that conformity to practices sometimes contains the element of voluntariness that may only be a fiction when it comes to the state. It can genuinely be said that one voluntarily chooses to participate in some practices. Consequently, it may be more broadly appealing to our ordinary moral intuition to claim that one ought to contribute to the continuation of such practices if one is going to benefit from them. Thus, some version of the fairness argument may have broader appeal outside the context of the argument for political obligation. Consider the following example.

In the small town in northern Wisconsin where the author grew up it snows often. People frequently become stuck in their automobiles. It is customary for people who come along, and are capable of doing so, to render assistance. The practice of rendering assistance to people stuck in the snow has the structure of a collective action problem. The person interested in promoting her narrow self-interest will want to receive help when she needs it but will also want to be able to avoid assisting others when she comes upon them. In other words, she would like to free ride on the practice. She is quite literally a free rider, as she is able to drive away without troubling to render assistance.

In this example, by the lights of local norms, the person who takes part in the practice to the extent of accepting aid from others is bound out of fairness to reciprocate when the occasion arises, if she is able bodied and no special circumstances exist, such as that she is rushing her spouse or companion to the hospital or that the stranded person appears dangerous. We see then that voluntary participation in practices that have the structure of an iterated collective action problem can, by the lights of ordinary morality, create a special relationship such that one has a duty to reciprocate that one would not otherwise have. Thus, the basic fairness or reciprocity intuition behind the Hart/Rawls argument appears to be ensconced in ordinary morality, at least in situations in which the participation is genuinely voluntary.

In the language of deontology, the moral relationship created here is a duty or obligation (these terms will be used interchangeably). What are the significant features of duties of this sort? First, they are created by specific acts rather than adhering to individuals simply in virtue of their moral personhood. They are thus not general duties one has simply in virtue of being a person capable of moral behavior interacting with persons deserving of moral treatment. Rather, they are duties created out of participation in a practice.

As Hart notes in the epigram that began this chapter, the notion that moral relationships can be created by consent is mysterious to some.[50] But they are not created by consent in the way, for example, that promises create duties out of consent. In the case of a practice such as the stuck-in-the-snow example, one could be described as consenting to take part in the practice when one accepts help when stuck in the snow and one knows that there is a practice in place that requires reciprocal participation when the shoe is on the other foot. But in so engaging the practice, one does not thereby consent to the creation of an obligation to reciprocate out of fairness. The obligation, or so the argument goes, arises regardless of one's consent. It is when one allows oneself to reap the benefits of the cooperative labors that constitute the practice that one takes on a special relationship toward those who participate in the practice.

A distinction often appealed to, to distinguish different types of duties, is that between positive and negative duties. Fairness of this sort would be a positive duty, for negative duties are simply duties not to harm others, and in the snow-pushing example, one has a more substantial duty than merely not to harm the other person. Rather, one may have a positive duty to benefit them by getting out and rendering assistance.

Whether duties of this sort will count within a deontological theory will depend on the theory. Different theories accept different sorts of duties. Perhaps the most minimal is a theory that recognizes only negative duties. Such a theory would not accept the fairness obligation as legitimate. It would say that you have a duty not to run the person off the road as they stand waiting for assistance, but there is no affirmative duty to stop and become involved, which after all may mean becoming enmeshed knee deep in snow, pushing while the back wheels spin mud. So what, this line of thinking goes, if you have been aided by others in the past, that means nothing now, for those were those people, and these are these? If you go out of your way and help these strangers, you are doing a good deed, period.

Nozick is a theorist who is known for having a spare deontological theory.[51] But his moral ontology of duties is more encompassing than just the duty not to harm others, for he recognizes that duties can be created by promising. In general, his account focuses on consent as the font of duties one creates, besides the basic duty not to harm others. It will be of interest to consider what he might say about examples such as the duty to reciprocate in helping people out of the snow. Remember that we are trying to see if popular morality holds that participation in norms and customs generates moral relationships of various sorts, and Nozick's theory is fairly seen as a philosophical interpretation of one strain of ordinary morality, the individualistic strain. As our society is popularly described as relatively individualistic compared to other societies, this strain clearly has some currency.

The snow example appears to escape Nozick's well-known criticisms of the fairness argument. Nozick's method of undermining the fairness argument is to present examples in which people receive benefits of the sort Nozick claims Hart and Rawls are committed to, and yet where common intuition is arguably pulled in the other direction, such that we would think the required contributions are coercive rather than fair. One of Nozick's most famous examples is that in which a neighborhood association sets up a program whereby public address broadcasts are made daily by members of the community who play music, tell stories, and the like.[52] Nozick argues that the mere fact that one benefits would not create an obligation to contribute one's time at the broadcast station doing a day of programming as one's share of the year's output.

Nozick's line of argument is effective because he creates a situation that fits the broad features of the fairness argument but that, where common moral intuition is inclined, at least strongly doubts whether the duty of contributing is owed simply because of the receipt of benefits of this sort. He offers a few other similar examples including one where a person has books delivered to his house by a stranger who does this as a practice.[53]

A feature of Nozick's examples that helps create his desired effect on our intuitions is that in each of them it is dubious whether the voluntariness condition is met. Rather, one is going about one's business and then the benefits are thrust upon one. Nozick's foes contend that this makes these examples inapropros Hart's and Rawls's argument, for these theorists envision persons who are more sanguine about the practices from which they accept benefits; hence, it is more intuitively plausible to contend that the voluntariness condition is met.[54] But Nozick has a ready retort available. Indeed, his examples are weak on the voluntariness condition, but in this they simply parallel the situation where the state provides public goods and extracts contributions from taxpayers, for the state does not perform a voluntariness test on particular persons to see if they wish to accept the benefits.[55] Even if this point is telling against Hart and Rawls, it is not telling against those norms and customs in which voluntariness is not at issue.

Another worry Nozick raises is that there is a problem if one person benefits from the scheme but others benefit much more.[56] How can this person be said to have an equal obligation to contribute? John Simmons considers this objection and properly observes that what seems intuitively fair is that, if there is a duty at all, it would be a duty to contribute roughly in proportion to the relative degree of one's benefit. There is no apparent reason Nozick could not accept this modification. And indeed, in the snow-pushing example, people need not suffer from a situation of a less attractive benefits/contributions ratio than their peers, for the practice is such that one can self-monitor one's own contributions. If one thinks one is giving more than one's share of assistance, one can simply reduce one's level of contribution, that is, drive by the stranded motorist with averted gaze if one feels oneself to be a burdened lender in the informal favor bank.

Nozick next worries that even if these conditions hold, one might still prefer that a different scheme existed.[57] But one will not be able to work to bring about one's new scheme if one is duty bound to contribute toward the present one. This objection is another version of casting the beneficiary as an outsider to the scheme. Nozick is correct here; this is a problem for the basic intuition. Fortunately again, for our purposes of establishing the existence of a minimal case for the moral intuition (a methodology, by the way, that drives *Anarchy, State, and Utopia*), we will be able to set aside such cases as admittedly troublesome, for there will still be many cases where the person has no problems of this sort with the practice, except, that is, that, other things being equal, she would prefer to receive its benefits for free. Often, there is no real issue about preferences for alternative practices because the extant practices seem to verge on being uniquely satisfactory; hence, there are no disgruntled citizens who prefer a shift to a new one. This seems to be a fair description of the snow-pushing practice for instance.

We see then that, despite Nozick's worries, making out the basic situation where a fairness obligation is attractive to ordinary morality is quite simple. The problem of course is that the further particular situations are from the paradigm example, the more cloudy the basic intuition will become. But to a basic case such as that outlined here, Nozick's worries do not apply. The principle of fairness or reciprocity appears, then, to be a sound moral intuition, by the lights of ordinary morality; just Hart and Rawls tried to get too much from it, as the principle appears clearly more attractive when applied to small groups as compared to serving as a grounding for political obligation.

To establish this point says nothing about why people actually conform to SD norms. For all the fairness argument says, it may still be the case that the Hobbesians are correct and all people are narrowly self-interested and only conform when it promotes their narrow self-interest to do so. But, as discussed earlier, predominant egoism may be the better assumption about human motivation; in which case the fact that ordinary morality appears to promote some forms of the fairness obligation may mean that some conforming behavior to SD norms is best explained as an expression of this moral impulse. In other words, some persons conform, and encourage others to conform, as a result of a belief in the moral propriety of contributing to practices one voluntarily takes part in and benefits from.

Some rational choice theorists have entertained the possibility that such fairness or reciprocity concerns might indeed motivate people to conform. Such conformers could still be predominantly self-interested, just not totally so to the point of defection on every possible occasion. What the account does is put more clothes on the bare skeleton of accounts such as those of Kavka and Margolis, who think that a concern for fairness is part of the makeup of the predominant egoist but who do not specify the workings of the principle in sufficient detail. Margolis, for example, spells out fairness in proportional terms such that one is fair to others by exhibiting some altruism when one has not done so in a while, or by exhibiting altruism when the cost to oneself is small and the benefit is great.[58] Margolis does not take account of the manner in which predominant egoists will adjust their other-regarding behavior in a reciprocal fashion to benefit those who made possible the norm under which they benefit.

C. The Morality of Coordination

The previous section explored the moral element that is most salient with SD norms. This section looks at the moral elements most salient in coordination norms. Fairness concerns arising in the context of the temptation to free ride appear not to arise as a result of the strategic structure of coordination norms. Recall that a coordination norm is maintained by persons seeking to achieve the coordination benefit. Sanctions are not required to maintain the norm because there is no natural inclination to free ride. Just the opposite, because others conform, it is also in one's interest to conform. The first question to ask then is whether there are any moral duties or other sorts of moral relationships that arise in such a context?

Lewis's discussion of the morality of conventions is relevant. As noted in Chapter Two, although Lewis talks about conventions, he has in mind the strategic structure of proper coordination equilibria. With proper coordination equilibria, others have an interest that one conform, that is, their payoffs are positively impacted by one's conformity. Lewis discusses the morality of conventions in the following terms.

[C]onventions may *be* a species of norms: regularities to which we believe one ought to conform. I shall argue that they are. There are certain probable consequences implied by the fact that an action would conform to a convention (whatever the action and whatever the convention) which are presumptive reasons, according to our common opinions, why that action ought to be done.[59]

Lewis goes on: "And we presume, other things equal, that one ought to do what answers to others' preferences, especially when they may reasonably expect one to do so."[60] We see here that Lewis is touching upon the issue of moral legitimacy for both preferences and expectations. With respect to the preferences of other conformers to conventions, Lewis's basic moral claim is that one ought to do what answers to these preferences, namely conform. Notice that Lewis refers to "we," as the holders of this view. In other words, he takes himself to be presenting a characterization of common sense or ordinary moral views.

Recall that for Lewis, conventions have the structure of proper coordination equilibria, which means that each of the conformers benefits from the conformity of each of the others. This explains why each will have a preference that each of the others conform. In addition, each person does better for himself by conforming, given the conformity of the others. Hence, conformity will be individually rational and so each will likely want to conform. Because each wants to conform, it will be rational for each to expect others to conform; all other things equal, it is reasonable to expect people to do what is in their interest. Because people expect one to conform, they will be likely to gear their behavior toward this expectation; hence, they may suffer a loss if one fails to conform as a result. This is an instance in which others' expectations of oneself bring their interests into play. And according to Lewis, other things equal, ordinary morality requires us to do what answers to other peoples' expectations. This is Lewis's basic account of how expectations generated in the context of conventions may take on moral properties.

Lewis here is making a very strong claim about the nature of ordinary morality vis-à-vis the moral fecundity of expectations, namely, that one always has a prima facie duty to meet the expectations of others. When stated minimally like this, it immediately appears to be a suspicious claim. It is suspicious because the moral impulse seems not to characterize ordinary morality so much as to reflect a particular critical moral viewpoint, utilitarianism.

It seems simply incorrect that by the lights of everyday morality one ought to seek to meet others' expectations, per se. Often times, one will disagree with the moral propriety or social worth of the preferences of another. In such circumstances, it is clear that ordinary morality does not require giving weight to the preference. If, for instance, a non-Christian lives in a community of fundamentalist Christians who prefer that certain sorts of activities not occur, such as the reading and writing of secular philosophy, she need not give these preferences weight in deciding whether or not to pursue her interest. It is clear why others would like one to conform to their preferences; they benefit. This pure desire is not enough by the lights of ordinary morality to create a duty or entitlement. I would like you to send me $1000 right now, but this does not mean that I think you are duty bound in this regard.

Everyday morality is fairly individualistic and places greater emphasis on the negative duties than the positive duties. One has a general duty to not harm others, but not a general duty to benefit them. Ordinary moral thinking does of course acknowledge the value of going out of one's way to benefit others. This is seen as satisfying what moral theorists label *supererogatory duties*, which are those duties that are not required to be carried out in particular circumstances.

Gerald Postema provides the following example to illustrate the negative rights perspective on the duties that flow from expectations. The example appears to capture an element of ordinary morality more closely than does the utilitarian account. He writes:

Tradition has it that Kant's daily walks through the streets of Konigsberg were as regular as clockwork. But the fact that Frau Schmidt put her pie in the oven with the expectation that she would be reminded to remove it by the sight of the philosopher walking past her window would not put Kant under any obligation to walk his accustomed route, even if he knew Frau Schmidt's plans. Frau Schmidt's expectations were reasonable enough – she had reason to expect Kant to pass by at the appropriate time – but she was not *entitled* to expect him to do so. She had, we might say, reasonable but not fully *legitimate* expectations.[61]

According to Postema, the implication here is that one does not have any prima facie duties to meet others' expectations. A bare expectation is not a "legitimate expectation." Note that in this passage Postema appears to be providing his own critical moral viewpoint rather than attempting to characterize ordinary morality. Though his critical viewpoint seems closer to ordinary morality than that of Lewis, he may have come too far in the other direction from the perspective of common moral intuition, as it would appear that in situations of a sort similar to that Postema describes, we would indeed recognize some sorts of moral relationships emerging. Should Kant have no concerns whatsoever about Frau Schmidt's pies?

Postema contends that expectations may take on an obligatory character where there is detrimental reliance on the expectation and the expectation was "induced."[62] This notion is closely related to the doctrine of promissory estoppel in contract law.[63]

Promissory estoppel is a doctrine whereby the law will enforce certain sorts of promises in which the usual requirement of consideration is not met and yet a promise or other relevant behavior that induced reliance by the promisee ended up working to her detriment.[64] Postema is not discussing the legal doctrine, however. Rather, his claim is that as a matter of morality, expectations of others that arise as a result of conventions will take on an obligatory character when there is induced detrimental reliance. Postema does not attempt to argue in great detail for the validity of this claim as a matter of critical morality. For his purposes, it is enough that the underlying moral intuition is of reasonable enough warrant to be incorporated into the law.[65]

What is striking about Postema's moral claim is its minimal character when compared to Lewis's utilitarian-inspired moral intuition. Whereas Lewis thinks all expectations have prima facie moral weight, Postema thinks that none do, save those cases where there is induced detrimental reliance. There are positions even less demanding than Postema's. For someone could ask, why should induced detrimental reliance create an obligation? For example, a critical moral theorist who only accepted the principle that one has a duty not to harm others might say that induced detrimental reliance does not create an obligation unless one thereby harms others, as presumably, these are cases where there is induced reliance that is detrimental but not to the point of harming another. In such cases, the negative harm theorist would say that there is no obligation despite the induced detrimental reliance.

Other critical moral viewpoints will be more demanding than either of these positions but still less demanding than the utilitarian position. For example, some theorists will acknowledge that some preferences and expectations, but not others, matter. They may have a sort of Parfitian objective list approach such that there is a list of things that are morally good and others that are morally bad.[66] Expectations regarding outcomes that are morally good are worthy of respect, but expectations for the morally bad are not.

Alternatively, one might adopt a proportionality principle of the sort that Margolis and Kavka contend is part of everyday morality. If one sees that, by failing to meet another's expectation, she would suffer great loss, but that going out of her way to satisfy their expectation can be done at relatively little cost, she may deem herself morally required to meet their expectations. These theorists implicitly disagree with Postema, holding that if we ever have moral obligations to be just flat out giving of ourselves, it is in cases where a little help on our part can do a great deal of good to a person innocently in a position to otherwise suffer a significant loss. A less demanding but similar position would hold that though one may not have a duty to meet others' expectations, one may nevertheless have a duty to inform the person of one's change of plan so that they can adjust their plans, if the cost of doing so is within reasonable bounds. Here the proportional cost to oneself versus the benefit to another may be small indeed. It seems as if Postema has identified an existent ordinary moral impulse or intuition in the duty that he shows arises in situations of induced detrimental reliance.

It will be helpful to go beyond discussion of conventions in Lewis's sense and to look at the more inclusive concept of a coordination norm, as this notion has been defined in Chapter Two. With one-directional norms, the coordination effect only impacts the putative new conformer, whereas, with two-directional coordination norms, there is a coordination effect for both the new conformer and the current conformers. For the current conformers, the coordination effect may be positive or negative, that is, they may either prefer or disprefer that the putative conformer conform.

Consider first the moral evaluation when there is only a one-directional coordination effect. Because it is only oneself who benefits, the question is really about whether there is a duty to benefit oneself. Some moral theorists do indeed contend that one has moral duties to oneself; nevertheless, judging by the relative dearth of literature on the topic, this is generally seen as a tangential issue in moral theory, which, for the most part, concerns itself with relationships between people and the types of moral relationships created by these interactions. And even within moral theory, to the extent that the issue is discussed, it is controversial whether one has moral duties toward oneself.

The main concern in this chapter is to explicate the ordinary morality of such situations and not their status by lights of critical morality. It appears to be more consonant with ordinary morality to reject the notion of duties to oneself as a needless interference with one's highly valued personal freedom. The presumption of freedom is a moral impulse whereby one is permitted by morality to take the freedom to do what one wants with one's life as long as, along the way, one takes time out to fulfill an often fairly modest set of duties to charity, special relationships, and the like. The presumption of freedom applied to coordination norms would focus on the basic structure of the situation and evaluate its implications for the freedom of the relevant participants.

With one-directional norms, the person considering conforming has the freedom to choose whether or not to conform. Because we are discussing coordination norms, it is by definition in the interest of the person to conform. But it is a basic element of freedom that one be free to maximally promote one's interests, or not, as one pleases. This strain of ordinary morality is clearly evident in the context of current social debate over issues such as the coerced use of motorcycle helmets, seat belts, airbags, and the like. Those who argue that they should be free to choose to use these safety items, or not, as they so please, typically do not ground their argument in the claim that indirectly such a rule will promote their interests. Rather, the position is grounded in the fundamental moral impulse that one should be free to act as one likes when it comes to what are seen as essentially self-regarding behaviors. Inasmuch as a presumption of freedom is a part of everyday morality, one appears not to have a duty to conform to the norm simply to achieve a coordination benefit for oneself. In a phrase, then, one-directional coordination norms generate opportunities not duties.

The next question is what duties, if any, are generated in the context of two-directional coordination norms. These have the strategic structure of the conventions discussed by Lewis in which both the potential conformer and the current conformers benefit from conformity. The foregoing discussion of the views of Lewis and Postema showed that indeed by both the lights of utilitarianism and ordinary morality, moral duties may arise in these situations.

It turns out, however, that the most central moral underpinning of coordination norms has not been discussed in the rational choice literature on conventions or coordination norms. This moral intuition is one manifestation of one of the most overreaching of all moral intuitions, the tort duty not to harm others. When moral and political theorists talk about the duty not to harm, usually they implicitly have a notion of intentional harm in mind. But the notion of unintentional harm is actually of greater interest when it comes to exploring the moral complexities of coordination norms.

Unintentional harms result from unintended causal chains leading from neutral or even beneficent acts to harmful consequences. By the lights of common sense morality, one test of whether you are morally culpable for these unintended consequences is whether you were careless or negligent in the behavior leading up to the action of yours that proved to be harmful to another.[67] For instance, you will be held culpable if though the harm was unintended, it nevertheless could have easily been foreseen, and if foreseen deserved to be stopped.

It appears, then, that the bare moral principle of harm avoidance implies two duties, one negative and the other positive. On the one hand, there is the duty to refrain from intentionally harming others. This is a negative duty in that it does not require an action but rather the forbearance of action. On the other hand, there is the duty to take reasonable precautions so as to avoid unintentionally harming others, which appears to be a positive duty because it requires positive behavior on one's part, namely, taking precautions.[68] Intentional harm is for many people easier to stop than unintentional harm. One can more or less decide never to murder, rob, and so on. One cannot just decide not to unintentionally harm others. In fact, as long as one is living and breathing, there is nothing one can do to rule out the possibility of unintentionally harming others. The best one can do is take steps to lower the risk of harming others.[69]

The important question for present purposes is whether forming expectations may aid one in better avoiding the negligent harming of others and thus whether there is some sort of obligation to pay proper attention to expectations. Much of negligent harming arises from social interaction gone awry, social collisions so to speak. The more in touch one is with the social practices of one's normative milieu, the more finely honed one's expectations of the future activity of others will be. This knowledge will allow for a higher degree of interactiveness and a smoother level of performance, and so less friction and, in the end, less social collisions. To interact at a higher level is to form expectations of others and to let them form expectations of you, so that coordination may occur. To be properly cautious, then, you may need to be apprised of the local community practices so that you know what to expect of others, and so that they in turn will know what to expect of you. Consequently, our ability to be moral by avoiding harming others depends in part on our ability to properly form and act on our expectations regarding extant norms and customs.

I postulate, then, the existence of a general moral duty (by the lights of ordinary morality) to form expectations about the behavior of those one is dealing with, that is, to form expectations about the general patterns of behavior extant in one's community. Because much of this is behavior that conforms to norms and customs, one has a duty to form expectations about others' conforming behavior. Not only is this plausibly seen as a duty of ordinary morality, but it would also likely be endorsed by a variety of critical moral theories because it is built on the bare moral principle that it is wrong to harm or injure others, which is a principle that is widely endorsed.

A striking feature of this moral assertion is its broad applicability. For although the injunction to be normatively sensitive to one's social environment may appear not to present an especially weighty consideration when compared to the injunction against murder, for example, yet its significance lies in the pervasiveness of relevant situations. For most people, injunctions against positive harms such as murder do not play a major role in their day-to-day lives because this behavior is not a usual temptation. But the issue of the negligent harming of others is one that all people must deal with on a regular basis. As long as one is in society, one must be vigilant not to harm others through negligence. This can be a challenge as one may often be thrust into new situations that require one to appraise anew what would be appropriate behavior.[70] This duty holds for all members of society for all other members.

We see then that expectations created by the existence of practices do indeed engender moral relationships by the lights of ordinary morality, although not for the reason championed by Lewis. It is not the moral impulse to maximize utility that undergirds the relationship. Rather, it is the harm principle. Note that this duty to take reasonable precautions not to inadvertently harm others applies to all structures of norms, for the moral relationship does not depend on strategic structure but simply on the fact that practices create expectations and that one may inadvertently harm others by failing to pay enough attention to what one may expect of them.

Conclusion

Section One developed the concept of predominant egoism in order to reconcile the rational choice and moral theoretic approaches. In Section Two, we saw that participation in particular norms may create various sorts of moral relationships. I have only explored the most basic ones. We saw that fairness and reciprocity relationships, obligations based on the creation of induced detrimental reliance, and a duty not to harm may all emerge. These emergent moral relationships will be of interest in the exploration of the law in Parts Two and Three. For although I have looked at informal practices solely here, when judges and juries look at these same sorts of practices in the context of legal disputes, we will see that they are also attuned to the moral relationships that such practices incorporate and give rise to. Thus, seeing how practices may give rise to moral relationships in Section Two of this chapter will help to make sense of the behavior of courts. First, however, it will be necessary to complete the development of the pattern conception of norms, which is the task of the next chapter.

5

Critical Moral Norms

Without such a convention, no one wou'd ever have dream'd, that there was such a virtue as justice, or have been induc'd to conform his actions to it. Taking any single act, my justice may be pernicious in every respect; and 'tis only upon the supposition, that others are to imitate my example, that I can be induc'd to embrace that virtue.[1]

David Hume

Introduction

Varieties of moral acts fall into two main types: outcome-oriented moral acts and action-oriented moral acts. Outcome-oriented moral norms are constituted by outcome-oriented acts, and action-oriented norms are constituted by action-oriented moral acts. An outcome-oriented act is one that is taken to be right insofar as it is the best means to some desired consequences. An action-oriented act is taken to be right for some reason other than, or in conjunction with, its role in the production of desired consequences. Both deontological and virtue-theoretic behavior may be considered action-oriented. Outcome-oriented norms will be examined in Section I, and action-oriented noms will be examined in Section II.

Prima facie, it is puzzling how action-oriented moral behavior might lead to norms. Kantian reasoning is the paradigm of action-oriented behavior. The notion of conformity necessary for norms seems alien to Kantian thought. For the Kantian, when duty calls for one to act in some particular manner, the fact that others are not acting in this manner does not negate one's duty. Nor does the simple fact that others are acting in some particular manner provide one with reason to act in the same manner. In both types of situations, Kantianism appears to exclude such empirical concerns from the domain of moral reasoning. Thus, if not downright hostile, Kantian morality, and so perhaps non-outcome-oriented morality generally, seems prima facie incompatible with a normative framework built on acts of conformity.

In contrast, it seems fairly obvious that outcome-oriented views might be reconciled to conformity. If it would maximize good outcomes to conform, then the outcome-oriented moral actor should conform. In the following discussion, outcome-oriented moral norms will be examined first, then I will take up the more difficult issue of how conformity to norms may make sense from an action-oriented moral point of view.

As with rational norms, moral norms are subdivided into types depending on the circumstances, strategic or otherwise, in which conformity arises. Surprisingly, the same general types of circumstance that exist for rational norms exist for moral norms, that is, there are coordination moral norms, sanction-driven moral norms, and epistemic moral norms. This indicates a certain unity of the normative. In addition, the strategic structure of the normative world is shown to be independent of the assumption of *Homo economicus*.

I. Outcome-Oriented Norms

The building blocks of outcome-oriented norms are outcome-oriented acts of conformity that are motivated by desires that are neither selfish nor irrational. These are *other-regarding* acts.[2] There are two dimensions along which an action may be other-regarding. It may be other-regarding with respect to the scope of concern and the degree of concern.

Scope of concern refers to the breadth of one's regard for others. One may have a very small scope of concern for others, say, for example, if one is concerned only with one's family and friends. On the other hand, utilitarians believe in a universal moral domain, that is, the scope of concern includes all moral agents. The actions that make up outcome-oriented moral norms may have a scope of concern anywhere between these extremes. For example, those who act in the national interest have a scope of concern that includes other citizens but not necessarily foreigners; teachers often act with genuine moral concern for their students; loyal employees sometimes act with regard for the interests of their companies.

Degree of concern refers to the weight attached to the interests of those who are included in the scope of one's concern. One may count others, for example, but count them very little. Utilitarians (and consequentialists generally) count all people equally, but many others who act with regard to their fellows do not count the interests of all to the same degree. Just as some consequentialists may take the interests of animals into account but discount their value relative to humans, others do the same with regard to their fellow humans. For example, a parent may weigh the interests of her family as greater than the interests of others. A member of Congress may weigh the interests of her constituents above the interests of other citizens, whose interests are in turn ranked higher than those of noncitizens. The concern of some people for their fellows has been characterized as a series of concentric circles. We have most concern for ourselves, then our family, friends, community, and so on.[3]

In principle, the possible number of other-regarding motivational types is the number of possible combinations of members in the scope of concern, multiplied by the possible combinations of degrees of concern. Of course, most of these possibilities are never realized. Mainstream moral theory has considered only a small number of these combinations as of legitimate interest. In the case of utilitarianism, only one combination counts (open scope, equal degree).

As noted in previous chapters, coordination norms and sanction-driven norms arise in situations of strategic interaction, and epistemic norms arise in situations of nonstrategic interaction. Sanction-driven norms arise in situations of strategic interaction in which sanctions are necessarily present, whereas they need not be present in situations in which coordination norms arise. Conformity in coordination situations produces coordination norms; conformity in sanctioned-coordination situations produces sanction-driven norms, and conformity in epistemic situations produces epistemic norms.

Each of these three situations has a moral analogue. In other words, conformity turns out to be in the spirit of outcome-oriented morality in coordination, sanctioned-coordination, and epistemic situations. In the following discussion, outcome-oriented morality will be subdivided into cases of motivation with a universal scope of concern and cases with a restricted scope of concern. The reason for this will become apparent. The strategic situations will first be examined for both universal and restricted scopes of concern. Next, the nonstrategic case will be considered.

A. Universal Scope of Concern: Utilitarian Teleology

I will restrict my remarks in this section to the case of utilitarian moral motivation, which is the paradigm of moral motivation with a universal scope of concern. It turns out that utilitarian norms may be maintained in each of the three types of norm-producing situations. This will first be seen for coordination norms, next for SD norms, and finally for epistemic norms. The first two are the coordination situation and the sanctioned-coordination situation.

Recall from Chapter Two that there are a variety of related strategic structures that tend to produce coordination norms among rational agents. Lewis and Ullmann-Margalit thought the class was restricted to situations of iterated coordination problems with a minimum of two proper coordination equilibria. We saw that, in fact, a wider range of situations may be sufficient for the generation and maintenance of coordination norms. As argued in Chapter Two, the crucial factor for determining whether something is a coordination norm turns out to be whether one may achieve a coordination benefit from coordinating with others, regardless of whether the strategic situation happens to have two proper coordination equilibria.

The same is true for utilitarian coordination norms. What matters is that, as a result of coordination, one is able to secure a coordination benefit. But it does not matter for whom the benefit is secured. It will not be necessary to consider the truth of this claim for all the various coordination structures considered in Chapter Two. I will look at only structures to make the general point, as their broader application out from here would be fairly straightforward. Consider first the simplest sort of coordination situation, labeled earlier as the Rock Quarry Game. The example was one of two children coordinating at a swimming hole. The same situation can be considered for utilitarian children.

The basic point of interest is that just as rational egoists will coordinate on the 1, 1 outcome, so too will utilitarians. For they are interested in choosing acts that produce the most utility. In this case, the utilitarian act is to coordinate with the other person at the rock quarry. Rational agents in strategic situations care about the array of payoffs for the other agent only because it contains clues as to what the other is likely to do. For utilitarians, in contrast, the payoffs to the other player matter in their own right.

In repeated situations of this structure in which norms develop, they will be conformed to by utilitarian agents working to achieve the coordination benefit. Thus we see that the notion of conformity to coordination norms makes sense from a utilitarian point of view. Whereas conformity made sense to egoists because it was rational, conformity to coordination norms makes sense to utilitarians because it is moral, that is, utility-maximizing.

Another distinct feature of utilitarian coordination is that the payoffs need not go to either of the participants. For example, the payoffs could represent the ranking of people other than the agents. In this case, suppose that the parents of each of the children want their child to learn to swim, and so the payoffs in Figure 5.1 characterize the parents' preferences. Note that although each of the children are neutral toward the different outcomes as far as their own utilities are concerned, as utilitarian junior achievers, they coordinate in order to please the parents.

Column-Chooser

		Goes	Doesn't Go
Row-Chooser	Goes	1, 1	0, 0
	Doesn't Go	0, 0	0, 0

Figure 5.1 The Rock Quarry Game for Utilitarians

Column-Chooser

		A	B
		A	B
Row-Chooser	A	2, 1	0, 0
	B	0, 0	1, 2

Figure 5.2 Coordination and Conflict Game

Column-Chooser

		Cooperate	Defect
Row-Chooser	Cooperate	3, 3	1, 4
	Defect	4, 1	2, 2

Figure 5.3 Artificial Coordination in the Prisoner's Dilemma

Recall that egoists may face situations of mixed coordination and conflict as shown in Figure 5.2. Though each egoist prefers disadvantageous coordination over noncoordination, each also prefers even more to coordinate at the outcome in which she rather than the other receives the higher payoff. For Row, this is choice A, while for Column, it is choice B. Each of the players faces a situation that combines coordination and conflict. This is not the case for utilitarians, however. A utilitarian will be indifferent toward either of the preferred outcomes. It does not matter who does better as long as the sum is equally beneficial because utilitarians care about total utility, not how it is distributed. Thus, for utilitarians no conflict can arise in these types of games.

Earlier, we saw that, for egoists, conformity to an SD norm is only rational owing to the presence of sanctions. Though sanctions may arise from many sources, we focused on those in the form of implicit threats on the part of others to discontinue cooperation if one defects in a single game of the Prisoner's Dilemma.

Figure 5.3 shows the payoff structure of a single game. When both cooperate, the outcome is 3, 3. It is in the self-interest of each of the agents, however, to defect. This results in the suboptimal outcome 2, 2, in which each does worse than she would have had both cooperated. As we saw in Chapter Two, when the game is iterated, it may be rational for each of the agents to choose to cooperate. The reason is that otherwise the other agent will cease to cooperate in order not to be suckered in future plays. Thus the threat of sanctions in the form of threats not to cooperate in the future may lead rational agents to cooperate.

Unlike the egoist, the utilitarian is interested in producing the optimal outcome for all concerned. The utilitarian will not defect when it is in her self-interest to do so. Rather she will cooperate when this will help lead to the production of the optimal outcome. For example in the matrix in Figure 5.3, if the numbers represent individual utilities, utilitarians will see that the 3, 3 outcome is optimal from a utilitarian point of view. Hence they should be able to coordinate on the cooperative choice to bring it about.

Unlike egoists, utilitarians will not have conflicts over the production of different outcomes because each will prefer the same outcome, the one that is socially optimal. Thus, utilitarians (and those with universal scopes of concern, generally) will not need to threaten one another with sanctions as a means of bringing about conformity. It would appear that this would imply that for the utilitarian there will be no situations in which the maintenance of the norm is the result of fear of sanctions of the type I have called situations of sanctioned coordination. A group of utilitarians, might, however, conform to a norm due to the threat of sanctions imposed from outside. Thus, utilitarians might have external sanction-driven norms but not internal sanction-driven norms, as these terms were used in Chapter Two. The same is not true for outcome-oriented moral motivation with a restricted scope of concern, as we will now see.

B. Restricted Scope of Concern: Nonutilitarian Teleology

Just as egoists and utilitarians may sometimes face each other in strategic situations that have a structure such that there is no conflict of interest, the same may happen to persons exhibiting nonuniversal teleological moral motivation. You may do what is best for your group and I for mine, but in the particular situation in which we find ourselves, there is a perfect coincidence of interests, that is, we both rank all the outcomes identically.

In a game with the coordination structure of Figure 5.4, we have a perfect coincidence of interests. In particular, we both desire that choice A, the 3, 3 outcome, be realized.[4] Thus, strategic interaction does not necessarily mean conflict for players with restricted scopes of concern. But in coordination games in which there is not an identical ranking of outcomes, there will be conflict.

In the strategic situation of Figure 5.5, each prefers coordination on the other's terms to noncoordination, but each prefers still more to coordinate on her own terms, that is, to coordinate on the outcome in which her family receives 2 rather than 1. Even though sanctions may not be necessary to bring about coordination in such an instance, there is conflict. This is in contrast to the case of universal scope of concern in which such situations do not generate conflict.

Column-Chooser

		A	B
Row-Chooser	A	3, 3	1, 1
	B	1, 1	2, 2

Figure 5.4 Pure Coordination with Ranked Alternatives

Column-Chooser's Family

		A	B
Row-Chooser's Family	A	2, 1	0, 0
	B	0, 0	1, 2

Figure 5.5 Conflict Resulting from Restricted Scope of Concern

Column-Chooser

		C	D
Row-Chooser	A	3, 3	1, 4
	B	4, 1	2, 2

Figure 5.6 Narrow Scope and the Prisoner's Dilemma

There also will be conflict in situations that have the strategic structure of a Prisoner's Dilemma (Figure 5.6). In this situation, each most prefers that the other cooperate and she defect, therefore suckering the other and producing the best results for her own family. In iterated play, however, mutual cooperation may be achieved through mutual threat to discontinue cooperation if the other defects. Thus the threat of sanctions may produce cooperation. Situations of this sort may produce sanction-driven norms, that is, those that are only sustainable as a result of the presence of sanctions internal to the conformers. Hence, whereas utilitarians will not have internal sanction-driven norms, those with restricted scopes of concern may.

There is an interesting intermediate case between norms that result from universal scope motivation and norms that result from restricted scope motivation. These are cases in which conformers have restricted scope motivation, but each has the same scope of concern. In such cases, even though each has a nonuniversal scope of concern, if each shares the same scope, they will not conflict in their preferences. Examples arise in a number of different circumstances. The circumstances vary according to the relation between the group of conformers and the group for which concern is being shown, the beneficiaries.

For example, teachers of a grammar school might have certain norms, conformity to which is motivated by the desire to promote the interests of the school's underprivileged students. Here the beneficiary group is distinct from the group of conformers. In the following example, the group of conformers and the group of beneficiaries partially overlap. Suppose that the beneficiaries of nonsexist language norms are women, and the group of conformers to these norms consists of men and women. Then there is a partial overlap between the group of conformers and the group of beneficiaries, namely, the female conformers. Alternatively, the norm group may be a subset of the benefit group, or vice versa. An example of the first would be a group of politicians all devoted to the same constituency. Examples of the second might be norms among the president and her White House staff, which have the goal that she be cast in the most favorable light. All these examples share the feature that, because all the conformers aim at the same outcome (just as utilitarians do), there will be no conflict in their norm-conforming behavior and hence no need for sanctions. Consequently, in such circumstances, sanction-driven norms will not form.

To summarize this section, the difference between universal and restricted scope motivation appears to be the following. Agents who are motivated by a universal scope of concern will never conflict over outcomes when interacting with other agents with the same universalistic motivation. Agents with restricted scopes of concern may or may not conflict, depending on whether the others in the interaction situation have the same or different nonuniversal scopes of concern. For example, utilitarians will never conflict with other utilitarians in strategic situations, whereas nationalists may or may not conflict with other nationalists, depending on whether the other nationalists in the strategic situation are nationalists of the same or of a different nationality. Thus, for utilitarians, internal sanction-driven norms will not arise because conflict is required to create the need for artificial coordination, and as we see, utilitarians will have no conflicts of this nature. Those who hold nonuniversal scopes of concern will run into conflict with others who hold different nonuniversal scopes of concern. Having now considered how outcome-oriented moral actors will conform to norms in strategic situations, it is time to look at what they will do in nonstrategic situations.

C. Outcome-Oriented Epistemic Norms

In this subsection, the concern is whether conformity to norms is consistent with outcome-oriented moral acts in nonstrategic situations. Norms constituted by a preponderance of such acts are epistemic norms. In the last chapter, we saw that egoists will sometimes conform to norms as a short-cut to maximizing their welfare. In conforming, they bypass a great deal of the need for information and calculation that might otherwise be required to make the best choice. Thus, norms can be low-cost providers of information on how to act. In a particular instance, conformity might not prove to have been the best choice, but in the long run, conformity will often pay off, due to the overall savings in information and calculation costs.

The same possibility for economizing on the cost of information through conformity appears to hold for adherents to outcome-oriented moralities. They are in an analogous situation to egoists; they want to perform the right action, which for them is the one that will produce the best outcome, but they lack information to indicate what that action is. They may expend resources to determine what the best act is, but this cost must be subtracted from any additional gains the search garners. It may be the case that they are better off conforming to extant norms than acquiring more information and performing a calculation on each occasion.

The general idea at work here is as old as the notion of rules of thumb in utilitarian theory. One follows rules of thumb in order to avoid calculating before each decision. As we saw in Chapter One, however, the notions of conforming to rules and conforming to norms are not equivalent. As discussed there, it is often harmless to treat norms like rules, and indeed many norms are accompanied by what I call norm statements, which are essentially rules. For many norms, the behavior required to conform is fairly easily described in a few words. In these cases, talk of rule conformity versus norm conformity matters little, as long as one keeps in mind that there is a difference that may show up, especially when subtle and complex norms are at issue. But even when the case is complex and cannot be captured in a rule, one can still save on information by conforming to norms.

The following two examples show that the conformity necessary for epistemic norms is consistent with outcome-oriented morality. The first was discussed in Chapter Two. It is modified here to exemplify the outcome-oriented morality of those who have concern for the outcome of their children. The second example deals with the morality of concern for the environment. Thus the first is roughly a case of a restricted scope of concern, and the second is a case of universal scope of concern.

Recall the example of the neighbor who is a highly respected child psychologist who in general seems to exhibit good judgment and common sense in our occasional interactions. Under the circumstances, out of concern for my child's welfare, I might be sensible to conform to my neighbor's behavior regarding the treatment of children, especially if I am ill-informed and in search of guidance. There are no rules as such that I follow. Rather, I observe her behavior and conform to it. For example, if she talks to her young infant a lot in the backyard, I may take this as evidence that this is a preferred form of behavior. If she reprimands her toddler with a harsh tone of voice or an occasional mild swat, I may take this as acceptable behavior.

These are examples of conforming behavior. I do what my neighbor does because she does it. It is nonstrategic, as the outcome I wish to produce is not dependent on any choice of hers. And it is an outcome-oriented moral act because I act in order to promote a good outcome for another. As it stands, this is an example of a single act of morally motivated conformity in a non-strategic situation. It is not conforming to a norm but rather to the behavior of a single person. However, as discussed in more detail in Chapter Two, similar conforming acts might be performed by other parents in the neighborhood, also in response to the behavior of the respected child psychologist and also out of concern for their children's welfare. In such a manner, a norm may develop. One would no longer be conforming to a person but to a norm.

The second example deals with norms that may arise among those concerned for the environment. It takes a lot of information to determine the consequences of certain actions. Not all those with the desire to be environmentally conscientious should take it upon themselves to get the required information to make the most environmentally friendly choices. Better if the behavior of experts, and those in one's circle who are most expert, are imitated. Needless to say, it is also good if experts disseminate spoken and written directives, but the two processes are complimentary and mutually reinforcing. For example, paper-recycling plants are major producers of pollutants. How is one to know that, all things considered, it is better for the environment to recycle than not recycle paper? It is not economical for each person who is morally motivated to be environmentally conscientious to seek out the detailed information on such issues as the amount of pollutants produced by paper-recycling plants. Instead, such people are better off imitating the practices of the environmental cognoscente as to whether paper products are best recycled.

These last two examples are intended to show that conformity to norms to save on information costs is in the spirit of outcome-oriented morality. We see that when norms are present, moral actors may often desire to conform to them rather than determine the best outcomes on their own by seeking more information. It has now been shown that conformity to norms is in the spirit of outcome-oriented moral norms in both strategic and nonstrategic contexts.

Two qualifying points need to be added about conformity as a means to taking a moral short-cut. For simplicity, I have treated this phenomenon as if it would occur only in nonstrategic contexts, but in fact one could also take a moral short-cut and conform to the behavior of another in a strategic context. For example, one could imitate the behavior of a friend who was taking part in a coordination norm, and thus coordinate oneself with her. One may do so without being conscious that one is taking part in a coordination norm. Second, other cases we have been considering were pure in the sense that all the motivation was of a type. With epistemic norms, however, it would be hard, if not impossible, for all the participants to the norm to be taking a short-cut. Seemingly, someone would have to have better knowledge to justify conformity if the norm is to stay in existence.

II. Action-Oriented Norms

Not all action-oriented moral views sit equally comfortably with the notion of conformity necessary for the existence of moral norms. As discussed earlier, Kantian deontology seems ill-suited to an account of moral conformity. Perhaps with enough squeezing and repackaging, a fit might be brought about. But in the initial stages of inquiry, it is perhaps best to restrict discussion to the more straightforward results that may be achieved. Accordingly, I will set the very limited goal of demonstrating the initial plausibility of the thesis that norm conformity may be reconciled to action-oriented views. If this can be established satisfactorily, perhaps it will encourage in-depth examination of the particular action-oriented views at issue and their relationship to norms. Before this is attempted in detail for particular views, however, it is better to get an overall picture of the likely success of the general project. To examine action-oriented views at a sufficiently general level, I will take these views to be of two basic sorts: rule views and virtue views.[5] Not all nonconsequentialist views fit neatly into either side of this partition. But many do, and, for simplicity, these will be the concern here.

Rule views tell agents to act according to certain rules. These rules can be justified in a variety of ways: because they are derived by moral intuition; or because they pass the test of the Categorical Imperative; or because they are consented to or could be consented to; or because they issue from an authority of one sort or another, such as a deity, or an elected governing body. Virtue views, on the other hand, tell one to become virtuous. These views are less common and do not appear in the wide variety that rule views do. For the most part, I will not be concerned with the subtle differences that distinguish either rule or virtue views. Rather, the concern is to see whether normative views of these sorts, taken generally, are reconcilable with conformity.

In addition, I will be interested in looking at views that can only be called moral in the descriptive sense of the term. These views may not be capable of justification, but this does not gainsay the fact that they may command wide allegiance. The concern here is whether conformity makes sense on these views, not whether these views are ultimately defensible.[6]

A. Action-Oriented Epistemic Norms

This subsection examines epistemic norms and the following subsection examines strategic norms.

1. DIVINE COMMANDS. A divine command theory, as I shall understand it, is a theory that holds that the source of morality is divine revelation in the form of commands. Theories of this sort are action guiding in that the commands tell one how to act, not which outcomes to seek. Though it may be possible for individuals to receive their morality in this manner by means of direct revelation, I will consider divine command theory in its usual context, that is, as applying to religious groups. In the following discussion, we will see that whether divine commands lead to norms depends on a consideration external to the (first-order) divine commands themselves, namely, (second-order) religious doctrine regarding their proper application to concrete cases. This can be seen by contrasting the following cases.

Imagine a religious group whose morality is governed by a set of divine commands that are written down in the Holy Book. Because these commands are pithy statements and because the world is complex, adherents to the faith are often unsure how to apply particular commands to particular circumstances. Imagine further that the group is splintered into two sects, the Individualist Interpretation (I.I.) sect and the Authoritative Interpretation (A.I.) sect. Those in the I.I. sect are instructed to determine for themselves how to interpret all ambiguous situations by returning to the Holy Book and examining it for clues. For this group, it makes no difference in determining how to apply a command that others apply it in some particular manner, as individual interpretation is the path to the correct answer. Those in the A.I. sect, on the other hand, are told that interpreting the Holy Book is a complicated matter suited only to church authorities. Thus, they are instructed to follow the extant interpretations as captured in the officially sanctioned patterns of behavior monitored by the authorities.

Under these conditions, the A.I. sect will tend to form religious norms whereas the I.I. sect will not. In the A.I. sect, there will be patterns of behavior that are endorsed by the religious authorities. When an individual wants to know how to follow a command, she will be told to do as other members of the group do in like circumstances. For example, suppose one of the commands is, *Remember the Sabbath and keep it holy.* Suppose an individual in each sect is wondering whether it would violate this command to keep her convenience store open on Sundays. In the A.I. sect, she will know that this question may be answered by looking at what others in the sect are doing (assuming she has reason to believe the others are faithful). Suppose there are four other members of the sect who own convenience stores and all of them keep their stores open on Sundays. She might reasonably conclude then that were she to keep her store open, it would not violate a divine command.

The member of the I.I. sect, on the other hand, will read the Holy Book and follow her conscience. She may determine that it does not violate the command to keep her store open. Further, suppose that the other members of her sect who own convenience stores independently make the same determination. The difference between this scenario and the preceding one is that the pattern of behavior in the A.I. sect will count as a norm on my definition but not the pattern in the I.I. sect. Each is a pattern of rationally governed behavior instantiated in a group. It is a pattern of behavior, as all agents in like circumstances act in a like manner. The behavior is rationally governed because each of the constitutive acts is done from the motive of satisfying a divine command. The difference is that in the A.I. sect, the pattern is maintained as the result of agents conforming to the behavior of other agents in like circumstances, whereas in the I.I. sect, the pattern is not maintained as the result of conformity; it just so happens that each agent in similar circumstances acts in the same manner, thus resulting in a pattern. This would count as a bird's-eye-view pattern. From above, one can detect a pattern, but it does not result from agents on the ground acting in a concerted manner. The first pattern of behavior is maintained by conformity, and the second is not. Accordingly, the first is a religious moral norm and the second is not.

We see that a religious morality consisting of divine commands may lead to moral norms, but it need not. I have not actually shown how norms might emerge under such a regime, but rather how they might be maintained. In this example, the maintenance is due to a subsidiary doctrine regarding the proper interpretation and application of the commands. In simple cases, such as the foregoing, an emergence account might not be too difficult. Imagine, for example, that there was a time when no one in the A.I. sect owned a convenience store. The first member to acquire one could not then look to the extant patterns of the sect to determine the proper interpretation of the command regarding the Sabbath. Let us suppose that in such cases, the church-ordained procedure is that members appeal to the church council for an interpretation of the divine will. But after this first decision, later members with convenience stores will not have to appeal to the council as they will have the behavior of others to follow. In such a manner, a religious norm may emerge.

This scenario illustrates the manner in which conformity to norms may be a plausible feature of a divine command theory. Conformity of this sort is best placed in the category of epistemic conformity. One conforms to the behavior of others, not for strategic reasons, but because acting in a particular manner conveys information as to why one would be moral to act in a like manner.[7]

2. FREE-FLOATING MORAL RULES. The divine commands just examined have their source or authority in a deity. Next, consider rules at the opposite end of the extreme, those with no obvious source or authority. I will call these free-floating rules. There are rules current in subcultures or across the culture that are not connected in any direct and systematic manner with other rules.[8] Examples are the following: *Be patriotic*, *Be true to your school*, or the prescriptions hidden in the seemingly unprescriptive phrases, *A friend in need is a friend indeed*, and *Charity begins at home*. These are prescriptions that one might hear in certain situations offered as advice for action. Our normative world abounds with such free-floating rules or prescriptions. Though such rules might be made to fit into more theoretically coherent outlooks, it seems likely that, for the mass of people, these rules function autonomously. We are in general a fairly unsystematic jumble of normative pushes and pulls. This jumble has been reified and sometimes legitimated with the phrase *common-sense morality*. But this is misleading. Talk of a morality of common sense makes it sound as if there is a unified view, when in fact there does not seem to be one. Philosophers downplay the extent to which people can see particular rules as worthy of their moral allegiance without understanding how they fit into a larger, unified view.

Earlier we saw that conformity is only contingently a part of rule-following systems such as found in divine command theory. The contingent factor that was present in addition to the (first-order) rules themselves was a (second-order) rule regarding the proper application of the rules to particular instances. A similar point appears to hold in the case of free-floating rules. In principle, it could be that every individual applies the rule to particular cases on her own. Alternatively, however, the behavior of others may play a significant role in a particular agent's determination of the correct application of a rule. Unlike divine commands, conformity to free-floating rules is not ordained. What then might lead a rule follower to conform?

Consider an obvious answer. Conformity is often the best means by which to apply rules. For it does seem like a natural and epistemically reasonable procedure to follow. One might initially suppose that because the actual content of a rule is often minimal, one will necessarily need additional guidance for its application. So why not draw guidance from conformity? But, on the other hand, if the rule does not precisely specify behavior, it may just mean that there is some latitude inherent in the application of the rule. One may look to others to see what they are doing, but the rule is also minimal for them, so there is not really any reason to suppose that they apply it better.

What in fact often seems to happen is that if a standard interpretation comes about (for whatever reason), it then takes on a certain epistemological authority. There seems to be a background principle at work that one should not challenge a status quo interpretation without a reason. However, this does not imply that conformity to the pattern as such is demanded. For one can always argue against one's community that, contrary to appearances, what one is doing really does follow the rule. For example, the rule, *Be patriotic,* may be prevalent in a community, and it may be generally taken to imply, *Buy American.* There might, for example, be a norm against buying foreign automobiles. One might argue against one's community on economic grounds that buying foreign automobiles is really not unpatriotic. The point is that conformity to the rule, not the behavior as such is prescribed. Otherwise it would never be possible to go against the norm for behavior and claim that the rule really should allow it.[9]

The following appears to be at work in conformity to free-floating rules. When there is consensus in a community about the application of a rule, people will be pressured to interpret the rule in the standard manner. A reasonable moral justification for this pressure can be presented. In the absence of an argument to the contrary as to why her interpretation is to be preferred, a person has no reason to suppose that the prevalent interpretation is not acceptable, and the community will have a general reason to suppose that often self-interest is at least a partial motivation for the desire to deviate. For example, the rule, *Be true to your school,* may have different interpretations at different schools. At school A the rule might be commonly interpreted to prohibit athletes from dating athletes from other schools, while at school B the rule might be interpreted as not prohibiting this. At school A, if it is really the rule, *Be true to your school,* that is what people believe in, and not just certain behavior, as such, then the students should be open to reasoned arguments as to why a particular case of dating an athlete from another school is not a case of being untrue to one's school. But in the absence of such an argument, the linguistic community at the school may contend that the person has no reason to think her interpretation of the rule's application is better than the status quo interpretation. The person is not making a moral error but an epistemological error of contravening an accepted application of a concept without any ground to do so. They may say to her, "This is the accepted meaning of the rule, what grounds do you have for offering a differing interpretation?"

What are the implications of this discussion for the question of conformity? Recall that we are trying to determine whether the conformity required for epistemic norms is in the spirit of free-floating rules. It appears that there may exist an underlying epistemological dictate to conform to the common interpretation of rules as instantiated in behavior unless one can give a defensible reason for relying on one's own interpretation instead. I am not necessarily endorsing this epistemological principle about rule interpretation, rather I am suggesting that this is one plausible way of understanding how people actually behave. On such a view, conformity has nothing to do with free-floating rules as such. Rather, conforming to the status quo interpretations of such rules is dictated by an underlying epistemic principle that others accept and enforce. But enforcement is not necessary. For only the self-interested heed rules for their own benefit. One might genuinely accept the epistemological principle along with one's fellows. In fact, if sanctions are the reason one conforms, then this seems like a case in which conformity may not be in the spirit of the theory. If one does not accept the epistemic principle in good conscience, one has no reason to conform. Thus, conforming to avoid sanctions is conforming for the wrong reason. One should act out of allegiance to the free-floating rule based on the status quo interpretation, not out of the motivation to avoid sanctioning.

Compare this situation to that of divine commands. There is nothing about the commands themselves that necessitates conforming to the interpretations of others. Rather, what matters are the background interpretative principles of the particular sects. In the I.I. sect individualistic interpretation is encouraged, while it is prohibited in the A.I. sect. Both sects share the feature that, due to the existence of an accepted church hierarchy, the laity accept as gospel whatever underlying interpretive rules they receive. Thus, the I.I. sect interprets particular rules on their own because this is the rule, and the A.I. sect conforms to inscrutable interpretations because this is the rule.

In the case of free-floating rules, there are no experts to supply second-order rules for interpreting the rules. There are local authorities but nothing as well structured as a church hierarchy. For example, the head of the local Veterans of Foreign Wars hall may be taken as a local authority on patriotism, or the head of the pep squad may be taken as an authority on school loyalty, but neither of them appear to carry the same weight as the church high command. It seems possible, in principle, that either of the second-order interpretative rules could be in force in a community, even in the absence of an established hierarchy.

A background epistemic principle could exist that dictates compliance to the local authority's interpretations, or a background epistemic principle could dictate individualistic interpretation. Neither of these situations seems to hold, however. Rather, there appears to be a background epistemic principle that dictates conformity unless one can provide reasons for overriding the status quo interpretation. It is interesting to note that there could exist a third religious sect in which this epistemic principle is accepted.

It should be clear why conformity of the sort discussed in the last paragraphs should count as nonstrategic. Others performing an action does not increase one's payoffs for doing so. Rather one conforms because the behavior of others is good evidence as to the best application of the rule. Thus, this conformity is aptly characterized as epistemic.

In summary, we have seen that rule followers may become epistemic norm conformers for two reasons. Rule followers may look to norms for information about the authoritative application of rules, or they may use the norms to glean information about the consensus application of the rules. What the two cases have in common is that the extant norms carry information relevant to the best application of the rules. Although I will not consider the matter here, it would seem on the face of it that analogous claims may hold for other moral views that emphasize rules. For all rule-following accounts face the problem of accounting for the application of the rules.[10]

3. VIRTUOUS CONFORMITY TO EPISTEMIC NORMS. Next to be examined are instances of virtuous conformity to norms for epistemic reasons. Consider the following. Though some find the idea paradoxical, a standard claim of virtue theory is that you may learn what virtue is by observing the behavior of the virtuous.[11] What is the implication for practical reason of this epistemic claim? One plausible implication is that, if you want to be virtuous, act as the virtuous act. Here, in this single step, is the basic building block out of which an account of virtuous epistemic norms can be constructed. For what we seem to have is a moral reason why a virtuous person would be motivated to conform to the behavior of an accomplished person of virtue. It does not take much imagination to see how imitation of this sort might lead to a large-scale virtuous norm. For with each new imitator, the group grows in size and temporal continuity.

The following objection might be raised to the idea that a virtuous norm may grow through imitation. Such imitative behavior should not count as truly virtuous behavior because the imitator or conformer does not really act from an understanding of the requirements of virtue but rather from rote imitation. This objection, however, can be answered. Another widely held view in virtue theory is that, through practicing virtue, one may become virtuous. By adopting the behavior to the best extent possible, you may eventually come to see why the behavior is intrinsically appropriate. For example, if you were brought up in a family of liars but now believe that being honest would be better, if you make yourself refrain from lying, you may come to see over time why honesty is a virtue and thus come naturally to desire it. By imitation of virtuous behavior, you will come to understand what virtuousness is all about; consequently, your continued conformity will be informed, that is, motivated epistemically and not just causally by the requirements of virtue.

A second objection, however, arises at this stage. Once you become a person of accomplished virtue, conformity is no longer necessary. This objection seems legitimate, but it must also be taken into account that because we lack omniscience, even after one has attained a virtuous state, it will be advisable to look to what others are doing as a way of assuring oneself of one's judgment regarding particular modes of behavior. For example, honesty is a virtue, but one can be too honest, hurting others' feelings by providing too much information. Virtue might be better served by imitating the behavior of those with a more subtle understanding of how to handle such delicate situations. Thus, conformity still has a role to play.

It might be virtuous, then, to imitate the behavior of the virtuous as a means to becoming virtuous. The fact that people, who to all appearances are virtuous, act in a certain manner carries information about behavior of this sort, making conformity to their actions morally plausible. This is analogous to the rule follower who takes the behavior of others as evidence for the proper application of rules. Both cases, in turn, are analogous to the egoist or the consequentialist who conforms to norms to save on calculation costs. In all these cases, the fact that certain others are performing a type of action serves as evidence that it would also be right to perform this action oneself.

B. Action-Oriented Conformity in Strategic Circumstances

The examples considered in the previous section were instances of conformity by action-oriented moral theorists for epistemic reasons in nonstrategic contexts. The question remains: Are strategic norms possible in rule-following theory and virtue theory? Prima facie, one might think the answer would be no. When one reasons strategically, one takes into consideration the reasoning of others to determine how to act. Based on how one thinks they will act, one does so because outcomes that are jointly determined are at stake. Thus, these outcomes seem to drive the whole process. In contrast, action-oriented theorists focus on the quality of actions not the consequences that flow from those actions, and so their behavior would seem by definition to be nonstrategic. Despite this appearance, however, there is nothing in the notion of strategic action per se that is outcome oriented. It is just that up until now, only outcome-oriented theorists have worried about strategic action.

Strategic action requires that the right action depend on the behavior of others. There appears to be no reason in principle why action-oriented views cannot accept this condition. Some appear to reject it. For example, Kant is often interpreted as thinking that one should follow actions that accord with the moral law regardless of whether others are. But there is no reason to suppose that all action-oriented views need make this claim. Those that do not may lead to what I will call strategic coordination.

1. STRATEGIC COORDINATION. One can often best see how the correctness of one's actions depends on what others in the group are doing by looking at what happens when someone from another group migrates into the first group. For example, where I grew up, people who take driver's training are taught to leave a distance of one car length between vehicles for each ten miles per hour of speed being traveled. One is taught that this is the safe thing to do. In all naturalness, this would be called a rule of safe driving, and on most moral theories, it would count as a moral rule, as safe driving is surely a moral concern. Alternatively, it could be said that being a safe driver is a sort of virtuous behavior. In either case, the behavior consistent with these types of theories need not be outcome oriented. One might, for example, think it required to sometimes drive safely even when it would maximize utility not to.

With the example of keeping a proper distance between moving cars, notice what happens when you try to leave the requisite amount of car lengths in a metropolitan area in which such behavior is not the norm. It will be impossible to act in this manner because inevitably a car will cut in front of your vehicle to fill in the open space ahead. If you slow down in order to reopen the space, it will again be filled. The fact that others are not conforming to the norm will make it impossible for you to do so. Still worse, the very attempt will cause you to be a hazard on the road because slowing down to create a space will set in place a chain reaction such that those behind must either slow down or change lanes. In this example, the proper distance to keep between your car and the car ahead is the amount of space that is the local norm. More space and people will try to fill it; less space and you risk an accident. Thus, the behavior of the virtuous or rule-abiding person is dictated by whatever behavior is the norm.[12] Just to be clear that there is not something special about norms of the road, notice that other norms of the road do not have this strategic structure. For example, it is virtuous to dim your lights when passing a car regardless of whether others are doing the same.

This example is best seen as a virtue or rule that has a consequentialist component. What really drives the moral principle is a concern for good outcomes, that is, safety on the road as a means to preventing accidents. This is of course perfectly acceptable to deontological theories, which clearly may have consequentialist components. It is just that deontological theories cannot be purely consequentialist. Once we realize that though this virtue or rule arises from within an action-oriented perspective, it nonetheless has a strongly consequentialist component, we should not be surprised that the right action might be strategically determined.

Yet more interesting is the issue of whether there may be strategic action-oriented behavior in cases that are nonconsequentialist. The answer is yes. For example, what counts as friendliness will depend on what others are doing. In many small towns, it is the norm for people who do not know one another to have eye contact or strike up conversations when encountering one another. For instance, people from small towns may feel uncomfortable with strangers in elevators or in waiting rooms unless they strike up a conversation or at least have eye contact. Not to be open to conversation or eye contact is to be unfriendly, whereas, this is not true, or less so, generally speaking, in cities.

Consider a second example. In small towns, there has apparently long existed a gender-differentiated norm that dictates that it is more acceptable for women to interact with children who are not known to them than for men to do so. I have been told that in the past women were to some extent normatively encouraged to engage children in conversation and actively look out for their welfare in small ways. Now, however, perhaps in substantial part due to the media coverage of child abductions, the norm has changed such that it is no longer the norm to engage children in this manner.

Note that what the rule-following or virtuous person should do depends to some extent on the norm in the group. Why would it no longer be friendly to talk to strange children? The reason seems roughly to be that children are taught to resist such interaction. If there is a real or perceived danger of molesters, kidnappers, and the like, then parents may be reasonable in not wanting their children to be in the position of judging who it is safe to talk to and who it is not. Better not to talk to strangers. But it is not that one will never engage children in such conversation. Rather one will tend to do so in the situations in which others are doing so. The current situation seems to permit such discourse when parents are present, as for example in a supermarket line. Perhaps in small and isolated towns, the old, more friendly norm still holds. When there, if you do not follow it, others will think you unfriendly. They will be correct, though you are not to blame. In this example, it may be that no one is.

Conversely, small town people may be perceived as overly friendly when they come to the city. A person brought up to think that engaging strangers in small talk is part of the virtue of friendliness will soon come to see that urban denizens do not feel the same way. One will not be experienced as friendly but rather as intrusive and perhaps even threatening. Still, one will be within one's normative wherewithal in sometimes attempting to engage strangers in conversation. Roughly, one will tend to have those conversations permitted by the norm. For example, it has been my experience that in New York it is normatively permissible, though still not the prevailing practice, to engage strangers who live in one's building in conversation.

In these examples, which contrast norms from towns to cities, the moral quality of the act varies depending on what others are doing. Your act will be a friendly act only to the extent that it coincides with the like acts of others. The examples are not consequentialist in nature as was the case in the example of the proper distance to maintain on freeways. One need not be friendly to promote some further end. Friendliness may be thought to be morally desirable on its own terms. Accordingly, these are examples of action-oriented behavior for which the rightness is strategically determined and yet the promotion of good outcomes is not a driving motivation.

Consider the following examples of norms that vary from *traditional* to *progressive* subcultures. The practices of men opening doors for women, and both men and women referring to women as *ladies* are endorsed in traditional culture but rejected by progressive culture. Whether one goes from the progressive to the traditional culture or from the traditional to the progressive culture, if one is *well-mannered* (and manners are fairly seen as moral rules or character dispositions), one's reflections on what is the proper action will to some extent be affected by a consideration of what is considered to be the proper action in the context in which one is presently situated. To go against the norm may offend others or inadvertently cause doors to be slammed in one's face. Regardless of what one ends up doing, in general there will be a normative pull in the direction of the instantiated norm. In these examples, politeness is strategically determined. What counts as the polite act will depend on what others are doing.

The previous examples apply either to virtue theory or rule views. The following example is geared more specifically toward normative views that emphasize the importance of autonomy. Consider the norm regarding the practice of letting friends drive under the influence of alcohol. There is an effort currently in our culture to change this norm, as witnessed by the ad campaign with the slogan, *Friends don't let friends drive drunk*. Unfortunately, the very need for the slogan is evidence of the fact that it is more prescriptive than descriptive.

Suppose you are a person who believes in respecting the autonomy of others and a friend is about to leave your house under the influence of alcohol. Roughly the following competing considerations enter into your reasoning. On the one hand, there is the consideration of safety, both that of your friend and of other motorists. This consideration weighs strongly in favor of intervention. On the other hand, there is the consideration of respect for the friend's autonomy and good judgment. There is a strong norm in this culture against paternalism. To offer unwanted advice is in a sense to tell the friend that you have better judgment than she. If your friend is strongly intoxicated, the advice might perhaps be offered without imparting this implication. But the case I am discussing is one of mild inebriation; it would exaggerate the case to claim that the friend's rational faculties are impaired to such an extent that you would not be overriding her autonomy in attempting to intervene in any strong way. Thus, you are pulled in two directions.

Schematically, we can think of autonomy at one end of a continuum and concern at the other end. The level of inebriation will determine where on the continuum the person is in your mind. If she is very inebriated, she will be closer to the concern end of the continuum, and if she is hardly inebriated, she will be closer to the autonomy end. Let us assume that in a particular culture there is a level of inebriation (a point on the continuum) after which the norm would dictate concerned intervention. This level will vary from culture to culture and within subcultures. For example, one might reasonably guess that the level at which one could expect intervention among a group of moral theorists is much lower than among a group of members of the National Rifle Association or other groups known for their strong stand on individualism. The point I wish to make is that the norm extant in the culture will to some extent determine (in the view of most people) whether one should intervene. The point of the ad campaign is to move the general level such that it will take less amount of concern to tip the scale against autonomy toward intervention.[13]

In the preceding examples, I have sought to show that, in certain types of situations, the behavior of others will exert a certain gravity, causing one's own action to be pulled in the direction of theirs, that is, to conform to theirs. The examples considered involved friendliness, politeness, and autonomy. In each case, the right action was seen to be strategically affected by the behavior of others. The following normative view takes this rationale for conformity to an extreme.

2. TRADITIONALISM. Traditionalism, as it will here be understood, is the view that one should do what others have done in similar circumstances in the past. Such acts are clear-cut cases of acts that are proper not because of their instrumental role but because of the intrinsic features of the act. Given that others have acted in some specific manner in the past, the proper act must share the specific features of the earlier acts. Thus, the character of the act itself matters in determining its correctness. Patterns of behavior made up of traditionalist acts may not seem fitting subjects for a discussion on moral norms as there seems nothing especially moral about them. But recall that we are working with a broad definition of the moral, one that includes everyday notions of morality, even if they do not necessarily withstand the scrutiny of moral theorists.

The following characterization of tradition by W. R. Sorley lends weight to the claim that the everyday version of traditionalism has some currency.

There is a set of customs . . . and a set of beliefs intermingled with the customs; and to these he feels himself bound, and is bound, to conform. All this may be called his social heritage; it has been handed down to him from his elders; its source, that is to say, is tradition, and it comes to him with authority.[14]

This passage characterizes the basic elements of tradition as a set of customs and beliefs handed down by authority. There is no explicit mention of the justification for the customs and beliefs, although "authority" is ambiguous in this respect.

On any plausible view, the normative pull of tradition is morally more complex than requiring blind conformity to the past. Yet the everyday version of the traditionalist prescription may capture one piece of the confused mosaic of ought-claims that make up the everyday normative world we inhabit. The phrase, *You will do it that way because that's the way its always been done,* is, after all, sometimes offered as a reason for action. Thus, at a basic level, tradition, or the normative view I call traditionalism, may be said to exert a normative force to do acts of type X in circumstances Y simply because one's forebears did acts of type X in circumstances Y.

The question arises, what do acts dictated by tradition have to do with the study of conformity? The answer is that it is plausible to suppose that they may lead to norms. Notice that, in the case of the traditionalist prescription, the structure of the prescription itself seems to necessitate that acting in accordance with the prescription will result in norms. For the prescription tells one to do what has been done in the past in similar circumstances. But this is simply a prescription for conformity. The traditionalist prescription is then by its very nature norm producing, or at any rate norm maintaining. In some of the previous examples, conformity was justified as an informational short-cut, but with tradition, conformity is not a shortcut but a destination; hence, it is closer to deontological and virtue-theoretic approaches than to teleological approaches.

3. SANCTION-DRIVEN CONFORMITY. Sanction-driven moral norms may also exist among action-oriented theorists. Initially, it is puzzling how sanctions could cause action-oriented moral theorists to alter their behavior in a manner necessary for the existence of sanction-driven moral norms. Sanction-driven norms are such that agents would not conform were it not for the sanctions. Sanctions affect the cost of actions. Agents who previously did not want to conform may now want to because nonconformity has been made more expensive. This makes it sound as if these agents perform cost–benefit calculations before acting, which surely does not sound in the spirit of action-oriented moral views. In spite of this initial appearance, however, conformity to sanction-driven norms is in the spirit of action-oriented moral views.

In the previous section, we saw that action-oriented views sometimes contain consequentialist components. These mixed views were the most straightforward cases in which strategic factors come into play. Mixed theories that contain consequentialist components, and particularly examples in which only a consequentialist rule with a restricted scope is engaged, will be the best place to start in looking for cases where sanctions may lead to norms for action-oriented moral actors.

For example, it may be a principle of a group that one should show favor toward other members of the group relative to nonmembers. Among the members of a religious sect, for instance, it may be decreed that other members of the sect, even if strangers, should be shown favor over nonmembers. If members of this sect are hegemonic in a political community, this principle might come to be interpreted as meaning that members of this sect should be favored in hiring in the public sector. This is an example of a prescribed form of behavior that is largely consequentialist, although it may be part of a nonconsequentialist moral outlook, as for example, a divine command view. It is consequentialist because there is nothing intrinsically special about the act of showing favoritism in hiring. Rather, what matters is that showing favoritism is a means to promoting the interests of the members of one's sect.

Because this behavior is consequentialist in inspiration, it appears especially susceptible to alteration by the application of sanctions. For example, suppose the group has hegemony over one of the states of a federation, but not over the federation as a whole. Suppose further that a federal court or national legislature has declared that favoritism in hiring is illegal and that those who practice it are subject to sanctions. This may change the behavior in the state with the hegemonic group into one of impartiality in public sector hiring. The resulting regularity of behavior would appear to be a sanction-driven norm because the change in behavior is motivated by a desire to avoid sanctions. Contrary to appearances, however, this does not count as a sanction-driven norm because the conformity is not motivated by sanctions. Each bureaucrat stops the favoritism regardless of what others are doing. The behavior happens to fit into a regularity, but each act is not at all caused by other acts of a similar type.

A simple example that fits this description follows. Imagine a number of religious groups that all hold to the rule, *Help members of your own church.* This rule is consequentialist in its inspiration and its effect even though it is part of a deontological system. It has a restricted scope in that the maximization principle applies to only a subset of the population. These groups might find it in their interest to cooperate on a new rule that required impartial treatment of all members of the community. In other words, one could not help a member of one's own congregation if a member of another congregation could be helped to a greater extent. This rule might be agreed upon by all the groups as a means to satisfy the original rule, as it might be that by all taking part in the new rule, each is actually more effective at aiding the members of her own congregation. In addition, it might take a sanctioning mechanism to make the new rule effective. This example would count as sanction-driven conformity. The members of the various groups conform to the norm to avoid sanctions. Their behavior is conforming behavior in that part of the explanation for their behavior is the behavior of others. For if others were not acting in a like manner, the sanctioning scheme would not be in place.

The next question is whether sanctions might cause conformity for actions that are not importantly consequentialist. An often cited type of behavior that is squarely deontologically justified is that of not taking the life of an innocent person. For certain deontologically oriented moral actors, it may always be wrong to take the life of an innocent person, no matter what the consequences. For other deontologists, however, there may be situations in which the potentially negative consequences may be so significant that the stricture against killing is trumped. If one is a nonabsolutist of this sort, it may be possible to influence one's behavior by the imposition of sanctions.

For example, it is sometimes said that early Christians had an absolute prohibition against killing, even in war.[15] Suppose the Romans had threatened the Christians saying that unless the Christians fought alongside the Romans, innocent Christians would be killed. Suppose the Romans calculated how many of the enemy would be killed on average by each Christian serving in the army and declared that for each of these potential deaths, the Romans would kill twenty innocent Christians as a sanction against the Christian unwillingness to serve.

Under such conditions, it may become a norm among the Christians to serve in the Roman army. This will count as a sanction-driven norm, depending on how the situation is described. If each Christian decides on his own to serve as a result of the threatened sanctions to the group, the requisite conformity is not present. But serving in the army under these conditions may become a normatively governed practice, maintained by conformity and encouraged by official teachings and doctrine.

Essentially, this same distinction was discussed earlier with the distinction between the Individual Interpretation sect and the Accepted Interpretation sect. In the case of the A.I. sect, conformity is properly said to be present because the individual applications of rules take place after consulting a second-order interpretative rule. Suppose the Christian sect in the current example has such a second-order interpretative rule. Individuals do not interpret the rule, *Do not kill,* on their own but rather conform to the dictates of the church hierarchy as to how this rule shall apply. The circumstance in question is one in which by refusing to kill one innocent person, twenty innocent persons will be killed. Suppose that, in reaction to the sanction, the church decides that serving in the Roman army is the morally appropriate action.

In the actual case, the rule against killing was reinterpreted so as to no longer include killing in *just wars.* Suppose instead that the church determined that such killing was still proscribed by the rule, but allowable under the circumstances; the wrong being outweighted by the consequentialist considerations. Hereafter, the laity conform to the church-sanctioned norm that Christians are to serve in the Roman army. In such a case, a sanction-driven norm is present, although it is sanction driven only at a second remove. The sanctions cause the individuals to conform to a norm to which they otherwise would not, but the causal path is that the Roman application of sanctions causes the Christians to promote conformity and sanction nonconformity to the laity.

Finally, the question arises, can there be cases of sanction-driven norms among moral absolutists who are not at all susceptible to countervailing considerations of consequences? It appears that, even in these cases, something like sanction-driven norms may be possible. We must expand the notion of a sanction-driven norm, however: there is a more general feature of such situations than is captured by a consideration of sanctions per se. It may be the case that one can alter the environment in which the moral behavior arises so as to alter the moral quality of the action. It turns out that sanctions are but one means of altering the moral quality of an action.

Consider the action-oriented theorist who believes in respect for the law. A situation might arise in which behavior that accords with a norm that this type of moral actor thinks is morally required behavior may become illegal due to a change in the law. For example, the Fugitive Slave Law may have made the virtuous behavior of aiding fugitive slaves morally out of bounds for some. Suppose a group of individuals existed who had previously had a group norm to aid fugitive slaves, but who changed norms as a result of the change in the law. Suppose that they were not afraid of being sanctioned by the law, but rather, they believed in respect for the law as a trump against most other considerations, even ones as weighty as aiding fugitive slaves.

In such a case, a norm against aiding fugitive slaves might be established among those who previously had supported such behavior. It would not be established as a result of sanctions, but rather as a result of a more general phenomenon. The more general feature is that the environment is changed in some manner that has the effect of altering the moral worth of the act types that made up the previous norm. Norms brought about in such a manner might be called extrinsically imposed norms, in contrast to intrinsically generated norms, for which conformity comes about as a result of features intrinsic to the situation. With intrinsic norms, no one needs to attempt to alter the situation in some manner to bring about conformity because the behavior occurs naturally given the other features of the situation already present.

Extrinsic norms are like sanction-driven norms in that an external influence brings about conformity that would otherwise not be forthcoming. Sanctions bring about conformity by affecting the costs and benefits of performing certain actions. But this is only one of a variety of means of affecting the surrounding conditions of an act to affect the moral quality of the act. In the example of making aid to fugitive slaves illegal, the moral quality of the act is not affected by means of altering the payoff structure. Rather, the act of aiding slaves itself is no longer a morally desirable action, all things considered, in a regime in which such actions are illegal.

In this example, the requisite conformity condition is met only if we assume that the law is passed only because the authorities expect a high level of compliance. It cannot be maintained otherwise. Thus, one's conformity is indirectly the result of the conformity of others, in the sense that the law would not continue to exist if not for their conformity. Thus, this is an example of an unwelcome, externally driven norm.

Conclusion

For the study of norms, morality was seen to be usefully partitioned into outcome-oriented and action-oriented views. First, universal and nonuniversal outcome-oriented views were considered. Comparable to the case of self-interested rationality in Chapter Two, there are three types of circumstance in which conformity to norms may be moral from an outcome-oriented moral point of view. The results are outcome-oriented coordination norms, epistemic norms, and sanction-driven norms. Next, the trickier issue of whether conformity could be made sense of on action-oriented moral views was considered. The details of particular views were not considered. Instead, the two overarching types of nonconsequentialist views, rule views and virtue views, were examined. Prima facie, there were good reasons for being particularly suspicious as to whether these outlooks could be made compatible with conformity to norms. Despite initial appearances conformity was seen to be in the spirit of these views for a variety of reasons. What is even more interesting is that conformity will be justified in the same three types of circumstances as it was for the egoist and the consequentialist, that is, action-oriented moral actors will participate in coordination norms, epistemic norms, and sanction-driven norms. Thus, we see that there is a compatibility, indeed a unity, between the rational choice and moral-theoretic approaches and within different moral-theoretic approaches.

This evaluation completes the present attempt to develop a philosophical conception of norms. The first chapter rejected the received view of norms and replaced it with a reformed view on which norms are patterns of normatively governed behavior that are instantiated in groups and maintained by conformity. Chapter Two demonstrated that the pattern conception did not fall prey to the important criticism that conformity to norms violates the canon of methodological individualism. A tripartite typology of norms resulted from this examination. Chapter Three began the moral analysis of norms. Discussion was limited to the utilitarian approach as it is consistent with the Hobbesian assumption of narrow self-interest as the driving factor in human motivation. We saw that utilitarians, if they are to best serve their critical normative goals, should replace a rule conception of norms with a pattern conception. Chapter Four then sought to reconcile the rational choice and moral-theoretic approaches. We saw that by the light of ordinary morality, participation in certain rationally governed practices may create sui generis emergent moral relationships. The existence of these relationships was shown to be consistent with an account that starts from a rational actor assumption. The blended approach was called predominant egoism. Predominant egoism is not overly reductive in the way that the narrow rational actor model is, but it is not a closet aspirational account either. Rather, it represents the most realistic account of human motivation. I argued that this account, in fact though not in name, is acceptable to a wide variety of theorists who have less disagreement with one another than is ordinarily supposed.

This chapter completes the examination of the pattern conception of social norms. In law, the past matters; what judges have done in the past matters to what judges should do in the present in deciding cases. But what judges have done in the past is not a straightforward matter that can be simply read off from the black-letter case law. Rather, we in the present must interpret past legal decisions. And part of doing this inevitably involves considering the normative elements that were incorporated in the legal outcomes. This procedure involves providing what I will refer to as a normative interpretation of particular legal outcomes. Parts Two and Three of the book will perform normative interpretations of the role of norms and customs in tort law generally, and in specific detail, with regard to privacy in cyberspace.

PART TWO

NEGLIGENT NORMS

Law embodies and enforces fundamental social norms, and it would be surprising to find that those norms were inconsistent with the society's ethical system.[†]

Richard Posner

[†] RICHARD POSNER, *Economic Analysis of Law* 23 (4th ed., 1992). This epigram expresses a deep truth about the relationship between social norms and the law. As will become clear by the end of Part Two, Judge Posner forgets this truth when he develops his own theory of norms and torts.

6

The Traditional Rule of Custom

In country life a multitude of acts are habitually committed that are technically trespasses. Persons walk, catch fish, pick berries, and gather nuts in alieno solo without strict right. Good-natured owners tolerate these practices until they become annoying or injurious, and then put a stop to them. Little practical inconvenience results from the state of things, which the courts may well leave to regulate itself.[1]

Albright v. Cortland

Introduction

Part One developed the pattern conception of social norms. Part Two will apply this framework in the context of tort law. This application will test the value of the pattern conception; the more it illuminates tort law, the more valuable it is proven to be. As discussed in the book's Introduction, tort law is at the core of a liberal theory of social order. Liberalism begins with a brute conception of the intrinsic moral worth of the individual. From this starting point, the theory of human rights and personal autonomy follow. Free people may do as they please, so long as others are not injured in the process.[2] When others are injured, however, tort law may be implicated. As Part One indicated, free people characteristically choose to conform to social norms. When they do, and when others are injured in the process, meaningful solutions must take place at the intersection of norms and torts.

The present chapter begins the examination of the role of social norms in tort law. The focus in this chapter is on the historical development of the concept of legally valid custom, or what is sometimes referred to as the *rule of custom*. The first section will begin at the beginning with a brief discussion of the jurisprudence of custom. As will become clear, custom in the law is closely related to the concept of a social norm.[3] Essentially, a custom is a social practice that is obligatory. Only these two features – practice and obligation – are found in all cases that invoke custom. Section II will look more closely at the concept of legally valid custom, understood as obligatory social practices. Finally, Section III will discuss the most significant historical example involving the rule of custom – trespass norms and customary easements in land. The emergence of easements will be seen to put the positive efficiency thesis to the test. I will argue that customary easements are best explained as due in important part to a normative impulse akin to induced detrimental reliance rather than due simply to an impulse toward welfare maximization.

The following five chapters will then examine the important and misunderstood role that customs play in modern negligence law. Chapters Seven through Nine will consider custom's potential to serve as a mechanism for welfare maximization. I will seek to determine which of the possible versions of the rule of custom judges should choose when attempting to produce the most efficient outcomes. Chapters Ten and Eleven will then engage in a normative interpretation of the role of informal social norms with regard to the determination of liability. I will argue that heterogeneous norms of ordinary jurors are in part constitutive of the de facto liability standard is negligence. This finding gives additional reason to doubt the adequacy of the traditional economic interpretation of tort.

I. The Jurisprudence of Custom

Historically, there have been two importantly different conceptions of custom. On the older conception, customs of a certain sort were law themselves, so-called customary law. Custom was the unwritten law, the so-called lexis non scriptus, found in the practices of communities. Coke considered custom as one of the points of the triad of English law, along with statutes and the common law.[4] On the dominant modern conception, customs are not law in themselves but rather potential sources of law. It is only when courts give judicial recognition to these community practices that they become so-called valid custom.[5]

This latter conception can be fairly understood as corresponding to a form of positivist approach. The former conception can be understood as a form of natural law approach. According to a standard positivist approach, a rule, no matter how laudable, is not law unless it arises through an accepted process of law making.[6] It appears to be entailed by this conception that customs, no matter how important to a group or how deeply felt their obligatory force, are not law unless they have been made into law by an accepted law-creating process, such as when a court recognizes a custom as valid.[7] On a positivist approach, then, there is no customary law per se, but rather informal customs and legally validated customs. On a natural law approach, however, law and custom cannot be so clearly distinguished, as law may be defined so as to include all rules and practices of a group for which conformity is expected or required as one's obligation.[8]

The relationship between custom and law has changed over time in a manner not accounted for by either positivism or natural law theory. Early on, when there was little enacted law, custom was clearly accepted as a type of law.[9] Though the idea of custom as law made sense in early English history, it no longer describes the real judicial attitude toward customs, which are now typically treated as "persuasive sources of law," but not law itself.[10]

Carleton Allen contends that valid custom is law.[11] His main argument is that when judges recognize a custom, it does not henceforth become law but is recognized to have had legal force, that is, the judicial act does not give custom legal force, it had it all along.[12] Support for this view is found in the well-known Tanistry Case.[13] The opinion states: "A custom, in the intendment of law, is such a usage as hath obtained the force of a law, and is in truth a binding law to such particular places, persons and things which it concerns. . . . [I]t is ius non scriptum."[14] To the contrary, Brown's explanation of this phenomenon is that customs, like many other legal rules, have retroactive force. The idea that customs recognized by judges were law all along is, according to Brown, but a legal fiction whereby judges mask the fact that they are making law.[15]

It is not obvious what precisely is at issue in this debate as to the true relation between law and custom. On one view, this is a jurisprudential debate for which progress might be made by first arriving at a true understanding of law and then determining law's relation to custom. On another view, however, the issue is ultimately one of the history and usage of the concepts law and custom. My own view is that there is no deep, unchanging truth regarding the nature of law. Law is not a natural kind like uranium or hydrogen with an ontological status apart from the meaning people have given to the term and the particular configuration of institutions people have built up that embody the term. Over the course of its existence, a linguistic community plays a language game with the word *law*, and thus it becomes culturally defined.[16] There is no essential core to the concept of law that need remain uniform from era to era or culture to culture.

The lack of an essential definition does not imply, however, that the meaning of the term *law*, or its relationship to the term *custom*, are transparent. The goal then is to determine the contingently created historical notion of law and then further determine its relation to custom, also historically and culturally determined. This may mean, for example, that the role custom has played in the United States may differ from the role it has played in England. There may be a strong family resemblance between these accounts of the relationship between custom and law, but there is not necessarily an identity.[17] It may make sense to refer to customary law in the English system but refer to custom as a source of law in the American system. For example, custom receives constitutional recognition in England,[18] while American courts have rejected custom based on state constitutional principle.[19]

As the positivist holds that customs do not acquire legal force until recognized by judges, the crucial issue for the positivist is to specify the criteria that entitle customs to legal recognition. For natural law theory, however, the question of criteria for legal recognition appears not to arise; customs need not audition to become law as they are law already. But this appearance is deceiving. A custom, as the word is used in ordinary language, was not a custom in the natural law theorist's sense, unless it fulfilled certain criteria. Such a test was inevitable unless all community practices were to be given legal effect. Thus, the same question that arose for the positivist is seen inevitably to arise for the natural law theorist; what are the features of certain patterns of social behavior such that they may qualify as legally valid custom? Section II seeks to answer this question.

II. Custom as Obligatory Practice

The role of custom in promoting social order precedes the emergence of the common law. The rise of the English common law came about through the gradual usurpation of the informal power exerted by informal social customs.[20] Common law was the beginning of English law that was national in scope.[21] Early customary law by contrast was local.[22] Customary law grew up around the practices of groups and so the scope of the law was dependent on the size and geographical reach of the group. The medieval manorial system of land use constituted the predominant form of social organization out of which these early customs arose.[23] Agrarian life was simple, and travel was difficult. Manors were semiautonomous social worlds unto themselves, governed by sets of informal customs. Sometimes these customs were written down in customals.[24] As English judges began riding circuit in an attempt to create a law common to this multitude of minijurisdictions, they at the same time went about the work of supplanting the power of these jurisdictions. One of the means by which the common law grew was by absorbing customary practices.

As Part One of the book indicated, a norm is a social practice, and as Section I claimed, a custom is, for present purposes, synonymous with a norm or, to be more precise, a norm of not insignificant duration. A practice implies at least four things, a group of people who practice, a segment of time over which they practice, a place where they engage in the practice, and a subject matter – a type of behavior – that constitutes the particular practice. Each of these elements of a practice has received discussion in the cases involving legal custom.

Consider first the group of people who have a practice. Courts historically distinguished between general customs on the one hand, and local, particular or special customs on the other hand.[25] General customs were said to be those that represented the practices of the people of England. These were practices said to be common to all; thus, the general custom was the common law.[26] By contrast, local customs were the practices of smaller groups, such as the members of a parish, vill, manor, borough, or county, or those who belonged to professional or commercial groups. Sometimes, local customs were restricted in their application to members of these sublocal groups, and others would not have similar rights extended.[27] References were often made to "customs of the countryside,"[28] "customs of the realm,"[29] or "popular custom."[30] In addition, an important part of English custom were the so-called "customs of the court," which were customs developed among the judges regarding both procedural and substantive matters.[31]

There appears to be no group size too small to make up a group of conformers to a custom, although the smaller the group the harder it sometimes was to have the custom recognized as having legal force.[32] Though commentators have not explicitly noted the fact, the number of people who partake of a custom in relation to the number of people in the community appears to have mattered as well. Thus, it is not always the absolute number of people who are conformers that is relevant, but the percentage of people in the community. This matters with regard to the notice requirement for a legally valid custom. In other words, customs must be public so that members of a community who may be obligated to conform to them will have notice of their existence.[33] General notice of a custom's existence will vary with the percentage of members of the community that conform to the custom.

The overall size of the group or community where a custom was practiced also mattered. In general, it appears that the larger the town, the greater deference it could expect toward its local customs.[34] In many cases, this deference was the result of royal charters secured by boroughs or towns, or charters granted by local lords in imitation of the royal charters.[35] The county of Kent for example received a charter from the early Norman rulers allowing it relative autonomy.[36]

It is natural to think that a custom is made up of all the acts of conformity by those who share a practice of a particular sort. For example, those who customarily walk along a beach would be thought to make up the group who participate in the relevant custom as they share a distinctive sort of behavior, namely, beach walking. But for legal purposes, the participants in a custom may be a larger group. For example, with the custom of public use of a beach, the owner of the property is legally a participant in the custom, as she may have obligations toward those who customarily walk along the beach, although she herself may not use the beach in the customary manner.[37]

Next, consider the amount of time required for a practice to count as a legally valid custom. The orthodox view is that the older the custom the better; that is, the longer the custom has been in existence, the stronger the claim it has to legal validity. This is captured in the venerable phrases that the custom must have existed since "time out of mind," or since "time immemorial," or since the "memory of man not runnith to the contrary."[38] The often-stated rule in the old cases was that the custom must have existed uninterrupted since 1189.[39] Not surprisingly, this rule was not strictly followed.[40]

In spite of the general tendency to prefer the old to the new, many old customs were not given legal recognition, while many relatively new customs were recognized. In addition, the preference for antiquity mattered less, or not at all, if the custom had a contractual or commercial underpinning.[41] Immemorial usage also was not required in towns.[42] Boroughs could adopt new customs.[43]

Third, the element of place also has mattered regarding the legal validity of custom. It is sometimes said that local customs pertained to a particular place and not particular people.[44] Over time the particular set of persons who conform to a specific custom will typically change; what remains the same and makes for the same custom is that the same behavior takes place in the same location.

Commercial customs were an exception to the requirement that a custom must be maintained by a group of people sharing a particular geographical place. A group of merchants could share a custom despite the fact that they did not share a geographical space.[45] What appears to matter is that the group share a community.[46] Being in the same place is usually what allows a group of people to share cultural understandings and practices and so constitute a community, but commercial groups are an important exception. So perhaps are the communities sprouting up on the Internet.

Finally, regarding the subject matter of the practices that make up custom, there does not seem to be a subject matter or type of social practice that was excluded from possible legal recognition. Different subject matters appear to have received different treatment under the rule of custom, however. For example, practices regarding property in land were particularly subject to the centralizing influence of the early common law courts, while practices related to the family appear to have been given greater scope for more localized customary law development.[47] Customs of the commercial class were also given greater deference from the centralizing influence of the common law.[48]

Customs are practices of a particular sort, ones that are obligatory. Frederick Pollock states that customs must be regarded by those concerned as binding, not as a matter of individual choice.[49] In the words of another commentator, the thing done becomes the thing which must be done.[50] This is sometimes expressed in terms of the requirement of opinio necessitatis, or alternatively, that customs are "prescriptive."[51] The requirement of the opinio necessitatis has been defined as: "[T]he conviction on the part of those who use the custom that it is obligatory, and not merely optional."[52] Some community practices are obligatory, but others are not. Doctrinal accounts contend that only obligatory customs may be subject to acquiring legal validity. When it is said that custom is prescriptive, what is meant is that there exists an expectation of conformity among members of the community and usually sanctions of one form or another for nonconformity.

Contrary to the explicit views of commentators, however, the conformity need not be obligatory for all persons. In fact, at the extreme, it is only necessary that one person be obligated by the custom. This is true of the customary right to beach access, for example. The users are not obligated to use the beach so it is not literally true that the thing done becomes the thing that must be done.[53] The owner of the property, however, is obligated to permit access.

The early doctrine was that customary law trumped common law when there was a conflict.[54] Over time, however, the common law got the upper hand in this relationship. The common law usurped the primacy of custom by impinging both means by which customs may serve as sources of law.[55] First, the autonomous legal power of small jurisdictions such as that of manors and villages was curtailed and eventually choked off.[56] Second, the test by which customs could enter the common law was made more difficult.[57] The best-known test that a custom must pass in order to be a "source" of law was stated by William Blackstone.[58] According to Blackstone, a legally valid custom was a usage that had been practiced in a community without interruption from time immemorial. The Blackstonian test for custom was used by common law courts to narrow the influence of local jurisdictions in favor of their own.[59]

This section described the historical shift in the legal understanding of custom. In the early period, customs were plausibly understood as law itself – customary law. In modern law, however, customs are more appropriately understood as potential sources of law rather than as law itself. In the next and last section, the role of custom as a source of property easement law will be explored. Through the recognition by courts of customary uses of land, what would otherwise be an instance of the intentional tort of trespass may instead become a permanent easement in land.[60]

III. Trespass Norms and Customary Easements in Land

Beach users sometimes seek easements over the dry sand portion of the beach, which is part of the adjacent landowner's property. The public has a right in the wet sand in most jurisdictions as it is owned by the state. If people could only use the wet sand, there would undoubtedly still be beach use. Given the fact that the wet sand portion of the beach is accessible to the public, however, there is much social benefit to be gained in addition if people are able to use the adjacent dry sand. For example, small children can be more easily watched and kept away from the water with the extra girth added by dry sand access. Not only can the benefits of such use be great, but the countervailing damage may be small, for beach sand is strikingly impermeable to damage over a broad range of uses, and beach property is often purposefully left undeveloped. Likewise, in cases involving customary pathways over private land, courts sometimes note that it is possible for people to merely pass over the owner's property, leaving the land substantially as it was.[61]

Courts have paid particular attention to easement situations involving the so-called taking of profits. A profit is some physical part of the land such as grass, soil, lumber, or firewood. For the most part, courts have frowned upon the taking of profits.[62] When courts have allowed taking of profits, they usually pointed to the minimal loss to the owner. In some cases, the main loss to the owner was not what people took away or consumed but what they left behind, trash. In some cases in which easements have been granted, courts have pointed out that trash was picked up by the local municipality, apparently as evidence of the workability of the easement.[63]

If a permanent easement is granted, it can stop the owner from making improvements on her land in the future, which may cause her great loss. Nevertheless, courts sometimes cause owners to suffer such losses.[64] Proponents of the positive law and economic thesis can with some plausibility claim that the court is reacting to the fact that great utility or welfare may be produced if beaches remain free to the public, despite the substantial loss to the property owner.

In City of Daytona Beach v. Tona-Rama, the Florida Supreme Court waxed poetic about the valuable uses to which the public had put the beaches over the years: "There is probably no custom more universal, more natural or more ancient, on the sea-coasts, not only of the United States, but of the world, than that of bathing in the salt waters of the ocean and the enjoyment of the wholesome recreation incident thereto. The lure of the ocean is universal; to battle with its refreshing breakers a delight."[65] The court recognized the customary use of the adjacent land.

The beach cases are a departure from earlier easement doctrine, which tended to disrespect recreational pursuits as a valid category of land use to be accorded privileged treatment. But in cases such as Gion, the courts explicitly recognized recreation as a legitimate interest to promote.[66] This orientation toward a broad conception of the good comports well with utilitarianism, which does not draw a principled distinction between recreation and other sorts of welfare-enhancing activities. Likewise, the economic approach would not draw a distinction between different types of land usages, as long as they are of a sort that people would in principle be willing to pay for.

The economic account would apply the Coasian model to claims for customary easements.[67] Users of a beach or path face a classic coordination problem in getting together to represent their interests in a bargain with the owner to gain usage of the land. The law, then, should do its best to provide a rule that creates an outcome closest to that which would have resulted if such a bargaining process had been feasible. In other words, in cases in which judges think the conformers have the requisite interests, such that if capable of expression in a bargaining process with the owner, these interests would have been sufficiently strong so as to garner an easement by contract, then the law should validate the practice by creating the easement. By such a process, the law is able to simulate the results of an ideal bargaining process.[68]

In their discussions, courts often focus on the benefits to the public of particular customary practices when finding a custom, and focus on the loss suffered by the owner when rejecting a custom.[69] The more benefit to the public the better, and the less loss to the owner the better. Courts pay particular attention when a whole community can be said to benefit. The beach access cases have long been replete with mentions of the great value to the public of expanded beach use.[70]

While courts appear to have paid a good deal of attention to the efficient promotion of interests of the affected parties in their decisions involving customs, it would be rash to conclude that considerations of interests alone were the sole or predominant normative impulse motivating courts in customary easement cases. What has been seen so far is that consequentialist or interest-based considerations have been important in easement cases. No grounds have been established for thinking that such concerns play any greater role than this, however. To show that the positive efficiency thesis is not the whole story, one must demonstrate the significant role of other normative impulses besides the desire to promote efficiency. If other normative impulses play a significant role, their tracks should be discernible. And, indeed they are; the most important one is discussed next.

The most significant reason why an efficiency interpretation of easement doctrine looks attractive is that courts in easement cases have paid a good deal of attention to the interests of the involved parties. Precisely because courts have been relatively open in their discussions of the role of interests, it is all the more apparent that even though considerations of interests have been important, their role is not best interpreted in a straightforwardly efficiency-maximizing manner.[71]

Courts look to more than interests, and when they do look at interests, they do not treat the interests of all participants equally. This latter notion bears elaboration. Taking account of consequences, but weighing them differently depending on whose they are and other features of the situation, may seem foreign to normative analysis. But that is because doing so may not correspond precisely with any of the leading critical normative theories. The goal here, however, is to understand what has gone on descriptively or positively, not whether what has gone on is justifiable or reconcilable with any of the better known moral theories.[72] Consider the following example.

Courts have shown a sensitivity to a special normative relationship that may arise between the conformers to a practice and the owner on whose property the practice takes place. The relationship arises when property owners acquiesce in the usage over a period of time, allowing the group to develop a pattern of behavior and form expectations around it. The longer the practice is allowed to go on and the more the expectations and habits of the community form around it, the more inclined the courts are to validate the practice as a permanent easement.[73] Over time the relative weighing, normatively speaking, of the owner's interests shifts vis-à-vis those of the conformers. The more longstanding the practice, the more weight the conformers' interests are accorded relative to those of the owner. On the face of things, an efficiency account cannot make sense of this for it is forward-looking, and this normative impulse looks to the particular history between the parties and attaches moral significance to it. No doubt, there might be good interest-based reasons for judicial recognition of such ensconced practices as well, but the normative impulse that appears to motivate courts is distinct from this.

In a well-known passage, Lon Fuller has enunciated a basic moral intuition that appears strongly similar to the one lying behind situations of this sort, although Fuller was not discussing easements. Fuller writes:

Where by his actions toward B, A has (whatever his actual intentions may have been) given B reasonably to understand that he (A) will in the future in similar circumstances act in a similar manner, and B has, in some substantial way, prudently adjusted his affairs to the expectation that A will in the future act in accordance with this expectation, then A is bound to follow the pattern set by his past pattern of actions toward B. This creates an obligation by A to B.[74]

Fuller's position can be summarized by saying that a moral obligation is created in A toward B based on detrimental reliance by B on A. Though Fuller brings up moral intuition in the context of contract law,[75] a moral intuition of this sort appears to be the key to understanding the normative subtleties of what courts have been doing in easement law when they have given increased weight to the practices of groups as a function of the longevity of these practices.

It is ambiguous whether Fuller means to say that a genuine moral obligation is created by such detrimental reliance or rather that, as a matter of description, our culture and our legal system happen to be cognitively constituted such that they take events like these to create an obligation. It is perhaps the best interpretation of the text to say that Fuller does not have this distinction clearly in view, so his remarks are best not taken as evidence of a claim one way or the other. The present discussion, however, will avoid the question whether detrimental reliance creates a moral obligation, in the moral realist or Platonic sense of this term. Rather, the concern is over the best positive account of the practices. For this, Fuller's insight, understood as a moral-sociological characterization, is of great interest.[76]

Consider some of the main features of the moral impulse. Courts pay particular attention to whether owners could have done something to stop the practice and whether the users relied on the continuation of the practice. In Gion, for example, the court was quite explicit in its use of language connoting reliance: "If the open and known acts are of such a nature as to induce the belief that the owner intended to dedicate the way to the public and individuals act on such conduct, proceed as if there had been in fact a dedication and acquire rights that would be lost if the owner were allowed to reclaim the land, then the law will not permit him to assert that there was no intent to dedicate, no matter what may have been his secret intent."[77] Having allowed the use of their land over a long period such that people have formed their expectations accordingly and would suffer from a disruption of the status quo, it would be unfair, courts appear to think, for owners to unilaterally snatch away the physical underpinnings of the practice.[78] Thus, a legal obligation to continue to allow the usage is created and enforced.[79]

In easement cases, courts have typically employed a stricter test than that enunciated by Fuller. The test is usually stated so as to require conformity to the practice performed under a claim of right. Courts often do not say precisely what they mean by this requirement. Roughly, the idea is that courts find it significant that conformers thought they had a right or entitlement to use the land in question and accordingly did not seek permission.[80] In Gion, for example, the court wrote:

What must be shown is that persons used the property believing the public had a right to such use. This public use may not be "adverse" to the interests of the owner in the sense that the word is used in adverse possession cases. If a trial court finds that the public has used land without objection or interference for more than five years, it need not make a separate finding of "adversity" to support a decision of implied dedication.[81]

The test, then, is that the general public must be acting, if only implicitly, under the assumption that the usage was open to the public. In other words, people must act under the assumption that the public was entitled to use the land in question.[82] In the beach cases, it was natural for people to assume that they had a right of access to the beaches. After all, one typically comes and goes to the beach as one likes. No one takes a ticket, puts up a fence, or stops one from laying one's blanket on the dry sand portion of the beach. Because members of the general public think they have a right to such usages, they will more naturally tend to come to rely on them, as it would not occur to them that the usages could be curtailed by the unilateral acts of one private party.

The contracts literature on detrimental reliance forms the background to Fuller's discussion.[83] Part of the test for one's being responsible for another party's detrimental reliance is that one induced it. Inducement is a causal notion. The same condition appears to apply in easement law. Owners must be in some sense causally connected to the detrimental reliance of the customary users. Reliance gone bad cannot be laid morally on the shoulders of any random person who happens to be nearby when the detrimental reliance occurs. He or she must have played some special role in bringing the reliance about.

Though one must be causally connected to the detrimental reliance, courts have a number of options in terms of choice of rules for determining what connections between the owner's actions and the detrimental reliance of the conformers will have adverse legal consequences for the owner. The courts might have created a very difficult test to pass whereby owners had to intentionally attempt to create detrimental reliance. Or courts might have required that owners have acted negligently in creating the reliance. The rule courts in fact adopted can be seen as approaching a sort of strict liability standard.

Owners are seen as causally connected to the reliance by virtue of their ability to stop the reliance from naturally occurring. This is true even though stopping the reliance from occurring may require positive acts on the owner's part such as putting up a fence or posting signs. If owners fail to take these steps and people use the land for easements for long periods such that they come to rely on the usages, owners will be held liable for the reliance of the group, in the sense that the practices will be given the status of permanent easements.

In Gion, one of the owners had posted signs and had even put a log across the access road to the beach that ran across his land.[84] The court held that this was not enough.[85] So owners need not cause the reliance except in the very weak sense that they fail to take positive steps to stop detrimental reliance from naturally occurring. Thus, in effect, courts have placed a positive duty on the owner to either take serious steps to stop the usage, or sit back and watch a few sticks fall out from her bundle of property rights onto the common.

Summing up the discussion to this point, an examination of case law on property easements has explicated an interesting moral relationship that may develop between conformers to a practice and the owner on whose land the practice takes place. A moral relationship may develop that displays features making it strongly akin to the sort of obligation that arises (descriptively speaking) in situations of induced detrimental reliance in contract law. Overall, what was seen was that the best interpretation of the common law of easements sees judges as rewarding practices of groups with legal recognition when the practice took place under a claim of right and with the owner's acquiescence. It is in such circumstances that reliance of a detrimental sort may easily be induced. This relationship affects the extent to which the interests of the various parties are counted by courts.

The question remains as to the relationship between this moral impulse and the economic interpretation of easement doctrine, which was looked at earlier. The important role played by induced detrimental reliance is plausibly seen as showing that the positive efficiency thesis does not hold true for this particular corner of the common law. This finding would only be fatal to the strong claim that the common law always and only promoted efficiency.[86] Few theorists appear to defend this strong position however. Judge Posner, the scholar most associated with the positive thesis, in fact makes room for exceptions. Indeed, he provides a list, albeit a short one, of some legal doctrines that are best understood as not promoting efficiency.[87] An implication of the foregoing normative interpretation is that the role of custom in property easement law should be added to the list.

The preceding normative interpretation of easements is best understood as posing a more fundamental threat to the positive efficiency thesis than simply adding another entry to the list of its exceptions. In the process of performing the interpretation, we uncovered a type of normative feature that Judge Posner's remarks on the topic are inadequate to deal with. Posner puts all normative

concerns into two categories: wealth-maximization and redistribution.[88] Posner
then attacks the feasibility of redistribution. Posner says that judges are not
well equipped to redistribute but offers little discussion as to why this is so.
A number of scholars have questioned this claim.[89] The worry here is of a
different sort. Judicial recognition of a moral impulse flowing out of situations
of induced detrimental reliance demonstrates that it is not illuminating to label
all normative impulses that are other than efficiency promoting as falling under
the heading of redistribution.

For example, consider some of the thick moral features one sees in the
everyday world, such as the special duty that arises when one makes a promise,
or the special duty one may have toward those who have helped one in the past.
It is a core tenet of modern moral theory that such impulses cannot be reduced
to instrumentalist concerns, for it can always be the case in a particular situation
that one may have to choose between maximizing welfare or efficiency, on the
one hand, and showing fidelity to the demands of one of these duties, on the
other hand, that is, between doing what is good and doing what is right. These
duties are not helpfully seen as redistributive. It is apparent then that neither
these moral principles nor the moral impulse that arises in situations of induced
detrimental reliance fit well into Posner's categories. Once one actually looks
into the complexity and the moral nuances of this relationship, it is simply not
descriptively accurate to label it as redistributive. Even if one accepted Posner's
assertion that judges are largely incapable of affecting distribution, it would not
necessarily matter for normative impulses such as these, for as we have seen,
judges are indeed capable of affecting the law so as to promote the impulse
whereby obligations are created through induced detrimental reliance under a
claim of right.

In addition, Posner argues that other normative impulses lack the social
consensus that efficiency or wealth maximization have.[90] This may or may not
be true for the generic impulse toward income redistribution, but it certainly is
not true for customs, which by definition have some degree of social consensus.
There is no reason to suppose that a moral impulse such as the one created in
situations of induced detrimental reliance is any less a feature of our shared
moral outlook than is a concern for social efficiency. The opposite seems more
likely to be the case.

In passing, Posner suggests that, for practical purposes, the issue is not of
great concern because other normative impulses are more of less consistent with
the dictates of efficiency.[91] Consistency does not mean, however, that sui generis
moral impulses can be reduced to efficiency. Consistency here just amounts to
the fact that the thick moral features also happen to be welfare-enhancing for
some noticeable portion of all possible situations of the relevant sort. The crucial
situations are where the principles are inconsistent or clashing, not where they
are consistent.[92] In particular situations, a judge may be in a position in which
efficiency points in one direction and thick normative features of the situation

in another. And even when they are consistent, other normative impulses ought not automatically be characterized as reducible to efficiency. Any reduction to efficiency concerns will fail to appreciate the intentional content or internal moral logic of such principles, and plausibly, this is what judges and juries are motivated by, either because they personally hold to such principles or, as may be the case for some judges, desire to accommodate public sentiment for some instrumental reason, such as the prospect of reelection.

The preceding discussion sheds light on the processes whereby informal moral or normative impulses enter into the law. What appears to happen with customary practices that involve detrimental reliance is that over time the group develops a sense of entitlement to a continued usage of the land. Courts appear to share the moral outlook, or at any rate they choose to pay respect to it. If this is so, and if the community is normatively heterogeneous, then one would expect the same heterogeneity to be found in the best interpretation of what judges have been doing. In such a manner, normatively heterogeneous informal customs come to have legal backing.

Conclusion

This chapter focused on the historical development of the concept of legally valid custom. The first section explored the changing jurisprudential status of custom. Early on, certain customs attained the status of customary law. In more recent times, customs may serve as sources of law but are not law itself. In the second section, the more modern conception of custom was examined in greater detail. On this conception, customs are best understood as obligatory social practices. Finally, the third section performed a normative interpretation of the role of custom in property easement law. It was seen that the emergence of easements is best explained as due in important part to a normative impulse akin to induced detrimental reliance, rather than simply to an impulse toward welfare maximization.

7

The Evidentiary Rule of Custom

If the defendants had proved that in every mining establishment that has existed since the days of Tubal-Cain, it has been the practice to cut ladder-holes in their platforms, situated as this was while in daily use for mining operations, without guarding or lighting them, and without notice to contractors or workmen, it would have no tendency to show that the act was consistent with ordinary prudence, or a due regard for the safety of those who were using their premises by their invitation. The gross carelessness of the act appears conclusively upon its recital.[1]

Mayhew v. Sullivan Mining Co.

Introduction

This chapter continues the examination of the role that social norms and customs play in tort law. The last chapter concluded with an examination of how customary easements have arisen in situations that might otherwise constitute a trespass, owing to the recognition of community norms of land use. The present chapter extends the analysis beyond the specific context of trespass to tort law generally. Custom's role in tort is pervasive.[2] When people injure one another while conforming to social norms and customs, it is the duty of tort law to determine which of these injuries may merit legal redress.

Modern tort law mainly follows the *negligence standard* according to which one will be found liable for an injury only if one acted negligently in causing it. Leading early cases established the connection between negligence and "ordinary care"[3] While *ordinary care* and *due care* are often used as synonymous terms in tort law, note the linguistic peculiarity of referring to ordinary care in a circumstance in which there is a lack of relevant customary activity. Ordinary behavior is customary behavior. Courts look to whether an injurious action conformed to an accepted custom or social norm in determining whether the action was either negligent or an expression of due care.[4] In other words, common law doctrine recognizes that conformity to custom may have evidentiary or epistemic value with regard to the issue of negligence.

In negligence litigation, injurers attempt to establish their conformity to custom as evidence of due care, while victims attempt to establish the injurer's failure to conform as evidence of negligence. When conformity is used defensively, the injurer in effect asks: "How could I have done wrong, as I was simply doing what others do in similar situations? How could all the conformers to this widespread social custom be negligent?" This was the sort of defense offered by the defendant railroad in Texas & Pacific Railway v. Behymer, one of two leading cases establishing the modern rule of custom in tort.[5] When the rule of custom is used offensively, the victim in effect complains: "Surely the injurer was negligent as she failed to exhibit the degree of caution that is so obviously required that it has become customary." The rule of custom was used offensively in *The T. J. Hooper*, the other leading case establishing the modern rule.[6]

Modern tort law has alternatively endorsed two main rules of custom, which I label the *per se* and the *evidentiary* rules.[7] The introductory doctrinal discussion in Section I focuses on the manner in which the older per se rule, whereby conformity to custom established the fact of due care, was replaced by an evidentiary rule, which holds that conformity may be evidence of, but is not dispositive of, due care. Understanding these rules in greater detail, and particularly why the evidentiary rule won out, will be essential to gaining a larger perspective on the relationship between customs and tort law.

An adequate account of why courts have gravitated toward the evidentiary rule has remained elusive.[8] Section II initially considers the two most plausible candidates for such an account. The first, developed in the classic article, *Custom and Negligence*, by Clarence Morris, argues that juries will be less biased against defendants in their deliberations when they are made to appreciate that the defendant's injurious behavior conforms to widespread industry practices.[9] The second account is the traditional, positive economic account of Landes and Posner, which predicts that the per se rule will be found in situations in which there is actual or potential bargaining between the parties, but not otherwise.[10] When parties are able to bargain, they will be able to reach welfare-maximizing agreements on their own, and these agreements will be represented in customary practices. Accordingly, courts should insulate the practices by means of the per se rule.

Each of these accounts must be rejected, however, for failing to explain the emergence of the evidentiary rule as the dominant modern rule. Morris's account, while a fine early legal realist attempt to explore the sometimes jarring realities of jury psychology, nevertheless fails to explain why there may be genuine reasons that conformity to custom has epistemic value with regard to the issue of negligence, once concerns regarding jury bias have been taken into account. Landes and Posner's account fails because it wrongly predicts that the per se rule will prevail in bargaining contexts. In fact, the evidentiary rule is the dominant modern rule in both bargaining and nonbargaining contexts.

In the process of evaluating Landes and Posner's account, it will become apparent that informal game theory promises a better explanation of negligence law's use of social custom. Chapter Eight argues that a game-theoretic account that is adequate for the purposes of tort law necessarily encompasses the tripartite typology of norms and customs that was discussed in Part One: sanction-driven customs, coordination customs, and epistemic customs. Sanction-driven customs are closely related to the collective action problem or Prisoner's Dilemma, which has received a good deal of attention in recent law and norms literature.[11] Scant attention has been paid, however, to customs with the structures of coordination customs or epistemic customs. These latter two types of customs, while potentially beneficial to their participants and to society in general, often involve activities that create serious injuries. Accordingly, they are of great interest to tort law. We will see that understanding the tripartite typology is essential to fully appreciating the subtleties of a number of important cases, leading to the conclusion that courts, if they are to do their job, must better understand the varieties of rational structure that undergird legally relevant social norms and customs.

Chapter Nine will then begin by offering a chart that systematically presents the most important factors that welfare-maximizing courts must consider when dealing with norms and customs. The chapter will next provide an explanation of how courts can use the chart: They can first determine which type of rational norm is at issue in a particular case and then consider each of the markers of welfare-maximization – such as whether the underlying community is *close-knit* or whether the conformers to the custom have *superior epistemic warrant* – in order to arrive at the appropriate rule of custom. The remainder of Chapter Nine will then demonstrate the value of the enhanced structural account by utilizing it to reinterpret *The T. J. Hooper* and Behymer. Among other things this analysis will show that while *Hooper* is conventionally considered to be the leading case of custom in tort, this description better befits Behymer. Finally, Chapters Ten and Eleven move outside of a wealth-maximization framework. I will argue that the reasonable person standard, as it presently exists, and as it has previously existed in the law, is not best understood in terms either of wealth or welfare maximization.

From the perspective of welfare maximization, there is both an upside and a downside to the more complex account of custom developed in this and the next four chapters.[12] The upside is that the other two types of customs do not face the same constraints on efficiency that are faced by sanction-driven customs. The efficiency of an SD custom will depend on whether the participants are able to use the threat of sanctions to incentivize one another into cooperative behavior.[13] For example, with regard to the Prisoner's Dilemma, Ellickson argues persuasively that participants may be able to solve this problem when the underlying community is "close-knit."[14] The potentially disastrous implication of Ellickson's hypothesis, however, is that all norms not arising in close-knit communities will fail to be efficient.

Fortunately, the same dire implication may not pertain to coordination customs and epistemic customs that are maintained by communities that are not close-knit. In contrast to sanction-driven customs, there is no natural incentive to free ride on coordination customs or epistemic customs. Participants conform to these customs because it is in their direct interest to do so. With coordination customs, people conform to achieve a *coordination benefit*. Accordingly, efficient coordination customs may be maintained in communities that are not close-knit. Consequently, courts will not be able to look to close-knitedness as the sole, sufficient indicator of efficiency when it comes to coordination customs. The same will hold for epistemic customs. Participants freely conform to these customs to economize on the cost of information, not to avoid the sanctioning forces of others. Accordingly, such customs may be maintained by groups that are not close-knit.

The downside to the more complex account of custom is that each of the three types of custom faces its own characteristic inefficiencies. In other words, simply because epistemic customs and coordination customs may be efficient in groups that are not close-knit does not mean that they are always efficient. Coordination customs may be inefficient because the participants get locked into a practice in which individual conformity continues to be rational, even though the overall practice could itself be replaced by a better practice. With epistemic customs, inefficient practices may be maintained simply as a result of the fact that all the conformers to the practice think that conformity is welfare maximizing based on their mistaken expected-utility calculation.[15]

The complexity of custom's role in tort law is best understood by beginning with an examination of the leading doctrinal accounts of this relationship.

I. Holmes and Hand: Creators of the Modern Rule of Custom in Tort

There have been two main rules of custom in modern negligence law, which I have labeled the per se and the evidentiary rules. In addition, courts sometimes give no legal weight whatsoever to the fact of conformity to custom, which could be characterized as yet a third rule, the no-priority rule.[16] The per se rule holds that conformity to custom is a complete defense to negligence.[17] The evidentiary rule holds that conformity to custom may serve as evidence of nonnegligence, but it does not conclusively establish the fact of due care. Rather, it will be for a jury to decide whether a customary act exhibited an appropriate degree of caution.

The leading case promoting the per se rule was Titus v. Bradford, which, in an often-cited phrase, referred to this rule as the "unbending test of negligence."[18] The court stated: "[T]he unbending test of negligence in methods, machinery and appliances is the ordinary usage of business. No man is held by law to a higher degree of skill than the fair average of his profession or trade, and the standard due is the conduct of the average prudent man."[19]

This passage indicates that, according to the per se rule, "ordinary usage" amounts to a basically statistical notion, the "average." Average people are by definition doing what most others are doing, that is, conforming to widespread customs. When one conforms to custom, one provides ordinary or due care by definition, for as the preceding passage states, the "standard due" is the conduct of the "average" prudent man who will not be held to a higher standard than that prevailing in his profession.

In Webber v. Bank of Tracy, the court bluntly stated that juries should not be in a position to have such a dramatic impact on an industry as might result from a decision adverse to the industry, involving a prominent industry custom.[20] The court stated: "Juries must necessarily determine the responsibility of individual conduct, but they cannot be allowed to set a standard which shall, in effect, dictate the customs or control the business of the community." Here, the court used the per se rule to protect industry against the possibility of liability for standard practices. With the coming of the Industrial Age, the per se rule provided powerful protection to a variety of industrial entities engaged in activities that produced serious injuries to employees and third parties.

The practical effect of the per se rule in the courtroom is substantial; a judge will direct a verdict in favor of the injurer charged with negligence upon a finding of conformity to custom. The jury will not be given the opportunity to find the injurer negligent.[21] By contrast, the procedure of the evidentiary rule is such that judges will allow facts regarding conformity to custom to be introduced as evidence going to the issue of due care. Under this latter approach, the important task is to determine the criteria for deciding when conformity is probative of due care. As we will see, neither courts nor commentators have displayed a good grasp of these criteria, characteristically saying very little of substance as to why a particular custom should or should not be accorded evidentiary weight, or what the relevant custom is.

Despite cases such as Webber, the evidentiary rule has in large part won out over the per se rule. Two important decisions by two of the century's leading jurists – Oliver Wendell Holmes and Learned Hand – were influential in bringing about the rejection of the per se rule in favor of the evidentiary rule. Both decisions essentially turn on the same key point: The standard of reasonableness is analytically distinct from the test of conformity to custom, such that there is no rational ground on which one should expect all conforming acts to be reasonable acts. Whether conformity is reasonable depends on whether the practice itself is reasonable. There is nothing about the existence of a customary practice, per se, that makes it reasonable. Each practice must be judged on its own merits.

In Texas & Pacific Railway Co. v. Behymer, Justice Holmes stated: "What usually is done may be *evidence* of what ought to be done, but what ought to be done is fixed by a standard of reasonable prudence, whether it usually is complied with or not."[22] The case involved a railroad employee who was seriously injured when he slipped from the top of an ice-covered railroad car that was moving about in a train yard. The train hit a bump and the worker slid and caught his trouser leg on a protruding nail, causing him to fall. The railroad sought to use conformity to industry custom as a per se defense so that the question of negligence would not go to the jury. The railroad claimed that it was operating in its "usual and ordinary way," and so by application of the rule of custom, it had a proper defense to the charge of negligence.

Holmes rejected this argument, holding that if the underlying social practice was unsafe, there should be a determination of negligence in tort. In other words, mere conformity to a custom cannot be a per se defense to negligence when the underlying practice is itself negligent. Holmes ruled that the lower court had not been in error in rejecting the per se defense and allowing the issue of negligence to go to the jury, as the railroad's practice was, according to Holmes, "obviously dangerous."[23] In this decision, Justice Holmes rejected the per se version of the rule of custom in favor of the evidentiary version.

From an historical perspective, we can view Holmes's decision in Behymer as an attempt to respond to a dramatic increase in the number of grave accidents that had been wrought by the instrumentalities of the Industrial Age. In Holmes's day, the case law contained numerous instances in which defendants attempted to escape liability for injuries resulting from patently dangerous practices by appeal to the defense of conformity to custom. In Mayhew v. Sullivan Mining, for example, the injurer was a mining company that had failed to place a guard rail around a hole in an underground mining platform that was unlighted.[24] The mining company in addition had also neglected to warn plaintiff of the hole's existence. The plaintiff did not see the hole in the unlighted platform and fell approximately thirty-five feet through the dark shaft before crashing down onto another platform. The worker was seriously injured and sued to recover for damages.

In seeking to introduce evidence of industry practice, the defendant pleaded: "This mining company was bound to keep up to the average. The plaintiff was entitled to ordinary care on its part. How can the jury tell whether the lack of a railing was a lack of *ordinary* care unless they are told how it is ordinarily in other mines?" Outraged, the court rejected in no uncertain terms the defendant's attempt to use custom as a cover:

If the defendants had proved that in every mining establishment that has existed since the days of Tubal-Cain, it has been the practice to cut ladder-holes in their platforms, situated as this was while in daily use for mining operations, without guarding or lighting them, and without notice to contractors or workmen, it would have no tendency to show that the act was consistent with ordinary prudence, or a due regard for the safety of those who were using their premises by their invitation. The gross carelessness of the act appears conclusively upon its recital.[25]

Patently dangerous situations such as the one that outraged the Sullivan Mining court in this passage probably were on Holmes's mind when he decided Behymer.

Along with Behymer, the second modern case that did the most to undermine the per se rule was *The T. J. Hooper*, decided by the Second Circuit in 1932.[26] Writing for a three-judge panel, Learned Hand famously remarked:

Indeed in most cases reasonable prudence is in fact common prudence; but strictly it is never its measure; *a whole calling may have unduly lagged in the adoption of new and available devices.* It never may set its own tests, however persuasive be its usages. Courts must in the end say what is required; there are precautions so imperative that even their universal disregard will not excuse their omission.[27]

As is well known, the case involved the issue of whether it was negligent for a tugboat, *The T. J. Hooper*, not to have been equipped with radio equipment that might have allowed it to receive notice of an impending storm. Judge Hand found there to be no custom either way with respect to radio use. According to Hand, the special master could conclude that the absence of a working radio on *The T. J. Hooper* rendered it not seaworthy and that this defect was a proximate cause of the loss of the loaded barge it was towing. It did not matter that other tugs were also generally not equipped with radios (if in fact they were not so equipped). They too were courting disaster.

Hand concluded that because not all conforming acts are reasonable acts, there cannot be a per se defense to negligence based on a showing of a conforming act. Courts, he said, must instead engage in an inquiry as to whether the particular act at issue was one that conformed to a custom, but also as to whether that custom lagged behind what was reasonably required. In Hand's view, radios were so inexpensive and their potential benefits so great that the owners of *The T. J. Hooper* were likely negligent for not having this equipment in place, regardless of the fact that such devices were a recent invention that had yet to dominate the tugboat industry. Thus, like Justice Holmes, Judge Hand rejected the notion that conduct was immune from negligence liability merely because it accorded with what others in the occupation or practice did in similar circumstances.[28]

Holmes and Hand would be the first to acknowledge the fact that, across a wide range of human activity, what is ordinarily done is evidently prudent behavior as little injury results.[29] Ordinarily, people display a good deal of prudence. But this is not always the case; there is nothing magical about ordinary behavior that makes it prudent by definition. As Clarence Morris states: "Since customs may be venal, conformity to them may constitute outrageous misconduct."[30] Conversely, if individual acts may be imprudent, a set of individual acts of a similar sort constituting a custom may also all be imprudent. In fact, the instantiation of the per se rule in a particular jurisdiction may serve as a perverse incentive for negligent behavior by providing it a safe harbor.[31] In this vein, an early commentator noted:

The harmful results that would in all probability follow the adoption of the common usage, and the safe results that would be assured by the substitution of a different method might, in a particular case, be so apparent that a prudent man would reject the former, and adopt the latter course. But in doing this he would depart from the rule laid down by the "unbending test" and of his own accord adopt the wiser and safer rule. Yet the rule of the "unbending test" constrains him to adopt the unsafe method in order to bring himself within the rule and escape the charge of negligence.[32]

Miller's point in this passage is that the per se rule will have the perverse effect of causing people to stay in the safe harbor created by the rule when they otherwise might have acted on their belief that the customary practice was faulty, and instead have performed the nonconforming action that appeared to be safer. Perhaps in part due to an implicit appreciation of this sort of argument, along with that of Holmes and Hand, the per se rule lost a good deal of prominence. Nevertheless, it survived. In apparently all jurisdictions, the two rules lived side by side, though sometimes uncomfortably.[33] Because jurisdictions had decisions going in either direction, a court could choose to employ either rule in any given case.

The durability of the per se rule against the critiques of Holmes and Hand may have owed in part to the fact that courts saw it as providing a salutary "policy" check on potentially vast liability. Thus, in the period between the 1930s and the 1960s, one tends to find the rule invoked in cases where courts seem anxious to provide protection for certain industries.[34] Nevertheless, by the 1970s, the majority of courts and commentators had opted for the evidentiary rule and, accordingly, it has become the dominant rule of custom in modern tort law.[35]

The practices of medical doctors (and other professionals) are, however, subject to an exception to the modern evidentiary rule. Conformity to customary medical practices by a physician is generally a complete defense to negligence.[36] In the past, it was enough that a physician conformed to a local customary practice. Many modern jurisdictions require, however, that the custom be regional or national.

It is striking, however, that while the evidentiary rule has won out over its rival, courts and scholars have been content to rely on the negative arguments of Holmes and Hand and have not offered a positive justification as to why the mere evidence of a practice made up of the actions of nonparties to a lawsuit has anything whatsoever to do with whether a particular defendant's actions in some particular circumstances constitute negligence. If a whole industry can lag behind, then in order to know whether or not the particular industry at issue is lagging, a judge seemingly must make an independent evaluation of the particular act of conformity involved in the situation. But if the act is evaluated independently, then the practice is analytically posterior and apparently irrelevant to the evaluation of the particular act.[37] In other words, why should compliance with custom have any role to play in the negligence determination? The silence of Holmes and Hand may not be surprising, as courts are not required to give a rationale for the rules they apply if they apply them more or less correctly. This, however, leaves scholars with the task of articulating the evidentiary connection between conformity to custom and nonnegligence.

II. Two Faulty Rationales for the Evidentiary Rule of Custom

In Section I, we saw that while the evidentiary rule has largely supplanted the per se rule, making it the dominant modern rule of custom in tort, courts have not adequately articulated the rationale behind this rule. Previously, the most sustained academic remarks on the subject were to be found in *Custom and Negligence*, by Clarence Morris.[38] Following on the heels of Behymer, decided in 1903, and *The T. J. Hooper*, decided in 1931, this article, published in 1941, is fairly seen from an historical perspective as the leading scholarly exploration of the twin attack on the per se rule of custom by two of the leading common law judges from that era.

While Morris's account proves ultimately to be unsatisfying, it is nevertheless the best place to initiate a deeper understanding of the competing virtues of the two rules. The next place to turn is the law and economic account, which naturally suggests itself, as Holmes and Hand are claimed to be two of the law and economics movement's early progenitors. Landes and Posner's account of efficient custom will be examined. After rejecting it as failing in predictive power, we will then see in Chapter Eight whether an informal game-theoretic account may provide better predictions.

A. Morris's Jury Bias Interpretation

Morris argued that evidence of conformity to custom is relevant and should go to the jury because it tends to reduce natural jury prejudice against businesses that injure individuals.[39] He contended, however, that there should be no per se rule protecting all injurers simply because they were conforming to an existent practice.[40] Morris gave two main reasons in support of his view that evidence of conformity should go to the jury, beginning with the following: "Evidence of conformity induces objective thought; it counteracts sympathy for an injured plaintiff; it highlights the need for care in weighing the defendant's conduct; and inhibits the tendency to hold the defendant on the suspicion that he is able to absorb the loss better than the plaintiff."[41]

Note that the thrust of Morris's point in this passage is not about the probative or epistemic value of custom but rather about its value with regard to reducing jury bias. Starting from the plausible assumption that jurors will naturally be sympathetic with regard to the personal injuries of individual plaintiffs, Morris claims that evidence of conformity will serve to counteract the biased outcomes that are likely to result from such sympathies.[42] Jurors, he supposes, will be more sympathetic toward a particular company if they are brought to realize that it must compete with other companies, and that doing so requires making expenditures on safety commensurate to that of other companies. In addition, jurors may be less prone to slight the interests of whole industries if they are reminded of the potentially dramatic impact on an industry if it is forced to change its manner of doing business due to a finding of liability in a particular case. While only the particular defendant at trial is in jeopardy of suffering damages directly as a result of the lawsuit, the stakes are nevertheless higher in cases involving industry custom than in a case that does not involve custom because the entire industry may be forced to adopt a different practice in order to avoid future liability. Morris thinks juries will be less blinded by their sympathy for plaintiffs if they have in the back of their minds these high stakes, both for a whole industry and for the particular company that is a party to the lawsuit.

These points have the ring of truth so far as they go, but their plausibility depends on the assumption that the defendant was following a reasonable or nearly reasonable custom. If the custom was flagrantly unreasonable, juries would be unlikely to worry that their verdict will make the defendant less competitive. It is more plausible to suppose that a jury would instead think that, as all industry participants in the practice were acting wrongfully, each should make changes in its behavior (and pay for failing to do so). In other words, the fact that the whole industry engages in an odious practice might well make a jury more sympathetic toward the victim of such a practice. It is clear then that Morris's first point about the relevance of conformity to custom on the part of the injurer does not contribute toward establishing the general value of evidence of conformity but at most explains why evidence of conformity with reasonable customs will counter jury bias against business defendants.

Morris's second point with respect to the evidentiary rule of custom also concerns the connection between custom and jury prejudice rather than its connection to due care. Morris states this justification for preferring the evidentiary rule as follows:

Evidence of conformity sharpens attention on the practicality of caution greater than the defendant used. It puts teeth in the requirement that the plaintiff establish negligence. Judges and jurymen seldom know much about the defendant's business. When the defendant's craft is palpably esoteric, the courts require the plaintiff to prove by experts that a feasible way of avoiding the plaintiff's injury was open to the defendant. But unfortunately men do not always appreciate their ignorance. Those not in the know are prone to set impractical standards when they judge conduct that has caused injury. Evidence that the defendant has followed the ways of his calling checks hasty acceptance of suggestions for unfeasible change.[43]

Note that Morris's second point in defense of the evidentiary rule again speaks to the effect of the information on the jury's ability to arrive at a less prejudicial perspective on a situation, rather than to the intrinsic, epistemic value of the evidence. Morris says the information regarding custom "sharpens attention on the practicality of caution greater than the defendant" exhibited and "checks hasty acceptance of suggestions for unfeasible change."[44] The implication is that, for a sharp jury not acting in haste, evidence of custom would be redundant. A jury's attention might just as well have been sharpened by the well-honed trial skills of an accomplished litigator. We are looking, however, for an explanation as to why conformity to custom might be substantive evidence relevant to the issue of negligence – evidence that matters apart from the cognitive foibles of particular jurors, such as their hastiness or lack of attention. We see then that just as with Morris's first rationale for the evidentiary rule, here too the argument, while of interest to the overall study of norms, does not increase our understanding as to why conformity to custom has independent, evidentiary value.

B. Landes and Posner's Economic Interpretation

The traditional law and economic approach is a natural place to look for a better understanding of why conformity to custom may be of evidentiary value in tort law, as Holmes and Hand wrote the key opinions ensconcing the evidentiary rule and they have been declared precursors of the law and economics approach.[45] There are two related theses to the law and economic approach to the common law: the *positive thesis* and the *normative thesis*. The positive thesis holds that the common law has in fact developed so as to promote efficiency, and the normative thesis holds that the law should promote efficiency. It is the positive thesis that is of present interest because our concern is to understand the battle for dominance in the common law of tort between the per se rule and the evidentiary rule, and this is a factual or positive issue.

Richard Posner is the leading expositor of the "efficiency theory of the common law," which he describes as "a system for maximizing the wealth of society."[46] Consistent with this general thesis, one would expect Posner to account for the shift from the per se rule to the evidentiary rule in terms of how this shift promoted more efficient outcomes. Posner discusses the rule of custom in tort in *Economic Analysis of Law*, and in *The Economic Structure of Tort Law*, written with William Landes.[47] In the former work, Posner considers "Custom as a Defense," while in the latter work, Posner and Landes analyze both the defensive and offensive uses of the rule of custom.

Based on an application of the Coase Theorem, Posner and Landes predict that when transaction costs are sufficiently low, conformity to custom will be recognized as a defense to negligence.[48] They write: "If transaction costs are low, an optimal allocation of resources to safety as to other activities will be achieved by negotiation regardless of the liability rule in force. *In these circumstances whatever is customary is, at least prima facie, optimal*."[49] According to Posner, transaction costs will be low when the parties stand in an "actual or potential" bargaining relationship. In such circumstances, "compliance with the standard of safety that is customary in its industry should be recognized as a defense."

When transaction costs are high, however, we should not expect to see optimal customs. Landes and Posner write that "[i]nsofar as the benefits of a safety device or practice will inure to people with whom the potential injurer does not have an actual or potential contractual relationship, he will have no incentive, in the absence of law, to provide the benefits. There is no presumption in such a case that the customary level of care is efficient."[50]

Based on this analysis, Landes and Posner formulate the following hypothesis about the common law: "We are led to predict that compliance with custom will not be a defense in accident cases where transaction costs are high but will be where those costs are low."

Consider how Landes and Posner's prediction applies to the two versions of the rule of custom. The per se rule provides a strong defense to negligence claims for conforming firms. On this strong defense, if the judge was satisfied that there was a proper custom, the question of negligence would not go to the jury. As discussed previously, the evidentiary rule does not serve as a per se defense to negligence, but rather the issue of negligence will remain a fact question for the jury. So the per se version of the rule of custom corresponds to the description of the rule Landes and Posner predict to be operative in situations in which the injurer and victim are in an actual or potential bargaining relationship. Landes and Posner clearly have in mind a rule whereby the fact of conformity means the defendant has made a defense with no chance that the issue of negligence will go to the jury.

Note the startling result when we apply Landes and Posner's prediction based on the positive thesis of efficiency of the common law to the leading cases that have shaped the modern rule. Their analysis does not explain the rise of the evidentiary rule; indeed it predicts the opposite result whenever the injurer and victim stand in an actual or potential contractual relationship. However, as we saw in Section I, the case law has not developed in this manner. Rather, thanks to the early leading cases of Behymer[51] and *The T. J. Hooper*,[52] there is little left to the per se defense despite the fact that in both of these cases, and a large number of their progeny, there exists a bargaining relationship between injurer and victim.

In support of the efficiency thesis, Posner cites the rule for medical malpractice, which usually entitles medical practitioners to the per se rule as a defense. This is deceptive, however, for, as mentioned earlier, professional malpractice is the most prominent exception to the modern rule. Because he treats the exception as the exemplar, Posner cannot explain why the common law treats conformity by medical doctors and other professionals differently than conformity to custom by nonprofessionals. Subsequent discussion will demonstrate, however, that the treatment of these cases in tort law results from the fact that doctors' customs are nonstrategic epistemic customs in which the conformers have superior *epistemic warrant* as compared to nonconformers (including both the victims and the courts).

In *The Economic Structure of Tort Law*, Landes and Posner acknowledge that economic analysis cannot explain the rise of the evidentiary rule. Indeed, they concede that Hand's analysis in *The T. J. Hooper* represents a rejection of the Coase Theorem.[53] There, Hand remarked, "a whole calling may have unduly lagged in the adoption of new and available devices."[54] On Landes and Posner's account, however, a whole industry such as the one involved in coastal shipping should never be lagging behind, for this is precisely the sort of setting in which an efficient practice should emerge, as there is a contractual relationship between the tug boat owner and the barge owner (and possibly the party whose goods are being transported).

Landes and Posner attempt to explain away Hand's decision in *The T. J. Hooper* as a mistake. They claim that an efficient practice was in place but that Judge Hand got the facts wrong. Alternatively, they contend that Hand may have been confused about the meaning of custom. It is beside the point to put too much weight on the particular factual dispute in *The T. J. Hooper*, however, because there are a large number of cases in addition to *Hooper* that contradict Landes and Posner's analysis. In fact, they concede that *Hooper* provides the "classic statement" of the modern rule of custom, but they do not consider cases before or after it.[55] Thus, they refuse to acknowledge that in *Hooper* Hand cited to two Supreme Court cases as precedent – Behymer and Wabash Railway Co. v. McDaniels,[56] a decision written by Justice Harlan which was cited by Holmes as precedent in Behymer. In each of these cases, the Supreme Court rejected the per se rule despite the fact that the parties had an actual or potential bargaining relationship.

As discussed in Section I, Behymer involved a worker who was seriously injured as a result of being ordered to work on top of an ice-covered railroad car that was moving uphill. On Posner's account, the facts in Behymer present a low transaction cost situation in which the Coase Theorem would predict the emergence through bargaining of an efficient industry custom; hence, conformity should count as a defense. We see, then, that the Coase Theorem, as applied by Posner, gives no explanation of Behymer, for Justice Holmes did emphatically think the evidence of conformity was merely probative, not dispositive.

While Landes and Posner acknowledge that *Hooper* is a problem for their positive economic account, Behymer and McDaniels are devastating because they are Supreme Court cases that, in a time of federal common law, represented a rejection of Landes and Posner's analysis not only in the Second Circuit but across the land. These cases each involved torts arising in the context of an employee/employer relationship, which is a relationship between bargainers that should, according to Landes and Posner's analysis, produce efficient results through bargaining. We see then that a tidy set of three leading cases have brought about the modern rule of custom in tort. All of them contradict Landes and Posner's analysis.

Conclusion

It will be useful to conclude with a summary of the discussion of this chapter. Section I examined the historical competition between the per se rule and the evidentiary rule. We saw that while the per se rule has not disappeared entirely, the evidentiary rule has become the dominant modern rule. Having led this transition, Holmes and Hand nevertheless had precious little to say regarding the rationale for preferring the evidentiary rule to the per se rule or to the rule that accords custom no deference whatsoever. To better understand this historical transformation, we then considered the two most prominent scholarly accounts in Section II.

Each of these accounts was seen to be lacking. Morris provided an interesting account of the jury psychology of the rule of custom, arguing that juries will tend to be less biased in favor of injured plaintiffs when they are made aware of a defendant's conformity to industry custom. Morris's account did not, however, speak to the issue of why a court should properly allow evidence of conformity to custom to go to a jury after concerns regarding jury psychology are factored in.

Landes and Posner's law and economic analysis of custom was considered next. Their account yielded a hypothesis that was seen to be at odds with the modern rule; it incorrectly predicted the appearance of the per se rule in situations of actual or potential bargaining between the parties, when in fact the evidentiary rule is dominant across the board, and courts do not apply separate rules in bargaining and nonbargaining situations. Moreover, Landes and Posner's account did not explain the main exception to the modern rule of custom. This exception inures to the benefit of professionals such as physicians. But these groups are neither more nor less likely than nonprofessionals to engage in the sort of bargaining discussed by Landes and Posner.[57]

In one important respect, however, Landes and Posner's analysis was correct. This was their focus on choosing an appropriate rule of custom depending on an assessment of the degree of efficiency of the underlying social practice. They considered only two modalities, however, when in fact there are four of interest. The per se rule will make more sense when the custom at issue is thought to be efficient because this rule will protect the conforming action from going to the jury where the injurer might be found to be negligent, despite the fact that the injurious act conformed to a welfare-maximizing custom. The evidentiary rule will make more sense when the custom at issue is not optimal but welfare-enhancing because this rule encourages juries to give deference to the custom, while allowing the jury to find negligence if a superior custom appears attainable. The evidentiary rule may take a weak form under which conformity is evidence of due care or a strong form under which conformity serves as a rebuttable presumption of due care. Finally, the rule that accords conformity no priority may be suitable if sanction-driven customs are either neutral or detrimental to the production of welfare.

The problem then is to determine the efficiency conditions for social norms and customs. Unfortunately, this task is much more complex than suggested by Landes and Posner's analysis, for not only are there four rules of custom, but there are also three importantly different types of customs to which these rules may apply. To determine whether a particular custom in a particular case is, or might be, efficient, courts will want to know which type of custom is involved. This is because different, though overlapping, sets of *welfare-maximization markers* apply to each of the three types of custom. When courts have an estimation of the welfare-producing capabilities of particular customs, they are then in a position to choose the most applicable rule of custom. The safest possible world will be the one in which courts are best able to perform this function.

In the next chapter, simple payoff matrices of informal game theory will be used to model the different types of custom. It will be necessary to go outside of game theory proper because it exclusively examines strategic structures and an important class of customs that are of interest for negligence law have nonstrategic yet rational structures. As the discussion in Part One indicated, strategic and nonstrategic social practices must be analyzed within the same framework for a comprehensive account of norms and customs to emerge.

8

A World of Dangerous
Norms and Customs

[M]embers of a close-knit group develop and maintain norms whose content serves to maximize the aggregate welfare that members obtain in their workaday affairs with one another.[1]

Robert Ellickson

Introduction

As set out in Part One, there are three distinct types of customs: *epistemic customs, coordination customs*, and *sanction-driven customs*. Epistemic customs solve nonstrategic, informational problems, while coordination customs and sanction-driven customs solve strategic problems of two different sorts.

The Prisoner's Dilemma, when iterated and solved by a social practice, is actually a subset of the broader category of sanction-driven customs and norms. A sanction-driven custom is maintained due to the existence and casual efficacy of sanctions. Along with Prisoner's Dilemma (hereinafter alternatively PD) games, games such as iterated Chicken[2] or Ellickson's Specialized Labor Game may also be solved – or not – depending on the ability of participants to sanction one another effectively.[3] Nearly all applications of informal game theory to law, to date, have focused on the Prisoner's Dilemma or collective action problem.[4] One would naturally suppose that tort law would take an interest in PD-structured customs because tort law is concerned with injuries, and many PD customs present a situation in which a person is repeatedly in a position to cause injury to others, either by failing to conform to a safe PD custom or by conforming to a dangerous PD custom.

Although PD customs, and sanction-driven customs more generally, are indeed of great interest, it will be demonstrated that epistemic customs and coordination customs may be important sources of injuries as well, and so are equally of interest to tort law. In the following discussion, these rational structures will be explored in greater depth so that we can better understand how different customs may have an impact on social welfare in different ways. As will be discussed in the next two chapters, it is this framework that courts will need to apply in order to choose an appropriate rule of custom in particular cases.

I. Tortious Sanction-Driven Customs

As noted in Chapter Two, the literature on iterated Prisoner's Dilemmas is helpful for understanding the broader category of sanction-driven customs.[5] Even though a one-shot Prisoner's Dilemma is thought not to be solvable, many theorists have discussed the manner by which iteration or repeat play may make it possible to solve PDs.[6] Examples are legion of social situations that are best understood as solved iterated PDs. Early in the development of the literature on the topic, Russell Hardin, for example, presented case studies from the environmental movement and women's movement in which these groups were able to solve their collective action problems in order to pursue group ends.[7] More recently, Elinor Ostrum has studied a large number of commons situations that were successfully solved.[8]

The fact that these situations may be solved does not mean, however, that they represent outcomes that are optimal. As already discussed in Chapter Two, Ellickson has developed the leading argument in the legal literature for the efficiency of social norms that function as solutions to iterated Prisoner's Dilemmas. Ellickson's account has recently come under fire from Eric Posner, who contends that there is little reason to think that such norms will be efficient.[9] It will be useful to briefly examine this debate.

Ellickson develops his position at greatest length in *Order Without Law*. In the context of a modern-day ranching and farming community, Ellickson examines damage to crops, motorists, and automobiles by wandering cattle, and damage to cattle by motorists.[10] One of Ellickson's main examples involves practices that have developed with regard to boundary fences that are erected to control wandering animals. Each party will benefit from the provision of a boundary fence, but each prefers that the other party bears the cost of erecting and maintaining it.[11] Ellickson calls this the "Specialized Labor Game" and characterizes it with the payoff matrix in Figure 2.16 in Chapter Two.

The residents of Shasta County are able to reach the welfare-maximizing social practice as represented in the northeast quadrant. Ellickson argues that it is the "close-knitedness" of the community that allows it to solve its fencing problem. Neighbors who share a common fence may be especially close-knit since they live physically close together and are thus likely to have repeated interactions over a variety of everyday concerns. Such multiplex[12] social relationships allow members of the community to sanction one another so that conformity to the socially preferred practice becomes individually rational.[13] Ellickson contends that "the more close-knit a group, the more successful it will be at generating and enforcing utilitarian norms to govern informal disputes."[14]

Eric Posner argues that social norms of the sort Ellickson discusses are inefficient. The relevance of the disagreement between Ellickson and Posner is significant for the present context because the stronger Ellickson's argument for presuming the efficiency of custom is, the wiser will be a court's choice to adopt the per se rule of custom (at least for collective action customs). On the other hand, the stronger Posner's argument, the better the grounds for adopting the evidentiary rule – or perhaps even the rule that accords sanction-driven customs no special status.

For purposes of argument, Posner assumes that customs may sometimes be efficient. Nevertheless, external circumstances can be relied upon to change such that the custom will no longer be efficient. Posner considers the Coasean railroad sparks story and Demsetz's account of the development of property rights in land among native tribes in Canada. He argues that, even if there are processes at work in these types of examples to move the custom in an efficient direction, such processes take time, and in the meantime the custom will be inefficient. With regard to the fact pattern in Coase's original article, Posner poignantly observes that perhaps customs are always left in the wake of ever-changing circumstances:

[T]he farmer and the railroad would abide by the deal for such a long time that gradually the village gossips would forget about the old norm and accept the new pattern of behavior as reflective of a new norm (perhaps without even realizing that this norm or the pattern of behavior is new). Still, this story must be highly unsatisfactory for the believer in efficient norms. For during the periods of transition the reigning norm is an inefficient one. Furthermore, one would expect that even as the old norm is gradually replaced by the new norm, continuing changes in the economy and in technology will render even the emerging new norm inefficient.[15]

In this passage, Posner implicitly understands the norm to be the linguistic item shared among the third-party "village gossips." It is the norm that has not changed sufficiently quickly, Posner argues, so as to keep up with the change in behavior that has already occurred between the railroad and the farmer. The conception of a norm at play here is problematic, however. With regard to the production of social welfare, it does not matter that the linguistic item bantered about by the village gossips is lagging, for it is not this linguistic bit that produces welfare – it is the behavior. And, by assumption, the railroad and the farmers have changed their behavior in a welfare-maximizing manner.[16]

In the example borrowed from Demsetz, however, Posner presents a more compelling challenge to the Ellicksonian framework, as here the practice itself represents a failure to solve a commons problem. Once the traders arrived and began to offer valuables for furs, each native gained an incentive to seize animals at a much higher rate. This produced a common-pool problem: No one had an incentive to ensure that the furs remained a renewable resource.

As Posner discusses the situation, the parties are able to remedy the commons problem by adopting new customs. As Posner notes, however, the problem is that it took them a few hundred years to do so. With regard to Demsetz's example, Posner writes:

Demsetz's theory may be correct. But note that the system of property rights did not emerge until the middle of the 1700s. Fur trading had begun in the early 1500s and had reached significant proportions by the middle of the 1500s. Thus, the efficient norm may have lagged by *two centuries*. State intervention at any time in the interim (if it had been possible) would have promoted efficiency.[17]

While Posner's observation that there was an inefficient gap of two centuries is significant, we cannot merely assume that state intervention in the interim would have been efficient.[18] With this caveat in mind, Posner's point is well taken; Ellickson should pause at this example in which order without law emerged, albeit at a snail's pace. Even if Ellickson accepts the force of this example, however, he may fairly respond that such lags are evidently not preordained, as witnessed by Shasta County where the norms did not lag in this manner.[19]

At this point, we must conclude that the debate between Ellickson and Posner is inconclusive. Posner has given good reason to suppose that PD customs in close-knit communities may sometimes be inefficient, but his argument cannot be interpreted as applying to all such customs in all such situations. On the other hand, Ellickson has provided a strong argument based on his analysis of close-knit communities for supposing that norms will sometimes be efficient. But his argument does not in any obvious way counteract the problem raised by Posner.

Both Ellickson and Posner qualify their arguments in ways that remove some of the distance between their positions; Ellickson acknowledges that close-knittedness is a matter of degree,[20] and Posner acknowledges that what matters is relative efficiency.[21] In effect, Ellickson acknowledges that social norms will not always be the product of completely close-knit groups and, therefore, will not always be fully efficient; Posner, in effect, acknowledges that less than optimal customs are nevertheless of interest to welfare-promoting legal institutions.

Consider the implications of these two theorists' analyses in terms of the rule of custom. In those situations in which there are no "social imperfections," the implication of Ellickson's analysis is that the per se rule should be applied because the customs at issue are likely to be efficient. By contrast, the implication of Posner's analysis is that the evidentiary rule should be applied, as the practice is suboptimal and hence the jury should be afforded room to incentivize change to status quo practices.

Ellickson is agnostic as to whether social norms may be welfare-maximizing in groups that are not close-knit.[22] Posner similarly restricts the application of his conclusions to close-knit groups.[23] The whole force of the literature on the collective action problem would strongly suggest, however, that when groups

Driver B

		Not Speeding	Speeding
Driver A	Not Speeding	3, 3	1, 4
	Speeding	4, 1	2, 2

Figure 8.1 The Custom of Speeding in Automobiles

are not close-knit, the resulting customs will not be welfare-maximizing.[24] In such circumstances, there would appear to be clear reason not to prefer the per se rule. The question would remain, however, whether the evidentiary rule or the no-priority rule were preferable.

To answer this question, it will be necessary to consider customs arising in a non-close-knit environment in more detail. The familiar examples of collective action problems do not involve tortious situations and so do not directly concern us.[25] There are many social practices, however, that have the structure of collective action problems but ones in which a failure to reach a solution may produce serious injuries. Some of the leading threats to one's health in civil society have the structure of failures to solve n-person collective action problems. Carrying handguns, failing to practice safe sex through condom use, and speeding in automobiles all have a similar structure: significant numbers of individuals prefer that others engage in the safer practice, but they themselves want to be able to free ride by performing the more dangerous practice when it suits them. The result is that there are socially significant amounts of each of these activities.

In the example of speeding in automobiles modeled in Figure 8.1 failure to solve the collective action problem leads to a dangerous situation because – as public service ads are fond of saying – speed kills. The world we live in is one in which this collective action problem goes largely unsolved; people speed with frequency, and others are injured or die because of it.

A rational actor prefers that others adhere to a custom of not speeding in automobiles because this actor will thereby be subject to less risk.[26] But the actor will want to be able to speed when it is desirable to do so. This puts others at risk, however, so they prefer that the actor not defect from the practice of observing the speed limit. The strategic situation presented by speeding is represented with the game-theoretic matrix shown in Figure 8.1.

Both Driver A and Driver B most prefer the situation in which other people cooperate in conforming to the safer driving speed, while the driver is able to defect from the practice by speeding when it is desirable to do so. The southwest quadrant represents the payoffs to the parties when A is the speeder, and the northeast quadrant represents the payoffs to the parties when B is the speeder. If A defects (that is, fails to conform to the cooperative practice and instead speeds) while B does not (the southwest cell), then A receives 4, her most preferred outcome, and B receives 1, her least preferred outcome. A is happiest, as she benefits from others' safe driving but gets to speed herself when she so desires. Likewise, if B speeds while A does not (the northeast cell), B receives 4, her most preferred outcome, and A receives 1, her least preferred outcome. If both speed, each receives the second least preferred outcome of 2 (the southeast cell), while if both refrain from speeding, each receives the second most preferred outcome of 3 (the northwest cell). This is true if we make the plausible assumption that each would prefer to live in a world in which no one is speeding rather than in a world in which all are speeding.

The problem these drivers face is that, if rational, each will notice that it is in each driver's interest to speed when the driver desires to, no matter what other drivers do. In other words, speeding is the dominant strategy.[27] The result is that each of the drivers will speed when it is desirable to do so. This will put them in the southeast cell, giving each the second worst outcome. If they had both refrained from speeding, each would have ended up in the northwest cell, with the second best outcome. Thus, when each chooses the individually rational strategy, both end up worse off than if they had been able to restrain themselves and choose the strategy that would provide for the jointly preferred outcome. We end up with a custom that represents a failure to solve an n-person Prisoner's Dilemma and thousands of people die on the roads every year because of this failure.

Speeding is a situation in which there is a lack of close-knitedness between the participants to the practice. They are not credibly able to threaten sanctions against one another in future interactions because the nature of driving is such that under most plausible scenarios, it is a largely anonymous activity. This anonymity encourages free riding because actors will be unable to make credible threats to sanction malfeasants in the future, as anonymity means there is no shared future. The result is a custom that represents a failure to solve a collective action problem. There is a social practice of speeding even though safety would dictate that this practice not exist. Because this custom is not welfare-maximizing, a court that sought to maximize welfare would surely not apply the per se rule in order to insulate this custom. The court must then choose between the evidentiary rule and the no-priority rule. If speeding is hazardous, the fact that others speed would appear not to affect the danger of the injurer's action and accordingly the no-priority rule is better.

In sum, this section has performed an initial exposition of sanction-driven customs in a negligence context by considering examples in which such customs are welfare-maximizing and examples in which they are not. Before going into greater detail in examining the importance of these examples for the rule of custom, however, it is necessary to first examine in greater detail the other two types of custom.

II. Tortious Coordination Customs

As explicated in Part One, coordination customs may emerge in situations of iterated coordination problems or games. In contrast to the iterated collective action problems discussed in Section I, players in coordination games do not have defection in their hearts. Rather, given the conformity of others, each wants to conform to the prevalent practice, even in circumstances in which the player could defect without fear of detection.

The most widely known game of coordination is that made by societies deciding which side of the road on which to drive. This custom appears to pass the Pareto test. An outcome is Pareto superior when it makes at least one person better off and no one else worse off.[28] With the example of driving on the right-hand side of the road, this situation is obtained. The driver from England, accustomed to driving on the left-hand side of the road, benefits from the choice to conform to the American practice when in America, and no one will be worse off due to this conformity. The same is true for the other drivers who choose to conform to the practice of driving on the right-hand side of the road – they will be made better off and no one will be made worse off. As this practice currently exists, with full conformity more or less in force, can altering this practice make anyone better off without also making someone else worse off? It would seem not. This coordination custom appears, then, to be efficient.

The best known analysis of coordination problems of a sort that may lead to coordination customs is that of David Lewis, who argues that "conventions" have the structure of "proper coordination equilibria."[29] Lewis defines a proper coordination equilibrium as a combination of actions such that no one would have been as well off had any one agent acted differently.[30]

For present purposes, the important aspect of Lewis's account is the claim that not only does the actor have a rational interest in conforming to the convention, but the other conformers have an interest in each other actor's conformity as well. An important implication of the particular strategic structure that Lewis examines is that, because other conformers have an interest in one's conformity, they will use sanctions to make this conformity more likely.[31] On Lewis's model, then, sanctions will be as pervasive in a world of coordination customs as they are in a world of customs that serve as solutions to iterated Prisoner's Dilemmas.

In fact, however, the minimal condition for the maintenance of a coordination custom is simply that each conformer receives a *coordination benefit* for conforming, given the conformity of others. Other conformers may be indifferent or even suffer detriment due to one's conformity. To adapt an example from Chapter Two to the present context, consider the norms and customs that govern how law students should dress when interviewing for jobs in various sectors of the legal profession. These are coordination customs: Individuals receive coordination benefits for conforming to the applicable dress code, unwritten though it may be. Such customs will be maintained by acts of conformity despite the fact that others are either indifferent to one's conformity or may even prefer that one fail to conform. Because of these facts, others will not use sanctions to incentivize conformity; rather, conformity will be driven by the pursuit of coordination benefits.

If most others wear a suit to job interviews, then I will benefit from doing so too. And if most others do not wear a suit to job interviews, then I will benefit from not doing so. For if I do not do what most others do, I will be conspicuous, and this could hurt my chances of being hired. Thus, I benefit from coordinating with the behavior of others. But most others who also wear suits to interviews may be indifferent to my doing so, as it has no effect on them; that is, they receive the same payoff whether I coordinate with them or not. Accordingly, this situation has the structure of a coordination equilibrium but not that of a proper coordination equilibrium.

In Figure 2.9, the conformers were represented as being indifferent to the conformity of any particular newcomer, but they may as well actively disprefer that this person fail to conform. This sort of strategic structure is seen even more clearly in another example from Chapter Two.

I have a friend who works for a Washington law firm where, although the nonpartners officially have three weeks vacation, the norm is to take two. Inspired by my friend's example, Figure 2.10 was called the Associates Vacation Game.

In this situation, I prefer to do whatever others do. If they all take two weeks vacation, then I also want to take two weeks so as not to stand out as a slacker. If they take three weeks, I will prefer three weeks as well, so as to enjoy the longer vacation and so as not to be ostracized as obsequious. My co-workers, on the other hand, prefer that I do whatever they are *not* doing. If they take two weeks, they prefer that I take three weeks so as to stand out as a slacker, making them look better. And if they all take three weeks, they prefer that I take two weeks so as to stand out as obsequious. Thus, my best choice of action is dependent on that of the others. I will receive the coordination benefit for taking two weeks if they take two weeks or for taking three weeks if they take three weeks. The others lose out due to my coordination, however; they suffer a coordination loss.

The current situation at my friend's firm is that nonpartners take two weeks. This situation is in equilibrium because each person could not have done better, given what the others did. Given that the others are taking two weeks, each prefers to take two weeks as well. Thus, the regularity will persist; the lawyers have reached equilibrium. But this is not a coordination equilibrium because it is not the case that no agent wishes any one agent – either herself or someone else – to have alone acted differently. Rather, each agent wishes any other agent to alone act differently from the rest. Yet such a game is a coordination norm in my account. It is a pattern of normatively governed behavior instantiated in a group and maintained by conformity. The conformity is explained by the desire to achieve the coordination benefit. Intuitively, it is clear that the lawyers' conforming practice at my friend's law firm should count as a norm and, thus, it is a virtue that an account denominate it as such.

Political and legal theorists have not paid adequate attention to games of coordination such as those just examined, apparently due to the view that these games are unimportant for social theory.[32] The idea appears to be that because it is in everyone's interest to participate in socially beneficial coordination games, people will freely do so of their own accord, and hence, by implication, there will be no reason for legal intervention. As the following examples will demonstrate, however, coordination customs merit review for potential judicial intervention based on the potentially suboptimal level of injuries flowing from them.

Consider first an example of a coordination custom in which the injuries are shared more or less equally among the participants. In New York, people often cross streets by first going to the center (double-yellow) line and then crossing to the other side at the first chance. This behavior occurs both at crosswalks and between them. It is not the custom for cars to stop to let pedestrians cross to the other side. Rather, pedestrians are responsible for spotting an opening in the stream of cars and making the crossing on their own. In San Francisco, the custom is strikingly different. Pedestrians mostly walk at crosswalks with the traffic light (though deviations occur with some frequency). When a pedestrian does cross to the center line, the practice is for motorists to stop to let the pedestrian cross all the way, even if this means stopping or slowing down in the middle of the block.[33]

To act contrary to the established practice of each community creates dangerous situations. When New Yorkers go to San Francisco and attempt to cross the street between crosswalks, they are surprised to discover that cars stop to let them pass to the other side. For motorists to suddenly stop is dangerous, and yet the pedestrian-friendly ethic is so strong that it is nevertheless the motorist norm in such situations. Pedestrians accustomed to the New York custom soon learn of this difference in motorist behavior and appear to modify their behavior accordingly, by not crossing to the center strip in the middle of the block, or at least by doing so less often.[34]

Now consider the New Yorker driving in San Francisco. This driver will at first expect pedestrians to know that motorists do not stop for pedestrians. Because pedestrians do in fact expect motorists to stop, a dangerous situation results. The pedestrian in San Francisco who walks to the center line – say, a newly arrived New Yorker or a San Franciscan in a hurry – maintains an expectation that she will be able to continue. The San Franciscan driving in New York is similarly dangerous if he acts like he is back home and hits the brakes for pedestrians attempting to make the dash between vehicles. Because hitting the brakes is contrary to local custom, the driver behind him will not be expecting it, which is dangerous. Under either scenario then, unless a traveler immediately conforms to resident custom, this traveler threatens to be the but-for cause of serious collisions. Once there is but-for causation, this driver may be one jury decision away from being found the proximate cause of any resulting injuries.

Coordinating with the behavior of others is paramount in this situation. One has reason to conform to the custom that is extant in one's community. Because others behave in a certain manner, one has additional reason to act in the same manner. Thus, as a practical matter, informal convergent social practices importantly influence what is reasonable because they importantly influence the sorts of actions that will in fact harm others.

This example makes graphically clear how important it is to pay attention to the coordination customs of the community in which one finds oneself. The behavior of others will often exert a gravitational pull such that one is well advised to do as others are doing. The august adage that one should do as the Romans when in Rome is often well-heeded. In the preceding example, the gravitational pull of the convergent social practice is so strong that it is dangerous to act against it. This example demonstrates, then, how dramatically coordination customs may affect the concrete, day-to-day substance of what it means for people to take due care.

For present purposes, the important question to ask with regard to this practice is which rule of custom would be most appropriate. For the reasons just discussed, conformity to local customary practices clearly deserves some degree of judicial support. The question then is which rule of custom is most appropriate. The per se rule appears to make the most sense because not only is conformity a good idea, but also failure to conform will actually be highly dangerous. Not all coordination customs have this last feature. In some situations, there may be a coordination effect in place such that others' conformity, to some extent, incentivizes one's own conformity; nevertheless, the risk from defection may be small or the loss slight.

This is the situation with the custom involved in the well-known case of Brown v. Kendall.[35] In Brown, the parties' dogs were fighting. The defendant was beating the dogs with a wooden stick in order to separate them, while plaintiff looked on. The defendant moved back from the dogs, striking them while he backed up. He moved toward plaintiff with his back toward him. Defendant raised the stick high to make another swat and in so doing accidentally struck plaintiff in the eye with the tip of the stick, inflicting a severe injury.

To modern ears, Brown may seem quaint. Yet, to the rural and village inhabitants of times past, dogs served a variety of important functions such as hunting, protection of livestock and poultry, and protection of the homestead from rootless men.[36] These dogs were necessarily less domesticated than today's pets and more likely to fight. In this context, it is not strange that practices would emerge around such activities as keeping dogs apart and having recognized means, such as the use of walking sticks, for breaking up fights that did erupt. In a community where people often carried walking sticks and it was accepted to use them to break up dog fights, such facts would bear significantly on the reasonableness of the manner in which Mr. Kendall used his walking stick.

There is an element of coordination in this example such that once the custom is established, villagers will wish to conform and will care that others conform. With convergent social practices, doing things in one manner often precludes doing things in another manner. Once social practices are underway, expectations develop among people that strangers they meet will act with the practice in mind. An important part of why it is reasonable for an individual to break up a dog fight with a stick is that this is the custom and so others' expectations will be formed with some degree of cognizance of this prospect. The reasonable individual action, then, is the one that conforms to the established practice.[37] It is not the fact that the custom is efficient that makes the individual conforming act desirable, but rather the fact that the custom has a coordination structure and that it is instantiated.

There is nevertheless an important difference between the customary practice in Brown and the varying pedestrian practices found across the two coasts. With these latter practices, failure to conform is dangerous. This is not true with the custom in Brown. If the defendant had not used a stick to break up the fight, a dangerous situation would not have been created. Thus, the evidentiary rule may be more appropriate as it recognizes that conformity was in fact made more reasonable by the conformity of others, while not creating a safe harbor for conforming activity which would have the effect of deterring individuals from ever experimenting with other potentially preferable practices.

Note that both the New York/San Francisco ("NY/SF") pedestrian custom and the custom of using sticks to break up dog fights in Brown are situations in which a possibly suboptimal social practice may be maintained through an extended series of individually rational conforming actions. It may be the case that, for example, New Yorkers would all be better off in a world in which the San Francisco norm was instantiated, and yet individual New Yorkers cannot reasonably act as if it is, given the background in which other New Yorkers do not. Because of the manner in which expectations of community members are shaped by extant practices, it may be the case that it is rationally justified for the defendant to conform to the extant practice even though the practice is suboptimal, such that all members of the community would prefer that all members of the community instead observed a different practice.[38] Assume for purposes of argument, for example, that the New York pedestrian and driver practice is not welfare-maximizing (See Figure 8.2).

For each NY resident, such as NY Resident A, it is the case that this resident receives a higher payoff, 2, for conforming to the NY custom, given that others are also conforming to the NY custom, than she would receive for conforming

Other NY Residents

		NY Custom	SF Custom
	NY Custom	2, 2	1, 1
NY Resident A	SF Custom	1, 1	3, 3

Figure 8.2 Inefficient New York Pedestrian and Driver Custom

to the SF custom, for which she would receive 1. Conforming acts of this sort work, however, to maintain the suboptimal NY custom, as represented in the northwest quadrant in which all conformers receive 2, as compared to the southeast quadrant in which conformers to the SF custom would all receive 3.

We see, then, that the mere fact that all the individual conforming acts that serve to maintain a coordination custom are individually rational is no guarantee that the custom itself is socially preferable. Furthermore, just because there is no collective action problem in maintaining the custom, and the risks created by such a practice are borne by the participants to the practice (and not by third parties), there is no reason to assume that the optimal custom will result.

The question, then, is: What is the relevance of this for courts that want to choose welfare-maximizing customs? In the discussion of sanction-driven customs in Section I, we saw that when a custom is optimal, there is reason to apply the per se rule, but not otherwise. The reason is that when the custom is optimal, then it should be insulated from the jury. In the type of situation just discussed, however, the situation is different. The custom is suboptimal, and yet it may not make sense to allow the custom to go to a jury. For unlike the situation in the SD case, here it would not have been welfare-promoting for the particular injurer to have acted otherwise. And it will not work to try to incentivize future actors to behave differently by altering their incentives. Given that most people will still be conforming to the established custom, suboptimal though it may be, we do not want particular individuals to act differently (even though were all others to also do the same, the result would be welfare-promoting). Given that the suboptimal practice is instantiated, it may be as welfare-promoting to insulate it with the per se rule as with the evidentiary rule. Under the evidentiary rule, if a court finds a particular litigant liable, future actors might be incentivized to act differently, even though doing so would be unlikely to promote social welfare.[39]

Consider next an example in which the suboptimality results from injuries to third parties. In Rhine v. Duluth, plaintiff, who was traveling in an automobile, collided with defendant's locomotive as plaintiff's car crossed defendant's train tracks on a foggy night. Rhine charged the Duluth Railroad with negligence for not using warning flares at the intersection.[40] Plaintiff claimed he could not see the train because of bad weather but could have avoided the accident if defendant had issued a minor warning. Plaintiff claimed that there was an extant custom of flare use and the Duluth railroad had negligently failed to conform. Defendant denied the existence of the custom. The court found that although flares were sometimes used by this railroad, there was not enough evidence to establish the existence of a custom, but had a custom been established, it would have been dispositive in favor of the plaintiff.

The practice of flare use has the structure of a coordination game. Just as a person wants to drive on the same side of the road as others, a railroad has reason to do what others are doing when it comes to using flares. If others are using flares, then people will expect to see flares and will tend to drive faster and with less attention than if the practice is not to use flares. Because people will expect flares, a particular railroad had better use them. Whereas, if other railroads are not using flares, then a particular railroad also wants not to use flares. This saves the railroad some expense, but more importantly, it might easily confuse drivers if a particular railroad used flares, contrary to custom. This coordination custom has the structure shown in Figure 8.3.

The other railroads besides the Duluth either receive 2 or 1 depending on whether or not they use flares. Other things being equal, they prefer not to use flares because it is costly to use them. Their payouts are not affected by the Duluth railroad, however, because they are indifferent as to what it does individually with regard to flare use.[41]

The Duluth, on the other hand, wants to do what the other railroads do. It has four rankings of preferences. It would most like not to use flares in a situation where others are not using them. All would save on the cost of using flares and the Duluth does not stand out as the lone defector (and so is not creating exposure to damages that may result because a driver was confused by the

Other Railroads

		Flares	No Flares
Duluth Railroad	Flares	2, 1	0, 2
	No Flares	1, 1	3, 2

Figure 8.3 Railroad Flare Use Custom

railroad's nonconforming behavior). The Duluth's next preference is to use flares when the other railroads are using them. When other railroads use flares, cars may drive faster near intersections, which makes not using flares relatively more dangerous; accordingly, it makes the Duluth more open to exposure.

The Duluth's third preference is not to use flares when the others are using them. And finally, it least prefers to use flares when the others are not. In each of these situations, the Duluth increases exposure to liability by doing an activity that will go against general expectations and so will increase risk. Of the two choices however, the railroad least prefers to incur the expense of flare use. Note the coordination effect; being careful is a function of coordinating with the behavior of others.

Duluth is an example of the second sort of potentially inefficient coordination norms, those in which the suboptimality may result from the fact that the coordination custom creates risks for third parties. These third parties are motorists who will be unlikely to be in a position to have an impact on whether railroads use flares or not. In situations involving injuries to third parties, the appropriate test to apply for purposes of determining welfare maximization is the Kaldor-Hicks Test, which asks whether, in principle, the cost of the risks borne by third-party highway users could be compensated out of the gains acheived by the conformers.[42] Prima facie, there is no reason to suppose that coordination customs will always, or even frequently, pass this test. Hence, there is no reason to think coordination customs of this sort will typically be efficient.

Courts, then, need to consider two issues to determine whether these customs are likely to be efficient: first, whether the class of injuries to third parties that results from these customs is relatively minor in comparison to the benefits obtained by the conformers due to the existence of the custom; second, if the first condition does not hold, whether the class of injured third parties are close-knit so as to be in a position to influence the behavior of the conformers to the coordination custom. Note that close-knittedness matters for coordination customs but for a different reason than discussed by Ellickson. Unlike PD customs, coordination customs may be efficient in communities that are not close-knit, that is, in those situations in which the Kaldor-Hicks criterion happens to be satisfied despite the lack of close-knitedness of the community.

The question, then, is: Which rule should courts apply? From the bare fact that a coordination custom is at issue, courts will not be able to determine which of the three rules to apply. The coordination custom could be strongly welfare-promoting, strongly welfare-decreasing, or anything in between, depending on the outcome of the Kaldor-Hicks Test.

III. Tortious Epistemic Customs

With epistemic customs, people conform in order to take a short-cut in terms of the amount of information they gather before making decisions. Rather than gather all the information necessary to make a fully informed decision, people often instead conform to convergent social practices of the communities in which they live. Though such actions are based on less information, they may nevertheless be rationally justified on balance if the savings achieved in the cost of gathering information are likely to be greater than the loss from making decisions with less investment in information. Customs are obvious candidates for rational epistemic conformity, as customs provide for repetitive behavior so that people can learn about the consequences that have flowed from similar sorts of actions in the past.

For example, the recently emergent norm of wearing bicycle helmets has an epistemically motivated maintenance structure. This is clearly a safety norm because one can easily imagine parents prescribing bicycle helmet use to their children, or bicycle shops displaying posters depicting the virtues of helmet use.[43] This norm is maintained by nonstrategic conforming acts, as the payoffs helmet wearers receive will be unaffected by whether others are also wearing helmets (except, perhaps, in the unlikely circumstance of a head-on collision; and then, perversely, the nonconformity of others might actually turn out to be a good thing for the narrowly rational helmet wearer). Rather, people plausibly are seen to conform out of a sense that, by doing so, they are taking advantage of emerging social knowledge to the effect that the bother and expense of helmet use is merited by the increased personal safety produced by such use.

The general idea that one might conform to prevailing social practices in order to economize on search costs has its roots in the rule utilitarianism of John Stuart Mill, as discussed in Chapter Three.[44] The idea has been endorsed by leading economists of both the Chicago and Austrian schools.[45]

Some epistemic customs involve no material risk of harm to others and so are of no direct interest to tort law. This is true of wearing bicycle helmets, which serves the interests of the bicyclists themselves without material third-party effects. Other epistemic customs create risks of injury mainly for parties not directly involved in the practice. This is true, for example, of customs in the medical profession, which are maintained by doctors' conformity to medical procedures that are prevalent in their community. Under such practices, the patients of the conforming doctors are put at risk.[46] Yet other epistemic customs create risks for participants in the practice and third parties as well. For example, use of cellular phones in automobiles is becoming a customary social practice despite some indication of increased hazard of auto accidents, which pose a threat to all.[47]

The sort of situation in which epistemic conformity has the most obvious appeal is where complex or arcane factual elements would need to be much better understood before a fully informed decision would be possible. Tort suits involving industry standards are often clear examples of complex conformity motivated by the concern to economize on the cost of information. In Sledd v. Washington Metropolitan Area Transit Authority, for instance, the plaintiff charged the Washington, D.C., metro system with negligence for having an unsafe train platform.[48] The plaintiff was injured when her foot became stuck between the platform and the train. Plaintiff argued that the distance between the train and the platform was too great. Defendant pleaded conformity to design custom as a defense. This is an epistemic custom because the conformity is best understood in nonstrategic terms. Agents conform to save on the costs of determining on their own the optimal sort of platform to build. The practice is not strategic, as the other conformers do not care if the D.C. Metro conforms to the custom or not.

Note that because agents want to conform to epistemic customs, sanctions are not needed for the maintenance of such customs. This is important to keep in mind because as already noted many theorists consider sanctions to be at the heart of social norms and customs. Sanctions, in turn, are an important element in the efficiency account of norms. Ellickson argues that social norms will be efficient when they are the product of close-knit groups.[49] As we have seen, sanctions play a crucial role in Ellickson's argument. The close-knitedness of groups allows people to credibly threaten sanctions against noncooperators.[50]

Epistemic customs raise the issue of whether or not social norms and customs might be efficient, despite being maintainable in a sanction-free environment.[51] It would appear that epistemic customs may sometimes be efficient as judged by the Pareto criterion. Pareto efficiency is the test by which an action is deemed efficient if at least one person is made better off by it and no one is made worse off.[52] A simple example of an individual conforming to an epistemic practice would appear to satisfy this criterion: I conform to a prevalent social practice in the belief that it is more sensible to do what others are doing than to figure out on my own what the best choice is. This is true, for example, of the norm of wearing bicycle helmets. If helmet use has become a norm among a particular social group I admire and whose judgment I generally respect, I may simply begin wearing a helmet myself, rather than expend the effort to research whether doing so is, in fact, cost-justified. I benefit from the epistemic conformity, and no one loses, thus satisfying the Pareto criterion. A practice maintained by a set of such acts might plausibly be seen as efficient.

With SD practices, people will free ride when they think they can get away with it. When they do, inefficient norms will result. But people conform to epistemic customs because it is in their direct interest to do so, and accordingly they have no desire to free ride. Hence, were an epistemic custom efficient in the first place, there is no reason to suppose it would degenerate as a result of the free-rider problem. Nor is there a danger of getting locked into suboptimal coordination equilibria, a problem that may arise with coordination customs, as discussed in Section II. If one wishes to act differently from the prevailing epistemic custom, one may simply do so; one must drive on the same side of the road as others (a coordination custom), but one can wear a bicycle helmet, or not, and others will be indifferent.

Given that epistemic customs may clearly be efficient and given that they are not susceptable to the pitfalls of sanction-driven customs or coordination customs, there would appear to be good reason for courts to apply the per se rule to insulate these customs. In fact, however, things are not so simple. Despite examples such as that of wearing bicycle helmets, there is clear and compelling evidence that epistemic customs may sometimes be inefficient.

There are two important classes of situations in which epistemic customs may be inefficient. The first is where the custom is efficient for the participants in the custom but where third parties are adversely affected by the custom and the losses to these parties are not compensated by the gains to the participants. Such an epistemic custom would fail to pass the test of Kaldor-Hicks efficiency. The second is where the practice that is conformed to happens to be less welfare-producing than another possible practice, but no one knows it as each adherent fails to gather enough information to make an independent determination.

Consider the following example of the first sort of potential inefficiency. If buying German automobiles had become a norm among a particular social group whose judgment I generally respect, I may simply "buy German" myself rather than expending the effort to read *Consumer Reports* or other comparable sources of information. I benefit from the conformity, and none of the other conformers loses, so, from the perspective of this group, the Pareto criterion is satisfied. But if American automobile dealers, manufacturers, and workers lose out in the process, then the custom is not Pareto efficient, although it may still turn out to be Kaldor-Hicks efficient.

As an example of the second manner in which epistemic customs may be inefficient, consider the medical custom of performing tonsillectomies, which has the structure shown in Figure 8.4.

A doctor might reasonably choose to perform tonsillectomies given that the prevailing medical custom in the doctor's professional community is to perform tonsillectomies.[53] Note that the payoffs in such a situation are not strategic; other doctors do not do better or worse *for their patients* depending on the choice made

Other Doctors

		Tonsillectomies	No Tonsillectomies
Doctor A	Tonsillectomies	3, 2	0, 1
	No Tonsillectomies	1, 2	2, 1

Figure 8.4 The Tonsillectomy Game

by doctor A.[54] But the *expected* utilities for A's patients are, however, affected by what other doctors do. If they generally perform tonsillectomies, then A expects that her patients will fare better by having a tonsillectomy (northwest cell), and if other doctors do not perform tonsillectomies, then A expects that her patients will do better by not having the procedure (southeast cell).[55]

This example highlights a deeply troubling feature of epistemic medical customs, namely that, though they may be maintained by the conduct of doctors who justifiably believe that conforming to them will maximize expected utility, the resulting custom may nevertheless be less welfare-enhancing than an alternative. Note further that the existence of close-knit groups might perversely facilitate a sanctioning regime that worked to perpetuate such inefficient practices. With epistemic customs, then, not only are close-knit communities not required for efficiency, but they may also be an impediment.

Evidence strongly suggests that tonsillectomies may not be a health-justified practice.[56] Yet, it seems clear that in the model whereby epistemic customs are maintained by acts justifiably believed to maximize expected utility, such customs may be maintained for significant periods of time.[57] While the potential for suboptimality will be present for all epistemic customs, the epistemic customs of doctors are nevertheless the most striking examples because these are typically contexts in which the custom represents the combined efforts by the conformers to take the utmost care. Despite these sometimes heroic efforts, the resulting customary practices may nevertheless fail to be welfare-maximizing.

In sum, then, we see that even though epistemic customs may not be susceptable to all of the suboptimality problems of the other types of custom, they are nevertheless susceptible to two problems of this sort. The final question to address is: What rule of custom makes sense given all the features of epistemic customs just considered?

Consider first the rule that best addresses the fact that whole groups may conform to customs that are in reality suboptimal due to the incorrect belief that the custom is optimal. On first appraisal, one would expect this fact to argue strongly in favor of the evidentiary rule over the per se rule. The per se rule would insulate the rule from change despite the fact that a court might think the group of conformers was wrong such that a better custom was possible. The evidentiary rule would allow the jury to give deference to the custom while allowing it to find liability and thereby incentivize a shift toward an alternative if it deemed the current practice suboptimal.

The per se rule may be appropriate, however, when the conformers have "superior epistemic warrant" for their view regarding the welfare-enhancing properties of the epistemic custom. No one may know with certainty at a particular moment in history whether medical procedure A is better than medical procedure B, but doctors may nevertheless be better situated than anyone else – courts included – to make educated guesses. From an epistemic perspective, their guesses may be more warranted.

If doctors have difficulties in determining welfare-maximizing customs, how are courts going to be in any better position to do so? In fact, one would expect courts to be in a worse position. Epistemic customs, then, raise the issue of institutional competence of the courts to make determinations regarding the welfare-producing propensities of particular customs.[58] The issue of institutional competence is sometimes raised in comparing the courts versus other branches of government.[59] But here the issue emerges in comparing the relative competence of informal, social processes of professionals versus the competence of formal, legal processes.[60]

The determination of who has superior epistemic warrant should properly be taken into account by courts in applying a rule to epistemic customs. The per se rule naturally suggests itself in situations in which a conforming group such as doctors or other professionals have a superior epistemic warrant in comparison to courts, as this rule would insulate the custom from changes that cannot be warranted as welfare-enhancing. When the court is in as good of a position as the conformers to make an educated guess regarding efficiency, however, then the evidentiary rule may be justified because it allows courts to take account of the conformers' combined judgment regarding efficiency, but the court also maintains the option to substitute its judgment for that of the conformers. Note that doctrine draws the line with professionals versus nonprofessionals, but that the logic of the analysis draws the line at those with superior epistemic warrant. In principle, any group of conformers could argue that their appraisal of the welfare-enhancing value of one custom over another has superior epistemic warrant and therefore deserves the protective status afforded by the per se rule.

Courts may also compare the professional customs of various local communities. A court may then criticize one group's customs on the basis of another group's customs. In other words, courts may implicitly hold that one group has superior epistemic warrant to another group. In the past, courts applied the "locality rule." Under this rule, the actions of doctors would be judged by a local standard; that is, courts would ask whether the particular action conformed to the local medical custom when considering the question of negligence. Modern courts have, for the most part, however, done away with the locality rule; instead, they require doctors to conform to national medical practices in order to come within the safe harbor of the per se rule.

Recall that two types of suboptimality situations may arise with epistemic customs. The second type of situation may arise with regard to third parties injured by the custom. The example involving the Washington, D.C., metro has this structure. The various mass transit authorities conform to a complex design custom to economize on information costs. If they fail to maintain an optimal practice, third-party users of the metro system will suffer. In principle, these third-party potential victims will be in a better position when they are close-knit, because they will be able to use sanctions to incentivize the conformers to take due precautions. The problem, however, is that it is not enough for the third parties to be close-knit with one another; they must be close-knit with the conformers as well. This will be a difficult criterion to meet in the context of the present example because the various metro systems are spread out geographically, not only across the United States but also across the world. In other situations, however, third parties will be close-knit with the group of conformers. In these circumstances, the potential victims should be able to incentivize the conformers to internalize the risks.

Conclusion

Chapter Two developed a tripartite account of the rational structure of custom. Chapters Three, Four and Five demonstrated the relevance of this account for moral and political theory, both under the Hobbesian motivational assumption and the more normatively expansive Humean motivational assumption. In the chapter, we saw that the tripartite account also has relevance in tort law as conformity, or lack of conformity, to all these types of custom may produce the sorts of injuries that are the subject matter of tort. We saw that whether customs may be maintained in a safe and efficient manner will depend on a number of features. The broad lesson is that courts will need to pay greater attention to these features of the various types of customs if courts are to best promote welfare. The next chapter looks in greater detail at the tasks faced by courts.

9

Regulating the Rule of Custom to Create Safe Social Norms

What usually is done may be *evidence* of what ought to be done, but what ought to be done is fixed by a standard of reasonable prudence, whether it usually is complied with or not.[1]

Oliver Wendell Holmes

Introduction

In Chapter Seven, we saw that while courts nominally consider the evidentiary rule as the proper rule of custom in negligence cases, their actual treatment of customs is more complex. Courts sometimes give customs greater deference (by means of the per se rule) and other times give custom no deference (by means of the no-priority rule). The analysis in Chapter Eight demonstrated that each of the three types of rational custom has distinctive welfare-enhancing capabilities. Factors – such as whether the incidence of injury falls on conformers or third parties, whether these groups are close-knit, whether the conformer has superior epistemic warrant, whether the Kaldor-Hicks Test favors conformers, and whether an optimizing alternative practice is available – matter differentially depending on the type of custom at issue.

In this chapter, I will argue that in order to account adequately for the structured complexity of the relevant social phenomena, it will be necessary for courts to implement a more fine-grained rational actor account than is suggested by those game-theoretic accounts that focus on the Prisoner's Dilemma or collective action problem. In terms of the general analysis, thirty-seven distinct modalities of rational custom will be identified. In particular, the tripartite model of rational custom will be used to explicate the role of custom in the leading cases of Behymer and *Hooper*. Looking closely at these cases calls into doubt the basic justification of the dominance accorded to the evidentiary rule by Holmes in Behymer and Hand in *The T. J. Hooper*. After all, only eight of the thirty-seven applications of the rule of custom call for the evidentiary rule. The per se rule is preferable for nineteen of the situations; and the no-priority rule, for ten of the situations.

I. Judicial Determination of a Rule of Custom: Thirty-Seven Subtypes of Rational Custom

An implication of the fact that the rational structure of customs is complex is that courts must apply a more fine-grained approach to their application of the rule of custom in tort cases than has occurred in the past if courts are to take best advantage of the welfare-enhancing capabilities of customs. It will be useful to organize the factors that courts should consider into a graph for use by courts that deal with parties pleading custom in tort cases. By providing a graphical display of the set of relevant factors, it is hoped that courts will be more self-aware and purposeful when choosing from among the competing rules of custom. See Figure 9.1.

The chart in Figure 9.1 is meant to be a tool for welfare-maximizing courts when they deal with a litigant who seeks to introduce the fact of conformity or lack of conformity to a custom as having probative value regarding the issue of negligence. To use the chart, a court must first identify which of the three types of custom is at issue: a sanction-driven custom (column A, rows 1–10), a coordination custom (column B, rows 11–25), or an epistemic custom (column C, rows 26–37). This choice is made by determining whether conformity is due to the desire to avoid sanctions, the desire to reap a coordination benefit, or the desire to economize on the cost of information. After a court has determined which sort of custom it is dealing with, it can then apply the appropriate set of "Welfare-Maximization Markers" from among the total set represented in columns D–N of the chart, in order to arrive at an applicable rule of custom (columns R–U).

A. Ten Subtypes of Sanction-Driven Customs Rationalize Four Distinct Rules of Custom

After a court has determined that it is dealing with a sanction-driven custom, its focus will be restricted to rows 1–10 on the chart. Rows 1 and 2 capture the situation where the sanction-driven custom only produces injuries to the conformers themselves (column D). When this is the case, the most important efficiency consideration is whether the group is close-knit. When the group is close-knit (row 1, column F) then the applicable rule of custom is the per se rule (column R), as close-knitedness should allow this group to solve its strategic problem in order to produce an efficient outcome. However, if the conformers are not close-knit (row 2, column G) and there is no reason to think they would solve their problem, then the applicable rule of custom is the no-priority rule (row 2, column U) because it properly affords conformity no privileged status.[2]

	Types of Custom			Incidence of Injury		Welfare Maximization Markers									Rules of Custom			
	Collective Action Customs	Coordination Customs	Epistemic Customs			Close-Knittedness				Conformer has Superior Epistemic Warrant		Kalder-Hicks Test Favors Conformers			Per Se Rule	Evidentiary Rule		No-Priority Rule
				Conformers	Third Parties	Conformers		Third Parties								Regular	Presumption Shifting Rule	
						Yes	No	Yes	No	Yes	No	Yes	Uncertain	No				
	A	B	C	D	E	F	G	H	I	J	K	L	M	N	R	S	T	U
1	X			X		X									X			
2	X			X	X		X	X										X
3	X			X	X	X	X								X			
4	X			X	X	X			X						X			
5	X			X	X	X			X			X			X	X	X	
6	X			X	X	X		X	X				X	X				X
7	X			X	X		X	X				X						
8	X			X	X		X	X	X			X	X			X	X	
9	X			X	X		X	X						X				X
10	X			X	X		X	X	X						X			
11		X		X	X		X					X						
12		X		X	X	X	X								X			
13		X		X		X	X		X				X					
14		X		X	X	X	X	X					X			X	X	X
15		X		X	X	X		X				X			X			
16		X		X	X	X	X	X	X				X		X			
17		X		X	X	X	X	X	X					X	X			
18		X			X	X		X	X			X			X	X	X	X
19		X			X	X	X	X	X						X			
20		X			X	X	X	X	X					X	X			
21		X			X	X	X	X	X				X					
22		X			X	X	X	X	X									X
23		X			X	X	X		X						X	X	X	
24		X			X		X		X									
25		X																X
26			X	X		X	X				X	X			X	X	X	
27			X	X			X				X		X		X			
28			X	X		X	X				X		X					
29			X	X		X	X				X			X	X			X
30			X	X	X	X		X			X	X			X	X	X	
31			X	X	X	X		X			X		X		X			
32			X	X	X	X		X			X		X					
33			X	X	X	X	X		X	X			X	X				X
34			X	X	X	X	X		X	X			X		X	X	X	
35			X	X	X	X	X		X	X			X		X			
36			X	X	X	X			X	X			X		X			
37			X	X	X	X			X	X			X		X			
															19	8	8	10

Figure 9.1 Judicial Determination of a Rule of Custom by Application of Welfare-Maximization Markers to Various Types of Custom

200

Rows 3–10 represent sanction-driven customs in which the risks of injury fall on third-party nonconformers to the custom (either as well as, or in addition to, injuries to the conformers). The eight different possible outcomes depend on whether the conformers or third parties are close-knit and on how the Kaldor-Hicks Test applies to the situation,[3] given the various costs and benefits of these groups.

When the conformers and the third parties are close-knit (row 3, columns F, H), the custom should be efficient because the third parties should be able to use various sanctioning devices to incentivize the conformers into conforming with optimal practices. Accordingly, the per se rule will be appropriate (row 3, column R). When the conformers are close-knit and the third parties are not (row 4, columns F, I), however, we should not expect the custom to be efficient. But we cannot necessarily think it inefficient either. What we know is that the conformers are not forced to internalize the costs of their conformity. But this does not gainsay the possibility that the overall benefit to the conformers might win out in a Kaldor-Hicks Test over the losses to the third parties. Consequently, a welfare-maximizing court will need to perform a Kaldor-Hicks Test.

After performing the test, if a court thinks that the practice is such that the benefits to conformers outweigh the costs to third parties (row 4, column L), it will be inclined to support the custom by means of the per se rule (row 4, column R). Alternatively, because of the need to perform a Kaldor-Hicks Test, a court might feel that there is a significant fact issue regarding a balancing of risks and benefits and so let the issue of the merits of the custom go to a jury, on the theory that twelve heads are better than one.[4] Accordingly, the court will apply the evidentiary rule or the presumption-shifting rule (row 5, columns S, T). If a court thought, however, that the benefits to conformers clearly did not outweigh the costs to third parties, the court might utilize the no-priority rule (row 6, column U) in order to avoid supporting the custom.

The last four situations involving sanction-driven customs are ones in which the conformers are themselves not close-knit (rows 7–10, column G). Other things equal, we should expect customs maintained in this type of strategic situation to be inefficient as the custom represents a failure by the conformers to solve their strategic problem. Surprisingly, however, the efficiency of the practice may turn on whether the third parties are close-knit. If third parties are close-knit (rows 7–9, column H), they may be able to pressure the conformers into customs that serve the interests of the third parties.

The best rule of custom will depend on an application of the Kaldor-Hicks Test. If the Kaldor-Hicks Test favors the conformers, the court will not lend support to the practice, and so the no-priority rule will be appropriate (row 7, column U). But if the Kaldor-Hicks Test favors the third parties, a court will support the custom with the per se rule (row 9, column R). If the court is uncertain as to the results of the Kaldor-Hicks Test, however, it will let the issue go to the jury (row 8, columns S, T). The last situation is where neither the conformers nor the third parties are close-knit (row 10, column G, I). Here, there is no reason to treat the custom specially because the lack of close-knitedness means that conformers will not be incentivized to internalize costs. Accordingly, the no-priority rule is appropriate (row 10, column U).

B. Fifteen Subtypes of Coordination Customs Rationalize Four Distinct Rules of Custom

Courts will be able to identify coordination customs by the feature that participants in the practice conform because of the conformity of others and not because of the sanctions of others. Courts should next consider incidence of injury, that is, which group or groups suffer injuries under the custom. If only the conformers suffer injuries (rows 11–14, column D), then the next question is whether the group is close-knit. If it is (row 11, column F), then a court can expect the group's coordination custom to be efficient. This will be true because the close-knitedness will promote a cost-justified level of injuries within the group. Accordingly, a court will be justified in choosing the per se rule (row 11, column R) as there are grounds for believing that the practice is welfare promoting and no distinct grounds for supposing that it is not.

When the conformers are not close-knit (rows 12–14), then a court will need to take account of the possibility that the injuries to the conformers outweigh the benefits to the conformers. Because the group is not close-knit, the incidence of injuries will be disconnected from the attainment of coordination benefits from the custom, as each participant conforms as a result of the coordination benefits this participant receives and with disregard for the risks created for others. It will be necessary to perform a Kaldor-Hicks Test to compare the benefits against the costs. Usually, when this test is applied to groups, the group of beneficiaries and the group of victims are distinct groups. Here, however, the membership of the groups will be significantly overlapping.[5]

Courts will choose an appropriate rule of custom depending on their assessments of how the Kaldor-Hicks Test comes out. If a court determines that the benefits clearly outweigh the costs (row 12, column L), it will opt for the per se rule, and if it determines that the costs clearly outweigh the benefits (row 14, column N), then it will opt for the no-priority rule. If the court is uncertain, however, as to whether the costs outweigh the benefits (row 13, column M), it may once again give the issue to the jury to decide (row 13, columns S, T).

In the next set of cases, the incidence of injuries is shared by both the conformers and third parties (rows 15–18, columns D, E). When both groups are close-knit (row 15, columns F, H), circumstances most favorable to the per se rule obtain. Because both groups are close-knit, only those risks that are cost-justified should be present (row 15, column R). When either or both of the groups are not close-knit, however, then a court will need to consider whether the losses or the gains are greater, that is, apply the Kaldor-Hicks Test. Courts will want to take account of the benefits to the conformers, on the one hand, and the losses to both the conformers and third parties combined, on the other hand. When the Kaldor-Hicks Test appears to strongly favor conformers (row 16, column L), the per se rule will be justified (row 16, column R), and when the test strongly favors third parties (row 18, column N), the no-priority rule will be justified (row 18, column U). And when the test bears an uncertain result (row 17, column M), a court may once again leave the issue for a jury to decide (row 17, columns S, T).

The last category of coordination customs are those in which the incidence of injuries falls solely on third parties (rows 19–22, column E). Under these conditions, it may matter whether the group of conformers are close-knit. If both the conformers are close-knit and the third parties are close-knit (row 19, columns F, H), then the third parties may have a chance of incentiving the conformers to internalize the cost of injuries such that the level of risk to third parties that results will be cost-justified, and accordingly the per se rule will be applicable (row 19, column R).

If the conformers are not close-knit but the third parties are (row 20–22, columns G, H), then the third parties may incentivize conformers not to take part in the practice or to take part in a manner that is less injurious to third parties. The resulting custom may have a lower level of injuries to third parties than would be cost-justified. A Kaldor-Hicks Test will be needed to determine if the benefits to the third parties from avoiding injuries outweigh the costs to the conformers from not being able to follow the custom that would otherwise be preferable. If the test favors supporting the custom (third-party benefits outweigh conformers' costs), the per se rule will be justified (row 20, column R). If the test favors rejecting the custom because the benefits to third parties do not outweigh the losses to the conformers, then the no-priority rule is appropriate (row 21, column U). But if the test results are uncertain, the issue is best left to a jury (row 22, column S, T).

Finally, if both the conformers and the third parties are not close-knit (rows 23–25, columns G, I), a court will have no reason to think the level of injuries is optimal. Once again, it will choose a rule of custom depending on whether the Kaldor-Hicks Test favors supporting the custom (row 23, column R), rejecting the custom (row 24, column U), or giving an indeterminate answer (row 25, columns S, T).

C. Twelve Subtypes of Epistemic Customs Rationalize Four Distinct Rules of Custom

Welfare-maximizing courts will be able to pick out epistemic customs from the fact that the dominant motivation for conformity is to economize on search costs. Just as with the two strategic types of custom, actors pay attention to what others are doing, but they do so for the nonstrategic reason that they take others' conformity as providing them with information as to the wisdom of their own conformity.

Injuries are not inherent to the structure of epistemic customs. Nevertheless, in the process of conforming to these customs, people may be injured. Courts will naturally worry least about injuries that befall the conformers themselves as a result of their own actions, as these are most likely to be internalized into the cost structure of the individual conformer. Injuries that befall either second-party conformers or third-party nonconformers are more problematic.

The first item to consider on the chart's welfare-maximization menu bar is on whom the incidence of injury falls. When injuries fall solely on other conformers (rows 26–29, column D), the group will be most likely to have efficient practices when it is close-knit (row 26, column F) because then members will be able to incentivize one another to internalize the costs of injuries to other conformers by means of the multitentacled sanctioning power close-knitedness provides. Thus, the per se rule is appropriate (row 26, column R). When injuries fall on conformers and the group is not close-knit (rows 27–29, column G), there should be no expectation that the custom is efficient, however. If the benefits of conformity clearly outweigh the costs (row 27, column L), a welfare-maximizing court will apply the per se rule so as to protect the practice (row 27, column R). But if a court is clearly convinced of the opposite (row 29, column N), it would apply the no-priority rule (row 29, column U). Perhaps more often than not, however, judges will be uncertain and will defer to a jury, in which case either the evidentiary rule or the presumption-shifting rule will be appropriate (row 28, columns S, T).

Next are those coordination customs in which both conformers and third parties suffer injuries (rows 30–33, Columns D, E). When the third-party victims are close-knit (row 30, column H), they should be able to use informal sanctioning powers to incentivize the conformers to internalize the cost of the injuries. Accordingly, the per se rule will be appropriate (row 30, column R). When the third parties are not close-knit, however, the choice of rule will turn on the results of a Kaldor-Hicks Test comparing benefits to conformers versus costs both to third parties and conformers. Once again, the appropriate rule will turn on whether the judge thinks the test goes strongly toward either one side of the equation or the other (row 31, column L or row 33, column N), or whether instead there is uncertainty best resolved by a jury (row 32, column M).

As noted earlier, the customs of professionals are accorded the main exception to the dominant evidentiary rule. We can make sense of this exception in terms of the superior epistemic status that professionals may possess. It is often difficult to know which of a number of choices will best promote social welfare. Inevitably, courts must engage in a guessing game, although these guesses will be more or less well grounded, depending on the amount of effort courts and the parties expend to produce and evaluate the available information.[6] Nevertheless, courts may see themselves as in at least as good of a position as the litigants to evaluate the welfare-producing capabilities of various practices.[7] Because courts see themselves in as good of a position as the parties to determine if a custom is optimal, they employ the rule that makes most sense depending on their evaluation of whether a more optimal rule is feasible. But with the customs of professionals, particularly doctors, courts are inclined to show deference, out of respect for the relative disparity in their degrees of epistemic warrant.

Courts have recognized the privileged epistemic status of professional customs as grounds for extending the per se rule to the custom. The question then is how does the consideration weigh against the other welfare-maximization markers applicable to epistemic customs that were just considered. The relevant cases are represented in rows 28–29 and 32–33, which are cases in which courts would otherwise not choose the per se rule.[8]

The efficiency markers that are most relevant are "close-knitedness" and the Kaldor-Hicks Test. When a group lacks superior epistemic status, the fact that it is close-knit may hurt it, as the group will be less exposed to superior practices that it might otherwise consider adopting.[9] If the group is in an epistemically superior position, however, the fact that the group is close-knit may allow it to more effectively maintain the practice while continuously monitoring to ensure that the practice continues to be what, in their opinion, is the best practice.[10]

With regard to the Kaldor-Hicks Test (columns L–N), note the peculiar situation that obtains for professionals bound by fiduciary duties to their patients or clients. The professionals will tend to act in ways that promote the injured parties' interests, due to their fiduciary obligations. Thus, there will not be an issue of balancing the gains to conformers versus losses to injured parties as has been the case with the earlier applications of the Kaldor-Hicks Test. What matters is not a balancing of competing interests, but a judgment regarding which type of action is in fact the welfare-maximizing one. Thus, we are back to the question of superior epistemic warrant. Accordingly, the per se rule may be the appropriate choice for the situations represented in rows 34–37 (which are identical to rows 28–29, 32–33, respectively, except that the conformers have superior epistemic status).

II. Rational Reinterpretation of *The T. J. Hooper*

Of the thirty-seven modalities of rational customs, the per se rule is preferable in nineteen modalities, the evidentiary rule in eight modalities, and the no-priority rule in ten modalities. Note that the evidentiary rule is not the best choice in a majority of these situations. This fact should make courts call into question the predominance of the evidentiary rule. Instead of reflexively applying the evidentiary rule when custom is pleaded, courts must instead look more closely at the rational structure of the custom. As demonstrative examples of how courts may better promote efficiency when applying the rule of custom, the rational choice account of norms and customs developed in Section I will be applied to *The T. J. Hooper* and Behymer in the final two sections.

In Behymer, there were two overlapping customs; in *The T. J. Hooper*, there is debate over whether there even was a custom. This is a striking fact given that this is the case that famously established the modern rule of custom in tort. Learned Hand contends that there was not: "But here there was no custom at all as to receiving sets; some had them, some did not; the most that can be urged is that they had not yet become general."[11]

Richard Posner argues that there was a custom: "It *was* customary for coastal tugboats to be equipped with radios; 90 percent of such boats were equipped with them, and one of the tugboats involved in the case had a radio – it just was not in working order."[12] Posner claims that there is a discrepancy between the lower court opinion and Hand's opinion regarding the existence of a custom, and that the lower court got it right. Posner claims that Hand was confused.[13] There is, however, a better explanation than the one provided by Posner; Hand had a definite purpose in mind in controverting the finding of the lower court regarding the presence of custom, which was to use the case to promote the evidentiary rule. Hand had the flexibility to do so because the social situation at issue, radio use among ocean-going tugs along the Atlantic coast, was in the gray area between custom and noncustom.[14]

The lower court had implicitly supported the per se rule by finding that the defendant was negligent for not having done what many others in its line of commerce were doing. In other words, the lower court had accepted conformity to custom as a per se defense to negligence but found that, on the facts, defendant could not establish this defense as it had failed to conform. In applying the per se rule, the lower court was following a respectable line of Second Circuit authority on the subject.[15] In contrast, by allowing that there may have been a custom, Hand could then go on to make the point that despite the existence of a custom, the defendant could still be negligent, as a whole industry may lag behind in the provision of due care. As result of this fact, the evidentiary rule is preferable to the per se rule. Hand explicitly attacked the per se rule and promoted the evidentiary rule by playing up the fact that a whole industry may lag behind in the provision of due care so that it can never be enough to look to a particular agent's conformity to industry custom.[16] We see, then, that Hand used this case as an opportunity to bring the Second Circuit in line with Holmes' decision in Behymer.[17]

The Second Circuit's handiwork is best understood by examining the rational structure of the underlying situation in *The T. J. Hooper*. When embarking on such an analysis, the first question to ask is whether the practice has a naturally sanction-driven maintenance structure, or a completely voluntary maintenance structure. In other words, is the practice one that the conformers, other things equal, want to conform to, or is it the sort of practice in which people only conform out of fear of sanctions? If the former, the next question is whether voluntary conformity is for coordinational or epistemic reasons.

The first question amounts to asking whether a tugboat would want to free ride on the practice of other tugs with respect to the use of radios. Consider first the scenario in which either there is no custom or the custom in place is that tugs are not outfitted with radios. In either of these situations, is there a reason why a particular tugboat would want to defect from the custom? One plausible answer is that a tugboat would want to be outfitted with a radio in order to be able to offer its customers better, safer service than competing tug companies. This is a Prisoner's Dilemma because, if all the tugboats could coordinate on not having a radio, they would all be better off. But there will be a plausible incentive to defect from this practice to be the one tug operator who is able to offer safer service at little expense.

Now consider if the custom is to have radios. Would there be reason to wish to defect from the practice? One reason to do so would be to economize on the cost of doing business. Such a possibility might plausibly obtain if, due to general compliance to the custom, potential customers naturally assumed that, as such safety precautions were standard, this tug offered them as well. Business plans such as this may well backfire, however. The other tugs benefit from promoting a better, safer service at a very inexpensive cost, while this business could quickly suffer if it developed a reputation as a business that cuts corners. Given the inexpensive cost of radios, it seems highly unlikely that a tug would choose a business strategy whereby it failed to equip itself with a radio in order to economize, in an environment in which other tugs were equipped with radios.[18] Installing and using radios appears, then, as if it was probably the dominant choice.

Notice that, because there is a natural incentive to do the type of action that in conglomeration will constitute a non-negligent custom, there is no need for a legal rule to create incentives to nudge the custom in a safer direction. Accordingly, even if the per se rule of custom were in place, there would be no fear that the law would function so as to maintain a safe harbor in which an inefficient custom would be protected from change. This can be seen by supposing the per se rule is in effect such that a tug will not be liable for injury due to lack of a radio if other tugs also did not have radios. This would not cause a tug to refrain from installing a radio, for as mentioned above, a tug might nevertheless want to offer the radio as a safety feature that the other tugs are not offering.

In *The T. J. Hooper*, then, the lag in the practice whereby some – but by no means all – tugs had radios, is better explained by the time it takes for social change to come about. It is certain that over time nearly all the tugs would have been retrofitted with radio receivers even if the decision in *The T. J. Hooper* had not come along. It is not surprising that an industry might lag in the adoption of a safer, new technology. Change takes time; even in the field of health care where lives are at stake, such lags occur.[19]

Compare *Hooper* to Behymer. We saw in Section I that, in *Behymer*, the per se rule would allow an inadvertent safe harbor in which coordination customs that have dangerous effects on third parties could develop. The shift from the per se rule to the evidentiary rule was necessary to overcome a strategic situation in which once a suboptimal situation obtained, individual railroads that conformed enjoyed a safe harbor in the dangerous activity. By contrast, the tug owners in *The T. J. Hooper* had no use for a safe harbor in which tugs failed to equip themselves with radios. We see, then, that while *The T. J. Hooper* is often cited as a paradigm case whose facts regarding industry lags serve to justify the evidentiary rule, Behymer better illustrates the sort of problematic social situation in which the evidentiary rule was truly necessary, namely, one in which the strategic structure allowed for the maintenance of suboptimal customs. In other words, contrary to conventional wisdom, Behymer, not *Hooper*, is the leading case establishing the logic of the modern rule of custom in tort law.

III. *Texas & Pacific Railroad Co. v. Behymer:* The True Leading Case

Recall that in Behymer, the railroad workers participated in a dangerous practice which involved working atop a railroad car moving over uneven terrain under icy conditions. This railyard custom may plausibly be seen as having the same strategic structure as the dangerous custom of speeding in automobiles represented in Figure 8.1. If a worker wished to remain employed, this worker did not have the freedom to not participate in the dangerous practices, just as an individual driver cannot be free from a custom that allows speeding in automobiles. Judging by the behavior of other workers, the railroad would have been able to find a replacement willing to work under the dangerous conditions. In these circumstances, each employee who preferred to work in a safer work environment was adversely affected by the willingness of others to cooperate in the dangerous practice, and would have been better off if other workers had refused to participate.[20]

The railroad workers each face an n-person Prisoner's Dilemma. If the workers could band together, they may be able to collectively bargain with the railroad in order to bring about the safe practice as a concession without significantly lowering their compensation. But bringing about this cooperative result will be difficult because of the free-rider problem. This situation has the strategic structure shown in Figure 9.2.

Defection from the cooperative outcome, performing the dangerous activity, is the dominant strategy. If the other workers are willing to conform to the dangerous practice, then a particular worker will want to as well, so as not to be fired for substandard work performance. But if others refuse to perform

Other Workers

		Safe Practice	Dangerous Practice
	Safe Practice	3, 3	1, 4
Worker A			
	Dangerous Practice	4, 1	2, 2

Figure 9.2 The Worker's Custom in Texas & Pacific Railroad v. Behymer

the dangerous activity, a worker will nevertheless want the option of sometimes performing this activity in order to either be among those who keep their jobs or be among those who get newly hired due to their willingness to work under such conditions. Thus, regardless of the choice made by other workers, a particular worker will want the option of performing the dangerous practice when it is suitable, just as each of the drivers wants the option of speeding when it is suitable.[21] In terms of the matrix presented in Figure 9.2, the workers will end up in the southeast cell with each receiving her second least preferred outcome, instead of ending up in the northwest cell with each receiving her second most preferred outcome.

Given the strategic situation of the workers, consider how Holmes's decision promoting the evidentiary rule over the per se rule helped their position vis-à-vis the railroad. Note that the per se rule creates a safe harbor, which precludes injured workers from prevailing in a lawsuit. The fact that other railroads besides the Texas & Pacific are each individually conforming, such that the custom is maintained, will mean that any particular railroad may successfully invoke the custom as a defense to negligence. By contrast, the evidentiary rule favors the injured workers – as a dangerous custom such as the one at issue in Behymer would have gone to a jury where a victim might well have done better than under the per se rule, and could certainly have done no worse.

Under the evidentiary rule, courts allow the fact of conformity to custom (or deviation from it in the case of the offensive use of the rule) to be introduced as evidence that may go to a jury. But, the fact of conformity will not as a matter of law constitute a per se defense to negligence. Accordingly, the evidentiary rule does not provide a safe harbor that would allow for the maintenance of a dangerous coordination custom. The fact that other railroads are performing one practice rather than another will not have a strategic effect on whether a particular railroad should rationally do so as well. If some particular railroad does a dangerous act and an injury results, it knows that it will not win on summary judgment due simply to its conformity to industry custom, but may instead have its actions evaluated by a jury. The possibility that the case may

Other Railroads

		Dangerous Practice	Safe Practice
	Dangerous Practice	2, 2	0, 1
Texas & Pacific R.R.	Safe Practice	1, 2	1, 1

Figure 9.3 The Railroads' Custom in Texas & Pacific Railroad v. Behymer

go to a jury if an injury occurs to one of its workers is an unwelcome prospect for any firm in any industry.[22]

To better understand the importance of the shift from the per se rule to the evidentiary rule, it will be helpful to model the manner by which the strategic relationship between the parties changes depending on the legal rule in place. What will be seen is that the legal rule affects the strategic structure of the underlying situation, which in turn might be expected to affect the custom that results. In particular, the per se rule creates ripe conditions for the emergence and maintenance of a coordination custom, whereas the evidentiary rule encourages an epistemic custom.

With coordination customs, such as driving on the right or left side of the road, one wants to do what others are doing as there is a positive coordination effect in coordinating with others. Under the per se rule, a railroad wants to have its employees working on top of icy railroad cars if other railroads are, and not if other railroads are not. This is like the example of driving on the right or left-hand side of the road; each wants to do what others are doing. The previous matrix represented the strategic structure among the railroad workers. Now consider the strategic structure of the railroads themselves.

If other railroads are pursuing the dangerous practice, then the Texas and Pacific Railroad prefers to do the same (northwest quadrant) because each railroad has more freedom to move its railroad cars about as it pleases. But if other railroads are following the safe practice, then the Texas & Pacific Railroad prefers to do the same (southeast quadrant). This is true because, if other railroads are performing the safe practice, then for a particular railroad to perform the dangerous practice is to expose itself to serious risk of liability because it will stand out from the other railroads. In contrast to the example of driving on the right or left side of the road, however, the railroads are not neutral between the dangerous and safe cooperative outcomes; their payoffs are greater under the dangerous practice.

Notice that, because it is in the interest of each to do what others are currently doing, whichever of the two practices happens to prevail initially will be self-maintaining. In other words, even if all the railroads would prefer to follow the dangerous practice, if the safe practice is in place, it will be in the interest of each particular railroad on each particular occasion to conform to the safe practice.

An implication of this effect is that if a suboptimal practice somehow becomes instantiated, it will be self-perpetuating.[23] This will be true despite the fact that if all the railroads could coordinate, they would all be better off switching to the dangerous practice. In such a circumstance, the railroads face a collective action problem of their own as each of the railroads would do better if they were all performing the dangerous practice, but each acting alone will always choose to conform to the safe practice. Therefore, the safe practice will be perpetuated. This collective action problem may be difficult to solve because there will be significant transaction costs involved in organizing a wholesale change in a practice of this sort among a group of railroads (not to mention antitrust concerns). Practically speaking, then, the railroads may get stuck in the suboptimal practice.

In fact, however, the railroads in Behymer were not locked into a suboptimal practice. Instead, the railroads had a custom in place that was efficient for them but put their employees at great risk. Given that the per se rule would perpetuate the dangerous practice once it existed, Holmes had reason to support the evidentiary rule because it would incentivize railroads to reevaluate the practice of putting employees in dangerous situations. Holmes's decision in Behymer may, therefore, plausibly be seen as evincing an intuitive appreciation of the different possible structures of customs and, in particular, the manner in which coordination customs may provide a safe harbor for dangerous activity when they are allowed to flourish under the per se rule.

Note that the custom of the railroads that will emerge under the evidentiary rule will be nonstrategic.[24] Just because the custom is nonstrategic, however, does not mean that a particular railroad will not have a reason to conform to the custom; it is just that the reason for doing so will be nonstrategic. A railroad may well conform to the customary practice for epistemic reasons. The fact that the other railroads do not allow their employees to work under dangerous conditions might be taken as evidence that this course of action is also preferable for the Texas & Pacific Railroad. In other words, instead of undertaking a detailed cost–benefit analysis of the two competing practices, a railroad might forego the expenditure and instead conform to the prevailing practice. A custom maintained by conforming acts of this sort, motivated as they are by the desire to save on information costs rather than due to strategic considerations, is an epistemic custom.

We have seen, then, that to understand the structure of Beyhmer fully, it is necessary to appeal to all three of the possible rational structures of norms and customs. The workers face a collective action problem that may preclude bargaining for a safe railyard practice, while the railroads themselves are in a game of coordination under the per se rule of custom. Finally, under the evidentiary rule, the railroad may develop an epistemic custom.

Conclusion

The book began with an epigram from Bacon that emphasized the important extent to which people's behavior conforms to their surrounding customary practices. We have seen that courts will need to pay attention to the rational structure of these surrounding customary practices if they are to promote social welfare. In particular, there are thirty-seven possible situations for the three rational structures of customs all combined. We saw that courts will be able to determine which rule of custom to apply to each situation by applying the welfare-maximization markers to the three types of custom.

Chapter Seven first explored the doctrinal battle that took place during the first half of this century between the per se rule of custom and the evidentiary rule of custom. We saw that under the lead of Holmes and Hand, the evidentiary rule emerged as dominant. This raised the issue of why, on the merits, custom should have this elevated role in negligence law. Chapter Seven began to consider this question by examining Clarence Morris's classic account of custom in tort. Morris argues that juries should be apprised of relevant customs because such knowledge would incline jurors to be less prejudicial in their deliberations. Morris does not, however, provide an explanation for why conformity is relevant to due care, once the issue of jury bias is taken into account. The remainder of Chapter Seven explored the traditional economic approach to this issue. In Landes and Posner's analysis, courts should employ the rule of custom in situations of actual or potential bargaining, and not otherwise. This hypothesis failed, however, to predict the emergence of the evidentiary rule as dominant in both bargaining and nonbargaining situations.

In Chapter Eight, we saw that to account adequately for the complexity of the relevant social phenomena, it is necessary to utilize the tripartite model of the structure of social customs and norms. In particular, courts must implement a more fine-grained rational actor account than is suggested by those game-theoretic accounts, which focus on the Prisoner's Dilemma or collective action problem, because potentially dangerous social practices may come in the form of coordination customs or epistemic customs. In this chapter, thirty-seven distinct modalities of rational custom were first identified. Next, the tripartite model of rational custom was used to explicate the role of custom in the leading cases of Behymer and *Hooper*.

According to the orthodox analysis, courts seeking to maximize welfare should focus on the close-knitedness of the communities that produce the customs at issue. In this vein, we saw that sanction-driven customs served to further confirm the Ellicksonian hypothesis. We also saw, however, that with both epistemic customs and coordination customs, conformers may maintain efficient customs despite a lack of close-knitedness. This is a very important finding because many pivotal social norms and customs that bond societies together are not maintained within close-knit groups.[25]

With epistemic customs, close-knittedness could actually be detrimental if close-knit groups become isolated from gains in knowledge achieved in the wider world. Rather than looking to the close-knittedness of the communities that produce epistemic customs in order to see if an effective sanctioning regime is in place, courts instead need to appraise the epistemological features of these customs in order to determine if conformers are incorporating information in an optimal manner. With coordination customs, conformity is rationally justified due to each person's ability to achieve a coordination benefit. As participants conform of their own accord and not because they have been incentivized to do so, such customs may be maintained in groups that do not provide the close-knitedness necessary for effective sanctioning.

Coordination customs and epistemic customs may nevertheless be inefficient. Coordination customs may be inefficient because it is individually rational to conform to a suboptimal equilibrium after it is in existence. A court may be unable to do anything to remedy this situation. The sort of case-by-case incrementalism that is the cornerstone of common law legal process may then simply not be suited to creating the sort of shock to a customary practice that will sometimes be necessary to shift the equilibrium in order to move a community to a more preferable practice. Similarly, epistemic customs may be maintained for reasons that have nothing to do with close-knitedness. A close-knit group, just as well as a group that is not close-knit, may wrongly think it is following the best practice.

We see, then, that welfare-maximizing courts will need to pay attention to a number of features of customs, and not simply whether there was a bargaining situation between the parties or a close-knit community surrounding the parties,[26] à la Landes and Posner (the elder) or Ellickson, McAdams, and Posner (the younger), respectively. As indicated in the Figure 9.1, there are thirty-seven rational modalities of social customs for courts to consider. Looking closely at this complexity is important because it calls into doubt the basic justification of the dominance accorded to the evidentiary rule by Holmes in Behymer and Hand in *The T. J. Hooper*. After all, only eight of the thirty-seven applications of the rule of custom call for the evidentiary rule. The per se rule is preferable for nineteen of the situations; the no-priority rule, for ten of the situations; and the presumption-shifting rule, for eight of the situations.

The rational complexity of custom gives us good reason to suppose that the story of the emergence of the evidentiary rule of custom as the dominant modern rule is more complex than has been previously understood. With regard to sanction-driven customs, a general explanation for the historical transition from the per se rule to the evidentiary rule might be that the world is becoming more anomic, less close-knit, and that this means these norms and customs, on average, are less likely to be efficient.[27] This account will not work for the other types of customs, however, because they do not have the same reliance on the power of sanctions. Given the rational complexity of social norms, then, the dominance of the evidentiary rule of custom remains in need of explanation.

A defender of the evidentiary rule might contend that because of the structural intricacies of various types of customs and how they may have an impact on efficiency, it makes sense for the sake of simplicity to have one dominant rule that works best in the overall run of cases. Given that all three types of custom are sometimes efficient and sometimes inefficient, the evidentiary rule may be preferable to the per se rule or the no-priority rule because it does not provide a safe harbor for dangerous activity but nevertheless accords customary social practices some degree of favorable treatment. Accordingly, it serves as a reasonable intermediate position. Such a response is a thin rationalization, however, for a legal rule that is clearly only roughly equipped to do the important task to which it is assigned. Instead, the suggestion of this chapter is that the way to create safe social norms and customs in a dangerous world is to first understand their rational structure; then, courts should use this knowledge to develop more fine-grained legal rules.

The analysis of the last three chapters was built on the assumption of welfare-maximizing courts. Courts are in a position to promote welfare when it comes to their application of the rule of custom. We saw, however, that courts that take this task seriously will need to work hard to discern the presence of all the factors relevant to the welfare properties of each of the three types of custom, and then after weighing the relative merit of each factor, choosing the appropriate version of the rule of custom. It is then the task of judges to determine the appropriate law to apply. Therefore, the choice of the appropriate version of the rule of custom falls on the judge. The next two chapters examine an important impact exerted not by judges, but by jurors, on the norms and customs that play a role in tort law. We will see that the heterogeneous norms of jurors are in important part constitutive of the de facto liability standard. This juror effect is not best interpreted in terms of welfare maximization. Thus, the dominant Hand Test paradigm for negligence is shown to be an inaccurate characterization of the actual case law liability standard.

10

Juror Norms and the Reasonable Person Standard

It is true that we think of that common-law duty as though it were imposed before the event, because it demands only "reasonable" care; but that does not specify the conduct required and creates a duty incapable of being known in advance, and it is ascertained and imposed only retroactively. Our excuse is that it is fair to exact conformity to such a standard because it should be the inherited portion of the actor; although never formulated before – being measured by a unique occasion – he will divine it by intuition. Nor is it derived alone from forecasting the probable course of events, though that enters into it. It involves a matching of human interests: it is "legislation" in parvo [in little].

Stronelli v. United States Gypsum

Introduction

The focus in this chapter and the next is on the dominant two paradigms of negligence and their relation to the substantive, real-world norms of jurors.[1] The two paradigms I have in mind are the economic account of tort and the corrective justice account of tort. I will explore one important problem that is shared by these accounts. This problem arises with respect to their treatment of the jury. The dominant paradigms marginalize the jury. The effect is to badly skew the account of how the negligence standard receives its content. In particular, the dominant paradigms fail to explain the essential role that the norms of jurors play in filling out the reasonable person standard. In so doing, these paradigms run afoul of the sound jurisprudential tenet that the best explanations of key legal concepts are those that provide a pragmatic explanation of the underlying legal practices.[2]

The power of either litigant to request a jury is both a practically universal and a practically unique feature of America tort law.[3] Despite the fact that most cases settle, the prospect of a case going to trial is always in the background, influencing litigation tactics, expected outcomes, and therefore settlement negotiations. In other words, litigants bargain in the shadow of the jury.[4] Legal practitioners understand the importance of the jury to the outcome of legal disputes, which is why litigants who are in a position to do so will often perform complex and expensive jury studies when developing legal strategies, and expend significant additional resources to affect the composition of the jury.

Given the jury's important role in the actual practice of tort law, there is a puzzle; why so little attention to the jury in the dominant conceptions? One commentator has suggested that the jury's role is so significant that legal scholars in general tend to avoid discussion of it for that very reason. Mark Gergen writes that "[t]he jury has a great deal of normative discretion in deciding what is reasonably prudent. Most academic scholarship on negligence law passes over this feature of the law, I think, because it makes theorizing about how negligence cases ought to be decided seem academic."[5] A less cynical explanation may simply be that scholars have sought to provide accounts of the structure of tort that transcend the particularities of any one country's tort regime and, consequently, have avoided extended discussion of the tort jury because of its uniquely important role in American law.[6]

I will argue in favor of a third explanation, that the dominant paradigms exhibit a bias that in another context Robert Ellickson has labeled "legal centralism."[7] Ellickson defines legal centralists as those holding the view that "the state functions as the sole creator of operative rules of entitlement among individuals."[8] Legal centralists wrongly focus on top/down formal explanations of the source of liability entitlements at the expense of bottom/up explanations that would take account of the casual impacts of informal social norms (such as those that might flow from the deliberations of juries).[9]

The concept of legal centralism, explicitly or implicitly, has served as a fulcrum in the emerging norms literature. In her leading early article, Lisa Bernstein demonstrated the predominantly informal character of the regulation of the diamond industry.[10] In response to the bottom/up accounts set out by Ellickson and Bernstein, Larry Lessig, Richard McAdams, and Cass Sunstein have separately argued that government may have an important role to play as a *norm manager*.[11] They cite examples such as the regulation of cigarette smoking in which government has played a significant role as a shaper of emerging social practices.

In the context of entitlements created through the process of tort litigation, the important question is whether a *legal-centralist* account as compared to a *legal-peripheralist* account provides the best explanation of the emergence of these entitlements, or perhaps instead whether a hybrid account combining both bottom/up and top/down causal forces provides the best explanation.[12] In Section I, I develop a five-stage account of the jury's role in a tort suit that makes its way through trial. I will argue that the practice of tort law gives the informal social norms of jurors an essential role in constituting the actual substance of the negligence standard. As a causal matter, it is this de facto standard, serving as an instantiation of the abstractly formulated formal standard promulgated by the judge via the jury instructions, that determines the final outcome in tort suits. Because the de facto standard plays an essential role in the outcome of tort litigation, the litigation entitlement is causally influenced in its creation from below by the norms of jurors, as well as from above by the jury instructions conveying the formal liability standard. In the following discussion, the bottom/up component of this bidirectional causal process will be referred to as the *jury norm effect.*

Section II will provide an account of the particular substantive normative forces that are typically unleashed by means of the jury norm effect. These forces will be seen to include everyday analogues of strict liability and direct causation, comparative negligence and redistribution. In their efforts to provide a unified normative account, the dominant paradigms fail to notice these sui generis normative forces that fill out the substantive content of negligence determinations.

The economic paradigm, which receives its most important expression in the *Restatement*, will be considered first, and in greater depth.[13] Discussion of social norms is relegated to Section 1 of the *Restatement*, entitled "Custom," which deals with the rule of custom in determining negligence. The *Restatement* follows *The T. J. Hooper* in holding that conformity to custom may count as evidence of due care but is not dispositive with regard to due care.[14] The *Restatement* only countenances a role for social norms in the special situation in which there is an instantiated custom in place, such that either the defendant pleads conformity as a defense or the plaintiff seeks to demonstrate lack of conformity as evidence of negligence. What is missing is any acknowledgment of the pervasive role that social norms play in providing grist for the jury's concrete application of the reasonable person standard. This process may occur not only in situations in which custom is explicitly introduced as evidence by one of the parties but also in all situations in which lay juries deliberate.

I will argue at length that the *Restatement*'s account is misguided, apparently due to its legal centralism, which leads the restaters to assume, largely without argument, the dominant causal efficacy of the Hand Test interpretation of the reasonable person standard on the deliberations of juries, and hence on the outcomes of negligence suits.

Based on the analysis and empirical evidence examined in this chapter, I will argue in Chapter Eleven that there is every reason to suppose that jurors do not engage in Hand Test analysis but instead draw from their motley array of everyday norms and customs when providing concrete substance to the abstract reasonable person standard in order to come to a decision on the issue of negligence. By marginalizing the role of the jury – treating jurors as puppets on strings controlled by an overarching Hand Test rationale – the *Restatement*, as standard bearer for the economic paradigm of negligence, fundamentally misconstrues the important role played by jurors in negligence law. The discussion in Chapter Eleven will then turn to an innovative attempt by Stephen Gilles to insulate the *Restatement* from the sort of criticism I offer. Finally, Chapter Eleven will examine Jules Coleman's corrective justice approach to see how it handles the role of the jury in determining negligence outcomes.

I will conclude that there is a need for a new negligence account that accords the jury conceptual space commensurate with its role in the actual legal institution of tort law as practiced in America. The jury norm effect allows the norms of ordinary people to exert a direct casual effect over formal, legal outcomes. From the perspective of democratic theory, this is an antielitist, liberal feature of American tort law, which distinguishes it from its counterparts abroad.[15] According to one core tenet of pragmatist jurisprudence, important legal practices should be analyzed in order to uncover the normative principles embodied in the practices.[16] In addition to the substantive norms of jurors that will be set out in Section II, tort jury practices arguably embody important liberal principles of political participation, value pluralism, and separation of powers. In their focus on welfare or corrective justice, the dominant paradigms fail to countenance any of these important values embodied in American tort law.

I. The Five Stages of Jury Activity

Jury activity in negligence suits can be conveniently broken down into five stages. These stages are formal in the sense that jurors, regardless of the particular norms to which they conform, will go through them. Figure 10.1 represents these stages in chronological order, with the exception of the first box, which

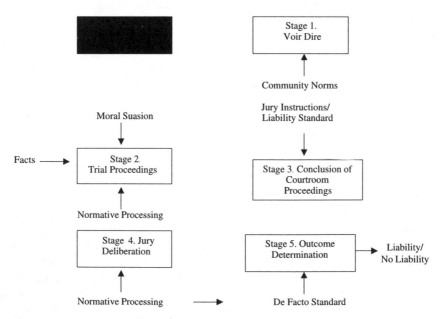

Figure 10.1 Stages of Jury Activity

represents the role of the jury as characterized in many leading theories of tort. Those theories typically do not explicitly claim that the jury plays no role. Rather, they say little about this role, thereby effectively treating the jury as a black box.[17] The specific content of the deliberations of particular juries will likely remain a mystery, and for good reason; nevertheless, there is information available about the role played by juries.

Stage 1: Voir Dire

The second box in Figure 10.1 represents Stage One, Voir Dire. In this stage, a group of (usually twelve) jurors is chosen by lawyers for the parties to participate in the trial. Jurors do not come to their task as blank slates, but rather as individuals, each of whom will have a set of social norms that she accepts and prescribes, or at any rate conforms to, and expects others to conform to as well.[18] These preexisting normative commitments are likely to be drawn upon by jurors in their deliberations. Thus, these commitments might cause one prospective jury to be more attractive than another to the lawyers in the case with the power to choose or exclude jurors.

Different jurisdictions have placed a variety of stipulations on those who may serve on a jury. Jurors have been required to be of "sound judgment" and "good moral character."[19] Jurors have been required to be male or white or property holders.[20] Jurors are required to be residents of the jurisdiction.[21] One of the main justifications that has been given for the civil jury is its ability to infuse "community values" and norms into the legal process.[22] By restricting jury service to whites, or property holders, clearly some values would be more likely to find expression in outcomes than other values.

Beginning with Stage One, each party's legal counsel will seek to shape the narrative that she will create in order to put the facts into a coherent normative framework. Throughout the trial, the lawyers will seek to push the jury's normative buttons. Their ability to do so will depend on the normative starting points of each of the jurors.

Stage Two: Trial Proceedings

In the second stage, the jury observes the trial proceedings and thereby becomes exposed to the facts of the case. In the third box in Figure 10.1, the arrow representing the introduction of facts is drawn from the left side because the input of facts does not seem readily characterized as either a formal, legal influence from above, or an informal normative influence from below.

Advocates for each party will continue to present a narrative throughout the conduct of the trial. As new facts are presented, each advocate will seek to weave the new fact into the each lawyer's competing narrative. The lawyer for the plaintiff will seek to establish that the facts indicate the defendant acted unreasonably by the lights of reigning community norms, and the lawyer for the defendant will seek to establish that the defendant's behavior conformed to accepted norms of reasonable behavior.[23]

The lawyerly component of influence is best represented as coming from above because the advocates are officers of the court. But this influence will be effective, or not, depending on the moral mental states and dispositions of the jurors, who will perform *normative processing* of all the information they receive, according to the thick set of norms to which they subscribe.[24] Thus, the element of normative processing is correctly represented as coming from below.

Stage Three: Conclusion of Courtroom Proceedings

After the conclusion of courtroom testimony, the jury receives instructions and the liability standard from the judge. Through these communications, law as a formal institution can be expected to have a causal impact on the normative deliberations of the jury. Both the liability standard and the instructions are intended to guide and constrain the deliberations of the jurors.

For example, juries sometimes receive an instruction telling them that they should not take account of the wealth of the parties. It is of course an open empirical question how effective this instruction will be in actually affecting the norm of redistribution that may happen to reside in the jury. But assuming that the instruction is at least somewhat effective, this will serve as a partial bound on the ambit of the normative processing that is likely to ensue.

In negligence suits, the injury instruction regarding the liability standard is typically stated in terms of the reasonable person test.[25] There is typically little further instruction telling the jury how to interpret this test or determine the meaning of the crucial concept of reasonableness.[26] The result is that the normative processing engaged in by the jury during its Stage Four deliberations will not be constrained by any specific legal test for the application of the concept of reasonableness.

Stage Four: Jury Deliberation

The jury has a fact-finding function. The jurors are meant to discuss their views and seek to persuade one another so as to reach a consensus.[27] The jury is given relatively little instruction on how to deliberate; nevertheless, it is expected to deliberate. And if these deliberations result in a hung jury, the judge will often tell the jury to deliberate harder. Deliberation is a process value. What matters is that deliberation of a sufficient quality occurs, not that any particular verdict is reached. In the absence of a specific legal test for negligence, it is predictable that jurors, when attempting to engage in good faith deliberations, will fall back on their ordinary moral intuitions regarding the demand of reasonableness. These intuitions will in turn be importantly influenced by the set of norms conformed to by the group of jurors empanelled.

For example, take the basic facts of the venerable old case, Vaughn v. Menlove, and suppose the following two scenarios.[28] In scenario 1, there is a norm in the region to build hayricks with apertures. In scenario 2, there is a norm in the region to build hayricks without apertures. In scenario 1, it is completely plausible to suppose that the jury might decide very quickly that Menlove was reasonable in building his hayrick with an aperture; however, in scenario 2, it is completely plausible to suppose that the jury might decide very quickly that Menlove was not reasonable in building his hayrick with an aperture. Thus, there is a de facto standard that results from the jury's application of the formal standard through the lens of its normative vision. The evidence for the existence of a de facto standard is that different jurors with different sets of norms can be expected to produce different outcomes, as a result of their normative processing of the same facts and the same formal standard. A neutral, objective application of the standard to the facts simply does not exist. Any application will be the application of some particular set of jurors.

Given the crucial role played by social norms in shaping their intuitions, the jury's determination regarding liability is not accurately characterized as "fact finding" in the usual sense. It is frequently noted that reasonableness is not a fact in the way that the question of whether, for instance, one of the parties was wearing her seatbelt is a fact. Frances Bohlen describes liability as a mixed question of law and fact.[29] Other commentators have characterized jury deliberation as a process whereby the jury decides an "ultimate question" or makes little bits of law. Catherine Wells writes, "[I]n negligence cases, the line between the judge's sphere and the jury's does not separate an area of normative, law-like matters from one that is purely factual. It is a misconception to say that the jury simply applies the law. Its role is to decide the ultimate question of liability in the individual case before it."[30] Similarly, Learned Hand says that the jury in effect makes little laws, legislation in parvo.[31]

These explanations may create as much mystery as they dispel, however, as talk of ultimate questions or legislation writ small is no less opaque than is the notion that "reasonable" is a factual predicate that may be truthfully asserted regarding a potential tortfeasor's actions. It is more straightforward to simply acknowledge that some facts are more complex than others. In the present context, this complexity is due to the inherent normative dimension of the concept of "reasonable" behavior.[32]

Importantly, despite this complexity, jurors are generally able to perform their appointed task. While tort theorists may spend infinite keystrokes fighting over the preferable conception of reasonable behavior, nothing stops an ordinary person, that is, a juror, from making a quick decision as to the reasonableness of the actions of other ordinary people (victims and injurers). The sure evidence for this is that juries reach verdicts all the time. Some juries reach their decisions in a very short period of time.[33] Hung juries are the exception to the rule.[34]

Stage Five: Outcome Determination

In Stage Five, the final stage, the jury produces a general verdict. The jury need not provide an explanation for how it reached its result, or seek to justify or provide a rationale for the result.[35] Does this mean that the jury is free to reach its verdict in any manner whatsoever? No, even though the jury is not constrained in the substantive outcome that it may produce, it is constrained in the way by which it is supposed to reach the outcome. Specifically, the outcome must be the result of deliberation. The secrecy of jury deliberations means that outsiders have no way of knowing that the outcome was produced through deliberation, as compared to say flipping a coin, but this does not change the fact that due process demands that the outcome be produced in a deliberative manner.

II. Substantive Jury Norms

The account developed in Section I dissected tort litigation into five stages in order to provide a more nuanced understanding of the role of juror norms. Legal centralists write as if all entitlements are created in the shadow of the law. The examination of the five stages told a different story, as informal social norms were seen to play an essential role in all the stages except Stage Three. Overall, norms play an essential role in determining the outcome of the negligence inquiry and hence in determining whether plaintiff is entitled to a recovery.

As noted earlier, the five-stage account of the role of the jury is formal in the sense that each of the five stages may be passed through regardless of the particular substantive norms adhered to by any given set of jurors. The following discussion will consider a few of the more important attempts to uncover some of the more important substantive normative elements that appear to exert a casual influence on jurors during the various stages of their activity. Three sorts of normative influence will be considered: strict liability norms, comparative negligence norms, and redistributive norms. This account is preliminary and is meant to be suggestive of the complexity of juror normative processing. Much empirical study needs to be done before we can speak more definitively on the contours of normative processing by American jurors.

A. Strict Liability Jury Norms

As the following discussion demonstrates, considerations of strict liability and directness of injury appear to play a role in jury interpretations of the reasonable person standard. The orthodoxy is of course that the reasonable person standard is not a strict liability standard. Strict liability is liability without fault, and the reasonable person standard requires fault.[36] As long as the injurer was acting reasonably, taking due care, the reasonable person will not be liable for injuries. In Wagon Mound II, the Privy Council famously observed that the fault standard is a morally superior standard, claiming it to be "immoral and unjust" to hold an injurer liable in a situation in which the injury was not reasonably foreseeable.[37]

There is evidence, however, that everyday people who comprise juries may see the issue differently.[38] There is evidence that strict liability intuitions have long played a role in negligence, as indicated by the following remarks from Bohlen:

> The general utility of such conduct in not likely to receive much consideration from a jury who sees before them a plaintiff whose vital interests have been harmed by a particular instance of it. A court might emphasize to the jury *ad nauseam* the social value of the act, but the jury would only see one man injured by another. And only the most confirmed optimist would dare to hope that they would judge the defendant's conduct by what the ideal creature, the "reasonable man" would do. . . . The concept universal among all primitive men, that an injury should be paid for by him who causes it, irrespective of the moral or social quality of his conduct, while it has disappeared from legal thought, still dominates the opinion of the sort of men who form the average jury.[39]

Bohlen's remarks indicate that in his experience, the actual outcome of jury decisions applying the reasonable person standard will reflect the tendencies of juries to find liability based on whether the defendant "caused" the injury rather than on some other criteria such as whether the defendant was acting to maximize "social value" at the time he caused the injury. In other words, actual court decisions sometimes reflect an implicit strict liability standard rather than a negligence standard.

There is reason to believe that juries continue to apply a strict liability standard. One particularly salient factor appears to be the *directness* of the injury. Juries appear more likely to find liability when the causal nexus between defendant's injurious act and plaintiff's injury is more rather than less direct. The most famous directness case is Polemis.[40] In this case, the court held that because of the directness of the injury, there could be a finding of liability, even without consideration of whether there was reasonable foreseeability on the part of the defendant.[41] This case is often contrasted with Wagon Mound II, in which, as noted earlier, the Privy Council rejected the directness test as "immoral and unjust."[42] The elite Privy Council exhibits a value judgment that evidently is at odds with ordinary morality, however, as across most jurisdictions, directness and reasonable foreseeability have each commanded respect from jurors.[43]

The "sort of men who form the average jury," to use Bohlen's elitist remark, are presumably still the same sort of men, ordinary people, that is. It is inaccurate then to characterize jury determinations of liability that reflect a strict liability norm as "legislation writ large." Rather, these are simply instances of normative processing in which juries plug their more concrete norms of reasonable behavior into the abstract reasonable person standard.

B. Comparative Negligence Jury Norms

There is evidence that juries have a normative predilection in favor of comparative negligence. It is not clear whether this is a matter of jury nullification or simple jury normative processing. Wells describes the facts of Li v. Yellow Cab Co. and describes the sort of deliberation everyday people such as she and the jury might go through.[44] In Li, the plaintiff was injured when struck by an oncoming motorist as the plaintiff attempted to make a left-hand turn in her automobile. Prior to this case, California had applied the rule of contributory negligence. Wells argues persuasively, however, that regardless of the formal rule in place, fact finders will be inclined to take account of the degrees of fault of both parties.[45] In Li, the California Supreme Court replaced the contributory negligence rule with the comparative negligence rule such that the defendant was held responsible for his portion of the fault, despite the fact that plaintiff was also at fault in making the left-hand turn. Wells notes: "Only the lawyers among us will think that this responsibility should depend on whether the law of California looks to contributory or comparative negligence."[46] In other words from an ordinary moral point of view, people will do the functional equivalent of a comparative negligence approach, as they will tend to reach a result that apportions partial fault or responsibility to each party and lets the outcome split the difference as it were. With comparative negligence, the informal social norm played a significant causal role in the emergence of the formal legal rule. The Li court acknowledged its decision to switch to comparative fault reflected its perception that this is what juries are inclined to do anyway.[47]

C. Redistributive Jury Norms

Commentators have long claimed that juries are predisposed toward redistribution.[48] Empirical research suggests that the story of normative impulses toward redistribution is more complex than one might at first suppose.[49] Valerie Hans argues, for example, that jurors hold corporations to higher standards.[50] Thus, it may not be a redistributive norm but a norm regarding elevated duties of firms that may explain the observed outcomes.

Other observers have noted the influence of redistributive norms.[51] Leon Green, for instance, argues that courts will be inclined to "place the loss where it will be felt the least and can best be borne."[52] Wells argues that juries tend to attempt to make negligence decisions in order to bring about an outcome that is "fair," "all things considered," which may involve taking account of the "defendant's ability to absorb or spread costs," which is fairly seen as a redistributive impulse.[53]

D. *Jurors as Providers of Total Justice*

The preceding examination indicates that there are a plurality of distinguishable normative influences that may have a casual impact on the de facto standard. Based on empirical work on the tort jury, Neil Feigenson finds that jurors do "total justice."[54] What is meant by total justice is that jurors decide liability not solely on either a welfare-maximizing criterion or on a corrective justice criterion, but rather, they take account of a plurality of factors. Some of these factors may be dubious from the perspective of prevailing critical moral frameworks, such as the wealth of the defendant or the likelihood that the defendant is insured. Nevertheless, these factors may play a role in ordinary morality and this is what matters when presenting the best positive account of juror behavior.

Conclusion

In Section I, I developed a five-stage account of the jury's role in a tort suit that makes it to trial. I argued that the picture of tort law gave the informal social norms of jurors an essential role in constituting the actual substance of the negligence standard. Causally speaking, it is this de facto standard that determines the final outcome in tort suits.

Because the de facto liability standard plays an essential role in producing outcomes, the litigation entitlement is causally influenced in its creation from below by juror norms and from above by the jury instructions conveying the formal liability standard. In the foregoing discussion, the bottom/up component of this bidirectional causal process has been referred to as the jury norm effect.

Section II provided an account of some of the substantive normative forces that may be unleashed through the jury norm effect, such as strict liability and direct causation, comparative negligence, and redistribution. In the next chapter, I will argue that, in their efforts to provide a unified normative account, the dominant paradigms fail to notice these sui generis normative forces that fill out the substantive content of negligence determinations.

11

Rejection of the Dominant Paradigm of Negligence

Cases come to the courts through formal pleadings cut to some pattern or patterns of legal theory. Evidential data are offered to support these and the opposing theories. There is no suggestion that the tenor of the Restatement is designed for these purposes. After the evidence is heard, the theories insisted upon by the parties through their lawyers are translated to the jury by instructions in terms of formulas. Certainly the black letter statements are not intended to supplant the formulas already worked out and utilized by the courts in tort cases. These are too ponderous and elaborate for such a purpose. Assuming that a judge would know which ones to give, no jury would comprehend them.[1]

Leon Green

Introduction

In this chapter, I will argue at length that a failure to properly characterize the jury norm effect leads the *Third Restatement* account of negligence astray. Apparently due to the bias of legal centralism, the *Third Restatement* assumes, without little by way of argument or evidence, the dominant causal efficacy of the Hand Test interpretation of the reasonable person standard on the deliberations of juries, and hence on the outcomes in negligence suits.

Based on the empirical support and analysis presented in Chapter Ten, I will argue to the contrary that there is good reason to suppose that juries do not engage in Hand Test normative processing but instead draw from their diverse array of everyday norms and customs when providing concrete substance to the abstract reasonable person standard in order to come to a decision on the issue of negligence. By marginalizing the role of the jury, the *Third Restatement*, as the embodiment of the dominant paradigm, misconstrues the important role played by jurors and their norms in negligence law. In this important respect, the Restatement fails to restate the law.

Section I will critically examine the approach followed in the *Third Restatement*. Section II will consider an innovative attempt by Stephen Gilles to inoculate the *Third Restatement* from the sort of criticism developed in

Section I, by arguing that the social values of jurors will reflect a "Hand Norm." I will argue that both the *Third Restatement* and Gilles's attempt to save it are importantly flawed in their understanding of the role played by juror norms.

I. The Hand Test Interpretation of Juror Normative Processing

Negligence is the breach of a legally recognized duty.[2] The *Restatement* fails to state duty as an overt element.[3] It would thus seem incapable of defining negligence as the breach of a duty.[4] The *Restatement* ducks this thorny issue by proceeding directly to a discussion of negligence or fault.[5]

The *Restatement* sets forth a "risk-benefit test" for negligence which it explicates as follows: "the 'risk' is the overall magnitude of the risk created by the actor's conduct and the 'benefit' is the advantages that the actor or others gain if the actor refrains from risk prevention measures."[6] The *Restatement* notes that in a "cost-benefit test," the "'cost' signifies the cost of precautions and the 'benefit' signifies the reduction in risk those precautions would achieve."[7] The *Restatement* concludes, "[M]ore simply, this can be referred to as supporting a 'balancing approach' to negligence."[8] The *Restatement* explicates the balancing approach in the following terms:

The balancing approach rests on and expresses a simple idea. Conduct is negligent if its disadvantages exceed its advantages, while conduct is not negligent if its advantages exceed its disadvantages. The disadvantage in question is the "magnitude of risk" that the conduct occasions: the phrase "magnitude of risk" includes both the foreseeable likelihood of harm and the foreseeable severity of harm, should the incident ensue. The "advantages" of the conduct relate to the burdens of risk prevention that are avoided when the actor while engaging in conduct declines to incorporate some precaution. The actor's conduct is hence negligent if the magnitude of the risk exceeds the burden of risk prevention.[9]

In this passage, the *Restatement* evinces an explicitly utilitarian or economic conception of balancing, as "disadvantages" are weighed against "advantages." In particular, this is a quantitative conception, one in which these values are to be measured on a single scale by comparing their respective "magnitudes" in order to determine whether the advantages "exceed" the disadvantages. This is a Hand Test formulation that emphasizes the "burdens of risk prevention," rather than the overall utility of the defendant's act.[10] The Hand Test focuses on the burden that must be expended in order for a tort defendant to avoid liability. If $B < P \times L$, then one will be liable if one's action results in injury to another.[11] The *Restatement* gives the "reasonable care" standard a gloss that implicitly reflects the Hand Test formulation.[12]

The *Restatement* claims that the best way to understand the case law is for courts to attempt to implement the balancing approach described earlier.[13] The *Restatement* explicitly equates its suggested balancing approach with the Hand

Test approach,[14] and cites a long string of cases that purportedly utilize the balancing or Hand approach.[15]

The *Restatement* notes that a number of federal appellate courts have explicitly endorsed the Hand formula.[16] This is loosely presented as evidence for the claim that the Hand Test has really played a pervasive role in the case law, despite the failure of trial courts to mention explicitly cost-benefit analysis in jury instructions.

This argument is flawed. From the mere fact that some federal appellate courts have been influenced by the normative account of breach contained in the Hand Test, there is no reason to conclude that trial courts have been similarly influenced. If explicit mention of the Hand Formula is taken as evidence of the influence of this formula in federal appellate courts, then by parity of reasoning, one would more naturally conclude that the failure of the formula to receive explicit mention by trial courts is evidence of its lack of influence there.[17] Certainly, in the absence of explicit discussion of the Hand Test by trial courts, the initial presumption, albeit a rebuttable one, should be that it has not played a role.[18]

The fact that negligence is a fact question determined by jurors is additional reason to think that trial court decisions do not result from cost-benefit analysis. Under settled American practice, juries are under no obligation to explain or justify their decisions.[19] The jury simply applies the "reasonable person standard" to the facts as it finds them and issues a general verdict.[20] Contemporary jury instructions typically tell the jury to apply the reasonable person standard, without explaining or defining this standard.[21] In particular, juries do not receive instructions to apply the Hand Test, the risk-utility test, or the risk-benefit test. This is straightforward and powerful evidence for the supposition that juries do not apply any of these tests.

In cases in which defense attorneys might seek Hand Test instructions, they nevertheless typically choose not to. Gary Schwartz argues that this is because they fear jury nullification.[22] In other words, seasoned trial lawyers intuit that typical jurors would find a cost-benefit mode of reasoning morally unattractive. If this claim turns out to be true, it is additional evidence that juries do not think in Hand Test terms in the usual case.[23] Moreover, even if they were morally inclined to do so, typical juries may be practically incapable of such reasoning.[24]

The *Restatement* notes that "while the concept of 'probability' is more technically precise, it will utilize the concept of 'likelihood,' instead, as the word is in common usage with a clear meaning."[25] In this passage, the *Restatement* seeks to suggest that the cost-benefit test is capable of being performed by ordinary people. The *Restatement* presumably means to suggest by this appeal to ordinary language that the negligence standard is a test capable of application by ordinary persons, such as jurors. This only establishes the hypothetical that if juries were to apply the Hand test, the use of "likelihood" as compared to "probability" would make the test more easily applicable by ordinary people.

Even if this is correct, the point does nothing to establish the proposition that jurors who are not told to apply the Hand Test, either in terms of probability or likelihood, will somehow be more inclined to apply the test.

In fact, one can more readily utilize an ordinary language argument against the legal centralism of the *Restatement*.[26] The ordinary language phrase "reasonable person" does not in any way suggest a utilitarian or economic approach of the sort conventionally read into the Hand Test. According to Webster's, "reasonable" simply means "sensible," not "extreme," "immoderate," or "excessive."[27] Based on the mere fact of their hearing jury instructions, then, there is simply no reason to think that juries, composed as they are of everyday people, would somehow insert a technical mode of reasoning such as cost-benefit analysis into their untutored deliberations regarding the behavior of reasonable persons.

It will be the atypical juror who will have had more than a passing acquaintance with cost-benefit analysis specifically, or utilitarian reasoning more generally.[28] Even when jurors are exposed to utilitarian thinking, however, this exposure probably will not influence their actual behavior. There are two separate reasons, each grounded in a competing conception of human nature, for thinking that welfare-maximizing actions will not be forthcoming from typical jurors.

To the extent that jurors are narrowly self-interested rational actors, mere exposure to utilitarianism would not cause them to act according to the dictates of utilitarianism. Rather they would support the outcome that best served their own interests. It is arguably more plausible to assume that people are predominantly, rather than narrowly, self-interested rational actors.[29] In other words, people are, at least to some extent, morally motivated. The jury system appears ideally designed to take advantage of jurors' moral propensities because jurors typically have little to gain one way or another from the outcome of a trial. Thus, their propensities toward self-interest will be unlikely to interfere with their admittedly limited propensities toward moral behavior.[30]

The implication of this finding is not, however, that jurors will therefore act as utilitarians. It is more plausible to suppose that under these conditions, jurors will simply make decisions based on their ordinary moral understanding of the world. In other words, the determination of liability will depend largely on whether the behavior in question conformed to community norms.[31] Ordinary morality bears little resemblance to utilitarianism.[32] Therefore, we should not expect that morally motivated jurors applying the reasonable person standard in light of their norms would act in a utilitarian manner.[33]

This section rejected a number of arguments for thinking real-world juries apply the Hand Test version of the reasonable person standard. The fact that some federal circuit courts explicitly discuss cost-benefit analysis is no reason to think that juries implicitly appeal to this analysis. The opposite would appear more likely, as the fact that there is no explicit mention is reason to think there is not an implicit appeal. Furthermore, even in products liability cases when lawyers might seek Hand Test jury instructions, they typically do not. Most important in understanding juror behavior is the fact that juries do not receive jury instructions regarding cost-benefit analysis. Nor do jurors typically learn about cost-benefit analysis elsewhere so as to be able to appeal to it intuitively in their deliberations. Finally, even if jurors happen to learn about cost-benefit analysis, there is no reason to think that they will be inclined to promote it. Instead, it is much more likely that they would either act in a narrowly self-interested manner or conform to extant social norms, neither of which is likely to coincide with global welfare maximization.

II. A "Social Values" Approach to Juror Norms

In an important recent article, Stephen Gilles endorses the legitimacy of community values as a source of objective legal standards.[34] Gilles argues that the negligence test is best understood as incorporating a "Hand Norm." According to Gilles, "[t]he Hand Norm tells us that it is negligent to omit a precaution if the reduction in expected accident costs would have been greater than the costs of the precaution."[35] The Hand Test, then, is not merely an arid academic formulation but also one important component of the set of norms that characterizes the community morality of jurors. If Gilles is right, the task of the economist is potentially rendered more tractable. The Hand Test is no longer merely a functionalist description of what juries do. Instead, it attempts to give center stage to cost-benefit balancing by explaining that such balancing is itself a moral norm held by jurors.

Gilles refers to the community norms that juries consult as the "common coin of 'social value.'"[36] He further explains that "human beings have various interests, and those interests have more or less social value."[37] Thus, for Gilles, talk of community morality and norms shifts to talk of values on a uniform scale in which interests have "more or less social value," and all values may be reduced to a "common coin."[38]

As Gilles notes, his approach derives from that of the *First Restatement*. The *First Restatement* conceived of courts as being influenced by the "social value[s]" of the surrounding community in making determinations of the standard of care required of the reasonable person under the particular circumstances of the case at bar.[39] In contrast, the *Restatement* merely says that courts should determine reasonableness "under all the circumstances."[40] The *First Restatement* approach thus gives the reasonable person standard a more determinate content. The content comes from the thick moral norms of the actual communities out of which the pool of jurors are drawn. Jurors, being ordinary members of the community untrained in utilitarian reasoning, have nothing else to appeal to but their social sense of how ordinary moral members of the community would have acted in parallel circumstances.

In an influential article written during the era that produced the *First Restatement*, Warren Seavey sought to legitimate community norms as an objective source of legal decisions.[41] Gilles cites to the following passage from Seavey as evidence that the Hand Test is incorporated into the negligence standard via *community values* or *social values*. Seavey writes:

In this computation there are involved two distinct kinds of problems. The first is purely mathematical, namely the ascertainment of the degree of likelihood that certain events will or will not occur. As to this, the result would be the same under any system of law; it is achieved by purely intellectual processes. The complete answer can be obtained, however, only by solving the other type of problem, that is the comparative values of the conflicting interests of the actor and the one whose interests are threatened. This evaluation calls for the so-called moral qualities. To the extent that the solution of these problems involves standardized elements, or, phrasing it differently, to the extent that the actor's conduct is determined with reference to the community valuations, we may say that an objective test applies.[42]

In this passage, Seavey first notes that the process of discounting for the uncertainty of particular injuries is a process that will not vary with particular communities. Speaking anachronistically, this is the "P," or probability, component in the Hand Formula. Regarding the values to be imputed to the benefit received by the tortfeasor and the loss inflicted on the victim, "community valuations" are to serve as the measure. Although these valuations may vary from community to community, the fact that they will be standardized within particular communities nevertheless allows for the conclusion that "an objective test applies."

Returning to Gilles's argument, the following consideration weighs heavily against the Hand Norm argument. Recasting balancing as a moral norm does not establish the primacy of a welfarist conception of fault or breach. This is because there is no logical connection between factor balancing, generically understood, and the cost-benefit approach. Gilles takes too literally the metaphors of "balancing" and "weighing" of utility. A set of scales can balance weights at either end, but ordinary usage also permits a more general sense of the words "weigh" and "balance" to mean simply that rational actors may take account of numerous factors in their practical reasoning with regard to a particular issue. Practical reason itself typically involves taking account of numerous factors. There is nothing intrinsically utilitarian or consequentialist in practical reasoning. A deontologist can engage in practical reasoning by balancing various considerations, every bit as much as a utilitarian can.[43]

For example, a deontologist may balance freedom of action against security.[44] Doing so in no way transforms the deontologist into a utilitarian. When the U.S. Supreme Court performs its multipart balancing tests in deciding cases involving basic constitutional rights, it would be implausible to suggest that the Court has first reduced all the competing rights-based considerations to some "common coin" of consequentialist value. Likewise, there is no reason to think that when the ordinary juror weighs or balances various community-based moral factors, that she is therefore somehow transformed into a utilitarian.

Hand himself was not deluded into thinking that the Hand Test implied weighing in anything more than a metaphorical sense. Nor did Hand have any illusions that values could be quantified. He wrote: "[O]f these factors care is the only one ever susceptible of quantitative estimate, and often that is not. The injuries are always a variable within limits, which do not admit of even approximate ascertainment; and, although probability might theoretically be estimated, if any statistics were available, they never are; and besides, probability varies with the severity of the injuries."[45] This can be seen by imagining a community of deontologists.

Gilles's argument appears to provide support for the utilitarian thesis, due to its conceptualization of the social values at stake as "Hand Factors."[46] Stripped of rhetoric, however, the so-called Hand factors are simply the core factors of any account of negligence. These factors will be present under any theoretical conception of the reasoning processes engaged in by jurors. For example, the first of Gilles's Hand factors concerns the utility of the defendant's action. Any theoretical approach to torts must take account of the defendant's actions. The Kantian will hold this action to the test of the categorical imperative.[47] The corrective justice theorist will consider the sort of wrongfulness contained in the action.[48] In a general sense of the term, each of these can be seen as "factors" looked into by courts.

The third Hand factor is based on the fact that, ex ante, the injury to the plaintiff was not certain to occur. Gilles and the *Restatement* describe this factor in terms of "risk," "probability," or "likelihood," of the injury occurring. Once again, there is nothing that is particularly utilitarian about factoring in risks, probabilities or likelihoods. Because outcomes that are probable, rather than certain, are an unavoidable part of life, any theory of practical reason, and any normative theory of liability in negligence, must account for them.

With regard to all three of the so-called Hand factors, then, there is nothing inherently utilitarian about any one of them. Any normative approach will necessarily involve the balancing of these considerations.[49] What is distinctively welfarist is putting all such considerations on one scale of value. But as we have seen, there is no evidence that this is what juries do, and there is, in fact, good reason to think this is not what they do.

At times, the *Restatement* echoes Gilles's approach in emphasizing the multiple considerations that enter into the assessment of fault, as, for example, when it discusses the idea of "ethical particularism" in commentary to Section 5.[50] Reviewing the famous Holmes/Cardozo debate regarding the appropriateness of bright-line negligence rules, the *Restatement* endorses Cardozo's position and describes it as an approach favoring "ethical particularism."

Despite the invocation of Cardozo, the *Restatement* understands ethical particularism in utilitarian terms. Its claim is simply that each fact pattern giving rise to a negligence claim in tort litigation presents particular factual details that distinguish it from other similar factual situations. Thus, rather than having a bright-line rule to deal with similar situations, courts allow the negligence question to go to the jury, which can then perform more fine-grained Hand factor analysis based on all the details of the case.[51] The *Restatement*'s error is to reduce all the ethical particularities of specific fact patterns to their consequential value, that is, how they are to be quantified in terms of cost-benefit analysis. In fact, however, the argument from ethical particularism to which the *Restatement* cites has nothing to do with making a full count of utilities. Rather, the ethical particularities thought to be implicit in specific situations cannot be reduced to any particular critical normative framework, be it consequentialist or nonconsequentialist.[52] As Section I indicated, the moral judgments rendered by juries are often based on a variety of moral factors such as directness of the injury, which cannot be reduced to consequentialist factors to be measured by their relative magnitudes.

The *Restatement*'s misconception regarding the prospect of quantifying all factors relevant to negligence has an important practical implication. The *Restatement* notes that directed verdicts for negligence, per se, should increase as more exact measurement of utilities becomes feasible.[53] In other words, the role of the jury in tort law will diminish over time, as utilitarian science displaces lay juror guesses regarding the exact utilities to be attached to the Hand factors. Given the important and unique role that juries have played in American tort law, this aspect of the *Restatement* deserves greater attention from future scholars.

The discussion in this section demonstrated that the attempt to assimilate factor balancing and cost-benefit analysis is misguided. Section I demonstrated that the *Restatement*'s attempt to read cost-benefit analysis into the reasonable person standard was implausible. Combined, then, earlier discussion has shown that the *Restatement*'s cost-benefit conception of fault understates the role of nonutilitarian negligence norms in filling out the actual substance of the reasonable person standard.

III. Corrective Justice Norms

The previous section examined the leading instantiation of the economic approach to tort in terms of its ability to account adequately for the juror norm effect in determinations of negligence. This section does the same for the corrective justice approach. I will focus my attention on the metaphysically and epistemologically grounded new defense of corrective justice vis-à-vis the economic approach contained in Jules Coleman's recent book, *The Practice of Principle*.[54] In the short space that can be devoted to the complex topic here, only an initial exploration will be possible. This will still be of value, however, if it indicates that Coleman's account of the role of juror norms is inadequate and, further, that it is plausible to believe that his account may be typical of corrective justice approaches in this regard.

Coleman contrasts the economist's functionalist explanation of tort with his pragmatist explanation.[55] Coleman seeks to develop a set of commitments about the semantic contents of theories and about the criteria of theory justification. A pragmatist account should answer the question of what is to count as an explanation of a particular area of the law, such as tort law. Coleman presents the corrective justice account as an instance of a pragmatic conceptual explanation.[56] According to Coleman, satisfactory "explanations of [legal] practices typically take the form of analyses of the concepts that figure prominently in those practices."[57] Coleman begins the analysis with middle-level concepts. He asks "what principles, if any, are embodied in the legal practices we are presently engaged in?"[58] Coleman's goal is to identify the "normatively significant elements of the practice and to explain them as embodiments of principle,"[59] that is, to satisfy the titular quest of uncovering the *practice of principle*.

According to Coleman's pragmatic methodology, it is crucial to look at the practical inferences that are drawn from the central concepts of a practice. Of particular importance for tort law is the inference of liability. Coleman argues that the economic account is inadequate owing to its faulty account of the inference of liability. Most important, the economic account fails to explain the "bilateral structure" of tort law, that is, the existence and significance of tort suits in which a plaintiff demands redress of a defendant on the basis of having been injured by the defendant. Coleman reinforces the argument he has developed elsewhere to the effect that the bilateral party structure, while at the core of the practice of tort law, has no intrinsic justification in the economic approach.[60] The identities of the victim and the injurer, and the normative relationship between the two, are of only contingent importance to the economic account. All that ultimately matters for efficiency is that future actors are optimally incentivized to minimize the cost of accidents. It is a contingent matter whether the bilateral party structure serves this larger social purpose.

The intuitive attractiveness of Coleman's argument can be attributed to the idea that the central features of tort law hold together in a tight manner that bespeaks a coherent enterprise of delivering corrective justice. One question that deserves more attention than Coleman has given it is this: On what basis does a feature of tort law count as sufficiently important such that it should be accounted for within a pragmatic conceptualist account? The particular question of interest here is whether the jury should play a role in Coleman's account. It currently does not. The jury poses two questions for Coleman: First, what is the intended breadth of his interpretive account? Second, does it apply to Commonwealth tort law, which generally does not rely on the jury? If the answer to the second question is yes, then whose "practice" is being interpreted? Coleman's account is in danger of sliding from interpretation of an actual legal practice into pure analytic philosophizing about an ideal form of law. If the answer to the second question is no, that is, if the account is meant to be an interpretive account of American tort law, on what basis can Coleman exclude the jury from his account?

It is an important element of Coleman's pragmatist approach that practice and principle are to be understood in light of one another. Accordingly, the introduction of an additional component of practice raises the question as to whether some further principle is thereby implicated. By the lights of his own theory, the question posed to Coleman in this regard is whether the jury's role is "normatively significant" and, if so, whether this role can be fairly said to "embody" principle.[61] These two questions will be the focus of the following discussion. How they are answered will determine the importance of the jury to Coleman's account. If the jury's role is not "normatively significant," there is no need to consider the second question as to whether the jury somehow embodies principles. On the other hand, the answer to the first question may be yes, the jury is normatively significant, while the answer to the second question is no, the jury does not embody principle. A third possibility is that the jury's role embodies a principle of special interest, corrective justice. In this case, inclusion of jury practice in the overall account of negligence may support a corrective justice interpretation. Finally, jury practice may embody norms or principles other than, or in addition to, corrective justice.

As earlier discussion indicated, the jury's role in American tort litigation is normatively significant in a number of respects, both substantive and procedural. Most importantly, juror norms give content to the reasonable person standard. Courts do not tell jurors how to interpret the concept of reasonableness. Consequently, jurors must draw on their own understanding of reasonable behavior, based on their experience of the world. When an action in question is an instance of an extant social practice of a community, the jury will be able to consult their personal knowledge of the general functioning of the practice and, equally important, consult their knowledge of the extent of community acceptance of the practice.[62] For purposes of evaluating Coleman's theory, a definitive account of the role of jurors is not necessary as the five-stage account examined earlier is sufficient to establish that the jury's role is normatively significant. The analysis may accordingly proceed to a consideration of Coleman's second criterion, which is whether the jury's role in negligence law embodies principle.

Coleman does not discuss the jury's role in any detail so it is necessary to draw inferences from his theory. The obvious first question to ask is what is the result, in terms of the embodiment of principle, when Coleman's corrective justice account is extended to encompass the role played by the jury? Coleman would likely contend that the jury's role is simply to follow the judge's instructions by applying the legal standard that is handed down to them to the facts of the case. Because the fault standard applied in the context of bilateral adjudication embodies the principle of corrective justice, when the jury finds on the question of negligence under this standard, it is participating in the production of an outcome that embodies corrective justice. Specifically, the jury is redressing a "wrongful loss" that occurred when defendant injured plaintiff.[63] Thus, Coleman has a plausible account as to how the jury's role in tort practice may be compatible with his corrective justice account.

There is a problem with this account, however. Simply because jury outcomes may be compatible with corrective justice does not imply that they will always be compatible, as the jury may also act in a manner that would not plausibly be deemed correctively just. The important question, then, is what reason is there to suppose that juries are typically acting to promote corrective justice rather than some broader set of norms? Coleman does not directly address this question. He does, however, note the existence of "our ordinary intuitions about corrective justice."[64] If Coleman is correct that corrective justice intuitions are commonplace, then when a situation arises in which people are capable of carrying out corrective justice, such as when they find themselves serving on a jury in a tort suit, they will be able to do so, and they will be inclined to do so.

Thus, it appears that Coleman's corrective justice explanation of tort law depends on an implicit premise to the effect that people are characteristically inclined to act based on a natural inclination to redress wrongful losses when it is in their power to do so. This empirically based premise, if it is one on which he relies, is worthy of further exploration. Perhaps this exploration will end up lending support to the corrective justice account. Empirical studies have indicated that people acting in many different contexts may display fairness motivations under certain circumstances. There clearly appears to be more evidence that people are motivated by fairness than by the motivation to promote aggregate wealth or efficiency. Whether this suggests that they would be motivated by corrective justice concerns as well is not certain.[65]

For all we know, when given the chance, jurors may also correct for unjust income disparities, a history of chattel slavery, or other injustices that go beyond simply correcting for the defendant's imposition of a wrongful loss on plaintiff. Suppose, for instance, that the jury determined liability in a particular case primarily because of the "deep pockets" of the defendant in combination with the ethnicity of the plaintiff. Presumably, Coleman would not wish to claim that this outcome embodied corrective justice, despite the bilateral structure of the litigation or the fact that the judge had instructed the jury to apply the reasonable person standard. These possible scenarios compel the conclusion that a jury's finding on the issue of liability may be, but is not necessarily, an instance of corrective justice.[66]

In defense of Coleman's account, it could be replied that the judge's instructions will often tell the jury not to take account of factors such as the parties' wealth or whether the defendant is likely to be insured. Coleman could plausibly claim that these instructions serve as structural features that support his claim that tort law embodies corrective justice rather than some broader set of norms. Other features of courtroom activity may, however, support the claim that a broader set of norms may come into play. For example, during the trial, lawyers for either party will try to shape the jury's sympathies toward their own client along any promising normative dimension that serves their client's interests and not just with respect to a concern for redressing wrongful losses.

Coleman may respond that he has never claimed that corrective justice is the only normative principle embedded in tort. Rather, his claim is that corrective justice is at the core. Coleman notes that "corrective justice . . . expresses important moral values."[67] More broadly, Coleman argues that tort must be understood within a broader context of liberal political theory.

Arguably, looking at the jury's normatively complex role may support Coleman's claim, as it does appear that even if other normative influences are at play, the impulse toward redressing the wrongful loss to the plaintiff because of the defendant's injurious act may nevertheless be the dominant impulse. Further, Coleman may argue that even if jurors do not have a natural inclination solely toward duties of repair for wrongful losses, perhaps they might deliver corrective justice because that is what they are instructed to do by the judge. A look at pattern jury instructions, however, shows that this is not the case. These instructions make no mention of duties of repair for wrongful losses. The jury is instructed on the reasonable person standard. There is nothing in the meaning of the words *reasonable, person,* or *standard* that tells a group of jurors who would not otherwise be disposed to redress wrongful losses to go ahead and do so.

In his attack on the economic account for failing to capture the structure of tort, Coleman observes that were the economic model true, "the judge would instruct the jury to find against the party who is in the best position to reduce harm in the future."[68] Coleman continues, "In other words, were the concept of efficiency embedded in tort law, we should expect to have an entirely different structure and content to the practice of reasoning."[69] It is not clear that Coleman's corrective justice account can pass this test. Coleman opens himself up to the same criticism he uses against the economist: If his is the best account, then why is it not the case that judges instruct juries in terms of "duty to repair" for "wrongful losses"? What is needed is an account connecting the language used by judges in their instructions and the calling forth of jury actions that serve to redress wrongful losses. In other words, Coleman needs an explanation for why what the jury does somehow tracks what would be called for by the substantive conception of responsibility for wrongful losses that Coleman argues to be operative.

Summing up, then, the jury's role in American tort law may embody both substantive and procedural principles in addition to the principle of corrective justice. Depending on the relative importance of these principles in comparison to the principle of corrective justice, Coleman may still be correct that corrective justice nevertheless forms the core of tort law. This further examination may as well prove him wrong, however. This important issue bears greater discussion than may be pursued here.

Conclusion

This chapter explored one important respect in which the dominant paradigms of negligence are misguided. This is with respect to their treatment of the jury. We first saw that the *Restatement* provides an incorrect account of the substantive content of the reasonable person standard. The *Restatement* presented a picture in which jurors perform the Hand Test to determine whether the defendant acted reasonably and hence whether the defendant will be held liable. This normatively driven picture fails as a descriptive account, however, owing to the lack of empirical support.

Coleman's account is not so obviously incorrect. While it may be quite implausible to suggest that the norms of ordinary jurors track the demands of cost–benefit analysis, it is less implausible to suggest that these norms might somehow track some ordinary conception of doing justice between victims and injurers. Nevertheless, Coleman owes us an explanation as to why the norms that appear to affect jury deliberations somehow lead to outcomes that are accurately characterized as instances of corrective justice, given the heterogeneity of the normative inputs.

Coleman's account and the proposed *Restatement* are leading examples of the dominant corrective justice and economic approaches. If we are to make full progress toward an account of negligence that adequately countenances the jury norm effect, it will be necessary in the future for scholars to expand the scope of examination to other accounts of negligence as well. All in all, a new theory of negligence may be needed, one that provides a more accurate account of the jury's important role in the practice of tort law in America. While the beginnings of this project are contained in the foregoing discussion, much remains to be done.

The preceding remarks bring to a close the discussion of the role of norms and customs that has transpired over the six chapters that make up Part Two. The goal of Part Two was to apply the theory of norms developed in Part One to tort law. Part Two began in Chapter Six with a look at the historical and jurisprudential underpinnings of the rule of custom. Chapter Six then looked in detail at the historically important example of customary easements in land. We looked at the strategic structure of some prominent examples of customary land usages. We saw that the norms motivating the decisions appear to be a mixture of welfarist and nonwelfarist impulses. The specific nonwelfarist side constraint we uncovered in the normative interpretation was one that arose in situations of induced detrimental reliance.

Chapters Seven through Nine explored the rule of custom from within a welfarist perspective. In particular, the one holding that courts seek to maximize welfare. I first discussed the historical shift from the dominance of the per se rule of custom to the evidentiary rule of custom. I argued that courts will want to apply different versions of the rule of custom depending on the welfare factors in play, and the rational structure of the underlying custom. We saw that the same three types of customs from Part One are salient in Part Two as each of these types has distinctive welfare markers. The analysis indicated that there were thirty-seven different types of rational custom. The evidentiary rule was the best choice in only eight of the thirty-seven possibilities. This has the practical implication of calling into question the dominance of the evidentiary rule of custom.

Finally, Chapters Ten and Eleven moved outside of the welfarist framework. We saw that the heterogeneous norms of jurors are in important part constitutive of the de facto liability standard. This juror norm effect is not best interpreted in terms of welfare maximization. Thus, the dominant Hand Test paradigm for negligence is shown to be an inaccurate characterization of the actual case law liability standard. Next, Part Three will apply the pattern conception of norms to the more specific topic of Internet privacy.

PART THREE

CYBERSPACE PRIVACY NORMS

Information privacy is a social goal, not a technological one. To achieve information privacy goals will require social innovations, including the formation of new
norms and perhaps new legal rules to establish boundary lines between acceptable
and unacceptable uses of personal information.[†]

Pamela Samuelson

[†] PAMELA SAMUELSON, "Privacy as Intellectual Property?," 52 *Stan. L. Rev.* 1125, 1126.

PART THREE

CYBERSPACE PRIVACY NORMS

12

Harmful Online Personal Data Practices

[Nonconsensual website interactions are] particularly likely when incentives are asymmetrically distributed in the community, as when buyers and sellers have their own conflicting norms. The norm that results from this conflict may represent a variety of things besides consensus: superior bargaining power on the prevailing side, collective action problems on the other side, or the use of strategic behavior.[1]

Mark Lemley

Introduction

There is a burgeoning privacy crisis caused in large part to the explosive growth of the Internet.[2] In large measure, this crisis has emerged in a legal vacuum, as there is little positive law that directly regulates the private collection of personal data. Because of this legal vacuum, informal social norms have the potential to play an especially important role in the regulation of data collection online.[3] This chapter begins an examination of the emergence of website norms pertaining to data collection that have emerged in the past decade.[4] This examination will provide another occasion to test the pattern conception of norms developed in Part One and further explored in Part Two. This case study will also be instructive regarding the possibilities for more effective regulation of online privacy, on a going forward basis.

The vast majority of commercial websites use their interactions with consumers as the occasion to collect personal data about these consumers.[5] The connection between the collection of personal data and personal privacy is straightforward; the more personal data that websites collect, store, and use, the less privacy that data subjects have. This reduction in privacy may be justified if the data subjects agree to exchange their personal information for something they prefer more.[6] Typically, however, personal data has been taken by websites without the subject's knowledge or consent.[7] Commercial websites behave in this morally dubious, but commercially reasonable, manner for two reasons. First, personal data is not owned; hence, it is not unlawful to collect it without consent. Second, in the emerging digital economy, personal data is becoming

increasingly valuable.[8] Given these facts, it is no surprise that commercial websites collect and use as much personal data as possible, and at a growing rate.[9]
Due to a torrent of media exposure, there is a growing public awareness of the
data-collection norms of the website industry and the ramifications of these
norms for personal privacy.[10]

Public awareness of this erosion in privacy has precipitated public outrage.
Opinion polls show increasing public concern with respect to online privacy.[11]
This outrage sets the stage for rapid policy shifts by private industry and lawmakers alike. The U.S. Congress increasingly has shown an interest in enacting
omnibus privacy legislation.[12] The Federal Trade Commission (FTC) repeatedly has articulated an interest in regulating online data collection.[13] Although
increased governmental regulation of online privacy likely will ensue, norms
and customs will continue to play a significant role as a result of the continued
strength of the norm favoring Internet self-regulation.[14]

Because of the importance of informal social and industry norms in regulating privacy in cyberspace, this topic presents a natural arena for the application
of law and norms theory. As discussed earlier in the book, based on empirical
studies of ranching and farming communities in Northern California, Ellickson
developed the hypothesis that efficient norms will emerge in "close-knit
communities."[15] These norms will serve as solutions to the iterated "collective-
action problems" faced by the group.[16]

With regard to Ellickson's hypothesis, the Internet may present an especially
difficult context for the emergence of efficient norms, however, because online
participants would appear to be anything but close-knit.[17] The apparent implication is that website privacy norms are inefficient because they are the product
of communities that are not close-knit.[18] Thus, even though these norms indeed
are emerging rapidly, there is reason to conclude that they are not moving toward greater efficiency. The task at hand, then, is not only to examine how and
why website privacy norms are emerging, but also to evaluate and hopefully
improve their efficiency, as well as other normatively desirable properties, such
as their ability to promote respect for Internet users.

The concept of privacy is itself generally understood in rights-based terms.[19]
In an online context, there is frequent discussion of the need for greater respect
for privacy. Phrased simply, respect is a deontological concept. Despite the
rhetorical focus on deontological concepts, the emergence of online privacy
norms that has occurred over the last decade is equally well described as a
move toward a more efficient regime of regulation of the flow of personal data.
One of the goals of the following discussion will be to establish a *compatibility
thesis* with regard to privacy and utility.[20] The crucial norms that have begun
to emerge in the website industry are both more efficient and more respectful
of privacy.

The compatibility between efficiency and privacy has been possible because
respect for data privacy has been cashed out in terms of autonomy. Respect for

privacy does not require minimizing the amount of personal data that is collected and processed.[21] Rather, it requires that data collection and processing not violate the autonomy of the data subject. Data collection that is respectful of autonomy is accomplished through the mechanism of consent.[22] When data subjects consent to the use and collection of their data by websites, then the websites are collecting data in a manner that respects the autonomy of the data subjects. These exchanges of data for valuable consideration are also productive of social utility because through exchange each party is able to receive something it prefers more by trading away something it prefers less.

This chapter will first look at the original privacy norms that emerged at the Web's inception in the early 1990s.[23] Two groups have been the main contributors to the emergence of these norms; the thousands of commercial websites on the early Web, on the one hand, and the millions of users of the early Web, on the other hand. The main structural feature of these norms was that websites benefited through the largely unrestricted collection of personal data, while consumers suffered injury due to the degradation of their personal privacy from this data collection. In other words, degradation of consumer privacy resulted as a third-party externality of free-market data-collection norms of the website industry.[24] Broadly speaking, then, these injuries occurred in a tort context as the injurers and victims were not in a bargaining relationship with regard to the injurer's procurement of the victim's personal data.[25]

Next, the chapter will examine the strategic structure of the relationships between websites and consumers that allowed these highly exploitative norms to flourish. Analysis will indicate that consumers faced a large-scale collective action problem. There is a collective good that consumers potentially could have achieved, namely, the abatement of disrespectful data-collection practices by websites. Web users would have great difficulty in organizing to secure this collective good, however, because of their large numbers and lack of repeat play and overlapping relationships.[26]

Reacting to this suboptimal but stable social situation, "norm entrepreneurs" entered the picture.[27] Three main types of norm entrepreneurs have been involved: public-interest advocates, website industry advocates, and governmental actors, particularly the Federal Trade Commission. Chapter 13 will examine how new, more respectful website privacy norms recently have begun to emerge, due largely to the efforts of these norm entrepreneurs. In the short history of the Internet, there has been a major shift – a "norm-cascade" – toward more respectful privacy norms.[28] The transition has been from a wild-west world in which websites did almost whatever they wanted with impunity to a world in which a significant percentage of websites are explicitly addressing privacy concerns. Norm entrepreneurs, in particular, *privacy norm proselytizers,* have been the prime movers in this transition.[29] Overall, an aspirational grundnorm of respect for website data privacy has begun to emerge in American culture generally.[30] Only time will tell whether this grundnorm can become more adequately instantiated in actual online practices.

It is important that the policy community better understand the mechanics whereby more respectful website privacy norms have emerged. If better norms are already emerging through informal social processes and minimalist governmental guidance, there may not be a need for sweeping legislation of the sort currently being proposed by the FTC, as well as by many privacy advocates who suggest that the United States adopt the comprehensive European model of privacy regulation, despite its evident tension with sacred free speech principles.[31]

I. The Original Website Privacy Norms

The first message sent across the Internet occurred one month after the moon landing in late 1969.[32] In theory, from that moment onward, the Internet could have been used by one person to gather personal data about another person impermissibly. There is nothing in the historical record to suggest, however, that the invasion of data privacy was a problem in this early stage of the Internet's development. One reason may be that, in this early period, the Internet was mainly used by academic researchers working in shared disciplines. Such groups tend to have fairly small numbers and overlapping, multiple interactions. In Ellickson's terms, these were close-knit communities in which there would have been internal incentives to deter opportunistic behavior.[33]

It took the occurrence of two events in the 1990s to set in motion the series of developments that would lead to the current privacy crisis. The first was the invention of the World Wide Web in the early 1990s by Tim Berners-Lee.[34] Once the core features of the Web were in place, the Internet became dramatically easier to use, and a vast flowering of websites spurted up spontaneously and rapidly. These were not electronic-commerce sites, however, as the National Science Foundation did not then permit commercial use of the Internet.[35] The Web was not available for consumers until the first Bush Administration zoned cyberspace for commercial use.[36] The commercialization of cyberspace is the second event that precipitated the privacy crisis, as commercial websites have been the main users of personal data collected under questionable circumstances.

Early commercial website norms facilitated data collection in two ways. First, many websites explicitly requested user information. Second, many websites collected data that was produced as a byproduct of website/consumer interactions, such as when consumers provided their credit card numbers or mailing addresses to sites. With the introduction of these online techniques of data collection, the commodification of personal data entered a phase of rapid acceleration, as each of these initial means of data collection was soon improved upon by websites.[37]

Regarding explicit requests for data, websites soon began conditioning access to their sites, or to prized pages within their sites, on the provision by website visitors of some personal data. For example, one who wanted to receive the *New York Times* online had to fill out a detailed data questionnaire first. Alternatively, users might receive discounts, coupons, or free entry in contests as an inducement for the provision of information.

Regarding the collection of data without consumer notice, websites soon began to deploy sophisticated technological means of data gathering, such as cookies.[38] Cookie technology allows a website's server to place information about a consumer's visits to the site on the user's computer in a text file that only the website's server can read. In the early period especially, because cookies were planted secretly and subsequently operated seamlessly, Web users were typically unaware of the fact that data about them was being gathered.[39] In other words, there was no bargain between the parties; the data was simply spirited away.[40]

When using cookies, a website assigns each consumer a unique identifier[41] so that the consumer may be recognized in subsequent visits to the site.[42] In this manner, the site engages in "passive tracking" of the consumer.[43] On each return visit, the site can call up user-specific information, which typically will include the consumer's preferences or interests, as indicated by pages the consumer accessed in prior visits, items the consumer clicked on while at the site, or information downloaded.[44] Cookies make it easier for firms to engage in highly targeted marketing.[45] Cookie technology has proven to be extremely valuable to online companies because it not only enables merchants to target products and services that are increasingly tailored to consumer preferences but it also permits other companies to boost their revenues by selling more highly valued advertising space on their web sites.[46] As Michael Froomkin says, cookies are the tip of the iceberg.[47] Once firms collect personal data, they may then aggregate it, or sell it to others who aggregate it, into databases containing profiles of named individuals. For example, a firm named Acxiom currently holds personal and financial information about nearly all U.S., U.K., and Australian consumers.[48] The personal-data norms of the early website industry are characterized in the following list.

PERSONAL-DATA NORMS OF THE EARLY WEBSITE INDUSTRY

1. Websites may freely gather as much personal data as desirable from consumers.
2. Websites need not ask permission to gather personal data.
3. Websites need not inform consumers of their data-gathering practices.
4. Websites may use personal data in any manner they prefer, such as selling or licensing it to third parties.
5. Websites need not allow consumers access to their data.
6. Websites need not provide security for personal data in their possession.

The most striking feature of these early website personal-data norms is that they were completely geared toward serving the interests of the website industry. They reflect the fact that most websites felt neither legal nor social pressure to respect the data privacy of the visitors to their sites. There was no legal pressure because there were no laws on the books that clearly prescribed these practices, and there was little social pressure because most people had little or no awareness that these practices were taking place.[49] In other words, these norms did not reflect any informal bargaining taking place between websites and consumers.

The fact that they emerged in a context in which there was a lack of bargaining is the most salient feature of the personal-data norms of the early website industry. Despite a lack of bargaining, there may be reason to think that these norms were efficient. They are potentially justifiable from an economic perspective, as websites take something from the public domain that was under utilized and put it to productive use. Like campers in a wooded area who collect fallen branches for use in their campfires, websites, on this view, are simply making use of a common resource that would otherwise be left lying in an unproductive state. After all, great quantities of personal data are produced as a by-product of other online activities. If not collected, this data would simply go unused. In fact, the economic argument in favor of shared use of personal information is stronger than it is for downed wood. Personal data is a *nonrival* good in the classic economic sense of the term; collection and use of personal data by one website does not diminish the amount available, either for other websites or for the data subject herself to use.[50] Because data is nonrival, arguably it should be left unregulated so that the greatest number of users will have free access to its use.

In this regard, note the important difference between personal data and creative expression of the sort protected by copyright law. Creative expression – original works of authorship – received legal protection, pursuant to Article I of the U.S. Constitution, in order to create incentives for authors to produce works.[51] Such an incentive is not necessary for the production of personal data, however, because it is produced as a by-product of living a life. Thus, there would appear to be a presumption in favor of treating personal data as a public good available to all.

There is an important disanalogy, however, between personal data and other shared goods such as fallen branches in a national forest. No one need suffer an injury when downed wood is burned, whereas data subjects often suffer significant harm when their personal information is used by others. Commentators have noted a wide variety of harms that may arise due to improper online data collection and use.

One type of harm is *identity theft*. Identity theft occurs when one person intentionally assumes another person's online identity. Thus far, identity thieves have typically gone on shopping sprees at the expense of their victims, but the possibilities for abuse through identity theft will grow as the functionality of the Internet expands.[52] Another type of harm that has received a good deal of attention is predation on children. Prior to recent legislation, children were especially vulnerable to questionable website practices.[53] A wide variety of detailed personal information has been collected online from children through various stratagems, such as encouraging a child to register for a contest, enroll in an electronic "pen pal" program, complete a survey, sign up for informational updates, or play a game. Still other sites used "imaginary" characters to request information from children, or had them sign a "guest book."[54] Data-gathering norms of the early website industry, however, did not distinguish children from adults. All visitors were equally disrespected.

Alternatively, harms may result as the foreseen but unintended consequences of mundane business operations, such as when firms use private medical information of potential employees in making hiring decisions. For example, one-third of Fortune 500 companies use personal medical information in hiring, promotion, or termination decisions.[55] This has the significant policy consequence that many people are failing to seek medical diagnosis and treatment.[56]

Some commentators have used the fact that personal data has a public-goods structure to argue that website/consumer interactions will be inefficient.[57] The mere fact that websites need not internalize the costs they create for third-party Web users does not, by definition, mean that the resulting website privacy norms are inefficient. The determinative factor will be a Kaldor-Hicks Test.[58] This test makes a hypothetical comparison of whether the websites' benefits from the activity could in principle more than compensate Web users for their losses. As a practical matter, this determination is often exceedingly difficult to make with any degree of certainty.

In the eyes of many privacy advocates, the calculation is not even close, because the loss to individual privacy is thought to be so grievous and fundamental as to outweigh any claim based merely on the prospect of more efficient electronic commerce. The website industry sometimes makes pronouncements to the effect that the benefits to industry, and therefore to consumers indirectly, are great, while privacy-related harms, although not insignificant, are nevertheless relatively small and greatly exaggerated. The fact that the website industry makes this claim cannot be taken as evidence of the industry's true estimation of the likely result of a Kaldor-Hicks Test, however, as industry speakers can be expected to seek to maximize profit, not candor. Because of the lack of a parallel profit motive, there may be less reason for cynicism with regard to the distance between the expressed views and the actual views held by public-interest privacy advocates. Accordingly, there is some reason to suppose that a Kaldor-Hicks Test may favor consumers over websites.

Some consumers, however, may be in a position on their own to sanction misuses of their personal data.[59] If it is the sort of site that one might visit on a repeated basis, then users can sanction these sites by withholding their visits and instead visit competing websites. In addition, disaffected users may sanction sites through negative gossip or criticism. Consumers also may adopt self-help measures such as supplying false information to the site.[60] Under typical circumstances, this behavior would be ruled out by a widely shared norm against deception and lying. But there is a competing norm of turnabout-is-fair-play, which may prove dispositive for numerous people who might otherwise not be given to deception.

The problem, however, is that all of these self-help measures assume that consumers have knowledge of the data extraction practices of offending websites. It is precisely for this reason that websites have generally sought at all costs to avoid explicit disclosure of their personal-data practices. Even when the consumer is aware that personal data is being collected, there is still the potential for abuse because consumers may be unaware of the uses to which their data is being put. For example, a user might be passively aware that personal data, such as credit card number or mailing address, are being collected but have no idea that this data is then being used by a website for purposes other than processing payment or mailing a product. In particular, many sites furtively sell data to third parties.[61]

The website industry did not trumpet the fact that the website industry data-collection norms discussed previously characterized its behavior with regard to the collection of personal data. The industry maintained these norms because it was profit maximizing and legal for individual websites to conform to them, not because the managers of the various online firms, acting as a coherent group, wished to establish justified norms of obligatory behavior for their industry. Thus, it served the website industry's interests that these norms in general remained unarticulated. This highlights the fact that norms, at their core, are patterns of behavior as opposed to rules, statements, or other linguistic entities.[62]

The early website norms are fairly described as *permissive norms*. They create normative freedom for their conformers rather than obligations or constraints.[63] This is noteworthy because norms theorists often write as if norms by definition express obligatory behavior.[64] One illuminating way to conceive of the project of privacy norm proselytizers, then, is that their goal is to shift website norms from permissive norms to obligatory norms.

II. Game-Theoretic Structure of the Original Website Personal Data Norms

The purpose of informal game theory is to model the strategic structure of social situations. The most famous and perhaps pervasive strategic structure of interest to social scientists and policymakers has been the structure variously known as the Prisoner's Dilemma, collective action problem, public good problem, or Tragedy of the Commons.[65] As the following discussion will demonstrate, the collective action problem is applicable to the topic of online privacy.

Much less understood than the collective action problem is the coordination game. While political scientists, economists, and philosophers have been developing a deeper understanding of strategic coordination for a generation, legal theorists have only recently come to appreciate its significance. The following discussion will demonstrate that coordination games have an important role to play in modeling the strategic structure of some of the social situations that undergird the online privacy debate.

This section has three parts, each of which will explore a strategic situation of concern to the privacy debate. Once these distinct strategic structures are understood, it will be easier to proceed on a path toward more respectful and efficient online personal-data norms. Section II.A considers whether the original permissive norms of the website industry can be accurately modeled as failed solutions to an iterated collective action problem. This question arises because the FTC has remarked that it intuitively views the situation in these terms. I argue in Section II.B, however, that this characterization is incorrect. Instead, the original, permissive norms of the website industry are best modeled as a multiparty coordination game. Getting clear on this distinction matters tremendously because it affects how various norm entrepreneurs should approach the task of bringing about more respectful practices in the website industry. Section II.C demonstrates that there is a significant collective action problem. It is website users, not the websites, however, who face a collective action problem. Their collective action problem arises with regard to organizing themselves to demand more respectful privacy norms.

A. Purported Website Industry Collective Action Problem

The FTC contends that it would be in the interest of the website industry to provide better privacy protection for consumers. The idea is that by showing more respect for the data privacy of consumers, websites will gain their trust and confidence. This in turn will lead to substantial growth in electronic commerce as trusting consumers will be more inclined to use the Internet to conduct their business. In its 1999 *Report to Congress*, the FTC stated that, "The Commission's efforts have been based on the belief that greater protection of personal privacy on the Web will not only benefit consumers, but also benefit industry by increasing consumer confidence and ultimately their participation in the online marketplace."[66] In testimony before Congress, Marc Rotenberg of the Electronic Privacy Information Center (EPIC) made a similar assertion: "Users of web-based services and operators of web-based services have a common interest in promoting good privacy practices. Strong privacy standards provide assurance that personal information will not be misused, and should encourage the development of on-line commerce."[67]

As these remarks indicate, both the FTC and EPIC think that it would be in the interest of the website industry to be more solicitous of the privacy concerns of consumers, in order to bring about greater user trust, which in turn will lead to a more robust online marketplace. This shared assumption by these leading online policymakers is crucial because of the policy implications that the FTC appears to think flow from it. Specifically, if it is in the industry's interest to respect privacy, bringing about more respectful practices will be a task of creating recognition across the website industry of the importance of privacy for consumers and why it is in the industry's interest to be solicitous of this concern of consumers. Not surprisingly, then, the FTC has sought to promote more respectful industry practices by means of educating the website industry. The FTC has held a number of workshops and related events with the goal of raising industry consciousness of the importance of data privacy.[68]

The problem with the FTC's education program, however, is that it implicitly treats the website industry as if it were a unitary actor capable of behaving in a concerted fashion so as to promote its collective goals. In its belief that its education program could achieve this result, the FTC unwittingly falls prey to the so-called *fallacy of composition*.[69] This is the fallacy of thinking that because a group, considered as a whole, would benefit from some particular political outcome, that therefore it is in the interest of each of the particular members of that group to do its part to help bring about this political outcome. It is simply false to assume that a typical website would have such an interest.[70]

The benefit of a particular website's individual contribution to the collective good, for all but the largest sites, will be marginal. Whether the collective good comes about almost surely will not depend on the additional contribution of the particular site. Thus, from a narrowly rational, economic perspective, the site is better off to free ride on the contributions of the other sites. Either enough other sites cooperate and the collective good is provided, or enough other sites do not cooperate, and the collective good is not provided. Either way, the behavior of the particular website will have but a marginal impact. Thus, it might as well refrain from incurring the expense of cooperating, that is, it might as well free ride. The problem is that all the other websites are similarly situated. Each will have a dominating preference to free ride. The result is that all will free ride and the collective good will not be produced.

The strategic structure of this situation may be represented as shown in Figure 12.1.

Figure 12.1 displays the strategic relationship between a particular firm, call it Website A, and all other websites (as based on the FTC's assumption described at the outset of this section). As indicated by the payoffs in the southwest cell, A's first preference is that other firms respect privacy so that it will be able to free ride on this set of practices and disrespect privacy. For the time being, *disrespect privacy* should just be taken to mean that the site will conform to the set of personal-data norms of the early website industry listed above, and *respect privacy* should be taken to mean that the site will refrain from conforming to

Website Industry

	Respect Privacy	Disrespect Privacy
Respect Privacy	3, 3	1, 4
Disrespect Privacy	4, 1	2, 2

Website A

Figure 12.1 Website Industry Respect Game

these norms. Chapters Thirteen and Fourteen will provide greater content to the notion of respecting consumer data privacy.

In the circumstance in which A free rides on the respectful behavior of the other sites, A receives the highest payoff, 4. According to the FTC, when other firms respect privacy, consumers will be less fearful of the Internet and consequently more prone to participate in electronic commerce. This will make it easier for website A to benefit from its own disrespectful practices, as consumers will be less leery of providing personal data to the site, based on their generally positive experiences with other sites.

The problem is that the same strategic situation pertains for the other websites as well. Each website would like all the other websites to be respectful so that it alone can take advantage of the more trusting consumers. Because defection is the dominant strategy for all, however, the southeast cell will be the result. Note that in the southeast cell, each website receives 2, its second lowest payoff. If, however, the website industry were to be successful in solving its collective action problem, the situation as characterized in the northwest cell would obtain instead. In this situation, each website would receive 3, its second highest payoff.

Note the distressing result that even though all parties would do better by cooperating and thus ending up in the northwest cell, because of the fact that each is compelled by narrow self-interest to perform the noncooperative action, the mutually dispreferred group outcome as represented in the southeast cell is the actual result.[71] We see then that individually maximizing behavior leads to a collectively suboptimal result – the classic collective action problem.

Uncovering this strategic structure inherent in the relationship among websites has important policy implications. Recall that one of the FTC's initiatives to promote online privacy was to educate the website industry about the connection between treating consumers with respect and the expansion of electronic commerce. In light of the preceding discussion, however, it is clear that things are not so simple; educating the industry participants as to their collective interest will in no way address the collective action problem faced by each of the particular members of the industry with regard to the supply of this collective good. Education may enhance the appreciation of each of the members as to the value of the potential collective good available to the group, but it will not change the incentives of individual members so as to bring the group any closer to realizing the collective good.

It will be difficult for the website industry to solve this collective action problem on its own. According to Ellickson's hypothesis, close-knit communities may produce solutions to collective action problems because they provide opportunities for repeat play and multiplex relationships among "neighbors."[72] When there is repeated interaction, parties may have an incentive to reach a mutually preferable manner of interaction because they will take their long-term interests into account, and these will often favor cooperation in current games in order to foster cooperation in future games. In the present context, this would mean individual websites not defecting on the cooperative behavior necessary to bring about a higher level of consumer trust in online commerce.

It may not be possible to apply Ellickson's hypothesis in the present context, however, because it is unclear whether the notions of "close-knittedness" or "neighbor" have any reference in cyberspace. Ellickson provides an extended discussion of land-use practices of the close-knit ranching and farming community that inhabits Shasta County in northern California. This community's norms concern issues such as liability for damage done by cattle and allocation of the costs of fencing, so as to avoid damage from cattle. This discussion implicitly assumes that the space in which interaction was taking place was physical space, not virtual space. What allows the ranchers and farmers to be close-knit was their physical proximity, as the subtitle of Ellickson's book – "How Neighbors Settle Disputes" – indicates.[73]

If the notion of close-knittedness is to have meaning online, then the term must be cashed out in nongeographical terms. The Internet promotes communication, par excellence, and thus is a boon to the formation and maintenance of social relationships. There is no reason those online relationships cannot involve repeat play and be overlapping, and there is no reason they cannot involve sanctions. Thus, the core preconditions for Ellickson's hypothesis may in principle be satisfied. More research is needed on the extent to which mechanisms such as hyperlinking may provide the foundation for close-knit communities in cyberspace. Despite the potential significance of this suggestion for our understanding of cyberspace generally, the implication for website privacy norms is untoward, as the relevant relationships at issue – those between websites and other websites, websites and users, and users and other users – are typically not close-knit. It is simply not the case that all the numerous sites on the Internet have repeated and overlapping interactions with one another.[74] The unavoidable conclusion appears to be that the website industry will not be able to solve its collective action problem on its own.

The collective action problem is a classical justification for governmental intervention.[75] Websites could simply be required to adopt more respectful practices.[76] This would have the effect of forcing websites to produce the cooperative outcome represented in the northwest cell in Figure 12.1. It is doubtful, however, whether the FTC has the authority to demand that websites change their behavior.[77] Even if the FTC had the authority, if one takes their remarks at face value, this is not authority they would care to exercise in this manner. As discussed earlier, the FTC has all along avowed an interest in promoting industry self-regulation to the extent possible. If the agency is to remain faithful to this goal, it must somehow indirectly encourage websites to solve their industry-wide collective action problem. Collective action problems, however, are notoriously difficult to solve. Thus, the FTC would face an especially daunting task in seeking to do so in an indirect manner.

B. Website Industry Coordination Norms

As noted at the outset of Section II.A, the analysis was based on the assumption of the FTC that the website industry has an overriding interest in bringing about more respectful privacy norms, if only the constituent websites could coordinate their efforts to bring about the cooperative result. It is more plausible to suppose, however, that the benefit of increased electronic commerce is not worth the high cost that providing respect for privacy might impose on websites.

The most significant cost for many sites of course will be the fact that consumer personal data will no longer be theirs to use and manipulate at will for free. In addition, for small sites, the very act of creating privacy policies imposes a cost that may be significant.[78] For large sites, these development costs are of marginal importance. But sites of successful or well-funded companies face a much larger cost: the increased exposure to litigation they face as a result of making explicit representations to site visitors regarding the site's data-collection practices.[79] Even if there is some marginal increase in their online traffic due to heightened consumer trust, it is more plausible to think that most sites would forego this benefit in order to avoid exposure to legal liability. Thus, the problem the FTC has in seeking to foster respect for privacy by self-regulatory means is not best modeled as the problem of helping an industry group that is not close-knit procure a collective good. Instead, as the following discussion demonstrates, the strategic structure faced by the website industry is actually that of a coordination problem. Its solution could potentially result in a desirable coordination norm.

As set out in Chapter Two, a coordination norm is a practice in which each conformer receives a *coordination benefit* for conforming to the norm. A coordination benefit is the added benefit an actor receives for conformity, given the conformity of other participants. To take a simple example, if the norm is to walk on the right side of the sidewalk, such as it is in America, then a particular conformer to this norm receives a benefit when others conform to the norm as well, as she is less likely to be involved in a pedestrian collision.

A coordination norm may be "an equilibrium," a "coordination equilibrium" or a "proper coordination equilibrium."[80] An equilibrium is a combination of choices in which each actor has done as well as the actor can, given the choices of the other actors. No actor will regret her choice given the choices of the others. A coordination equilibrium is a combination of choices such that no one would have been better off had any one actor, either the actor or someone else, behaved differently. A proper coordination equilibrium is a combination of choices such that no one would have been as well off had any one actor behaved differently, either the actor or someone else.[81]

Details aside, the crucial feature of coordination norms is that actors conform to them because it is in their direct interest to do so. This contrasts with collective action problems in which each actor's direct preference is not to conform but instead to defect, or free ride. With collective action problems, conformity will be forthcoming only if the participants are able to incentivize one another to conform due to the possibility of repeat play that results as a by-product of the overlapping social relationships of close-knit communities. With coordination norms, by contrast, actors want to conform, given the conformity of others. Hence, efficient coordination norms may emerge in communities that are not close-knit.[82]

The present concern, then, is whether personal-data practices are best modeled as coordination norms. The core feature of a coordination norm is that an actor receives a coordination benefit from performing the conforming action, given the conformity of others. This condition is met with regard to the permissive data-collection practices of the early website industry. As already noted, particular websites have a direct interest in not showing respect for consumers. By this means, they gain use of valuable user data at less expense and effort and they avoid the worry of exposing themselves to legal liability by making explicit representations to consumers as to how their data will be used.

In addition, it is plausible to suppose that websites prefer that other websites also fail to show respect for consumer privacy. First, websites will be able to collect data more successfully when consumers are left in the dark. Thus, all websites will be hurt to the extent that some particular website takes it upon itself to be more forthcoming in telling consumers about its data-gathering activities. The greater the public awareness of website data-gathering activities in general, the more likely it is for consumers to be wary of the activities of any particular website, and the more the site will be made to feel public pressure to alter its practices in the direction of greater respect.

The second reason why websites prefer that other websites conform to disrespectful privacy norms is that in privacy law, reasonable expectations of privacy matter.[83] An action in tort for invasion of privacy may be brought in civil litigation by aggrieved parties.[84] In such cases, a central consideration is whether the

Website Industry

	Respect Privacy	Disrespect Privacy
Respect Privacy	2, 2	1, 3
Disrespect Privacy	3, 1	4, 4

Website A

Figure 12.2 Website Industry Coordination Game

plaintiff had a reasonable expectation of privacy. If most websites are collecting data at will, with no safeguards and no notice, then the website-defendant will have a colorable defense based on the claim that the plaintiff did not have a reasonable expectation of privacy.[85]

For both of these reasons, then, it is to be expected that industry insiders will discretely promote disrespectful norms among their number on whatever occasions present themselves, such as through trade association meetings and the like, as doing so strengthens the norm and consequently solidifies their safe harbor. This means that these disrespectful website coordination norms will tend to be stable. Particular websites will have no internal motivation to change their behavior, and further, each site will have an incentive to motivate the other sites to continue their disrespectful behavior.

The original website data collection norms appear then to be proper coordination equilibria, as it is the case with each particular website that it would not have been as well off had either it or some other website acted differently by not conforming to the disrespectful privacy practices. This situation is represented by the payoff matrix in Figure 12.2.

The payoff matrix in Figure 12.2 displays the outcomes received by websites depending on whether each of them, as well as the other websites, participate in personal data collection practices that either respect privacy of Web users, on the one hand, or disrespect privacy of Web users, on the other hand. Note that the payoff to a typical website, call it Website A, is affected by whether other websites respect privacy or disrespect privacy. The dominating preference is to disrespect privacy. Website A prefers to disrespect privacy regardless of what other sites are doing. Thus, A's payoffs are higher in either of the southern cells as compared to either of the northern cells. But A receives a coordination benefit when other sites also disrespect privacy. Thus, the payoff for A is higher in the southeast cell as compared to the southwest cell. A least prefers the situation represented in the northeast cell in which it respects privacy and other sites disrespect privacy. In this situation, there will be no noticeable increase in electronic commerce and yet A has lost all the benefits from the free receipt of user data.

Like A, other sites prefer to disrespect privacy, so their highest payouts come in the eastern cells. They prefer, however, that A also disrespect privacy, due to the coordination benefit of keeping consumers in the dark. Thus, the other sites do better in the southeast as compared to the northeast cell. If the other sites are respecting privacy, however, then they will likely prefer that A do so as well, so that A is not at a competitive advantage. Thus, their payoff is higher in the northwest as compared to the southwest cell.

Note that the outcome as represented in the southeast cell in which all web-sites are disrespecting privacy is a stable equilibrium. No website has any in-centive to change its behavior, nor does any website have any incentive to get another website to change its behavior. Just the opposite, each website has an incentive to encourage each other website not to change its behavior. As should be obvious, this is not a happy outcome from the perspective of consumers or the FTC.

C. Web User Collective Action Problem

Note that the data-collection coordination norms of the website industry dis-cussed in Section II.B may function efficiently from a point of view internal to the conformers themselves. The harm resulting from these practices – the degradation of personal privacy – is successfully externalized onto the Web-surfing public.[86] Because these data-collection practices are bad for consumers as a group, there is the potential for this group to secure an important col-lective good, the abatement of these practices. As the current section demon-strates, however, there is a severe practical problem in consumers securing this good.[87] Consumers will face a collective action problem in seeking as a group to bring about the collective good of more respectful website pri-vacy practices. Thus, when the analysis of this section is combined with that of the previous two sections, the surprising result is reached that while the website industry does not face a collective action problem, the users of their websites do.

As discussed earlier in the context of website practices, standard game the-ory teaches that groups will stand their best chance of pursuing collective goods when their membership is close-knit such that members have repeated interac-tions across a number of dimensions.[88] This is more likely for smaller groups than larger groups, for groups that are close to one another in geographical space, and for groups that share similar interests, preferences, and histories. For exam-ple, the civil rights protestors who fought for months and ultimately prevailed in integrating Nashville's downtown restaurants in 1960 were African-American students of Fisk University, who had together participated in extensive group training in Gandhian methods of passive resistance.[89]

The Internet, however, makes collective action of this sort difficult. In theory, privacy militants might electronically enter previously targeted sites and all request downloads at the same time, such that the site's servers might be overwhelmed.[90] Clearly, this technique would require a good deal of coordination and effort among a large number of people. Thus, although possible in theory, such collective action is unlikely in practice.[91] Visitors to a website are the opposite of close-knit – they are globally interspersed strangers. Thus, a solution to the Prisoner's Dilemma of the sort outlined by Ellickson is unlikely because of the larger numbers of web users who lack overlapping or close-knit relationships. Accordingly, we can predict that extant website practices will represent a failure by consumers to solve collective action problems regarding the abatement of the degradation of their data privacy.

Moreover, the mere existence of a collective action problem does not imply that a norm, or set of norms, has been identified to deliver the potential collective good. A particular consumer who wanted to do her part to bring about the collective good of greater respect for consumers would not know where to start. There are no previously identified norms of behavior which, if conformed to by consumers, would help force websites into more respectful behavior. Because there is no cooperative norm under way, there is no form of cooperative behavior to *internalize*,[92] no issue of loss of *esteem* for failing to be cooperative,[93] and no concern to *signal* to others that one is a cooperative online activist.[94] It seems unlikely, then, that better website practices will emerge as a result of consumer collective action along the lines of any of the other leading models for solving collective action problems.

Conclusion

It will be useful to summarize the preceding discussion in order to see how the last finding regarding the dismal prospects for consumer collective action fits in with the earlier findings. The key fact on which the whole analysis thus far is predicated is that the original data-collection norms adopted by the website industry demonstrated a good deal of disrespect for consumer privacy. Essentially, the vast majority of websites have done whatever they wanted with regard to the use of personal information on consumers, with complete disregard for the impact of these activities on the privacy interests of these consumers. Despite growing complaints about this significant threat to individual privacy, the government was reticent to regulate this activity directly, apparently in response to the widespread norm that, as much as possible, the Internet should be left free to self-regulate.

Internet self-regulation, at least in the context of website practices with regard to the personal data of consumers, has been widely regarded as a failure.[95] In the preceding discussion, informal game theory was utilized in order to better understand why self-regulation has failed to produce a set of online practices that better respect consumer privacy. Generally speaking, self-regulation failed due to the strategic structure of the underlying social situations that obtained regarding the relationships between consumers and websites, on the one hand, and websites with one another, on the other hand. Specifically, websites are in a coordination game with one another, not an iterated collective action problem. Thus, efforts to educate websites on the importance of privacy to consumers, and on the connection between allaying consumer privacy fears and the promotion of consumer confidence, will not work to change website behavior in the manner desired by the FTC. Nor will consumers be able to band together to demand more respectful privacy practices on the part of websites due to the large-scale collective action problem they face.

A number of commentators concluded that the failure of self-regulation to overcome these hurdles mandated that the government step in and take a direct role in requiring more respectful informational practices on the part of websites. In the discussion in the next two chapters, however, it will be shown that direct government regulation of website practices has in fact not been required to bring about more respectful privacy practices, at least on the part of some websites.

13

The Emergence of Online Privacy Entitlements

Companies used to think of customer data as theirs. They're starting to realize they're really custodians, and the customer controls the information.[1]

Peter Brondmo

Introduction

Over the past few years, the norms governing personal data interactions between consumers and websites have changed dramatically. There is an increasing moral sensitivity regarding the commercial collection and use of personal data.[2] The social meaning of personal data collection has changed from a morally neutral to a morally charged status.[3] Consumers now perceive a general right to privacy in cyberspace that includes respectful treatment of personal data. This change arose not by accident or necessity but from the intentional actions of actors possessing an interest in promoting online privacy. I will designate these actors as *privacy norm proselytizers*.[4]

Social meanings attach to social norms; one method of changing social norms is to alter their social meanings.[5] For example, changing the social meaning associated with smoking is one way to regulate cigarette smoking among teens. As long as smoking retains a cool and rebellious mystique, it will be difficult to eradicate the practice.[6] Analogously, privacy norm proselytizers are in the process of changing the social meaning associated with websites' collection and use of personal data.[7]

The set of normative concepts that increasingly surround the practice in popular discourse is evidence that consumers are developing a more complex normative understanding. Notably, interactions between websites and their visitors are increasingly framed in terms of privacy. Privacy is among the most potent normative concepts of the modern age.[8] Proponents of personal data privacy have won a substantial victory now that data is widely understood to raise concerns for a new species of privacy: informational or data privacy. Not long ago, these expanded privacy concepts did not exist in either popular discourse or the moral theory lexicon.

Privacy is generally conceptualized as a right.[9] In ordinary moral understanding, rights function differently than preferences. Our preferences do not imply the existence of desired rights. By contrast, we have rights even if we do not prefer to exercise them. This is true for many individuals regarding their right of religious expression. Although they may have no desire to express their religious views, they may nevertheless place value in their right to do so. The same is true for personal data. Many people may not desire to actively control their personal data online; however, they may be inclined to support such a moral entitlement.

Increasingly, a consumer's entitlement to control her personal data is recognized.[10] Where does this growing sense of entitlement come from? It is primarily the result of the efforts of privacy norm entrepreneurs proselytizing to consumers regarding their entitlement to exercise control over personal data.[11] The word *proselytize* is appropriate because it would be unhelpfully reductionist to describe these entrepreneurs as merely fostering preferences for data privacy in the manner that Madison Avenue seeks to create preferences. Instilling a sense of moral entitlement to data privacy is fundamentally different from instilling a preference for Coke over Pepsi. Privacy norm proselytizers seek to arouse the moral consciousness of consumers vis-à-vis websites' collection and use of their personal data.[12]

As consumers increasingly perceive an entitlement, there is a corresponding tendency for them to feel moral outrage at websites that fail to respect data privacy. In terms of the emerging moral framework for governing online personal data, websites ought to respect the data privacy entitlements of consumers.[13] Websites that do so may earn the trust and confidence of consumers.[14] Consumers who think that they are disrespected, however, may seek to punish websites by taking their business elsewhere, reciprocating the disrespect by providing the website with false personal information,[15] or sanctioning the website through negative gossip.[16]

Commercial websites are profit-maximizing entities, and thus morality has no intrinsic relevance for them. Nevertheless, they must engage in interactions with consumers who do have complex moral psychological states. Woe be unto the website that blithely carries on as if consumers merely have a preference for data privacy in the same manner they have a preference for, say, price discounts or free gift-wrapping.[17] Thus, while websites are not themselves moral, they may nevertheless need to address moral concerns to effectively interact with consumers. They may even hire a morally oriented executive: a chief privacy officer.[18]

It may appear naive to assume that consumers could have a pseudomoral relationship with a distant, uncaring, and profit-maximizing website. In other areas, however, the law is available to create relationships that simulate moral relationships: this is the notion of the fiduciary. Ideally, doctors, lawyers, and accountants would legitimately care about their clients' well-being. At the very least, their clients expect and pay for these professionals to act as though they care. The reason clients may trust their fiduciaries to take their interests to heart is that this is part of their contractual agreement. Similar relationships may potentially be achieved via informal social norms rather than formal legal structures. We may be moving into a world where this occurs with respect to the relationships between websites and their visitors. Many websites now expressly promise to respect their users' privacy in statements loaded with moral language. This moral language arguably creates consumer expectations that may subsequently be interpreted as constituting special, legal relationships.

Among the strongest privacy guarantees are those found on financial services firm websites. Citigroup states that it is "committed to the Citigroup Privacy Promise for Consumers."[19] Note that Citigroup designates its assertions as a promise. Other websites typically entitle their commitments as a privacy "statement" or "policy."[20] The risk of making such statements is having the language used adversely against the firm should litigation ensue. Citigroup likely calculated that the positive value of the moral language offset the potential risk. The Citigroup Privacy Promise contains additional language that would be useful to a plaintiff's class-action attorney in arguing that a legally enforceable promise was made.[21]

The legal enforceability of privacy policies is currently an unsettled area of the law.[22] Some websites claim that users who use the website agree to the terms of the website.[23] This language may promote contractual interpretations of the privacy statement. Others expressly disavow any contractual reading of the document.[24] Even if not contractually interpreted, these promises may still have legal significance. The Federal Trade Commission has used its jurisdiction to regulate unfair and deceptive trade practices by prosecuting failures to comply with the terms of privacy policies.[25] Websites' representations may arguably create privacy expectations such that promiscuous uses of customer data are tortious.[26] More generally, Congress has regulated particularly sensitive categories of personal information, including medical and financial data and information collected from children.[27] The more that websites treat all consumer personal data in a similar fashion under their privacy policies, the more they invite Congress to formally treat all personal data on par with the most sensitive categories.

Why would websites expose themselves to potential liability and increased prospective regulation? In other words, what economic forces have fostered a situation where websites are the dominant suppliers of more respectful Internet privacy norms? What benefits do they receive as suppliers of these norms that have caused them to assume the costs associated with their supply? This chapter addresses these questions and examines the role of privacy norm proselytizers in changing the social meaning of data collection. These changes in social meaning have increased consumer demand for privacy and, correspondingly, website supply.

The previous chapter examined the original data-collection practices that emerged at the World Wide Web's inception in the early 1990s. The social meaning of these practices was nonmoral. Websites benefited through the largely unrestricted collection of personal data, while consumers, more or less unawares, absorbed a third-party externality in the degradation of their personal privacy.[28] These practices emerged as the first norms of online data collection. The persistence of these norms created a norm gap between the actual practices and the practices norm proselytizers judge to be preferable.[29]

This chapter will examine methods by which norm proselytizers endeavored to moralize the social meaning of online data collection to close this norm gap. These privacy proselytizers precipitated a norm cascade toward more respectful privacy norms.[30] Following in their wake, other norm entrepreneurs promoted the emerging moralized data norms. This chapter will conclude by examining the activities of two of these new entrepreneurs – the FTC and creators of new software privacy solutions.

The current situation is far from ideal because many websites have failed to adopt more respectful privacy practices. Other firms have endorsed such practices in word but not deed, either by posting deceptive privacy policies or by regularly violating the terms of their posted policies.[31] On the whole, improvements in consumer/website interactions have been realized. Through the efforts of norm proselytizers, a grundnorm of respect for consumer data privacy has generally emerged in American culture. American society is only at the beginning of the difficult task of incorporating this grundnorm into its social and business practices.

I. Privacy Activists Moralize the Social Meaning of Data Collection

The emergence of the grundnorm of industry respect for consumer privacy by websites is the story of how privacy activists working in their capacity as norm proselytizers have successfully changed the social meaning of data collection from a predominantly nonmoral to a morally charged activity. Consumers increasingly feel entitled to respectful treatment from those who handle their precious personal data. This dramatic change in the consumer/website relationship did not emerge spontaneously but was the result of the conscious efforts of privacy activists.

Subsection A examines the relationship between social meanings and social norms. Subsections B and C explore methods through which privacy activists have moralized the social meaning of data collection and the dimensions of this new morality. Subsection D examines the impact of this change in social meaning on the strategic relationship between consumers and websites. Finally,

Subsection E looks at a causal feedback loop that leads toward a pooling equilibrium.

A. *Social Meanings and Social Norms*

Among the key insights of recent law and norms literature is the connection between norms and their social meanings. The best approach to changing a social norm may be to change its social meaning. To illustrate this, Larry Lessig discusses dueling by the aristocratic class in the Old South.[32] The dueling norm was resistant to legal prohibition, but making dueling illegal left intact its social meaning: participation was perceived as honorable; refusal, as cowardly. A more promising approach was to change dueling's associated social meaning by making it illegal for duelers to hold the honorable position of public office.[33] This changed the social meaning such that potential participants were able to decline duels without losing honor because of the credible claim that the refusal was motivated by the esteemed prospect of holding public office.

With other social norms, however, the affiliated social meaning may be very difficult to change. With gun possession by juvenile members of street gangs, the challenge is to shift the social meaning from one in which gang members enhance their relative status by challenging authority through handgun possession.[34] The perverse logic of the illicit handgun possession norm and its affiliated social meaning is that the greater the legal sanction against the activity, the greater the peer status for continued participation.[35]

With personal data collection, the goal of norm entrepreneurs has been to shift the social meaning from a morally neutral to a morally loaded content. Two differences exist between data collection norms and norms such as gun possession and dueling, both of which uniquely complicate the privacy activists' task. In the previous examples, the norm conformers are also the primary intended beneficiaries of the proposed new norm. With data collection, however, website visitors are the main group of intended beneficiaries, not the websites themselves.

A second difference is that the goal in the preceding examples was to reduce or eliminate behavior. With personal data collection practices, however, the goal is more complex. The purpose is not to eliminate completely the collection and use of personal data by websites but rather to put this practice on firmer moral ground. Balancing websites' benefits from disrespectful collection practices and the desire not to eradicate data collection entirely, it seems especially difficult for privacy norm entrepreneurs to bring about a more respectful and nuanced result.

The next subsection addresses the manner by which privacy proselytizers have approached the difficult task of changing the meaning of personal data collection in cyberspace. As this section demonstrates, the logical first step was to fit the relevant practices into a broader normative framework. Privacy proselytizers were then in a position to evaluate potential demands placed on websites that respect privacy. Finally, the activists proselytized to convince the public to accept their moral position.

B. Internet Privacy Activists' Proselytizing Efforts

Privacy regulation in the United States has consisted of applying the concept of privacy to new situations that resulted from emerging technologies. Brandeis and Warren's famous article, for example, was a response to the new privacy threat posed by the invention of the camera and its subsequent use by the media.[36] The seminal Supreme Court cases, Olmstead v. United States[37] and Katz v. United States,[38] resulted from the development and use of telephone wiretapping technology by law enforcement officials.

A generation ago, the pre-Internet electronic privacy advocates highlighted the threat that government computers posed to privacy.[39] The threat arose from U.S. government plans to use computers to construct a comprehensive personal information database on its citizens. While privacy activists continue to perceive government as a threat to personal privacy, the focus of attention has changed in recent years to the private domain. The single most significant impetus for this change has been the emergence of the Internet and the associated website industry.[40]

When government was the perceived threat, privacy activists invoked the Fourth Amendment of the U.S. Constitution with some degree of success. When the main threat to privacy came from private entities such as websites and Internet companies like DoubleClick, legal claims in favor of data privacy have had little success. It has been argued that these websites violated one or more privacy torts,[41] or engaged in unfair trade practices. Attorneys have proposed that when websites plant cookies on the hard drives of consumers they commit trespass to chattels.[42] On the whole, however, none of these legal arguments has provided much protection against the majority of website data practices. Privacy activists instead place great reliance on claims that website practices are immoral.

In recent years, a number of public-interest organizations have identified online privacy as an important public-policy concern. These groups include the Electronic Privacy Information Center, the Electronic Frontier Foundation (EFF), and the Center for Democracy and Technology (CDT). Particular individuals, notably Marc Rotenberg and Richard Smith, have become highly visible advocates for online privacy. Rotenberg, the Director of EPIC, is the best known "inside-the-beltway" proponent of electronic privacy. Smith is a so-called *ethical hacker*, who works to expose new forms of privacy invasion.[43] As online privacy has become a highly publicized topic, shapers of public opinion, such as *New York Times* columnist William Safire, have also recently begun to proselytize.[44]

The privacy activist community has employed several strategies to further its goals: activists have functioned as industry watchdogs and legislative proponents and worked closely with the media. Through these activities, privacy activists have pursued the related aims of education and effecting a change in moral perspective. They have sought to educate the public, politicians, and the media regarding factual issues relating to data collection *and* have striven to change these groups' moral perspective regarding their personal data.

Activists have sought to inform the public of the causal connection between privacy and website data collection activities because the potential harms resulting from an inability to control personal data are not readily apparent.[45] It is sometimes noted that consumers are not significantly harmed by identity theft because fraudulent credit card billing is insured beyond a $50 deductible.[46] In fact, the real danger from identity theft is the potential for serious harm to consumer credit records.[47] The lack of education also frustrates public appreciation of the connection between private medical data and potential damage to public health. The media presented stories connecting the flow of medical information with harms that include failure to seek medical treatment for fear of an electronic trail that could later affect employment opportunities.[48]

The bare knowledge of potential consumer harm does not inherently carry any moral implication. No moral implication follows, for example, from dental-hygiene advocates informing the public of the harmful results of plaque. Thus, establishing a moral connection between website activities and consumer harms was a core goal of the privacy norm proselytizers. Norm entrepreneurs have advocated a moral relationship of responsibility between the data practices of websites and consumers' loss of privacy and have not dismissed consumer privacy loss as a necessary casualty of the emergence of electronic commerce. This is a moral criticism that has a distinct deontological or Kantian flavor: websites are effectively charged with treating people as mere means to an end. First, consider briefly a broad survey of the steps that privacy proselytizers have taken to promote their goals.

Ethical hackers and corporate watchdogs have been highly successful in discovering dubious website practices. The best examples of privacy activists targeting private companies surrounded DoubleClick's acquisition of Abacus Direct. Its intention was, contrary to earlier representations, to combine the online and offline personal data from both enterprises. The advocacy community brought the plan to the attention of the media, which gave generous attention to the story. The price of DoubleClick's stock dropped precipitously as the story unfolded in the press, destroying billions of dollars of the company's market capitalization.[49] The company has subsequently been embroiled in lawsuits and subjected to a heightened level of scrutiny from privacy activists and the FTC.[50]

Other examples of successful privacy activism occurred when ethical hackers discovered that Microsoft was building a tracking utility into its software and RealNetworks was tracking the online activities of its customers.[51] The media coverage of these stores typically included a quote from a privacy advocate regarding the threat to personal privacy posed by the technology.[52] Once under the media spotlight, these companies quickly backed away from their planned activities.[53]

In an effort to promote laws that will create greater compatibility between positive law and the personal data norms that they promote, privacy activists have engaged in legislative activities. Marc Rotenberg, for example, has repeatedly testified before Congress in support of privacy legislation.[54] Rotenberg is credited with the Digital Millennium Copyright Act provision that could serve as a loophole if the act fosters a regime of content licensing that requires unduly invasive monitoring.[55] Privacy activists were also instrumental in lobbying for the enactment of COPPA.[56] More recently, they have pushed for an extension of this regulatory framework to adults.[57]

As with their watchdog activities, privacy activists have effectively utilized their media contacts to draw public attention and support for their legislative initiatives. The activists' efforts have generally been geared toward bringing media attention to online data issues and then converting the media to their normative positions. Both efforts appear highly successful. In the recent past, the *New York Times* has contained at least one story per week touching on issues of electronic privacy. More conservative publications such as *The Economist* and *Forbes* have also given sympathetic treatment to the activists' views.[58] Because electronic privacy is currently a leading policy concern, the media's hunger for news stories is steadily growing, making it increasingly receptive to the story tips and press releases provided by the public interest advocacy groups.

The success of first-generation privacy norm proselytizers is reflected by the attention of a second generation of privacy entrepreneurs, public "opinion leaders," to online privacy.[59] William Safire, columnist for the *New York Times*, recently authored an editorial strongly endorsing the need for online privacy.[60] Remarkably, no particular privacy-related news event motivated the editorial – the topic itself has become newsworthy. Unlike many privacy activists, Safire did not either call for a legislative solution or explicitly promote a self-regulatory approach. Rather, he addressed the issue at a more theoretical level, arguing that Internet privacy is an issue of growing concern to all "lovers of freedom." As this example suggests, a second success of the first generation of norm proselytizers is that online privacy is perceived as so urgent and morally cogent that it transcends ideological faction.

C. The Moral Meaning of Internet Privacy: Reasonable Control Over One's Personal Data

Norm proselytizers, including those advocating privacy norms, promote norms because they morally support them. The bare fact that privacy proselytizers accept similar moral principles does not mean that they agree on the application of abstract moral principles to actual circumstances. Unless they take the untenable position that privacy trumps all other concerns, even strong believers in data privacy must balance this value against other values. Thus, the privacy proselytizer who has realistic hopes of winning converts among ordinary people must develop a position supporting increased online privacy that coheres with ordinary morality.

Two factors present in the early online environment should have deterred privacy proselytizers from quick conclusions about greater online privacy: the suspect website behavior was legal, and consumers were indifferent toward online data privacy issues. Typically, seriously immoral behavior is illegal. Because website data collection practices were not illegal, one implication was that websites were behaving in a morally acceptable fashion. This is not dispositive, however, because when new types of behavior arise, often there is some delay before the law reacts.

The second factor of consumer indifference is more troublesome for the privacy proselytizer. As discussed in Chapter Twelve, consumers did not appear concerned about website data collection practices when they first emerged. If the consumers themselves were indifferent, could norm proselytizers intervene without appearing as norm paternalists?[61]

Paternalism is a suspect form of activity that morally coherent norm entrepreneurs might seek to avoid, as it conflicts with the widely accepted principle of autonomy.[62] To act paternalistically is to fail to respect individuals' ability to make decisions that they believe will best serve their interests. The privacy activist must sometimes recognize that many people may not care what websites do with their personal data.[63] In fact, many individuals may favor free use of their personal data because they prefer the resulting personally tailored marketing over privacy.[64]

The paternalist seeks to assert parental authority against the inclinations of the subjects, while the proselytizer seeks to change the moral consciousness of autonomous subjects. Impressionistic evidence indicates that norm entrepreneurs have functioned in both capacities.

It is the mark of a savvy norm entrepreneur to spot a situation that is ripe for the emergence of a new norm. A norm may sometimes receive widespread yet weak social support, while the latent support for a potential replacement norm is strong. Cass Sunstein discusses the attack on apartheid in South Africa, the use of the term *liberal* as a term of opprobrium, and the current assault on affirmative action, as examples of this phenomenon.[65] Eric Posner provides a similar analysis of the norms that bolstered regimes of the former Soviet republics.[66] In Poland, the population was ripe for a new regime incorporating more democratic norms because the support for the old norms was more apparent than real.[67] Similarly, contemporary online privacy activists intuitively sensed that widely held moral concepts would assist them in quickly shifting public views from a position of indifference to moral concern.

The task of the privacy norm proselytizer varies depending on the community. In countries with generally weak commitments to privacy values, it is more difficult to proselytize for data privacy. In the United States, however, the privacy norm activists have an easier task because there is already a strong commitment to privacy.

The goal is to extend the scope of the concept of privacy to cyberspace. This is analogous to the task of animal rights proselytizers seeking to extend moral principles applicable to humans across species to other sentient creatures. Electronic privacy advocates do not extend moral principles to new species but rather to new types of situations involving the online collection of personal data. In either case, the goal is the same: to make people see a commonality where before they saw a distinction. The privacy proselytizer's core normative assertion is that individuals have a right to data privacy – though privacy activists rarely discuss why this right should exist. Indeed, it is not the task of privacy proselytizers to establish the right as an objective moral truth. Their task is to convince others to adopt their position; effective proselytizing need not involve reasoning from first principles.

The website industry accepts the proposition that consumers have some right to data privacy.[68] This is a striking admission. One might have expected the industry to take the more aggressive position that because personal data is in the public domain, websites are just as entitled to use it as the data subjects are. Instead, the typical posture of industry is to acknowledge that data subjects have some special entitlement to their personal data, despite a dearth of legal protection. The website industry's conflict with public-interest privacy advocates is over the proper conception of privacy, how much privacy is appropriate, and which thick behavioral practices should invoke the grundnorm of privacy respect. In other words, the disagreement is not over the grundnorm, per se, but which second-order norms and which thick behavioral norms should be established to promote privacy. The website industry has predictably proffered a fairly minimalist framework of practices to promote the grundnorm.

There is no monolithic view as to what the right to data privacy encompasses.[69] On one extreme, the less personal data that is collected and used, the better.[70] This position may have trouble winning widespread support, however, because this appears to go against consumer preferences.[71] Many consumers seem willing to trade away personal data as long as they receive valuable consideration in return.[72] Most privacy proselytizers do not seek to minimize data collection and use but rather to change the nature of the relationship between websites and consumers from a morally problematic to a morally acceptable situation.

Norm proselytizers espouse a number of concrete norms to support the second-order norms of data privacy respect: notice, consent, access, security, and enforcement. Least controversial is the notion that data privacy rights include a right to receive notification of the uses to which websites will put personal data. At least in its public discourse, the website industry widely accepts the requirement of notice.[73] Some notion of consent or agreement is the second most often mentioned component of data privacy rights. There is, however, deep division regarding the definition and implication of consent in the context of website data gathering.[74]

The concept of consent is ambiguous in distinguishing between opt-in and opt-out regimes. In an opt-out regime, personal data will automatically be collected unless a consumer specifically indicates otherwise. Industry groups such as the Online Privacy Alliance have also promoted an opt-out policy.[75] The alliance is a coalition of more than eighty companies and trade associations and was formed in early 1998 to encourage self-regulation of data privacy.[76] In an opt-in regime, the default is that personal data will not be collected unless the consumer explicitly agrees. Privacy advocates are typically advocates of opt-in.[77]

Privacy is often defined as the right to be left alone.[78] Website respect for consumer privacy cannot mean that websites should literally leave consumers alone because consumers are the ones who visit websites. Instead, the core meaning of privacy in the context of website personal data practices is that the website should leave the visitor's data alone, except to the extent the visitor consents to her personal data being collected and used. When a consumer allows her data to be collected and used, she will have less informational privacy as a result. Note that even though this collection and use would reduce privacy, it would not be an instance of the website disrespecting the visitor because the collection and use occurred with the visitor's consent. The central moral imperative is not to minimize collection and use of personal data but rather to gather and use a visitor's personal data in a manner that does not violate her ability to control the flow of her personal data. When a website surreptitiously collects personal data from a consumer, this bypasses her rational capacities and treats her as incapable of choosing to supply her data.

In addition to notice and consent, norm proselytizers have promoted a right of access to personal data residing on the databases of websites or related entities like DoubleClick.[79] Generally, the claim is for access and the additional ability to contest or correct incorrect data.[80] The industry has generally opposed these measures, claiming that they would be unduly expensive to implement.[81] Some websites, however, have begun to make explicit offers of consumer access to data.[82]

A fourth element of the general right to data privacy is security for personal data residing in databases of commercial firms.[83] If personal data is easily accessible by hackers, the website may be causally implicated in injuring the consumer whose data is stored by the website, even if the website is not guilty of any active wrongdoing.

Finally, the effectiveness of the foregoing privacy protections is dependent upon implementation of an enforcement principle, which requires that governmental and/or self-regulatory mechanisms impose sanctions for non-compliance with fair information practices.[84] These five aspects of the general right to data privacy are accurately grouped under the notion that people have a right of reasonable control over their personal data.[85] Note that a right to reasonable control does not entail a consumer right to ownership of individual personal data.[86] If consumers own their personal data, they presumably can sell it. Once alienated, the consumer has no more claim to it than a piece of real property. The right to access personal data and secure data storage discussed previously may be rights that are preferably inalienable.[87]

There is a logic of ordinary morality that applies by extension to the normative language of data privacy. For example, there are important differences between preferences and entitlements. Websites that mistreat personal data are not merely subverting consumer preferences but are violating consumers' perceived rights. This is morally offensive. Many consumers prefer that Amazon charge less for shipping and handling, but they do not feel morally outraged when Amazon fails to oblige because they are not entitled to this treatment. Consumers increasingly feel entitled to the specific respectful treatment of their data.[88] One Internet entrepreneur summarized Internet firms' growing recognition of consumer feelings: "Companies used to think of customer data as theirs. They're starting to realize they're really custodians, and the customer controls the information."[89]

Consumers currently have little legal recourse, but they may nevertheless possess a moral response that is, from the website's perspective, functionally equivalent. Morally speaking, consumers will disdain disrespectful websites. They will view such websites as less reputable, trustworthy, and worthy of continued business relationships. More aggressive consumers may feel that disrespectful websites deserve to be sanctioned or otherwise reciprocally ill-treated.[90]

We are now in a better position to understand the distinct and interrelated functions of privacy proselytizers. First, proselytizers sought to educate the public about the causal connection between website data collection activities and individual privacy. Advocates then sought to highlight the fact that websites were morally harming the public through their activities. Activists further taught that consumers have a moral entitlement to a reasonable degree of control over their personal data. The following subsection will discuss a consequence of this moral connection: consumers utilize their strategic leverage over websites to further their moral rights and entitlements to privacy.

D. Data Privacy Rights Create a Strategic Interaction of Respect and Trust

An important strategic implication follows from the activities of privacy activists in creating a sense of consumer entitlement to personal data. As previously discussed, consumers did not view their relationship with websites as strategic until they perceived it as a moral relationship. But once consumers perceive websites as either respecting or disrespecting them, they will respectively trust or distrust websites. The more strongly consumers feel a data privacy entitlement, the more they will be morally affronted by instances where websites disrespect their privacy. Accordingly, they will be slower to trust websites and more inclined to punish those that fail to show respect. Retaliation may take the form of negative gossip or providing false or misleading information to the website.[91]

The notion of website visitors choosing to trust is similar to Richard McAdams's idea that actors can choose whether to esteem another party with whom they are interacting.[92] Note, however, that whereas McAdams plausibly contends that the desire for esteem is a brute preference that a rational actor might prefer for its own sake, I am not asserting that trust is something that websites would independently desire. Rather, a website would prefer to gain the trust of its visitors because this trust will be positively correlated with these visitors choosing to interact with the website in the future. In other words, websites hope to signal to consumers that they are desirable partners with whom to cooperate.[93] The situation becomes strategic because the website is then in a position to choose whether to respect the consumer and engender consumer trust.[94] Part of the website's choice to show respect, or not, will depend in part on its calculation of how much its choice will cause the consumer to trust the website, and how much the resultant cooperative opportunities are worth to the website.[95] The strategic structure of the situation is represented in Figures 13.1 and 13.2.

Each party has two choices, each affecting the utility of the other party. Thus, each party needs to think about how its choice and the choice of the other party will affect its payoff. This means that each party considers whether it can affect the other's choice. Specifically, the website will consider whether it should attempt to foster consumer trust, and the consumer will consider whether she can influence the website's choice to provide a privacy policy.[96] Once the consumer appreciates that the website's actions will affect her outcomes, she will either withhold or bestow trust to incentivize the website to show respect.

Large Website

		Privacy Policy	No Privacy Policy
	Trust	3, 3	1, 4
Visitor			
	No Trust	3, 1	1, 2

Figure 13.1 Large Website/Consumer Strategic Interaction

Small Website

		Privacy Policy	No Privacy Policy
	Trust	2, 2	1, 4
Visitor	No Trust	2, 1	1, 3

Figure 13.2 Small Website/Consumer Strategic Interaction

Because of these mutually affecting choices, a greater number of websites may find it in their interest to respect privacy in order to maintain the trust of the increasingly educated, and demanding, consumer.[97] Indeed, the number of websites that show respect for privacy has continued to grow as public consciousness of the issue of online privacy has grown.[98] Note that as recently as a few years ago, only a minority of websites – the larger and better-known websites – offered privacy policies.[99] This makes sense because these websites are most likely to have overlapping, multifaceted interactions with consumers, thus making it crucial for these websites to have respectful and trustworthy reputations.

That websites place a premium on consumer confidence is readily indicated by the extent to which they attempt to acquire it deceptively. Many firms have deceptive privacy policies. In other words, the firm wraps itself in a cloak of respect by means of the privacy policy, and yet the actual terms of the policy are *lawyered* such that the firm does whatever it pleases with personal data.[100] For example, Toysmart.com explicitly promised not to sell data: "[p]ersonal information voluntarily submitted by visitors ... is never shared with a third party."[101] In bankruptcy, Toysmart then attempted to sell this data.[102] Despite the sense of consumer entitlement, many small websites may still prefer to avoid the expense of providing privacy policies. As illustrated in Figure 13.2 many small websites may still prefer the outcome of mutual noncooperation (southeast cell) to that of mutual cooperation (northwest cell).

As a result of privacy proselytizers, a situation has emerged in which there are two types of norms. Previously, there were simply permissive norms whereby websites did whatever they wanted with personal data without regard for consumers. Now new, more respectful, norms are emerging. For simplicity's sake, the previous discussion focused solely on the provision of privacy policies. But as already mentioned, there are many actions websites may undertake in order to demonstrate their respect. Although this represents significant moral progress from a privacy activist perspective, a major problem remains. New, more respectful norms are now in play, but so, too, are the old nonrespectful norms.

The following discussion will demonstrate that while the privacy activists may not themselves have the resources to push for universal conformity to respectful norms, these norms have taken on a life of their own. The result is that other norm entrepreneurs find it is their interest to get involved in promoting these norms. Both the FTC and various private companies have come to have an interest in further promoting those more respectful data norms first proselytized by the privacy activists. Before examining these norm entrepreneurial activities, however, consider briefly one additional force that may cause websites at the margin to switch to more respectful norms as a consequence of the initial efforts of the privacy activists.

E. Causal Feedback Loop Leading Toward Pooling Equilibrium

There is an apparent causal feedback loop operating: as more respectful practices emerged, consumers have become informed about online privacy and, consequentially, increasingly demanding of their privacy.[103] In a criminal law context, Dan Kahan observes a parallel phenomenon whereby a rise in crime makes social sanctions less powerful, which leads to more crime.[104] In the situation described by Kahan, the causal feedback loop leads to normative breakdown. Richard McAdams describes a similar dynamic involving social norms pertaining to wearing fur and smoking cigarettes.[105] McAdams observes that as more people shun the behavior, the remaining participants in the activities will experience an increasingly negative impact. This puts greater pressure on these remaining participants to abandon the activity. Depending on the utility functions of the remaining participants, the greater pressure may induce some to abandon the activity. Through continued iterations of this causal loop, all participants may, over time, defect from the activity. Alternatively, some stalwarts may have strong preferences that continuously outweigh all pressures to defect. After a time, a new equilibrium may result such that there are stable populations of conformers and nonconformers.

A parallel dynamic in website privacy practices seems to be under way. As the number of websites providing privacy policies increases, the more intense will be the perception that the remaining websites are disrespectful of consumer interests. Increasingly, websites without a policy will be outliers in their disregard for consumer privacy interests. This will likely cause an increasing number to alter their behavior, possibly leading to a tipping point where most websites begin to take privacy more seriously.[106]

Whether such a feedback loop is in operation is an important question. The previously described process is self-regulating in the sense that the impetus toward the new norms comes from informal social forces rather than formal legal methods. One criticism occasionally made of self-regulation is that while it may work to motivate many, or even most, players to act in a cooperative fashion, there will still be some players – the *bad actors* – who fail to conform.

Due to the causal feedback mechanism, there may be the potential for the *bad actors* to become cooperators. For example, this may already be occurring among the participants in the Network Advertising Initiative, an industry group formed to agree on acceptable forms of privacy protection. A commentator suggested that the 10 percent of advertisers who did not initially comply with the industry guidelines might be led by "centrifugal force" to go along, or risk losing both respect and business.[107]

II. Strengthening the Privacy Entitlement for Nonmoral Reasons

A. The FTC's Threat Model of Privacy Entrepreneurship

The FTC has recently acted to reinforce the privacy promoting efforts of the privacy activists. Privacy activists are motivated because they care deeply about privacy. What could motivate a federal government agency to promote more respectful online personal-data practices? Elsewhere, I have argued that public choice theory provides a plausible answer: the FTC has sought to become the leading federal agency regulating online activities as a means of extending its regulatory grasp to the fertile new domain of the Internet.[108] The FTC's role in helping to moralize the social meaning of data collection can also be understood in public choice terms as an effort to extend the agency's purview over the burgeoning website industry.

As an indirect result of privacy advocacy, Congress asked the FTC to examine online privacy issues.[109] Voters are increasingly contacting their congressional representatives and voicing concerns about online privacy.[110] These concerns have translated into increased agitation on Capitol Hill regarding online privacy. This agitation has resulted in proposed legislation and calls for FTC involvement. The FTC acts pursuant to its authority under the Federal Trade Commission Act, which mandates that the agency address "unfair" and "deceptive" trade practices.[111] In particular, the agency has borrowed the various specific privacy protection measures supported by the privacy activists and shrouded them in the rhetoric of fairness.[112] The FTC refers to standard proposed privacy measures as the fair information practice principles (FIPPs).[113]

The FTC contends that these fair practices are best promoted through website privacy policies. In other words, websites should address the elements of notice, consent, access, security, and enforcement in the representations that they make to consumers in their privacy policies. A privacy policy that accurately and completely states the website's personal data practices would be in accordance with the principle of notice/awareness because once the consumer has notice of the website's practices, she can consent to the data exchange or exit the website. In addition, stipulations concerning access/participation to the user's personal data on file with the website can be set out in the privacy policy, as can stipulations concerning integrity/security and enforcement/ redress.

Note that whereas the privacy activists promoted respect for privacy as the core moral concern, the FTC has shifted the moral focus from respect for privacy to a concern for fair practices. When websites take up the FTC's suggestion and seek to implement the FIPPs via privacy policies, the FTC's regulatory grasp is enhanced. Once websites make representations to consumers regarding their practices, the FTC has a claim to jurisdiction if the websites behave differently. From the FTC's perspective, the website has engaged in unfair and deceptive trade practices, which is directly within the FTC's jurisdiction.[114]

As a norm entrepreneur, the FTC faced a problem not confronted by the privacy activists: an unreceptive audience. As discussed earlier, privacy activists' audience is consumers. Consumers were naturally disposed to accepting the extension of the general right to privacy to the domain of data privacy in cyberspace and were thus generally receptive to such ideas. By contrast, the audience for the entrepreneurial efforts of the FTC were websites. Different websites had differing interests when it came to the provision of privacy protection for the online consumer. Generally, larger and more established websites had an incentive to provide privacy protections while smaller websites did not.[115] Importantly, the FTC's preference for websites to incorporate the FIPPs into online privacy policies provided no additional incentive to the smaller websites to provide such protections. The FTC addressed this impediment by creatively utilizing the unique resources available to it as a federal agency: it issued a threat to the website industry.[116]

In 1998, the FTC threatened to recommend to Congress that it enact privacy legislation if more respectful industry customs were not forthcoming through industry self-regulation. The threat was highly credible and particularly salient due to the commission's recent success in shaping legislation to protect children's online privacy.[117] This threat was a shock to the normative equilibrium of the website industry, causing many firms to alter their behavior. Generally, the impact of the FTC's threat could be expected to correlate with website size and structure. The larger and more multifaceted a website's activities, the more likely it would be to react to the FTC's threat by providing more respectful privacy practices.

Some large websites felt so threatened that they personally attempted to incentivize smaller websites into compliance with more respectful norms. Under this threat, the major websites are no longer indifferent to the actions of the smaller websites. The failure of these smaller websites to adopt privacy-respecting practices might lead to privacy legislation, which would adversely affect *all* websites. The large websites in particular would have the most to lose from onerous legislative requirements. Faced with this situation, large websites devised methods to bring small websites into conformity

Large Websites

	Privacy Policy	No Privacy Policy
Privacy Policy	4, 4	3, 2
No Privacy Policy	2, 3	1, 1

Small Website

Figure 13.3 Intraindustry Strategic Threats

with more respectful data collection practices. Large websites threatened to withhold advertising from websites that did not demonstrate adequate respect for privacy.[118] As represented in Figure 13.3, this action changed the strategic structure of the relationship between large websites and small websites.

The threats issued by some key large websites likely contributed toward the desired outcome, as an increasing number of small websites are now offering privacy policies. As indicated by the *1999 FTC Report to Congress*, the number of websites providing privacy policies has increased significantly. Regarding the issuance of threats by large websites, the FTC stated that "[c]ompanies like IBM, Microsoft and Disney, which have recently announced, among other things, that they will forego advertising on websites that do not adhere to fair information practices are to be commended for their efforts, which we hope will be emulated by their colleagues."[119]

Note that when large websites threaten to withhold advertising from small websites, the effectiveness of the threat does not depend on repeated interaction between the parties. Even if the small websites only interact once with Microsoft or IBM, they will typically prefer that this interaction permit advertising. In the terminology of informal game theory, the instrumental allocation of advertising is functioning like a "selective incentive" that rewards cooperative behavior on an individual basis.[120] Selective incentives allow the party seeking to incentivize conformity to provide incentives to individuals in order to elicit their conformity. This is in contrast to the collective good itself, which by definition is a public good: when provided for one, it is provided for all, and thus is open to free riders.

This type of selective incentive cannot be expected to work for all small websites. Some small websites will have little prospect of receiving advertising revenue from large websites and benefit extensively from the unfettered use of personal data. These websites may continue to have a dominating preference to free ride on the growing practice of providing privacy policies. Thus, the net result of the FTC threats was still a bi-normative world in which many large websites and some small websites were respectful of privacy, while other small websites were not. More recently, however, a growing number of the recalcitrant websites do appear to be conforming to more respectful privacy norms.[121] The final section will explore another important process that appears to be contributing toward this development.

B. Software Makers Promote Privacy for Profit

A new type of privacy norm entrepreneur has recently emerged. These are software vendors marketing so-called privacy solutions.[122] Privacy solutions are software that users or websites can install to create a more privacy-respecting online environment. The following discussion provides an examination of the advertisements placed by some of these software vendors for their products in tech-oriented magazines. Looking at the text of these advertisements serves two purposes: it provides strong evidence of privacy proselytizers' success in moralizing data privacy and suggests new methods by which these moralized norms may be further entrenched.

The ultimate audience for this growing type of advertisements is often websites, as they are the direct purchasers of these products. Due to the viral nature of norms, it is also integral that these advertisements impact consumers. The more the advertisements are successful in fostering moral concern among consumers, the greater the social pressure toward increased privacy protection that will be exerted on the website industry. As the price of not providing privacy increases, the number of websites that will have the balance favoring of respectful over nonrespectful norms will increase.

Particularly striking is the overt normative language used in the advertisements that dramatically inform consumers that they are being disrespected by many websites. For example, consider the representative advertisement by the firm, ZeroKnowledge.[123] It depicts an average Internet user, unremarkable except for the bar code emblazoned on her neck. The text consists of a small number of rhetorical statements made by a representative online consumer to the website industry: "I am not a pair of eyeballs to be captured or a consumer profile to be sold.... I am not a piece of your inventory.... I will not be bartered, traded or sold."[124] These phrases play on current website industry jargon, in which customer visits are referred to as "capturing eyeballs," and personal data is amassed into "consumer profiles."

The theme of these statements is aptly viewed in everyday Kantian terms. The consumer is demanding more respectful treatment. As portrayed, these firms equate her with her data in contravention of the Kantian maxim that actors should not treat persons merely as a means to their own ends.[125] The import of the advertisement is that typical websites currently treat people not as individuals, but instead as "inventory" that can be bar-coded and bartered, or as "eyeballs" that can be "captured."

The advertisement then contrasts these industry attitudes with the normatively acceptable position as portrayed by a representative consumer speaking rhetorically to the website industry: "I am an individual and you will respect my privacy."[126] This brief statement contains three normatively loaded words: "individuals," "respect" and "privacy."[127] The final claim is that "On the Net, I am in control."[128] This statement is, of course, aspirational, as the whole force of the advertisement is that the woman is not presently in control of her personal data. By demanding her moral rights when it comes to online privacy, she in effect admonishes the reader of the advertisement to do the same.

The advertisement by the company Netcreations, a provider of a permission-based e-mail marketing system, similarly invokes an everyday Kantian theme.[129] Netcreations promotes itself as providing consumers with only the information they have asked for. As contained in this chapter's epigram, the advertisement features a picture frame with the following tenets set out as its "Code": "This is not Cattle. This is a human being. We do not spam human beings. We respect human beings. Respecting human beings is good business. This is the code."[130] The advertisement strives to convince the website industry that privacy-respecting practices are also good for business. As the advertisement says, "[w]hat is right is also effective."[131]

A similar effort is made by a firm named PrivaSeek.[132] In a series of advertisements, PrivaSeek promotes technology that will give consumers control over their online profiles.[133] The advertisement notes that, "[c]onsumers are becoming more savvy about protecting their personal information online."[134] PrivaSeek's product is geared toward this changing privacy environment because it promises to increase the "confidence" of customers.[135] *Confidence* is a term that is often used in the business-to-business software market that supports secure online transactions. PrivaSeek plays on websites' desire for consumers to have confidence in them so that consumers will readily interact with websites on a repeated basis.

In conclusion, each software privacy solutions provider will likely influence privacy norms by further stoking consumer privacy concerns and the corresponding entitlement to personal data. In other words, the advertisements will further advance the shift in the social meaning of personal data collection toward a more normatively charged interpretation.[136] Although there is no hard data, these advertisements will likely have an effect as well in further galvanizing public opinion in the direction of greater demand for more respectful website privacy practices. For websites at the margin, it may now make sense to switch to more respectful norms. Thus, while companies selling privacy solutions may lack the lobbying savvy of organizations like EPIC or the coercive power possessed by the FTC, they may nevertheless be powerful shapers of public norms regarding online privacy due to their ability to reach millions directly through their print media campaigns.

Conclusion

There have been important changes in informal online privacy regulation over the past few years – primarily the recognition of a moral entitlement to privacy in cyberspace. This chapter has argued that privacy norm proselytizers are the leading contributors to this development. These activists have taken an interest in online privacy because they believe Internet users are morally entitled to, and desperately in need of, increased protection. Other norm entrepreneurs have subsequently supported an entitlement to privacy for reasons less moral, but no less efficacious in stimulating demand for increased privacy protections.

As a result of these efforts, Internet users are increasingly conscious of moral entitlements to respectful treatment by websites. The general social demand for privacy respect in cyberspace is half of a broader supply and demand model documenting the emergence of Internet privacy norms. While this chapter has begun to address the response on the part of websites to the growing demand for privacy, a more detailed analysis of the supply side is necessary in order to address a puzzle that has been created by the foregoing account.

Privacy activists have not been impressed with the response by websites to the increasing demand. They allege that websites have only made reluctant and ineffectual efforts to respect users' privacy interests. The puzzle is why the substantial increase in demand for online privacy has not resulted in a corresponding increase in the supply of online privacy, as a market model would naturally suggest. This puzzle is explored in the next and last chapter.

14

Website Privacy Respect:
Real and Feigned

This is not cattle.
This is a human being.
We do not spam human beings.
Respecting human beings is good business.
This is the code.[1]

Introduction

As the previous two chapters indicated, the threat to personal privacy due to the ever-expanding flow of personal data online is the most significant pubic policy concern that has yet to be spawned by the Internet. In the past few years, however, websites are increasingly claiming to address this concern adequately.[2] Privacy advocates have generally been unimpressed with these efforts by websites. Some commentators have claimed that the website industry's new data norms are pathetic and insincere attempts to address burgeoning privacy concerns. Jessica Litman states that industry self-regulation has been an "abject failure."[3] Whether the new website norms really do increase the supply of privacy is a contentious matter that will be addressed later. What is not contentious is that the website industry has responded to demands for greater online privacy with a new set of industry norms regarding the collection and use of consumer data. This chapter will seek to better understand what has motivated websites to adopt these new norms. This chapter completes the supply-and-demand model of the emergence of website privacy norms that was initiated in the last chapter. Chapter Thirteen considered the demand side of the equation,[4] looking at the role that has been played by norm proselytizers and other norm entrepreneurs in stimulating consumers to demand online privacy with respect to their personal data.[5]

This chapter will examine the response to this increased demand, which has been an apparent increase in the supply of privacy-related norms by websites.[6] In the view of their critics, the vast majority of websites have to date displayed no genuine regard for the privacy interests of users. If the critics are right, this raises an interesting question; why has an increase in demand not created an increase in supply?

One possible answer is that most websites have thought it to be in their interest to simulate privacy respect rather than provide the real thing. Section II will consider two competing accounts as to why many websites might think it sensible to simulate respect for their users' privacy. The two accounts are derived as applications of two competing theories of norms. On one theory, norms are patterns of rationally motivated conforming behavior.[7] On the other theory, norms are sets of individual signaling acts, each of which is meant to communicate that the signaler has a low discount rate and so is a good type with whom to enter into cooperative relationships.[8] As later discussion will demonstrate, each of these conceptions of a norm provides a distinct explanation of the dubious quality of many extant website privacy norms. I will argue that the pattern conception provides the more satisfying account. I will note as well that other potential emergence accounts do not even get off the ground; the online data collection world is not a close-knit community and so Ellickson's efficiency account is inapplicable, and websites are businesses, not people, and so McAdams's account based on the human desire for esteem is inapplicable.

Section II will conclude with a consideration of the normative implications of the preceding analysis for privacy proponents of various stripes. Advocates for all the competing substantive views regarding online privacy will find it useful to better understand what has caused websites to pay more attention to consumer privacy. With this knowledge in hand, privacy activists will be in a better position to further influence the course of website activities toward the provision of greater privacy protections. Cooperative websites will be in a better position to understand the efficacy of their past response to the privacy demands of consumers, with an eye toward adapting this response. Unfortunately, however, this will also be true for websites that adopt a deceptive strategy. The supply-side account of Internet privacy will also be of interest from a more general, social-scientific perspective because there is a dearth of case studies on the emergence of norms in an online setting.[9]

I. Meeting the Demand for Online Privacy?

In the previous chapter, it was seen that owing to the efforts of norm proselytizers and other norm entrepreneurs, the demand for privacy among consumers has surged. This section will examine the impact that this increase in demand has had on the level of supply. Generally, when demand for a good or service goes up, the supply will go up as well. This will not always be true. If there is a set amount of lakefront property, the supply will not go up when the demand goes up. Similarly, demand may rise for a good or service among a population, but this demand may not be backed up by a level of willingness to pay that will support the marginal cost of additional supply. Generally speaking, however, for most goods and services, increased demand leads to increased supply. Thus, barring special circumstances, one would expect that the increase in demand for personal data privacy online would produce an increase in supply.[10]

Other things equal, websites that could cheaply supply privacy would be more inclined to do so, while websites for which it was more expensive would tend to provide less privacy. Some relevant factors here are the extent to which the use of personal data plays a central role in the business model of a particular website, or the site's relative cost structure for collecting, storing, processing, and manipulating data.[11] In addition, other things equal, websites whose customers are more demanding of privacy will be more likely to provide greater privacy protections.[12]

Unlike the functioning of a formal market, however, it is unlikely that the supply of privacy respect will come via explicit monetary transactions. The fact that data privacy in increasingly conceived of as an entitlement of consumers makes it increasingly unlikely that most websites will seek to conduct explicit monetary transactions with consumers regarding their data. In other words, despite the fact that many sites have de facto control over the data of a set of consumers and that some of these consumers may want to assume control over their data, it is unlikely that many sites will begin selling this data to consumers.[13] Those firms currently providing privacy protections are not doing so as part of a monetary transaction.

Despite the increase in demand for respect for online privacy, there is great controversy as to whether there has been an increase in the supply of privacy respect. The industry claims to be responsive to user demand for a heightened level of respect.[14] Many privacy advocates, however, strongly disagree. As noted in the introduction, Jessica Litman has stated that industry attempts at self-regulation have been an "abject failure."[15] Similarly, Jason Catlett of Junkbusters, a privacy advocacy firm, has remarked that "[t]he stated policies of most big shopping sites run the gamut from bad to atrocious."[16]

Not all commentators sympathetic to consumer privacy concerns are this critical, however. In the same symposium in which Litman made her remarks. Pamela Samuelson noted that privacy policies are getting better.[17] Are Litman and Samuelson really disagreeing, and if so, who is right? Or are both wrong, and the industry is right in its more upbeat assessment? This chapter will seek to come to a better understanding of these central questions of the online privacy debate. Section A will examine the data-regarding norms that have been adopted by websites in their privacy policies. Section B will discuss the recent emergence of the chief privacy officer. These efforts constitute the main response of the website industry thus far to the chorus call for online privacy. Finally, Section C will critically evaluate these efforts by websites in order to better judge the merit of the critic's charges of duplicity. Following this discussion,

Part II will examine signaling theory in order to see whether it may lend insight into website behavior.

A. *The Features and Content of Current Website Privacy Policies*

Website privacy policies are a recent phenomenon, having come into existence in the late 1990s. The universal feature of website privacy policies is that they are accessible as a link from the homepage of many websites. Many sites also have links to the privacy policy from areas within the site, such as from internal pages that request customer data. Privacy policies range from a half-page to ten pages in length. In terms of their apparent intent and rhetorical structure, privacy policies are hybrid documents that reflect both public relations and legal concerns. On the one hand, privacy policies often have a chatty and disarming tone that clearly seems motivated by an attempt to create an air of closeness and intimacy between the site and its users. On the other hand, privacy policies are becoming more legalistic in tone.

Privacy policies typically begin with some warm and fuzzy language about the online entity's respect for its users' privacy. Typical in this regard are statements such as, "At 1-800-flowers.com, we recognize and respect the importance of maintaining the privacy of our customers and members."[18] The National Geographic privacy policy begins, "Nationalgeographic.com respects and protects the privacy of our users."[19] Some of the more scrupulous sites explicitly acknowledge the privacy rights of users in their opening remarks. Walmart's privacy policy states, "We believe that you have a right to know, before shopping at Walmart.com or at any other time, exactly what information we might collect from you, why we collect it and how we use it."[20] Nike's privacy policy begins, "Nike is committed to respecting the privacy rights of all visitors to our web site."[21]

In the opening statements of their privacy policies, some sites are explicit in stating that their goal is to create a relationship of confidence and trust with consumers. The Walt Disney privacy policy begins, "The Walt Disney Internet Group is committed to helping you make the most of your free time on the Internet within a trusted environment. . . . We hope that this disclosure will help increase your confidence in our sites and enhance your experience on the Internet."[22] The Walmart privacy policy begins with the remark that, "We realize that making purchases at Walmart.com, or any other Web site, requires trust on your part. We value your trust very highly, and pledge to you, our customer, that we will work to protect the security and privacy of any personal information you provide to us and that your personal information will only be used as set forth in this policy."[23] Sears.com states, "Sears, Roebuck and Co. values the trust its customers place in the company. Accordingly, Sears adheres to the highest ethical standards in gathering, using and safeguarding customer information that is entrusted to the company."[24]

Some sites make it apparent that they judge the moral relationship be-tween website and consumer to be a two-way street. The first paragraph of the MadonnaFanClub.com privacy policy states that the site, "always respects the privacy of Fan Club members and visitors to our site."[25] The last paragraph of the short document states that, "All information contained on this site is copyrighted. Your cooperation in respecting these copyrights is appreciated."[26] Here, a core normative principle is at play. Because the site holds itself out as respectful, it is appropriate – by the lights of the ordinary moral principle of reciprocity – to ask for respect in return. Privacy policies that are more legalistic in tone would be unlikely to make the same request for reciprocal treatment.

On the whole, however, privacy policies are increasingly employing more overtly legalistic formulations.[27] For example, Weather.com states, "This statement and the policies outlined here are not intended to and do not give you any contractual or other legal rights."[28] The Toyota privacy policy in part reads, "Toyota does not assume responsibility for the accuracy, completeness or authenticity of any information contained on this site. This site and all in-formation and materials contained herein, is provided to you 'as is' without warranty of any kind."[29] Toyota further states, "Toyota shall not be respon-sible for any harm that you or any person may suffer as a result of a breach of confidentiality in respect to your use of this site or any information you transmitted to this site."[30] Toyota's harsh legalistic tone illustrates the tension between a privacy policy crafted as a document meant to create trust in users, and as a legalistic document meant to protect the company against potential liability. The use of more legalistic language is perhaps not surprising, given that privacy policies are starting to play a role in lawsuits.[31] If privacy-related lawsuits become more prevalent, privacy policies may become even more legalistic.[32]

In the past few years, most websites have begun to address privacy con-cerns to one extent or another.[33] There are a number of common practices that websites are beginning to adopt. To some extent, these practices track the fair information practice principles that are being promoted by the privacy en-trepreneurs. The FTC has noted that it is not possible to specify in detail how the privacy principles should be implemented, as the meaning of the principles will vary depending on the particular activities of the site in question.[34] Indeed, the following brief survey of the terms of a number of website privacy policies will indicate just how complex and varied the personal data practices of websites are becoming. It will be necessary to examine these practices in some detail so that it will be possible in a later section to better understand the extent to which these practices are susceptible to, or indeed constituted of, either false signaling actions or acts of mimicry.[35]

1. NOTICE/AWARENESS. The provision of notice of a site's personal-data-related activities is the first of the fair practice principles. The principle of notice is a second-order principle that supports each of the other principles. It is only when a user has knowledge of the data-related activities of a website that the user can make informed decisions about how to interact with the site regarding each of the other privacy principles. At first glance, notice might seem like a straightforward requirement with which to comply. A site simply writes down a description of its data-related practices and creates a link to this text. For some sites with simple and minimal data-related practices, the provision of straightforward notice is possible. For example, the Official Madonna Fan Club site privacy policy, when printed out, is only half a page long and contains three short paragraphs.[36] The site is able to state straightforwardly, "We do not sell, rent or trade your personal information with others."[37] This site uses personal data to process commercial transactions, such as merchandise sales and membership dues. The site claims not to use cookies or other passive means of data gathering.[38]

Notice becomes difficult to provide, however, when a site has complex data-related practices. The problem is that the data-related practices of websites are becoming increasingly complex. The first layer of complexity is introduced by means of the manner in which data is collected. Users of course understand that data is being collected from them when this data is explicitly provided by them. More opaque is data collection by means of cookies and other means of so-called passive tracking of user online activities. Many sites provide definitions of arcane terms such as "cookies" and "IP addresses," and explanations of their importance for privacy purposes.[39]

For many sites, how the personal data is gathered is the determining factor in whether the data becomes "personally identifiable information," or "personal information," as compared to, "anonymous information." The information that people explicitly volunteer to the website such as name, address, social security number, and age is personally identifiable in the sense that it can be traced back to particular individuals. By contrast, websites collect information through the use of cookies on such activities as the users' visitation to various sites. Sites typically state that this information is not personally identifiable.[40] In other words, though the sites keep records of cookie-generated information, the site claims not to keep track of which personally identifiable person is attached to this information.

Perhaps the most significant challenge to adequate notice arises regarding the relationships that sites have with third parties of various sorts. Privacy advocates and consumers are especially concerned about the fact that personal data may be transferred to these third parties. Privacy policies refer to these entities as, "trusted third parties,"[41] "reputable third-parties,"[42] and so on. The main challenge to giving effective notice is the complexity and diversity of the relationships that sites have with these third parties. The difficult issue is determining how much description is necessary in order to provide adequate notice. Some sites are moving in the direction of providing fuller descriptions of their relationships with third parties. This means, however, that their privacy policies are becoming increasingly long and complex.

2. **CHOICE/CONSENT.** The second of the fair information practice principles is choice/consent. The intuitive idea is that users should have some say when it comes to the use of their personal information by websites. The FTC has interpreted the norm of choice so as to include making a choice among a number of alternatives.[43] Some sites, however, treat choice in the narrowest sense so as to mean simple consent or assent. Toyota writes, "By using this site, you signify your assent to the Toyota Online Privacy Policy. If you do not agree to this policy, please do not use this site."[44] Under the heading of, "Your Consent" on its site, Nike simply states, "By using our web site, you consent to our privacy policy."[45]

Many sites, however, do offer users choices other than the option of leaving. The most common choice made available to users is whether they want to have their personal data stored with, and used by, the site. Many sites give the user the option of removing their personal data from the site. For example, Kinkos.com states, "You can easily change any of the information you have been asked to provide by Kinko's. You can also permanently remove your information from the Kinko's database."[46]

As already mentioned, websites offer two types of consent or choice, which are widely referred to as opt-in and opt-out. With opt-out, the user must take some positive step in order to stop what would otherwise be a default process whereby her data would be available for use by the website. Typically, the user cannot simply opt-out without consequence. Sites often condition access to the site or to some portion of the site on the provision of data by consumers. Thus, opting out of the provision of data entails opting out of receiving some or all of the site's services.[47] Other sites, however, simply allow consumers to opt out of at least some of the site's collection practices without adversely affecting the consumers' abilities to benefit from the site.

Until recently, it has been very uncommon for websites to provide opt-in as a choice to users. A small but growing number of sites are now offering users the choice to opt-in to some or all of the site's data practices. With opt-in, personal data will not be collected or used unless the user provides her explicit permission. In particular, sites that deal with more sensitive data are beginning to offer opt-in for this data.

3. **ACCESS/PARTICIPATION.** The third fair information practice principle pre-scribes that websites provide users with access to their personal data stored with the website. This principle is often discussed in conjunction with the principle of allowing consumers to contest data stored at the site that they deem to be incorrect. It is getting increasingly common for sites to allow users to access their data. For example, microsoft.com states, "If you ever want to review or

update your profile, simply visit the Profile Center and edit your personal information. We'll ask you to disclose your Microsoft Passport (e-mail address and password) so that only you can access your profile."[48] Fewer sites offer the ability to contest data, however. One that does is nokia.com, which states, "Nokia will on its own initiative, or at your request, replenish, rectify or erase any incomplete, inaccurate or outdated personal data."[49]

4. INTEGRITY/SECURITY. A solid minority of sites now address the issue of security in their privacy policies. Under the heading of "Security" in its privacy policy, Sun Microsystems unhelpfully states merely that "[w]e will take appropriate steps to protect the information you share with us from unauthorized access or disclosure."[50] Many sites employ Secure Socket Layer (SSL) technology to protect the security of credit card information as it is transmitted to the site.[51] With SSL, the website's server scrambles the data as it travels from the user's computer to the website. It is much less common, however, for sites to make remarks in their privacy policies regarding the security of the user's data as it resides on the site's server. This latter form of security is more important than protecting the data while in transit, as most significant breaches of website security have involved hackers gaining access to databases in storage on a firm's website.[52] Increasingly, websites are addressing the issue of the security of data stored by the site. Some sites are limiting the number of employees with access to personally identifiable data as well as employing security systems to protect the data from external intruders.[53]

5. ENFORCEMENT/REDRESS. The fifth fair information practice is that of enforcement/redress. According to this principle, the user should be provided with some means of enforcing the preceding principles or of receiving redress in cases of injury resulting from a failure to provide protective practices that instantiate the fair information practice principles. Websites have done very little to promote this norm.[54]

6. STOPPING DATA TRANSFERS TO THIRD PARTIES. It is important to note that the fair information practice principles do not prohibit data transfers by websites to third parties. The first two principles, notice/awareness and choice/consent, are essentially an informed consent requirement. They do not prescribe a particular substantive set of privacy protections but rather stipulate that whatever data-related practices a website engages in, the site should receive the informed consent of its users as to these practices (with failure to opt-out counting as a form of consent). The latter three fair information practices provide more substantive requirements of access, security, and enforcement. None of these five principles, however, prohibits data transfers to third parties. Nevertheless, a small number of sites do promise that they will not sell or trade data to third parties. For example, Walmart states that, "We never sell or rent your personal information to any third parties under any circumstances."[55]

For sites with complex data activities – even sites with no intention to sell or trade data to third parties – it will be difficult to promise to make no data transfers whatsoever. The reason is that simple corporate efficiency may require outsourcing various data-related activities necessary to a firm's own internal usage of the data. Some firms are making a serious effort to protect the integrity of user data despite these third-party transfers. Walmart, for example, promises to transfer data only for specific purposes and then under contract.[56] This achieves a similar function to a complete prohibition on data transfers. Hallmark.com treats information in the site's address book as highly confidential and states that the information will not be disclosed to third parties.[57]

B. Chief Privacy Officers

The chief privacy officer (CPO) is a new and rapidly growing position in corporate America. Estimates vary but there are now CPOs at a growing number of firms, particularly larger firms. There is a newly created organization of CPOs and a nonprofit organization run by the dean of privacy advocates, Alan Westin, to train CPOs.[58] The emergence of the CPO is a practical solution to a growing problem; as technology develops, even firms that have the desire to provide privacy are finding it increasingly difficult to do so owing to the growing complexity of the task.[59]

So far, most chief privacy officers appear to have legal backgrounds. In addition to understanding the law of privacy, however, CPOs must be able to interface with their firm's software engineers and architects to create technical solutions to the demands of privacy. Unless someone at a firm is in a position to understand basic privacy concepts and also have knowledge of new developments at a company, there will always be the prospect that a new activity involves gathering or using data in a potentially problematic manner.

C. Spies in the House of Online Privacy

In the last two sections, we saw that websites have been active to one degree or another in the past few years in implementing various sorts of privacy-regarding practices. These activities have come about in response to the increased demands of consumers and various privacy advocates. While these practices are uncontroversially privacy-regarding, it is very controversial whether they are privacy-respecting or -enhancing. The practices have been subject to harsh criticism from privacy advocates, who have in general claimed that the level of protection provided by websites is far too low to provide adequate respect for consumer data privacy rights.

It is perhaps to be expected that privacy advocates, who are, after all, privacy advocates, would be hard to satisfy in this regard. But in addition to expressing dissatisfaction with the general level of protection, privacy advocates have sharply attacked websites for acting in a duplicitous fashion by seeking to create a false impression in consumers. Nearly all the criticism has been leveled against the main form of protection to be offered so far, the privacy policy. The general drift of criticism leveled by commentators is that privacy policies are vague, unintelligible, and incomplete. They are long and full of lawyerly language. They contain lots of respectful sounding language but little by way of substantive protection.[60] Readers are naturally led to believe they are getting greater protection than they in fact are. In terms of the potential cooperative bargain between users and websites whereby trust is exchanged for respect, this criticism can be recast in terms of seeing websites as trying to get something for nothing; seeking to obtain trust by exchanging not privacy protection but the illusion of privacy protection.

This criticism of the emerging website privacy norms is typically painted with a broad brush, dismissing in its entirety the effort by websites to provide respect for privacy. If these critics are right in the categorical dismissal of the efforts of websites, a puzzle arises when this dismissal is considered in light of the discussion in the preceding chapter. The puzzle is to explain why no supply of privacy has been forthcoming, given the increase in demand. As noted earlier, unless there are special circumstances, an increase in demand should bring about an increase in supply. If the critics are right, this has not occurred. What then are the special circumstances that occasion this outcome?

In spite of the widespread rejection of privacy policy protections by privacy advocates, or perhaps because of it, there has been little detailed examination of the particular norms that have been promoted in privacy policies to better evaluate whether the categorical rejection is accurate. Accordingly, further progress in understanding this important issue will necessitate closer examination from a critical perspective of the industry norms that have emerged thus far. Following is a discussion of the various aspects of privacy policies that highlights their most troubling features.

As noted earlier, the one principle that is most often addressed by websites is *notice*, so discussion may usefully begin here. All privacy policies, to one degree or another, describe the website's data practices. The question is When do such descriptions constitute adequate notice? The better websites make statements telling the user that the notice provided by the website is exhaustive of the uses to which the consumer's data will be put. The Walmart.com policy states, "We value your trust very highly, and pledge to you, our customer, that we will work to protect the security and privacy of any personal information you provide to us and that your personal information will only be used as set forth in this Policy."[61] On the other hand, more lax websites merely note, at most, that they will make an effort to inform users. For instance, MTVi.com says it makes "good faith efforts to make it clear why the information is being collected and what it will be used for." In the event of litigation against MTV, the firm will always be able to assert that it made a good faith effort, under the circumstances. Walmart's promise is more concrete; it either is, or is not, the case that the user's data was used by the website in a manner not set forth in the policy.

Even for websites such as Walmart.com, which appear genuinely interested to provide fair notice, this requirement is not without difficulties. There will inevitably be some deficit of reader comprehension simply because privacy policies may present a host of new terminology and a set of descriptions of varying and complex practices. This is a familiar problem from consumer contracts, leases, disclaimers, and the like.[62] With privacy policies, however, the failure of comprehension may be more due to unfamiliar technical processes than complex legal constructions, although, as noted earlier, privacy policies are becoming more legalistic as well.

There is no neat solution to this difficulty, which is inherent in giving notice to ordinary people of complex activities with significant legal implications. Even websites making their best effort will need to make difficult judgment calls regarding the proper level of information to provide. If the notice is too detailed, the reader may become lost or distracted, and if the notice is too pithy, the reader may not receive adequate information.[63]

Many websites appear not to make a best effort, however, or anything close to it. For example, many websites state that they reserve the right to change their data practices without prior notice. These websites typically instruct users that they should periodically consult the site's privacy policy in order to stay apprised of the site's current data policies. The obvious problem with this suggestion is that in the time between the time the user checks the policy and the time of the policy change, she will be misinformed as to the website's practices. In addition, this practice creates an incentive for websites to promise respectful treatment to users in order to lure them in, only to then change practices in midstream.[64]

Some websites do better in terms of providing notice. They inform their users by e-mail when they change their policies.[65] Given the presumably minimal cost of doing this – just one more piece of spam – it is hard to resist the inference that websites that fail to do so are attempting to avoid highlighting their changes in policy. These websites may credibly fear that their users would be alarmed by the changes in policy. Nevertheless, these websites do not act in a way that will properly provide notice. A reasonable user may easily be imagined to view this business practice as disrespectful, particularly in light of the ease with which better notification might occur.

The deepest fear of consumers arises regarding the use of their data by unknown third parties using their data in unknown ways. People expect that their data will be used only for the purpose for which it was collected. By the lights of ordinary moral logic, this would imply that websites have a duty to inform users adequately of uses of their data that go beyond these internal uses. It is thus here that websites have their greatest opportunity to either display respect, or not. It is also here that websites have perhaps been most guilty of providing inadequate notice. Websites commonly note that they will deal with third parties in order to promote the interests of the users. This vaguely fiduciary language is likely to be misleading, however. The warm and fuzzy labels and phrases used by websites to describe their relationships with unnamed third parties deceptively hide the fact that most websites use language that leaves them completely open to deal with anyone in any manner that they please. There is no evidence and little reason to believe that many websites restrict their activities with third parties to those that promote their users' interests.[66] Here, websites that were more genuinely interested in providing full notice to users would provide more detailed explanations of their dealings with third parties.[67] Some of the better websites are beginning to do so.[68]

The second fair information practice principle is choice/consent. This principle is connected to the first principle of notice in that when notice is inadequate, consent will be inadequate as well. One cannot consent to what one does not know about. Thus, as a matter of the normative logic of privacy policies, unless a website demonstrates a reasonable degree of respect with regard to the provision of notice, the website cannot demonstrate a reasonable degree of respect with regard to the principle of choice/consent.

As discussed previously, the crucial issue regarding the principle of choice/consent is between opt-in and opt-out.[69] The criticism of opt-out is that it puts the default in the wrong place. The reality of opt-out is that most users do not read and study privacy policies. Thus, most users will not in fact opt-out. But this does not mean that they have actually consented to the data policies of the website but merely that they have not read the privacy policy. Thus, it can be argued that if websites were really respectful, they would not go about the collection and use of user data unless they had actual consent from the user.

Websites can argue with some plausibility, however, that opt-in is unduly restrictive in that most consumers do not mind having their data collected and used by websites. Thus, opt-in would create an artificially high burden to all those users who prefer receiving the benefits that various websites have to offer but who do not bother to read privacy policies. In an early article discussing junk mail, Richard Posner argued that opt-out was more efficient than opt-in.[70] Similarly, the website industry might argue that it is actually doing consumers a favor to have opt-out instead of opt-in as the former policy will promote efficiency.[71]

This example nicely illustrates the important point that one's view regarding the proper scope of the demands of privacy respect may turn on one's higher-level normative theory. If one is a consequentialist such as Posner, then respect will be – to proffer a term that may be apt despite its dated coinage – cashed out in terms of wealth maximization.[72] From a deontological perspective, however, respect will not be defined in terms of efficiency but rather independently, or as part of an interrelated set of moral concepts such as autonomy. To respect people is to treat them as autonomous beings. For adherents to everyday Kantian morality, this may entail a prohibition on using their data without explicit notice and consent, even if it may be productive of social utility, or a particular user's utility, to do so.

Some sites arguably frustrate true consent by making choices more difficult than need be. For example, flowers.com states, "If you prefer not to have us provide information about you to third parties, please let us know by either: [e-mailing or writing]." Note that the website does not say to call despite the fact that the name of the company is 1-800-flowers. The site appears not to want to make it easy to opt-out.

The third fair information principle is that users should have access to their data and the ability to remove incorrect data. As discussed earlier, a growing number of websites are allowing users some version of these features. What these websites do not typically explain, however, is that this access is nearly always only to data explicitly gathered from the user. This means that the click-stream data collected on the user by means of cookies is not available to the consumer to access or remove. A website might say in its own defense that click-stream data is not personally identifiable and so there is no basis for user concern and thus no reason to provide access or the ability to remove the data. But there is always the possibility that clickstream data can be linked back to users, either by the website that collects the data or by some other website that cares to gain possession of such data.[73] Thus, even though the clickstream data is not currently personally identifiable, it may later come to be so. Thus, respectful websites might provide access to clickstream data (not to mention notice of the potential hookup of so-called anonymous data and user personal identity).

The fourth fair information practice is security. As noted earlier, some websites provide SSL protection for personal data while in transit to the website. Other websites provide some protection for the data while in storage at the website, such as by encrypting the data or restricting employee access to the data. While these protections cannot hurt, nevertheless, for most websites, these protections in no way address the main threat to the security of user data. This threat is due to the loss of control over the data owing to voluntary alienation of the data to third parties. In addition, other sites allow third parties to collect user data but take no responsibility for the actions of these third parties.[74] It is as if websites padlock the backdoor to keep the illegal hackers out but leave the front door wide open for any third party with the means to walk in, conduct a transaction, and leave with the data in hand.

II. Discount-Rate Signaling Versus Privacy Disposition Signaling

The apparent dearth of substantive privacy protections as evidenced by the preceding discussion raises the question as to why the increased demand for privacy has not had the effect of bringing about a more robust supply of privacy protections on the part of websites. One possible answer is that the level of demand thus far has not been sufficiently strong to elicit greater supply. In other words, despite the best efforts of privacy entrepreneurs, consumer demand has simply not been sufficient to drive websites into a more aggressive posture in terms of providing more respectful practices.

While this is one possible answer, it suffers from the fault that it appears to leave unexplained the deceptive nature of the response on the part of many websites. If there is so little demand for online privacy, why go to the bother of attempting to create the impression in one's visitors that one's website is committed to respect for user privacy? Why not just avoid dealing with the topic all together, as any firm must do with a myriad of issues that have a marginal impact on its business? Thus, a more satisfactory explanation of the website industry response must explain why websites bothered to respond at all.

One type of explanantion that naturally suggests itself is a signaling model. Signaling models seek to explain the manner by which words and deeds can serve a signaling function.[75] Signals are used to communicate information regarding something about which there is *nonverifiable information*.[76] For example, warranties may be used to communicate that a product is of high quality. The signal works because the sellers of the higher-quality products are able to more cheaply send the signal.[77]

Perhaps the reason that the words and deeds of many websites appear to be motivated by the desire to deceive rather than to actually provide respect is that indeed they are motivated by the desire to falsely signal privacy rather than actually provide it. The following discussion considers two competing signaling accounts, each of which may contain the resources to explain the deceptive, nonrespectful actions of the bulk of websites.

A. Signaling Discount Rates

As discussed in Chapter Two, in his recent book, Eric Posner develops an important new theory of norms that sees them as essentially constituted of attempts to signal.[78] Posner argues that social norms are sets of rational acts whereby individuals seek to signal to others that they have low discount rates and hence that they would be good cooperative partners.[79] Individuals seek to signal that they value the future sufficiently such that they are willing to forego the immediate benefits of defecting in order to derive the future benefits of a sustained cooperative relationship. Posner makes clear, however, that signaling is a distinct form of activity from cooperative behavior itself. He writes,

Defection in cooperative endeavors is deterred by fear of reputational injury but the signaling behavior independently gives rise to forms of collective action that can be of great significance. People who care about future payoffs not only resist the temptation to cheat in a relationship; they signal their ability to resist the temptation by conforming to styles of dress, speech, conduct, and discrimination.[80]

As this quote indicates, on Posner's account, signaling allows actors to communicate to others that they have the "ability to resist the temptation" to defect in the current game. Thus, signaling is logically prior to actual rational acts of cooperation. It is signaling that may afford actors better opportunities for future cooperative relationships.[81]

Whether cooperation occurs will depend on the discount rates of the various actors. The more one discounts the future, the less likely one is to forego the immediate one-time benefit gained from the defection in favor of the delayed benefit of future cooperation. Posner refers to those with low discount rates as "good types" and those with high discount rates as "bad types."[82]

The goal in searching for cooperative partners is to find people with low discount rates. Accordingly, actors will seek to convince others that they have low discount rates. Thus, reputation plays a crucial role in Posner's account just as it does in the standard account of cooperation.[83] Posner writes, "One wants a general reputation as a "cooperator," a person with a low discount rate, and one establishes that reputation both by declining to cheat in repeated games and by sending signals at every opportunity."[84] People will attempt to signal that they are good types and attempt to discern that others are good types, based on the signals that these others are sending.

Recall that on Posner's account, any behavior may come to serve as a signal as long as the behavior is observable and has an associated cost.[85] Because the signal is costly, it will mean that some actors – the bad types – will be prudentially excluded from sending it. The result will be a *separating equilibrium* in which good types act in one manner and bad types act in another manner.[86] For example, a good type may be willing to incur a greater cost from giving a gift in the early period of a relationship.[87] The less one discounts the future benefits of the relationship, the more one is willing to spend early on in order to signal one's low discount rate in order to foster a cooperative relationship. Social norms then on Posner's account are simply the patterns of behavior that result as the equilibrium outcomes of various signaling games such as the game of gift giving.

Posner gives a sense of the dynamism of norms. Once norms have been established, there will continue to be forces at play that push toward new norms. In short, on Posner' account, bad types will often seek to *pool* with good types in order to benefit from the signal's power to make others think that the bad type is in fact a good type. But this in turn may lead to good types attempting to migrate to new norms in order to avoid the muddying of the old signal by the bad types.[88]

A possible explanation of the apparently deceptive actions of websites is suggested by Posner's signaling theory of norms. In brief, on this account, the emerging website privacy norms are best explained as being constituted of sets of attempts to signal to users that a website is a good type. Recall that for Posner, a norm is simply a pattern of behavior constituted of the set of individual signaling behaviors of the actors seeking to signal that they are good types. In the online privacy context, the relevant norms are the patterns of behavior whereby websites are addressing user privacy concerns by offering privacy policies with varying elements of notice, choice, access, security, and enforcement and by instituting chief privacy officers. Good types have low discount rates, that is, they do not much discount the value of future utility in comparison to present utility. Thus, they are more likely to enter into cooperative relationships that promote future utility despite a sacrifice of present utility.

Posner's good types desire a situation in which they are able to establish a separating equilibrium whereby good types participate in one practice and bad types participate in another practice, as it is only when there exists a separating equilibrium that the behavior of the good types will be able to serve effectively as a signal of their type.[89] Consider how this condition applies in the context of website personal-data practices. The situation appears to vary depending on the particular norm in question.

Regarding the practice of providing a privacy policy with a simple notice of the website's data practices, it appears that instead of a separating equilibrium, there exists a pooling equilibrium in which most websites follow this norm or are inclined to do so in the future.[90] Website behavior appears to be moving in this direction as well for the practice of providing choice, at least when choice is understood in a less demanding sense so as to include opt-out. Thus, a pooling equilibrium has formed for these two norms. The good types are not able to distinguish themselves from the bad types by means of the signals created by participating in these norms.[91]

Note, however, that for the norms of opt-in, security measures, access, redress, and no sales to third parties, it does appear that separating equilibria have formed whereby some websites conform to these norms while other websites do not.[92] One way to interpret these new norms is that they are attempts by good types to find signals that are more costly and so not susceptible to becoming pooling equilibria whereby good types and bad types pool into uniform signaling practices.

The websites that are conforming to the more demanding norms are actors who are willing to expend costs in signaling at a level that is apparently not sustainable by most websites. Indeed, one conspicuous feature distinguishing these latter norms is that they are costly. For example, an opt-in policy is costly in terms of opportunity costs, which are the costs from not gaining access to the data for free unless the consumer explicitly opted out, which is the situation with opt-out as the default instead. With providing access and ability to contest data, the costs are more direct. With providing security, the costs are also direct and come from the cost of supplying the security.[93]

Thus, some websites conform to norms that really cost them significantly. Posner's account would have an explanation as to why some websites have shown an interest in providing these more costly forms of regard for consumer data. The motivation is to signal that they are good types and to signal in a manner that is not easily duplicated by bad types, thus enabling the good types to establish a separating equilibrium for each of the more costly practices.

B. Signaling a Respectful Disposition

Things may not be so simple, however, for the application of Posner's model to the present set of facts regarding the response of websites to the heightened concern for consumer online privacy. There appears to be an important difference between the norms as characterized in Posner's model and the norms that arise in the context of website privacy-regarding activities. Contrary to Posner's model, some websites are not seeking to signal that they are good types; they are in fact taking steps that would be required of good types. Thus, their behavior is not best understood as signaling future cooperative acts but as actually engaging in cooperative acts. Posner's model is, in effect, always looking ahead to a future of cooperating after all the signaling is done. But in fact some websites have already taken significant steps to begin cooperative relationships with users. Posner goes wrong, then, by using signaling of discount rates as the sole explanation for norms.[94]

1. AN ITERATED PD MODEL OF USER/WEBSITE COOPERATION. The heart of cooperative solutions to iterated Prisoner's Dilemmas is that the parties incur short-term costs to engender long-term gains. Each party has the opportunity to defect in the first round of a game. Defection is the dominant strategy in a single-shot game, that is, each party does best by defecting regardless of the choice made by the other party. When there is an opportunity for the parties to interact over time in a repeat game situation, however, then it may be rational for each party to adopt a cooperative strategy in which each defers the immediate gain from defection in order to attempt to realize the long-term gain that may result from cooperation.[95]

Cooperation in a repeat game is a better description of what occurs with some websites, for they do sometimes incur significant short-term costs in order to provide privacy protections. Websites find themselves in a situation with consumers in which consumers feel entitled to respect and also will trust websites that can demonstrate that they are worthy of it. Thus, there is the prospect for a cooperative relationship in which users and websites exchange trust for respect.

Consumers did not view their relationship with websites as strategic until they perceived it as a moral relationship. But once consumers perceive websites as either respecting or disrespecting them, they will respectively trust or distrust websites. The more strongly consumers feel a data privacy entitlement, the more they will be morally affronted by instances where websites disrespect their privacy. Accordingly, they will be slower to trust websites and more inclined to retaliate against those that fail to show respect.[96]

For example, when a website offers an opt-in policy, guarantees that it will not transfer data to third-parties, provide access and redress, or provides heightened security, the website incurs real costs with the apparent goal of meeting consumer demand. These costs are distinct from the costs that may be incurred by websites that are only interested in signaling a low discount rate. With Posner's signaling account, there is no cost associated with actually engaging in the cooperative relationship, as the actual cooperation is in the future. Websites that are currently incurring real costs as part of an already ongoing cooperative relationship have moved beyond merely signaling their type and are actually playing out the cooperative endeavor characteristic of their type.[97]

The situation is strategic because websites are in a position to choose whether to respect the consumer and engender consumer trust.[98] Part of the website's choice to show respect, or not, will depend in part on its calculation of how much its choice will cause the consumer to trust the website, and how much the resultant cooperative opportunities are worth to the website.[99] The strategic structure of the situation is represented in Figures 14.1 and 14.2.

Each party has two choices, each affecting the utility of the other party. Each party must consider how its choice and the choice of the other party will affect its payoff. This means that each party will consider whether it can affect the other's choice to improve her own outcome. Specifically, the website will consider whether it should attempt to foster consumer trust, and the consumer will consider whether it can influence the website's choice to provide a privacy policy.[100]

Because of these strategically interactive choices, a greater number of websites may find it in their interest to respect privacy in order to maintain the trust of the increasingly educated, and demanding, consumer. As recently as a few years ago, only a minority of websites – the larger and better-known

Large Website

		Privacy Policy	No Privacy Policy
	Trust	3, 3	1, 4
Consumer			
	No Trust	4, 1	2, 2

Figure 14.1 Large Website/Consumer Interaction

Small Website

	Privacy Policy	No Privacy Policy
Trust	2, 2	1, 4
No Trust	4, 1	3, 3

Consumer

Figure 14.2 Small Website/Consumer Interaction

websites – offered privacy policies.[101] This makes sense because these websites are most likely to have overlapping, multifaceted interactions with consumers; thus making it crucial for these websites to have respectful and trustworthy reputations. The number of websites that show respect for privacy has continued to grow, however, as public consciousness of the issue of online privacy has grown.[102]

Despite the growing sense of consumer entitlement, many small websites may still prefer to avoid the expense of providing privacy policies. As illustrated in Figure 14.2, many small websites may still prefer the outcome of mutual noncooperation (southeast cell) to that of mutual cooperation (northwest cell).

2. MIMICKING RESPECT FOR USER PRIVACY. While earlier discussion indicated that Posner's signaling model failed to account for the genuinely cooperative behavior taking place between some websites and their users, nevertheless, an alternative signaling account may be appropriate. As noted, warranties are a standard example of a signal. In the case of online privacy, the privacy policy may serve a parallel role to a warranty. If the analogy is to work, there must be some parallel to the nonverifiable information the seller possesses about some good, such as a television, that is protected by a warranty. In the privacy context, however, it is not necessarily or typically the case that one purchases a product from the website one visits. This may be true in some circumstances such as if one purchases a book from Amazon and Amazon collects data pursuant to this transaction, but most website visits do not result in a transaction. The privacy relationship between websites and users, then, is not inherently part of any transaction between these parties. A better analogy may be drawn between the online experience and the experience of customers while in the store of a seller. For example, is the customer surreptitiously monitored while trying on apparel in the dressing room?[103]

The nonverifiable information that the website has and the user does not is the website's *privacy disposition*. In other words, the level of its commitment to respecting consumer privacy, and its competence to fulfill this commitment. While such dispositions on the part of a firm may be less sticky than the dispositions of persons, what matters is not that such dispositions are immutable but that they are relatively stable.[104] Walmart.com's disposition to be concerned for user privacy is stable in the sense that Walmart, the parent corporation, will continue to have an important interest in its reputation with its customers.[105] This disposition is not readily knowable to the website's users, however. Accordingly, there is the possibility that the privacy policy may be used to signal that this website has good privacy dispositions.[106]

The reason warranties may work as signals is because firms with high-quality products will be able to provide warranties more cheaply than firms with low-quality products. Is the same true for privacy policies? In other words, will websites with more respectful privacy dispositions be able to offer privacy policies more cheaply? The answer appears to be yes, at least some of the time.

One can imagine two websites that each offer the same fairly rigorous privacy policy. Imagine further that one of these websites, call it Walmart, has more respectful privacy dispositions than another website, call it Toysmart. Walmart will be able to live up to the policy's commitments more cheaply than Toysmart. The implication is that websites such as Walmart that have more respectful dispositions, will be able to provide privacy policies more cheaply than websites such as Toysmart that have less respectful dispositions.

By analogy with the example of warranties, one might expect that the Walmarts of cyberspace would offer privacy policies while the Toysmarts of cyberspace would not. This is not what happened, however. Instead, privacy policies have become ubiquitous. The reason appears to be that the less respectful websites do not duplicate the signal with exactitude but rather mimic it with an inferior substitute, yet one that is not readily discernable as inferior by the typical user. As was seen in Section I.C, many websites use deceptive language to create an impression in users that they are being accorded a higher level of respect than in fact is the case. To the average consumer, these privacy policies are not readily distinguishable from the privacy policies of the more genuinely respectful websites such as Walmart.

This attempt by some websites to offer privacy policies that superficially mimic the better privacy policies but that are inferior in their details, is, then, a plausible explanation for privacy policies that are characterized by privacy activists as deceptive.

C. Normative Implications

The preceding discussion presented an account of a complex regulatory system comprised of both informal social processes combined with legal support. It is important that those interested in privacy, from whatever normative perspective, have the best possible understanding of the detailed workings of this system. Like it or not, this is the system currently in place. The job of any advocate is to evaluate this system in terms of the goals of privacy. Is this system the best system for promoting online privacy by the lights of each particular advocate? If the answer is no, then what would a better system be? A better system must build on what is currently there, seeking to improve or replace some features while perhaps simply fine-tuning others.

As a matter of moral logic, one cannot derive a normative conclusion from factual premises without the addition of a normative premise. Thus, raising the question of normative implications immediately raises the further question, normative implications for whom and based on what normative assumptions. The supply-and-demand model of the emergence of website privacy norms implies no categorical imperatives, but rather hypothetical imperatives that will depend on the particular normative assumptions that are combined with the positive analysis. In the interest of maintaining the objectivity of the positive analysis, no normative assumptions will be given priority here.

Of the actors who bring different normative assumptions to the table, two broad categories of such actors may be distinguished; those that are publicly interested and those that are privately interested. Of the preceding cast of characters, those who are publicly interested are the privacy norm activists. Those who are not intrinsically publicly interested, but who may nevertheless act in a manner that promotes the public interest for instrumental reasons, are the other norm entrepreneurs, namely, the FTC and software firms, as well as the websites.

Within the group of actors with intrinsically publicly interested motivations, there may be principled disagreement. Different actors have different moral conceptions of privacy. It will matter, for example, whether one is a privacy deontologist or a privacy consequentialist. Deontologists will be willing to trade off welfare in order to reduce the amount of privacy disrespect, when privacy concerns are judged to trump efficiency concerns, while consequentialists will not. Even within deontology, there will be divergent normative positions. Some privacy advocates appear to want to reduce the flow of personal data as a normative goal in itself. Other advocates have what can be characterized as an autonomy-based conception of privacy regulation. Reducing the amount of data flowing is not a per se goal on this conception. What matters is that all personal data flows pursuant to principles that respect the autonomy of the participating parties. On this view, while one may indeed have dramatically less privacy if one lives in a glass house, this is not a problem as long as one autonomously chooses to live in a glass house.

It is of interest to ask whether there is common ground among the various normative positions. There is in fact a growing consensus in support of the proposition that online privacy should be promoted. This is the hypothetical imperative that will be taken as operative in the following brief analysis of the normative implications of the foregoing account. In other words, an answer to the following question will be sought: what are the normative implications of the positive account, given the general hypothetical imperative that respect for consumers' online privacy should be promoted? The normative implications fall into two broad categories, implications for the demand side and implications for the supply side.

On the demand side, the goal will be to maintain and increase the level of demand by consumers for more respectful treatment of their data by websites and third parties. This is the demand that creates an incentive for suppliers of privacy, websites, to reflect on whether it is in their interest to supply greater privacy. On the demand side, we saw that norm entrepreneurs and particularly norm proselytizers have done a good job to stimulate the emergence of a sense of entitlement in consumers to a reasonable level of control over their personal data. As the foregoing discussion indicated, a large number of websites are now beginning to incur real costs to enter into cooperative relationships with users. The more demand that can be created for respectful treatment, the more websites at the margin that will find it in their interest to begin making cooperative gestures. Generally, then, the normative implication on the demand side would appear to be simply that there should be an effort to continue to stimulate demand for online privacy. There is reason to think that there is more room for consumers to increasingly come to have this sense of entitlement.[107]

On the supply side, one might initially suppose that if indeed demand is increased, then supply should naturally take care of itself, rising to meet the higher level of demand. As the foregoing discussion has made clear, however, such an assumption may not hold true. The efforts of those websites that want to be more respectful will be hampered by the existence of websites with inferior privacy dispositions that make efforts to mimic the websites with higher-quality privacy dispositions.

For privacy activists, then, the general task on the supply side is to reduce the incidence of false signaling in the hope that this will increase the incidence of genuinely cooperative behavior. What is needed is for websites with cooperative dispositions to find a way to signal exclusively. For this, the signal must be costly so that the websites with inferior dispositions cannot send it.

This raises the question as to whether there are norms that make it easier for cooperative websites to distinguish themselves. For example, if opt-in became a more dominant norm, this might make it easier for good types to distinguish themselves. It would force many websites to either adopt an opt-in practice in order to be in the vanguard of respectfulness or else live with the consequences of being seen as less respectful.

Consider a second example. Earlier discussion indicated reasons why it may not be possible to have a norm that prohibits transfers to third parties under all circumstances. This seems as though it is not a possible norm because even websites with no core interest in transferring data for profit-based reasons, may sometimes need to do so in order to better perform the site's functions. This has caused some sites to note explicitly that they only transfer data for this purpose. This is indeed a norm that bad sites cannot easily mimic.[108]

Clearly, then, there may be room for creative solutions to the problem of how cooperative websites can distinguish themselves from bad sites. Note that while false signaling may be bad, it need not stop good types from conforming to cooperative norms. Even though bad websites promise notice and consent but do not deliver, it may still be rational for good types to perform these actions, as they are part of cooperating.[109]

One response to the notion that privacy proselytizers should help make it easier for websites with high-quality privacy dispositions to signal this fact is to say that this will not make any difference because it will still be true that people do not read privacy policies. Privacy policies are just a click away from being observable by users. Nevertheless, it still may be the case that privacy policies are not much accessed by users. Any discussion of normative implications must take account of the important fact that people do not read privacy policies.

This does not mean, however, that websites cannot develop reputations. The reputation system is more complex and circuitous. Consider Walmart. Even though most people will not read their privacy policy, Walmart nevertheless has an incentive to make the policy statement a respectful one. Doing so is a central means for Walmart to foster a reputation as respectful of privacy. Privacy activists may have a significant influence in the general reputations of large firms such as Walmart, and these activists are better informed about Walmart's practices, such as whether it has a respectful privacy policy.

A general lesson, then, is that privacy proselytizers should seek to publicize the reputations of websites. Privacy proselytizers may help to channel website activity into more defined forms to further aid in public comprehension of website reputations. How more defined forms may be advantageous is best understood by comparison with a similar argument made by Posner.

Posner provides an interesting account of marriage laws that lends insight into one possible task for privacy proselytizers. He notes that whereas in contract law generally the contractors are allowed almost complete freedom to determine the terms of the deal, this is not true for marriage contracts, which are highly specified by the government.[110] Posner argues that this promotes the emergence of uniform social norms surrounding marriage. A similar point may be made about the role of the FIPPs. Privacy entrepreneurs have engaged in an effort to channel the privacy-regarding practices of websites into a small number of specific forms. Reduction to these specific forms may have an effect of making it easier to signal.[111]

For example, privacy proselytizers may be able to promote more effectively the norm of consent due to the articulation of the categories of opt-in and opt-out. The fact that there are precise names for these activities and that a number of websites are engaged in them allows consumers to attach a fairly precise meaning to these behaviors.

While an increasing number of websites may find it in their interest to be respectful, many sites continue to provide false signals of their willingness to cooperate. These are the bad actors that perhaps only a statute will deter. Note that this is a different position from the one that says that self-regulation has been an abject failure. One can acknowledge that a growing number of websites are acting in a more respectful fashion and yet contend that, on the whole, the amount of disrespect is too high to tolerate. The normative implications are not clear, however, as one might also conclude that some amount of false signaling was a negative but tolerable cost to bear, given the set of alternatives and their associated costs.

Conclusion

This chapter completes the supply-and-demand model of the emergence of website norms that was initiated in the last chapter. Chapter Thirteen considered the demand side of the equation, looking at the role that has been played by norm proselytizers and other norm entrepreneurs in stimulating consumers to demand online privacy with respect to their personal data. The present chapter examined the response to this increased demand, which has been an apparent increase in the supply of privacy-related norms by websites. But for a large number of websites, this response has been more apparent than real, more hype and spin than genuine. The preceding discussion sought to account for this situation. Section II considered two competing explanations as to why many websites might think it sensible to go to the bother of simulating respect for the users' privacy. The first was an application of Eric Posner's signaling model of norms and the second was an application of the pattern conception of norms developed in Part One. As the discussion indicated the latter account of norms provided the more plausible explanation. I noted in passing as well that the norm origination accounts of other law and norms scholars are inapplicable. The online data collection world is not close-knit so Ellickson's account is inapplicable. Websites, not being humans, do not value esteem or suffer guilt from violating internalized norms, so the accounts of McAdams and Cooter are inapplicable. The chapter concluded with a consideration of the normative implications of the preceding analysis for privacy proponents of various stripes.

Conclusion

The book began with the observation that while social order may be regulated from above by the law, its foundation is built on norms and customs. The law's ability to promote a just and effective social order can never be fully understood without taking account of the concurrent influence of these informal social practices. In spite of this, as noted at the outset, much jurisprudential writing has been devoid of sustained discussion of norms and customs, focusing instead on individuals and governments. In concentrating on the small individual below and the vast, looming state above, those intermediate objects of the social world – norms and customs – were long neglected by mainstream legal analysis.

The recent law and norms literature has begun to fill this gap. This emerging literature draws on important work emanating from the social sciences as well as from moral and political philosophy, and to a lesser extent from evolutionary biology and anthropology. Nearly all the new work by legal scholars utilizes rational choice methodology. The foregoing discussion also presented an analysis in the rational choice tradition albeit one that incorporated irreducible moral elements into the analysis. One of the underlying themes of the book was the compatibility of rational and moral analysis. The demonstration of this compatibility promises to be important in paving the way to an interdisciplinary norms account.

Chapter One defended what I referred to as the pattern conception of norms against the dominant rule conception. I argued that the traditional conception of norms as rulelike linguistic entities was faulty. Even though rulelike linguistic entities or "norm statements" still play a role in the pattern conception, I claim to have demonstrated that patterned, conformative behavior is the essence of a norm.

Because norms and customs are behavioral patterns rather than linguistic rules, they have rational structures rather than grammatical structures. Chapter Two developed an account of these structures based on a Hobbesian assumption of narrow self-interest. Chapter Three maintained this motivational assumption but examined the various norm structures from the perspective of utilitarian moral theory. Chapter Four then developed an account based on a broader Humean conception of rationality, one that I argued was consistent with the existence of genuinely moral motivation. On the Humean motivational assumption, genuinely moral norms were shown to be capable of emerging as a result of norm conformity. Finally, Chapter Five examined the potential for norm maintenance based on the motivational assumptions of leading critical moral-theoretic approaches.

In combination, the chapters of Part One explicate and defend an original theory of norms as rationally and morally governed patterns of behavior maintained in groups by acts of conformity. In developing this theory, the goal was not to defend one particular set of normative assumptions over others. Quite the opposite, the goal was to develop a conception of norms and customs that was independent on any particular set of normative assumptions, either assumptions regarding the normative motivations of the actors or assumptions regarding the critical normative goals of the overall system.

Informal game theory was utilized in the development of the pattern conception. Peoples' patterns of behavior were modeled as iterated games among players. By showing how these players might rationally conform to certain practices, informal game-theoretic models offer a mechanism for explaining how norms and customs may be maintained over time. This is significant as plausible mechanisms of this sort are in short supply in social science and social theory. Structurally speaking, norms are either strategic or nonstrategic. I divided strategic norms into two groups: those consisting of patterns of behavior maintained by sanctions and those consisting of patterns of behavior maintained as a result of the coordination benefit. The former are sanction-driven norms, and the latter are coordination norms.

The sanction-driven norm was demonstrated to be a broader structure than the well-known Prisoner's Dilemma norm. I argued that each type of norm may potentially serve as a solution to one of the fundamental paradoxes of rationality. The paradox is thought to reside in the fact that there is a divergence between individual and collective rationality; the collective of individuals will each do better if all contribute toward the production of certain important collective goods than if no one does, and yet for each individual it is rational to defect from cooperation. Although norms and customs are not goods in the usual sense, nevertheless, their provision may constitute a strategic problem of this sort. I argued that sanction-driven norms may solve problems of this sort. They may solve a wider array of problems as well, such as the Game of Chicken, or Ellickson's Specialized Labor Game.

The second type of strategic norm in my tripartite schema was the coordination norm. I set out the account of the coordination norm by comparing and contrasting it with David Lewis's well-known account of convention. According to Lewis, conventions have the strategic structure of proper coordination equilibria because everyone benefits from participating, and everyone benefits still more from the participation of others. Lewis claimed to capture the idea of conventions as first discussed at length by David Hume. I argued, however, that Hume's fundamental insight about the deeply conventional structure of social institutions must be formalized in a more complex manner than Lewis suggests. According to the account developed in Chapter Two, proper coordination equilibria are but a subset of coordination norms. Coordination norms are patterns of behavior made up of act-types performed to achieve a coordination benefit. I demonstrated that the flow of these benefits to a group of conformers may be maintained, even though a pattern of behavior is not a proper coordination equilibrium, a coordination equilibrium, or even an equilibrium.

Finally, epistemic norms were the third category of norms on my account. These norms were best understood in terms of informational economy rather than in strategic terms. People often conform for epistemic reasons, that is, they conform to a preexistent social practice, rather than expend the effort to gather new information in order to economize on the cost of information. Other theories have not incorporated strategic and nonstrategic norms into a single account. In particular, I argued that the accounts previously preferred by leading law and norms scholars are all deficient in this respect. Each of these accounts focuses exclusively on norms that have a sanction-driven structure.

Another intended contribution to the general theory of norms developed in the book was its attempt to reconcile the sociological notion of conformity with rational choice and moral choice. A fundamental if implicit tenet of much social theory is that conformity to prominent social customs substantially explains human conduct; *Homo sociologicus* is a conforming animal. But, as was noted in the main text, the notion of conformity scarcely makes an appearance in the work of rational choice theorists. The instinct of these theorists is to view conformity as suspect. I argued, however, that the appeal of the rational choice approach is substantially diminished if it cannot be shown to be compatible with the supposition of widespread conformity to norms, as conformity is a fairly straightforward social phenomenon. The pattern conception of social norms reconciles rational choice with conformative behavior by demonstrating that conformity to norms may be rational under a variety of conditions. In other words, *Homo economicus* was also shown to be a conforming animal.

Along with rational choice theorists, moral theorists have neglected to acknowledge the importance of conformity in the lives of ordinary people, for whom Kantian, Aristotelian, or utilitarian reflection is rare, while conformity to dominant moral practices is pervasive. The result is a sterile formalistic conception of morality with only a glancing connection to the complex normative texture of ordinary people's lives. Under traditional moral theory, conformity is suspect. It is as if conformers are not moral at all; they are merely conforming. The fundamental question then is whether moral actors can consistently confrom to norms. I argued that ordinary morality does indeed allow for conformative behavior. I made this argument for the first best world from the perspective of the critical theorist, which is the world in which the population of actors share her moral outlook, and for the second best world, the real world, in which the moral actor must come in constant contact with heterogeneous norms constituted of conforming actions by people who represent a variety of moral and nonmoral outlooks diverse from her own.

In addition to arguing that rational choice and moral choice are compatible with conformative behavior, the main text sought to integrate moral motivation into the rational choice model of norms. The vast majority of moral theorists and sociologists appear to reject the rational choice approach outright, apparently because they have assumed that after moral motivation is postulated, the rational choice framework loses coherence. At root, people are either moral or egoistic, but the twain shall never meet. These theorists may have gotten themselves too tangled up in their own normative framework, however; for in ordinary morality, it is completely acceptable to behave over a wide range of activities in a self-regarding manner. As long as one minds one's general duties and other more particularized moral relationships such as role-based responsibilities, one is allowed the space in ordinary morality to pursue one's own interests simply because they interest one. There is then a significant overlap between self-interested behavior and moral behavior.

The traditional economic account recognizes this fact for the wrong reason. On this account, morality and rational choice are compatible because a person's utility function may happen to encompass the interests of others. In other words, compatibility is possible because, for particular persons, their self interest is – as an empirical not a conceptual matter – the general interest, or some portion of it. This model is, however, distinct from and inferior to the model developed in the book. The economic model is faulty in that it solely countenances instrumentalist moral reasoning, whereas ordinary morality is quite transparently not in the least restricted in this manner. On nonconsequentalist normative approaches, one must think in the correct manner or act in the correct manner in order for one's actions to count as being moral. It is not sufficient that desirable outcomes result. On the account developed in the book, a broader heterogenous, normative perspective was demonstrated to be capable of encompassing self-regarding behavior in such a manner that noninstrumentalist, action-oriented views were shown to be compatible with self-regarding behavior. Overall, the theory developed in the book allowed deontological, virtue-theoretic, and everyday moral motivation into the model of norm functioning, alongside consequentialist motivation.

The analysis in the text led to a typology of moral norms that paralleled the one that emerged from the study of rational norms. We saw that moral norms come in three basic types: coordination moral norms, sanction-driven moral norms and epistemic moral norms. This parallel structure demonstrated unity of the normative.

After developing a theory of norms and customs in Part One, the remainder of the book put this theory to the test by applying it to substantive legal debates. I began with the assumption that if the theory was a good one, it should work well in these applied contexts, serving to illuminate important areas of the law. Alternatively, if the account contained errors that needed to be corrected, or was fundamentally wrongheaded, these defects should have become apparent as well.

A number of scholars have drawn attention to dysfunctional properties of norms. In Parts Two and Three, the legal norms I examined were seen to display some significant dysfunctional characteristics. In Part Two, I explored the manner by which norms of significance to tort law, that is, norms that revolve around injury-producing behavior, may emerge and be maintained, despite possessing significantly dangerous characterstics. Part Three looked at a different sort of dysfunctionality: norms that allow for websites to falsely signal respect for user informational privacy, thereby fooling consumers.

Part Two examined two intimately connected issues: the important role for custom in determining negligence and the important role played by the jury in injecting its norms into substantive applications of the reasonable person test for negligence. I argued that these are the two most significant roles played by norms and customs in negligence law.

Part Two began with a discussion of the puzzle as to why custom should matter at all in tort, particularly today. In this epoch of accelerating change, it might be thought that custom was no longer capable of playing a prominent role in the maintenance of a safe social order, for how can customary practices evolve quickly enough to keep pace with the rapid changes that characterize modern society. In law in particular, it might seem that traditional, informal solutions should be rejected in favor of more rationalized and centralized means of affecting social order. Despite this initial appearance, however, the discussion demonstrated that custom continues to play a foundational role in negligence law.

Part Two began in Chapter Six with a look at the historical and jurisprudential underpinnings of the so-called rule of custom. The shifting jurisprudential relationship between custom and law was first examined. At one time, certain customs were law itself – customary law. While custom no longer has this exalted status, nevertheless, customs may serve as sources of law. Chapter Six then examined the historically important example of customary easements in land. Looking at the strategic structures of some prominent examples of customary land usages, we saw that the norms motivating the courts' decisions regarding these usages appeared to be a mixture of consequentialist and nonconsequentialist impulses. In particular, in certain sorts of situations involving induced detrimental reliance on the part of customary users of land, courts have been inclined to find customary easements. The role of custom in this instance is striking; what would otherwise be a tortuous trespass instead becomes a use by right.

Chapters Seven through Nine explored the development of the modern rule of custom. Modern tort law mainly follows the negligence standard according to which one will be found liable only if one acted negligently in causing an injury. Negligence is the failure to exhibit due care or ordinary care. Leading early cases established the connection between "ordinary" behavior and "customary" behavior. Ordinary behavior was simply customary behavior. Courts looked to whether an injurious action conformed to an accepted custom or social norm in determining whether an action was negligent. Injurers attempted to establish their conformity to custom as evidence of due care, while victims attempted to establish the injurer's failure to conform as evidence of negligence.

Leading decisions by Holmes and Hand expanded the role of custom by holding that custom not only may be dispositive regarding the question of negligence but also might convey less powerful yet relevant evidence regarding negligence. This finding in effect expanded the options of courts to apply the rule of custom in a more nuanced fashion. As the examination of the case law indicated, modern tort law has alternatively endorsed two main rules of custom, which I labeled the per se and the evidentiary rules.

The introductory doctrinal discussion in Chapter Seven focused on the manner in which the older per se rule was replaced by the evidentiary rule. Discussion began with an examination of two initially plausible explanations for this transition. The first, developed by Clarence Morris in his classic work, *Custom and Negligence*, argued that juries will be less biased against defendants in their deliberations when they are made to appreciate that the defendant's injurious behavior conformed to widespread industry practices. The second account considered was the traditional, positive economic account of Landes and Posner, which predicted that the per se rule would be found in situations in which there was actual or potential bargaining between the parties, but not otherwise. On this theory, when parties are able to bargain, they will be able to reach welfare-maximizing agreements on their own, and these agreements will be represented in customary practices. Accordingly, courts should insulate the practices by means of the per se rule.

I argued that each of these accounts failed to explain the emergence of the evidentiary rule as the dominant modern rule. Morris's account failed to explain why there may be genuine reasons that conformity to custom has epistemic value with regard to the issue of negligence after concerns regarding jury bias have been factored in. Landes and Posner's account wrongly predicted that the per se rule would prevail in bargaining contexts, as I demonstrated to the contrary that the evidentiary rule is the dominant modern rule in both bargaining and nonbargaining contexts.

Moreover, Landes and Posner's account did not explain the main exception to the modern rule of custom, which applies the per se rule to the injuries caused by physicians and other professionals, despite the fact that they are neither more nor less likely than nonprofesionals to engage in the sort of bargaining discussed by Landes and Posner. By contrast, I offered an explanation for this phenomena that drew on the rational structure of the underlying practices. I argued that the norms of physicians and other professionals are often given strong deference by courts, as a result of the superior epistemic warrant possessed by those knowledgeable in a field requiring expert training. In other words, my account relied on the supposition that certain important norms of professionals have epistemic rational structures.

In the process of evaluating Landes and Posner's account, it became apparent that informal game theory helped to provide a better understanding of negligence law's use of social custom. On the account that I set out, there were four relevant modalities of the rule of custom. The per se rule would be justified when the custom at issue was thought to be efficient, as this rule would protect the conforming action from going to the jury where the injurer might be found to be negligent. The evidentiary rule would make more sense when the custom at issue was not optimal but welfare-enhancing nevertheless because this rule would encourage juries to give deference to the custom, while allowing the jury to find negligence if a superior custom appeared attainable. Alternatively, the evidentiary rule might take a weak form under which conformity was evidence of due care or a strong form under which conformity served as a rebuttable presumption of due care. Finally, the rule that accorded conformity no priority might be suitable if the custom at issue was either neutral or detrimental to the production of welfare.

The goal was to determine the efficiency conditions for the sorts of norms and customs that matter to tort law. This task was complex for not only were there four versions of the rule of custom, but there were also the three different rational structures of customs to which these versions may apply differentially. Practically all previous applications of informal game theory to law have focused on the Prisoner's Dilemma or collective action problem. One would naturally suppose that tort law would take an interest in PD-structured customs because tort law is concerned with injuries, and many PD customs present a situation in which a person is repeatedly in a position to cause injury to others, either by failing to conform to a safe PD custom or by conforming to a dangerous PD custom. While PD customs, and sanction-driven customs more generally, are indeed of great interest, the examples I considered in Part Two demonstrated that epistemic customs and coordination customs may also be important souces of injuries and so are equally of concern to tort law.

I argued that in order to determine whether a custom in a particular case was efficient, courts would need to know which type of custom was involved, as different sets of welfare-maximization markers applied to each of the three types of custom. Factors such as whether the incidence of injury fell on conformers or third parties, whether either or both of these groups were close-knit, whether the conformer had superior epistemic warrant, whether the Kaldor-Hicks test favors conformers, and whether an optimizing alternative practice was available, each mattered differentially depending on the type of custom at issue.

Combining the various possible rules of custom, the various possible rational structures of custom, and the various welfare markers, thirty-seven distinct modalities of tort custom were identified in Chapter Nine. The development of this schema called into doubt the basic justification of the dominance accorded to the evidentiary rule by Holmes, Hand, and their modern followers. After all, only eight of the thirty-seven applications of the rule of custom called for the evidentiary rule. The per se rule was preferable for nineteen of the situations; the no-priority rule, for ten of the situations; and the presumption-shifting rule, for eight of the situations.

The conclusion was irresistable, then, that welfare-maximizing courts must pay attention to a number of features of customs, and not simply to whether there was a bargaining situation between the parties or a sanctioning situation surrounding the parties. In general, courts have not demonstrated a sophisticated understanding of the relevant complexities of customs. While courts have to some extent accorded different legal treatment to some of the different types of custom, to all appearances, they have done so by means of an intuitive methodology that failed to articulate explicitly the rationale for applying particular rules to particular structures.

The analysis in Chapters Seven through Nine labored under the assumption that courts were intent to maximize welfare in their decisions regarding the choice of a particular version of the rule of custom to apply in particular cases. Notice that this assumption was neutral regarding the motivations of the various other actors besides the judges. The lay members of the community may all be narrowly self-interested utility maximizers, they may be predominant egoists, or they may exhibit some other species of motivation entirely. The last two chapters of Part Two developed a more substantive account with regard to the motivations of at least some of the participants other than judges, namely, the jurors. I argued that jurors, and in particular their norms and customs, play a crucial yet generally underappreciated role in negligence law, at least as judged by the two dominant accounts, the economic account, and the corrective justice account.

The power of either litigant to request a jury is both a practically universal and a practically unique feature of America tort law. Despite the fact that most cases settle, the prospect of a case going to trial is always in the background, influencing litigation tactics, expected outcomes, and therefore settlement negotiations. In Chapter Ten, I developed a five-stage account of the jury's role in a tort suit that makes its way through trial. I argued that the practice of tort law gave the informal social norms of jurors an essential role in constituting the actual substance of the negligence standard. As a causal matter, this de facto standard, serving as an instantiation of the abstractly formulated formal standard promulgated by the judge via the jury instructions, determined the final outcome in tort suits.

Because the de facto standard played an essential role in the outcome of tort litigation, any entitlement created by the litigation was causally influenced in its creation from below by juror norms, as well as from above by the jury instructions conveying the formal liability standard. I referred to the bottom/up component of this bi-directional causal process as the *jury norm effect*. Chapter Ten provided an account of the particular substantive normative forces that appeared to be most often unleashed by means of the juror norm effect. These forces included everyday analogues of strict liability and direct causation, comparative negligence and redistribution. I argued that, in their efforts to provide a unified normative account, the dominant paradigms failed to notice these sui generis normative forces that fill out the substantive content of negligence determinations.

Given the jury's important role in the actual practice of tort law, a question arose: why was so little attention paid to the jury in the dominant accounts of negligence? I argued that the answer to this question was probably that these accounts exhibited a bias that in another context Robert Ellickson has labeled "legal centralism." Legal centralists wrongly focus on top/down formal explanations of the source of liability entitlements at the expense of bottom/up explanations that would take account of the casual impacts of informal social norms, such as those that might flow from the deliberations of juries.

Chapter Eleven looked in greater detail at the dominant accounts of tort – the economic account and the corrective justice account – and the fact that each has failed to pay proper attention to the important role played by juror norms. The economic conception received its fullest expression in the *Restatement (Third) of Torts*. As the discussion indicated, the *Restatement* only countenanced a role for social norms in the special situation in which there was an instantiated custom in place, such that either the defendant pled conformity as a defense or the plaintiff sought to demonstrate lack of conformity as evidence of negligence. What was missing was any acknowledgment of the pervasive role that social norms play in providing grist for the jury's concrete application of the reasonable person standard. This process might occur not only in situations in which custom was explicitly introduced as evidence by one of the parties but also in all situations in which lay juries deliberated.

I argued that the *Restatement*'s account was misguided, apparently as a result of its legal centralism, which led the restaters to assume, largely without argument, that the dominant causal efficacy of the Hand Test interpretation of the reasonable person standard on the deliberations of juries, and hence on the outcomes of negligence suits. Based on the analysis and empirical evidence examined in Chapter Ten, I argued to the contrary that there was every reason to suppose that jurors do not engage in Hand Test analysis but instead draw from their heterogeneous array of eveyday norms and customs when providing concrete substance to the abstract reasonable person standard in order to come to a decision on the issue of negligence. This discussion concluded with an examination of an innovative attempt by Stephen Gilles to insulate the dominant conception from the line of criticism I offered. Gilles argued that, properly understood, the Hand Test actually involves a morally attractive Hand Norm that ordinary jurors would find attractive. Despite the attractiveness of Gilles's Restatement (First) approach as compared to the Restatement (Third) approach, it was in the end rejected as well.

Chapter Eleven next examined the corrective justice approach to negligence, focusing on Jules Coleman's influential account. Throughout much of his writing, Coleman set out to provide a pragmatic explanation of tort law that would be sensitive to the two-party structure of litigation and the justice concerns raised by one party's injury of the other party. The jury has played no role in Coleman's account, however. I argued that it thus remains to be explained why real-world juries would promote solely or mainly corrective justice norms.

I drew the conclusion that there is a need for a new negligence account that would accord the jury conceptual space commensurate with its role in the actual legal institution of tort law as practiced in America. The jury norm effect allows the norms of ordinary people to exert a direct casual effect over formal, legal outcomes. From the perspective of democratic theory, this is an antielitist, liberal feature of American tort law, which distinguishes it from its counterparts abroad. According to one core tenet of pragmatist jurisprudence, important legal practices should be analyzed in order to uncover the normative principles embodied in the practices. Tort jury practices arguably embody important liberal principles of political participation, value pluralism, and separation of powers. In their focus on welfarist concerns or justice between the litigants, the dominant accounts failed to countenance these important values embodied in American tort law.

As indicated throughout, law and norms theory is developed in the book at three levels: pure theory, intermediate-level, and micro-level analysis. Part Three took the analysis down to a micro level, looking at the specific issue of online personal-data collection. Because this is one of the most pressing contemporary public policy concerns, it poses a serious challenge to the theory of law and norms. Norms and customs are patterns of behavior. Patterns of behavior have traditionally existed in physical space. With the creation and ongoing construction of cyberspace, an increasingly rich new world is coming into being. Physical space plus cyberspace together create a wired world in which manifold social norms will emerge in the future. Injuries will increasingly occur in this world. The most significant type of injury to emerge thus far is injury to one's interest in personal-data privacy. Incursions on one's online privacy do not currently rise to the level of a tort. This will almost surely change over time, however, either because of increasingly intrusive activities or because sensibilities change.

As the discussion in Part Three indicated, the paucity of formal regulation of online personal-data collection has been conducive to the emergence of informal online norms to regulate this activity. Part Three examined the emergence of these norms. Over the past few years, the norms governing personal-data interactions between consumers and certain websites have changed significantly, albeit unevenly. There is an increasing moral sensitivity on the part of many websites regarding the commercial collection and use of personal data. In general, the social meaning of personal-data collection has changed from a morally neutral to a morally charged status. Consumers now perceive a general right to privacy in cyberspace that includes respectful treatment of personal data. I argued that this change arose not by accident or necessity, but as a result of the intentional behavior of actors possessing an interest in promoting online privacy. Some of these actors sought to maximize their own welfare, and consumer privacy was merely a means to this end, while other actors appeared to have genuine moral regard for the data privacy of others. The former were privacy norm entrepreneurs. I designated the latter actors as privacy norm proselytizers.

In Part Three, I developed a supply and demand model of the emergence of website privacy norms. Chapter Twelve first examined the industry's initial efforts at self-regulation. These efforts, by and large, failed. Self-regulation failed at first because of the strategic structure of the relationship between consumers and websites, on the one hand, and websites with one another, on the other hand. Specifically, websites were in a coordination game with one another, not an iterated collective action problem. Efforts to educate websites on the importance of privacy to consumers, and on the connection between allaying consumer privacy fears and the promotion of consumer confidence, did not work to change website behavior in the manner desired by the Federal Trade Commission. Nor were consumers able to band together to demand more respectful privacy practices on the part of websites because of the large-scale collective action problem they faced in organizing their efforts. A number of commentators concluded that the failure of self-regulation mandated that the government step in and take a more direct role in requiring respectful informational practices on the part of websites. As the discussion in Chapters Thirteen and Fourteen indicated, however, little direct government regulation of website practices occurred. Nevertheless, norms between websites and consumers have emerged. Some sites have begun genuine efforts to provide respect for user privacy, but many more sites have taken no substantive action whatsoever, or worse, have simulated respect in a cynical effort to get something for nothing.

Chapter Thirteen developed the demand-side analysis. The chapter looked at how privacy norm proselytizers changed the social meaning of data collection through education, legislative efforts, and changing consumers' moral outlook on the practices of websites. The set of concepts that increasingly surround the practice in popular discourse is evidence that consumers have developed a more complex normative understanding of data collection issues. Notably, interactions between websites and their visitors are now frequently framed in terms of privacy. Not long ago, the concept of informational privacy did not exist in either popular discourse or the moral theory lexicon, but, increasingly, a consumer's entitlement to control her personal data is generally recognized. In economic terms, these events can be viewed as an increase in the demand for personal-data privacy. The increase in demand in turn led to an increase in supply. This development was the topic of Chapter Fourteen.

As consumers increasingly perceived an entitlement, there was a corresponding tendency for them to feel moral outrage at websites that failed to respect data privacy. Consumers who felt that they were disrespected sought to punish websites by taking their business elsewhere, reciprocating the disrespect by providing the website with false personal information, or sanctioning the website through negative gossip. As a result of this pressure, numerous websites were inclined to increase the supply of respectful privacy treatment. I utilized the account of rational norms developed in Part One of the book to model these interactions between websites and consumers. This analysis uncovered a strategic interaction of respect and trust, in which some websites were interested to exchange respectful treatment toward consumers for trust on the part of these consumers.

While some websites have begun to cooperate, we saw that the vast majority of websites have to date displayed no genuine regard for the privacy interests of their users. This raised an interesting question: why had a substantial increase in demand for respectful treatment not created a substantial increase in supply? In answer to this question, I argued in Chapter Fourteen that the *simulation* of respect was plausibly in the narrow self-interest of many sites, as compared to their provision of genuine respect.

Chapter Fourteen examined two initially plausible explanations for why many websites might think it was sensible to simulate respect rather than provide the real thing. These accounts were derived as applications of two of the theories of norms explored in Part One. On Eric Posner's theory, norms are sets of individual signaling acts, each of which is meant to communicate that the signaler has a low discount rate and so is a good type with whom to enter into cooperative relationships. On my theory, norms are patterns of rationally motivated conforming behavior. Each of these conceptions of a norm was seen to provide a distinct explanation of the dubious quality of most extant website privacy norms. Posner's signaling model would hold that websites were signaling their cooperative type but that all actual cooperation would occur in the future. On my theory, depending on the sorts of strategic considerations outlined in Part One, many websites were best viewed as already engaging in the cooperative activity of providing genuine respect for user privacy in exchange for trust on the part of their users.

The case study of the emergence of website privacy norms was of interest for a few reasons. First, norm theories have not been applied in cyberspace in a sustained fashion previously. This raised the issue of whether norms function in cyberspace in the same manner that they function in real space. Though the investigation was preliminary, the answer to this question appears to be yes. Second, one of the common themes of much of the law and norms literature has been the topic of bottom/up law formation. The emergence of website privacy norms was of interest in this regard, as the account that I provided has tracked these norms from their earliest, prelegal formative stage in which the practices were not yet recognized as putatively tortuous. Finally, the case study allowed us to test the general applicability of the emergence accounts of Ellickson, Cooter, McAdams, and Posner. First, the world of online data collection is not a close-knit community, so Ellickson's account is not applicable. Second, websites are not motivated by guilt or esteem, so the cooperative outcomes are not explained by either Cooter's or McAdams's accounts. Nor is there mere signaling of future cooperation but an element of real cooperation, so Posner's account is not applicable.

Overall, norms are patterns of behavior that have rational structures not grammatical structures. This was seen throughout the applied analysis in Parts Two and Three. It is because patterns are extant they they are shared by community members. This gives customs a definite form and shape that, for example, jurors can draw on in their group deliberation. It will matter to the typical juror that a custom is in fact followed by members of the community. As Part One indicated, however, courts should be willing to overturn dominant customs when the structural features of the custom provide reason to believe that it may be dysfunctional for one reason or another. In Part Three, the relevant norms were conspicuously seen to be actual practices rather than mere linguistic rules, as was evidenced by the fact that website privacy norms could be measured and studied social scientifically. One could, for example, empirically determine the percentage of sites that were observing certain benchmarks of privacy respect, such as providing written notice of the site's privacy policies.

In sum, then, the pattern conception of norms has served to illuminate the substantive areas of the law explored in Parts Two and Three. Pragmatically speaking, this is an indication that the pattern conception has value. Just how much will depend on whether the pattern conception turns out to illuminate other areas of law and social order as well.

Notes

Introduction

1. The terms *norm* and *custom* are used here as near synonyms. Custom is the term that typically appears in legal discussions. While both are rationally governed patterns of behavior, norms may come to exist over a short period of time, while customs may not. Similar to norms and customs, but little discussed as such in this work, are *folkways*, *mores*, and *traditions*. See STEVEN HETCHER, "*Norms*," *Encyclopedia of Ethics* (2ⁿᵈ ed., 2001).

2. The first sustained analysis of social norms by a legal theorist appears in ROBERT ELLICKSON, *Order Without Law: How Neighbors Settle Disputes* (1991). Jeffrey Rosen refers to Ellickson's book as "[T]he harbinger of the new interest in law and social norms." JEFFREY ROSEN, "The Next Crimebuster: The Social Police," *New Yorker*, Oct. 20 & 27, 1997, at 173. Ellickson views law and norms as representing a new paradigm within the traditional law and economic approach. See ROBERT C. ELLICKSON, "Law and Economics Discovers Social Norms," 27 *J. Legal Stud.* 537 (1998). Perhaps, not surprisingly, Judge Richard Posner instead views law and norms theory as second-generation law and economics. See RICHARD A. POSNER, "Social Norms, Social Meaning, and Economic Analysis of Law: A Comment," 27 *J. Legal Stud.* 553 (1998). Social norms theory has been the subject of a number of important recent symposia. *See* SYMPOSIUM, "The Informal Economy," 103 *Yale L. Rev.* 2119 (1994); SYMPOSIUM, "Law, Economics, and Norms," 144 *U. Pa. L. Rev.* 1643 (1996); SYMPOSIUM, "Law and Society & Law and Economics," 1997 *Wis. L. Rev.* 375 (1997); SYMPOSIUM, "The Nature and Sources, Formal and Informal, of Law," 82 *Cornell L. Rev.* 947 (1997); SYMPOSIUM, "The Legal Construction of Norms," 86 *Va. L. Rev.* 1577 (2000).

3. Leading nonlegal scholarship on social norms and customs includes: DAVID LEWIS, *Convention* (1969); EDNA ULLMANN-MARGALIT, *The Emergence of Norms* (1977); RUSSELL HARDIN, *Collective Action* (1982); JOHN MAYNARD SMITH, *Evolution and The Theory of Games* (1982); ROBERT AXELROD, *The Evolution of Cooperation* (1984); ROBERT SUGDEN, *The Economics of Rights, Co-operation and Welfare* (1986); JON ELSTER, *The Cement of Society* (1989); JAMES S. COLEMAN, *Foundations of Social Theory*, Chapters 10, 11, 30 (1990); RUSSELL HARDIN, *One for All: The Logic of Group Conflict* (1995).

4. Over the past forty odd years, law and economics has developed on twin tracks. On the one hand, it has developed at a theoretical level; on the other hand, it has developed by being persuasively applied to explain an ever-expanding set of specific social institutions and

practices. In the decade-old development of law and norms theory, it has begun to develop along theoretical and applied tracks as well. Although there have been numerous notable applications of the new law and norms theory, there is much room for more work in applying these theoretical accounts to new situations, both to illuminate the concrete situation and to help better understand the strengths and weaknesses of the competing theories of norms. Ellickson has noted the importance of case studies for the further development of the law and norms approach. See ROBERT C. ELLICKSON, "Law and Economics," supra note 2. Recent law and norms literature has included a number of significant case studies. See, for example, LISA BERNSTEIN, "Merchant Law in a Merchant Court: Rethinking the Code's Search for Immanent Business Norms," 144 *U. Pa. L. Rev.* 1765 (1996); ROBERT COOTER AND JANET T. LANDA, "Personal Versus Impersonal Trade: The Size of Trading Groups and Contract Law," *Intl. Rev. L. & Econ.* 15 (1984); RICHARD H. McADAMS, "Cooperation and Conflict: The Economics of Group Status Production and Race Discrimination," 108 *Harv. L. Rev.* 1003 (1995); MARK D. WEST, "Legal Rules and Social Norms in Japan's Secret World of Sumo," 26 *J. Legal Stud.* 165 (1997); ANN E. CARLSON, "Recycling Norms," 89 *Cal. L. Rev.* 1231 (2001); EDWARD B. ROCK AND MICHAEL L. WACHTER, "The Enforceability of Norms and the Employment Relationship," 144 *U. Pa. L. Rev.* 1913 (1996); ANN BARTOW, "Electrifying Copyright Norms and Making Cyberspace More Like a Book," 48 *Vill. L. Rev.* 13 (2003) MICHAEL P. VANDENBERGH, "Beyond Elegance: A Testable Typology of Social Norms in Corporate Environmental Compliance," 22 Stan. Environmental L. J. 55 (2003). None of these case studies, however, has applied law and norms methodology in an online context.

5. Reflective equilibrium is the name for an approach developed by John Rawls to help guide theory elaboration. JOHN RAWLS, *The Theory of Justice* 48 (1973). ("From the standpoint of moral philosophy, the best account of a person's sense of justice is not the one which fits his judgments prior to his examining any conception of justice, but rather the one which matches his judgments in reflective equilibrium. As we have seen, this state is one reached after a person has weighed various proposed conceptions and he has either revised his judgments to accord with one of them or held fast to his initial convictions (and the corresponding conception.").

6. See generally, BRIAN BARRY AND RUSSELL HARDIN, *Rational Man and Irrational Society* (1982). The rational choice account explains how groups may share norms yet avoids postulating a *social mind*. See BENJAMIN CARDOZO, *The Paradoxes of Legal Science* (1928) (" '[the] term ["social mind"] is simply an expression for the mass of ideas operative in a society, communicable from man to man, and serving to direct the actions of individuals'" (quoting L. HOBHOUSE, *Social Evolution and Political Theory* 96–97 [1911])); see R. POSNER, *Cardozo: A Study in Reputation* 99 (1990) ("there is no social mind"). While instantiated norms may create a set of shared understandings that can loosely be called a social mind, this fact is consistent with methodological individualism and does not imply the existence of any new metaphysical entities.

Broadly speaking, there have been two camps in the academic war over the proper understanding of the role and importance of social norms. In one camp are the traditional sociologists, anthropologists and learning theorists and in the other camp the economists, rational choice political scientists, philosophers and legal theorists. The former camp have typically been methodological holists while the latter camp have been methodological individualists. The present work is resolutely in the methodological individualist tradition. What is not often recognized is that methodological individualism is consistent with moral-theoretic analysis.

7. See BARRY & HARDIN, supra note 6.

8. See ELLICKSON, *Order Without Law*, supra note 2.

9. See LEWIS, supra note 3.

10. Even in the context of strategic norms, conformity will sometimes come from persons seeking to save on information costs. In other words, both strategic and nonstrategic motivation may co-exist as forces helping to maintain the same norm.

11. LEWIS, supra note 3; ULLMANN-MARGALIT, supra note 3; ELLICKSON, supra note 2; RICHARD MCADAMS, "The Origin, Development, and Regulation of Norms," 96 *Mich. L. Rev.* 338 (1997); ERIC POSNER, *Law and Social Norms* (2000). There appears to be a conceptual nexus between rational choice theory, law, and philosophy. Leading works have developed two sides of the trilogy of core subjects; Lewis and Ullman-Margalit (philosophy/rational choice) and Ellickson, McAdams, and Posner (rational choice/law). The present analysis is an interdisciplinary work that combines all three subjects. More than two hundred years ago, Thomas Hobbes and David Hume took the first, intuitive steps toward establishing a game-theoretic framework for modeling practices constitutive of social order. These theorists did not use the payoff matrices characteristic of modern game theory, yet it is clear that they had in mind the same underlying strategic situations that these matrices help elucidate. The following analysis will examine the foundational insights of Hobbes and Hume as well. See generally, THOMAS HOBBES, *Leviathan*; DAVID HUME, *A Treatise of Human Nature* (2nd ed., L. A Selby-Bigge ed., 1978).

12. JAMES COLEMAN, "Norms as Social Capital." In *Economic Imperialism: The Economic Approach Applied Outside the Field of Economics* 133 (Gerard Radnitzky and Peter Bernholz, eds., 1987).

13. *Id.* POSNER, supra note 11 ("Most people refrain most of the time from antisocial behavior even when the law is absent or has no force. They conform to social norms. The question left unanswered by law and economics is why people conform to social norms. Without an answer to that question, one cannot understand the effect of laws on people's behavior.").

14. See, for example, id. at 39.

15. Hobbes famously thought that spontaneous cooperation among groups or communities would be nearly impossible because it requires people to make personal sacrifices, which, being self-interested, they would be disinclined to do. Social order will emerge only when there is a strong sovereign – a Leviathan – with the power to force cooperative acts through the promulgation of laws backed by sanctions. Early rational choice theorists noticed that the well-known Prisoner's Dilemma or collective action problem can be aptly applied to the strategic structure Hobbes thought characterized an individual's relation to other individuals and to the state.

16. Hume was more sanguine than Hobbes regarding the prospects for informal social groups to sustain cooperative practices. His approach stresses the importance of informal, processes percolating from below that may result in cooperation. On the Humean account, law plays only a partial role in the creation of social order, often working in tandem with informal efforts to stimulate cooperation. The theory I develop is closer to Hume than Hobbes in the importance it ascribes to the informal domain in helping shape social practices.

17. Hume outlined a two-stage process of the evolution of social norms whereby moral features may emerge out of the rational machinations of a collective of actors who have some degree of natural sympathy. See HUME, supra note 11.

18. Cited in MCADAMS, supra note 11.

19. 60 F.2d 737 (2d Cir. 1932).

20. Id. at 740.

21. See Brown v. Kendall, 60 Mass. (6 Cush.) 292 (1850) ("ordinary" care). See also Vaughan v. Menlove, 3 Bing. (N.C.) 468, 132 Eng. Rep. 490 (C.P. 1837) ("ordinary prudence").

22. Texas & Pacific R.R. v. Behymer, 189 U.S. 468 (1903). *The T. J. Hooper*, supra note 19. A surprising result of the analysis of Part Two is the finding that Behymer, not Hooper, should be by all rights the leading case, since the underlying facts of Behymer have a structure that better exemplifies the core strategic problems that the rule of custom is meant to address.

23. CLARENCE MORRIS, "Custom and Negligence," 42 *Colum. L. Rev.* 1147 (1941).

24. See RICHARD A. POSNER, *Economic Analysis of Law* 153 (4th ed. 1992). See also WILLIAM M. LANDES AND RICHARD A. POSNER, *The Economic Structure of Tort Law* 132–3 (1987).

25. See, for example, CASS R. SUNSTEIN, "Social Norms and Social Roles," 96 *Colum. L. Rev.* 903, 918 (1996) ("Good social norms solve collective action problems by encouraging people to do useful things that they would not do without the relevant norms.").

26. In other words, litigants bargain in the shadow of the jury. LAWRENCE M. FRIEDMAN, "Some Notes on the Civil Jury in Hisotrical Perspective," 48 *DePaul Law Rev.* 201, 204 (1998).

27. ELLICKSON, *Order Without Law*, supra note 2, at 4. (Ellickson defines legal centralists as those holding the view that "the state functions as the sole creator of operative rules of entitlement among individuals.")

28. *Restatement (Third) of Torts: General Principles* § 21–5 (Restatement Apr. 5, 1999) [Hereinafter *Restatement*].

29. Liberalism – modern and classical – begins with a brute conception of the intrinsic moral worth of the individual. See generally, JOHN STUART MILL, *On Liberty* (1859). From this starting point, the theory of human rights and personal autonomy follow. Free people may do as they please, so long as others are not injured in the process. Free people characteristically choose to conform to social norms. When they do, and when others are injured in the process, tort law and social norms may be implicated.

30. See generally, JULES L. COLEMAN, *The Practice of Principle* 5–6 (2001); BENJAMIN ZIPURSKY, *Pragmatic Conceptualism*, Legal Theory 614 (2000); JOHN C. P. GOLDBERG AND BENJAMIN C. ZIPURSKY, "The Moral of MacPherson," 146 *U. Pa. L. Rev.* 1733, 1734–44, 1821–32 (1998).

31. See also VICTOR GOLD, "Covert Advocacy: Reflections on the Use of Psychological Persuasion Techniques in the Courtroom," 65 *N.C. L. Rev.* 481, 499 (1987) ("In a democracy, the government is ruled by people. The jury is comprised of people from the community who are expected to use community values in making their decision. The use of the jury prevents judicial tyranny.").

32. See LAWRENCE LESSIG, "The Regulation of Social Meaning," 62 *U. Chi. L. Rev.* 943, 951 (1995) ("Any society or social context has what I call here social meanings – the semiotic content attached to various actions, or inactions, or statuses, within a particular context.").

33. See, for example, "The End of Privacy," *The Economist*, May 1, 1999, at 21; REP. ASA HUTCHINSON AND REP. JIM MORAN, "Industry Needs to Take the Lead on Protection,"

Roll Call, Jul. 10, 2000, available at 2000 WL8734799; ADAM L. PENENBERG, "The End of Privacy," *Forbes*, Nov. 29, 1999, at 182; JARED SANDBERG, "Losing Your Good Name Online," *Newsweek*, Sept. 20, 1999, at 56; CELIA SANTANDER, "Web-Site Privacy Policies Aren't Created Equal," *Web Fin.*, Dec. 11, 2000. Opinion polls show increasing public concern with respect to online privacy.

34. Norm entrepreneurs are actors who promote the change of norms. SUNSTEIN, supra note 25.

35. Traditional economic analysis has eschewed the topic of preference formation. This is changing, however. See GARY S. BECKER, *Accounting For Tastes* 3 (1996).

36. See GEORGE R. MILNE, "Privacy and Ethical Issues in Database/Interactive Marketing and Public Policy: A Research Framework and Overview of the Special Issue," 19 *J. Pub. Pol'y & Mktg.* 16, 16 (2000). Milne succinctly summarized several studies: "When Web sites require consumers to provide information to register, many consumers provide false information. Surveys report that half the Internet users report false information about a quarter of the time." *Id.* (citation omitted). See also DOMINGO R. TAN, "Personal Privacy in the Information Age: Comparison of Internet Data Protection Regulations in the United States and the European Union," 21 *Loy. L.A. Int'l & Comp. L.J.* 661, 664–5 (1999) (citing a Boston Consulting Group consumer study stating that "40% of Internet users have provided false information at least once when registering at a website"); JERRY GUIDERA, "Online Shoppers Often Lie To Guard Privacy, Survey Says," *Wall St. J. Europe*, Mar. 16, 2000, at 28.

37. ELLICKSON, *Order Without Law*, supra note 2, at 213–14.

38. See PAMELA SAMUELSON, "Privacy as Intellectual Property?," 52 *Stan. L. Rev.* 1125, 1163 (2000) ("The more enlightened private sector firms are coming to realize that fuller adherence to privacy principles will promote consumer trust which will, in turn, promote commerce").

Chapter One

1. SAMUEL JOHNSON, *Selected Writing* 122 (R. T. Davies ed., 1965).

2. See JOHN FINLEY SCOTT, *Internalization of Norms: A Sociological Theory of Moral Commitment* (1971). (Although this model is associated with Max Weber, John Finley Scott argues persuasively that the ultimate origin is Kant).

3. Although the occurrent thought model is the most straightforward notion of what a verbal or linguistic entity might amount to, others are possible. For example, there is a research program in cognitive science that takes all information stored within the brain to be linguistically encoded. Perhaps the rules that guide our behavior are linguistically encoded in such a manner but not excisable as occurrent thought, just as the rules of grammar are presumably internally represented in some manner, although not readily accessible. This might still fairly be called a rule view, although this view will not plausibly hold that the linguistically encoded information is readily accessible to the agent, which is the first tenet of the rule conception. This is a possible view, but it should be stressed that it is not the received view.

4. But see RICHARD HARE *Moral Language* 12 (1952) (claiming that "commands, however much they may differ from statements, are like them in this, that they consist in telling someone something, not in seeking to influence him.").

5. MAX WEBER, *Economy and Society: An Outline of Interpretive Sociology* Part 2, Chapter 1 (Guenther Roth and Claus Wittich, eds., 1979).
6. TALCOTT PARSONS, *The Structure of Social Action* 75 (1937).
7. GEORGE HOMANS, *The Human Group* 124 (1950).
8. Id. at 7.
9. ROBIN WILLIAMS, *American Sociology* 207 (1961).
10. FRANCESCA M. CANCIAN, *What Are Norms?* 5 (1975).
11. MICHAEL TAYLOR, *Anarchy and Cooperation* 29 (1976).
12. See SCOTT, supra note 2 at 72.
13. ALLAN GIBBARD, "Norms and Human Evolution," 3 (unpublished manuscript) (1986).
14. Id. at 3.
15. EDNA ULLMAN-MARGALIT, *The Emergence of Norms* 12 (1977).
16. ROBERT ELLICKSON, *Order Without Law: How Neighbors Settle Disputes* 126 (1991).
17. See id. at 131.
18. RICHARD MCADAMS, "The Origin, Development, and Regulation of Norms," 96 *Mich. L. Rev.* 338, 381 (1997).
19. Id. at 350.
20. Id. at 382 ("Within the broad category of neighbor norms is a subcategory of no-littering norms, one of which is 'cleanup after your dog.' When this is true, little is lost by ignoring the broad norm and focusing only on *the norm that most directly governs behavior*" (emphasis added); but see, RICHARD MCADAMS, "Conventions and Norms: Philosophical Aspects," 4 *International Encyclopedia of the Social and Behavioral Sciences* 2735–41 (Neil J. Smelser & Paul B. Baltes, eds., 2001) ("In the sense pursued here, however, a norm describes a regularity of behavior among a population of individuals, the central feature of which is that most or all of the individuals approve conformity to the regularity and/or disapprove nonconformity.").
21. Although his remarks on the issue are brief, Allan Gibbard appears to understand rules along the lines of this retrenched view. He writes: "In one respect the rules are in the eyes of the beholder: Neither the beast nor the human can state them, but they can be formulated – with considerable ingenuity and effort – by a sophisticated human observer. In another respect, the rules are really in the actor: if they were not somehow represented internally, it would be mysterious how these patterns of behavior could be maintained.... By the norm itself, I suggest, we should mean simply a prescription or imperative that gives the rule a sophisticated observer could formulate." See GIBBARD, supra note 13 at 11–12.
22. SAUL KRIPKE, *Naming and Necessity* (1972).
23. The norms of professionals such as doctors are discussed in greater detail in Part Two.
24. One theorist who does recognize this distinction is Edna Ullmann-Margalit. She notes: "A typical feature is useful for explicatory purposes if it is sufficiently common in the class characterized by it, if it applies to its paradigmatic cases, and if, moreover, it requires a certain degree of ingenuity to provide counterexamples to it." See ULLMANN-MARGALIT, supra note 15 at 12.
25. CANCIAN, supra note 10 at 9.
26. This feature of British culture is richly portrayed in British works of fiction such as the novel *Daniel Martin* by John Fowles, or the BBC television series with the metaphorical

title, *Upstairs, Downstairs*. See JOHN FOWLES *Daniel Martin* (1977); *Upstairs, Downstairs* (British Broadcasting Corp., 1971–2001).

27. STEVEN HETCHER, *Norms* (Ph.D. dissertation, 1991); STEVEN HETCHER, "Norms", *Encyclopedia of Ethics* (1992); ERIC POSNER, *Law and Social Norms* (2000) (norms as behavioral regularities constituted of attempts to signal the signaler's low discount rate). Some of Posner's remarks may also be read as endorsements of the rule conception. See Chapter Eight, note 19; Chapter Twelve, note 64.

28. GIBBARD, supra note 13 at 12.

29. DAVID LEWIS, *Convention* 43–44 (1969) (discussing the problem of determining which criteria constitute an act type).

30. Ordinary language appears to allow that a group as small as two persons may be enough for a norm or custom. See, for example, JACK KEROUAC, *The Portable Jack Kerouac* (Ann Charters, ed.) 1995 (In an amusing letter to John Clellon Holmes, Kerouac begins to relay a story based on events that occurred during his stay with William Burroughs in Mexico City in 1952 as follows: "Dig this, peotl eaters of the hip generation: It was only a customary (I'm writing this as I go along) week in the life of Bill and I when all of a sudden, to break the calm or paralysis . . . ") (Boldface deleted).

31. These transhistorical groups would appear to be able to have *traditions*, however; thus, norms and traditions are not identical to one another.

32. DAVID S. SHWAYDER, *The Stratification of Behavior* (1965). (Shwayder uses *conformity* in a similar manner.)

33. ROBERT NOZICK, *Philosophical Explanations* (1981).

34. This does not gainsay the fact that many of the subtleties of eating behavior are often governed by norms.

35. As the analysis in Parts Two and Three of the book will indicate, in the law, attenuated causal connections are sometimes sufficient to constitute *conformity* to custom, as the term is used by judges.

36. HILARY *Putnam, Mind, Language and Reality*, 227 (1975).

Chapter Two

1. ARISTOTLE, *Nicomachaen Ethics* viii.9.1160a (H. Rackman, trans., 1975).

2. JAMES COLEMAN, "Norms as Social Capital." In *Economic Imperialism: The Economic Approach Applied Outside the Field of Economics* 133 (Gerard Radnitzky and Peter Bernholz, eds., 1987).

3. A parallel problem arises with regard to reconciling conformity to norms with moral theory, which characterizes moral action as resulting from moral deliberation. Such deliberation is, on its face, in tension with the sort of nondeliberative conformity involved in the maintenance of many norms.

4. EDNA ULLMAN-MARGALIT, *The Emergence of Norms* (1977).

5. DAVID LEWIS, *Convention* (1969). Both Lewis and Ullmann-Margalit acknowledge that their conceptions derive from Thomas Schelling's discussion of games of pure coordination. The *locus classicus* of the idea is David Hume. See DAVID HUME, *A Treatise of Human Nature* (2d. ed., L. A. Selby-Bigge ed., 1978). Lewis's work is often and rightly touted as a model for analytic philosophy. Ullmann-Margalit's work, though less widely known, deserves a place in the same category.

6. This and the following matrices (unless otherwise noted) are to be read such that the highest number represents the most preferred outcome of each player and the lowest number represents the least preferred outcome of each player. Each of the four pairs of numbers represents the payoffs to each party in each of the four possible outcomes, the left-hand number is the payoff to the row-player and the right-hand number is the payoff to the column-player.

7. See Lewis, supra note 5.

8. See id. at 24; Thomas Schelling, *The Strategy of Conflict* 83–118 (1960).

9. See Lewis, supra note 5.

10. Shelling uses the term *focal points* for these salient outcomes. See Schelling, supra note 8 at 57. For a view that is critical of the notion of salience, see Margaret Gilbert, *On Social Facts* 334–6 (1989). See also David Gauthier, "Coordination," *Dialogue* 4, 195–221 (1975).

11. See Lewis, supra note 5 at 25.

12. See id. at 36–42.

13. See id. at 36.

14. Ullmann-Margalit uses "convention" for coordination norms with a certain origin, namely, those that emerge informally. "Decree" is her term for coordination norms that arise as a result of explicit attempts at norm construction. See Ullmann-Margalit, supra note 4 at 97. In terms of the terminology developed in Chapter One, note that Ullmann-Margalit is falling into rule theorist language when she invokes the notion of a decree. The formal rule or decree that may have been the initial impetus to the coordination norm may bear no precise relationship to the actual practice that is extant, just as *Brush after every meal* does not accurately describe a practice in which the actual pattern of behavior is that people brush shortly after waking and shortly before bed.

15. Lewis, supra note 5; Ullmann-Margalit, supra note 4.

16. It is unclear what Lewis takes to be the ultimate reach of the notion of convention. As an off-hand remark, he mentions that his is a theory of convention "along the lines of Hume's." Lewis, supra note 5 at 3. This comparison is not developed in the text, however. I will argue later that Hume had a broader notion of convention in mind, one along the lines I develop. It is also unclear what the intended range of Ullmann-Margalit's coordination norms is supposed to be. On page one of her book, she says, "This study attempts to provide a rational reconstruction of the formal features of states of social interaction in which norms are generated" (Ullmann-Margalit, supra note 4). This passage lends itself to the interpretation that Ullmann-Margalit is dealing with the types of formal features in which all norms are generated. See Ullmann-Margalit, supra note 4. The formal feature of concern in the present section is the coordination problem and the resulting type of norm, the coordination norm. It is reasonable to interpret Ullmann-Margalit as believing she has found in coordination norms the essence of one of the basic norm types, those dealing with coordination. See Ullmann-Margalit, supra note 4. This is speculative as she does not explicitly say that she is exhaustively characterizing norms as they emerge from various types of strategic situations. But to the extent that it is fair to interpret her in this way, and to the extent that my account is convincing in arguing for a conception of coordination norms that is broader than hers, it will serve as a criticism of her account as being less than the full picture of what deserve to be called coordination norms.

17. Other problems in coordinating are relevant to understanding coordination norms though they will not be labeled *coordination problems*. For example, in the case of subtle and complex norms already in existence, one might have a problem simply determining what conforming to the norm requires. This is not a problem in coordinating with others to solve a novel coordination problem, but rather a problem of coordinating on performing the same subtle action that others already are performing. This is a problem in coordinating that may keep someone from achieving the benefits of coordination, though not a coordination problem in my sense, or the sense of Lewis or Ullmann-Margalit.

18. For reasons different than those provided below, Margaret Gilbert also argues against Lewis that unique coordination equilibria are not necessarily trivial. See GILBERT, supra note 10 at 63–5.

19. Ullmann-Margalit discusses a game with this structure and incorrectly dismisses it as "no genuine problem of coordination." ULLMANN-MARGALIT, supra note 4 at 80.

20. LEWIS, supra note 5 at 6, 45; ULLMANN-MARGALIT, supra note 4 at 84.

21. There are circumstances in which one may sometimes expect to see some sanctioning and prescribing in each of these games, as the discussion at the end of the chapter will indicate.

22. LEWIS, supra note 5.

23. For a discussion of various possible responses to this so-called paradox, see BRIAN BARRY AND RUSSELL HARDIN, *Rational Man, Irrational Society* (1982); RUSSELL HARDIN, *Collective Action* (1982).

24. See id.; BRIAN BARRY, *Sociologists, Economics and Democracy* (1978).

25. The precise details as to when cooperation in iterated Prisoner's Dilemma situations may be rational are varied and complex. The literature on the topic is vast. See especially HARDIN, supra note 23. Whatever the precise details, sanctions play a key role. What is presently at issue is the relationship between Prisoner's Dilemmas and sanction-driven norms. In scenarios of this sort, cooperation is rational only due to the presence of sanctions. Because we threaten to sanction one another by withdrawing from future interactions, cooperation may be preferred over defection. Pairs of agents may rationally choose to follow cooperative norms in such circumstances. Norms arising in these circumstances will be sanction-driven norms; the acts of conformity are motivated by the desire to avoid sanctions. How such norms might actually emerge is not well understood. Following, however, is a schematic account of how a sanction-driven norm might come about.

26. HUME, supra note 5 at 490. In this passage, two factors are at work for Hume (though elsewhere he acknowledges that the agreement may be "tacite." See HUME, supra note 5 at 505. First, one has to be smart enough to be capable of appreciating the fact that there is the possibility of mutual gain, and second, there has to be communication between the parties so that each will know that the other realizes there is a mutual gain to be had through cooperation. In the accounts in the literature regarding the emergence of cooperation among egoists in iterated Prisoner's Dilemmas, the first of these two factors does all the work. Actors are rational and thus are capable of realizing that there is a prospect for mutual gain. In general, communication is disallowed. Rather, the models try to account for cooperation among actors who do not communicate. For example, in the original Prisoner's Dilemma, the prisoners are not allowed to communicate.

27. PAUL A. SAMUELSON, "The Pure Theory of Public Expenditure," 37 *Review of Economics and Statistics* 350–6 (1955). Neither of these features need hold in their pure form for the cases of interest here. The jointness of supply may be restricted to subgroups within the larger population. These are so-called *shared goods*, or *collective goods*. Similarly, exclusion from consumption need not be impossible, just infeasible. See MANCUR OLSON, *The Logic of Collective Action* 14n (1965); MICHAEL TAYLOR, *Anarchy and Cooperation* 6 (1976). Hardin argues that the public goods problem is a Prisoner's Dilemma. See HARDIN, supra note 23.

28. THOMAS HOBBES, *Leviathan*.

29. See, for example, TAYLOR, supra note 27.

30. See OLSON, supra note 27 at 50.

31. HUME, supra note 5 at 538. Hume appears to contemplate a single-shot situation but one might just as easily imagine a meadow that needed repeated draining, such that the proper solution might call for a practice or norm of meadow maintenance.

32. TAYLOR, supra note 27; HARDIN, supra note 23.

33. H. L. A. Hart talks about the "internal point of view." H. L. A. HART, *The Concept of Law* 86 (1961). Characterizing the Parsonian view, Karl-Dieter Opp writes: "A norm is said to be internalized if it becomes 'part of the personality' i.e. if the conformity to a norm becomes a motive of its own." KARL-DIETER OPP, "The Emergence of and Effects of Social Norms: A Confrontation of Some Hypotheses of Sociology and Economics," 32 *Kyklos* 777 (1979). See also JOHN FINLEY SCOTT, *Internalization of Norms: A Sociological Theory of Moral Commitment* (1971).

34. For a discussion that draws on a number of varied sources, see ROBERT FRANK, *Passions within Reason* (1988).

35. My apologies to epistemologists who use the term *epistemic norm* in an unrelated sense.

36. The basic idea at work here is familiar both to rational choice theory and utilitarian moral theory. To the extent that economists talk about norm following or kindred notions at all, it tends to be in terms of economizing on information costs. Gary Becker, for example, writes, "the assumption that information is often seriously incomplete because it is costly to acquire is used in the economic approach to explain the same kind of behavior that is explained by irrational and volatile behavior, or traditional behavior, or 'nonrational' behavior in other discussions." GARY BECKER, *The Economic Approach to Human Behavior* 7 (1976). In utilitarian moral theory, the problem of acquiring information is addressed in terms of the notion of *rules of thumb* by which to guide one's utility maximizing behavior.

37. This example illustrates a fact about norms that is not often noticed, namely, that they do not always involve publicly observable behavior.

38. ROBERT ELLICKSON, *Order Without Law: How Neighbors Settle Disputes*, 1 (1991).

39. Ellickson notes that the subject matter of his case study was in part motivated by the Coasean parable. See id. at vii. The main example in Coase's famous article is that of damage done to crops by sparks thrown by a passing locomotive. See RONALD H. COASE, "The Problem of Social Cost," 3 *J.L. & Econ.* 1 (1960). Coase's and Ellickson's examples share the core feature that the underlying activity will, with some regularity, cause significant damage to the interests of others (either due to sparks or cattle that will not stay put). See id. See also WAYNE EASTMAN, "How Coasean Bargaining Entails a Prisoner's Dilemma," 72 *Notre Dame L. Rev.* 89 (1996). A virtue of Coasean analysis is

that it highlights the situation of these third parties and the transaction cost problems they may face. The special problem that customs present is that the injured third parties will typically be groups of people who are strangers to one another and disbursed throughout various communities. Thus, they may face insurmountable collective action problems in getting together to represent their interests.

40. The Specialized Labor Game does not have the structure of a Prisoner's Dilemma. The Specialized Labor Game differs from the Prisoner's Dilemma in that the maximum total payoff is generated in the northeast quadrant, not the northwest quadrant. "Specialized Labor" situations are interesting because, in Ellickson's words, "they invite the generation of norms that impose duties *selectively* on those unusually well positioned to effect rescues or otherwise act pro-socially." Letter from Robert Ellickson, Walter E. Meyer Professor of Property and Urban Law, Yale Law School, to Steven Hetcher, Associate Professor of Law, Vanderbilt University School of Law (June 19, 1998) (on file with author). While Specialized Labor is not a PD, it is nevertheless maintained by sanctions, that is, it is a type of sanction-driven custom.

41. ELLICKSON, supra note 38 at 167. As the title of his book on the subject indicates, such interactions in communities, in toto, may be fairly said to constitute social order without law. Ellickson makes exceptions for "distributive norms," and "foundational norms." Id. at 174.

42. As Ellickson discusses, sociologists refer to such overlapping relationships as "multiplex." See id. at 55.

43. Ellickson refers to the "enforcement opportunities needed to establish norms." Id. at 177. Sanctions are a central element of Ellickson's description of norms: "[Norms] are evidenced by patterns of sanctions, patterns of primary behavior, and aspirational statements." Id. at 183.

44. ELLICKSON, supra note 38 at 250. Ellickson defines "close-knit" groups as follows: "A group is *cose-knit* when informal power is broadly distributed among group members and the information pertinent to informal control circulates easily among them." Id. at 178. Ellickson induces close-knittedness from features of repeat play in PDs. See Id. at 177–8. Ellickson's definition of close-knittedness implies "group members . . . having both continuing reciprocal power over one another and also a bank of shared information." Id. at 238. Ellickson notes that close-knittedness is inversely related to group size – the smaller the group, the greater the degree of close-knittedness. See id. at 182. However, "a group does not necessarily have to be small to be close-knit." Id.

45. See generally, ROBERT D. COOTER, "Law and Unified Social Theory," 22 *J. L. & Socy.* 50 (1994).

46. ROBERT D. COOTER, "Decentralized Law for a Complex Economy: The Structural Approach to Adjudicating the New Law Merchant," 144 *U. Pa. L. Rev.* 1643, 1665 (1996).

47. Id. at 1668.

48. RICHARD H. MCADAMS, "The Origin, Development, and Regulation of Norms," 96 *Mich. L. Rev.* 338, 354 (1997). McAdams does not claim that his account explains all norm emergence: "My thesis, however, is not that the esteem theory of norm origin is strictly necessary to explain any norm, but that the esteem model solves the origin puzzle in a way that explains more of what we observe about norms."

49. See generally, RUSSELL HARDIN, "The Emergence of Norms" (review essay of, Edna Ullmann-Margalit, *The Emergence of Norms*), 90 *Ethics* 575 (1980).

50. Id. at 355, 342. See also PHILIP PETTIT, "Virtus Normativa: Rational Choice Perspectives, Symposium on Norms in Moral and Social Theory," 100 *Ethics* 725 (1990). See also MCADAMS, supra note 48 at 365 ([C]ommunication of approval is rarely costly and is often pleasurable."; "The key feature of esteem is that individuals do not always bear a cost by granting different levels of esteem to others.").

51. Id. at 342.

52. McAdams plausibly speculates that the smallness of these costs may be why mainstream economic theories ignore these costs completely. Id. at 342.

53. Id. at 380.

54. Id. at 357.

55. Id. at 358.

56. Id.

57. Id.

58. Id.

59. Id.

60. Id. at 365.

61. Id. at 366.

62. Id. at 366.

63. Id. at 366.

64. Id.

65. Id.

66. In addition, according to McAdams, esteem processes can lead to norm internalization. Id. at 376.

67. ERIC POSNER, *Law and Social Norms* (2000). Posner's book develops a "general model of nonlegal cooperation," which consists of a "signaling game in which people engage in behavioral regularities in order to show that they are desirable partners in cooperative endeavors." According to Posner, "social norms" are the result of these behavioral norms constituted of collections of signaling activity. Id. at 5. As this quote indicates, Posner appears to believe that his signaling account provides a general account of social norms.

68. See, for example, D. BAIRD, R. GERTNER, AND R. PICKER, *Game Theory and the Law*, Chapter Four (1994).

69. Id. at 123 ("Signaling takes place when those who possess nonverifiable information can convey that information in the way they choose their actions").

70. Id. at 124 ("Assume, for example, that buyers have no direct way of knowing whether a seller makes a high- or low-quality product. High quality sellers may be able to signal their type by selling goods with a warranty. Because their goods break down less often, these sellers can offer a warranty more cheaply than low-quality sellers.").

71. See POSNER, supra note 67 at 5.

72. Id. at 18 ("Holding everything else equal, a good type is more likely to cooperate in a repeated prisoner's dilemma than a bad type is, because the good type cares more about the future payoffs that are lost if cooperation fails.").

73. Id. at 15 ("Then as long as each player cares enough about his payoffs in future rounds – that is, he has a low discount rate – he will cooperate rather than defect in each round."). This bi-polar typology is, as Posner notes, a methodological convenience. Clearly, in reality there are not simply two types of preferences when it comes to discounting the

future but rather there will be a continuous set of preferences. See id. at 19. Interestingly, Posner implicitly draws a positive correlation between good and bad types in his sense of these terms and in the ordinary moral sense of these terms. He writes: "The reader should be reminded that a "good" or "bad" type is not necessarily a good or bad person; the label refers to the beliefs of those within the group about the hidden characterstics of others."). Id. at 25.

74. Id. at 21.
75. Id. at 29, at 22–3 ("All these elements follow from the signaling model, according to which signals are costly and observable actions with no necessary or intrinsic connections to the beliefs that they provoke.").
76. MCADAMS, supra note 48 at 5.
77. See POSNER, supra note 67 at 19.
78. Id., Chapter Five.
79. TALCOTT PARSONS, *The Structure of Social Action* (1937). *See also* ROBERT FRANK, supra note 34 (arguing that adherence to norms of fairness might sometimes be irrational).
80. It is a bit misleading to speak of irrational reasons, as such. Rather, this should be understood as a convenient term for all the desires for objects, states of affairs, and the like, that we take to be irrational, as well as irrational beliefs, inferences, and so on. Thus, an irrational conforming act is motivated by a desire or inference of a type we consider irrational, or that is explained by an irrational belief or inference.
81. This is just what economists accuse sociologists of believing in. BRIAN BARRY, *Sociologists, Economists and Democracy* Chapter IV (1978); RALF DAHRENDORF, "Homo Sociologicus: On the History, Significance, and Limits of the Category of Social Role," *Essays in the Theory of Society* (1968).
82. GARY BECKER, "Habits, Addictions and Traditions," *Accounting for Tastes* 118, 127 (1996). J. ELSTER, *The Cement of Society: A Study of Social Order* (1989).

Chapter Three

1. RICHARD BRANDT, *A Theory of the Good and the Right* 181 (1979).
2. John Austin takes the calculation problem to be the most pervasive and fundamental criticism of utilitarianism. See JOHN AUSTIN, *Lectures in Jurisprudence* 111 (1885). Mill considers it at some length. See JOHN STUART MILL, *Utilitarianism* 275 (Mary Warnock ed., 1962).
3. This is a central theme in the writings of Friedrich A. Hayek. See, for example, FRIEDRICH A. HAYEK, *Law, Legislation and Liberty, Vol. 1 Rules and Order* (1973).
4. As Alfred North Whitehead remarks, "Civilization advances by extending the number of important operations which we can perform without thinking about them." ALFRED NORTH WHITEHEAD, *Introduction to Mathematics* 61 (1911).
5. See MANCUR OLSON, *The Logic of Collective Action* 83–118 (1965).
6. JOHN P. STEVENS, "The Life Span of a Judge–Made Rule, 58 *N. Y. L. Rev.* 1, 9 (1983). PETER L. STRAUSS, *"Bowsher v. Synar: Formal and Functional Approaches to Separation-of-Powers Questions – A Foolish Inconsistency?"* 72 *Cornell L. Rev.* 488 (1987). WILLIAM N. ESKRIDGE, JR., "Relationships Between Formalism and Functionalism in Separation of Powers Cases," 22 *Harv. J. L. & Pub. Poly.* 21, 29 (1998).

7. In Urmson's reading of Mill, matters that only marginally impact utility are not of concern to utilitarianism. See J. O. URMSON, "The Interpretation of the Moral Philosophy of J. S. Mill," 3 *Philosophical Quarterly* 35 (1953).

8. In the following, I will consider representative passages from the major classical and modern utilitarians, most notably Mill and Brandt. See ANTHONY QUINTON, *Utilitarian Ethics* 24–5 (1973) (references minor classical utilitarians such as Tucker and Hartley who also emphasize rules). It can be stated with little exaggeration that all utilitarians see an important role for rules.

9. This recalls David Lyon's argument for the extensional equivalence of act utilitarianism and rule utilitarianism. See DAVID LYONS, *Forms and Limits of Utilitarianism* 115–18 (1965).

10. See URMSON, supra note 7.

11. MILL, supra note 2 at 279.

12. AUSTIN, supra note 2 at 115.

13. BRANDT, supra note 1 at 181.

14. RICHARD HARE, *The Language of Morals* 59 (1952).

15. MILL, supra note 2 at 277.

16. Id. at. 276.

17. BRANDT, supra note 1 at 164. Brandt allows for some exceptions to universality. Id. at 192.

18. Id. at 181.

19. MILL, supra note 2 at 276.

20. Id. at 275.

21. Id. at 275–6.

22. QUINTON, supra note 8 at 48.

23. BRANDT, supra note 1 at 288.

24. Id. at 293.

25. Id. at 182.

26. Id. at 186.

27. LYONS, supra note 9 at 276, 279.

28. See, for example, BRANDT, supra note 1 at 287 (learning through imitation is mentioned); RICHARD HARE, "Ethical Theory and Utilitarianism," *Essays in Ethical Theory* 201 (1989) ("self-education" is discussed).

29. LYONS, supra note 9 at 279, italics in original.

30. AUSTIN, supra note 2 at 115.

31. My explication of the Commandment conception might be criticized for failing to discuss *practices*, which are sometimes mentioned by utilitarians and which are, on their face, similar to norms as I define them. See R. F. HARROD, "Utilitarianism Revised," XLV, No. 178 *Mind* 137–56 (1936); STEPHEN TOULMIN, *Reason in Ethics* 153 (1961); and, JOHN RAWLS, "Two Concepts of Rules," 64 *Philosophical Review* 24 (1955). Utilitarians consider practices to be the result of instantiated rules. Rawls, for example, writes: "It is the mark of a practice that being taught how to engage in it involves being instructed in the rules which define it, and that appeal is made to those rules to correct the behavior of those engaged in it. Those engaged in a practice recognize the rules as defining it." The problem, however, is that neither Rawls nor any utilitarians have developed an illuminating account of practices or how they function to promote utility. Rather, they treat them only as the

causal downstream of the rule account of utility generation. We will now see why this move is inadequate – both for norms and practices.

32. It is possible that subcultures may evolve with the capacity to comprehend the complex rules. The law seems to be a case in point. This appears to be a counterexample to my claim that complex rules are not susceptible to being understood, memorized, or taught. But the counterexample fails because my claim is that these rules cannot be *easily* understood, memorized, or taught. When we consider the time and energy that must be exerted to become a law professional, it is clear that an analogous set of rules are not learned, memorized, or taught within the general population as a prelude to the everyday functioning of these rules.

33. Some norms may receive their start by means of an explicit formulation of a rule, which is then promoted. But if the rule takes hold, it becomes a norm, which then takes on a life of its own. For a similar view, see HAYEK, supra note 3 at 45.

34. See RONALD HAMOWY, *The Scottish Enlightenment and the Theory of Spontaneous Order* (1987) (discussion and full set of references).

35. See OLSON, supra note 5; DAVID LEWIS, *Convention* (1969); HAYEK, supra note 3; MICHAEL TAYLOR, *Anarchy and Cooperation* (1976); EDNA ULLMAN-MARGALIT, *The Emergence of Norms* (1977); ROBERT SUGDEN, *The Economics of Rights, Co-Operation and Welfare* (1986).

36. Social conventions may spontaneously emerge in the absence of rule transmission. For example, Robert Sugden's emergence account works in the absence of transmitted rules. See SUGDEN, supra note 35 at Chs. 1–3. It does seem, however, that rules will help rational agents' choices as rules reduce information costs. The easiest means to social coordination is for agents to share rules explicitly to make the desired behavior as clear as possible. In the absence of explicit rules, rational agents should happen on these behaviors anyway, as following the convention is rational given that others are following. But it will take longer, and the result will be less precise. One plus of coordination sans explicit prescription is that the process is freer of the possible coercion of social opinion.

37. Moral realists and virtue theorists have advanced similar lines of thought regarding the objectivity of moral perception in the presence of "thick" moral concepts or in "moral communities." See, for example, BERNARD WILLIAMS, *Ethics and the Limits of Philosophy* 140, 147, 152 (1985); ALASDAIR MACINTYRE, *After Virtue*, 236, and passim. (1981).

Chapter Four

1. H. L. A. HART, "Are There Any Natural Rights?" 64 *Phil. Rev.* 175, 185 (1955).

2. For discussion, see, BRIAN BARRY, *Sociologists, Economics and Democracy* Chapter IV (1978); RALF DAHRENDORF, "Homo Sociologicus: On the History, Significance, and Limits of the Category of Social Role," *Essays in the Theory of Society* (1968).

3. THOMAS AQUINAS, *Summa Contra Gentiles* Book II, Chapter 47 (Burns, Oates, and Washbourne, eds., 1923); THOMAS AQUINAS, *Summa Theologiae* (1981); THOMAS AQUINAS, *De Veritate* (1954).

4. H. L. A. HART, "Positivism and the Seperation of Law and Morals," 71 *Harv. L. Rev.* 593, 614 (1958).

5. JON ELSTER, *The Cement of Society: a Study of Social Order* 111–24 (1989). I reject Elster's distinction between moral and social norms as artificial. Though the criteria for the distinction are not specified, evidently, the domain of the moral is overly narrow as the following norm types are listed within the nonmoral: "Norms against 'behavior contrary to nature,'" "Norms of reciprocity," "Medical ethics," "Codes of honor," "Norms of retribution," "Norms of cooperation," and "Norms of distribution."

6. No doubt there are difficulties in trying to characterize ordinary morality, for the normative realities of a society do not come in one uniform bundle, but rather themselves come in a variety of types. Nevertheless, one can fairly provide a characterization that accounts for this complexity and diversity while yet giving a picture of dominant features. After all, nontheorists do not shrink from making broad characterizations of this sort, such as when American culture is described as more individualistic than Asian cultures, or when commentators note the distinction between harming and failing to benefit, both in ordinary morality and in the law. See, for example, J. FINNIS, *Natural Law and Natural Rights* (1980); MARTIN K. WHYTE AND WILLIAM L. PARISH, *Urban Life in China* (1984); SETSUO OTSUKA, "Why Do Asians Do Well at School?" 2(1) *Deep South* (1996).

7. MANCUR OLSON, JR., *The Logic of Collective Action* (1965); BARRY, supra note 2; OLIVER E. WILLIAMSON, *Introduction to Organization Theory: From Chester Barnard to the Present and Beyond* (1990); ROBERT C. ELLICKSON, *Order Without Law: How Neigbors Settle Disputes* (1991).

8. Terms like *rational* and *moral* do not have simple and largely agreed upon definitions such as terms like *chair* or *table*. Rather, these are *fundamentally contested concepts*. G. W. GALLIE, *Essentially Contested Concepts* (1956). Meeting of the Aristotelian Society at 21, Bedford Square, London W.C.1 on March 12th, 1956, XI 169–98. Thus, when applying one of these terms, it will sometimes be necessary for purposes of precision to specify which contested conception is being assumed. Nevertheless, all these terms have a home in ordinary language and so it must be meaningful at least to ask in a general sense whether a particular person, group of persons, or people in general, are either rational, irrational, moral or immoral, some of the time, or all of the time. In ordinary language, a particular person can be a combination, such as rational and moral. And a person can be different at different times, such as generally moral but sometimes immoral, or moral but sometimes irrational.

9. RUSSELL HARDIN, *Collective Action* (1982) (comments on the high degree of rationality assumed by economists).

10. For a broad and illuminating treatment of irrationality from a perspective friendly to the rational choice approach, see JON ELSTER, *Sour Grapes: Studies in the Subversion of Rationality* (1983).

11. Whether notions such as evil have a positive role to play in a theory depends on whether conceiving of them as positive forces provides for a better explanation than seeing them merely as the lack of something. An example of such a positive role is the theodicy whereby the existence of evil is seen as indispensable for the development of admirable character traits such as self-control and courage. See generally, ALVIN PLANTIGA *God, Freedom, and Evil* (1974); RICHARD SWINBURNE *The Existence of God* (1979).

12. See, for example, DAVID GAUTHIER, *Morals By Agreement* 5 (1986) ("[W]e claim to generate morality as a set of rational principles for choice. We are committed to showing why an individual, *reasoning from non-moral premises*, would accept the constraints of morality on his choices." (Italics added)). See also RICHARD A. POSNER, *The Problems*

of Jurisprudence (1990). On the issue of whether Hobbes was a psychological egoist, see GREGORY KAVKA, *Hobbesian Moral and Political Theory* 44–51 (1986).

13. HOWARD MARGOLIS, *Selfishness, Altruism & Rationality: A Theory of Social Choice* 7 (1982). Elster draws the same distinction I have in mind in the following terms: "[W]e may usefully contrast *rational man* with *economic man*. The first involves – in the thin sense which we are discussing now – nothing but consistent preferences and (to anticipate) consistent plans. The second is a much better-endowed creature, with preferences that are not only consistent, but also complete, continuous and selfish. To be sure, economists have constructed a large variety of models involving non-selfish preferences, but their reflex is nevertheless to attempt to derive all apparently non-selfish behavior from selfish preferences." ELSTER, supra note 5 at 10, n 21.

14. In economics, there is a long tradition of attempting to incorporate a broader motivational conception with the basic economic framework. (There is an even longer tradition in utilitarian theory, which is the precursor of welfare economics in this regard). See, for example, PHILLIP WICKSTEED, *The Common Sense of Political Economy* (1910); LIONEL ROBBINS, *On the Nature and Significance of Economic Science* (3rd ed., 1984).

15. DAVID HUME, *A Treatise of Human Nature* (2nd ed., L. A. Selby-Bigge, ed., 1978). This was also the view of Adam Smith, whose account is deeply indebted to Hume. See ADAM SMITH, *The Theory of Moral Sentiments* (D. D. Rapheal and A. L. Macfie, eds., 1976). While acknowledging moral motivation, Smith perceptively argues that some of what appears moral is better seen as a form of self interest. For recent accounts, see RUSSELL HARDIN, *Morality Within the Limits of Reason* (1988); AMARTYA K. SEN, "Rational Fools: A Critique of the Behavioral Foundations of Economic Theory," 6. *Phil. & Pub. Aff.* 317 (1977).

16. *Rational Man and Irrational Society?* 21 (Brian Barry and Russell Hardin, eds., 1982) ("Part of the appeal of the assumption of narrow rationality is almost methodological: it is easy to accommodate in analysis and it is relatively easy to assess in generalizable behaviors. An additional appeal might be, as is sometimes claimed, that it explains a very large fraction of behavior in certain realms. One can too easily overrate the size of that fraction even in the most explicitly economic contexts. But often the assumption of narrowly rational motivation yields predictions that are the most useful benchmark against which to assess the extent and the impact of other motivations. Occasionally it yields predictions that so nearly fit behavior that investigation need to go no further to satisfy us that we have understood why certain outcomes occur and others do not.").

17. MARGOLIS, supra note 13 at 44.

18. Harsanyi proposes that people possess two sets of preferences: one set that consists of the usual preferences assumed by economists, and a second set that concerns social welfare. Harsanyi refers to the second set of preferences as the person's social welfare function. JOHN HARSANYI "Cardinal Welfare, Individualistic Ethics, and Interpersonal Comparisons of Utility," 63 (4) *J. Pol. Eco.* 309–21 (August 1955). See also JOHN HARSANYI, "Rational Choice Models of Political Behavior vs. Functional and Conformist Theories," 21 *World Politics* 513–38 (July 1969).

19. MARGOLIS, supra note 13 at 6. Practically all rational choice theorists who incorporate morality have a strong consequentialist bent, such that even a nonutilitarian notion such as fairness is cashed out in terms of weighing quantities of cost to oneself as compared to benefits produced. Many fairness theorists will scoff at such an account because it fails to capture the distinctive moral reasoning that is concomitant to the varied particular fairness

accounts. There is a greater tension between Kantianism and the assumption of narrow self-interest. If people are unchangeably self-interested, then the Kantian may well throw her hands up in despair. In fact, if the Hobbesian assumption were literally true, there could not even exist one such Kantian to be in despair because Kantian accounts require that one must reason morally and develop moral practices for oneself. For the Kantian, moral behavior is never determined simply by looking at the outcomes of the behavior. Rather, the person must reason and act according to the categorical imperative.

20. Id.

21. Id.

22. KAVKA, supra note 12 at 64. See, also, STEVEN HETCHER, "Hobbesian Moral and Political Theory," 98 *Mind* 435 (1989) (review essay of Kavka).

23. Id. at 3.

24. Id. at 65.

25. See, for example, JOHN RAWLS, *A Theory of Justice* (1971). SAMUEL HOLLANDER, "Adam Smith and the Self-Interest" 20 *J. L. & Econ.* 133 (1997); RICHARD A. POSNER, "The Problematics of Moral and Legal Theory," 111 *Harv. L. Rev.* 1637, 1662 (1998).

26. DAVID LEWIS, *Convention* 98 (1969). See also ROBERT SUGDEN, *The Economics of Rights, Co-Operation and Welfare* (1986) (arguing that conventions will become norms).

27. Id.

28. EDNA ULLMAN-MARGALIT, *The Emergence of Norms* 88 (1977).

29. Id. at 89.

30. With Lewis, it is not clear whether he includes himself in those who hold "our common opinions," in the preceding quote. I will assume that he does.

31. ULLMANN-MARGALIT, supra note 28 at 90.

32. LEWIS, supra note 26 at 99.

33. ULLMANN-MARGALIT, supra note 28 at 89.

34. Some of his comments, however, implicitly assume that prescriptions may exist. For example, in the example of the convention of what to do when two parties are cut off during a telephone conversation (which happened after three minutes of conversation in Lewis's hometown of Oberlin, Ohio for ten years), Lewis mentions that "new residents were told about the convention or learned it through experience." LEWIS, supra note 26 at 43.

35. ULLMANN-MARGALIT, supra note 28 at 86.

36. Id. at 87.

37. Id.

38. This may not be true in all cases. One might wish to punish a defector as a means of curbing defections by others. Though it is doubtful that individuals would sanction for such a reason, perhaps groups would. The issue of when sanctions might be forthcoming seems worthy of investigation, but not within the scope of the present chapter.

39. HART, supra note 1; JOHN RAWLS, "Legal Obligation and the Duty of Fair Play." In *L. Phil.* 9–10 (S. Hook, ed., 1964); ROBERT NOZICK *Anarchy, State and Utopia* (1974); see also C. D. BROAD, "On the Function of False Hypotheses in Ethics," 26 *Intl. J. Ethics* 377–97 (1916).

40. Hart has a conception of obligation that is important to understand. He writes: "To some philosophers the notion that moral phenomena – rights and duties or obligations – can be brought into existence by the voluntary action of individuals has appeared utterly mysterious; but this I think has been so because they have not clearly seen how special

the moral notions of a right and an obligation are, nor how peculiarly they are connected with the distribution of freedom of choice; it would indeed be mysterious if we could make actions morally good or bad by voluntary choice. The simplest case of promising illustrates two points characteristic of all special rights: (1) the right and obligation arise not because the promised action has itself any particular moral quality, but just because of the voluntary transaction between the parties; (2) the identity of the parties concerned is vital – only this person (the promisee) has the moral justification for determining how the promisor's freedom of choice is diminished, so that if he chooses to release the promisor no one else can complain." HART, supra note 1 at 184.

41. HART, supra note 1.

42. Explicit consent is on its face not a plausible justification for political obligation for the obvious reason that we do not give such consent. Implicit consent may at first appear promising but attempts to spell it out inevitably to lead back to real consent or to fictional consent. SANFORD LEVINSON *Constitutional Faith* 113 (1988); A. JOHN SIMMONS, *Moral Principles and Political Obligations* (1981).

43. JOHN RAWLS, "Two Concepts of Rules," 64 *Phil. Rev.* 3–32 (1955).

44. Id.

45. BARRY AND HARDIN, supra note 16.

46. HART, supra note 1; RAWLS, supra note 43.

47. See M. B. E. SMITH, "Is There a Prima Facie Obligation to Obey the Law?" 82 *Yale L. J.* 950 (1973).

48. This is not to say that defense might not be provided by practices, as, say, was the case for groups who lived in camps or forts for whom defense consisted of practices such as doing guard duty by rotation.

49. NOZICK, supra note 39; SIMMONS, supra note 42.

50. HART, supra note 1.

51. NOZICK, supra note 39.

52. Id.

53. Id.

54. RAWLS, supra note 43; HART, supra note 1.

55. It is difficult to understand how else to understand benefits of a public goods sort that the state creates and one has little choice but to benefit in. As Simmons says, the only way to avoid the rule of law, protection by the armed forces, pollution control, and other public goods is to immigrate. JOHN SIMMONS, "The Principle of Fair Play," 8 *Phils. & Pub. Aff.* 307, 328 (1979).

56. NOZICK, supra note 39.

57. Id.

58. MARGOLIS, supra note 13.

59. DAVID LEWIS, supra note 26 at 97 (italics in original).

60. Id. at 98.

61. GERALD J. POSTEMA, "Coordination and Convention at the Foundations of Law," XI *J. Legal Stud.* 165, 180 (1982).

62. Id. at 181.

63. Id.

64. Hoffman v. Red Owl Stores, Inc., 133 N.W. 2d 267 (Wis. 1965).

65. See, for example, Greenfield v. Terminal Ry. Ass'n., 289 Ill. App. 147, 6 N.E. 2d 888 (1937); *Prosser on Torts* 339 (3d ed., 1964).

66. See DEREK PARFIT, *Reasons and Persons* (1984).
67. As Chapter Eleven will argue, ordinary moral intuition also recognizes an everyday parallel of strict liability.
68. Whether this last duty is best seen as positive or negative can be debated. It is a duty to do some actions rather than just avoid doing some actions, and so it seems positive. But it is not directly a duty to do something vis-à-vis a particular person, so this seems to preclude it from being a positive duty.
69. See generally, JULES COLEMAN, *Risks and Wrongs* (1992).
70. This is seen in tort cases where people are held to have the duty to learn about a new community.

Chapter Five

1. DAVID HUME, *A Treatise of Human Nature* 498 (2nd ed., L. A. Selby-Bigge, ed., 1978).
2. Usually, when we speak of other-regarding acts, we have in mind acts that benefit others. But one might act in a non-egoistical, nonirrational manner so as to harm others. Such acts seem fairly labeled as other-regarding. A sequence of such acts in a group could turn into a norm. One might conform to such norms out of spite, malice, or hatred. These norms, though formally in the class under consideration, will not be discussed.
3. RONALD DWORKIN, "Law, Community and Moral Reasoning," 77 *Calif. L. Rev.* 479, 503 (1989).
4. Note that the payoffs are for the families in question. In contrast, with the utilitarian norms considered in Figures 5.1, 5.2, and 5.3, the payoffs were not for the group that the utilitarian is concerned with but rather for the egoistical payoffs. If these payoffs are transformed to group payoffs, it becomes clear why games for a utilitarian are always coordination games. Compare, for example, the Prisoner's Dilemma with egoistical payoffs as shown in Figure 5.3 and the same strategic situation with payoffs for the group as characterized here.

		Column-Chooser	
		A	B
Row-Chooser	A	6, 6	5, 5
	B	5, 5	4, 4

In this matrix, we see clearly why Prisoner's Dilemmas are, for the utilitarian, just coordination games, and, hence, why utilitarians will never have internal sanction-driven norms.

5. The literature that touches upon this distinction is large and far flung. Especially interesting are BERNARD WILLIAMS, *Ethics and the Limits of Philosophy* Chapter 6 (1985); ALASDAIR MACINTYRE, *After Virtue* (1981).

6. Failure to draw this distinction leads Elster to characterize non-outcome-oriented, non-moral (in the justified sense) norms as irrational, though many of the examples he considers seem clearly moral from the point of view of the groups in question. JON ELSTER, *The Cement of Society: A Study of Social Order* 36, 98, 100–1 (1989).

7. On first glance, it appears as if conformity to norms for epistemic reasons could have no appeal to the action-oriented moral theorist for this model of conformity seems inherently consequentialist and thus irrelevant to the action-oriented agent, who, by definition, is not trying to maximize utility (whether hers or everyone's) by choosing economically from among an array of possible outcomes.

8. J. C. NYIRI, "Wittgenstein's Later Work in Relation to Conservatism." In *Wittgenstein and His Times* 44, 58 (A. Kenny, B. McGuinness, J. C. Nyiri, R. Rhees, and G. H. Von Wright, eds., 1982).

9. A quick aside is in order to note the following point. As discussed in Chapter One, I do not think the model assumed here best captures the most common relationship between rules and norms. Rather it is often the behavior as such that is prescribed, and the rule is just a pithy means of summarizing the norm. For example, *Do not practice incest*, is not a free-floating rule that one is allowed to apply as one sees fit. Rather, one is to act in certain very complex ways that are then more or less summarized by the rule. In this subsection, however, I am assuming the rule theorist's point of view regarding the functioning of rules in order to better understand her views regarding conformity.

10. *See*, JOHN KEKES, *Moral Tradition and Individuality* 128–9 (1989); CHARLES LARMORE, *Patterns of Moral Complexity* 4 (1987); BARBARA HERMAN, "The Practice of Moral Judgment," 82 *J. Philos.* 414–35 (1985).

11. *Seedbeds of Virtue: Sources of Competence, Character and Citizenship in American Society* (Mary S. Glendon and David S. Blankenhorn, eds., 1995).

12. A weaker condition may hold such that though the actions are not enough to determine one's decision, they provide positive reason to act in the conforming manner. In such cases, it will still be true that the virtuous or rule-abiding person will be more inclined to act in a certain manner purely because others are doing so. This will be all it will take to establish the claim that there is some moral reason for conformity. Metaphorically, we might say that the norm exerts a gravitational pull. With strong enough countervailing forces, one may resist being drawn into conformity, but the pull is present nonetheless.

13. I am not making a claim that it is normatively defensible that one's decision be influenced by the general norm in this example. One might plausibly say that this is an example in which what others are doing is irrelevant; there is simply a point after which it is not good to drive when one has been drinking or to let others do so. And this may be the correct answer, although I am not occupied at this juncture with this important issue for here *morality* is being considered in a broader, sociological sense.

14. W. R. SORLEY, *Tradition* 9 (1926).

15. WALTER GUEST KELLOGG, *The Conscientious Objector* (1919).

Chapter Six

1. 64 N.J.L. 330, 338 (1900).

2. See generally, JOHN STUART MILL, *On Liberty* (1859).

3. Although the term *custom* is a legal term of art, its usage in the law retains a strong affinity with both its ordinary language meaning and its meaning in other academic disciplines. In the following discussion, the terms *custom* and *social norm* will be used synonymously, except in those contexts in which it may matter to specify divergences in meaning. Most importantly, *custom* is sometimes reserved for social practices that are long standing; customs require an element of obligation, while social norms do not.

4. Sir Edward Coke, *The First Part of the Institutes of the Lawes of England* 110b (1979) (1628). Salmond writes: "Custom is law, not because it has been recognized by the Courts, but because it will be so recognized, in accordance with fixed rules of law, if the occasion arises." John William Salmond, *Jurisprudence*, 154 (10th ed., Glanville Williams, ed., 1947). On one version of natural law theory, its key assertion is that only moral law is law. A natural law theorist could contend that only moral law is law and yet consistently claim that law must nevertheless come about by a legislative or common law procedure. On this view, morally acceptable custom is not law unless it has gone through this procedure. Despite this possibility, however, natural law theorists tend to have a more inclusive conception of law such that customs of a certain sort are customary law, rather than candidates for law, or persuasive sources of law. W. Jethro Brown, "Customary Law in Modern England," 5 *Colum. L. Rev.* 561, 567 (1905). *Black's Law Dictionary* 347 (5th ed., 1979) appears intent on not choosing sides as to whether customs are law or instead sources of law. The definition that specifies the criteria for valid customs does not refer to them as "customary law." Rather, they are said to be "compulsory" and have the "force of law."

5. A leading early modern case, Goodwin v. Roberts, L.R. 10 Exch. 351–2 (1875) states: "The Law Merchant is neither more nor less than the usages of merchants and traders in the different departments of trade, ratified by decisions of Courts of Law, upon such usages being proved before them, having adopted them as settled law with a view to the interests of trade and the public convenience. . . . By this process, what before was usage only, unsanctioned by legal decision, has become engrafted upon, or incorporated into, the common law, and may thus be said to form part of it."

6. John Austin, *Lectures On Jurisprudence*, vols. I and V (1904); Jules L. Coleman and Brian Leiter, "Determinacy, Objectivity, and Authority," 142 *U. Pa. L. Rev.* 549 (1993).

7. Id. Though the incorporation of customs into law is almost exclusively discussed in the context of case law, legislatures and administrative agencies can also incorporate custom into the law.

8. Sir William Blackstone, *Commentaries on the Laws of England*, vol. 1, 67 (1979); Carleton Kemp Allen, *Law in the Making* 66–7, 148–51 (6th ed. 1958) (1927); L. L. Fuller, "Human Interaction and the Law." In *The Principles of Social Order* 212–21 (Kenneth I. Winston, ed., 1981).

9. Theodore Plucknett, *A Concise History of the Common Law* 290 (5th ed., 1956).

10. Brown, supra note 4 at 581 ("The theory recalls the period in our legal history when competent lawyers doubted whether a statute had any authority to overrule usage, and regarded usage as a law-creating power co-ordinate with Parliament rather than subordinate to it. In our own day it is not custom as such which is enforced, but custom as satisfying certain tests which the judges themselves have fixed, and which they may vary if in their wisdom they think it desirable to do so."). See id. at 577.

11. Allen, supra note 8 at 148–51.

12. Allen, supra note 8 at 66–7, 1498–51. See also THOMAS E. HOLLAND, *The Elements of Jurisprudence* 57 (9th ed. 1900). ("To such customs as come up to a certain standard of general reception and usefulness the Courts give operation, not merely prospectively from the date of such recognition, but also retrospectively; so far implying that the custom was law before it received the stamp of judicial authentication. The contrary view, supported by Austin, is at variance with fact.")

13. The Case of Tanistry, 80 Eng. Rep. 516, 520 (K.B. 1608).

14. *Ius non scriptum* means unwritten law.

15. BROWN, supra note 4 at 567. ("[T]he judicial theory of customary law seems to have been elaborated less to reveal facts than to conceal them. It has been, not a scientific analysis of custom, but a fiction to serve useful purposes. The judge, like the priest, has legislated, but whilst the latter has attributed his activities to a Supernatural origin, the former has been content to throw the weight of responsibility upon the very mundane shoulders of the community at large".)

16. For this general approach, see LUDWIG WITTGENSTEIN, *The Blue and Brown Books* (1958).

17. The first English settlers along the Atlantic seaboard adapted English social and legal traditions to their new surroundings. This included giving a significant role to custom in creating and maintaining social order. See RANDALL BRIDWELL AND RALPH WHITTEN, *The Constitution and the Common Law*, 30–2 (1977).

18. E. K. BRAYBROOKE, "Custom as a Source of English Law," 50 *Mich. L. Rev.* 71, 91 (1951).

19. See, e.g., Delaplane v. Crenshaw & Fisher, 56 Va. 457 (1860).

20. ALLEN, supra note 8.

21. Id.

22. Id.

23. ALBERT KIRALFY, "Custom in Medieval English Law," 9 *J. Legal Hist.* 26 (1988).

24. F. A. GREER, "Custom in Common Law," 9 *L.Q. Rev.* 153, 157 (1893).

25. BLACKSTONE, supra note 8. ("This unwritten or common law is properly distinguishable into three kinds: 1. General customs; which are the universal rule of the whole kingdom, and form the common law, in its stricter and more usual signification. 2. Particular customs; which for the most part affect only the inhabitants of particular districts. 3. Certain particular laws; which by custom are adopted and used by some particular courts, of pretty general and extensive jurisdiction.")

26. Id. at 67. ("General customs; which are the universal rule of the whole kingdom ... form the common law.")

27. See, for example, Fitch v. Rawling, 2 H. Black, 393, 396, 126 Eng. Rep. 614, 615 (K.B. 1795) (custom to play sports on a particular piece of property held for parish members, but not for outsiders).

28. See KIRALFY, supra note 23 at 26.

29. See GREER, supra note 24 at 157.

30. BRAYBROOKE, supra note 18.

31. Id. at 75; BROWN, supra note 4 at 564 (distinguishing popular from judicial usage).

32. BROWN, supra note 4 at 574.

33. Blackstone stated that "secret custom" was an impossibility. See ALLEN, supra note 8 at 133.

34. BROWN, supra note 4 at 574.
35. BRAYBROOKE, supra note 18 at 82–3.
36. Id. at 92; N. NEILSON, "Custom and the Common Law in Kent," 38 *Harv. L. Rev.* 482 (1925).
37. This was the situation in the well-known modern beach cases discussed at greater length in Section III.
38. BRAYBROOKE, supra note 18 at 72; 1 COKE, supra note 4. ("[I]n our law the goodness of a custom depends upon its having been used time out of mind; or in the solemnity of our legal phrase, time whereof the memory of man runneth not to the contrary.")
39. ALLEN, supra note 8 at 130–1. ("Our law, therefore, has set an arbitrary limit to 'legal memory', fixing it at A.D. 1189, the first year of the reign of Richard I. This was established by analogy with the period of limitation, fixed by the Statute of Westminster, 1275 for the bringing of Writs of Right.")
40. See, for example, Fitch v. Rawling, supra note 27 (custom of holding cricket matches upheld). KIRALFY, supra note 23 at 26, states: "In practice proof of long user was generally accepted without requiring the party to go back as far as 1189, unless a contrary user could be shown by the opposing party to have preceded it."
41. ALLEN, supra note 8 at 132.
42. KIRALFY, supra note 23 at 26.
43. Id. at 33.
44. BLACKSTONE, supra note 8 at 263 (a custom "is applied to the place in general, and not to particular persons"). To preview the discussion in Part Three of the book, the requirement of place begs the question as to whether there can be legally valid customs in cyberspace, as there are arguably no places in cyberspace.
45. Accordingly, merchant custom was often treated as general custom. See SALAT, "The Ambit of a Custom," *Cambridge Legal Essays* 279, 287–8 (Percy H. Wiefield and Arnold D. McNair, eds., 1926). Vanheath v. Turner, Winch 24, 124 Eng. Rep. 21 (1657): "[T]he custome of merchants is part of the common law of this kingdom, of which the judges ought to take notice." Merchant custom was also sometimes pleaded as local custom, however. See, for example, Oaste v. Taylor, Cro. Jac. 306, 79 Eng. Rep. 262 (1612). See also, BROWN, supra note 4 at 572.
46. See CAROL ROSE, "The Comedy of the Commons: Custom, Commerce, and Inherently Public Property," 53 *U. Chi. L. Rev.* 711, 740 (1986).
47. KIRALFY, supra note 23 at 32–3.
48. BRAYBROOKE, supra note 18 at 85; KIRALFY, supra note 23 at 32.
49. FREDERICK POLLACK, *First Book on Jurisprudence* 264–6 (1896); See also ALLEN, supra note 8 at 134 (glosses the requirement that a custom be obligatory in terms of the behavior being not optional).
50. BRAYBROOKE, supra note 18 at 84.
51. BROWN, supra note 4 at 562 (refers to prescriptivity as the "mental element" of custom).
52. Id. at 572.
53. Though not obligated to use the beach, users nevertheless are obligated to use it in a certain manner if they use it at all.
54. KIRALFY, supra note 23.
55. Id.
56. ALLEN, supra note 8.
57. Id. at 57.

58. BLACKSTONE, supra note 8. The Blackstonian test suggests that only a select and narrow category of customs were suitable for legal validity. This was not true in the early period of the common law, nor has it even been completely true.

59. ALLEN, supra note 8.

60. City of Daytona Beach v. Tona-Rama, Inc., 294 So. 2d 73 (1974); Gion v. City of Santa Cruz, 465 P. 2d 50 (1970).

61. See for example, Pearsall v. Post III N.Y. (20 Wend.) 124 (1838).

62. Legal doctrine has, however, allowed the taking of profits by prescription. The Pearsall court suggested that the difference between these sorts of situations was that the damage to the owner's interests was much more contained with the doctrine of prescription, as the easement went to a person or small group who usually were adjacent landholders. The lessened adverse impact due to smaller numbers is obvious and appears to be what the court had in mind. But it is probably true in addition that by restricting the usage to adjacent landowners, the impact was also controlled in that such owners were bound by their location to be in repeat play with the owner of the servient tenant. In all likelihood, such neighbors would also be involved in multiplex relationships. See ROBERT ELLICKSON, *Order Without Law: How Neighbors Settle Disputes* 275–6 (1991) (discussing the relationship between geographical location and multiplexity).

63. Seaway Company v. Attorney General, 375 S.W. 2d 923, 926 (1964); Gion, 465 P.2d at 53.

64. In Gion, the court held that early usage going back to the nineteenth century and before meant the rights created by the dedication would have vested long ago, and once given, could not be taken back. 462 P.2d at 60.

65. Tona-Rama, Inc., 294 So.2d at 75 (quoting White v. Hughes, 190 So. 446 (1939)). Similarly, in Gion, 465 P. 2d. at 54, the California Supreme Court wrote: "The public has used the beach and the road for at least 100 years. Five cottages were built on the high ground of the ocean beach about 100 years ago. A small cemetery plot containing the remains of shipwrecked sailors and natives of the area existed there. Elderly witnesses testified that persons traveled over the road during the closing years of the last century. They came in substantial numbers to camp, picnic, collect and cut driftwood for fuel, and fish for abalone, crabs, and finned fish. Others came to the beach to decorate the graves, which had wooden crosses upon them. Indians in groups of 50 to 75 came from as far away as Ukiah during the summer months. They camped on the beach for weeks at a time, drying kelp and catching and drying abalone and other fish. In decreasing numbers they continued to use the road and the beach until about 1950."

66. See generally, Gion 465 P.2d; Seaway Company, 375 S.W. 2d 923; Thornton v. Hay, 462 P.2d 671 (1969); Neptune City v. Avon-by-the-Sea, 294 A.2d 47, 55 (1972) (trend toward greater acceptance of recreation uses).

67. RONALD H. COASE, "The Problem of Social Cost," 3 *J. Law & Econ.* 1 (1960). The Coasean model of reasoning as a procedure for judges to use assumes that judges look to the interests of the parties as an indication of what these parties would be willing to pay. This is the connection between the criteria of willingness to pay discussed by economists and the interests of the parties discussed by utilitarians.

68. This model assumes Kaldor-Hicks efficiency, which does not require that the owners actually be compensated, but simply that they could be. The difficult task for the efficiency-minded judge is to determine which party would pay the most for the right. The question arises as to how judges make this calculation. Posner's view is that they should guess.

Commenting on involuntary transactions of this sort, Posner writes: "How is one to know when such transactions increase, and when they decrease, efficiency? The answer is that one cannot know with anywhere near the same confidence with which one can judge voluntary transactions to be efficiency enhancing. But if we insist that a transaction be truly voluntary before it be said to be efficient – truly voluntary in the sense that all potential losers have been fully compensated – we shall have very few occasions to make judgments of efficiency, for very few transactions are voluntary in that sense; we shall be back with pareto superiority. An alternative approach, which is in the spirit of Kaldor-Hicks and is used very heavily in this book, is to try to guess whether if a voluntary transaction had been feasible, it would have occurred." RICHARD POSNER, *Economic Analyis of Law* 15 (4th ed., 1992) (emphasis added).

69. Courts sometimes observed, for example, that use by the public of the beach did not preclude the owner's use of the beach. Regarding paths and roads, courts frequently pointed to the fact that the path took up only a small part of the land, and so the owner maintained effective use over the great portion of her property. Carol Rose refers to this as the "loss-minimization" policy of courts. ROSE, supra note 46. In line with the emphasis on marginal impact to the owner, in the beach cases, the doctrine courts frequently pointed to regarding paths was that entire parcels of land could not be taken. See, for example, Pearsall 111 N.Y. at 124 (distinguishing acquisition of path from use of entire plot on grounds of damage to owner's interests). According to Rose, there was a rule that only narrow paths could be taken. See ROSE, supra at 750–2. There have been exceptions, however, that often go uncited by courts. See for example, Commonwealth v. Alburger, 469 Pa. (1 Whart) (1836) (public square can be dedicated). But even in these cases, it is arguable that the great public benefit justified the result. Other cases rejected custom as too burdensome on the owner of the property. See Delaplane v. Crenshaw ("It is not an easement, or even a profit that is claimed, but a portion of the principal subject itself; and it seems where the claim is destructive of the subject matter it is held bad even if the party setting up the custom does not claim to carry away and appropriate it to his own use"). 56 Va. (15 Gratt.) (1860). The Pearsall court emphasized that a profit by custom opened up the usage for an indefinite period to an indefinite number of people and rejected the claim on these grounds. 111 N.Y. at 115–24.

70. In Knowles v. Dow, a New Hampshire case involving a custom of storing seaweed on the owner's land, the court stated: "Nor is it unreasonable because it is prejudicial to the interests of a private man, if it be for the benefit of the commonwealth; as the custom to turn the plough upon the headland of another, in favor of husbandry, or to dry nets upon the land of another, in favor of navigation." 22 N.H. at 404 (1851). Hammond, in his treatise on Nisi Prius, made the following related remark regarding the doctrine of dedication: "The simple act of throwing open the property to the public use, without more, is sufficient to create this right, and no other formalities are essential; the case, therefore, is anomalous, and general utility is the principle which sanctions this mode of conveyance." ANTHONY HAMMOND, *A Treatise on the Law of Nisi Prius*, 103 (Am. ed., 1832).

71. This would be apparent to anyone who tried to go to court to validate a prospective practice based entirely on the claim that future benefits to the group will be so great as to justify the small inconvenience to the owner. Though, from a strictly welfarist or wealth-maximizing point of view, validating such a practice would be justified, the claim would not be recognized in any U.S. jurisdiction.

72. Though mixed normative positions are anathema to many moral theorists, it is commonly acknowledged that such positions are coherent. In particular, it is coherent to hold a position such that one accepts constraints on global maximizing, and yet these constraints are not absolute. To exemplify this sort of position, moral theorists offer one of the following explanations: it may be wrong, all things considered, to torture a terrorist in order to make a moderate utility gain, but it may be permissible, all things considered, to torture a terrorist if this is the only means, for example, to discover a bomb planted by her that would otherwise kill many thousands of people. The prohibition against torture serves as a side-constraint here, although not an absolute one. This normative position weighs both consequentialist and nonconsequentialist considerations.

73. The law's venerable metaphor for rights that materialize on their own is that of ripening. For example, in County of Hawaii v. Sotomura, the Hawaiian Supreme Court discussed the manner in which an, "easily recognizable [beach] boundary . . . ripened into a customary right." 517 P.2d 57, 61 (1973).

74. LON L. FULLER, "Human Interaction and the Law," 14 *Am. J. Juris.* 1, 24, 66–7 (1969). In this article, Fuller provides an in-depth discussion of custom that is remarkable for its presentation of a proto-rational choice analysis. Fuller criticizes prevailing accounts of custom for their lack of an explanation for how such customs are maintained. He says it is because of their "interactive" properties that customs function as they do. Fuller's rough account is ultimately not fine-grained enough, however, as he runs together various sorts of strategic structures under the heading of "interactive" practices. Nevertheless, the article represents a path-breaking early fusion of game theory and law.

75. The so-called fee simple absolute is not so absolute then in the sense that rights may be compromised if the owner is complacent when it comes to dealing with developing practices by the public on her land. These burdens can be economically onerous. With large parcels of land, options for protection such as fencing, or posting notices can be expensive. In addition, owners cannot sue the public for trespass or ejectment.

76. Indicating that this sort of moral impulse has been with the law for a long time, an earlier commentator made a similar point regarding the rationale for implied dedication of roads. Hammond, in his early treatise on Nisi Prius, states: "Whatever may be his [the owner's] real intention, if his conduct is at variance with his purpose, he cannot afterwards contest the right of the public, who, perhaps, have embarked in projects and formed expectations upon the strength of the appearances he held out to them, which it would be ruinous to disappoint." HAMMOND, supra note 70 at 194. This passage is cited with approval in Pearsall, 111 N.Y. at 121. In President of Cincinnati v. Lesee of White, a case involving implied dedication of a square, the U.S. Supreme Court held that an inference that the public accepted the dedication of a square was good if the usage had lasted long enough such that the public would be, "naturally affected by an interruption of the enjoyment." 31 U.S. 431, 439 (6 Pet. 1832).

77. Seaway, 375 S.W.2d at 936.

78. Research in psychology attests to the fact that losing status-quo-sustaining practices can be particularly devastating. ROBERT ELLICKSON, "Bringing Culture and Human Frailty to Rational Actors: A Critique of Classical Law and Economics," 65 *Chi.-Kent L. Rev.* 23, 35–40 (1989) (discussing Tversky and Kahneman's prospect theory). See also, OLIVER WENDELL HOLMES, "The Path of the Law," 10 *Harv. L. Rev.* 457, 477 (1897).

79. Not all courts have had their moral heartstrings plucked in this manner, however. In some cases, judges have pointed to the unfairness of a situation where a landowner who is

generous enough to allow people to use her land is then in effect penalized by having her kindness turned into a right against her. Of this sort of situation, the Pearsall court said: "What is still worse in a moral point of view, it would be perverting neighborhood forbearance and good nature, to the destruction of important rights." 111 N.Y. at 113. In Albright, the court appeared sympathetic to the moral claim but hostile toward legal regulation of it, as indicated in the epigram to this chapter. 64 N.J.L. 330 (1900).

80. The requirement of acting under a claim of right is a familiar notion to lawyers as it is typically one of the elements of adverse possession. JON W. BRUCE AND JAMES W. ELY, JR., *The Law of Easements and Licenses in Land* (2001). The requirement is weaker, however, in cases involving easements.

81. Gion, 465 P.2d at 56. The Gion court was following the lead of the Seaway court. Seaway, 375 S.W. 2d at 936. ("[T]he thing of significance is that whoever wanted to use [the land] did so . . . when they wished to do so without asking permission and without protest from the land owners.")

82. United States v. St. Thomas Beach Resorts, Inc., 386 F. Supp. 769, 772 (1974). It was significant to the court in Gion that there was public maintenance of the beach and road, as this would be an additional reason why people would be more likely to implicitly assume the land was part of the public domain. Gion, 465 P.2d at 53; Department of Nat. Res. v. Mayor & C. of Ocean City, 332 A.2d 630, 641 (1975). ("The expenditure of government funds for the provision of services on the beach area at issue in this case is a circumstance indicating that the public, as well as the property owners, understood that the beach was dedicated to public use.")

83. Restatement of Contracts, §90 (1981) maintains that a "gratuitous" promise that induces detrimental reliance creates an obligation on the part of the promisor.

84. Gion 465 P.2d at 53.

85. The following passage from Gion is suggestive of the doctrine of attractive nuisance in tort law, which roughly is the doctrine that owners with attractive items on their property such as swimming pools may have special duties to try to keep people, especially young children, from coming onto their land. With beach property, the idea seems to be that since beaches are by nature attractive to people, it is only natural that the public will attempt to access them, and this creates special duties of a sort in the owner; duties she breaches at the peril of her fee. The court writes: "Whether an owner's efforts to halt public use are adequate in a particular case will turn on the means the owner uses in relation to the character of the property and the extent of public use. Although "No Trespassing" signs may be sufficient when only an occasional hiker traverses an isolated property, the same action cannot reasonably be expected to halt a continuous influx of beach users to an attractive seashore property. If the fee owner proves that he has made more than minimal and ineffectual efforts to exclude the public, then the trier of fact must decide whether the owner's activities have been adequate. If the owner has not attempted to halt public use in any significant way, however, it will be held as a matter of law that he intended to dedicate the property or an easement therein to the public, and evidence that the public used the property for the prescriptive period is sufficient to establish dedication." 465 P.2d at 58.

86. The title of Rubin's paper and a number of his remarks convey such a connotation, although his argument only establishes that efficiency is fairly seen as one driving force in the law. See PAUL H. RUBIN, "Why Is the Common Law Efficient?" 6 *J. Legal Stud.* 51 (1977).

87. POSNER, supra note 68 at 233.

88. Id. at 238.

89. Arthur Leff criticizes Posner for failing to explain why the judicial process is systematically less sensitive to distributive considerations than the legislative process. ARTHUR ALLEN LEFF, "Economic Analysis of Law: Some Realism about Nominalism, 60 *Va. L. Rev.* 451, 471–3 (1974). James Krier argues that judges may prefer distributive over allocative consequences. JAMES E. KRIER, Book Review, 122 *U. Pa. L. Rev.* 1664, 1696 (1974). See also NEAL A. ROBERTS, "Beaches: The Efficiency of the Common Law and Other Fairy Tales," 28 *UCLA L. Rev.* 169, 177–80 (1980) (author dubious of common law as solver of collective action problems).

90. ROBERTS, supra 89 at 232. ("The competing goals have mainly to do with ideas about the just distribution of income and wealth – ideas around which no consensus has yet formed.")

91. POSNER, supra note 68 at 238.

92. Based on his marginalizing remarks, Posner cannot be said to acknowledge fully the gravity and potential frequency of such normatively hard cases, for he says little more than the following: "Granted, adherence to moral principles sometimes reduces the wealth of society – "honor among thieves" illustrates this point." Id. at 239.

Chapter Seven

1. Mayhew v. Sullivan Mining Co., 76 Me. 100, 112 (1884).

2. This should not be surprising as customs are pervasive in our social lives, as the quote from Francis Bacon that serves as the epigram to Part One of the book indicates. All the individual actions that together constitute these customs are capable of being pursued safely on the one hand, or negligently on the other. Behavior of the latter sort raises the specter of actions sounding in tort.

3. See Brown v. Kendall, 60 Mass. (6 Cush.) 292 (1850) ("ordinary care"); Vaughan v. Menlove, 3 Bing. (N.C.) 468, 132 Eng. Rep. 490 (C.P. 1837) ("ordinary prudence").

4. While the "rule of custom" as it pertains to negligence will be the focus of this chapter, social norms and customs play a crucial role in other areas of tort law as well. For example, courts pay attention, explicitly or implicitly, to relevant community practices in determining whether the necessary elements for particular intentional torts (other than trespass) are present. In Jones v. Clinton, 990 F. Supp. 657 (E.D. Ark. 1998), for example, Judge Susan Webber Wright found that then-Governor Bill Clinton did not exhibit outrageous conduct rising to a level required for the tort of intentional infliction of emotional distress by likening the May 8, 1991, events in the Excelsior Hotel to a "sexual proposition or encounter," governed by the social norms of dating rather than those of workplace predation.

5. 189 U.S. 468 (1903). In Behymer, Justice Oliver Wendell Holmes affirmed a lower court ruling in which the court found the railroad negligent despite its conformity to an industry custom that required employees to work on top of moving trains under dangerous weather conditions. Behymer demonstrates that customs are not legally sacrosanct, as a victim may prove negligence despite the injurer's conformity to custom by showing that the custom itself was negligent.

6. 60 F.2d 737 (2d Cir. 1932). In *Hooper*, Judge Learned Hand affirmed a lower court ruling in which the court found the defendant tugboat owner negligent for failing to conform to an industry custom of having working radios aboard ship. Hand disagreed with the lower court, however, as to whether an industry custom with respect to the use of radios on ocean-going tugs in fact existed. In dicta, moreover, Hand addressed the defensive use of custom, articulating the evidentiary rule that compliance with custom is evidence of due care, but not dispositive.

7. See generally, STEVEN A. HETCHER, "Creating Safe Social Norms in a Dangerous World," 73 *S. Cal. L. Rev.* 1 (1999).

8. A possible explanation is that the shift really has nothing to do with the merits of competing rules of custom in tort law per se but instead is a reflection of the broader shift from rules to standards. The per se rule of custom functions like a bright-line rule of strict victim liability, while the evidentiary rule functions like a standard inasmuch as the fact of conformity will be balanced along with other considerations. There is controversy as to whether tort law is inexorably moving in one direction or another with regard to rules and standards. See JASON SCOTT JOHNSTON, "Uncertainty, Chaos, and the Torts Process: An Economic Analysis of Legal Form," 76 *Cornell L. Rev.* 341, 371 (1991) ("chaotic oscillation" between rules and standards).

9. CLARENCE MORRIS, "Custom and Negligence," 42 *Colum. L. Rev.* 1147 (1941). The need for new work on the theory of custom and negligence is highlighted by the fact that Morris's article, now over half a century old, is still the only general treatment of the topic courts and commentators are able to cite.

10. See RICHARD A. POSNER, *Economic Analysis of Law* 153 (4th ed., 1992). See also WILLIAM M. LANDES AND RICHARD A. POSNER, *The Economic Structure of Tort Law* 132–3 (1987); Letter from Richard A. Posner, Chief Judge, U.S. Court of Appeals for the Seventh Circuit, to Steven Hetcher, Assistant Professor of Law, Vanderbilt University School of Law (June 23, 1998) ("The economic analysis of custom predicts that customs will be dispositive *only* in cases in which injurer and victim have a pre-existing contractual relation, as in medical malpractice.") (on file with author).

11. See, for example, CASS R. SUNSTEIN, "Social Norms and Social Roles," 96 *Colum. L. Rev.* 903, 918 (1996) ("Good social norms solve collective action problems by encouraging people to do useful things that they would not do without the relevant norms.").

12. For the purposes of this chapter, it will be assumed that courts seek to maximize efficiency or social welfare. There is deep disagreement regarding the accuracy of this assumption. Under this assumption, when courts choose among the per se rule of custom, the evidentiary rule of custom, and the rule that accords custom no privileged status, they do so because they think that one of these rules will be likely to have a more beneficial impact on the production of social welfare. When a custom is efficient, welfare-maximizing courts may want to apply the per se rule to prevent the question of negligence from going to a jury, which might find liability. If a custom appears not to be optimal, but to promote welfare nevertheless, a court might apply the evidentiary rule to promote the custom, thereby allowing a jury the opportunity to find liability if the jury thought a better custom might be achievable. With customs that appear to produce either no utility or negative utility, however, welfare-maximizing courts will show customs no deference whatsoever and accordingly would apply the no-priority rule.

13. ROBERT ELLICKSON, *Order Without Law*, 124–6, 208–11 (1991). A number of important recent discussions of social norms by lawyers have endorsed the main outlines of Ellickson's account.

14. Id. at 251. The per se rule will be appropriate when collective action customs emerge in close-knit groups because the per se rule will insulate the customary practice from pressure toward change resulting from a finding of liability from a jury. But when the group is not close-knit, the evidentiary rule or the no-priority rule will be preferable. While courts appear to have inchoately varied their choice among competing rules of custom depending on the rational structure of the underlying social situation, a better articulated account of rational structures and customs will allow courts to go about the process of attempting to maximize welfare through the application of different rules in a more self-aware manner.

15. While this phenomenon may occur with any epistemic custom, the customs of doctors serve as particularly striking examples because epistemic failures by a medical community may result in deaths to the doctors' patients. With epistemic customs, courts will look to who has the best epistemic warrant for believing conformity is justified on welfare-maximizing grounds. When injurers are ordinary people, there is no prima facie reason to suppose that they have better epistemic warrant than judges or jurors. Accordingly, these injurers' conformity may deserve no special deference and the evidentiary rule may be appropriate. But when there is reason to believe that the conformers are in a position of superior knowledge, such as when the practices of medical doctors are involved, then the per se rule may be the appropriate means to privilege their acts of conformity.

16. Clarence Morris conceptualizes the cases involving customs in tort law on a "scale." At one end are cases where "the ordinarily prudent man is the average man; and that the defendant charged with negligence who proves that he acted as the other members of his craft act, establishes the *fact* of due care." MORRIS, supra note 9 at 1153. At the other end of the scale are cases in which the courts have taken the view that "negligence is a question of what people ought to do, and that what people actually do is irrelevant." Id. at 1154. Morris ascribes to the "intermediate position" according to which "evidence of conformity can be useful without being conclusive." Id. As I hope will become evident, Morris's device of a "scale" of cases is unnecessary. It is more accurate and conceptually fruitful to say that there have been two main rules that accord some weight to the fact of conformity to custom and a third rule that accords conformity no weight.

17. Note that the rule is per se only with respect to the defensive use. Failure to comply with custom is not treated as proving negligence as a matter of law.

18. Titus v. Bradford, B. & K. R.R. Co., 20 A. 517, 518 (Pa. 1890) (Decedent had leapt from a train car that had been derailed due to a lack of standard gauge railroad tracks. According to the court, the custom at issue was as follows: "In the operation of this road it has been customary, as with other narrow-gauge roads, to transfer broad-gauge cars, both loaded and unloaded to narrow-gauge tracks for transportation to the different points on the line of defendant's road."). Based on its conformity, the court held that the railroad could not be negligent. For an early attack on the rule of this case, see HENRY R. MILLER, JR., "The So-Called Unbending Test of Negligence," 3 *Va. L. Rev.* 537, 543 (1915). A large number of cases followed the per se rule. See, for example, McClaren v. G.S. Robins & Co., 162 S.W.2d 856, 858 (Mo. 1942). The court stated: "No one is held by the law to a higher degree of care than the *average* in the trade or business in which he

is engaged. . . . A man, in conducting his business in the way that everyone else in a like business does, has measured up to the standard demanded by the law and has exercised the *ordinary* care of prudent men engaged in the business." Id. (emphasis added).

19. Titus, 20 A. at 518.

20. Webber v. Bank of Tracy, 225 P. 41, 44 (Cal. Ct. App. 1924) (holding that a rural bank's failure to install a burglar alarm or employ a night watchman was an insufficient basis for inference of negligence in guarding the contents of safe deposit boxes in a burglarized vault where this was customary among rural banks).

21. See MORRIS, supra note 9 at 1155–6 (citing numerous cases in which defendants who had conformed to customs received directed verdicts).

22. Texas & Pacific Railway Co. v. Behymer, 189 U.S. 468, 470 (1903) (emphasis added).

23. Behymer, 189 U.S. at 470. The court stated: "No doubt a certain amount of bumping and jerking is to be expected on freight trains, and, under ordinary circumstances cannot be complained of. Yet it can be avoided if necessary, and when the particular and known condition of the train makes a sudden bump *obviously dangerous* to those known to be on top of the cars, we are not prepared to say that a jury would not be warranted in finding that an easy stop is a duty." Id. (emphasis added) (citation omitted).

24. Mayhew v. Sullivan Mining Co., 76 Me. 100 (1884). See also Kehler v. Schwenk, 22 A. 910 (Pa. 1891).

25. See supra note 1.

26. *The T. J. Hooper* v. Northern Barge Corp., 60 F.2d 737 (2d Cir. 1932).

27. Supra note 6.

28. Prior to *The T. J. Hooper*, a number of Second Circuit decisions had supported the per se rule. See, for example, Ketterer v. Armour & Co., 247 F. 921, 931 (2d Cir. 1917); Spang Chalfant & Co. v. Dimon Corp., 57 F.2d 965, 967 (2d Cir. 1932); Adams v. Bortz, 279 F. 521, 525 (2d Cir. 1922); The New York, 204 F. 764, 765 (2d Cir. 1913). In contrast, the following statement from Judge Freund is representative of Second Circuit sentiment in the wake of *The T. J. Hooper*: "Adherence to an industry standard is not necessarily conclusive as to the issue of negligence and does not of itself absolve the defendant from liability." Buccafusco v. Public Serv. Elec. & Gas Co., 140 A.2d 79, 84 (N.J. 1958).

29. See, for example, OLIVER WENDELL HOLMES, JR., *The Common Law*, passim (1881) (equating reasonable care with ordinary care throughout).

30. MORRIS, supra note 9 at 1160.

31. A number of early cases provided perverse safe harbors. See, for example, Hamilton v. Des Moines Valley R.R., 36 Iowa 31 (1872); Maynard v. Buck, 100 Mass. 40 (1868); Ault v. Hall, 164 N.E. 518 (Ohio 1928); G. C. & Santa Fe Ry. Co. v. Evansich, 61 Tex. 3 (1884); Hennessey v. Bingham, 58 P. 200, 202 (Cal. 1899).

32. MILLER, supra note 18 at 543. Along these same lines, Prosser states: "And if the only test is to [do] what has been done before, no industry will have any great incentive to make progress in the direction of safety." WILLIAM L. PROSSER, *The Law of Torts* 136 (2d ed., 1955).

33. Miller described the situation in the state courts with regard to the two rules as follows: "The authorities on the question are in hopeless conflict and it cannot be said that the majority is in accord with either view. The decisions have been abundant on each side and even the more recent cases seem in conflict." MILLER, supra note 18 at 539 (citation omitted). Recent cases involving contamination of the blood supply have been divided on

the issue of whether the per se rule or the evidentiary rule of custom will govern. Compare Osborne v. Irwin Mem'l Blood Bank, 7 Cal. Rptr. 2d 101 (Ct. App. 1992) (accepting compliance with custom as a complete defense) with United Blood Servs. v. Quintana, 827 P.2d 509 (Colo. 1992) (holding that compliance with custom merely establishes a rebuttable presumption of nonnegligence). Especially in older cases, even when custom did not serve as a per se standard, it was often nevertheless a strong factor. In some cases, the rule seems to have been that if the defendant proved conformity to custom, the plaintiff had a heavy burden in showing unreasonableness by pointing to feasible means by which the legitimate end could have been achieved. See, for example, Paris v. Stepney Borough Council, A.C. 367 (1951).

34. See, for example, Ellis v. Louisville & Nashville R.R. Co., 251 S.W.2d 577 (Ky. 1962). Plaintiff, a railroad employee suffering from a serious lung condition allegedly due to breathing silica while on the job, charged railroad with negligence for failing to provide breathing masks. The court found that the custom was not to provide masks, and so held that the railroad could not be found negligent. See id.

35. As the orthodox account would have it, there was an historical shift in tort law from strict liability to a negligence or fault standard, reflecting what some scholars have seen as a greater moral sensitivity of tort law. See HOLMES, supra note 29 at 79–80 (1881); JAMES BARR AMES, "Law and Morals," 22 *Harv. L. Rev.* 97, 99 (1908).

36. See, for example, Tant v. Women's Clinic, 382 So. 2d 1120, 1121 (Ala. 1980); Walton v. Jones, 286 N.W.2d 710, 714 (Minn. 1979). The well-known exception to this exception was Helling v. Carey, 519 P. 2d 981 (Wash. 1974) (finding breach of duty of physician based on failure to take precaution that was not customary). This case was subsequently effectively overruled by statute. See *Wash Rev. Code Ann.* § 4.24.290 (West 1988). See also PAGE KEETON, "Medical Negligence – The Standard of Care," 10 *Tex. Tech L. Rev.* 351, 354 (1979); JOSEPH H. KING, JR., "In Search of a Standard of Care for the Medical Profession: The 'Accepted Practice' Formula," 28 *Vand. L. Rev.* 1213 (1975); ELANOR D. KINNEY AND MARILYN M. WILDER, "Medical Standard Setting in the Current Malpractice Environment: Problems and Possibilities," 22 *U.C. Davis L. Rev.* 421, 439–42 (1989); ALLAN H. McCOID, "The Care Required of Medical Practitioners," 12 *Vand. L. Rev.* 549, 558 (1959); RICHARD N. PEARSON, "The Role of Custom in Medical Malpractice Cases," 51 *Ind. L. J.* 528 (1976). For discussion of the rule of custom with respect to other types of malpractice, see Kenney v. Oak Builders, Inc., 224 So. 2d 161, 168 (La. Ct. App. 1969) (architects); Lambert v. Soltis, 221 A.2d 173, 175–7 (Pa. 1966) (dentists); Elizondo v. Tavarez, 596 S.W.2d 667, 672–3 (Tex. Civ. App. 1980) (nurses).

37. See MORRIS, supra note 8. Morris stated: "If, in a negligence case, the defendant offers to prove that he followed the usages of his craft, he is generally permitted to do so. But the courts holding that such evidence is relevant and not likely to mislead do not go far in explaining how and why the evidence is relevant, and seldom expressly consider the likelihood of its misuse." Id. at 1147 (citation omitted).

38. See id.

39. See id. at 1147–8.

40. See id. at 1149–50.

41. Id. at 1148. Morris's remarks must be considered in light of the distinction the law draws between the probative and the prejudicial value of evidence. The "probative value" is the

real substantive value that some bit of information has in furthering knowledge of some proposition. The "prejudicial value" of some bit of information refers to its effect on the jury, understood as constituted of real-world people with cognitive foibles, prejudices, and the like. Probative evidence contributes to proving or disproving a material issue. In the Federal Rules of Evidence, the requirements of materiality and probativeness are combined into a single definition of relevance. Thus, Rule 401 provides that "relevant evidence" means evidence tending to prove (probativeness) any fact of consequence to the action (materiality). A trial judge has broad discretion to exclude relevant evidence if its probative value is substantially outweighed by the danger of unfair prejudice, confusion of the issues, misleading the jury, or by considerations of undue delay, waste of time, or needless presentation of cumulative evidence. See FED. R. EVID. 403: Exclusion of Relevant Evidence on Grounds of Prejudice, Confusion or Waste of Time. When a judge considers the prejudicial effect of evidence, she considers how the information might affect the jurors' passions such that they might be less impartial. Judges weigh the prejudicial value versus the probative value in deciding whether some piece of evidence should be allowed to go to the jury. With regard to evidence of conformity to custom, Morris makes the interesting claim that not only is such evidence probative but it will also work to reduce the prejudicial elements that may be contained in other evidence.

42. See MORRIS, supra note 9 at 1148. In addition, the evidentiary rule is plausibly viewed as generally pro-plaintiff inasmuch as the evidentiary rule implies balancing by juries, the prospect of which will raise the value of a lawsuit and encourage settlement. See JAMES A. HENDERSON, JR. AND THEODORE EISENBERG, "The Quiet Revolution in Products Liability: An Empirical Study of Legal Change," 37 *UCLA L. Rev.* 479, 515 (1990).

43. See MORRIS, supra note 9 at 1148 (citation omitted).

44. Id.

45. See POSNER, supra note 10 at 438 ("Holmes, Brandeis, Learned Hand, and Robert Hale prepared the ground for the reception of economics into American law.").

46. Id. at 23. The positive, economic thesis of the common law has been the subject of a spirited and continuing debate. See RICHARD A. EPSTEIN, "The Path to *The T. J. Hooper*: The Theory and History of Custom in the Law of Tort," 21 *J. Legal Stud.* 1, 21–2 (1992) (dubious of Landes and Posner's efficiency reading of custom in tort); ERIC POSNER, "Law, Economics and Inefficient Norms," 144 *U. Pa. L. Rev.* 1699, 1703 (1996) (stating that a plausible model reconciling efficiency with judicial maximizing behavior has yet to be proffered); GEORGE L. PRIEST, "The Common Law Process and the Selection of Efficient Rules," 6 *J. Legal Stud.* 65 (1977). While I will argue here that an examination of the role of custom in tort law serves as a refutation of Posner's positive efficiency thesis as applied to custom in tort, this does not gainsay the fact that this thesis is certainly one of the most important and influential theses pertaining to the common law to emerge in this century.

47. POSNER, supra note 10; LANDES AND POSNER, supra note 10.

48. According to the Coase Theorem, if transactions are costless, the initial assignment of a property right will not determine the ultimate use of the property. See R. H. COASE, "The Problem of Social Cost," 3 *J. L. & Econ.* 1 (1960). Coase looked at the example of fire damage to crops that abut railroad tracks as a result of sparks thrown by a train. Coase argued that regardless of which liability rule is in force, the same final outcome will come about

through bargaining by the involved parties. If the railroad is liable, it will either pay damages when injury results, install safety equipment such as a spark arrestor, or perhaps buy the property adjacent to the tracks. If the railroad is not liable, farmers will either accept the damage or try to abate it by getting together with other farmers in order to strike a deal with the railroad to install a spark arrestor or take some other form of preventive action. In other words, in the absence of transaction costs precluding people from doing so, they will naturally bargain their way to efficient outcomes. Coase was of course well aware of the fact that we do not live in a world free of transaction costs but rather a world of varying transaction costs. See id.

49. LANDES AND POSNER, supra note 10 at 132 (emphasis added). Similarly, Epstein holds that tort customs are efficient when arising out of "consensual arrangement." EPSTEIN, supra note 46 at 4.

50. LANDES AND POSNER, supra note 10 at 133. Posner notes that transaction costs may be high in situations of bilateral monopoly or when the number of transactors is large. See POSNER, supra note 10 at 153.

51. 189 U.S. 468 (1902).

52. 60 F.2d 737 (2d Cir. 1932).

53. See LANDES AND POSNER, supra note 10 at 134. "On the facts of *The T. J. Hooper* case as they appear in Judge Hand's opinion, this statement is a rejection of the Coase Theorem." Id.

54. *The T. J. Hooper*, 60 F.2d at 740.

55. See LANDES AND POSNER, supra note 10 at 133–9.

56. 107 U.S. 454 (1882). In Wabash, plaintiff, a brakeman, was injured by a train crash due to a young telegraph operator who fell asleep on the job and failed to inform the central dispatcher of the train's location. At issue was a custom regarding hiring and training of young telegraph operators. Justice Harlan wrote: "[A]nd to say, as [a] matter of law, that a railroad corporation discharged its obligation to an employee – in respect of the fitness of co-employees whose negligence has caused him to be injured – by exercising, not that degree of care which ought to have been observed, but only such as like corporations are accustomed to observe, would go far towards relieving them of all responsibility whatever for negligence in the selection and retention of incompetent servants. If the general practice of such corporations in the appointment of servants is evidence which a jury may consider in determining whether, in the particular case, the requisite degree of care was observed, such practice cannot be taken as conclusive upon the inquiry as to the care which ought to have been exercised." Id. at 461.

57. The relationship between doctors and their patients does not represent a standard bargaining situation as Posner's analysis would have us believe. As will become apparent later, the key consideration is that the injurers possess superior epistemic warrant, both to the victims and the courts. Epistemic warrant does not concern the bargaining situation between parties but rather the relative strength of the epistemological groundings for the beliefs of each.

Chapter Eight

1. ROBERT ELLICKSON, *Order Without Law* (1991).

2. See MICHAEL TAYLOR, *The Possibility of Cooperation* 35–49 (1976).

3. See Ellickson, supra note 1 at 177.
4. See, for example, Cass R. Sunstein, "Social Norms and Social Roles," 96 *Colum. L. Rev.* 903, 918 (1996). "Good social norms solve collective action problems by encouraging people to do useful things that they would not do without the relevant norms." Id. *Collective action problem* is a broad term for the set of related concepts: *free-rider problem, Prisoner's Dilemma, Tragedy of the Commons*, and *public-goods problem*.
5. For *single-shot* Prisoner's Dilemmas, it is generally agreed that no solution to the collective action problem is available. It is one of the cruel facts about the world that individually rational choices may lead to collectively suboptimal results. The Prisoner's Dilemma is the subject of a large, interdisciplinary literature, apparently resulting from the pervasiveness and importance of problems in the real world that embody this strategic structure. Leading works include: Ellickson, supra note 1; Jon Elster, *Ulysses and the Sirens* (rev. ed., 1979); David Gauthier, *Morals by Agreement* (1986); Russell Hardin, *Collective Action* (1982); Mancur Olson, *The Logic of Collective Action* (1965); Thomas Schelling, *The Strategy of Conflict* (1960); Robert Sugden, *The Economics of Rights, Co-Operation and Welfare* (1986); Michael Taylor, *Anarchy and Cooperation* (1976); Edna Ullman-Margalit, *The Emergence of Norms* (1977).
6. See, for example, Ellickson, supra note 1 at 220–9; Hardin, supra note 5. Prisoner's Dilemmas, when recurring, may contain the makings of their own solution; for although the Prisoner's Dilemma captures the strategic structure of the direct payoffs to agents, the fact that these situations recur may change the overall, long-term strategic structure, making cooperation the rational strategy. If I defect in a Prisoner's Dilemma and consequently my partner receives the worst payoff, he may decide not to cooperate with me in future play. This may be more costly to me in the long run than the immediate gain from defection on one occasion because, in future interaction, we will both defect. Thus, my defection in this round of play costs me the benefits to be had from mutual cooperation in future play. In other words, by defecting in an iterated Prisoner's Dilemma situation, I may gain in the short run but lose overall. All things considered, my best choice may be to cooperate. Nevertheless, I will have free riding in my heart and will seize upon every available opportunity to do so. Note that the repeat play allows the power of sanctions, reputation, and self help to come to fruition. Customs provide opportunities for repeat play because they are by definition interactions extended in time such that players have numerous opportunities to interact. People who share communities often interact on a number of fronts, resulting in sets of customs for which many of the same actors are found across many of the same customs.
7. See Hardin, supra note 5.
8. See Elinor Ostrum, *Governing The Commons: The Evolution Of Institutions For Collective Action* (1990).
9. See Eric Posner, *Law Economics and Inefficient Norms*, 144 *U. Pa. L. Rev.* 1699 (1996).
10. See Ellickson, supra note 1 at 1.
11. Ellickson notes that the subject matter of his case study was in part motivated by the Coasean parable. See id. at vii. The main example in Coase's famous article is that of damage done to crops by sparks thrown by a passing locomotive. See Ronald H. Coase, *The Problem of Social Cost*, 3 *J. L. & Econ.* 1 (1960). Coase's and Ellickson's examples share the core feature that the underlying activity will, with some regularity, cause significant damage to the interests of others (either due to sparks or cattle that will

not stay put). See id. See also WAYNE EASTMAN, "How Coasean Bargaining Entails a Prisoner's Dilemma," 72 *Notre Dame L. Rev.* 89 (1996). A virtue of Coasean analysis is that it highlights the situation of these third parties and the transaction cost problems they may face. The special problem that customs present is that the injured third parties will typically be groups of people who are strangers to one another and disbursed throughout various communities. Thus, they may face insurmountable collective action problems in getting together to represent their interests.

12. As Ellickson notes, sociologists refer to such overlapping relationships as "multiplex." See id. at 55.

13. Ellickson refers to the "enforcement opportunities needed to establish norms." Id. at 177. Sanctions are a central element of Ellickson's description of norms: "[Norms] are evidenced by patterns of sanctions, patterns of primary behavior, and aspirational statements." Id. at 183.

14. ELLICKSON, supra note 1 at 250.

15. Posner, supra note 9 at 1711–12.

16. Posner does not explain why village gossips would be involved in the custom in the first place. He appears to assume that they are motivated out of a desire to do good. See id. at 1713. "It seems more likely that in approving or disapproving conduct, the enforcers rely mainly on a sense of justice or of the common good." Id. While no doubt people are sometimes other-regarding in their motivations, it would surely be expecting too much of this limited and precious human resource that it account for the general run of sanctions as they power sanction-driven norms. It is more plausible to assume either that there will be sanctioning behavior that is in the interest of the sanctioners or that there will be no sanctions at all. When sanctioners have their own interests at stake, they will cease sanctioning when the situation changes, if it is in their interest to do so.

17. Id. at 1711.

18. See PAUL SAMUELSON, "The Pure Theory of Public Expenditure," 36 *Rev. Econ. & Stat.* 387 (1954).

19. Note that Posner's argument does not apply to epistemic customs or coordination customs, as they may be maintained without the need for sanctions. Therefore, we cannot assume that changes in circumstances that alter the sanctioning regime will throw the customs off keel. Posner's argument for how customs move toward inefficiency is that third-party sanctioners cannot keep up with changes in the external environment. This will obviously not pose a problem, however, if the custom does not depend on sanctions. Note that epistemic customs are plausibly seen as changing along with changes in external circumstances, for the simple but significant reason that learning typically tracks changing reality.

20. Ellickson writes: "The hypothesis predicts that departures from conditions of reciprocal power, ready sanctioning opportunities, and adequate information are likely to impair the emergence of welfare-maximizing norms. If these predictions were to be validated, analysts might call these departures 'social imperfections,' analogous to the 'market imperfections' identified in traditional economic theory." ELLICKSON, supra note 1 at 181.

21. For example, Posner examines the custom of dueling and discusses its efficiency-promoting, albeit not optimizing, properties. See POSNER, supra note 9 at 1736–40.

22. See ELLICKSON, supra note 1 at 177 ("The hypothesis predicts that welfare-maximizing norms emerge in close-knit settings but is agnostic about whether such norms can emerge

in other social settings."). Ellickson employs an inductive methodology. One senses that Ellickson is uncomfortable with the implication of his analysis as applied to groups that are not close-knit for the reason that common observation would appear to indicate that customs in groups that are not close-knit may nevertheless be efficient. As an inductivist, Ellickson's instinct would be to take this observation as a datum potentially worthy of explanation. Sections II and III demonstrate that there is indeed a good rational actor account for why some types of customs may be efficient despite a lack of close-knit social surroundings. This account does not apply, however, to the rational structure of custom examined by Ellickson.

23. See POSNER, supra note 9 at 1711. An important difference between Ellickson and Eric Posner on the one hand, and Richard Posner on the other hand, is that the former theorists do not subscribe to the positive efficiency thesis of the common law. Ellickson thinks that PD norms in close-knit communities will be efficient and, hence, it will make sense for the law to leave such practices alone. He does not, however, claim that the law has systematically done so. See ELLICKSON, supra note 1 at 168. Similarly, Eric Posner states that advocates of the efficiency thesis have not explained how the judicial actions necessary for such a utilitarian system are compatible with individual maximizing behavior. See POSNER, supra note 9 at 1703.

24. See, for example, ELSTER, supra note 5 at 12 (1986).

25. There are a few well-known examples of collective action problems in the literature. First is the problem posed by the free rider who defects from the practice of paying the metro fare in a situation in which fare collection is run on the honor system. Second is the problem faced by the two prisoners accused of a crime who can together cooperate in withholding information from the police, or who can each individually defect from this joint activity and unilaterally provide information to the authorities on the other prisoner. And third is the problem encountered by the villagers who each seek to use a commons for private purposes, such as for grazing cattle, even though the combined effect when all villagers do so is that the commons is damaged through overgrazing, such that it is less valuable to all concerned. These are, respectively, the free-rider problem, Prisoner's Dilemma, and Tragedy of the Commons. While each of these examples involves adversely impacting the utility functions of others through free riding, none of the examples involves causing injuries to others. This distinction between injuring others on the one hand and "dis-utiling" them, as it were, on the other is a categorical normative distinction that is both fundamental to tort law and completely nonsensical to the instrumentalist normative impulse that undergirds traditional economic analysis.

26. This is not to say that there may not be efficient speeding in the sense that there may be a speed greater than the legal speed limit that is nevertheless welfare-maximizing. Inefficient speeding occurs at speeds above this speed. As Figure 8.2 indicates, such speeding may nevertheless be individually rational.

27. One strategy is said to "dominate" if the first strategy always yields a payoff at least as good as and sometimes better than the second, no matter what any other player does. See PETER C. ORDESHOOK, *Game Theory and Political Theory* 341 (1986).

28. See ROBERT COOTER AND THOMAS ULEN, *Law and Economics* 499 (1988).

29. DAVID LEWIS, *Convention* 22 (1969). In Chapter Two, I argued that, contrary to Lewis's analysis, social structures that we intuitively understand to be norms and customs need not be proper coordination equilibria, coordination equilibria, or even equilibria.

30. See id. An *equilibrium* is a combination of choices in which each agent has done as well as the agent can, given the choices of the other agents. No agent will regret her choice given the choices of the others, although the agent may be indifferent. A combination of choices is a *proper equilibrium* if each agent *prefers* her choice to other choices she might have made, given the choices of the others. A *coordination equilibrium* is a combination of choices such that no one would have been better off had any one agent, either the agent or someone else, acted otherwise. A *proper coordination equilibrium* is a combination of choices such that no one would have been as well off had any one agent acted differently, either the agent or someone else. See also MARGARET GILBERT, "Game Theory and Convention," 46 *Synthese* 41 (1981).

31. Lewis writes: "So if [conformers] see me fail to conform, not only have I gone against their expectations; they will probably be in a position to infer that I have knowingly acted contrary to my own preferences and their reasonable expectations. They will be surprised, and they will tend to explain my conduct discreditably. The poor opinions they form of me, and their reproaches, punishment, and distrust are the unfavorable responses I have evoked by my failure to conform to the convention." LEWIS, supra note 29 at 99.

32. See HARDIN, supra note 5 at 48, 71 ("[l]ittle distinctly moral" about games of coordination). Hardin develops the important topic of coordination by convention in the latter chapters of *Collective Action*. See id. at 206–19. The underlying structure of these situations is that of the iterated PD, however, and not the coordination problem. Convention enters in with respect to settling on one among multiple equilibria.

33. The practice of either coast is suspect in as much as each is a custom that promotes jay walking. See George Gilmore Co. v. Garrett, 582 So. 2d 387, 395 (Miss. 1991) ("There can certainly be such a thing as customary negligence, as the unchecked habit of jay walking in some communities may support.").

34. The narrowly self-interested pedestrian accustomed to the New York practice might continue to cross streets in the accustomed manner, despite the risk created to others. Casual empirical observation and discussion indicates, however, that most people forego this potential benefit to themselves for the sake of others.

35. 60 Mass. (6 Cush.) 292 (1850). Brown v. Kendall is often described as the leading American case establishing negligence as the dominant liability standard in tort law.

36. See Roos v. Loeser, 183 P. 204, 205 (Cal. Dist. Ct. App. 1919). The court wrote: "Cuvier has asserted that the dog was perhaps necessary for the establishment of civil society, and that a little reflection will convince one that barbarous nations owe much of their subsequently acquired civilization to the dog. From the building of the pyramids to the present day, from the frozen poles to the torrid zone, wherever man has wandered there has been his dog." Id.

37. Unreasonable nonconformity to coordination customs may also arise in nontortious contexts.

38. One might naturally have thought a logical connection existed between efficient customs and the per se rule, but this is not so. Even though custom may not be optimal, it may not make sense to attempt to incentivize individuals to do anything different than conform to the extant practice.

39. A potentially disturbing implication of the analysis in the text is that some customs may not be amenable to change by gradual processes of a sort assumed by the economic approach to judicial decision making. Generally, the approach implicitly assumes that

close-knit groups will be able to incentivize actors to do their part in maintaining welfare-maximizing practices. With the custom in *Brown v. Kendall* and the NY/SF pedestrian and driver custom, however, sanctions are ineffectual with regard to promoting efficient outcomes. An actor cannot be incentivized into doing a more socially preferred act in either of these two situations because the actor is doing the socially preferred act already. As discussed earlier, given how others in the community break up dog fights, and given how others in New York drive and cross streets, particular actors are already acting efficiently when they conform, despite the fact that such individually efficient acts may serve to maintain inefficient social practices. Courts have begun to take notice of these kinds of network effects. See, for example, United States v. Microsoft Corp., 147 F.3d 935, 940 (D.C. Cir. 1998). See also Mark A. Lemley & David McGowan, "Legal Implications of Network Economic Effects," 86 *Cal. L. Rev.* 479 (1998) (argument for limiting the assumption that network effects produce suboptimal lock-in); S. J. LIEBOWITZ AND STEPHEN E. MARGOLIS, "Path Dependence, Lock-In, and History," 11 *J. L. Econ. & Org.* 205 (1995).

40. See Rhine v. Duluth, M. & I. R. Railway Co., 297 N.W. 852 (Minn. 1941).

41. Note that this custom has a parallel strategic structure to the custom represented in Figure 2.9 where particular law students wish to conform to the mode of dress of other law students who are interviewing for jobs while these other students are indifferent as to the conformity of particular law students. See also WILLIAM L. PROSSER, *Law of Torts* 339 (3d ed., 1964).

42. See J. R. HICKS, "The Valuation of the Social Income," 7 *Economica* 105, 110 (1940). See also NICHOLAS KALDOR, "Welfare Propositions of Economics and Inter-Personal Comparisons of Utility," 49 *Econ. J.* 549, 550 (1939).

43. In congressional testimony on the safety benefits of bicycle helmets, well-known bicyclist Greg LeMond stated: "[E]very bicycle helmet saves this country $395 in medical costs and other costs to society. It is the single most effective safety device available to reduce head injury and death from bicycle crashes. If 85 percent of all child cyclists wore bicycle helmets in one year, the lifetime medical cost savings could total more than $109 million." *Examining the Success of the Safe Kids Campaign After Its 10 Years of Implementation: Senate Hearing 105-554 of the Comm. on Labor and Human Resources*, 105th Cong. 30 (1998) (statement of Greg LeMond, professional bicycle racer).

44. See J. O. URMSON, "The Interpretation of the Moral Philosophy of J. S. Mill," 3 *Phil. Q.* 33 (1953). Rule utilitarianism is the view that utility or social welfare will best be promoted by acting according to a set of rules that are thought to maximize utility, rather than evaluating each action for its welfare-promoting capabilities.

45. See, for example, GARY S. BECKER, *The Economic Approach to Human Behavior* (1976); F. A. HAYEK, *The Constitution of Liberty* (1960); GEORGE J. STIGLER, "The Economics of Information," 69 *J. Pol. Econ.* 213 (1961). Hayek has written most extensively on the informational virtues of informal social networks. Epstein appears to subscribe to an exclusively epistemic conception of norm conformity. See RICHARD A. EPSTEIN, "The Path to *The T. J. Hooper:* The Theory and History of Custom in the Law of Tort," 21 *J. Legal Stud.* 1, 10 (1992) ("Custom ... offers a cheap and reliable source of information."). Hayek is the strongest and most persuasive proponent of the thesis that customary practices have great social value due to their informational character. Whereas Becker, for example, sees customs as essentially "satisficing" devices, Hayek develops a stronger

position that individuals could not possibly be in possession of all the information that gets incorporated into social practices. On the concept of satisficing, see JAMES G. MARCH AND HERBERT SIMON, *Organizations* (1958) (we satisfice when we do not maximize, but instead stop calculating and consider a merely adequate choice or action).

46. There has been ongoing controversy regarding the proper rule of custom for practices of the medical profession. The notion of an epistemic custom may go a long way toward explaining the rational structure of many of these practices. Doctors cannot do their own research into the medical wisdom of each possible choice for each action they take that may have important effects on the health of their patients. They must instead rely on conformity to what others are doing as a means of economizing on the resources they devote to researching alternative therapies.

47. An early study by the National Highway Traffic Safety Administration (NHTSA) reported that "there are trends that show that cellular telephone use is a growing factor in crashes." NHTSA, "An Investigation of the Safety Implications of Wireless Communications in Vehicles" (visited Nov. 1, 1999) http://www.nhtsa.dot.gov/people/injury/research/wireless/.

48. 439 A.2d 464 (D.C. Cir. 1981).

49. See ELLICKSON, supra note 1 at 167. Other law and norms theorists have followed Ellickson in focusing on close-knit groups.

50. See id. The question of the efficiency of social norms is pivotal for Ellickson because the efficiency of norms creates desirable order without law – the central thesis of his book.

51. Note as well that the Posnerian efficiency model of custom is not applicable. There is no need for bargaining between parties in order to maintain epistemic customs as agents unilaterally conform to them.

52. See COOTER AND ULEN, supra note 28 at 499.

53. Eugene Robin observes that doctors are often not well informed regarding new research in their practice areas. Consequently, they tend to imitate the treatment decisions made by those who are thought to be more knowledgeable. See generally EUGENE D. ROBIN, *Matters of Life and Death: Risks vs. Benefits of Medical Care* (1984).

54. The payoffs in Figure 8.4 are payoffs to the patients of the doctors, which is appropriate given that doctors have fiduciary duties to their patients. See, for example, Black v. Littlejohn, 325 S.E.2d 469, 482 (N.C. 1985) ("The relationship of patient and physician is generally considered a fiduciary one"). Revealingly, the fiduciary relationship arises out of the doctor's superior epistemic status. See 61 *Am. Jur.* 2D Physicians and Surgeons § 95, at 214 (1972). The section states: "The relation of physician and patient has its foundation on the theory that the former is learned, skilled, and experienced in those subjects about which the latter ordinarily knows little or nothing, but which are of the most vital importance and interest to him, since upon them may depend the health, or even life, of himself or family; therefore the patient must necessarily place great reliance, faith, and confidence in the professional word, advice, and acts of the physician." Id.

55. Evidence for the important role played by epistemic conformity comes from the fact that the rate at which tonsillectomies are performed has varied markedly across geographical areas. See JOHN WENNBERG AND ALAN GITTELSOHN, "Small Area Variations in Health Care Delivery," 182 *Science* 1102, 1104 (1973).

56. Burnum discusses doctors who focus on "bandwagon" diseases and fashionable treatments "primarily because everyone else is doing the same." JOHN F. BURNUM, "Medical

Practice A La Mode: How Medical Fashions Determine Medical Care," 317 *New Eng. J. Med.* 1220, 1220–2 (1987). Robin states that tonsillectomies were performed on millions of young persons for decades even though in most cases the operation was unnecessary. See ROBIN, supra note 53 at 75.

57. See ABHIJIT V. BENERJEE, "A Simple Model of Herd Behavior," 107 *Q. J. Econ.* 797, 798 (1992) (defining "herd behavior" as "everyone doing what everyone else is doing, even when their private information suggests doing something quite different" and concluding that such behavior leads to suboptimal resource allocation); SUSHIL BIKHCHANDANI, DAVID HIRSHLEIFER, AND IVO WELCH, "A Theory of Fads, Fashion, Custom, and Cultural Change as Informational Cascades," 100 *J. Pol. Econ.* 992, 994 (1992) (stating that "[a]n informational cascade occurs when it is optimal for an individual, having observed the actions of those ahead of him, to follow the behavior of the preceding individual without regard to his own information" and using this theory to explain "rapid and short-lived fluctuations such as fads, fashions, booms, and crashes").

Each of these accounts seems to suggest that each of the individual conformers could have somehow done better if the conformer's "own information" had only been taken into account. Unfortunately, the problem is not so easily remedied. It is both more theoretically interesting and more realistic to assume that epistemic conformers do fully take account of their own information and still decide, on balance, that it is better to conform than to expend additional resources on additional information retrieval prior to acting.

58. Willing conformity to such customs may be hazardous to the health of third parties. In Doe v. Cutter Biological, Inc., 971 F.2d 375, 383 (9th Cir. 1990), the court suggested that the blood bank industry in the early 1980s may have been negligent regarding transmission of the AIDS virus due to the fact that a small group were able to set the industry standard. The court wrote: "The possibility that industry standards may fall short of reasonable care is particularly acute, we believe, in a situation such as this where the entire industry is comprised of only four manufacturers. Here, the individual manufacturers may have a far greater influence and control over 'industry' standards than do members of industries with greater numbers of participants." Id.

59. See, for example, NEIL K. KOMESAR, *Imperfect Alternatives* (1994).

60. See ROBERT C. ELLICKSON, "Controlling Chronic Misconduct in City Spaces: Of Panhandlers, Skid Rows, and Public-Space Zoning,"105 *Yale L. J.* 1165, 1244 (1996) (discussing institutional competence of "city hall" versus "civil society" for regulating urban streets). Some commentators have suggested that perhaps small social groups would be more effective at regulating some social behaviors, since 'socializing forces' powers are directly related to their proximity to the socializing force." MARK D. ROSEN, "Defrocking the Courts: Resolving 'Cases or Controversies,' Not Announcing Transcendental Truths," 17 *Harv. J. L. & Pub. Poly.* 715, 733 (1994).

Chapter Nine

1. Texas & Pacific Railway Co. v. Behymer, 189 U.S. 468, 470 (1903) (emphasis added).

2. Note that in neither case does the issue go to a jury. In situations in which there was a fact issue as to whether the group was close-knit, a judge would give the issue to a jury.

3. The Kaldor-Hicks Test is, as Judge Posner observes, a guess. See RICHARD A. POSNER, *Economic Analysis of Law* 14 (5th ed., 1998). The guess is, with regard to a fact question,

about whether the loss to third parties is outweighed by the gain to conformers. When faced with such a guess, courts may be more inclined to give the decision to the jury. See infra note 4. Accordingly, a judge would instruct a jury that the fact of conformity should be taken either as evidence of due care or as creating a presumption of due care.

4. See, for example, Dace v. ACF Indus., 722 F.2d 374, 377 (8th Cir. 1983) ("When questions of fact are involved, common sense is usually more important than technical knowledge, and twelve heads are better than one.").

5. Most beneficiaries under the custom will also be victims, although some beneficiaries will manage to avoid any injuries and so simply be beneficiaries. A situation approaching this occurs with respect to driving where drivers in large, heavy cars or light trucks with many safety features create more risks and are subject to less risks than their counterparts in smaller, lighter cars with fewer safety features.

6. The consideration of close-knitedness of the surrounding community has a different relevance here in comparison to strategic customs. With epistemic customs, close-knittedness may be detrimental if it shelters a group from learning about welfare-maximizing practices of other groups.

7. See POSNER, supra note 3 at 13–16.

8. When courts would have chosen the per se rule anyway (rows 26–27, 30–31), the fact that the custom is maintained by professionals will simply add additional support for the per se rule. Note that the previous discussion assumed a lack of superior epistemic warrant on the part of the conformers (rows 26–33, column K).

9. This may be why the locality rule is on the wane.

10. This idealistic description may be best approximated in the medical community where important medical practices are heavily scrutinized.

11. *The T. J. Hooper*, 60 F.2d 737, 740 (2d Cir. 1932). As is often the case when the issue of custom arises in tort litigation, the court dispatched with any sort of close examination as to whether the particular practice at issue possessed the various criteria necessary to pass the traditional test for valid custom.

12. WILLIAM M. LANDES AND RICHARD A. POSNER, *The Economic Structure of Tort Law*, 134 (1987).

13. See id. Landes and Posner state: "In saying there was no custom, Hand may have been misled by the fact that the radio customarily was supplied by the captain of the tug rather than by the owner. He may have thought that 'industry custom' implied that the members of the industry, rather than their employees, customarily supplied radios." Id. (citation omitted).

14. It appears that most, but not all, tug boat operators had radios. See *The T. J. Hooper*, 53 F.2d 107, 111 (S.D.N.Y. 1931) (90 percent had radios from testimony before the court). Importantly, however, radios were not required for safety purposes. It is significant in this regard that the captain of the *Hooper* happened to have a radio on board, but it did not have working batteries. Id. Neither court discussed the issue of negligence in this regard. Posner makes the comparison with workers bringing their own tools to their places of employment in order to argue that the captain had a duty. See LANDES AND POSNER, supra note 12 at 134. This is not an apt comparison, however, for clearly the radio was not required for the tug to perform its usual functions, nor was there any evidence that tug boat captains were required as a general matter to bring radios aboard as part of their job.

In addition, there was no indication that the captain was punished or censured for failing to live up to the alleged duty of supplying a working radio. See RICHARD A. EPSTEIN, "The Path to *The T. J. Hooper*: The Theory and History of Custom in the Law of Tort," 21 *J. Legal Stud.* 1 (1992), for a carefully researched discussion of the historical backdrop to *The T. J. Hooper*.

15. Hand correctly noted that previous Second Circuit decisions had supported the per se rule. *The T. J. Hooper*, 60 F.2d at 740 (citing Ketterer v. Armour and Co., 247 F. 921, 931 (2d Cir. 1917); Spang Chalfant & Co. v. Dimon, Corp., 57 F.2d 965, 967 (2d Cir. 1932)).

16. See id. This was the perfect case for Judge Hand to move the Second Circuit away from the per se rule toward the evidentiary rule, as the outcome for the parties to the lawsuit was unaffected by the fact that Hand supplanted his reasoning for that of the lower court; the defendant tugboat operator was liable on either court's analysis.

17. Hand cites to Behymer as well as Wabash v. McDaniels, another Supreme Court case that supported the evidentiary rule.

18. See EPSTEIN, supra note 14 at 33 (discussing the rapid growth of the radio industry in the 1920s).

19. See Doe v. Cutter Biological, Inc., 971 F.2d 375, 383 (9th Cir. 1992) (suggesting entire industry may have been negligent regarding blood testing).

20. It is tempting to suppose that, by applying the Coase Theorem, employees demonstrate their preference for higher wages and higher risk as opposed to lower wages and lower risk. The railroad would be happy to offer the latter employment package without need for legal prodding were it to be preferred. The fact that the custom in place is the dangerous one, then, is evidence that employees prefer to take the former package of higher wages and higher risk. This position simply fails to appreciate the collective action problem these workers are plausibly understood to face, however.

21. John Stuart Mill demonstrates an intuitive appreciation of the difficult strategic situation that factory workers in his day faced with regard to the shift from the ten-hour to the nine-hour workday. JOHN STUART MILL, *Principles of Political Economy* 351 (Jonathan Riley, ed., 1994). Mill states: "Assuming then that it really would be the interest of each to work only nine hours if he could be assured that all others would do the same, there might be no means of their attaining this object but by converting their supposed mutual agreement into an engagement under penalty, by consenting to have it enforced by law." Id. Russell Hardin interprets Mill's point into more explicit rational choice terms: "Because factory workers as a class face a difficult collective action problem, in which the logic is for all to favor the nine-hour day as a general rule but to work ten hours in their particular cases, they will wind up working ten hours for a day's pay if they are not prevented from doing so. Hence, what they need is not the simple right to a nine-hour day but the inalienable right to a nine-hour day. Indeed, the force of the logic of collective action may make the simple right of little value. We might simply extend the freedom of contract to allow the members of such a class to contract among themselves to hold together in seeking their interest against another party." RUSSELL HARDIN, *Morality Within the Limits of Reason* 92 (1988). In this passage, Hardin examines one means by which legal intervention may solve a collective action problem. Holmes engaged in another in Behymer, that is, by changing the tort rule of custom from the per se to the evidentiary rule.

22. Modern firms have become accustomed to living under this threat, but things were not always so. The per se rule of custom in the past gave firms a degree of comfort not experienced by the modern firm.

23. Note that when a suboptimal practice is referred to here, the suboptimality is from the point of view of the conforming group, the railroads. From the point of view of the railroad workers, the persistence of the practice is a cause to rejoice.

24. To be more precise, the resulting custom will be predominantly nonstrategic, but not completely so. The fact that the jury would be instructed to give epistemic weight to conformity will create some coordination effect. That is, the fact of others' conformity will have some positive impact on one's own conformity as one will know it is a factor to be taken into consideration by a jury. Overall, however, this factor will be outweighed by the fact that a jury will be able to make liability decisions based on the reasonableness of the action, all things considered.

25. This may be especially true for cyberspace.

26. In general, courts have not demonstrated a sophisticated understanding of the relevant complexities of customs. Courts have, to some extent, accorded different legal treatment to some of the different types of customs, but as to appearances, they have done so by means of an intuitive methodology that fails to articulate explicitly the rationale for applying particular rules to particular structures.

27. See ROBERT ELLICKSON, *Order Without Law: How Neighbors Settle Disputes* 177–8 (1991).

Chapter Ten

1. See generally, JOHN C. P. GOLDBERG, "Rights and Wrongs," 97 *Mich. L. Rev.* 1828 (1999) (analyzing dominant paradigm as loose Holmesian/Prosserian/Posnerian synthesis).

2. See generally, JULES L. COLEMAN, *The Practice of Principle* (2001); BENJAMIN ZIPURSKY, "Pragmatic Conceptualism," *Legal Theory* 614 (2000); JOHN C. P. GOLDBERG AND BENJAMIN C. ZIPURSKY, "The Moral of Mac Pherson," 146 *U. Pa. L. Rev.* 1733, 1734–44, 1821–32 (1998).

3. CAROLINE FORELL, "Statutes and Torts: Comparing the United States to Australia, Canada, and England," *WMTLR* 36, 865, 872 (explaining that England, Australia, and Canada have almost eliminated the use of juries in tort claims). Regarding the important role of the jury, it is noteworthy that in the state courts, the civil jury is predominantly a tort institution. In Cook County from 1960 to 1979, "fewer than two percent of civil trials involved nontort issues." In San Francisco County during this period, nontort cases were in the range of 6 percent. One study provides a subject matter breakdown for civil jury trials in the early 1980s for state courts of general jurisdiction in six other metropolitan counties. Four have very similar patterns of almost exclusively tort juries; the two exceptions each have about 20 percent nontort juries. Statewide figures for court systems in six states suggest that the civil jury is not so exclusively confined to tort cases: the tort portions of civil jury trials from 34 percent to 65 percent. In the federal courts, the pattern of case types of civil juries is somewhat different. In 1985, 5,440 civil cases terminated by jury trial – of these 2,462 (45.3 percent) were tort cases. See BRIAN J. OSTROM ET AL., "A Step Above Anecdote: A Profile of the Civil Jury in the 1990s," *Judicature* 79,

233, 234–5 (1996). In the period examined by Ostrom, a large percentage of jury trials (approximately 17,000 out of 22,000) were in cases involving automobile accidents, premises liability, and medical malpractice. See id. at 234.

4. LAWRENCE M. FRIEDMAN, "Some Notes on the Civil Jury in Historical Perspective," *DePaul Law Rev.* 48, 201, 204 (1998).

5. MARK P. GERGEN, "The Jury's Role in Deciding Normative Issues in the American Common Law," 68 *Fordham L. Rev.* 407, 425 (1999). Gergen is wrong that theorizing about negligence becomes academic if it is acknowledged that the jury plays a substantial role. To the contrary, the important issue is raised as to whether the jury should be phased out altogether, which might be the fitting conclusion if it were thought that the jury's role is both substantial and undesirable. Gergen's diagnosis may be wrong, but his general claim about most academic scholarship passing over the jury is correct. A goal of leading scholars representing both the economic and corrective justice approaches has been to provide an account of, or an explanation of, the *structure* of tort law. For instance, William Landes and Richard Posner's treatise is entitled, The *Economic Structure of Tort Law*, and Jules Coleman's seminal article is entitled "The Structure of Tort Law." See WILLIAM LANDES AND RICHARD POSNER, *The Economic Structure of Tort Law* (1987); J. COLEMAN, "The Structure of Tort Law" 97 *Yale L. J.* 1233 (1988). Despite the broad scope of these works, neither places the jury in tort law's basic structure.

6. This explanation may be particularly apt in the case of Ernest Weinrib, a Canadian.

7. ROBERT ELLICKSON, *Order Without Law: How Neighbors Settle Disputes* (1991). As Ellickson notes, the refutation of legal centralism is so central to his thinking that it animates the title of his book. Id. at 4.

8. Id. at 4.

9. Id. (Norms may exert a stronger influence on certain behaviors than legal rules. Ellickson found that the formal rules that governed different property regimes in Shasta County, California, had little effect on the way neighboring ranchers resolved disputes because the prevailing norms that existed governed their behavior regardless of the legal rule in effect.)

10. LISA BERNSTEIN, "Opting Out of the Legal System: Extralegal Contractual Relations in the Diamond Industry," 21 *J. Legal Stud.* 115 (1992).

11. See LAWRENCE LESSIG, "The New Chicago School," 27 *J. Legal Stud.* 661 (1998) (arguing that a new school of social norms theorists believes that social norms present an alternative form of regulation that makes activist government more effective); see CASS R. SUNSTEIN, "On the Expressive Function of Law," 144 *U. Pa. L. Rev.* 2021 (1996) ("Law might attempt to express a judgment about the underlying activity in such a way as to alter social norms. . . . Through time, place, and manner restrictions or flat bans, for example, the law might attempt to portray behavior like smoking, using drugs, or engaging in unsafe sex as a sign of individual weakness."); RICHARD H. MCADAMS, "Cooperation and Conflict: The Economics of Group Status Production and Race Discrimination," 108 *Harv. L. Rev.* 1003, 1065–85 (1995) (discussing how the passage of the Civil Rights Act of 1964 facilitated the erosion of the social norm that kept white business owners from serving or hiring blacks for fear of social stigma, since white business owners who now hire or serve blacks could be doing so because discrimination is illegal).

12. ELLICKSON, supra note 7 at 137–55 (distinguishing legal centralism from legal peripheralism, and defining the latter as the extreme law and society claim that norms determine behavior to the exclusion of law).

13. See *Restatement (Third) of Torts: General Principles* § 4–5 (Restatement Apr. 5, 1999) [hereinafter *Restatement*].

14. See *The T. J. Hooper*, 60 F.2d 737, 740 (2d Cir. 1932).

15. On tort as an element of the liberal state generally, see GOLDBERG, supra note 1 (setting out principles of liberal tort theory); JULES COLEMAN, *Risks and Wrongs* (1992). See also VICTOR GOLD, "Covert Advocacy: Reflections on the Use of Psychological Persuasion Techniques in the Courtroom," 65 *N. C. L. Rev.* 481, 499 (1987) (In a democracy, the government is ruled by people. The jury is comprised of people from the community who are expected to use community values in making their decision. The use of the jury prevents judicial tyranny.).

16. COLEMAN, supra note 15 at 5–6.

17. LEON GREEN, *Judge and Jury* (1930).

18. As argued in Chapter One, to accept and endorse norms is to accept and endorse the patterns of behavior that undergird the normative statements. Thus, heterogeneity of norms is best cashed out in terms of heterogeneity of social practices – Manhattan as compared to an Amish village. Norm conformers are not lifeless automatons. Rather, they have character traits of a sort classically laid out by virtue theory ethics. Honest people conform to social practices that embody the principle of honesty. See HEIDI LI FELDMAN, "Prudence, Benevolence, and Negligence: Virtue Ethics and Tort Law," 14 *Chi-Kent L. Rev.* 1431 (2000).

19. See LAWRENCE M. FRIEDMAN, "Some Notes on the Civil Jury in Historical Perspective," 48 *DePaul L. Rev.* 201, 214 (1998) (explaining that jurors needed to be of "good moral character, of approved integrity, of sound judgment and well informed").

20. Id. at 214–16.

21. See, for example, 28 U.S.C. §§ 1865(b), 1866(c)(2) (1994). The statutes require that the juror be a citizen, be eighteen years of age, be a resident in the jurisdiction of the court for a year, be able to read, write and understand English, and be free of any pending charges or convictions carrying a sentence of more than one year. Id. § 1865(b).

22. GOLD, supra note 15. (The jury is comprised of people from the community who are expected to use community values in making their decision.). See also KIM FORDE-MAZRUI, "Jural Districting: Selecting Impartial Juries Through Community Representation," 52 *Vand. L. Rev.* 353, 356 (1999); DARRYL K. BROWN, "The Means and Ends of Representative Juries," 1 *Va. J. Soc. Poly. & L.* 445, 451 (1994).

23. NEAL R. FEIGENSON, "The Rhetoric of Torts: How Advocates Help Jurors Think about Causation, Reasonableness, and Responsibility," 47 *Hastings L. J.* 61, 100–1 (1995) (Lawyers will attempt to explain the characteristics of what a reasonable person is and they will show how the client acted reasonably.).

24. KENNETH S. ABRAHAM, "The Trouble with Negligence," 54 *Vand. L. Rev.* 1187, 1206 (2001). Outcomes vary because of the norm that the jury uses. The jury reacts to social change based on their social conditions.

25. STEPHEN G. GILLES, "On Determining Negligence: Hand Formula Balancing, The Reasonable Person Standard, and the Jury," 54 *Vand. L. Rev.* 813, 815 (2001) (explaining that contemporary jury instructions tell the jury to use the reasonable person standard). W. PAGE KEETON ET AL., *Prosser and Keeton on the Law of Torts*, Section 65 at 451 (5th ed., 1984). (explaining that the contributory negligence standard involves the same reasonable person standard as ordinary negligence).

26. GILLES, supra note 25 (Contemporary pattern jury instructions typically tell the jury to apply the reasonable person standard without explaining or defining it.).

27. NANCY S. MARDER, "Juries and Damages: A Commentary," 48 *DPLLR* 427, 444–5 ("But in this country, jurors are asked to deliberate. One reason is that we assume that there is a give-and-take that occurs so that jurors who might have entered the juryroom with one point of view might leave the juryroom persuaded of the correctness of a contrary point of view. Perhaps the best-known example of the transformative power of deliberations is the movie *12 Angry Men*, which depicts a fictional jury deliberation. Each of the jurors, with the exception of Henry Fonda's character, entered the juryroom convinced of the defendant's guilt. After hours of heated debate, sparked by Fonda's questions, doubts, and arguments, the jury, however, emerged with a unanimous verdict of not guilty. Although studies have shown that it is difficult, if not extremely unlikely, for one or two people to change the opinions of the entire group, as Fonda did, it is possible for three or four people, or a sizable minority, to produce such a change.").

28. 132 Eng. Rep. 490 (C.P. 1837).

29. FRANCES BOHLEN, "Mixed Questions of Law and Fact," 72 *U. Pa. L. Rev.* 111, 119 (1924). Terry argues that the issue of negligence turns on what a "standard man," not "an ideal or perfect man, but an ordinary member of the community," would have done under the circumstances. HENRY T. TERRY, "Negligence," 29 *Harv. L. Rev.* 40, 47 (1915). Questions of negligence are left to the jury "because the jury is supposed to consist of standard men, and therefore to know of their own knowledge how such a man would act in a given situation." Id. Moreover, Terry thinks this appropriate because these are questions of fact; "the inference of reasonableness or unreasonableness, of due care, of negligence, is in its nature one of fact, the data furnishing the minor premise and the major premise being drawn from common experience [i.e., the jury's knowledge of how an ordinary person would act], whereas in a true inference of law the major premise is a rule of law." Id. at 50. See also FRANCESCO PARISI, *Liability for Negligence and Judicial Discretion* 226–7 (2d ed., 1992) (suggesting that American courts at the turn of the century tended to define negligence in terms of the care the average person would take).

30. CATHERINE PIERCE WELLS, "Tort Law as Corrective Justice: A Pragmatic Justification for Jury Adjudication," 88 *Mich. L. Rev.* 2348, 2388 (1980).

31. In Stornelli v. United States Gypsum, Hand wrote: "It is true that we think of that common-law duty as though it were imposed before the event, because it demands only 'reasonable' care; but that does not specify the conduct required and creates a duty incapable of being known in advance, and it is ascertained and imposed only retroactively. Our excuse is that it is fair to exact conformity to such a standard because it should be the inherited portion of the actor; although never formulated before – being measured by a unique occasion – he will divine it by intuition. Nor is it derived alone from forecasting the probable course of events, though that enters into it. It involves a matching of human interests: it is 'legislation' in parvo [in little]." Stornelli v. United States Gypsum Co., 134 F.2d 461, 462–63 (2d Cir. 1943).

32. LARRY ALEXANDER, "Root of Formalism: 'With Me, It's All er Nuthin'': Formalism in Law and Morality," *U. Chi. L. Rev.* 66, 530, 531. "I have said that the members of this community generally agree about the content of their moral rights and duties at a high level of abstraction. Yet as the moral questions become more specific – Does a fetus have a moral right not to be aborted? Should one be liable for causing an accident without

regard to fault? Should a contractual obligation be extinguished when the purpose of the contract has been frustrated? Should resources be divided so as to reflect differences in welfare? and so on – they begin to disagree. Moreover, even when they agree about the formulation of moral rights and duties, they might disagree about the facts that govern when and how those moral rights and duties apply. For example, although they may agree that no one should put dangerous pollutants in the water supply, they may disagree over whether a certain pesticide is a dangerous pollutant. Or, if they agree that those in irreversible comas should be regarded as 'dead,' they may disagree over whether a certain physical condition constitutes an irreversible coma."

33. See HANS ZEISEL AND THOMAS CALLAHAN, "Split Trials and Time Saving: A Statistical Analysis," 76 *Harv. L. Rev.* 1606, 1607–8 (1963) (Juries on average take 3.7 hours to decide liability and damages.). See B. K. CARPENTER, "Effect on Verdict in Civil Case of Haste or Shortness of Time in Which the Jury Reached It," 91 A.L.R. 2d 1220 (1963) (gives examples of jury deliberations lasting only three minutes).

34. NANCY J. KING, "Silencing Nullification Advocacy Inside the Jury Room and Outside the Courtroom," 65 *U. Chi. L. Rev.* 433, 433 (1998).

35. DOUGLAS G. SMITH, "Structural and Functional Aspects of the Jury: Comparative Analysis and Proposals for Reform," 48 *Ala. L. Rev.* 441, 495–6 (1997) (Jury is not required to give an explanation for its decisions and generally gives no explanations.).

36. The "fault standard" is a rule under which victims bear the risk of nonnegligent injuries. While the fault standard is often contrasted with strict liability, Judge Guido Calabresi more accurately notes that the so-called fault standard is equivalent to strict liability of another sort, strict victim liability. In other words, when no one is at fault for an accident, the injury will lie with the victim upon whom it fell, rather than being shifted back onto the injurer who caused the injury. GUIDO CALABRESI, "Optimal Deterrence and Accidents," 84 *Yale L. J.* 656 (1975).

37. Overseas Tankship (U.K.) Ltd. v. Miller Steamship Co. ("The Wagon Mound No. 2"), [1967] 1 App. Cas. 617, 644 (P.C.) (appeal taken from Australia).

38. Jules Coleman argues that there may be solid moral grounds in support of strict liability. See COLEMAN, supra note 15 at 228–9.

39. Perhaps Bohlen (see n. 29) was emboldened to denigrate ordinary people as "primitive" because he thought he had modern science on his side. Bohlen was writing during a brief period of history when his brand of utilitarianism was considered by its adherents as not merely normatively superior but also epistemically superior. It was scientific, whereas other theories were based on superstition and bad metaphysics. Seventy years after Bohlen's remark, however, utilitarianism has been on the academic ropes for a quarter century, most leading normative theorists are not utilitarian, and even its adherents do not claim for it epistemic superiority.

40. In re Polemis, [1921] 3 K.B. 560.

41. Under the *Restatement*'s reasonable person standard, the risk must be "recognizable" (reasonably foreseeable).

42. See the Wagon Mound No. 2, supra note 37 at 644.

43. VICTOR E. SCHWARTZ ET AL., *Prosser, Wade and Schwartz's Torts: Cases and Materials* 350 (10th ed. 2000) ("There are two general approaches to the problem of proximate cause – the hindsight, or direct-causation approach and the foreseeability approach. Practically every jurisdiction has used both, at one time or another.").

44. Li v. Yellow Cab Co., 13 Cal. 3d 804, 811, 532 P.2d 1226, 1231 (1975).
45. WELLS, supra note 30 at 2385.
46. Id.
47. *Li* at 811. The California Supreme Court quoted with approval the following passage from Dean Prosser's well-known article on the topic: "Every trial lawyer is well aware that juries often do in fact allow recovery in cases of contributory negligence, and that the compromise in the jury room does result in some diminution in damages because of plaintiff's fault." WILLIAM PROSSER, "Comparative Negligence," 41 *Cal. L. Rev.* 1, 3–4 (1953).
48. See, for example, PETER KASTEN, *Heart Versus Head: Judge-Made Law in Nineteenth-Century America* 271 (1997).
49. See, for example, PHILIP CORBOY, "The Not-so-Quiet Revolution: Rebuilding Barriers to Jury Trial in the Proposed Restatement (Third) of Torts: Products Liability," 61 *Tenn. L. Rev.* 1043, 1081 ("A third myth that has been laid to rest by empirical research is the idea of the 'runaway jury,' swayed by sympathy for plaintiffs and antipathy toward deep–pocket defendants. Juries, it turns out, continue to do their job well, and damage awards in products cases generally tend to reflect the severity of injuries. Empirical research reveals no support for the assumption that juries tend to award large verdicts out of bias in favor of an injured plaintiff against a defendant who is able to pay. Indeed, studies reveal that jury awards are usually not greater than awards by judges in bench trials. Additionally, juries tend to be more skeptical of personal injury plaintiffs than of corporate defendants.").
50. See generally, VALERIE P. HANS, "The Illusions and Realities of Juror's Treatment of Corporate Defendants," 48 *DePaul L. Rev.* 327 (1998).
51. Aristotle's conception of corrective justice may be interpreted as requiring courts to ignore distributional considerations. See, for example, ERNEST WEINRIB, "Toward a Moral Theory of Negligence Law," 2 *Law & Phil.* 37, 39 (1983). But see POSNER, "The Concept of Corrective Justice in Recent Theories of Tort Law," 10 *J. Legal Stud.* 187, 190–1 (1981). Ames, on the other hand, clearly thought that distributional considerations could be relevant to a tort law based on morality. See, for example, JAMES BARR AMES, "Law and Morals," 22 *Harv. L. Rev.* 46, 100 (1915). (approving a German rule allowing recovery against insane defendants in cases where they have more than enough resources to meet their own needs).
52. GREEN, supra note 17 at 99.
53. WELLS, supra note 30 at 2360.
54. See NEAL FEIGENSON, *Legal Blame: How Jurors Think and Talk About Accidents* 104–11 (2000); Feigenson acknowledges that his conclusions are based on a small sample and that more emperical work would be desirable. See also GREEN, supra note 17; CATHARINE PIERCE WELLS, "Tort Law as Corrective Justice: A Pragmatic Justification for Jury Adjudication," 88 *Mich. L. Rev.* 2348, 2386–90 (1990) (arguing that jurors do basic justice).

Chapter Eleven

1. LEON GREEN, "The Tort Restatement," 29 *U. Ill L. Rev.* 582, 595 (1935).
2. See *Restatement (Third) of Torts: General Principles* § 4–5 (Restatement Apr. 5, 1999) [hereinafter *Restatement*]. There are four elements to a cause of action in negligence – duty, breach, causation, and damage. VICTOR E. SCHWARTZ ET AL., *Prosser, Wade and*

Schwartz's Torts: Cases and Materials 130 (10th ed., 2000) (describing the four elements as "[a] duty to use reasonable care . . . [a] failure to conform to the required standard . . . [a] reasonably close causal connection between the conduct and the resulting injury . . . [and] [a]ctual loss or damage resulting to the interests of another").

3. John Goldberg and Benjamin Zipursky argue that the structure and organization of the *Restatement* are determined crucially by its skewed normative vision of the role of duty. See generally JOHN C. P. GOLDBERG AND BENJAMIN C. ZIPURSKY, "The *Restatement* (Third) and the Place of Duty in Negligence," 54 *Vand. L. Rev.* 657 (2001). Whereas the common law gives duty a role that is both central and "relational," the *Restatement* pushes duty under the rug. In the cases, duty is the first question, not the last. As Cardozo famously argued in Palsgraf, until the duty threshold is passed, proximate cause is not even an issue. Palsgraf v. Long Island R.R., Co., 162 N.E. 99 (N.Y. 1928). In the *Restatement*, however, the element of duty is relegated to the status of a possible policy-based exception to the standard analysis in which duty is simply taken for granted. See generally GOLDBERG AND ZIPURSKY, id. Acting in this mode, a court may simply decide, for whatever reason, to deny liability by a finding of no duty. As Goldberg and Zipursky argue, this account misstates the "relational" role played by duty in the common law. Id.

4. Had the *Restatement* wished to highlight a utilitarian duty, it could then have defined negligence as the failure to act so as to maximize welfare. Apparently, however, the *Restatement* wishes to downplay duty in order to downplay debate over welfarism as the undergirding normative rationale for duty in tort. Nevertheless, The *Restatement* contains a conception of duty that is implicitly utilitarian. The utilitarian perspective on duty is that all people have duties to all other people all the time, a duty "to the world," as Judge Andrews long ago famously remarked in his dissent in Palsgraf. Palsgraf v. Long Island R.R., Co., 162 N.E. 99 103 (N.Y. 1928) (Andrews, J., dissenting); see also OLIVER W. HOLMES, JR., "The Theory of Torts," 7 *Am. L. Rev.* 652, 660 (1873) (duty "of all the world to all the world"). The *Restatement* contends that duty is a "non-issue," *Restatement*, supra note 2, § 6 cmt. a. because there is always a duty. The *Restatement* refers to the duty in tort as a "general duty." Id. This conception of tort duty is implied by the more general act-utilitarian conception of moral duty, according to which moral agents are obligated to seek to maximize social welfare in all their actions. See generally SHELLY KAGAN, *The Limits of Morality* (1989). Goldberg and Zipursky treat the utilitarian analysis of duty as a form of duty-skepticism because it fails to capture what it means for a person to be under an obligation to another.

5. *Restatement*, supra note 2 at § 4.

6. Id. § 4 cmt. d. See also *Restatement*, § 4 cmt. j ("By imposing the threat of liability, the law seeks to encourage the defendant to avoid negligence – that is, to adopt reasonable safety precautions. The defendant's adoption of these precautions improves the overall welfare of society, and thereby advances economic goals.").

7. Id. § 4. The *Restatement* notes that the cost-benefit factors make up the "primary factors" to consider, id., and the "factors that ordinarily play the primary role in making determinations on the negligence issue." Id. § 5 cmt. b. This crucial point is noted in passing without any further consideration of the nature of these other factors or under what circumstances judges or juries are to take them into account. This is a huge lacuna in the *Restatement*. This is fairly read as a subtle admission by the *Restatement* that its utilitarian account is not the whole story.

8. Id. § 4 cmt. d.

9. Id.

10. *Restatement*, supra note 2, § 4 cmt. d. The *Restatement* states that what matters is the burden of precaution issue, and not the overall value of the activity. Id. § 4 cmt. i ("In those cases in which a party does allege negligence in the actor's decision to engage in an activity, the overall utility of the activity is a factor the court needs to consider. For more ordinary negligence claims, however, the utility of the activity is of minimal relevance. Supplying electricity, for example, is of extraordinary value to the community. Even so, the transmission of electricity poses serious risks. If certain precautions can minimize those risks, it is the burden of those precautions, and not the value of the activity itself, that is of primary relevance in a negligence analysis.") See STEPHEN G. GILLES, "Causation and Responsibility After Coase, Calabresi and Coleman," 16 *Quinnipiac L. Rev.* 255, 257 (1996) (uncommon for courts to find entire activity negligent).

11. United States v. Carroll Towing Co., 159 F.2d 169, 173 (2d Cir. 1947) ("[I]f the probability [of an accident] be called P; the injury, L; and the burden [of adequate precautions], B; liability depends upon whether B is less than L multiplied by P: i.e., whether B is less than PL.").

12. *Restatement*, supra note 2, at § 4. ("An actor is negligent in engaging in conduct if the actor does not exercise reasonable care under all the circumstances. Primary factors to consider in ascertaining whether conduct lacks reasonable care are the foreseeable likelihood that it will result in harm, the foreseeable severity of the harm that may ensue, and the burden that would be borne by the actor and others if the actor takes precautions that eliminate or reduce the possibility of harm.").

13. Id., § 4 Reporter's Note cmt. c ("A balancing approach to negligence has been accepted in judicial opinions in a majority of jurisdictions.") The Hand Test, per se, was not developed at the time of the *First Restatement*. The articulation of the Hand Test in Carroll Towing is arguably seen as Hand's attempt to promote the risk-utility analysis of the *First Restatement*, as Hand was involved in developing the *First Restatement*. See STEPHEN G. GILLES, "The Invisible Hand Formula," 80 *Va. L. Rev.* 1015, 1029–32 (1994).

14. *Restatement*, supra note 2, § 4 cmt. g ("A famous exposition of the balancing approach was by Judge Learned Hand in United States v. Carroll Towing Co.").

15. Id. § 4 cmt. c.

16. Id.

17. *Restatement (First) of Torts* § 172 (Tentative Draft No. 4) ("The comparison between the social utility of the act and the magnitude of the risk is occasionally, but only occasionally, stated as the basis of decision in negligence cases."). See also STEPHEN G. GILLES, "On Determining Negligence: Hand Formula Balancing, the Reasonable Person Standard, and the Jury," 54 *Vand. L. Rev.* 813 (2001); MICHAEL D. GREEN, "Negligence = Economic Efficiency: Doubts," 75 *Tex. L. Rev.* 1605 (1997) (documenting lack of negligence cases explicitly adopting cost–benefit balancing approach as of adoption of the *First Restatement*.

18. One means by which a jury might be caused to act in accordance with the Hand Test would be if they received Hand Test instructions. Any torts teacher who has ever taught the Hand Test to law students would probably agree that with some instruction and working through some cases and examples, along with some general background on

consequentialist reasoning perhaps, people can be made to understand the sort of test that is envisioned by proponents of the Hand Test.

19. Stephen Gilles writes: "Under settled American practice, the jury applies the negligence standard to the facts it finds, and renders only a general verdict that does not explain or justify the outcome. Together with the rules effectively limiting judicial review of jury verdicts to cases of manifest error, these features of trial practice ensure that the operational meaning of negligence is largely determined by juries in particular cases, rather than by the doctrines stated in appellate decisions (and restated in Restatements of Torts)." GILLES, supra note 13 at 814.

20. Id.

21. Id.

22. See GARY T. SCHWARTZ, "The Myth of the Ford Pinto Case," 43 *Rutgers L. Rev.* 1013, 1038 (1991).

23. See GILLES, supra note 13 at 1049 (discussing rejection of model cost-benefit instruction by Los Angeles trial judges on grounds it would invade the province of the jury).

24. Leon Green attacked the *First Restatement* on the basis that its formulations were not suitable for jury instructions. There is no reason to think this situation has changed. See LEON GREEN, "The Tort Restatement," 29 *U. Ill. L. Rev.* 582, 595 (1935) ("Cases come to the courts through formal pleadings cut to some pattern or patterns of legal theory. Evidential data are offered to support these and the opposing theories. There is no suggestion that the tenor of the Restatement is designed for these purposes. After the evidence is heard, the theories insisted upon by the parties through their lawyers are translated to the jury by instructions in terms of formulas. Certainly the black letter statements are not intended to supplant the formulas already worked out and utilized by the courts in tort cases. These are too ponderous and elaborate for such a purpose. Assuming that a judge would know which ones to give, no jury would comprehend them.")

25. *Restatement*, supra note 2, § 4 cmt. f.

26. While ordinary language philosophy has rightfully been rejected as an approach to deriving metaphysical or epistemological conclusions, ordinary language is nevertheless valuable for more limited purposes for uncovering the internal point of view of particular linguistic communities. See ERIC VOGELIN, *The New Science of Politics: An Introduction* 27–31 (1952).

27. *Webster's Third New International Dictionary of the English Language Unabridged* 1892 (3d ed., 1993).

28. For the utilitarian in a potentially tortious situation, the duty of the reasonable person is to act so as to maximize social welfare, not just one's own welfare. In other words, when taking actions that create risks to others, the reasonable person acts to maximize the overall social welfare of the act. The actor takes account both of the value of the act to herself as well as the possible disutility the act creates for the potential victim. The act is justified only if the benefit outweighs the risk. The *Restatement* uses liability rules to enforce this moral standard, which it refers to as the "ethical norm of equal consideration." *Restatement*, supra note 1, § 4 cmt. j ("The defendant who permits conduct to impose on others a risk of harm that exceeds the burden the defendant would bear in avoiding that risk is evidently a party who ranks personal interests or welfare ahead of the interests or welfare of others. This conduct violates the ethical norm of equal consideration, and a

tort award seeks to remedy this violation."). The notion that utilitarians treat all people equally is an idea that has developed in utilitarian moral theory in response to the criticism that utilitarianism allows individuals to be sacrificed for the good of the whole. The complexities of this core metaethical debate cannot be explored here. It must be noted, however, that utilitarian tort theory faces a parallel problem as utilitarian moral theory because it is not the individual plaintiff, per se, whose interests are taken into account but rather the class of potential plaintiffs. See *Restatement*, supra note 2, § 6 cmt. h ("In conducting such an analysis, the court can take into account factors that might elude the attention of the jury in a particular case, such as the overall social impact of imposing some significant precaution burden on a category of actors."). Thus, indeed, it is possible for individual victims to be sacrificed to the utilitarian whole. The *Restatement*'s notion of "equal consideration" is then an ex ante conception. As is the case with utilitarian moral theory, such justifications are cold comfort to real plaintiffs who seek redress for real injuries because their claims may be subordinated to the overriding concern for aggregate welfare. See generally JULES L. COLEMAN, *Risks and Wrongs* (1992). The *Restatement* does make one superficial nod toward acknowledging the moral complexity of determinations of negligence. When providing a rationale for negligence liability, the *Restatement* notes "fairness" between the litigants as a factor. This is evidently an attempt to address the criticism of the utilitarian approach that it does not deal with the actual moral relationship between the injurer and victim. The problem, however, is that the notion of fairness as understood by the *Restatement* is completely reducible to utilitarianism for the reason just indicated. Fairness just means that, ex ante, liability rules are as likely to promote one's welfare as the welfare of others. This conception has no connection to the leading conceptions of fairness that animate modern tort theory, such as those of Fletcher, Keating, or Wright. Nor, of course, does it take account of broader conceptions of corrective justice that do not reduce to fairness. See, for example, id.

29. See generally, STEVEN HETCHER, "Hobbesian Moral and Political Theory," 98 *Mind* 435 (1989).

30. The genius of the jury system is that by compelling jurors to deliberate in an environment in which their actions are neutral in terms of their self-interest, the cost of moral behavior is reduced practically to zero. Thus predominately self-interested jurors might nevertheless act so as to promote morally desirable outcomes, as doing so can be done with almost no personal sacrifice.

31. See STEVEN HETCHER, "Creating Safe Social Norms in a Dangerous World," 73 *S. Cal. L. Rev.* 1 (1999); PATRICK J. KELLEY, "Who Decides? Community Safety Conventions at the Heart of Tort Liability," 38 *Clev. L. Rev.* 315, 353–63 (1990) (cost-benefit negligence is a distortion of traditional, normatively superior, reasonable person standard based on community norms); STEPHEN R. PERRY, "Responsibility for Outcomes, Risk, and the Law of Torts," *Philosophy and Tort Law* 7 (Gerald Postema, ed., 2000) ("Jointly-created risks are, very roughly, those that fall within the range of risks which is normally or customarily associated with a given pattern of social interaction.").

32. See, for example, ALASDAIR C. MACINTYRE, *After Virtue: A Study in Moral Theory* 20 (1984); BERNARD WILLIAMS, "Consequentialism and Integrity," 20 *Consequentialism and Its Critics* (Samuel Scheffler, ed., 1988).

33. Landes and Posner note that social efficiency is the dominant philosophy among judges and policy makers and that it is less controversial than other philosophical views, such as those that require redistribution of wealth. WILLIAM LANDES AND RICHARD POSNER,

The Economic Structure of Tort Law (1987). It should be clear, then, why these authors would not be in a position to discuss the role played by the jury as distinct from the court, as one cannot credibly claim that utilitarianism is the social philosophy among the class of ordinary people who typically fill the ranks of juries (the claim is equally implausible for judges as well, but this point is not a present concern). Efficiency proponents might not like the jury effect. They may suppose that it comes at the expense of efficiency. But this is not certain. If the informal norms are themselves efficient, then support for them might be efficient as well. Suppose, for example, we are dealing with a close–knit community and Ellickson is right that efficient social norms will emerge from the bottom up in close-knit communities. Then the juror instructions based on their experience of informal norms as these enter into outcomes of negligence trials via jury deliberations may indeed promote utility.

34. GILLES, supra note 17 at 833–4 ("Jurors can safely be presumed to be familiar with prevailing community values. Beyond that, in consulting community values the jury would in an important sense be applying the 'law' because the common law has designated those values as part of the reasonable person standard.").

35. Id. at 818.

36. Id. at 828.

37. Id.

38. Elsewhere, Gilles refers to "social value" as a "metric for weighing risk against utility." Id. Gilles believes that the reasonable person will sometimes explicitly apply the Hand Test. Gilles appears to conceive of this in the manner that *act utilitarians* conceive of the utility maximization test. Gilles also appears to believe that people will sometimes act like *rule utilitarians*, conforming to customs and social norms rather than performing Hand Test calculations on each occasion in which they act. Id. at 825. Here, Gilles falls unwittingly into the trap of thinking that customs are welfare-maximizing such that conforming to them will necessarily be a welfare-maximizing shortcut; however, customs are not always welfare-maximizing. The custom may be structured so as to allow for third-party externalities such that the custom is welfare–maximizing for the conformers but not for the overall community. Or the custom may be the result of a collective action problem such that a collection of individually maximizing actions serves to maintain a practice that is nevertheless suboptimal.

39. *Restatement (First) of Torts* § 292(a) (1934). The *Second Restatement* follows the *First Restatement* in this regard.

40. *Restatement*, supra note 2, § 4.

41. WARREN A. SEAVEY, "Negligence – Subjective or Objective?," 41 *Harv. L. Rev.* 1, 1 n. 1 (1927). On the influence of Seavey, and the history of the *First Restatement* generally, see GREEN, supra note 17.

42. Seavey, supra note 41 at 8.

43. During the ascendancy of positivism, a belief took hold that utilitarianism was a scientific theory, whereas other normative theories were based on empty metaphysics. In Bentham's oft-repeated quip, rights are nonsense on stilts. From an historical perspective, it did not take long for metaethical theorists to destroy the claim of utilitarianism's superior scientific status. Nevertheless, it was in this period that the *Restatement (First) of Torts* was promulgated. In other words, the initial Restaters had the misfortune to be working at a time when some bad moral metaphysics was going around. Early utilitarian approaches to tort law are found in OLIVER WENDELL HOLMES, JR., *The Common Law* 94–6 (1881);

JAMES BARR AMES, "Law and Morals," 22 *Harv. L. Rev.* 97, 110 (1908); HENRY T. TERRY, "Negligence, 29 *Harv. L. Rev.* 40 (1915). On Holmes' utilitarianism, see H. L. POHLMAN, "Justice Oliver Wendell Holmes and Utilitarian Jurisprudence (1984). See also GARY T. SCHWARTZ, "The Character of Early American Tort Law," 36 *UCLA L. Rev.* 641 (1989) (finding utilitarianism running through nineteenth century tort law). See generally PATRICK J. KELLEY, "Who Decides? Community Safety Conventions at the Heart of Tort Liability," 38 *Clev. St. L. Rev.* 315 (1990) (arguing that Terry's five-part negligence test was an improvement on Holmes' account, and that Terry's test formed the basis of the Hand Test).

44. KEATING, infra note 49.
45. Moisan v. Loftus, 178 F.2d 148, 149 (2d Cir. 1949). Hand noted elsewhere that the problem with "the appraisal and balancing of human values" is that "there are no scales to weigh" them on. Hand continued, "the difficulty here does not come from ignorance, but from absence of any standard, for values are incommensurable." LEARNED HAND, *The Spirit of Liberty* 161 (1963). Note how this contrasts with Posner's hope that, someday in the future, we will be able to attach dollar figures to the relevant factors. McCarty v. Pheasant Run, Inc., 826 F2d 1554, 1557 (7th Cir. 1987) (Posner, J.) ("Conceptual as well as practical difficulties in monetizing personal injuries" mean that "[f]or many years to come juries may be forced to make rough judgments of reasonableness, intuiting rather than measuring the factors in the Hand Formula."). For a recent defense of his view, see RICHARD A. POSNER, "Wealth Maximization and Tort Law: A Philosophical Inquiry," *Philosophical Foundations of Tort Law* 99 (David G. Owen, ed., 1995).
46. GILLES, supra note 17 at 818 ("The 'Hand Factors,' if you will, are thus the raw data to which the 'Hand Formula' is applied to determine whether there was negligence in accordance with the 'Hand Norm.' "); Id. at 817 n. 5 ("I use 'Hand Formula approaches' as a shorthand for the whole range of approaches that balance the costs and benefits, however defined, of taking greater care to avoid an accident.").
47. See KEATING, infra note 49; RICHARD W. WRIGHT, "The Standards of Care in Negligence Law" *Philosophical Foundations of Tort Law* 249 (David G. Owen, ed., 1995).
48. See COLEMAN, supra note 28.
49. The balancing test, per se, may remain, as such phraseology may adequately be used to characterize a theory-neutral, normatively pluralistic account of the reasonable person standard. See, for example, RONALD DWORKIN, *Law's Empire* 276–313 (1986); HEIDI M. HURD, "The Deontology of Negligence," 76 *B.U. L. Rev.* 249 (1996); GREGORY C. KEATING, "Reasonableness and Rationality in Negligence Theory," 48 *Stan. L. Rev.* 311 (1996).
50. *Restatement*, supra note 2, § 5 cmt. d. The Restatement makes a rare citation to a philosophical text on the topic: JONATHAN DANCY, "Ethical Particularism and Morally Relevant Properties," 92 *Mind* 530 (1983).
51. *Restatement*, supra note 1, § 5.
52. DANCY, supra note 50 at 530.
53. *Restatement*, supra note 1, § 5 cmt. b.
54. Coleman, The practice of principle: In Defence of a Pragmatist Approach to Legal Theory (2001). The following discussion draws from my review essay of Coleman's book. See STEVEN HETCHER, "Review of Jules Coleman, The Practice of Principle," *J. Econ. & Phil.* (forthcoming).

55. Coleman notes that he does not use the term pragmatism in the currently fashionable sense that eschews theory. COLEMAN, supra note 54 at xiii. Rather, Coleman describes his approach as an outgrowth of philosophical pragmatism of the sort developed by Wilfrid Sellars, W. V. O. Quine, and Donald Davidson. See id. at 6 n.6.
56. On pragmatic conceptualism, see generally Zipursky, supra note 2; Goldberg & Zipursky, supra note 2.
57. COLEMAN, supra note 54 at 3.
58. Id. at 5.
59. Id. at 5–6.
60. See, for example, COLEMAN, supra note 54 at 198.
61. See COLEMAN, supra note 54 at 5–6.
62. Incidentally, this shows why norms are best understood as extant patterns of behavior and not simply as linguistic entities or rules; this was a core theme of Part One.
63. See COLEMAN, supra note 54 at 332.
64. COLEMAN, supra note 54 at 21.
65. W. KIP VISCUSI, "Jurors, Judges, and the Mistreatment of Risk By the Courts," 30 *J. Leg. Stud.* 107 (2001); W. KIP VISCUSI, "Corporate Risk Analysis: A Reckless Act?," 52 *Stan. L. Rev.* 547 (2000); W. KIP VISCUSI, "How Do Judges Think About Risk?," 1 *Amer. Law & Econ. Rev.* 26 (1999).
66. This same criticism applies to Catherine Wells' corrective justice account of the role of the jury. CATHERINE PIERCE WELLS, "Tort Law as Corrective Justice: A Pragmatic Justification for Jury Ajudication," 88 *Mich. L. Rev.* 2348 (1990). Given the evident heterogeneity of the jury norm effect, one cannot simply assume, as Wells appears to do, that the final result of jury activity will be the production of an outcome that is correctively just.
67. COLEMAN, supra note 54, at 5.
68. Id. at 23.
69. Id.

Chapter Twelve

1. MARK A. LEMLEY, "The Law and Economics of Internet Norms," 73 *Chi.-Kent L. Rev.* 1257 (1998) at 1276.
2. Federal Trade Commission, Privacy Online: A Report to Congress (June 1998), *available at* http://www.ftc.gov/reports/privacy3/priv-23a.pdf [hereinafter *1998 FTC Report to Congress*] ("While American businesses have always collected some information from consumers in order to facilitate transactions, the Internet allows for the efficient, inexpensive collection of a vast amount of information. It is the prevalence, ease, and relative low cost of such information collection that distinguishes the online environment from more traditional means of commerce and information collection and thus raises consumer concerns."). Emerging online technologies make the transmission of data virtually costless, which has contributed to a situation in which dramatically higher levels of personal data are now flowing across the Internet. Peter Huber and Mark P. Mills have estimated that it takes "about 1 pound of coal to create, package, store and move 2 megabytes of data." PETER W. HUBER, "Dig More Coal – The PCs Are Coming," *Forbes* (May 31, 1999), *available at* http://www.forbes.com/forbes/99/0531/6311070a.htm.

3. See LAWRENCE LESSIG, *Code: and Other Laws of Cyberspace* 85–90 (1999) (distinguishing four principal regulators of human behavior in cyberspace: norms, law, technology, and the market); see also PAMELA SAMUELSON, "Privacy as Intellectual Property?," 52 *Stan. L. Rev.* 1125, 1126 (2000) (endorsing Lessig's four-part approach to regulation in context of privacy).

4. The government has sought to regulate online privacy at a distance, purportedly out of respect for the established norm of Internet self-regulation. The Federal Trade Commission has stated that "self-regulation is the least intrusive and most efficient means to ensure fair information practices, given the rapidly evolving nature of the Internet and computer technology." See Federal Trade Commission, Self Regulation and Privacy Online: A Report to Congress 6 (July 1999), *available at* http://www.ftc.gov/os/1999/9907/privacy99.pdf [hereinafter *1999 FTC Report to Congress*]; see LESSIG, supra note 3 at Chapter 1 (lengthy discussion of dominant antiregulatory outlook regarding governance of the Internet). Numerous commentators have taken the view that since the Internet is growing so rapidly and successfully, it is sensible to be cautious before adopting any significant regulatory measures that might curtail this development. See, for example, I. TROTTER HARDY, "The Proper Legal Regime for Cyberspace?," 55 *U. Pitt. L. Rev.* 993, 1054 (1994) (contending that rules of conduct in cyberspace should be governed by presumption of decentralization, using self-help, custom, and contract of cyberspace participants, and noting that because the Internet is changing so rapidly, the first answer to how a legal problem in cyberspace should be solved is to "do nothing"); HENRY H. PERRITT, JR., "Cyberspace Self-Government: Town Hall Democracy or Rediscovered Royalism?," 12 *Berkeley Tech. L. J.* 413, 419–20 (1997) (contending that as a general rule "self–governance is desirable for electronic communities"). In addition, because the Internet is an inherently transnational phenomenon, it may be improper and overreaching for particular nations to attempt to exert too great an influence over its development. See, for example, DAVID R. JOHNSON AND DAVID POST, "Law and Borders – The Rise of Law in Cyberspace," 48 *Stan. L. Rev.* 1367 (1996); see also JOHN PERRY BARLOW, A Declaration of the Independence of Cyberspace (visited Jan. 28, 2000), *available at* http://www.eff.org/~barlow/Declaration-Final.html; A. MICHAEL FROOMKIN, "The Internet as a Source of Regulatory Arbitrage," *Borders in Cyberspace* 129 (Brian Kahin & Charles Nesson, eds., 1997) (discussing the Internet's "resistance to control"); JAMES BOYLE, "Foucault in Cyberspace: Surveillance, Sovereignty, and Hardwired Censors," 66 *U. Cin. L. Rev.* 177, 178–83 (1997) (noting the cyber-utopian argument that "the technology of the medium, the geographical distribution of its users, and the nature of its content all make the Internet specially resistant to state regulation").

5. There are two broad information categories of personal data: information that can be used to identify consumers, such as name, postal or e-mail address ("personal identifying information"); or demographic and preference information (such as age, gender, income level, hobbies, or interests) that can be used either in aggregate, nonidentifying form for purposes such as market analysis, or in conjunction with personal identifying information to create detailed personal profiles. See *1998 FTC Report to Congress*, supra note 2 at 20. It is the first sort of threat that particularly raises privacy concerns, for the reason that once others have information about a person's identity, they may use the information in new ways that adversely affect the person.

6. See SAMUELSON, supra note 3 at 1128 (discussing utilitarian and autonomy-based rationales for regulation of data collection).

7. ANNE WELLS BRANSCOMB, *Who Owns Information?* 3–4 (1994) ("A great deal of information we consider to be highly personal, and of interest to ourselves and the town gossip – our names, telephone numbers, marital status, educational accomplishments, job and credit histories, even medical, dental, and psychiatric records – is now being sold on the open market to anyone who believes he or she might be able to use such information to turn a profit. These transactions usually take place without our knowledge or consent.").

8. See "Online Privacy," *Bus. Week*, Mar. 20, 2000, *available at* 2000 WL 7825258 (comparing the stockpiles of information to an Internet gold rush); Kathryn Kranhold & Michael Moss, "Companies Are Refusing to Share Their Cookies Tracking Devices' Consumer Data Is Too Precious," *Chicago Trib.*, Apr. 10, 2000, *available at* 2000 WL 3654616 (discussing how large Fortune 500 companies are protecting online tracking devices from Internet advertising companies because consumer data is a veritable "gold mine"); MELISSA PREDDY, "Metro Teenagers Take Bait, Hook Prize on the Net – The Yield on Privacy in Bid for College Cash," *Detroit News*, June 15, 2000, *available at* 2000 WL 348130 (stating "personal information is like gold," especially to "get paid to surf," profiling websites that entice Internet users to give up information about themselves for rewards).

9. See ERIKA S. KOSTER, "Zero Privacy: Personal Data on the Internet," *The Computer Lawyer*, May 1999 at 7–8 (noting that commercial activity involving personal data is growing rapidly).

10. See, for example, "The End of Privacy: The Surveillance Society," *Economist*, May 1, 1999, at 21 (covering privacy degradation in online environment); REP. ASA HUTCHINSON AND REP. JIM MORAN, "Commission Is First Step to Privacy," *Roll Call*, July 10, 2000, *available at* http://www.rollcall.com; ADAM L. PENENBERG, "The End of Privacy," *Forbes*, Nov. 29, 1999, *available at* 1999 WL 28466750; JARED SANDBERG, "Identity Thieves Online," *Newsweek*, Sept. 20, 1999, *available at* 1999 WL 19354964; CELIA SANTANDER, "Web-Site Privacy Policies Aren't Created Equal," *Web Finance*, Dec. 11, 2000.

11. See GLENN R. SIMPSON, "E-Commerce Firms Start to Rethink Opposition to Privacy Regulation as Abuses, Anger Rise," *Wall St. J.*, Jan. 6, 2000, at A24. A recent U.S. Business Week/Harris Poll found that 92 percent of Internet users were uncomfortable about websites sharing personal information with other sites. See "Online Privacy," supra note 8.

12. See JESSICA LITMAN, "Information Privacy/Information Property," 52 *Stan. L. Rev.* 1283, 1287 (2000).

13. See STEVEN HETCHER, "The FTC as Internet Privacy Norm Entrepreneur," 53 *Vand. L. Rev.* 2041, 2043 (2000).

14. Federal Trade Commission, Privacy Online: Fair Information Practices in the Electronic Marketplace, A Report to Congress (May 2000), *available at* http://www.ftc.gov/reports/privacy2000/privacy2000.pdf [hereinafter 2000 *FTC Report to Congress*] (recommending continued support of self-regulatory approach along with legislation); see also REP. BILLY TAUZIN, "How Can Congress Protect Online Privacy? Self-Regulation Is Key to Web Privacy," *Roll Call*, Feb. 22, 1999, *available at* http://www.rollcall.com (confident that Internet was moving in right direction to make self-regulation a reality).

15. ROBERT ELLICKSON, *Order Without Law: How Neighbors Settle Disputes*, 137 (1991).

16. RUSSELL HARDIN, *Collective Action* (1982).

17. See Reno v. ACLU, 521 U.S. 844, 851 (1997) (J. Stevens, dissenting) ("Taken together, these tools constitute a unique medium – known to its users as 'cyberspace' – located in no particular geographical location but available to anyone, anywhere in the world, with access to the Internet."); Am. Libraries Ass'n v. Pataki, 969 F. Supp. 160, 168–9 (S.D.N.Y. 1997) ("Typically, states' jurisdictional limits are related to geography; geography, however, is a virtually meaningless construct on the Internet."); DAN L. BURK, "Trademark Doctrines for Global Electronic Commerce," 49 *S.C.L. Rev.* 695, 716 (1998) ("Notwithstanding that the Internet is and will be segmented by economic, social, and technological divisions, those divisions will not necessarily map onto the geographic, political, and economic divisions already existing offline... the current technological structure of the Internet... ignores customary political and geographical boundaries on which much of our legal system is based.").

18. See MARK A. LEMLEY, "The Law and Economics of Internet Norms," 73 *Chi.-Kent L. Rev.* 1257, 1275 (1998) (author dubious of claim that Internet norms are efficient).

19. See, for example, SIMON G. DAVIES, "Re-engineering the Right to Privacy: How Privacy Has Been Transformed from a Right to a Commodity," *Technology & Privacy* 143–5 (Philip E. Agre & Marc Rotenberg, eds., 1997) (noting a change in society's approach from privacy protection to data protection); JOEL R. REIDENBERG, "Setting Standards for Fair Information Practice in the U.S. Private Sector," 80 *Iowa L. Rev.* 497, 497–8 (1998) (arguing that a citizen's right to participate in government depends "on the ability to control the disclosure of personal information"); PAUL M. SCHWARTZ, "Privacy and Democracy in Cyberspace," 52 *Vand. L. Rev.* 1609, 1611 (1999) (claiming that the absence of privacy norms threatens democracy); see also JULIE E. COHEN, "A Right to Read Anonymously: A Closer Look at Copyright Management in Cyberspace," 28 *Conn. L. Rev.* 981, 982–3 (1996) (arguing that digital copyright management technologies violate First Amendment Rights protecting speech and freedom of thought). The EU Directive is based on a conception of personal data protection as a fundamental civil liberty interest. Council Directive 95/46/EEC, art. 1.1, 1995 O.J. (L 281) 281 [hereinafter Privacy Directive].

20. SAMUELSON, supra note 3 at 1128 n. 18 ("It is therefore both unnecessary and counterproductive to choose between, e.g., the market-based and civil liberty-based visions of privacy.").

21. Minimization of data collection is sometimes stated as the goal of privacy regulation. See, for example, LITMAN, supra note 12.

22. See SAMUELSON, supra note 3 at 1156–8.

23. The Web is that portion of the Internet that runs HTTP and TCP/IP and utilizes uniform resource locators. TIM BERNERS-LEE, *Weaving the Web* (1999).

24. See PETER P. SWIRE AND ROBERT E. LITAN, *None of Your Business: World Data Flows, Electronic Commerce, and the European Privacy Directive* 8 (1998). Yet another feature of the complex normative story behind the convergence of Internet privacy norms has to do with the recognition of entitlements in personal data. At the beginning of the period under study there was a divergence between the legal recognition of entitlements to personal data and the informal social norms that existed with respect to this data. Over the decade, the law has come to more closely represent the informal norms of entitlement.

25. The tortious relationship between the parties is itself expressed in deontological terms of unfair competition and breach of confidentiality. See SAMUELSON, supra note 3 at 1154–7.

26. By the lights of standard game theory, large-scale collective action problems are the most difficult to solve. See generally HARDIN, supra note 16; ELLICKSON, supra note 15.

27. Norm entrepreneurs are actors who promote norms. CASS SUNSTEIN, "Social Norms and Social Roles," 96 *Colum. L. Rev.* 903, 909 (1996).

28. Id.

29. See PAUL M. SCHWARTZ, "Internet Privacy and the State," 32 *Conn. L. Rev.* 815, 823 (2000) (defining a privacy policy as a document that is often accessed through a hypertext link on a homepage which spells out how it collects and uses personal information).

30. A grundnorm is a basic norm. See JOHN R. CARNES, "Why Should I Obey the Law?," 71 *ETHICS* 14, 19 (1960).

31. See SOLVEIG SINGLETON, "Privacy Versus the First Amendment: A Skeptical Approach," 11 *Fordham Intl. Prop. Media & Ent. L. J.* 97, 98 (2000); DOMINGO R. TAN, "Personal Privacy in the Information Age: Comparison of Internet Data Protection Regulations in the United States and the European Union," 21 *Loy. L. A. Intl. & Comp. L. J.* 661, 665.

32. STEPHEN SEGALLER, *Nerds 2.0.1: A Brief History of the Internet* 92 (1998).

33. Ellickson specifically mentions academic communities as often close-knit. ELLICKSON, supra note 15.

34. BERNERS-LEE, supra note 23.

35. See SEGALLER, *supra* note 32 at 224–5.

36. See id. at 297.

37. See generally MARGARET JANE RADIN, *Contested Commodities* 15 (1996); MARGARET JANE RADIN AND R. POLK WAGNER, "The Myth of Private Ordering: Rediscovering Legal Realism in Cyberspace," 73 *Chi.-Kent L. Rev.* 1295, 1302 (1998). The term *commodification* is not inherently pejorative. Whether, and to what extent, the commodification of personal data is a negative development depends on one's normative theory. For utilitarian theories generally, and economic analysis in particular, "commodification," per se, has no sui generis moral meaning. The core idea of this type of moral theory is that all things of value may be put on a single scale. Thus, to commodify data, or anything else, is not to change its moral status. In fact, economic theorists may view commodification as an instrumental good, as commodifying data may promote efficiency by allowing this data to more easily reach the hands of those who will value it most. For some versions of deontological theory, on the other hand, personal data may not morally be made the subject of market exchanges. See SAMUELSON, supra note 3 at 1143 ("If information privacy is a civil liberty, it may make no more sense to propertize personal data than to commodify voting rights."). See generally PAMELA S. KARLAN, "Not By Money but By Virtue Won? Vote Trafficking and the Voting Rights System," 80 *Va. L. Rev.* 1455 (1994) (explaining rationale for public policies against vote trafficking). This type of deontological theory, however, is not the type that is implicit in most discussions of online privacy. Most deontologically oriented discussions of privacy implicitly accept the notion that under proper conditions, such as when there is informed consent, a data subject may morally alienate personal data in a market exchange.

38. NEIL RANDAL, "How Cookies Work," PC Magazine Online, *available at* http://www.zdnet.com/pcmag/ventures/cookie/cksl.htm (last visited July 4, 2000). There is a shortage of social scientific information about cookie use. In its survey of websites, the FTC staff did not ascertain whether sites use cookies, or other hidden electronic means, to collect personal information, but looked instead to sites' information practice disclosures as a

gauge of the extent of such practices. See 1998 *FTC Report to Congress*, supra note 2 at 45 n. 4.

39. Lessig, supra note 3, at 34–42.

40. See ANDREW L. SHAPIRO, "Privacy For Sale: Peddling Data on the Internet," *Hum. Rts.*, Winter 1999, at 10.

41. Generally, a unique identifier is connected to the machine and not to a named individual. The problem is that this is a small gap to bridge. Consequently, privacy advocates have been concerned about unique identifiers even when connected to machines and not individuals. See, for example, *Electronic Communications Privacy Policy Disclosures: Hearing Before the Subcomm. on Courts and Intellectual Property of the House Comm. on the Judiciary*, 106th Cong. (1999) (statement of Mark Rotenberg, Executive Director, Electronic Privacy Information Center). Recently, both Intel and Microsoft have made efforts to tie numbers to names. See EDWARD C. BAIG, "Privacy: The Internet Wants Your Personal Info. What's In It for You?," *Bus. Week*, April 5, 1999, *available at* 1999 WL 8226796; DON CLARK AND KARA SWISHER, "Microsoft to Alter Windows 98 So Data About Users Won't Be Sent to Company," *Wall St. J.*, March 8, 1999, *available at* 1999 WL-WSJ 5443409; ROBERT LEMOS, "The Biggest Computer Bugs of 1999!," *ZD Internet Magazine*, Dec. 23, 1999, *available at* 1999 WL 14538475 (discussing Intel's Pentium III serial number, global unique identifiers, and two Microsoft products, Office 97 and Windows 98, that attempted to match various numbers to personal information and names); see also In re the Matter of Intel Pentium Processor Serial Number, Compl., Case No. 982 (Federal Trade Commission, Feb. 26, 1999).

42. An industry has emerged to market a variety of software products designed to assist websites in collecting and analyzing visitor data and in providing targeted advertising. See, for example, RIVKA TADHER, "Following the Patron Path," *ZD Internet Magazine*, Dec. 23, 1997, at 95; THOMAS E. WEBER, "Software Lets Marketers Target Web Ads," *Wall St. J.*, Apr. 21, 1997, at B1.

43. "Passive tracking" refers to information collected by using navigational software. 1998 FTC Report to Congress, supra note 2 at 56.

44. See id. at 3, 45.

45. MICHAEL FROOMKIN, "The Death of Privacy," *Stan. L. Rev.* 52, 1461, 1487 (2000).

46. FORESTER RESEARCH, INC., *Media & Technology Strategies: Making Users Pay* 4–6 (1998).

47. FROOMKIN, supra note 45 at 1487 ("Cookies, however, are only the tip of the iceberg. Far more intrusive features can be integrated into browsers, into software downloaded from the Internet, and into viruses or Trojan horses. In the worst case, the software could be configured to record every keystroke."). A trojan horse is a "malicious, security-breaking program that is disguised as something benign, such as a directory lister, archiver, game, or . . . a program." FOLDOC, "Trojan Horse," *available at* http://wombat.doc.ic.ac.uk/foldoc/foldoc.cgi?query=+trojan+horse (last visited Mar. 25, 2001).

48. FROOMKIN, supra note 45 at 1473–4.

49. Ellickson emphasizes the important role that knowledge plays in the monitoring process that allows for successful solution of strategic problems. ELLICKSON, supra note 15.

50. PATRICK CROSKERY, "Institutional Utilitarianism and Intellectual Property," 68 *Chi-Kent L. Rev.* 631, 632 (1993).

51. See U.S. Const. art. I, § 8, cl. 8. In the landmark case, Feist v. Rural Telephone Service, the Supreme Court has said that facts are not subject to copyright protection. Rather, they must be left in the public domain – the intellectual commons – available for all to use. 499 U.S. 340 (1991). Feist involved facts of a particular sort, namely, personal data; the names and addresses of the residents of a particular region of Kansas, as contained in a regional telephone directory. See id. at 359–60. Lawyers are just beginning to grapple with special issues raised by the digital commons. See LESSIG, supra note 3; STEVEN HETCHER, "Climbing the Walls of Your Electronic Cage," 98 *Mich. L. Rev.* 801, 814 (2000). Law regarding personal data, indeed all data, is at sea. Some commentators have argued for heightened intellectual property status for personal data as a means to greater privacy protection. See PATRICIA MELL, "Seeking Shade in a Land of Perpetual Sunlight: Privacy as Property in the Electronic Wilderness," 11 *Berkeley Tech. L. J.* 1, 78 (1996) (advocating statutory recognition of property rights in a "persona" consisting of personal information about the individual); KENNETH C. LAUDON, "Markets and Privacy," *Comm. ACM*, Sept. 1996, at 92 (suggesting property rights in personal data as a way to protect privacy). There are First Amendment tensions, however, with this sort of proposal. For a discussion of the First Amendment and privacy, compare PAUL M. SCHAWRTZ, "Free Speech v. Privacy: Eugene Voloch's First Amendment Jurisprudence," *Stan. L. Rev.* 52, 1559 (2000), with EUGENE VOLOKH, "Freedom of Speech and Information Privacy: The Troubling Implications of a Right to Stop People from Speaking About You," 52 *Stan. Law. Rev.* 1049 (2000). The tension between privacy and free speech can be avoided if data-subject control, as opposed to ownership, of personal data, can be protected. A trend leading in an opposite direction from heightened intellectual property protection is "copyleft," which argues that the Internet radically undermines ownership concepts for intellectual goods in the online world. See IRA V. HEFFAN, "Copyleft: Licensing Collaborative Work in the Digital Age," 49 *Stan. L. Rev.* 1487, 1491–2 (1997); see also DAVID BRIN, *The Transparent Society: Will Technology Force Us to Choose Between Privacy and Freedom?* (1998) (arguing that personal data should be subject to open access rules).

52. See, for example, SANDBERG supra note 10. Indicating the seriousness of the problem, the FTC has recently appointed a person to handle the issue. See *The Prepared Statement of the Federal Trade Commission on "Identity Theft:" Hearing Before the Subcommittee on Technology, Terrorism and Government Information of the Senate Committee on the Judiciary*, 105th Cong. (1998) (Statement of David Mendine, Ass'n Div. for Credit Practices, Bureau of Consumer Protection, Federal Trade Commission). A recently passed Identity Theft and Assumption Deterrence Act, 18 U.S.C. § 1028(a), imposes a penalty of fifteen years of imprisonment and fines for theft of personal information with intent to commit an unlawful act. See KURT M. SAUNDERS AND BRUCE ZUCKER, "Counteracting Identity Fraud in the Information Age: The Identity Theft and Assumption Deterrence Act," 8 *Cornell J. L. & Publ. Poly.* 20 (1999); PETER P. SWIRE, "Financial Privacy and the Theory of High-Tech Government Surveillance," 77 *Wash. U. L. Q.* 461, 470–4 (giving examples); see also Laracuente v. Laracuente, 599 A.2d 968 (N.J. Law Div. 1991) (showing typical social security number identity theft).

53. Discussions pertaining to the special concerns regarding data collection from children often mention the inability of children to effectively consent to such data collection. This demonstrates a special concern for the autonomy, or lack thereof, of children.

54. See *1998 FTC Report to Congress*, supra note 2 at 4–5.
55. See JANE BIRNBAUM, "Here's How to Protect Your Medical Records," *Chicago Trib.*, Nov. 23, 1999, *available at* 1999 WL 2935001; DAVID F. LINANES AND RAY APENCER, "How Employers Handle Employees' Personal Information: Report of a Recent Survey," 1 *Employee Rts. & Employment Poly. J.* 153 (1997).
56. See PAUL M. SCHWARTZ, "Privacy and the Economics of Personal Health Care Information," 76 *Tex. L. Rev.* 1, 22 (1997) ("[W]ide disclosure of certain kinds of information may distort individual behavior in an inefficient fashion. Fearing loss of employment and social discrimination, people will either lie to their physicians or avoid seeking care that might lead to the creation of sensitive health care or genetic information."); Patent Confidentiality: Hearing Before the Subcomm. on Health of the House Comm. on Ways and Means, 105th Cong. (1998), *available at* 1998 WL 18089939 ("In the absence of such trust, patients will be reticent to accurately and honestly disclose personal information, or they may avoid seeking care altogether for fear of suffering negative consequences, such as embarrassment, stigma, and discrimination. Along the continuum, if doctors and other health care providers are receiving incomplete, inaccurate information from patients, the data they disclose for payment, research, public health reporting, outcomes analysis, and other purposes, will carry the same vulnerabilities.").
57. See SWIRE AND LITAN, supra note 24 ("Consider the incentives of a company that acquires private information. The company gains the full benefit of using the information in its own marketing efforts or in the fee it receives when it sells the information to third parties. The company, however, does not suffer losses from the disclosure of private information. Because customers often will not learn of the overdisclosure, they may not be able to discipline the company effectively. In economic terms, the company internalizes the gains from using the information but can externalize some of the losses and so has a systematic incentive to overuse it. This market failure is made worse by the costs of bargaining for the desired level of privacy. It can be daunting for an individual consumer to bargain with a distant Internet merchant . . . about the desired level of privacy. To be successful, bargaining might take time, effort, and considerable expertise in privacy issues.").
58. See J. R. HICKS, "The Valuation of the Social Income," 7 *Economica* 105, 110 (1940); NICHOLAS KALDOR, "Welfare Propositions of Economics and Inter-Personal Comparisons of Utility," 49 *Econ. J.* 549, 550 (1939).
59. Sanctions have the potential to promote efficient norms. The role that sanctions play is to incentivize actors to adjust their norm conformity so as to take account of the sanction in their overall calculation of the worthiness of conforming to the norm.
60. See GEORGE R. MILNE, "Privacy and Ethical Issues in Database/Interactive Marketing and Public Policy: A Research Framework and Overview of the Special Issue," 19 *J. Pub. Poly. & Mkt.* 1, 9 (2000) (summarizing studies: "When Web sites require consumers to provide information to register, many consumers provide false information. Surveys report that half the Internet users report false information about a quarter of the time . . . Many surfers do not fill in reports because they are concerned about their privacy and do not want to be spammed . . . As noted by Petty . . . , unwanted contact is a primary concern of many consumers and a reason that consumers balk at providing information. Sheehan and Hoy . . . provide empirical evidence that unwanted email contact is of high concern to online consumers."); JERRY GUIDERA, "Online Shoppers Often Lie To Guard Privacy, Survey Says," *Wall St. J.*, Mar. 16, 2000, *available at* 2000 WL-WSJE 2948132.

61. Studies indicate that consumers are particularly afraid of transfers of their personal data to unknown third parties. See 1999 FTC Report to Congress, supra note 4.

62. As argued in Chapter One, a norm need not be expressed in linguistic terms in order to have content, whereas a rule is by definition linguistic. A norm's content is defined in terms of its strategic structure. A norm, then, is behavior of a certain sort, which may or may not have an attached linguistic component. When characterizing a group's norms, it is necessary to keep in mind the difference between norms and rules because as it is important to be able to look at the actual practices of groups, rather than merely going by what they express linguistically. Talk is cheap; it is conforming behavior that creates benefits for conforming groups and externalities for third parties.

63. See generally, SHELLEY KAGAN, *The Limits of Morality* (1989).

64. ROBERT D. COOTER, "Expressive Law and Economics," 27 *J. Legal Stud.* 585, 587–8 (1998); ERIC POSNER, SYMPOSIUM, "Law, Economics & Norms: Law, Economics, and Inefficient Norms," 144 *U. Pa. L. Rev.* 1697, 1699 (1996) ("A norm can be understood as a rule that distinguishes desirable and undesirable behavior and gives a third party the authority to punish a person who engages in the undesirable behavior.").

65. See generally, HARDIN, supra note 16.

66. *1999 FTC Report to Congress*, supra note 4 at 2–3; *1998 FTC Report to Congress*, supra note 2 at 3–4.

67. ROTENBERG, supra note 41.

68. See, for example, Federal Trade Commission, The Information Marketplace: Merging and Exchanging Consumer Data, *available at* http://www.ftc.gov/bcp/workshops/infomktplace/index.html (March 13, 2001) (Public workshop notices posted on the FTC homepage at www.ftc.gov).

69. HARDIN, supra note 16 at 2 ("Although it can make good sense to say that an individual is rational, there is no obviously useful new sense in which we can typically say that a group is rational. Yet, one of the more widely accepted doctrines of modern political science – the group theory of politics – was based on a presumption from the fallacy of composition: that a group of people with a common interest will take action to further that interest. That doctrine has collapsed in the face of two major developments . . . Mancur Olson's logic of collective action and game theory's Prisoner's Dilemma. In the latter, there is a dilemma precisely because what it makes sense for an individual to do is not what would make sense for the group to do – if one could meaningfully speak of what the group should do.").

70. Lighthouses are a classic example of a collective good as there is a collective action problem with regard to the provision of the lighthouse. Each individual potential beneficiary would benefit from the provision of a lighthouse. Nevertheless, there is a collective action problem because once the lighthouse is provided, it is provided for all. In other words, the individual cannot be excluded from benefiting from the good even though she did not contribute toward its provision. Thus, each individual does best by defecting from providing her share toward its provision. But because all potential beneficiaries are similarly situated, each will free ride and hence the good will not be provided.

71. Based in part on its survey of over 1400 commercial websites, the FTC in 1998 concluded that there was not yet effective self-regulation: "The Commission's examination of industry guidelines and actual online practices reveals that effective industry self-regulation

with respect to online collection, use, and dissemination of personal information has not yet taken hold." 1998 FTC Report to Congress, supra note 2.

72. ELLICKSON, supra note 15 at 250. Ellickson defines "close-knit" groups as follows: "A group is *close-knit* when informal power is broadly distributed among group members and the information pertinent to informal control circulates easily among them." Id. at 177–8. Ellickson's definition of close-knittedness implies "group members" having both "continuing reciprocal power over one another and also a bank of shared information." Id. at 238. Ellickson notes that close-knittedness is inversely related to group size – the smaller the group, the greater the degree of close-knittedness. See id. at 182. However, "[A] group does not necessarily have to be small to be close-knit." Id.

73. ELLICKSON, supra note 15.

74. MARK A. LEMLEY, "Shrinkwraps in Cyberspace," 35 *Jurimetrics* 311, 314 (1995) ("In addition, the rapid growth in the number of network users has worked to transform cyberspace in important respects. With its forty or fifty million users, the Internet is no longer comprised of a limited set of close-knit communities in which private ordering can be based on shared values and understanding."); see also, "The Domain Name System: A Case Study of the Significance of Norms to Internet Governance," 112 *Harv. L. Rev.* 1657, 1676–80 (1999).

75. For the classic discussions, see WILLIAM J. BAUMOL, *Welfare Economics and the Theory of the State* (1952); ANTHONY DOWNS, *An Economic Theory of Democracy* (1957).

76. For example, the E.U. Privacy Directive has a complex set of requirements to which firms that use personal data of Europeans must adhere. See Privacy Directive, supra note 19.

77. Consumer Internet Privacy: Hearing Before the Senate Comm. on Commerce, Science, and Transportation, 106th Cong. (2000) (Marc Rotenberg, Executive Director, Electronic Privacy Information Center) ("The reliance of privacy guidelines on the FTC Act prohibiting unfair and deceptive business practices has not provided an adequate basis for the protection of privacy interests.").

78. Anecdotal evidence suggests, however, that some sites avoid this cost by simply, and illegally, cutting and pasting from the privacy policies of other sites that they find on the Web.

79. For example, RealNetworks recently admitted that its RealJukebox assigned a personal ID number to users and uploaded information about their listening habits to its server, contrary to its privacy policy. See SARA ROBINSON, "CD Software Is Said to Monitor Users' Listening Habits," *N.Y. Times*, Nov. 1, 1999, *available at* http://www.nytimes.com. The company was subsequently slapped with a $500 million class action lawsuit for violating California's unfair business practices law. See "Real Networks Is Target of Suit in California Over Privacy Issue," *N.Y. Times*, Nov. 9, 1999, *available at* http://www.nytimes.com.

80. DAVID LEWIS, *Convention* (1969); EDNA ULLMANN-MARGALIT, *The Emergence of Norms* (1977); see also MARGARET GILBERT, "Game Theory and Convention," 46 *Synthese* 41 (1981).

81. LEWIS, supra note 80. With a proper coordination equilibrium, other conformers receive a benefit when a particular actor conforms. It is this feature that causes David Lewis to claim that "conventions" are best modeled as proper coordination equilibria. Conventions, on Lewis' well-known account, are maintained in part by sanctions. Conformers sanction

one another for non-conformity because it is in the interest of others that each conform. The sanctions are meant to ensure the conformity of others. The economics literature on "network externalities" encompasses a similar but broader rational structure as not all networks with significant externalities are norms.

82. Coordination norms have similar structural features to "network effects." On network effects generally, see, for example, Mark A. Lemley and David McGowan, "Legal Implications of Network Economic Effects," 86 *Cal. L. Rev.* 479 (1998) (arguing for limiting the assumption that network effects produce suboptimal lock-in); S. J. Liebowitz and Stephen E. Margolis, "Path Dependence, Lock-In, and History," 11 *J. L. Econ. & Org.* 205 (1995).

83. See, for example, Dorothy Glancy, "Symposium on Internet Privacy: At the Intersection of Visible and Invisible Worlds: United States Privacy and the Internet," 16 *Santa Clara Computer & High Tech. L. J.* 357, 363–4 (2000) ("Assurances of privacy protection by e-commerce vendors and Internet service providers demonstrate that the commercial side of the Internet recognizes that respect for privacy is a significant expectation of Internet users.") (footnotes omitted).

84. See generally Fletcher v. Price Choppers Foods of Trumann, Inc., 220 F.3d 871 (2000); Cramer v. Consolidated Freightways, Inc., 209 F.3d 1122 (2000).

85. Andrew B. Buxbaum and Louis A. Curcio, "When You Can't Sell to Your Customers, Try Selling Your Customers (But Not Under the Bankruptcy Code)," 8 *Am. Bankr. Inst. L. Rev.* 395, 411–12 (2000) (arguing that the appearance of privacy policies would create an expectation of privacy).

86. The possibility of externalization of the costs of an industry custom is one reason why the established "rule of custom" in tort law is that conformity to industry custom may serve as evidence of due care, but is not dispositive.

87. Ullmann-Margalit, supra note 80 (recounting classic norm emergence and emphasizing that the first step is to identify underlying social situations in which an emergent norm would promote efficiency).

88. Sociologists refer to such relationships as "multiplex." See, for example, Ellickson, supra note 15 at 55. In the early days of the noncommercial Internet, online interactions were typically between members of particular research communities. The members of those communities often had "multiplex" relationships with one another. These researchers might see each other at conferences; they might be former classmates, or share advisors or mentors; or they might wish to seek future employment at one another's institutions. Accordingly, there would often exist ample opportunities to sanction noncooperative behavior, or reward cooperative behavior. Listservs such as *The Well* are of interest in this regard. *The Well* was pre-Web and noncommercial. In addition, many of its members were part of a relatively close-knit community, the Bay Area Internet cognoscenti. *The Well* nevertheless allowed members to interact anonymously if they wished. Predictably, serious problems arose with the community. See Esther Dyson, *Release 2.0: A Design for Living in the Digital Age* (1998).

89. See David Farber, *The Age of Great Dreams: America in the 1960s*, 76 (1994). "In Nashville, which became the focal point for the sit-in movement, the means by which a protester should politely refuse to accept the legal bounds set by civil society were carefully codified. James Lawson, a longtime student of Gandhian non-violence, explained: 'Do show yourself friendly on the counter at all times. Do sit straight and always face

the counter. Don't strike back or curse if attacked.' With discipline, the protesters were turning American society on its head." Id.

90. TOM KIRCHOFER, "Microsoft Networks Tap Akamai," *Boston Herald*, Jan. 30, 2001, at 29 (noting that "Denial of Service" attacks overwhelm a company's computer with information and prevent legitimate traffic from getting through); see also GREG MILLER, "Microsoft Hit by New Wave of Outages; Internet: Hackers Cripple Company's Most Popular Websites; FBI is Asked to Probe 'Denial of Service' Attacks," *L.A. Times*, Jan 26, 2001, at C3.

91. In addition, websites may have more ready access to technological means to remove protesters. See LESSIG, supra note 3 at 66–70 (noting that no protesters allowed in AOL space through restrictive coding).

92. ROBERT D. COOTER, "Decentralized Law for a Complex Economy: The Structural Approach to Adjudicating the New Law Merchant," 144 *U. Pa. L. Rev.* 1643, 1690–4 (1996).

93. RICHARD H. MCADAMS, "The Origin, Development, and Regulation of Norms," 96 *Mich. L. Rev.* 338, 342 (1997) ("theory of origin and growth of norms" in which "the initial force behind norm creation is the desire individuals have for respect or prestige, that is, for the relative esteem of others.").

94. ERIC A. POSNER, *Law and Social Norms* (2000); ERIC A POSNER, "Symbols, Signals, and Social Norms in Politics and the Law," 27 *J. Legal Stud.* 765, 780 (1998).

95. See ROTENBERG, supra note 77; see also BRENDAN MAHER, "Self–Regulation," Target Marketing, Dec. 1, 2000, *available at* 2000 WL 10932469 (arguing that consumers and businesses have little confidence in self-regulation and citing a survey claiming 24 percent of adults polled felt the federal government should set privacy rules).

Chapter Thirteen

1. Peter Brondmo, founder of Netcentives, Inc.

2. The connection between the collection of personal data and personal privacy is straightforward; the more personal data that websites collect, store, and use, the less privacy that data subjects have. See A. MICHAEL FROOMKIN, "The Death of Privacy," 52 *Stan. L. Rev.* 1461, 1465 (2000); JESSICA LITMAN, "Information Privacy/Information Property," 52 *Stan. L. Rev.* 1283, 1283–6 (2000). There are two broad categories of personal data: information that can be used to identify consumers (personal identifying information: including name, postal or e-mail address) or demographic and preference information (including age, gender, income level, hobbies, or interests). The latter can be used either in aggregate, nonidentifying form for purposes including market analysis, or in conjunction with personal identifying information to create detailed personal profiles. *Federal Trade Commission, Privacy Online: A Report to Congress* 20 (June 1998), *available at* http://www.ftc.gov/reports/privacy3/priv-23a.pdf [hereinafter *1998 FTC Report to congress*].

3. See, e.g., "The End of Privacy," *The Economist*, May 1, 1999, at 21; REP. ASA HUTCHINSON AND REP. JIM MORAN, "*Industry Needs to Take the Lead on Protection*," *Roll Call*, Jul. 10, 2000, *available at* 2000 WL 8734799; ADAM L. PENENBERG, "The End of Privacy," *Forbes*, Nov. 29, 1999, at 182; JARED SANDBERG, "Losing Your Good Name

Online," *Newsweek*, Sept. 20, 1999, at 56 (describing the "alarming prospect" of identity theft – " the worst kind of privacy violation"); CELIA SANTANDER, "Web-Site Privacy Policies Aren't Created Equal," *Web fin.*, Dec. 11, 2000. Opinion polls show increasing public concern with respect to online privacy. See infra note 88.

4. Norm entrepreneurs are actors who promote the change of norms. CASS R. SUNSTEIN, "Social Norms and Social Roles," 96 *Colum. L. Rev.* 903, 909 (1996). Norm proselytizers promote norms for moral reasons which they themselves accept. Norm proselytizers, then, are a subcategory of norm entrepreneurs. Robert Ellickson seeks to develop a richer vocabulary by distinguishing among a variety of specialists who supply new norms. See ROBERT ELLICKSON, "The Market for Social Norms," 3 *Am. Law & Econ. Rev.* 10–12 (2001). "Change agents" are actors or enforcers who are relatively early in supplying a new norm. Id. He distinguishes among these subcategories of change agents: self-motivated leaders, norm entrepreneurs, and opinion leaders. Id. The following discussion will indicate that these subcategories may be aptly applied to norm creation in cyberspace. In addition, I will suggest that the norm proselytizer is aptly viewed as a distinct type of change agent.

5. See LAWRENCE LESSIG, "The Regulation of Social Meaning," 62 *U. Chi. L. Rev.* 943, 951 (1995) ("Any society or social context has what I call here social meanings – the semiotic content attached to various actions, or inactions, or statuses, within a particular context.").

6. See id. at 950–52.

7. On some accounts, this process may come too late. In a now famous remark, the CEO of Sun Microsystems, Scott McNealy, advised the public, "[y]ou already have zero privacy – get over it." JOHN MARKOFF, "Growing Compatibility Issue: Computers and User Privacy," *N.Y. Times*, Mar. 3, 1999, at A5. McNealy's remark is self-serving, given that it was made at the launch of Jini software, which raised privacy concerns because it promised to enable all electronic devices to interconnect using an identification number. Id. One can imagine McNealy making a statement similar to that quoted here, albeit toned down in its rhetoric, as a defendant in a civil suit, or as a witness in a congressional hearing, with the implicit message that if privacy is gone already, Sun Microsystems cannot be accused of its further degradation.

8. See, for example, A. S. BERMAN, "Reports of Gates' Death Greatly Exaggerated," *USA Today*, Apr. 5, 2001, at 3D (noting that Microsoft spokesperson Beth Jordan stated, "[t]here's nothing more important to Bill [Gates] than the privacy of his family and children."); FRED H. CATE, "The Changing Face of Privacy Protection in the European Union and the United States," 33 *Ind. L. Rev.* 174, 179 (1999) ("Privacy will be to the information economy of the next century what consumer protection and environmental concerns have been to the industrial society of the 20th century." (quoting Marc Rotenberg)).

9. See LOUIS D. BRANDEIS AND SAMUEL D. WARREN, "*The Right to Privacy*," 4 *Harv. L. Rev.* 193 (1890); SIMON G. DAVIES, "Re-engineering the Right to Privacy: How Privacy Has Been Transformed from a Right to a Commodity," *Technology and Privacy: The New Landscape* 143, 144 (Philip E. Agre & Marc Rotenberg, eds., 1997) (noting a change in society's approach from privacy protection to data protection); JOEL R. REIDENBERG, "Setting Standards for Fair Information Practice in the U.S. Private Sector," 80 *Iowa L. Rev.* 497, 497–8 (1995) (arguing that a citizen's right to participate in government depends "on the ability to control the disclosure of personal information"). Some European Union

Parliament and Council Directives dealing with privacy are based on a conception of personal data protection as a fundamental civil liberty interest. *See* Council Directive 95/46/EC, 1995 O.J. (L 281) 31.

10. PAUL DAVIDSON, "Marketing Gurus Clash on Internet Privacy Rules," *USA Today*, Apr. 27, 2001, at 1B ("Such a system recognizes a 'subtle but important shift' in direct marketing".)

11. MATT RICHTEL, "When Computers Know What a Stranger Can't," *N.Y. Times*, Mar. 12, 2000, at C9. Marc Rotenberg "believes that Web sites should make clear what information they are capturing and give users a clear option to decline to participate." Id.

12. Traditional economic analysis has shied away from the topic of preference formation. This is changing, however. See GARY S. BECKER, *Accounting For Tastes* 3 (1996) (noting in his study of individual preferences that "preferences or tastes play a crucial part in virtually all fields of study in economics. . . . [b]ut with few exceptions, economists and political scientists pay little attention to the structure of preferences"); see also JON ELSTER, *Sour Grapes* (1983).

13. JERI CLAUSING, "Can Internet Advertisers Police Themselves? Washington Remains Unconvinced," *N.Y. Times*, June 14, 2000, at C10 (reporting that Marc Rotenberg, director of the Electronic Privacy Information Center stated "Internet users should be able to have their profiles deleted upon request"); DAVID COHEN, "Be Sure You Never Take a Cookie from Strangers," *The Guardian* (London), Apr. 1, 2000, at 22 ("Some of the UK's popular internet banks are eager to point out their respect for customer privacy. 'We do not passively track visitors to our website,' says Richard Thackray, UK country manager for first-e. 'Once a customer is signed up, we keep records of all communications and may use the information for special offers, but we don't trade customer information without their prior consent.'"); REP. EDWARD J. MARKEY, "We Must Act Soon to Protect Online Privacy," *The Hill*, Feb. 7, 2001 ("I believe that Congress must enact meaningful privacy protections to reflect the fundamental value that the overwhelming majority of Americans place upon this core element of freedom.").

14. See KATIE HAFNER, "Do You Know Who's Watching You? Do You Care?", *N.Y. Times*, Nov. 11, 1999, at G1. "That's not to say that L. L. Bean executives think that people are ready to give up their privacy. To the contrary, L. L. Bean believes that, as always, people are willing to share private information with those they trust, and it believes that it has its customers' trust. The company may be right. It reports that customers love the convenience. In fact, one recent caller was so charmed by the personal treatment that she thought the saleswoman recognized her voice. "That's a trusting relationship with that business," said Marc Rotenberg, executive director of the Electronic Privacy Information Center, a privacy advocacy group in Washington. Mr. Rotenberg said L. L. Bean's customers had faith that the company would not abuse the information by reselling it." Id.

15. See GEORGE R. MILNE, "Privacy and Ethical Issues in Database/Interactive Marketing and Public Policy: A Research Framework and Overview of the Special Issue," 19 *J. Pub. Pol'y. & Mktg.* 16, 16 (2000). Milne succinctly summarized several studies: "When Web sites require consumers to provide information to register, many consumers provide false information. Surveys report that half the Internet users report false information about a quarter of the time." Id. (citation omitted). See also DOMINGO R. TAN, "Personal Privacy in the Information Age: Comparison of Internet Data Protection Regulations in

the United States and the European Union," 21 *Loy. L. A. Int'l. & Comp. L. J.* 661, 664–5 (1999) (citing a Boston Consulting Group consumer study stating that "40% of Internet users have provided false information at least once when registering at a website"); JERRY GUIDERA, "Online Shoppers Often Lie To Guard Privacy, Survey Says," *Wall St. J. Europe*, Mar. 16, 2000, at 28.

16. ROBERT C. ELLICKSON, *Order Without Law: How Neighbors Settle Disputes* 213–14 (1991).

17. See "The Internet's Chastened Child," *The Economist*, Nov. 11, 2000, at 80. Kevin O'Conner, founder of DoubleClick, lost his job due to his insensitivity to the issue of privacy: "Consumer watchdogs were slow to grasp the implications of the Abacus deal – and of the fact that, in its wake, DoubleClick had quietly dropped from its website its pledge to keep users' data completely anonymously. But they woke up in January when the company announced that it had created profiles of 100,000 individual surfers and was planning to sell them to advertisers. The resulting outcry triggered an FTC probe into whether DoubleClick had engaged in deceptive trade practices, leading to a 25% drop in the group's shares in a single day and eventually, to a pledge that it would not sell the profiles after all. DoubleClick's subsequent promise not to integrate its own database fully with that of Abacus turns the acquisition, in the eyes of many, into a monumental flop." Id.

18. See JOHN SCHWARTZ, "First Line of Defense, Chief Privacy Officers Forge Evolving Corporate Roles," *N.Y. Times*, Feb. 12, 2001, at C1 (explaining that lawyers are good at making sure that a company complies with privacy laws "but being a chief privacy officer is a lot more than simply compliance. 'You have to have a fundamental commitment to – dare I say it? – morality.'"); see also DAVID BICKNELL, "Directors Face E-Laws Overload," *Computer Wkly.*, Feb. 24, 2000, at 16 (stating that the burdens of complying with European privacy policies has led some companies to be proactive and engage in "self-help" through "privacy specialists").

19. See Citigroup Privacy Promise, *available at* http://www.citibank.com/privacy (last visited Sept. 4, 2001) [hereinafter Citigroup Privacy Promise].

20. See PAUL M. SCHWARTZ, "Internet Privacy and the State," 32 *Conn. L. Rev.* 815, 823 (2000) (noting that a privacy policy is a document that is often accessed through a hypertext link on a homepage, which spells out how it collects and uses personal information).

21. The Citigroup Privacy Promise reads: "our most important asset is our customers' trust. Keeping customer information secure, and using it as our customers would want us to, is a top priority for all of us at Citigroup." Citigroup Privacy Promise, supra note 19. It later states: "We will continuously assess ourselves to ensure that customer privacy is respected." Id. In the space of a one-page privacy statement, then, this document uses the normatively loaded terms, "promise," "trust," and "respect." Id.

22. LARRY E. RIBSTEIN, "Law v. Trust," 81 *B.U.L. Rev.* 553, 588 (2001).

23. See http://www.jcrew.com (last visited Sept. 4, 2001) ("By visiting jcrew.com you are accepting the practices described in this privacy policy.").

24. See http://www.weather.com (last visited Sept. 4, 2001) ("This statement and the policies outlined here are not intended to and do not give you any contractual or other legal rights.").

25. See infra note 31; STEVEN A. HETCHER, "The FTC as Internet Privacy Norm Entrepreneur," 53 *Vand L. Rev.* 2041, 2056–9 (2000).

26. The tortious relationship between the parties is expressed in terms of unfair competition and breach of confidentiality. See PAMELA SAMUELSON, "Privacy as Intellectual Property?," 52 *Stan. L. Rev.* 1125, 1154–7 (2000).

27. NINA BERNSTEIN, "Welfare Officials to Search Records Of Drug Treatment," *N.Y. Times*, Sep. 25, 1999, at A1 ("Marc Rotenberg, executive director of the Electronic Privacy Information Center, a civil liberties advocacy group based in Washington, said: 'Welfare recipients are among the first to lose their privacy. But the unfortunate consequences of these tracking and matching technologies tend to make their way up the line.' A Federal law passed in the 1970's makes it a crime, with few exceptions, to disclose information about patients in drug and alcohol treatment programs without the patients' narrowly defined written consent. That consent does not allow re-disclosure for any other purposes. Experts on privacy law call the measure unique and exemplary, and contrast it to the blanket consent forms allowed in the gathering of other types of health care information."); HAFNER, supra note 14 at G1.

28. See PETER P. SWIRE AND ROBERT E. LITAN, *None of Your Business: World Data Flows, Electronic Commerce, and the European Privacy Directive* 8 (1998).

29. STEPHEN LABATON, "U.S. Is Said to Seek New Law to Bolster Privacy on Internet," *N.Y. Times*, May 20, 2000, at A1. ("'The bottom line is that the privacy gap between the safeguards in place and the intrusions seems to be growing not narrowing . . .' said Marc Rotenberg, director of the Electronic Privacy Information Center, a research organization that studies privacy issues and technology.").

30. SUNSTEIN, supra note 4 at 909 (stating that a norm cascade is a rapid shift in norms, perhaps as a result of fragile social conditions); see also RANDAL C. PICKER, "Simple Games in a Complex World: A Generative Approach to the Adoption of Norms," 64 *U. Chi. L. Rev.* 1225, 1227–8 (describing the function of the law in "norm seeding," which is the idea that norms adopted by a small group of people may produce a norm cascade, such that the norm spreads throughout society and replaces old norms).

31. For example, in bankruptcy proceedings, Toysmart.com recently moved to sell personal data it had collected pursuant to a specific privacy guarantee. See infra note 102.

32. LESSIG, supra note 5 at 968–73.

33. Id. at 971–2.

34. See generally DAN M. KAHAN, "Social Influence, Social Meaning, and Deterrence," 83 *Va. L. Rev.* 349 (1997).

35. Likewise, with cigarette smoking, the challenge is to shift the social meaning away from the current situation whereby teen smoking is considered cool. The more that authorities try to control smoking, the cooler it may seem. See LESSIG, supra note 5 at 1025–34.

36. See BRANDEIS AND WARREN, supra note 9.

37. Olmstead v. United States, 277 U.S. 438 (1928).

38. Katz v. United States, 389 U.S. 347 (1967).

39. The privacy advocacy community formed in the 1960s to fight against wide-scale personal data collection and aggregation by agencies of the U.S. government, newly armed with mainframe computers. See DAVID H. FLAHERTY, *Protecting Privacy in Surveillance Societies* 306–8 (1989); PRISCILLA M. REGAN, *Legislating Privacy-Technology, Social Values, and Public Policy* 70–1 (1995).

40. Because of the recent passage of the U.S. Patriot Act, however, the governmental threat to privacy is beginning to receive renewed attention.

41. See In re Doubleclick Inc. Privacy Litigation, No. 00CIV 0641 NRB, 2001 WL 303744 (S.D.N.Y. Mar. 28, 2001).
42. See SETH R. LESSER, "Privacy Law in the Internet Era: New Developments and Directions," 632A *Practicing Law Institute* 187, 217–18 (June 2001).
43. See, for example, "Privacy Champion Defeating Net Threats One by One," *San Diego Union-Tribune*, Apr. 18, 2000, at 10. Richard M. Smith is a software expert who does not fully trust his own kind. Id. As a result, he has launched a personal crusade to expose technology practices that threaten the privacy of millions of Internet users. Id.
44. Ellickson refers to "opinion leaders." See ELLICKSON, supra note 4 at 12–13.
45. See MARK A. LEMLEY, "The Law and Economics of Internet Norms," 73 *Chi-Kent L. Rev.* 1257, 1276 (1998). Nonconsensual website interactions are "particularly likely when incentives are asymmetrically distributed in the community, as when buyers and sellers have their own conflicting norms. The norm that results from this conflict may represent a variety of things besides consensus: superior bargaining power on the prevailing side, collective action problems on the other side, or the use of strategic behavior." Id. As the discussion in the main text indicates, there is an additional reason for nonconsensual website interactions besides the one Lemley lists, namely ignorance on the part of visitors of the data-collection practices of websites.
46. SUSAN WELLS, "When It's Nobody's Business But Your Own," *N.Y. Times*, Feb. 13, 2000, at C11.
47. HAL BERGHEL, "Identity Theft, Social Security Numbers, and the Web," 43 *Communications of the ACM* 17, 19 (2000), *available at* http://www.acm.org/pubs/citations/journals/cacm/2000-43-2/p17-berghel ("As any victim can attest, identity theft can destroy personal credit and potentially lead to very expensive litigation *that may take years*, or perhaps decades, to fully correct."); KEVIN G. DeMARRAIS, "Beware Thieves Who Steal Christmas," *The Rec.*, Dec. 8, 1996, at B3 ("[I]dentity thieves can establish new accounts in your name and run up big bills and debt. By the time you realize what has happened, your credit record can be in ruins and it can take months to unravel the mess."); MICHAEL A. GIPS, "Victims Describe Identity Theft," *Security Management Online*," *at* http://www.securitymanagement.com/library/000901.html (last visited Aug. 3, 2001).
48. DAN STIMSON, "Internet Security an Issue for Telemedicine Success," *Albequerque Trib.*, Aug. 16, 1999, at A6 ("Exposure of private medical information can affect a person's ability to acquire employment."); "President to Toughen Medical Privacy Rules," *The Sunday Gazette Mail* (Charleston), Aug. 20, 2000, at 6B ("Public opinion polls show that Americans are increasingly concerned about privacy in general and want greater protection for medical records, in particular. Some people say they shun testing for cancer, HIV infection and other conditions because they fear discrimination in . . . employment.").
49. See "The Internet's Chastened Child," supra note 17 at 80.
50. See JERI CLAUSING, "Privacy Advocates Fault New DoubleClick Service," *N.Y. Times*, Feb. 15, 2000, at C2; "Privacy on the Internet," *N.Y. Times*, Feb. 22, 2000, at A22; "Marketing the DoubleClick Way," *Industry Standard*, Mar. 13, 2000; WILL RODGER, "Activists Charge DoubleClick Double Cross," USA Today.com (June 7, 2000), *available at* http://www.usatoday.com/life/cyber/tech/cth211.htm.
51. See DAVID HAMILTON, "The Gadfly: Privacy Cop Richard Smith is Out to Keep Companies Honest Whether Or Not They Like It," *Wall St. J.*, Jul. 16, 2001 (advocacy against RealNetworks and Microsoft); "Music Software 'Listens In'/ Realjukebox Secretly

Reported Listeners' Tastes," *Newsday* (New York, NY), Nov. 2, 1999, at A47 ("One of the most popular software programs for listening to music on computers is secretly sending details back to a Seattle company about customers' music preferences, including the CDs they listen to and how many songs they copy, a security expert found. The company, RealNetworks Inc., acknowledged that information from its free 'RealJukebox' software, used by more than 12 million people, is sent via the Internet to its headquarters."). There were also other examples involving plans to sell data to third parties by Toysmart.com and AOL. See infra note 102 (Toysmart.com); MARCELO HALPERN AND AJAY K. MEHROTRA, "From International Treaties to Internet Norms: The Evolution of International Trademark Disputes in the Internet Age," 21 *U. Pa. J. Int'l. Econ. L.* 523, 536–7 (2000) (noting the reaction of AOL users to a potential change in AOL's privacy policy permitting personal data sales to third parties. AOL users protested strongly and AOL decided not to alter the privacy policy).

52. See, for example, STEVE PAIN, "Big Brother in Disguise to Play Internet-Spy," *Birmingham Post*, Mar. 13, 2001, at 24 (quoting Richard Smith).

53. "Online Ad Agency Gives Up Plan To Sell Data; DoubleClick Bows To Privacy Advocates," *St. Louis Post-Dispatch*, Mar. 3, 2000, at C6. "Bowing to intense pressure from government authorities, investors and privacy advocates, Web advertising firm DoubleClick on Thursday backed off plans to amass a giant online database of people's names and Internet habits. DoubleClick's reversal was applauded immediately by several leaders of the broad backlash against Web-privacy intrusions. Weeks of legal actions and government probes into DoubleClick Inc. have placed the online company at the center of a growing clash between businesses seeking to exploit the Internet's pervasiveness and those fearful of the consequences. 'This is a great step forward for Internet privacy,' said Ari Schwartz of the Center for Democracy and Technology, a Washington-based group that tracks civil liberties on the Internet." Id.

54. See, for example, "Relaxing Limits on Export and Encryption Software: Hearing on the Security and Freedom Through Encryption Act (SAFE), H.R. 695, Before the House Judiciary Committee, Subcommittee on Courts and Intellectual Property," 105th Cong. (Mar. 20, 1997) (testimony of Marc Rotenberg, Director, Electronic Privacy Information Center); *Computer Technology Security: Hearing on CyberAttack: The National Protection Plan and its Privacy Implications, Before the Senate Judiciary Comm., Subcomm. On Technology, Terrorism, and Government Information*, 106th Cong. (Feb. 1, 2000) (testimony of Marc Rotenberg, Executive Director, Electronic Privacy Information Center); *Electronic Privacy: Hearing on HR 5018 "Electronic Communications Privacy Act of 2000," HR 4987, "Digital Privacy Act of 2000," and HR 4908, "Notice of Electronic Monitoring Act"*, 106th Cong. (Sept. 6, 2000) (testimony of Marc Rotenberg, Executive Director, Electronic Privacy Information Center).

55. See PAMELA SAMUELSON, "Intellectual Property and the Digital Economy: Why the Anti-Circumvention Regulations Need To Be Revised," 14 *Berkeley Tech. L. J.* 519, 544 n.138 (1999).

56. See "Privacy Advocate Calls for Strict Rules from Regulator, Encourages 'Just Say No' Attitude from Parents Against Web Sites That Solicit Personal Data from Kids," *Business Wire*, Apr. 20, 1999 ("Junkbusters Corp. President Jason Catlett today urged Federal regulators and parents to stand firm against marketers who want to use the Internet to extract information from the nation's children. 'From Microsoft to the 'young investor' site that asked kids to report on their parents' financial assets, Internet companies have

demonstrated they cannot be trusted to respect anyone's privacy. Parents and regulators must vigorously defend our children against the electronic molestation of their identities,' Catlett said."); "Privacy, For the Sake of Children," *Capital Times* (Madison, WI), June 30, 2000, at 1D ("The Children's Online Privacy Protection Act – or COPPA, as its usually called – went into effect on April 21, 2000. Its 'enactment marked a triumph for children's advocates, who have agitated since the mid-1990s for basic protections for the Internet's youngest users.'"); "White House Starts Privacy Push," *Chicago Sun-Times*, July 31, 1998, at 31 ("'On the main privacy issues, the ones that confront the country today, the administration is still reluctant to make the hard decisions,' said Marc Rotenberg, executive director of the Electronic Privacy Information Center.").

57. See "New Serious Side to Child's Play on Web," *N.Y. Times*, Nov. 27, 1998, at A4 ("Privacy advocates have raised different concerns about the law. Marc Rotenberg, executive director of the Electronic Privacy Information Center, a privacy advocacy group in Washington, favors online privacy protections for adults, too, and would have preferred legislation based not on parental consent, but on the idea of privacy for all."); "Protecting Kids' Privacy Online," *Newsbytes*, Mar. 11, 1999 ("'It's a parental notification law, which has some pluses and some minuses,' says Marc Rotenberg of the Electronic Privacy Information Center. 'What we really need is a base-line privacy bill for all users of the Internet. If this bill helps us move beyond industry self-regulation, we're moving in the right direction.'").

58. See, for example, "The End of Privacy," supra note 3 at 21; PENENBERG, supra note 3 at 182.

59. ELLICKSON, supra note 4 at 12–13. Especially influential early on were the norms developed by the Organization for Economic Cooperation and Development (OECD), which endorsed eight "privacy guidelines." Id. Marc Rotenberg, Executive Director of the Electronic Privacy Information Center, has stated that OECD's eight principles for data protection are still the "benchmark for assessing privacy policy and legislation." "Oversight Hearing on Electronic Communications Privacy Policy Disclosures, Before the House Committee on the Judiciary, Subcommittee on Courts and Intellectual Property," 106th Cong. 78 (1999); OECD Guidelines on the Protection of Privacy and Transborder Flows of Personal Data (Sept. 23, 1980), *available at* http://www.oecd.org/dsti/sti/it/secur/prod/PRIV-EN.HTM.

60. WILLIAM SAFIRE, "Stalking the Internet," *N.Y. Times*, May 29, 2000, at A15.

61. A norm paternalist is one who seeks to enforce norms of behavior out of paternalistic motivations despite the fact that the subjects of the potential norm would not themselves prefer the change. It is typical to discuss paternalism in a legal context. The norm proselytizer has a wider scope of interest, however, one that includes both the formal legal domain and the informal social domain. Thus, the norm paternalist would seek to exert paternalistic authority against the inclinations of the norm subjects in both the formal and informal domains.

62. See JOHN STUART MILL, *On Liberty* (1859), reprinted in *On Liberty and Other Essays*, at 14 (John Gray, ed., 1991); RICHARD J. ARNESON, "Mill Versus Paternalism," 90 *Ethics* 470 (1980); JEAN BRAUCHER, "Defining Unfairness: Empathy and Economic Analysis at the Federal Trade Commission," 68 *B.U.L. Rev.* 349, 384–7 (1988); JOEL FEINBERG, "Legal Paternalism," 1 *Can. J. Phil.* 105 (1971); see DANNY SCOCCIA, "Paternalism and Respect for Autonomy," 100 *Ethics* 318 (1990).

63. "Laws Should Define Who Owns 'Our' Data," *Newsday* (New York, NY), Apr. 25, 2000, at A37 ("Who cares if once-intimate details of people's lives circulate from one databank to another? What important interest or principle is threatened by that?").

64. "A majority of Internet users (61%) say they would be positive toward receiving banner ads tailored to their personal interests rather than receiving random ads. This represents about 56 million adult users interested in such personalization. More than two-thirds of Internet users (68%) say they would provide personal information in order to receive tailored banner ads, if notice and opt out are provided. This represents about 63 million adult users." Excerpt from Dr. Alan F. Westin, *Personalized Marketing and Privacy on the Net: What Consumers Want*, (Nov. 1999), *at* http://www.pandab.org/doubleclicksummary. html.

65. Sunstein, supra note 4, at 912.

66. See Eric A. Posner, *Law and Social Norms* Chapter 8 (2000).

67. Id.

68. See, for example, Walmart.com Privacy Policy, *at* http://www.walmart.com/cservice/ca_sp_privacypolicy.gsp?NavMode=3 (last visited Aug. 13, 2001) (stating that "[y]ou have the right to control your personal information as you see fit.").

69. Robert MacMillan, "Congress to Air Public Concerns Over Privacy," *Newsbytes*, Sept. 5, 2000 (privacy advocates are split with some advocating very strong privacy protections).

70. See, for example, Litman, supra note 2 at 1287.

71. See Fred O. Williams, "Area Man Wins Cybercash," *Buffalo News*, Oct. 28, 2000, at C1 (noting that "consumers appear willing to exchange personal data for free prizes and cash").

72. "Websites with a Personal Touch," *Financial Times* (London), Mar. 15, 1999, at 6 ("Do consumers mind being asked to part with information in order to receive personalised goods and services? Most early research would suggest that they do not, so long as they perceive a benefit, such as reading a newspaper for free or saving time.").

73. See, for example, "Harold McGraw III Says Internet Has Sparked a Revolution on Multichannel Publishing," *Business Wire*, June 18, 2001; see also Schwartz, supra note 18 at 1688–91 (noting the concept of notice being equivalent to privacy protection seems to be capturing much of the policy debate).

74. See Dorothy Glancy, "At the Intersection of Visible and Invisible Worlds: United States Privacy and the Interent,"16 *Santa Clara Computer & High Tech. L. J.* 357, 370 (2000). "Whether Internet users in the United States must be asked to consent to each appropriation of information about their on-line activities (opt-in) or, rather, whether Internet users have implicitly consented to general use of digitized profiles of their Internet activities so that each Internet user must expressly withdraw consent to sale of such information (opt-out), remains a very contentious privacy issue." See generally Jeff Sovern, "Opting In, Opting Out, or no Options at All: The Fight For Control of Personal Information," 74 *Wash. L. Rev.* 1033 (1999).

75. See, for example, http://www.privacyalliance.org/resources/ppguidelines.shtml. "Individuals must be given the opportunity to exercise choice regarding how individually identifiable information collected from them may be used when such use is unrelated to the purpose for which the information was collected. At a minimum, individuals should be given the opportunity to opt out of such use." Id.

76. See Federal Trade Commission, Self-Regulation and Privacy Online: A Report to Congress 2 (July 1999) [hereinafter *1999 FTC Report to Congress*].

77. AMY BORRUS, "The Stage Seems Set For Net Privacy Rules This Year," *Business Week,* Mar. 5, 2001. "Instead, privacy hawks will push for so-called 'opt-in' rules that require companies to get users' prior consent before collecting or sharing personal info. Opt-in is a far higher hurdle than opt-out, which allows a company to gather data until a consumer orders it to stop. Privacy gurus hope President Bush will be their strongest ally. As a candidate, Bush said customers 'should be allowed to opt in to information sharing.' Says Rotenberg: 'This is one campaign promise we're not going to forget.' " Id.

78. THOMAS M. COOLEY, *A Treatise on the Law of Torts or the Wrongs Which Arise Independent of Contract* 29 (2nd ed., 1888). With respect to privacy, the specific right articulated by Cooley was the "right to one's person." Id. Cooley suggested that the personal right was that of "complete immunity from attacks and injuries." Id. This he characterized as the right "to be let alone." Id.; see also "Legislative Hearing on H.R. 3365 Drivers Privacy Protection Act of 1993 Before the United States House of Representatives Committee on the Judiciary, Subcommittee on Civil and Constitutional Rights," 103rd Cong. (Feb. 3, 1994) (statement of Mary J. Culnan, Associate Professor, School of Business, Georgetown University).

79. DREW CLARK, "Activists Unite To Push For Stronger Privacy Laws," *Nat'l. J's Tech. Daily,* Jan. 30, 2001. "For the privacy advocates, the proliferation of privacy-invading technology means that Congress should pass privacy legislation rather than forcing consumers to confront privacy questions each time a new technology is introduced. 'Every new service offering raises new privacy issues because Congress and the administration are reluctant to apply a new privacy standard,' said Rotenberg. He praised the Edwards bill, which would require companies that make online tracking software to inform users and give them the right to access their personal data, as 'probably higher up the curve in terms of good privacy legislation' than most." Id.

80. Seventy-nine percent of American consumers rate as "absolutely essential" that customers should be afforded the opportunity of seeing their transaction records so that their accuracy can be checked and any mistakes can be corrected. Excerpt from DR. ALAN F. WESTIN, *The Era of Consensual Marketing is Coming,* (Dec. 1998), *at* http://www.pandab.org/1298essary/html.

81. See, for example, Final Report of the FTC Advisory Committee on Online Access and Security, May 1, 2000, *at* http://www.ftc.gov/acoas/papers/finalreport.htm [hereinafter Online Access and Security], § 2.5.1 ("For businesses this approach would lead to a substantial increase in costs, including, among others, the costs of required modifications or new design requirements placed on existing systems, new storage costs, new personnel costs, new legal costs and losses due to disclosure of internal practices and proprietary information.").

82. See, for example, Citigroup Privacy Promise, supra note 19 ("We will tell our customers how and where to conveniently access their account information at http://www.citibank.com/privacy/, except when we're prohibited by law, and how to notify us about errors which we will promptly correct.").

83. STEWART BAKER, "Cyberterrorism, Industrial Espionage and Crime on the Internet, Regulating Technology for Law Enforcement," 4 *Tex. Rev. Law & Pol.* 51, 53 (1999). "If

you are going to protect communications from cyberterrorism, if you are going to prevent people from breaking into computers and stealing valuable information, and if you are going to trust your life and your personal data to a computer, you want guarantees that the information will be kept secure. Cryptography and encryption – the ability to scramble data – are some of the building blocks of security." Id.

84. The European Union (EU) has recognized that self-regulation may in certain circumstances constitute "adequate" privacy protection for purposes of the EU Directive's ban on data transfer to countries lacking "adequate" safeguards. The EU has noted, however, that nonlegal rules such as industry association guidelines are relevant to the "adequacy" determination only to the extent they are complied with and that compliance levels, in turn, are directly related to the availability of sanctions and/or external verification of compliance. See European Commission, Directorate General XV, Working Document: Judging Industry Self-Regulation: When Does it Make a Meaningful Contribution to the Level of Data Protection in a Third Country?, (Jan. 14. 1998), *available at* http://www.europa.eu.int/comm/internal_ market/en/media/data-prot/wpdocs/wp7en.htm.

85. The website industry views the norms proposed by the privacy proselytizers as unworkable and overly expensive to implement. Todd R. Weiss, *Bush Faces His First Privacy Challenge: Proposals from Industry, Advocates Differ, Computer World*, Jan. 22, 2001, at 7. The industry's response has been to promote less demanding norms.

86. Some proselytizers have advocated for ownership of one's personal data as the best means to secure the set of rights entailed by the second order right to data privacy. See Lawrence Lessig, "The Architecture of Privacy," 1 *Vand. J. Ent. L. & Prac.* 56, 63–5 (1999). Such a right would be in tension with the First Amendment, however. See generally Eugene Volokh, "Freedom of Speech and Informational Privacy: The Troubling Implications of a Right to Stop People From Speaking About You," 52 *Stan. L. Rev.* 1049 (2000).

87. See, for example, Samuelson, supra note 26 at 1143 ("If information privacy is a civil liberty, it may make no more sense to propertize personal data than to commodify voting rights.").

88. Opinion polls show increasing public concern with respect to online privacy. See Glenn R. Simpson, "E-Commerce Firms Start to Rethink Opposition to Privacy Regulation as Abuses, Anger Rise," *Wall St. J.*, Jan. 6, 2000, at A24. A recent poll found that 92 percent of Internet users were uncomfortable about websites sharing personal information with other sites. "Business Week/Harris Poll: A growing threat," Bus. Wk. Online, Mar. 20, 2000, *at* http://www.businessweek.com:/2000/00_12/63673010.htm?scriptframed.

89. "Sellers Try to Soothe Fears About Personal Data Safety," *USA Today*, Apr. 27, 2001, at 2B (quoting Hans Peter Brondmo).

90. See sources cited supra note 15.

91. See Scott Killingsworth, "Minding Your Own Business: Privacy Policies in Principle and Practice," 7 *J. Intell. Prop. L.* 57, 62 (1999). "The obvious product of this distrust is that people avoid disclosing personal information by opting against online transactions and website registration. Less obvious but equally troubling for online marketers is the 'garbage in' syndrome: in two recent surveys, over forty percent of Americans who registered at websites admitted to providing false information some of the time, mainly

because of privacy concerns; the figure for European registrants was over fifty-eight percent.... The message to marketers is clear: if you want useful and accurate data, earn it by assuring consumers that you will use it appropriately." Id.

92. See RICHARD H. MCADAMS, "The Origin, Development and Regulation of Norms," 96 *Mich. L. Rev.* 338, 355–72 (1997). Similarly, Cooter's internalization account appears not to play a role because websites are commercial enterprises that are not readily susceptible to the psychological phenomenon of internalization. See ROBERT D. COOTER, "Decentralized Law for a Complex Society: The Structural Approach to Adjudicating the New Law Merchant," 144 *U. Pa. L. Rev.* 1643, 1690–4 (1996).

93. See generally POSNER, supra note 66.

94. "Gallup Poll Uncovers Opportunities to Build Consumer Confidence in 2001 by Implementing Best Practices for Online Privacy," *PR Newswire*, Jan. 16, 2001.

95. Prior to the burst of the Internet bubble, the mere eventuality of future visits to the site in itself was money in the bank because Internet companies were valued in the market in important part based on the number of "hits" the site received.

96. As this discussion has indicated, there are different ways to respect privacy. A privacy policy will be used in the example as it is the most basic means.

97. See supra note 18 (discussing how some companies are hiring chief privacy officers).

98. See generally *1999 FTC Report to Congress*, supra note 76.

99. In the Federal Trade Commissions's 1998 study, only 14 precent of websites were addressing consumer privacy issues. *1998 FTC Report to Congress*, supra note 2. As the consumer sense of entitlement grows, the chances of plaintiffs' lawyers prevailing in lawsuits grows. See MATT FLEISCHER, "Lawyers Eye Privacy Cases Against Many DoubleClick Rivals," 22 (27) *Nat'l. Law J.* A1 (Feb. 28, 2000) (noting many lawyers are now searching for the next privacy lawsuit against DoubleClick competitors, such as Engage, 24/7 Media, MatchLogic, Flycast, and L90, each collecting over 100 megabytes of clickstream data-information per day).

100. See SCHWARTZ, supra note 20 at 824. "In light of these flaws, the true argument in favor of the Privacy Policy can only be as follows: when a Web site says something about its data processing practices – even if this statement is vague or reveals poor practice – the visitor to the site is deemed to be in agreement with these practices so long as she sticks around.... Thus, a site that said 'we reserve the right to do whatever we want with the information we collect' [is] deemed to have provided notice of information practices." Id.

101. Toysmart Privacy Statement, *at* http://www.ftc.gov/os/2000/07/toyexh1.pdf.

102. See "FTC Announces Settlement with Bankrupt Website, Toysmart.com, Regarding Alleged Privacy Policy Violations," (July 21, 2000) *at* http://www.ftc.gov/opa/2000/07/toysmart2.htm; "Judge Is Urged to Reject Toysmart.com Settlement," *Wall St. J.*, Jul. 26, 2000, at B2. In addition, Toysmart faced a lawsuit filed by TRUSTe, which contended that Toysmart was in violation of its online agreement not to sell consumer data to third parties. See ELINOR ABREU, "TRUSTe to File Antiprivacy Brief Against Toysmart," *Industry Standard*, June 30, 2000, *available at* http://www.thestandard.com/chapter/display/0,1151,16577,00.html. See generally SUSAN E. GINDIN, "Lost and Found in Cyberspace: Informational Privacy in the Age

of the Internet," 34 *San Diego L. Rev.* 1153, 1180 (1997). This example demonstrates how noninternalized the norm is for a website. This is a difference between humans and firms. Once internalized, a human conforms to a norm in a manner that cannot be readily changed. A firm's commitments can completely change with the installation of new management.

103. See ANDREW B. BUXBAUM AND LOUIS A. CURCIO, "When You Can't Sell to Your Customers, Try Selling Your Customers (But Not Under the Bankruptcy Code)," 8 *Am. Bankr. Inst. L. Rev.* 395, 411–12 (2000) (arguing that the appearance of privacy policies would create an expectation of privacy).

104. See DAN KAHAN, "Gentle Nudges vs. Hard Shoves: Solving the Sticky Norms Problem," 67 *U. Chi. L. Rev.* 607, 611–18 (2000).

105. See MCADAMS, supra note 92 at 366.

106. This is modeled by the critical mass phenomenon of "tipping." See THOMAS C. SCHELLING, *Micromotives and Macrobehavior* 102–4 (1978). Tipping occurs when the success of a social practice depends on the formation of a critical mass and enough actors sign on or sign off such that the practice succeeds or fails. If enough actors sign on, the activity is tipped in. If enough actors sign off, the practice is tipped out. Because a relatively small number of crossover actors may cause a norm to tip, social norms may shift relatively suddenly. Id.

107. DAVID STOUT, "Government and Internet Ad Group Reach Agreement on Data Gleaned from Web Surfers," *N.Y. Times,* July 28, 2000, at C6.

108. See HETCHER, supra note 25 at 2053.

109. In a series of hearings in October and November of 1995, the FTC reported to Congress on consumer protection issues, including privacy concerns. See "Prepared Statement of FTC on "Internet Privacy" Before the House Comm. on Judiciary" (Mar. 26, 1998) *at* http://www.ftc.gov/os/1998/9803/privacy.htm. BRIAN KREBBS, "IT Industry Council Signals Privacy-Law Advocacy," *Newsbytes,* Feb. 2, 2001 (due to public outcry lawmakers are suggesting federal electronic privacy protections); see also "PrivacyRight, Inc. Forms Strategic Equity Partnership with Venture Factory," *PR Newswire,* June 6, 2000; ROSALIND C. TRITT, "Privacy: A Threat to Free Speech?," *Presstime,* Jan. 2001, at 27.

110. REP. BILLY TANZAN, CATO Online Privacy Workshop, Washington, DC (May 1999).

111. 15 U.S.C. § 45(a) (1994). The FTC prosecutes "[u]nfair methods of competition . . . and unfair or deceptive acts or practices in or affecting commerce" under Section 45 of the Federal Trade Commission Act (FTCA). Id. Section 57(b) authorizes the prosecution of actions to enforce Section 45. Id. § 57(b). Section 57(a) permits the FTC to create rules to prohibit deceptive or unfair practices prevalent in certain industries. Id. § 57(a). Note that the FTC's framework for regulating unfair practices does not require ownership of personal data. The fact that data subjects may have de facto control over their data is enough to generate an instance of an unfair or deceptive trade practice. This means that the agency may gain jurisdiction over website activities without a change in the intellectual property status of personal data.

112. The FTC explicitly states that it takes its normative framework from the privacy policy community. See *1998 FTC Report to Congress,* supra note 2.

113. *1999 FTC Report to Congress,* supra note 76 at 3.

114. Lawsuits filed so far have involved more than simple unconsented data collection and use. See In re DoubleClick, Inc., Federal Trade Commission (filed Feb. 10, 2000), *at* http://www.epic.org/privacy/internet/ftc/DCLK_complaint.pdf; Judnick v. DoubleClick, No. CV-421 (Marin Cty. Sup. Ct., filed Jan. 27, 2000), *at* http://www. perkinscoie.com/resource/ecomm/netcase/complaint1.pdf; PAMELA PARKER, "Doubleclick's Legal Troubles Deepen," InternetNews.com, *at* http://www.internetnews. com/bus-news/chapter/0,,3_299771,00.html (discussing four different cases against Doubleclick, Inc.); The Perkins Coie LLP Internet Case Digest, *at* http://www. perkinscoie.com/resource/ecomm/netcase/Cases-18.htm (summarizing other cases against Doubleclick, Inc.).

115. Large sites are prominent, and they would run the risk of coming under FTC scrutiny for questionable, albeit legal, trade practices, were they to fail to make a respectable effort to show respect for user privacy, as newly spelled out by the FTC, in its fair information practice principles. In contrast, small websites would plausibly have a dominating preference to not provide privacy policies. Because they are small, they will be able to fly under the FTC's radar. With the FIPPs, the FTC had merely outlined the principles that it contends are fair. It did not mandate them.

116. See HETCHER, supra note 25.

117. In 1998, after finding self-regulation of children's online privacy to be inadequate, the FTC recommended to Congress that it create legislation, which Congress quickly did, enacting the Children's Online Privacy Protection Act (COPPA). On October 21, 1998, the President signed COPPA into law. Children's Online Privacy Protection Act of 1998 Title XIII, Omnibus Consolidated and Emergency Supplemental Appropriations Act, 1999, Pub. L. 105–277, 112 Stat. 2681, 2681–728 (codified at 15 U.S.C. §§ 6501–6506) (Oct. 21, 1998). "The stated goals of the Act are: (1) to enhance the parental involvement in a child's online activities in order to protect the privacy of children in the online environment; (2) to help protect the safety of children in online fora such as chat rooms, home pages, and pen-pal services in which children may make public postings of identifying information; (3) to maintain the security of children's personal information collected online; and (4) to limit the collection of personal information from children without parental consent." 144 Cong. Rec. S12741-04 (Oct. 21, 1998) (statement of Sen. Bryan).

118. See HETCHER, supra note 25 at 2047.

119. Id.

120. See generally MANCUR OLSON, *The Logic Of Collective Action* (1965); LESSIG, supra note 5 at 996.

121. 1998 *FTC Report to Congress*, supra note 2 at 17.

122. JOHN GRAUBERT AND JILL COLEMAN, "Consumer Protection and Antitrust Enforcement at the Speed of Light: The FTC Meets the Internet," 25 *Can.-U.S. L. J.* 275, 290 (1999) ("In the case of Internet privacy, several technologies potentially capable of protecting the online privacy of consumers are evidently already on the market or under development. Technology-based privacy solutions may eventually provide consumers with the confidence and security that they need to conduct business on the Internet on a global scale."); see "P3P: Just a Start," *ZDWire*, Jul. 17, 2000 ("There's no disputing that privacy has emerged as a leading issue of the Internet age. A whole industry is springing up around it, with software and service providers rushing to offer the latest

and greatest solution for protecting an individual's personal information and identity online.").

123. ZeroKnowledge, Inc., Advertisement, *Wired*, Aug. 2000, at 5–6. ZeroKnowledge Systems lets Internet users surf the net anonymously. See http://www.zeroknowledge.com (last visited Sept. 4, 2001). ZeroKnowledge Systems' Freedom software uses the encryption and several different computers to mask its users' identities even from itself. Id. The Freedom IP overlay network opens up an anonymous route, with encryption, from server to server. Id.

124. Id.

125. IMMANUAL KANT, *The Metaphysics Of Morals* 187–9 (Mary Gregor, trans., 1991) (1797).

126. ZeroKnowledge, Inc., Advertisement, *Wired*, Aug. 2000, at 5–6.

127. Id.

128. Id.

129. Netcreations, Inc., Advertisement, *Industry Standard*, July 10–17, 2000, at 150–1.

130. Id.

131. Id.

132. PrivaSeek, Inc., Advertisement (on file with the author).

133. Id.

134. Id.

135. Id.

136. The strong moral tone of these advertisements is seen by contrasting them with ads meant to alert users to security issues. Here the threatening activities are illegal, and the need is to protect oneself from theft. There is no attempt to create moral outrage on the part of consumers in the text of these advertisements.

Chapter Fourteen

1. Netcreations, Inc., Advertisement, *Industry Standard*, Jul. 10–17, 2000, at 150–1.

2. See SANDEEP JUNNARKAR, "FTC Faces Suit for Access to Privacy Complaints," CNET News.com, October 12, 1999 (quoting David Sobel, general counsel for EPIC, "A large part of the privacy debate in the last couple of years has centered around industry claims that there are adequate systems in place to deal with privacy problems.") The most pervasive industry response has been the emergence of the *privacy policy*, whereby websites provide a link from their homepage to text describing the website's practices with regard to consumer data. In addition to providing *notice* of their data-related practices, many websites allow users to *opt-out* of some or all of the site's practices. A smaller number of websites, particularly those dealing with *sensitive data*, are beginning to collect data only after the user has expressly chosen to *opt-in* to the site's practices. Some websites are beginning to provide consumers with *access* to their data stored on the firm's servers, and allowing these consumers to contest the accuracy of this data. In addition, a growing number of websites are representing that they will store user data in a secure manner. Occasionally, websites will promise to never sell data to third parties. Finally, in a very recent development, larger firms are beginning to employ a *chief privacy officer*, whose task it is to oversee the data practices of the firm's website to further ensure compliance with emerging privacy norms.

3. JESSICA LITMAN, "Information Privacy/Information Property," 52 *Stan. L. Rev.* 1283, 1287 (2000).

4. See also STEVEN HETCHER, "The FTC as Internet Privacy Norm Entrepreneur," 53 *Vand. L. Rev.* 2041 (2000). See generally, ROBERT ELLICKSON, "The Market for Social Norms," 3 *Am. Law & Econ. Rev.* 1, 2 (2001) (setting out supply and demand model for norm emergence generally).

5. Norm entrepreneurs are actors who promote the change of norms. CASS R. SUNSTEIN, "Social Norms and Social Roles," 96 *Colum. L. Rev.* 903, 909 (1996). Norm proselytizers promote norms, for moral reasons, which they themselves accept. Norm proselytizers, then, are a subcategory of norm entrepreneurs. The word *proselytize* is appropriate because it would be unhelpfully reductionist to describe these entrepreneurs as merely fostering preferences for data privacy in the manner that Madison Avenue seeks to create preferences. Privacy norm proselytizers seek to arouse the moral consciousness of consumers vis-à-vis website's collection and use of their personal data. Privacy activists have functioned as norm proselytizers. HETCHER, supra note 4 at 907. ELLICKSON, supra note 4 at 10–12, seeks to develop a richer vocabulary by distinguishing among a variety of specialists who supply new norms. "Change agents" are actors or enforcers who are relatively early in supplying a new norm. Ellickson distinguishes among these subcategories of change agents: self-motivated leaders, norm entrepreneurs, and opinion leaders. The following discussion will indicate that some of these subcategories may be aptly applied to norm creation in cyberspace. In addition, I will suggest that the norm proselytizer is aptly viewed as a distinct type of change agent.

6. See PAMELA SAMUELSON, "Privacy as Intellectual Property?," 52 *Stan. L. Rev.* 1125, 1163 (2000) ("The more enlightened private sector firms are coming to realize that fuller adherence to privacy principles will promote consumer trust which will, in turn, promote commerce"); SHAWN A. SPARKS, "The Direct Marketing Model and Virtual Identity: Why the United States Should Not Create Legislative Controls on the Use of Online Consumer Personal Data," 18 *Dick J. Intl. L.* 517, 549 (2000). ("In the practical terms of the online environment, however, consumers have the option of choice. Unlike forced commercial interactions with utility-like cable providers, consumers may interact only with those websites that are to their liking. Websites that post adequate privacy policies, and adhere to them, will earn consumer trust and consumer dollars. Online businesses are increasingly aware of that concern, and will compete in the arena of privacy service in the same manner in which they compete on terms such as price.").

7. See STEVEN HETCHER, "Creating Safe Social Norms in a Dangerous World," 23. *S. Cal. L. Rev.* 1, 78 (1999); STEVEN A. HETCHER, Norms (1991) (Ph.D. dissertation).

8. See ERIC POSNER, *Law and Social Norms* (2000) (signaling theory account of emergence and maintenance of social norms).

9. For a theoretical account touching on some of the general difficulties of norm emergence in cyberspace, see MARK A. LEMLEY, "Shrinkwraps in Cyberspace," 35 *Jurimetrics* 311, 314 (1995) ("In addition, the rapid growth in the number of network users has worked to transform cyberspace in important respects. With its forty or fifty million users, the Internet is no longer comprised of a limited set of close-knit communities in which private ordering can be based on shared values and understanding."). Ellickson has noted the importance of case studies for the further development of the law and norms approach. See ROBERT C. ELLICKSON, "Law and Economics Discovers Social Norms," 27 *J. Legal Stud.* 537, (1998).

Over the past forty odd years, law and economics has developed on twin tracks. On the one hand, it has developed at a theoretical level, and on the other hand, it has developed by being persuasively applied to explain an ever-expanding set of specific social institutions and practices. In the decade-old development of law and norms theory, it has begun to develop along theoretical and applied tracks as well. Although there have been numerous notable applications of the new law and norms theory, there is much room for more work in applying these theoretical accounts to new situations, both to illuminate the concrete situation and to help better understand the strengths and weaknesses of the competing theories of norms. Recent law and norms literature has included a number of significant case studies. See, for example, ROBERT COOTER AND JANET T. LANDA, "Personal Versus Impersonal Trade: The Size of Trading Groups and Contract Law," *Intl. Rev. L. & Econ.* 15 (1984); LISA BERNSTEIN, "Merchant Law in a Merchant Court: Rethinking the Code's Search for Immanent Business Norms," 144 *U. Pa. L. Rev.* 1765 (1996); RICHARD H. McADAMS, "Cooperation and Conflict: The Economics of Group Status Production and Race Discrimination," 108 *Harv. L. Rev.* 1003 (1995); MARK D. WEST, "Legal Rules and Social Norms in Japan's Secret World of Sumo," 26 *J. Legal Stud.* 165 (1997). None of these case studies, however, has applied law and norms methodology in an online context.

10. An increase in the supply of online privacy would not, by itself, mean that the online privacy problem is getting better, however. This can be illustrated with a comparison to the problem of greenhouse gas emissions. Increased demand for greenhouse-gas-reducing technologies may lead to increased supply of these technologies. Nevertheless, the net level of greenhouse gas emissions may continue to increase simply because the overall level is growing at such a rapid rate so as to more than offset the reductions due to the technological innovations – so too with personal data. Privacy protections may be on the rise; nevertheless, the overall amount of personal data collected and used may be growing so dramatically as to offset whatever gains in privacy are produced.

11. For example, despite its high profile, Amazon recently announced that it was changing its privacy policy in a manner that was less favorable to consumer privacy interests. "Amazon Draws Fire for DVD Pricing Test, Privacy Policy Change," *Wall. St. J.*, Sept. 14, 2000. Presumably Amazon calculated that, despite the possible negative impact on its reputation as a respecter of privacy, it was worth it to make the change of practice due to the important role that consumer data plays in its business model. Ebay also recently changed its policy in a consumer-unfriendly fashion. "Ebay Says It May Sell Information on Users in Event of Acquisition," *Wall St. J.*, Apr. 3, 2001, at B7. One commentator remarked that what hope could there be for online privacy if even a prosperous site such as Ebay would make such a move. This comment fails to appreciate the fact, however, that Ebay is in an unusual position in that, owing to its business model, Ebay has unusually rich access to valuable data on consumer preferences and buying activities and thus for it to provide respect would involve an unusually large sacrifice, one that Ebay apparently does not judge to be justified by the prospect of increased consumer trust.

12. For example, health-related sites and financial sites appear to provide higher levels of privacy. This appears to be responsive to consumer demand. See STEPHANIE OLSON AND PATRICK ROSS, "Studies Out to Debunk Privacy Legislation," May 8, 2001 CNET News.com (quoting Rep. Michael Doyle, D–Penn, "Consumers seemed more concerned with financial and medical privacy than with other types.").

13. A number of commentators have contemplated the creation of an explicit market in data transactions. Generally, this is taken to mean that individuals will be able to alienate their data to websites for valuable consideration. Much less often discussed is the flip side of a free market in personal data, which could involve firms collecting data about a person from other sources and then seeking to sell this data to the person. To some extent, such a market exists already. Currently data brokers have personal profiles for sale. The existence of these data brokers has already led to some well publicized and troubling results.

14. See JUNNARKAR, supra note 2.

15. LITMAN, supra note 3.

16. See STEPHANIE OLSEN, "Top Web Sites Compromise Consumer Privacy," CNET News.com, December 17, 1999 (quoting Jason Catlett).

17. SAMUELSON, supra note 6 at 1161 ("[T]here is some evidence that American-based commercial based Web sites provide more notice about privacy policies now than they did a year ago. Some progress also continues in implementation of the other principles.").

18. http://www.1800flowers.com/flowers/security/index.asp.

19. http://wwwnationalgeographic.com/community/privacy.html. Seeking to highlight its public-spirited nature, this statement continues, "We encourage other sites to join us in this effort."

20. http://www.walmart.com/cservice/ca_securityprivacy.gsp. Walmart has an exemplary privacy policy. Sites of old economy firms like WalMart are of particular interest because they demonstrate the penetration of the growing ethos of Internet privacy beyond the now outdated notion of the dot-com economy. The Internet was never a marketplace but rather a technology platform.

21. http://www.nike.com/info_policies_privacy.jhtml.jsessionid.

22. http://disney.go.com/investors/wdig/legal/wdig_privacy.html.

23. Id.

24. http://sears.com.

25. http://www.madonnafanclub.com/privacy.html.

26. Id.

27. FTC commissioner, Sheila Anthony, has stated, "[M]any privacy policies are beginning to look like complex legal documents."; *Time* Magazine, July 2, 2001, (cover story) (suggesting reading privacy policies but warning of "fine print.").

28. http://www.weather.com/common/home/privacy.html.

29. http://www.toyota.com/html/privacy/index.html.

30. Id.

31. See, for example, Judnick v. DoubleClick, No. CU-421 (Main Cty. Sup. Ct., filed Jan. 27 2000).

32. Currently, the legal status of privacy policies is ambiguous. See SCOTT KILLINGSWORTH, "Minding Your Own Business: Privacy Policies in Principle and in Practice," *J. Internet L.*, Oct. 1999, at 12. The weather.com privacy policy states, "This statement and the policies outlined here are not intended to and do not give you a contractual or other legal rights."

33. See FTC, Privacy Online: Fair Information Practices in the Electronic Marketplace, A Report to Congress at p. 10 (May 2000), *available at* http://www.ftc.gov/reports/privacy2000/privacy2000.pdf (discussing that the Commission's Survey findings

demonstrate continued improvement with 88% Web sites posting at least one privacy disclosure).

34. See *1998 FTC Report to Congress* at 7–8; *available at* http://www.ftc.gov/reports/privacy3/priv-23a.pdf.

35. Previous studies of privacy policies have provided quantitative measures of changing website practices. See *2000 FTC Report to Congress*; The Georgetown Internet Privacy Policy Survey *available at* http://msb.edu/faculty/culnanm/gippshome.html. While of general interest, these studies do not lend insight as to whether these changes represent true or feigned respect for privacy.

36. See supra note 25.

37. Id.

38. Id.

39. See, for example, http://www.motorola.com ("When you come into our site, our server attaches a small text file to your hard drive – a cookie. Your unique cookie tells us that it is you whenever you re-enter our site, so we can recall where you've previously been on our site, and what if anything, you have in your shopping cart. It is important to note that cookies are safe. They cannot be executed as code or be used to deliver a virus, and personal information is not gathered from them, or stored on them."); Hallmark.com ("An IP [Internet Protocol] address is a number that is assigned to your computer when you are using your browser on the Internet. The servers that serve our web site automatically identify your computer by its IP address. We do log IP addresses, but the addresses are not linked to individual customer accounts nor are they used in any other way to personally identify our customers.").

40. The kinkos.com privacy policy states, "Also, Kinkos uses a reputable third party to collect and accumulate other anonymous data that helps us understand and analyze the Internet experience of our visitors ... this information may be stored in a cookie on your computer's hard drive. However, none of this information is personally identifiable and we only share this information in the aggregate, reflecting overall web site or Internet usage trends."

41. Barnesandnoble.com/help/nc_privacy_policy.

42. http://nokia.com.

43. *1998 FTC report to Congress*, supra note 34 at 7.

44. See supra note 29.

45. See supra note 21.

46. See supra note 40.

47. See motorola.com ("You also have choices with respect to cookies. By modifying your browser preferences, you have the choice to accept all cookies, to be notified when a cookie is set, or to reject all cookies. If you choose to reject all cookies you will be unable to use those services or engage in activities that require registration in order to participate.").

48. See microsoft.com.

49. See supra note 42.

50. http://www.sun.com/privacy; see also Toyota.com ("This information, such as name, mailing address, e-mail address, type of request and possibly additional information, is collected and stored in a manner appropriate to the nature of the data by Toyota and is used to fulfill your request.").

51. See motorola.com ("Motorola users Secure Sockets Layer (SSL) encryption technology, the highest level of security on the Internet. The SSL protocol provides server authentication, data integrity, and privacy on the Web. This security measure helps insure that no imposters, eavesdroppers, or vandals get your personal information. SSL not only encrypts your personal and financial information transmitted, including credit card information, but also verifies the identity of the server and that the original message arrives safely at its destination.").

52. Recently, a Russian hacker, Maxim, succeeded in stealing the credit card information of a large number of consumers whose data was stored on a site. Maxim attempted to extract $100,000 from the site. When they refused to pay, he posted the information for public display on the Internet. See "Extortion on the Internet; A Daring Hacker Tries to Blackmail an e-Tailer – and Sparks New Worries About Credit-Card Cybertheft," *Time*, January 24, 2000, at 56.

53. For example, MTV's website, mtvi.com states, "We have taken steps to ensure that personally identifiable information collected is secure, including limiting the number of people who have physical access to its database servers, as well as electronic security systems and password protections which guard against unauthorized access."; barnesandnoble.com ("To insure that your information is even more secure, once we receive your credit card information, we store it on a server that isn't accessible from the Internet."; microsoft.com ("[D]ata is stored in password-controlled servers with limited access.").

54. For a token effort see barnesandnoble.com ("We're so certain that our online ordering systems are secure that we back it up with a guarantee. In the unlikely event that you are subject to fraudulent charges . . . we will cover the entire liability for you, up to $50, as long as the unauthorized use of your credit card resulted through no fault of your own from purchases made from Barnes & Noble.com while using our secure server.").

55. See supra note 20 at 3.

56. See id. ("Coremetrics is contractually prohibited from using, in any manner, information obtained in the course of providing these services to Walmart.com, other than to help us provide you the best possible shopping experience on our site."); see also Hallmark.com ("If you sign up to become a Hallmark.com affiliate partner, you will be directed to a third party web site who manages the affiliate process, and this third party is not allowed to use the information they collect for any other purpose." It is not indicated, however, what leverage Hallmark would have over these unnamed third parties.

57. Hallmark.com ("Address book information is considered highly confidential and will not be used for promotional purposes by Hallmark or disclosed to third parties.").

58. One might think it a puzzle that the FTC has not promoted CPOs. But this would be predicted by the public choice account of the FTC. The FIPPs promote the growth of the FTC's jurisdiction. CPOs do not.

59. Perhaps the best way for a website to make consumers think it respects their privacy is to really respect their privacy. This might involve having CPOs who really believe in privacy as a moral value. Moral perception and moral reasoning can be complex and subtle activities. Institutional response to moral complexity has best made its presence felt in the professional context in the form of professional ethicists working with Institutional Review Boards (IRBs) in hospitals and medical research facilities. One can view the creation of the CPO as a step in a similar direction. As technology develops, the challenges for privacy promise to develop in lock-step. It is likely that it

will become more complex to determine what privacy requires in particular concrete circumstances.

60. See, for example, PATRICK THIBODEAU, "FTC Official Faults Corporate Privacy Policies," May 7, 2001, Computerworld.com (paraphrasing U.S. Federal Trade Commissioner SHEILA ANTHONY, "Many corporate privacy policies are too hard to find, too long and too confusing."); SHEILA ANTHONY ("In short, many privacy policies are beginning to look like complex legal documents that do not give consumers real choice.")

61. Walmart.com; see also intel.com ("Intel is committed to user privacy in our products and services. This policy outlines our personal information handling practices. If you give us personal information, we will treat it according to this policy."); microsoft.com ("For material changes to this statement, Microsoft.com will notify you by placing prominent notice on the Web site.").

62. See generally "Some British Consumers Work at Plain English Campaign to Promote Simpler Language in Bureaucratic Paperwork," August 10, 2000, *Marketplace*, Anchor: Rachael Myrow; Reporter: Stephen Beard.

63. Citibank is dealing with this problem by offering two versions of its privacy policy, the technical one and the short form. http://www.citibank.com/privacy/.

64. Many sites note that they collect personal information using cookies but that this information is not connected up to personally identifiable information. For example, Kinkos.com states that, "Kinko's does not link your IP address with any information that could personally identify you." But Kinko's also states that, "Kinko's reserves the right, at its sole discretion, to make modifications, alterations or updates to this policy at any time." In other words, Kinkos could at any time change its policy and begin to link up cookie data with personal information. This is precisely what DoubleClick proposed to do before they changed their plans in the face of heavy criticism. See "FTC Lets DoubleClick Off the Hook On Info-Sharing Charge," *E-Business Law Bulletin*, March 2001 at 12.

65. Hallmark.com states, "We reserve the right to change and update the privacy policy; if there is a change in privacy practices, we will notify you via email to specifically tell you what these changes are, including giving you the option to unsubscribe."

66. Numerous sites have demonstrated a flagrant lack of discrimination in their dealings with third parties. The Electronic Frontier Foundation launched a campaign in early June 2001, against Macys.com for giving away information from its bridal registry to its business partners. Toysmart.com explicitly promised not to sell data: "[p]ersonal information voluntarily submitted by visitors . . . is never shared with a third party." Toysmart Privacy Statement, *at* http://www.ftc.gov/os/2000/07/toyexh1.pdf. In bankruptcy, Toysmart then attempted to sell this data. See "FTC Announces Settlement with Bankrupt Website, Toysmart.com, Regarding Alleged Privacy Policy Violations" (July 21, 2000) *at* http://www.ftc.gov/opa/2000/07/toysmart2.htm; "Judge Is Urged to Reject Toysmart.com Settlement," *Wall St. J.*, Jul. 26, 2000, at B2; "Toysmart.com's Plan To Sell Customer Data Is Challenged by FTC," at C8. In addition, Toysmart faced a lawsuit filed by TRUSTe, which contended that Toysmart was in violation of its online agreement not to sell consumer data to third parties. See ELINOR ABREU, "TRUSTe to File Antiprivacy Brief Against Toysmart," *Industry Standard*, June 30, 2000, *available at* http://www.thestandard.com/article/display/0,1151,16577,00.html. "[T]hird party cookies are placed by ad servers on 78 percent of the sites in the Most Popular Group. Of those sites, only 51 percent disclose to consumers that they have allowed third party cookies to

be placed (and they usually locate that disclosure at the end of the policy statement). Unless consumers are technically skilled enough to set their browser to alert them to cookies or to decline all third party cookies, the placement of third party cookies generally goes unnoticed by consumers." See "Prepared Testimony of Sheila F. Anthony, FTC Commissioner Before the Senate Committee on Commerce, Science and Transportation;" Subject – Privacy online: fair information practices in the electronic marketplace, Federal News Service May 25, 2000, *at* http://www.ftc.gov/09/2000/05/index.htm # 22.

67. Some commentators have sarcastically noted the limits of notice as a fairness principle. See, for example, PAUL M. SCHWARTZ, "Internet Privacy and the State," 32 *Conn. L. Rev.* 815, 824 (2000). "In light of these flaws, the true argument in favor of the Privacy Policy can only be as follows: when a Web site says something about its data processing practices – even if this statement is vague or reveals poor practice – the visitor to the site is deemed to be in agreement with these practices so long as she sticks around. . . . Thus, a site that said 'we reserve the right to do whatever we want with the information we collect' [is] deemed to have provided notice of information practices." Id.

68. Walmart, for example, describes its dealings with Coremetrics and other third parties. See infra note 112. Once users possess these fuller descriptions, they will be in a position to decide for themselves whether the data transfers are for their benefit.

69. Many website's privacy policies are drafted in such a manner, either intentionally or negligently, such that the reader cannot discern if the operative practice is opt-in or opt-out. For example, halmark.com states, "We do not currently share your individual customer contact information with third parties. With your prior approval, we reserve the right to share your customer contact information in the future with select companies that Hallmark believes will be of interest to you." It is not clear, however, whether "prior approval" means prior explicit approval or merely the failure to opt-out when notice is provided.

70. RICHARD A. POSNER, "The Right of Privacy," 12 *Georgia L. Rev.* 393 (1978).

71. Opt-out is used "to improve profitability, to improve targeting efficiency and reduce unwanted mailings." See "Web Ad Agency Purchase Letting It Profile Users," *Daily News* (New York), Jan. 27, 2000, at K7259.

72. The Elder Posner, along with the younger Mill, attempts valiantly yet unsuccessfully to reconcile consequentialism and libertarianism.

73. According to the complaint, in June 1999, DoubleClick acquired Abacus Direct Corp., a direct marketing company that maintains an enormous database of names, telephone numbers, addresses, and purchasing information on millions of people. DoubleClick has matched its "clickstream" data with personally identifiable information gleaned from the Abacus database, to form personally identifiable profiles of the Internet surfing and purchasing habits of millions of individuals. See *Computer & Online Industry Litigation Reporter*, March 7, 2000, at 7.

74. See, for example, Kinkos.com ("Some of Kinko's strategic partners, such as those with links on our website, also use cookies, but Kinko's is not responsible for the abuse or misuse of any information gathered through the use of cookies by such third parties.").

75. See, for example, DOUGLAS BAIRD, ROBERT GERTNER, AND RONDAL PICKER, *Game Theory and the Law*, Chapter Four (1994).

76. Id. at 123 ("signaling takes place when those who possess nonverifiable information can convey that information in the way they choose their actions.").

77. Id. at 124 ("Assume, for example, that buyers have no direct way of knowing whether a seller makes a high- or low-quality product. High quality sellers may be able to signal their type by selling goods with a warranty. Because their goods break down less often, these sellers can offer a warranty more cheaply than low-quality sellers."). In the warranty example, Baird, Gertner, and Picker explain, "High quality sellers may be able to signal their type by selling goods with a warranty. Because their goods break down less often, these sellers can offer a warranty more cheaply than low-quality sellers."

78. See POSNER, supra note 8.

79. Posner's book develops a "general model of nonlegal cooperation," which consists of a "signaling game in which people engage in behavioral regularities in order to show that they are desirable partners in cooperative endeavors." According to Posner, "social norms" are the result of these behavioral norms constituted of collections of signaling activity. Id. at 5. As this quote indicates, Posner appears to believe that his signaling account provides a general account of social norms. McAdams reads Posner as making this claim as well. See McADAMS, supra note 9.

80. See POSNER, supra note 8 at 5.

81. Id. at 18 ("Holding everything else equal, a good type is more likely to cooperate in a repeated prisoner's dilemma than a bad type is, because the good type cares more about the future payoffs that are lost if cooperation fails.").

82. Id. at 15 ("Then as long as each player cares enough about his payoffs in future rounds – that is, he has a low discount rate – he will cooperate rather than defect in each round.").

83. Reputation is a key element in the standard account of cooperation in PD games. While rational actors prefer to defect in a single-shot PD game, they may cooperate when repeated play is possible, in order to establish a reputation as cooperator such that others may feel safe in entering into cooperative relationships with them.

84. POSNER, supra note 8 at 21.

85. Id. at 22–23, 29 ("All these elements follow from the signaling model, according to which signals are costly and observable actions with no necessary or intrinsic connections to the beliefs that they provoke.").

86. See POSNER, supra note 8 at 19.

87. Id., Chapter 5.

88. Id. at 19.

89. Id.

90. It was earlier a separating equilibrium. According to the FTC's 1998 study, only 14 percent of websites provided privacy protections. According to the FTC's 1999 study, already 66 percent posted at least one disclosure about their information practices. (See *1999 FTC Report to Congress* at 7.) *2000 FTC Report to Congress* indicated that 90 percent of the surveyed sites posted at least one disclosure about their information practices. See *2000 Report to Congress* at 10.

91. Effectively carrying out the false signaling strategy depends on being able to look like one is a cooperator when in fact one is not being cooperative. Note that this activity appears to be especially easy in the context of website personal data practices owing to the complex nature of these practices and the fair extent to which such practices are invisible to consumers. These practices importantly differ from exemplars of the cooperative model in this respect. For instance, one of Ellickson's main examples involves interactions between neighbors over the provision of border fences. Implicit in this example is the

fact that one party's cooperation is verifiable by the other party. Each party knows whether the other party is doing its share to bring about the cooperative good because failure to cooperate will be readily apparent. With respect for online privacy, however, this is not the case. A user is not typically in a position to verify whether, for example, the notice provided by a site of its data-related practices is indeed an exhaustive account. This difficulty of verification allows room for false signaling. It may be difficult to signal that one will be a cooperative fence builder without actually building a fence, but one may signal that one is a privacy respecter without actually respecting privacy. Thus, in situations in which verification is difficult, it will be important for potential cooperators such as websites to be able to establish that they are trustworthy, as such trust may serve as a proxy for direct verification.

92. ELLICKSON, supra note 4 at 19 ("Signals do not always result in a separating equilibrium. Sometimes an action that served to separate types at time 1 will, because of an exogenous shift in costs, fail to separate them at time 2. If the cost of the signal falls, bad types might join in (they 'pool'), in the hope that good types will infer that they (the bad types) are in fact good; or good types will stop sending the signal, because they realize that the bad types can join in, and thus observers cannot distinguish the good from the bad on the basis of who sends the signal.")

93. *Final Report of the FTC Advisory Committee on Online Access and Security*, Policy Papers, May 15, 2000 ("Security – and the resulting protection for personal data – can be set at almost any level depending on the costs one is willing to incur, not only in dollars but in inconvenience for users and administrators of the system.")

94. Posner apparently intends his account of norms to be an account of all norms, that is, all norms can be explained as signaling equilibria. See RICHARD H. MCADAMS, "Signaling Discount Rates: Law, Norms, and Economic Methodology," 110 *Yale L. J.* 625, 654 (2001) (reviewing ERIC A. POSNER, *Law and Social Norms* (2000)) ("I think it is fair to read Posner as offering signaling . . . as a general account of social norms.").

95. This point was illustrated by Robert Axelrod's computer tournaments. ROBERT AXELROD, *The Evolution of Cooperation* (1984). MCADAMS, supra note 9 at 2. When a Prisoner's Dilemma game is repeated, and if the incentive to defect is no longer dominant because defection may provoke the other side into defecting in future rounds, cooperation may induce cooperation. If the parties care enough about the future, the discounted benefit from mutual cooperation in future rounds may exceed the immediate benefit from defecting. Cooperation is not the dominant strategy, however, because that strategy is easily exploited by strategies that always defect. Even conditional cooperation like the tit-for-tat strategy that won the Axelrod tournament is not dominant. But the well-established result is that repetition of the game makes cooperation possible; sustained conditional cooperation is one possible equilibrium for the repeated game.

96. Retaliation may take the form of negative gossip or providing false or misleading information to the website. See SCOTT KILLINGSWORTH, "Minding Your Own Business: Privacy Policies in Principle and Practice," 7 *J. Intell. Prop. L.* 57, 62 (1999). "The obvious product of this distrust is that people avoid disclosing personal information by opting against online transactions and website registration. Less obvious but equally troubling for online marketers is the 'garbage in' syndrome: in two recent surveys, over forty percent of Americans who registered at websites admitted to providing false

information some of the time, mainly because of privacy concerns; the figure for European registrants was over fifty-eight percent. . . . The message to marketers is clear: if you want useful and accurate data, earn it by assuring consumers that you will use it appropriately." Id.

97. The notion of website visitors choosing to trust websites is similar to Richard McAdams's idea that actors can choose whether to esteem another party with whom they are interacting. See McAdams, supra note 9 at 355–72. Note, however, that whereas McAdams plausibly contends that the desire for esteem is a brute preference that a rational actor might prefer for its own sake, trust is not an item that websites would independently desire. Rather, a website would prefer to gain the trust of its visitors because this trust will be positively correlated with these visitors choosing to interact with the website in the future. Similarly, Robert Cooter's internalization account of norm conformity appears not to play a role as websites are commercial enterprises that are not readily susceptible to the psychological phenomenon of internalization. See Robert D. Cooter, "Decentralized Law for a Complex Economy: The Structural Approach to Adjudicating the New Law Merchant," 144 *U. Pa. L. Rev.* 1643, 1690–9 (1996).

98. "Gallup Poll Uncovers Opportunities to Build Consumer Confidence in 2001 by Implementing Best Practices for Online Privacy," *PR Newswire*, Jan. 16, 2001.

99. Prior to the bursting of the Internet bubble, the mere eventuality of future visits to the site in itself was money in the bank, as Internet companies were valued in the market in important part based on the number of "hits" the site received.

100. As the preceding discussion has indicated, there are different ways to respect privacy. A privacy policy will be used in the example as it is the most basic means.

101. In the Federal Trade Commissions's 1998 study, only 14 percent of websites were addressing consumer privacy issues. *1998 FTC Report to Congress*, supra note 34. As consumer sense of entitlement grows, the chances of plaintiffs' lawyers prevailing in lawsuits grows. See Matt Fleischer, "Lawyers Eye Privacy Cases Against Many DoubleClick Rivals," 22 (27) *Nat'l Law J.* A1 (Feb. 28, 2000) (noting many lawyers are now searching for the next privacy lawsuit against DoubleClick competitors, such as Engage, 24/7 Media, MatchLogic, Flycast, and L90, each collecting over 100 megabytes of clickstream data-information per day).

102. See generally *1999 FTC Report to Congress*, *available at* http://www.ftc.gov/ 05/1999/9907/privacy99.pdf.

103. People v. Moreno, 135 Cal. Rptr. 340 (Cal. App. Dep't Super. Ct. 1976).

104. See generally, Robert Frank, *Passions Within Reason*. (1988).

105. This is not to say that Walmart.com could not be spun off, have a name change, and reemerge as a more aggressive data gatherer and user.

106. Some people claim to be indifferent to the use of their personal data by websites. They say things like, "I have nothing to hide," or, "I like the idea because it will lead to more personalized marketing." Even a user who does not care about whether her data is used by websites might still rationally prefer to be dealing with a website that took privacy seriously because such a site would be signaling that it was interested in long-term relationships generally.

107. For instance, the major ISP, EarthLink, recently began a television marketing campaign featuring its offer to provide its services while at the same time protecting consumer data.

108. TrustE was supposed to be a way for sites to certify that they were legitimate in their respect for privacy. TrustE has had limited success. It has been criticized for being too lax in its standards. Note that while TrustE as a firm has been heavily criticized, nevertheless, there has been support for the general plan of the firm.
109. See BAIRD, GERTNER, AND PICKER, supra note 75 (noting that there may be other reasons for taking an action in addition to its signaling function.)
110. POSNER, supra note 8 at 159–60.
111. Note that there is anecdotal evidence that many websites, small websites in particular, derive their privacy policies by means of cutting and pasting from the privacy policies they find on the Web. This form of copyright violation may serve the useful unintended purpose of helping further the uniformity of privacy norms.

Index